MADE IN IBIZA

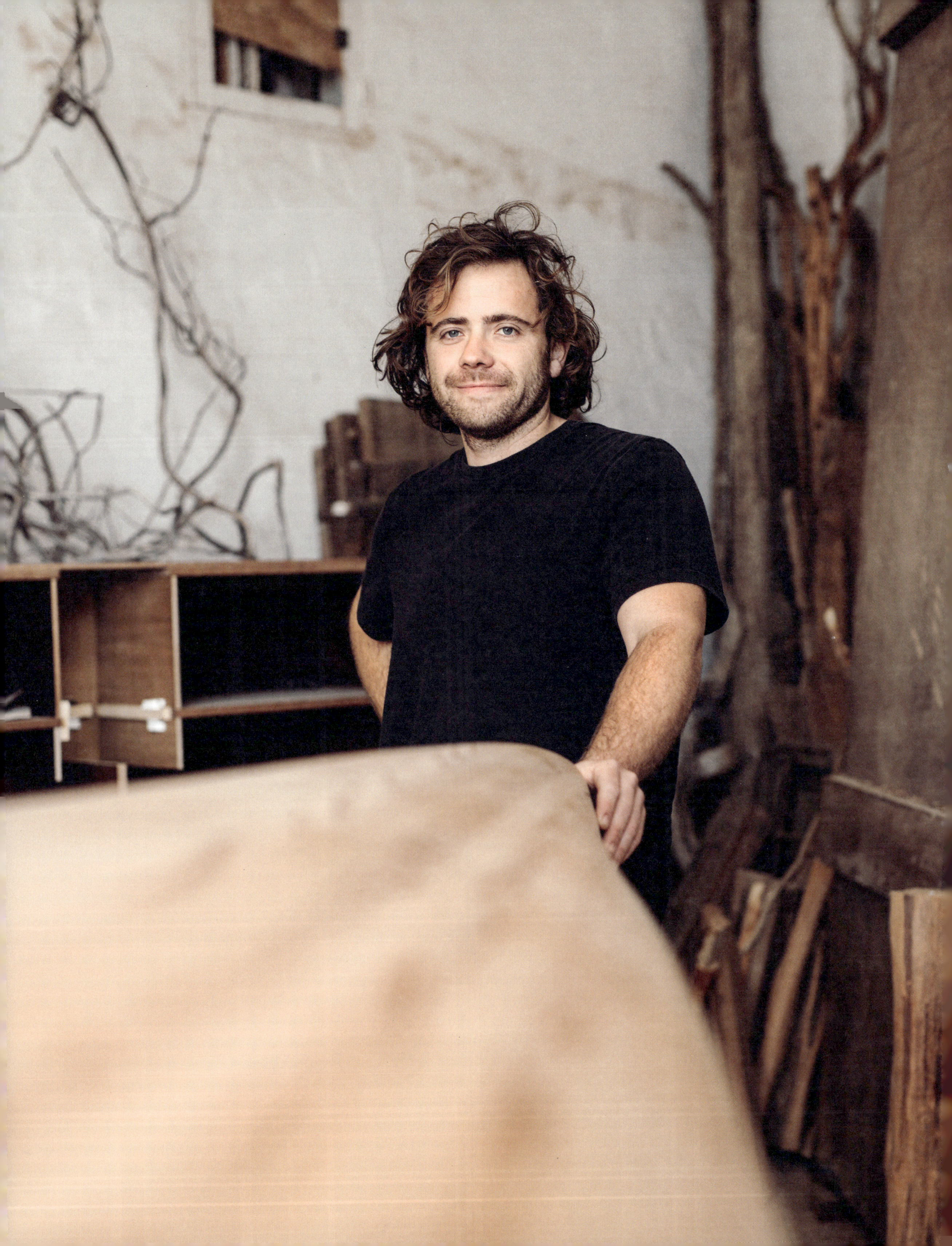

MADE IN IBIZA

A JOURNEY INTO THE CREATIVE HEART OF THE WHITE ISLAND

Texts by
LIAM ALDOUS
MAYA BOYD
MARTIN DAVIES
CLARE DOWDY
CHRISTOPHER ENGLISH

Photography by
ANA LUI & SALVA LÓPEZ

MERRELL
LONDON • NEW YORK

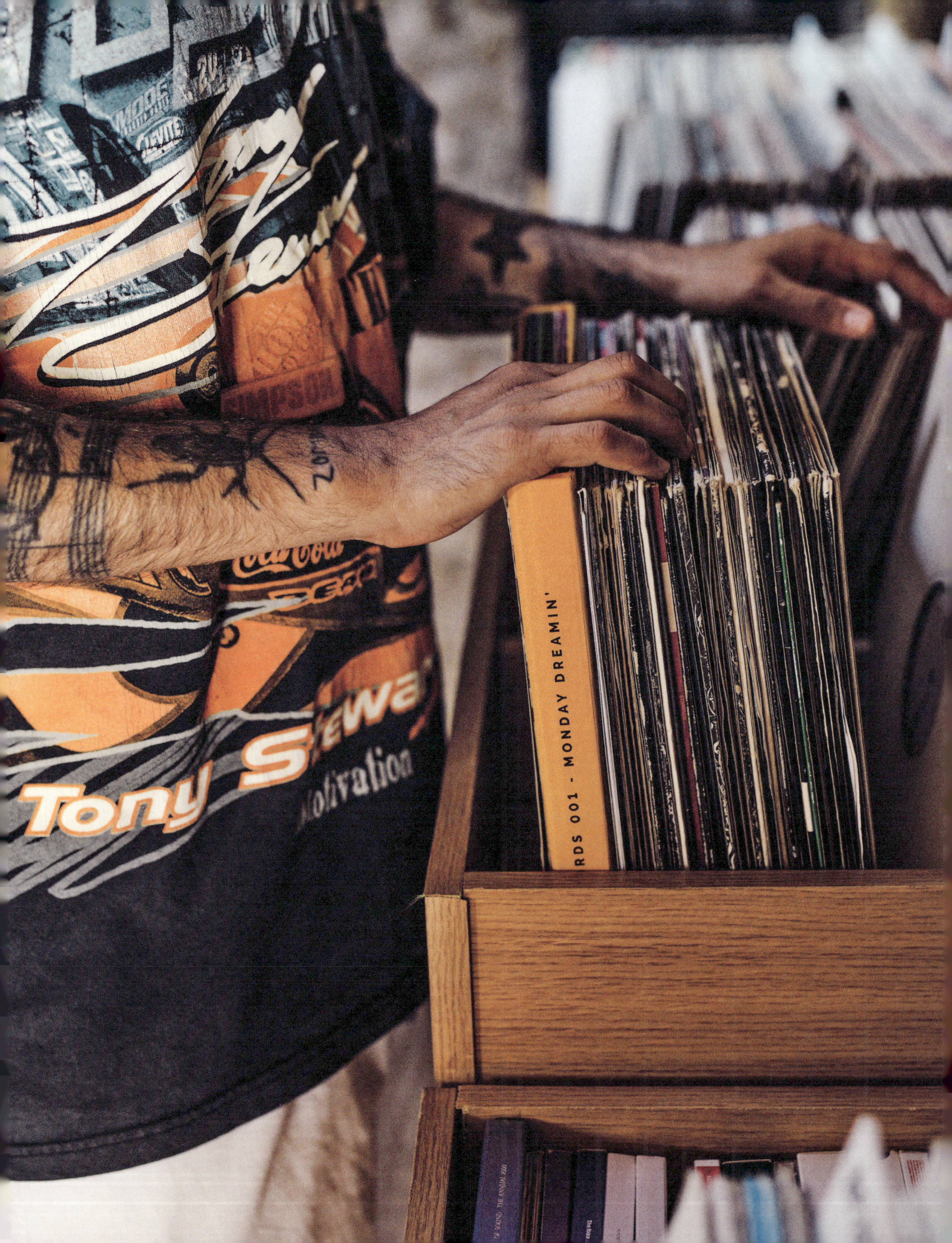
Tony
Motivation
RDS 001 - MONDAY DREAMIN'

CONTENTS

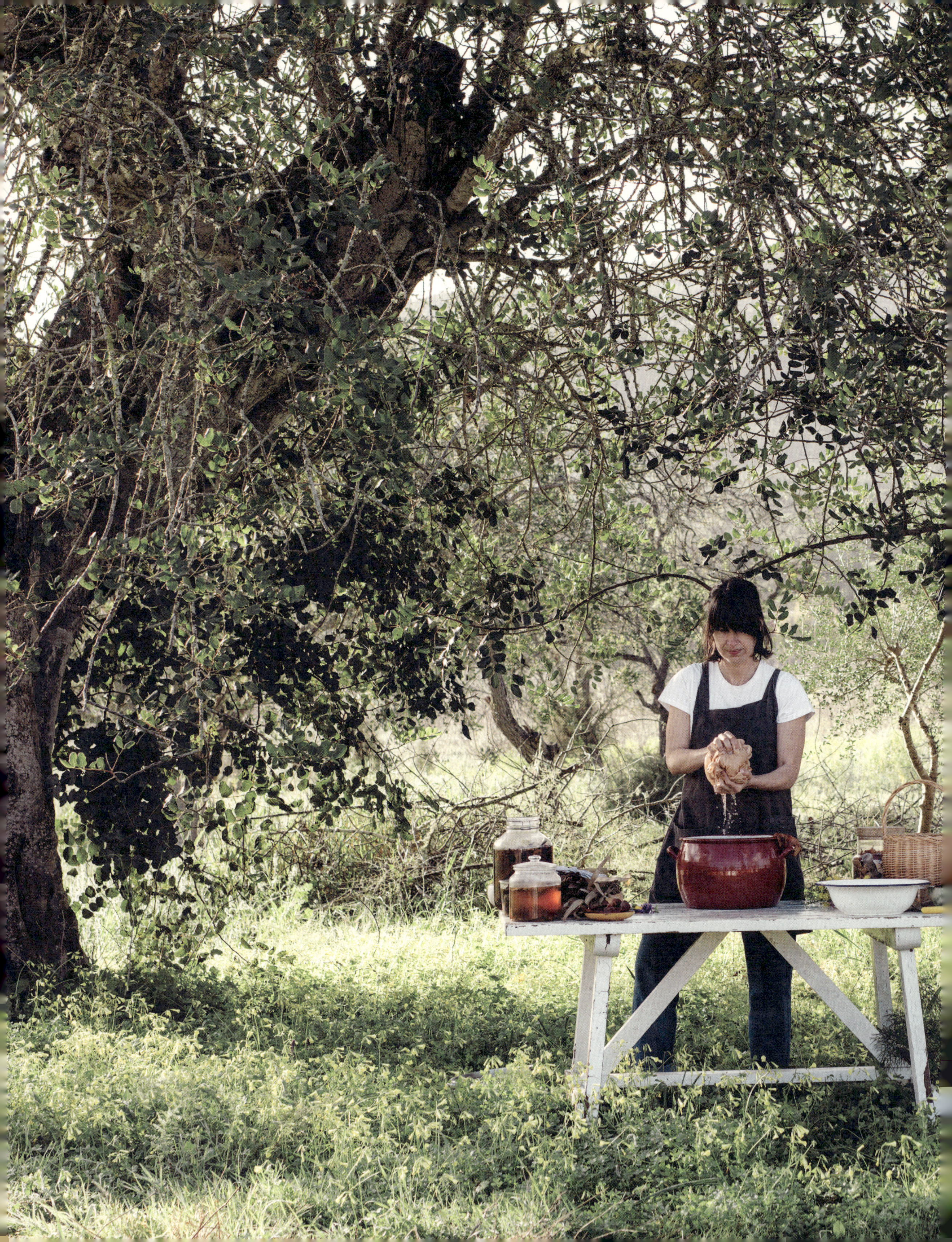

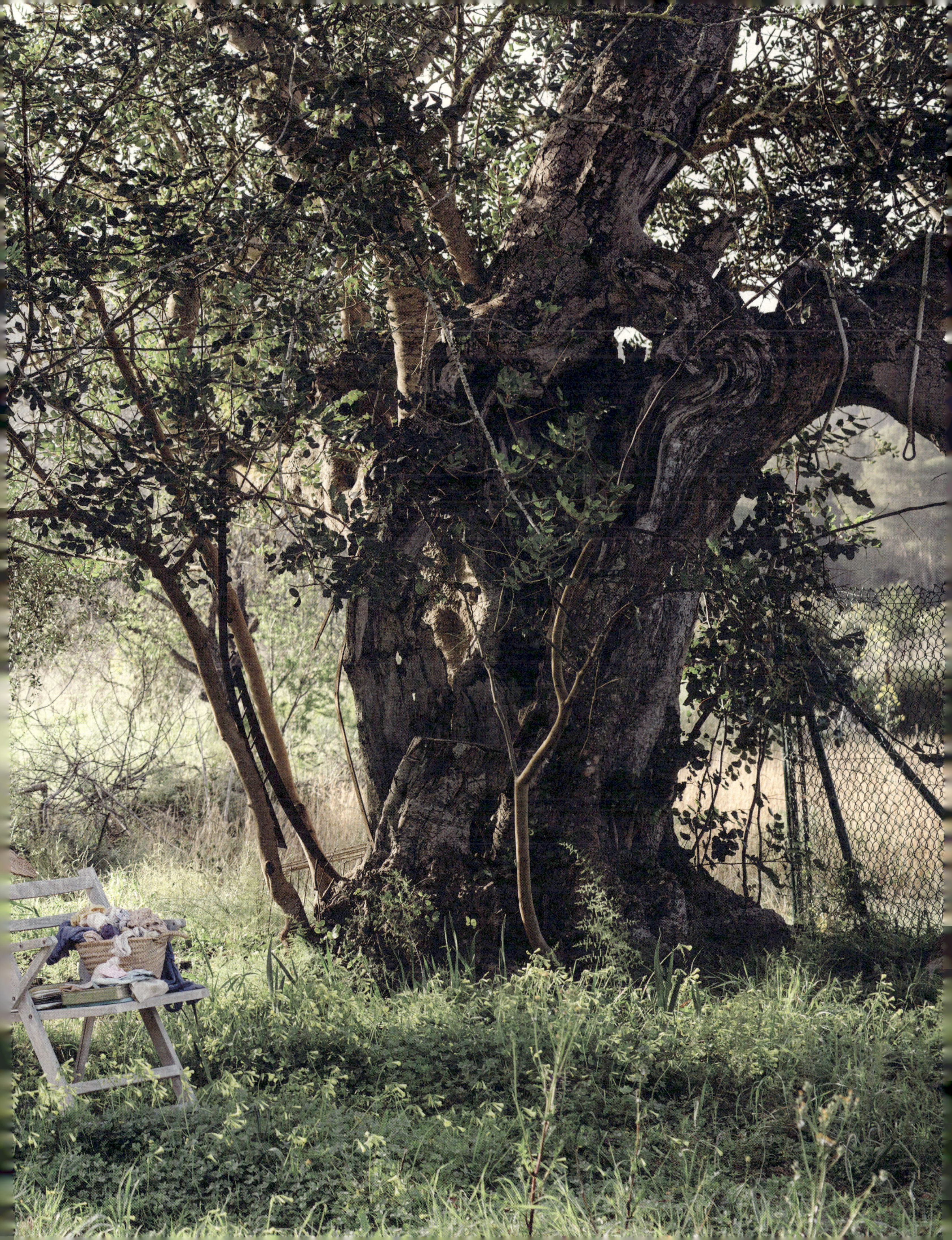

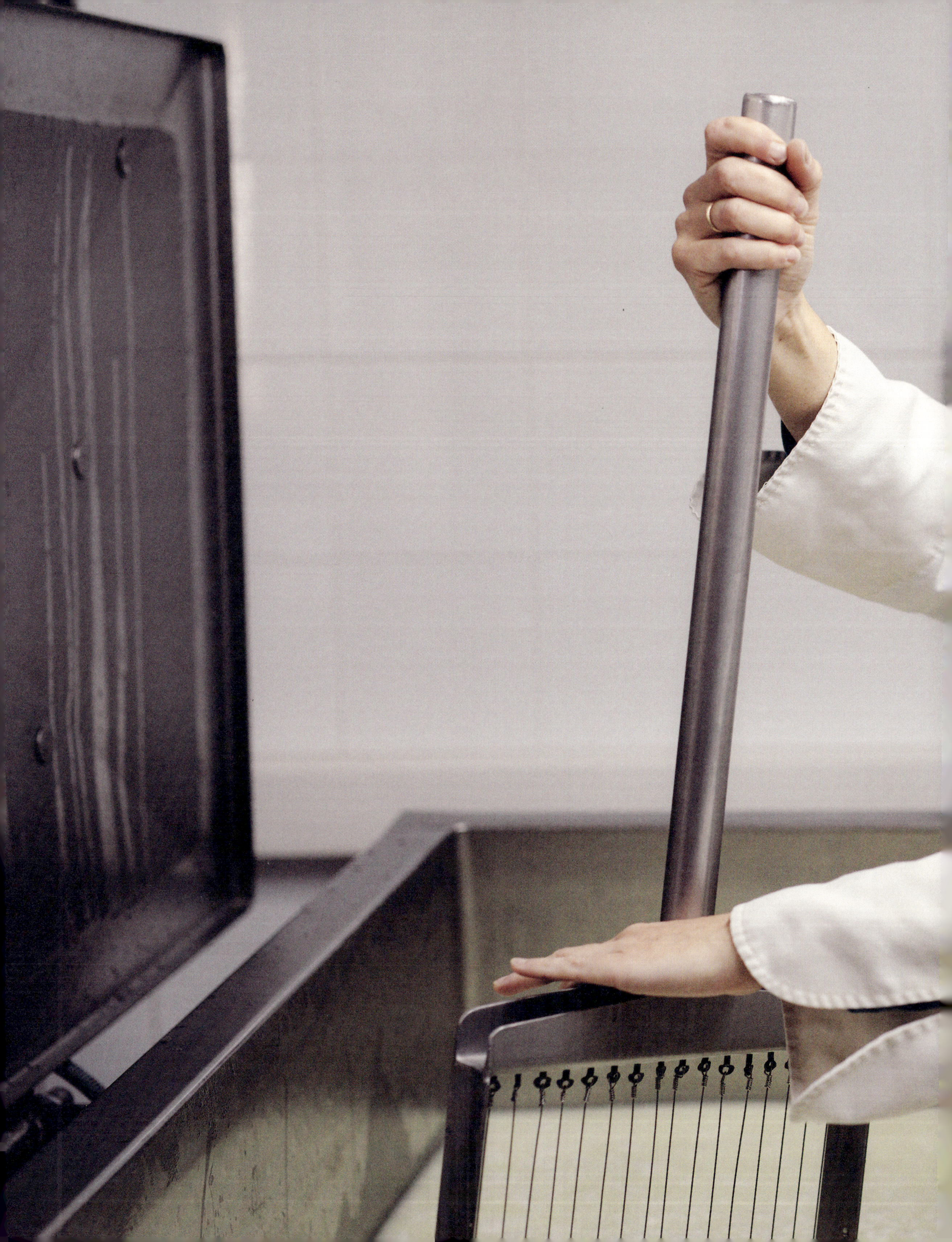

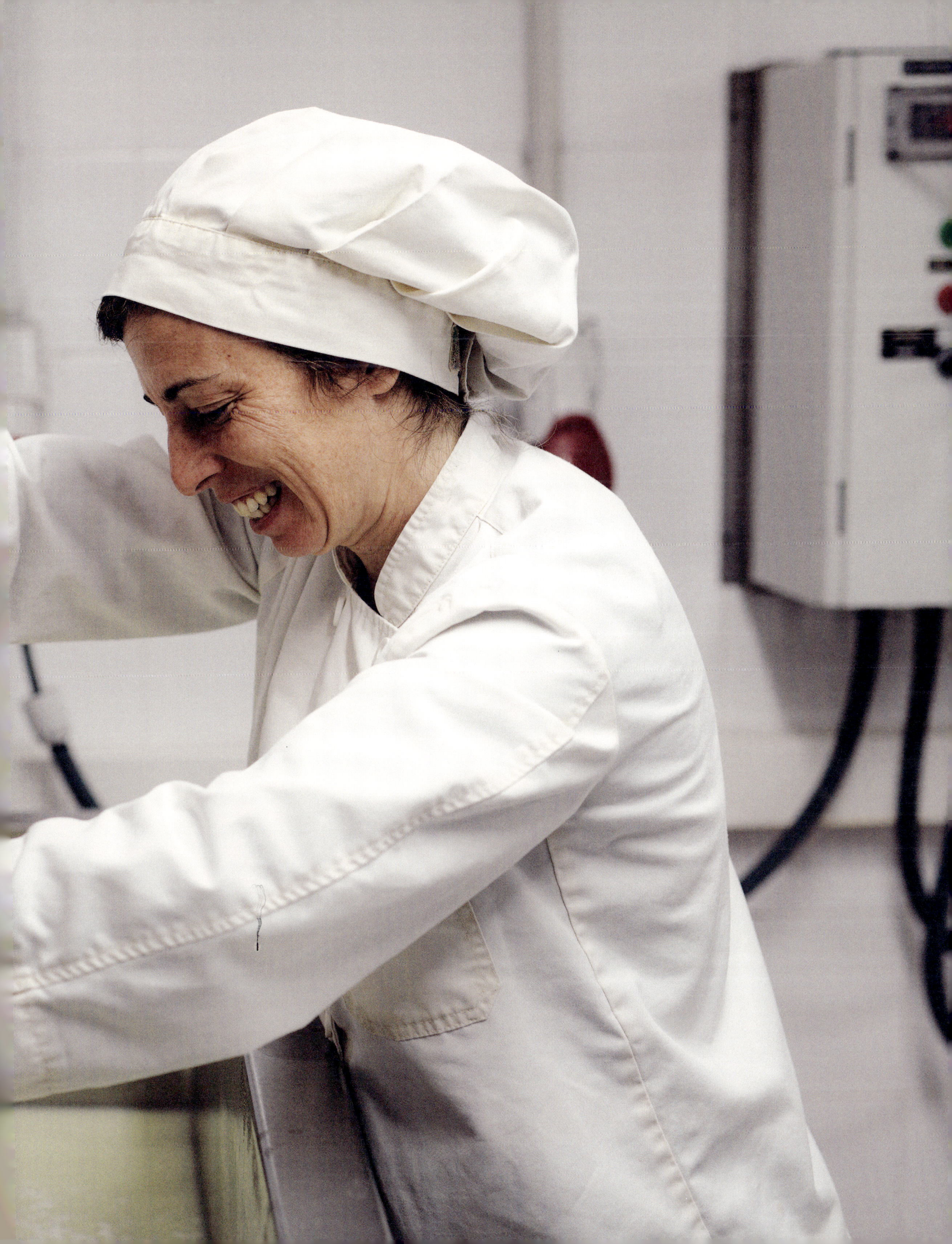

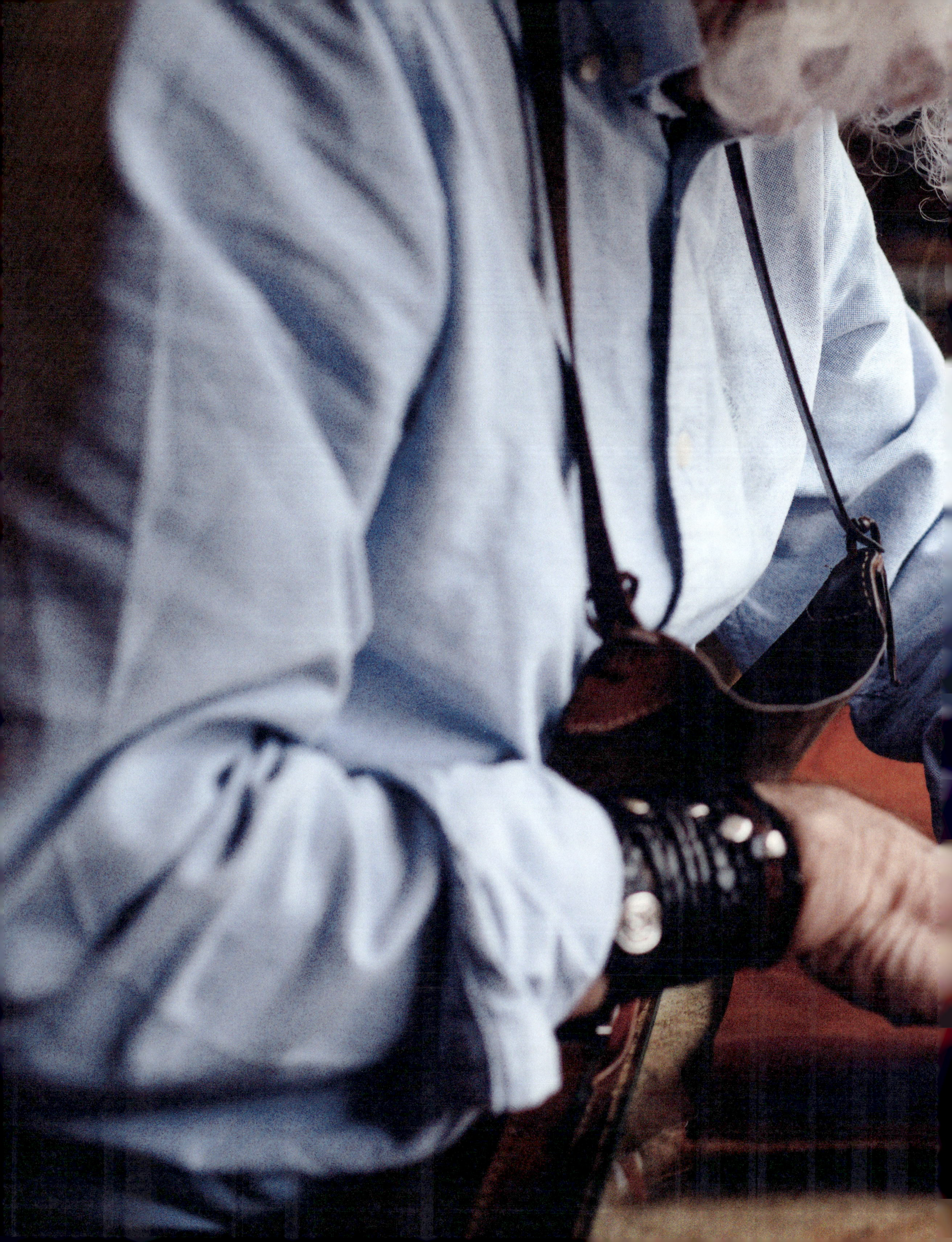

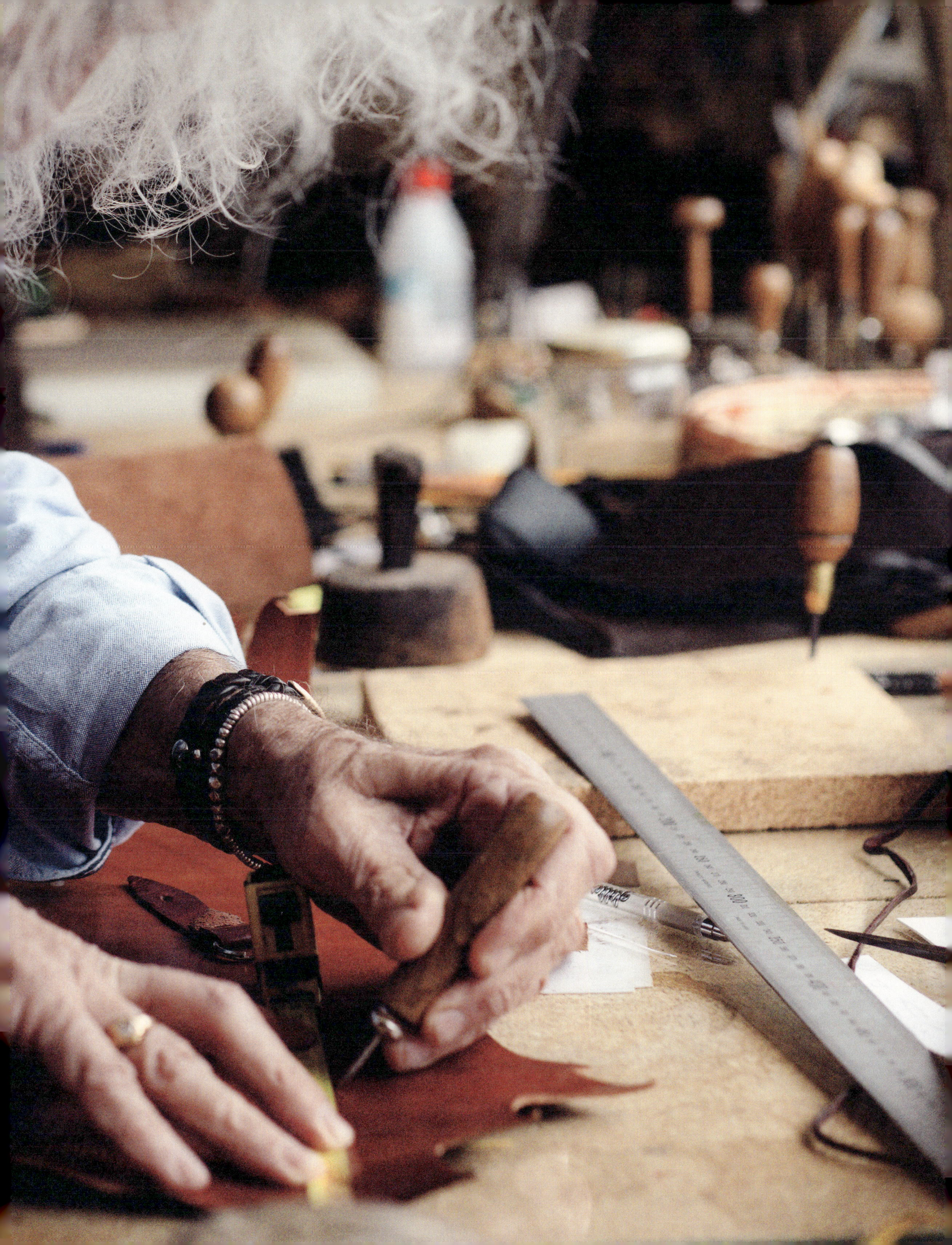

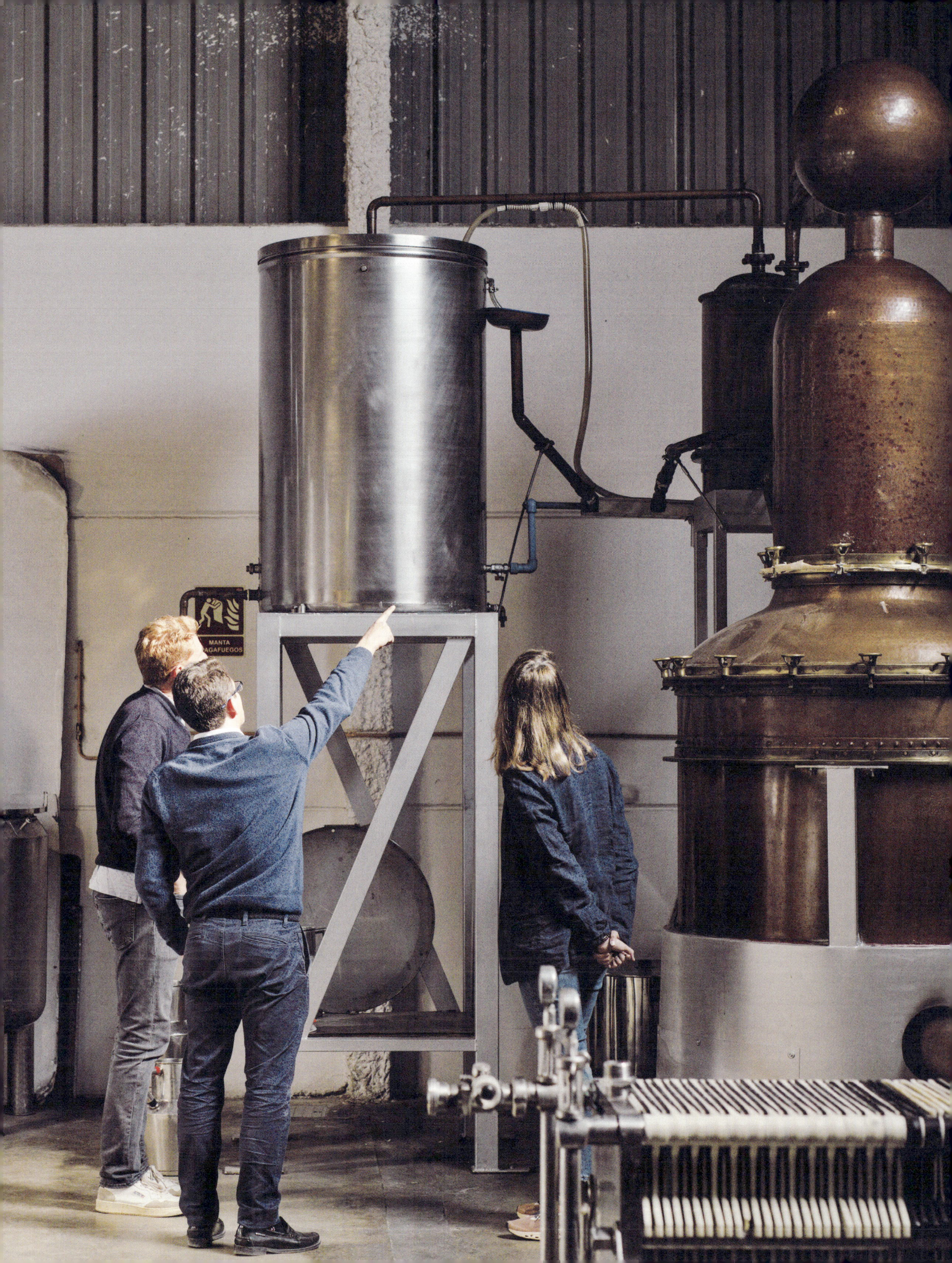
MANTA

PREFACE

SONJA & JAN VAN DER HAGEN

Creating this book was our way of shining a spotlight on the talented individuals and small companies that make Ibiza such a vibrant and fascinating place. Throughout months of research, we had the pleasure of travelling around the island, visiting numerous captivating locations and meeting so many interesting people. The endeavour provided confirmation that the spirit of Ibiza lies not only in its famous nightlife and stunning beaches but also in the creativity and passion of its locals.

We would like to extend our sincere thanks to everyone who contributed to this project. Your advice, contacts, photographic material, stories and time were invaluable and helped to make this book possible. We are deeply grateful to everyone who appears in *Made in Ibiza* for their participation in the photo shoots and text production. Your dedication to your craft is truly inspiring.

We would also like to express our appreciation to Hugh Merrell for publishing this book, and to the authors and photographers for their exceptional work in bringing the stories and images of Ibiza's local production and creativity to life. Nathalie Hummer, who is responsible for the layout design, has been part of the editorial board and has contributed to shaping *Made in Ibiza* from the very beginning. The talent and hard work of this creative team have given this project a voice and a presence that we hope will inspire others to explore and appreciate the unique offerings of their own communities.

At its core, this book is about supporting local endeavours. By supporting local projects and creative enterprises, we believe that we can help to maintain the unique character of a place like Ibiza and to create a more sustainable, diverse and interesting society. We can all play a role in preserving the character and uniqueness of our communities and in promoting growth and sustainability.

In conclusion, we wish to express our gratitude to everyone who helped us on this journey. Your support and contributions have made this project a remarkable success, and we hope that *Made in Ibiza* will have a lasting impact on the way we view and appreciate local production and creativity.

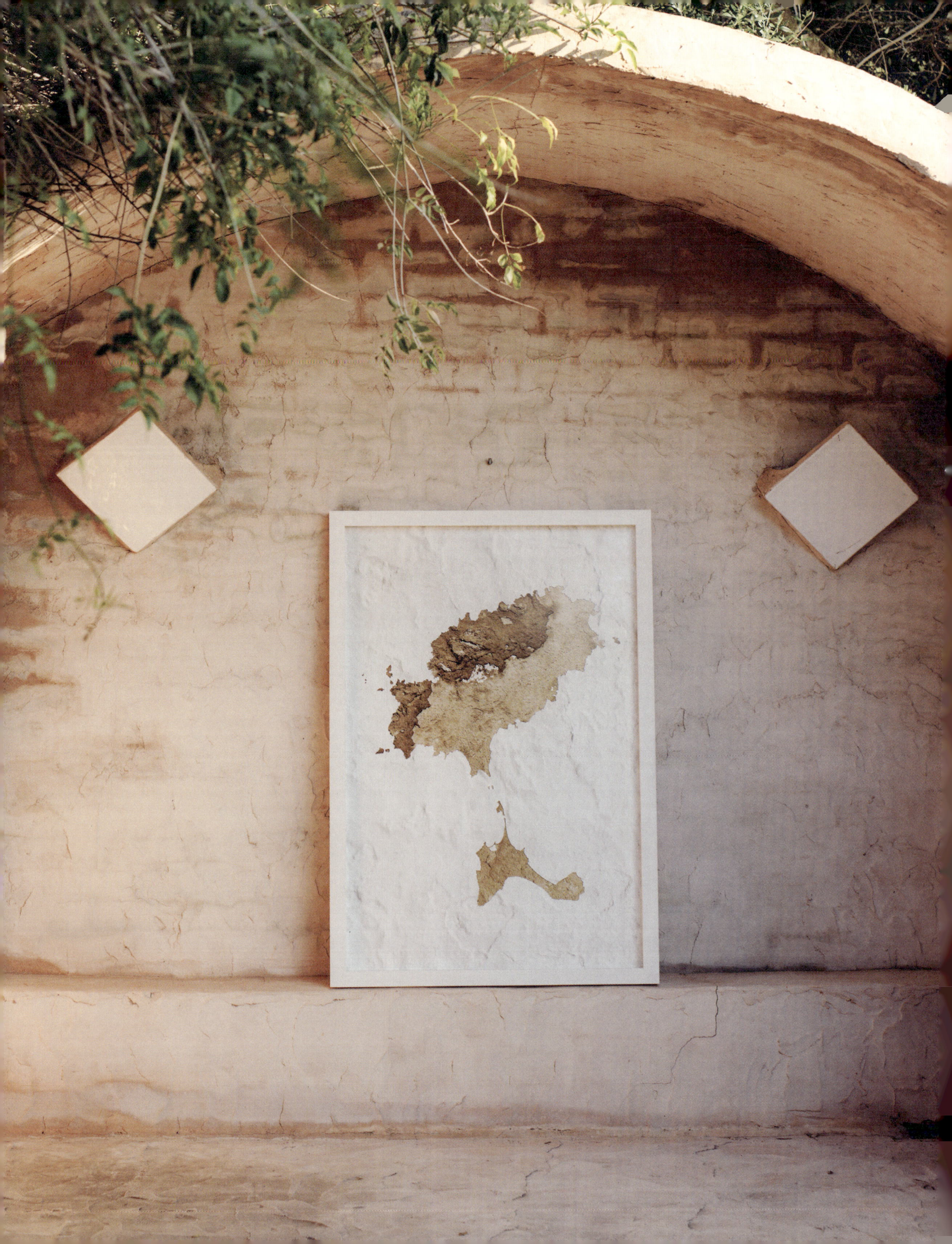

INTRODUCTION

LIAM ALDOUS

If Ibiza is the answer, what is the question? It is a mystery that has permeated cultures and minds for millennia. As always, the space in-between – the giant expanse that gives all life room to breathe – is where clues to the island's allure can be found. Steeped in experiences and expectations, Ibiza remains an immensely personal place. As an island of multiplicity, it is also a place where many things can be true.

The oft-mythologized soil provides a sensible enough starting point. Much of the island's lore seems to be born from beneath. Around the end of the seventh century BCE, the Phoenicians sent their illustrious fallen to be buried in the isle's sacred ground. Sea-faring ancient Greeks collected the same mineral-rich earth to be worn inside protective amulets, while the ancient Romans scattered Ibizan soil around encampments as an energetic shield before heading into battle. Hallowed by history, it is no wonder that the island became such a sanctuary during the last century. First came Europe's artistic vanguard, seeking refuge from the ravages of war. Then the influx of free-loving hippies in the 1960s and '70s mutated into the hedonistic pleasure-seekers of the 1980s and '90s. Indeed, every time the world wobbles, a new wave of émigrés set their sights on Ibiza as an idyll of peace and protection.

Over time, this plethora of perspectives and aspirations has embroidered the island's creative soul; from architects seeking to understand and emulate the agrarian vernacular to artists inspired by the abundance of nature. Artisans have sought to reconcile their own cultural canon with island life. Authors have superimposed their feelings on to fleeting fragments of time. This spirited interplay of imaginations has long bemused the local *payeses*, who in recent decades have gradually welcomed in the world. As the island has become more cosmopolitan, it has re-emerged as a global village.

Modular, rectilinear, peculiar – Ibiza's archaic-looking farmhouses, or *casas payesas*, have been the portals to new life. Within their storied walls, natives and newcomers, from farmers to foreigners, have sheltered and been shaped. Even the island's notorious party culture is rooted in these characteristic houses, with super-clubs such as Pacha and Amnesia beginning as makeshift fiestas inside remote rural fincas. Houses have hosted art movements, budding musicians and bold second-lifers hoping to redefine the meaning of modern life. Thankfully, the pared-back nature of Ibiza's fortified farmhouses has helped to humble any imported delusions of grandeur. As a template for new beginnings, their unabashed simplicity continues to capture imaginations.

Tethering a faraway past to the present day, Ibiza's traditional houses remind us that our connection with the island is reciprocal. Design features hint at nature having the upper hand, giving rise to houses that both sustain and harness the elements. Thick walls with tiny windows mediate seasonal heat and damp. Flat roofs collect rainwater that drains into a cistern for storage and survival. Living areas, or *porxos*, serve as a nucleus, prioritizing connection and the shared contribution to daily life. Over time, additional rooms, towers and walled patios have accommodated the inhabitants' growing needs. As a relic of functionality, the *casa payesa* stands out as a creative monument in symbiotic dialogue with the world around it.

This book is a conversation with the people who make Ibiza. A compendium of the island's inspired characters, their creations, homes and studios, the contents shine a bright Balearic light on a community that is often hidden in plain sight. The book is also about the art of making in Ibiza. This is an isle of abundant beauty, but there are inherent limitations to making things work. Geographic isolation, a lack of industry and a scarcity of materials remain perennial challenges. However, rather than constraining creativity, such friction fuels ingenuity and sharpens integrity. Lives dedicated to the process may become defined by projects. In Ibiza, where life's creative canvas often feels unfettered and fresh, creating art, architecture or artisanal goods can also be an opportunity. Many makers view their work as a locus for talking about, and toiling for, genuine change for the better.

Reset and renewal are the essence of creativity on the island. It is often said that Ibiza is a mirror, reflecting a person's intentions and inner-self back to them in myriad ways. This whimsical idea is grounded in reality by the choices people make. A yearning for connection manifests as a collective of painters, sculptors and poets. The desire for calm secludes the ceramicist. Legacies are safeguarded by honouring family values. A spirit of curiosity and community ensures that the generational chain of knowledge and wisdom endures. We, too, have a choice: to honour, appreciate and support the island's creators. In so doing, we make a contribution and keep the island in balance.

The island's allure may be personal, but universal themes abound. Escapism. Transformation. The pursuit of joy. Compelling stories embodied and enlivened by a magnetic mosaic of people and places. Which brings us back to that question about *the question*. Perhaps it does not need to be wholly defined, emerging instead as more of a promise. Any precinct for freedom becomes the natural province of creation. From the utilitarian handiwork of craft to the utopian visions of art, in Ibiza it is the wish to create a life on one's own terms that becomes the unifying thread. To be made in Ibiza is to make the world anew.

FASHION & JEWELLERY

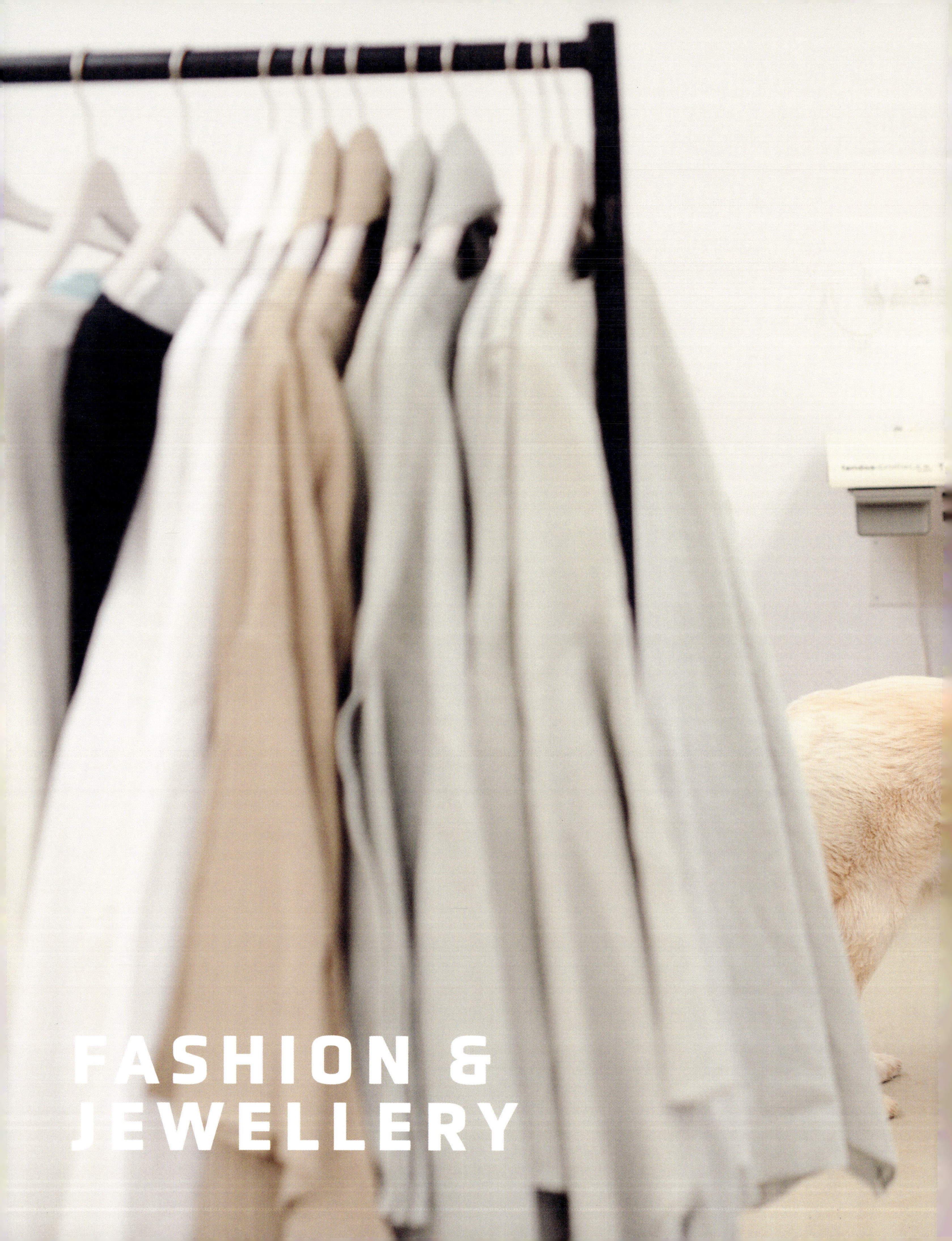

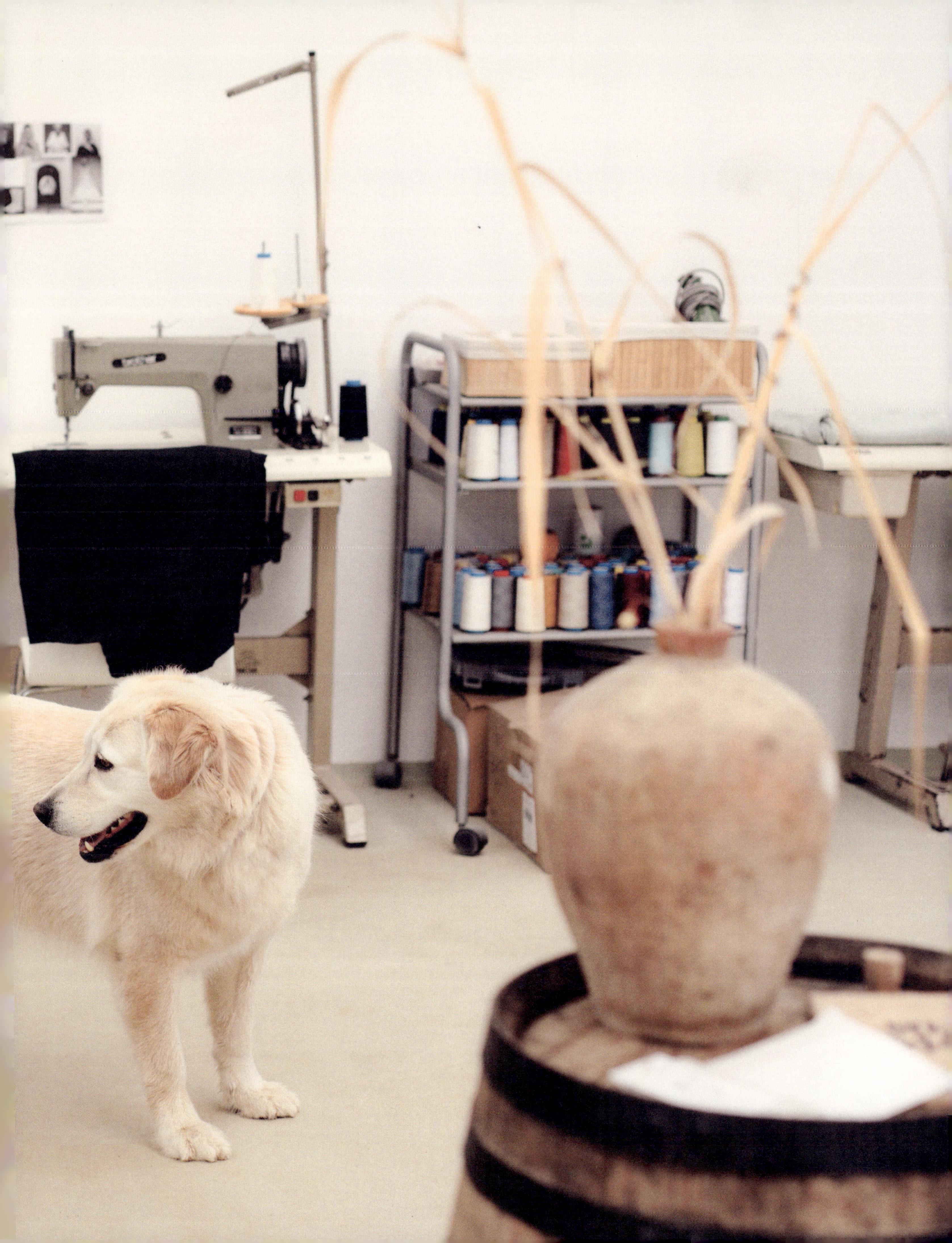

SAN RAFAEL
delbesibiza.es

DELBES IBIZA

FASHION INSPIRED BY TRADITIONAL DANCE

Sonia Ferrer took up traditional Ibizan dancing at the age of two, and still dances today. 'As a child, when I needed a new dress, I went to a seamstress who would take my measurements and make one for me', she recalls. Sonia still has all the dresses for these *bailes payeses* (peasants' dances) that she has worn over the years.

Traditionally, female dancers wore long-sleeved gowns with heavily gathered skirts. While most dresses were made of linen, cotton or wool, some were made of silk, brought back to the island by men who had left to work abroad. 'For a woman, wearing silk was a way of showing the world that her husband had returned', Sonia explains.

When Sonia was a fashion student at the Istituto Europeo di Design in Madrid, her love of the *baile payés* informed her final project. This eventually led to her setting up her fashion company, Delbes Ibiza, in 2018. But she was also driven by what she saw as a misconception of her homeland. She took a sabbatical during her studies and travelled abroad. 'I realized that very few people really know Ibiza. Only the parties are well known.'

On her return home, Sonia became aware that the name 'Ibiza' is often used as a marketing tool. 'A lot of fashion brands use marketing to justify their relationship with the island,' she says, 'but they are not born of any tradition or culture here.' In contrast, her idea was to rediscover the old patterns, techniques and craftsmanship associated with the island's traditional dress, and 'to make something authentic in Ibiza'.

Sonia launched her first collection on social media. 'People started coming to the workshop, and suddenly I'd sold the whole collection.' Initially, she made only one-off pieces. Then retailers approached her, and now Delbes is sold in the boutiques of the hotels Six Senses and 7Pines, in stores around the island, in Menorca, on the Greek island of Mykonos, and in Tulum in Mexico.

The name 'Delbes' comes from the ancient Egyptian god Bes, from whom the island's name is derived. 'Bes is rather ugly, but he has some very beautiful and important associations with protection of the family and with sexuality. By choosing this name, I hoped to draw attention to the lesser-known elements of the island, meaning the old traditions', explains Sonia.

Sonia's family has been in Ibiza for at least five generations, and the Delbes workshop is based in a converted farm building next to the family home, near the village of San Rafael. Sonia was born here, and lived with her parents, who are cattle farmers, her grandparents and her great-grandmother.

Using textiles she buys from the Spanish mainland, Sonia spends most of the time designing and sewing in the workshop. She also subcontracts to local tailors, but her plan is to have more people working from the atelier. Depending on how complicated and detailed the design is, a Delbes Ibiza dress takes between three and twenty-four hours to make.

Sonia's favourite design is the De Pou, which comes in three versions: a shirt, a short dress and a long dress. Made of linen, it has a row of buttons down the front and on the long cuffs of the puffed sleeves. 'It's inspired by an original Ibizan design', Sonia explains. 'We've been making it since 2018, and it's still very popular.'

Sonia imagines that her company will extend beyond fashion: 'One day, I would like Delbes to become a world of Ibizan craftsmanship and to feature more crafts such as ceramics and carpentry.' ***CD***

Sonia Ferrer draws inspiration from traditional Ibizan dance costumes. One of her most popular designs is the De Pou (on the mannequin at far right), which has been part of her collection since she started Delbes Ibiza in 2018.

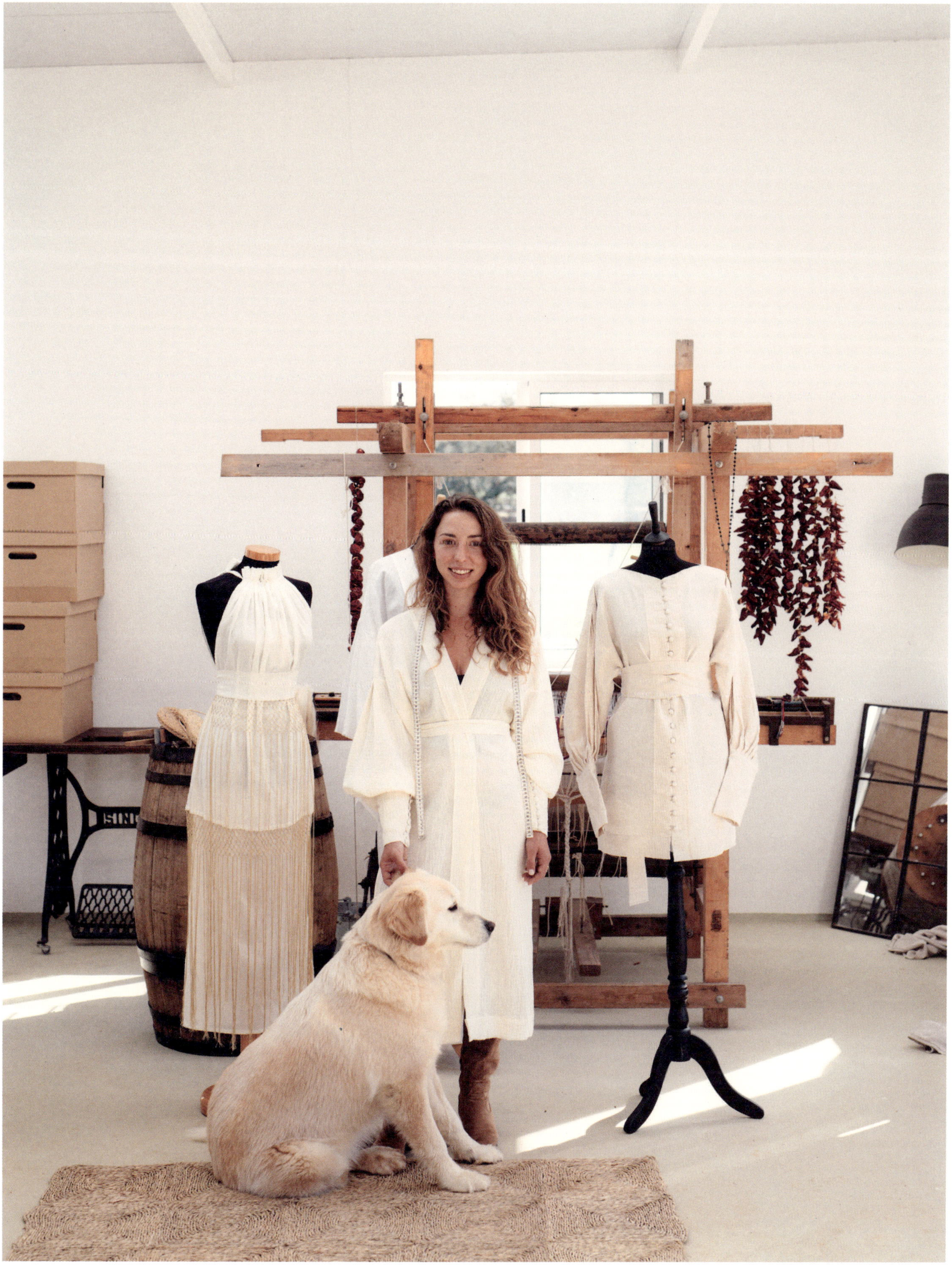

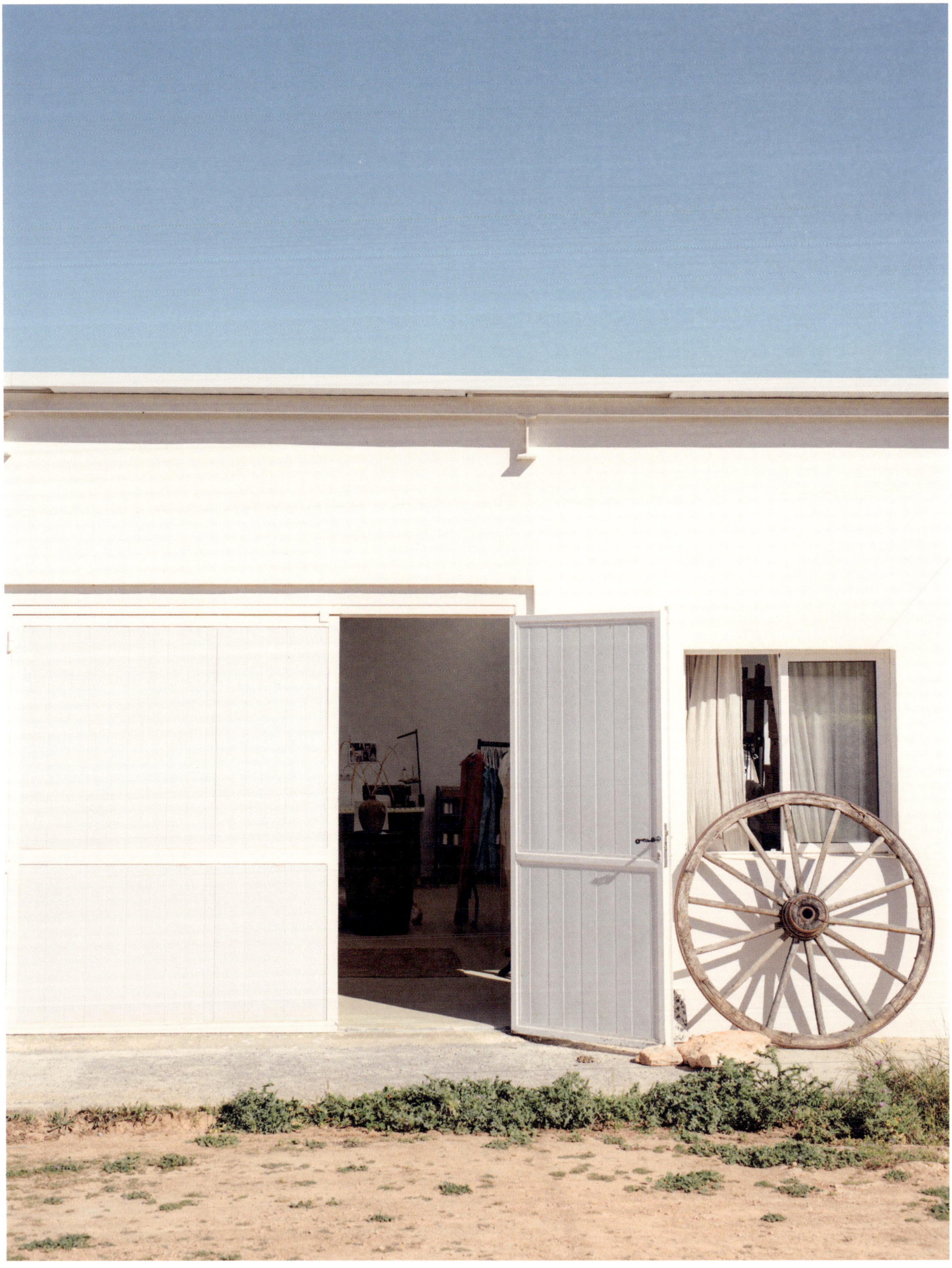

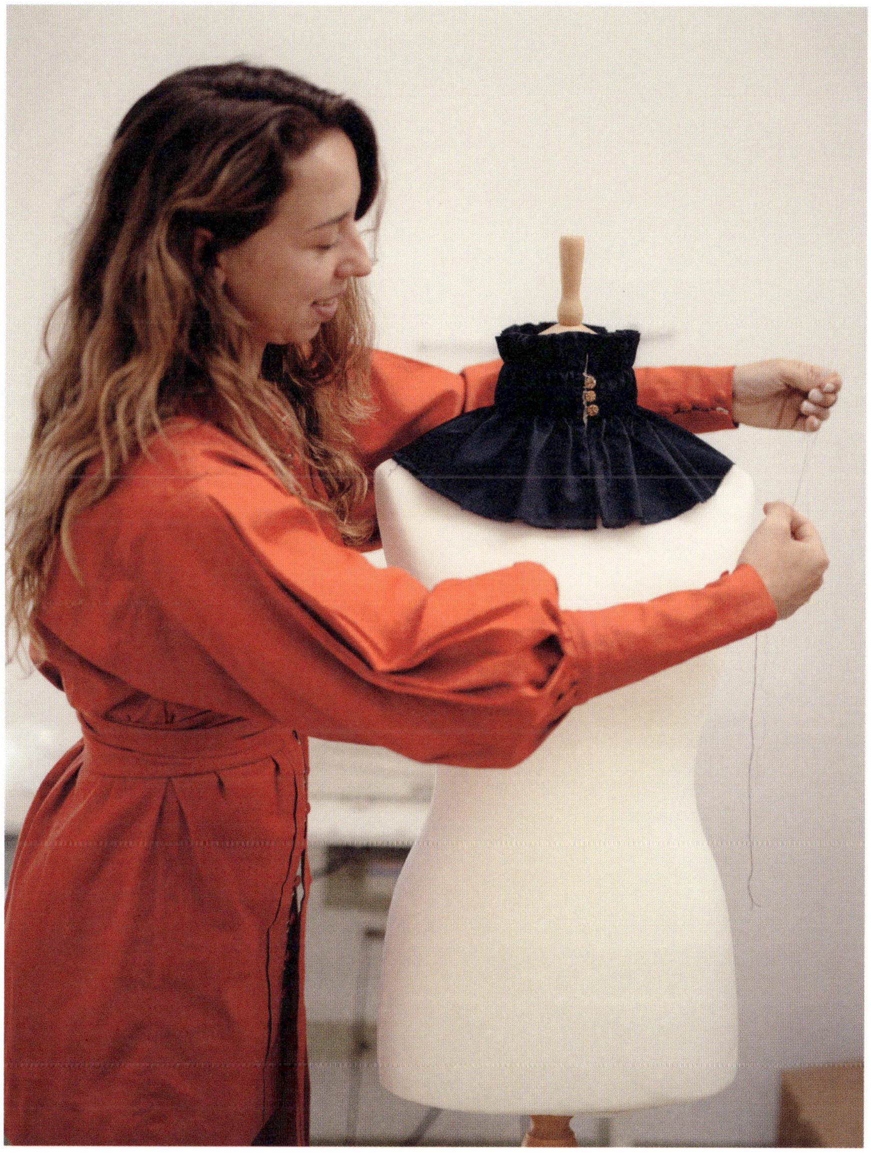

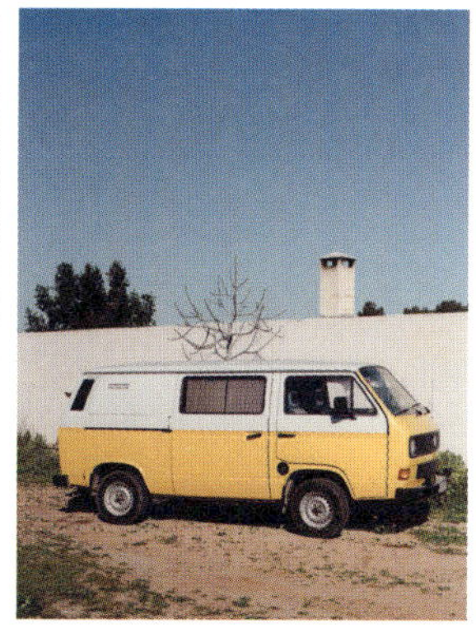

Delbes Ibiza's studio is in a converted stable block on the Ferrar family's cattle farm, in the countryside near San Rafael. Customers can visit by appointment.

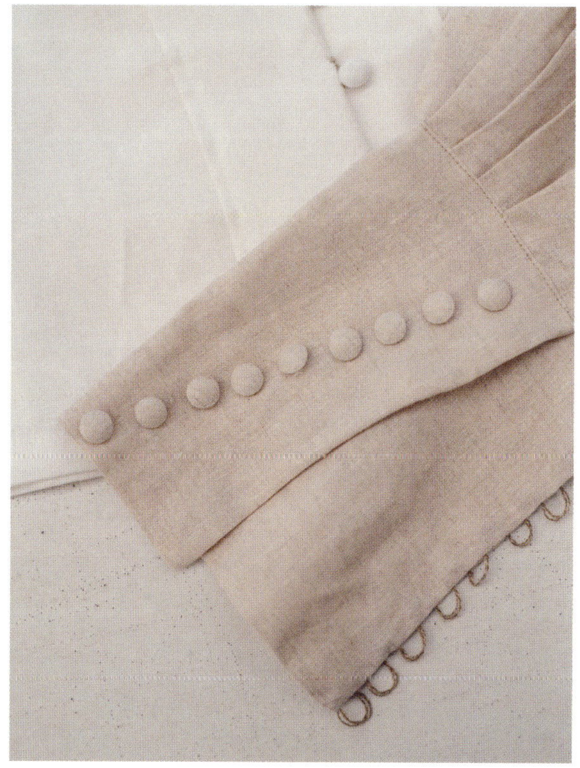

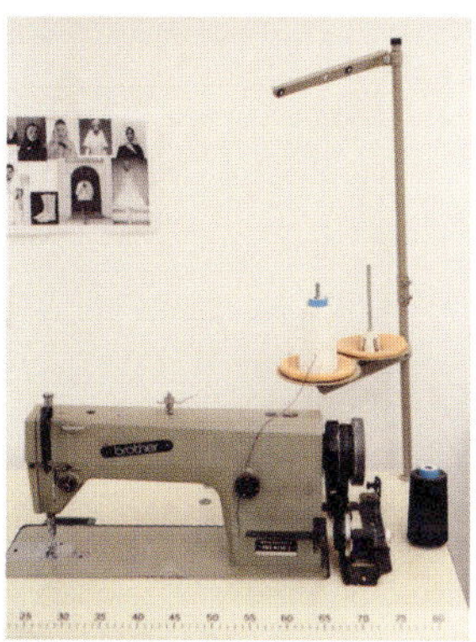

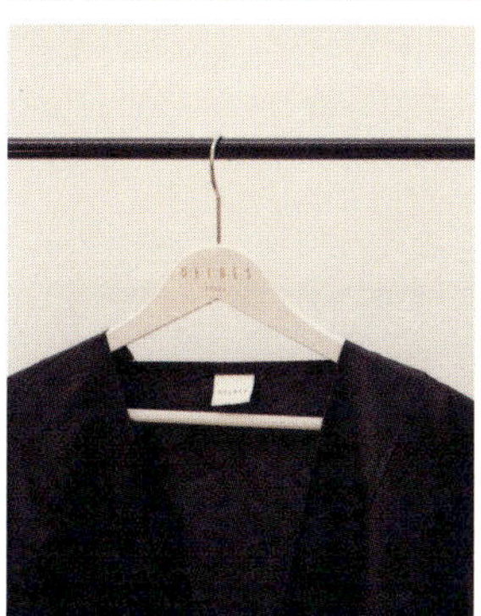

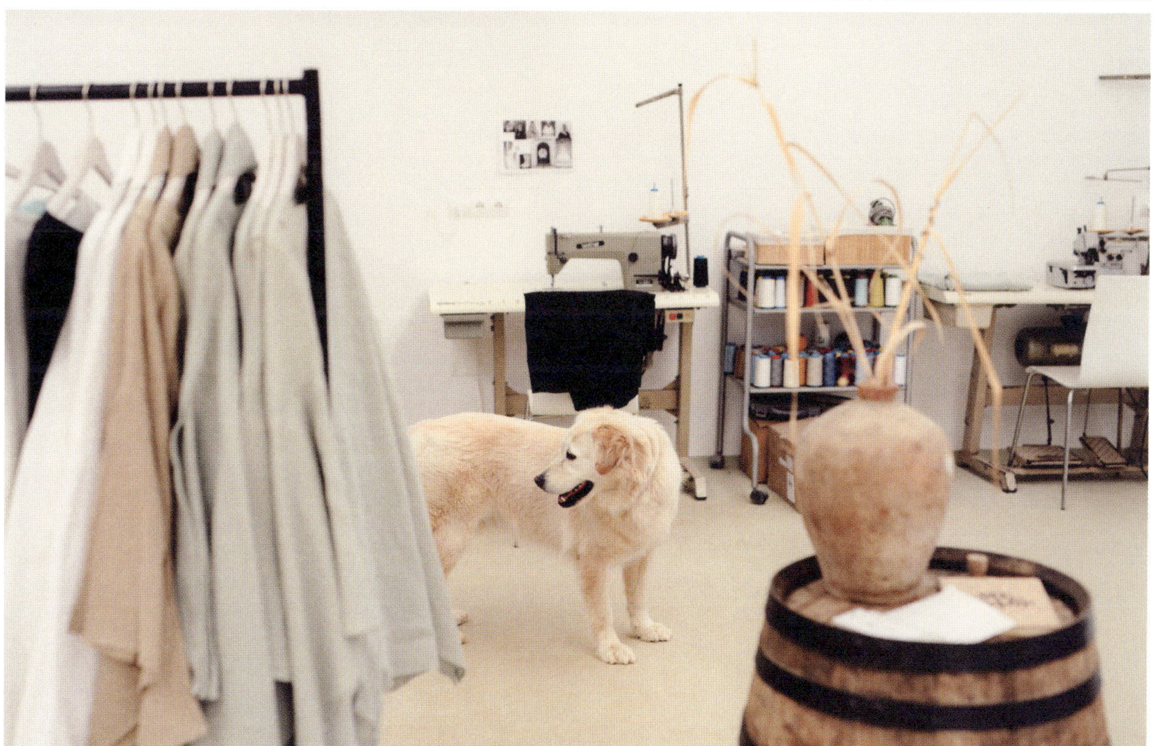

Sonia, who studied fashion in Madrid, combines the island's traditional patterns and dressmaking techniques with her own painted or printed designs and motifs. These appear on items such as bags and limited-edition clothing.

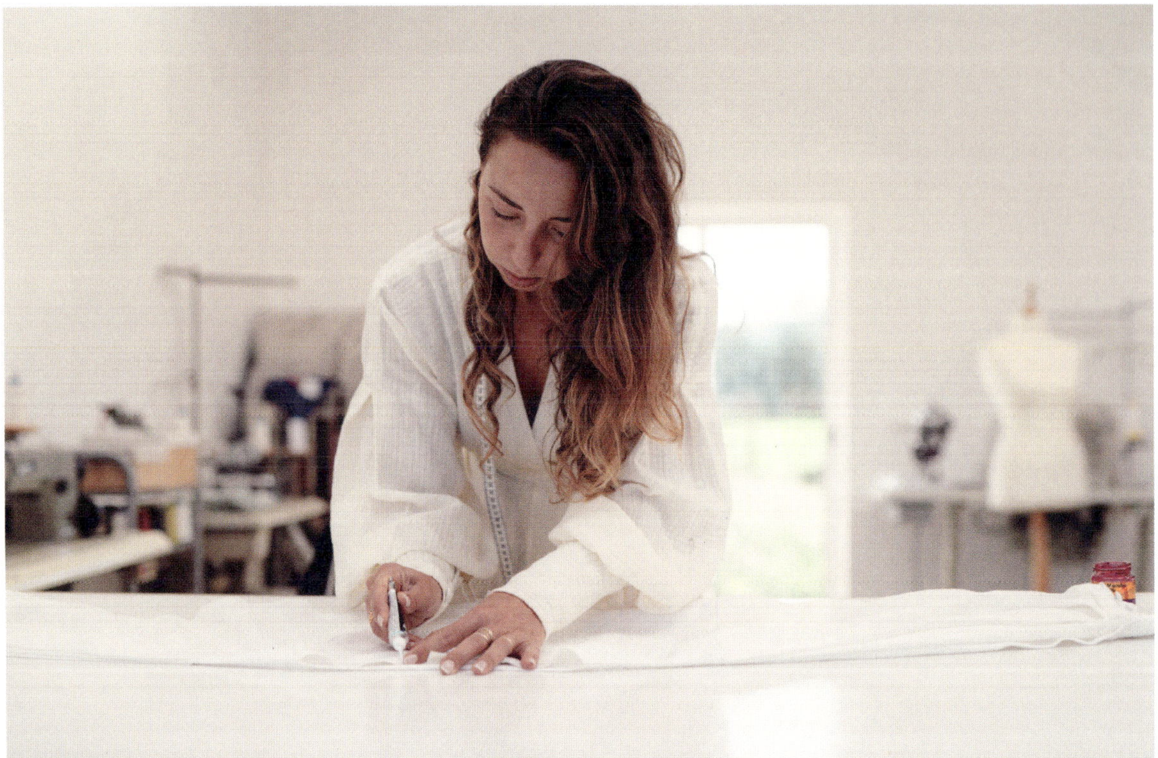

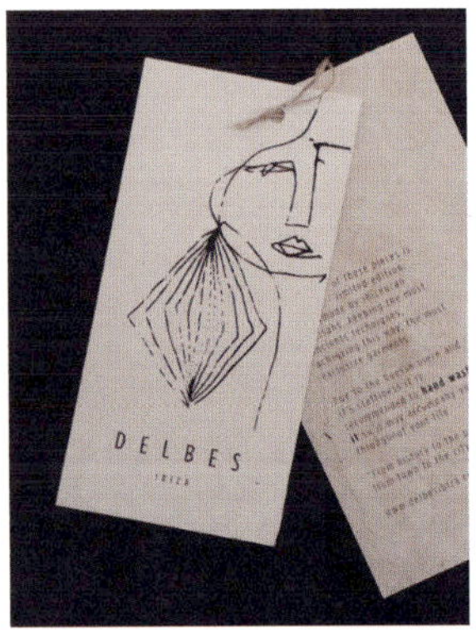

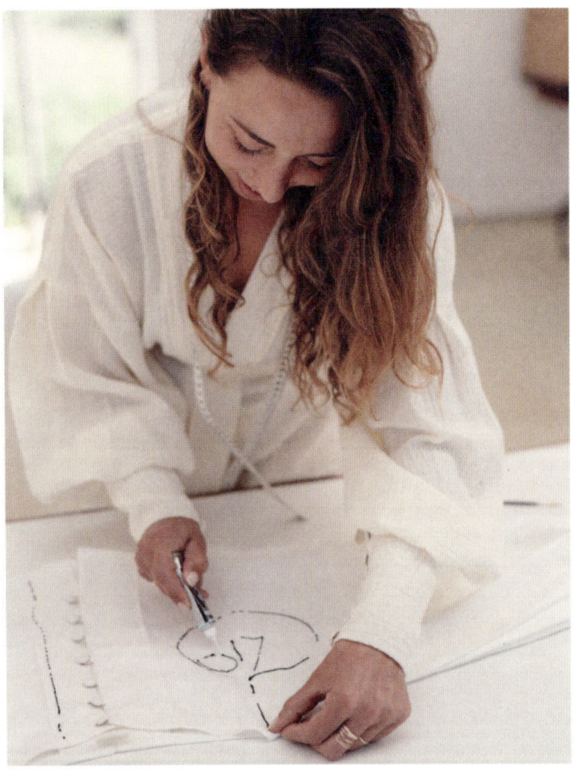

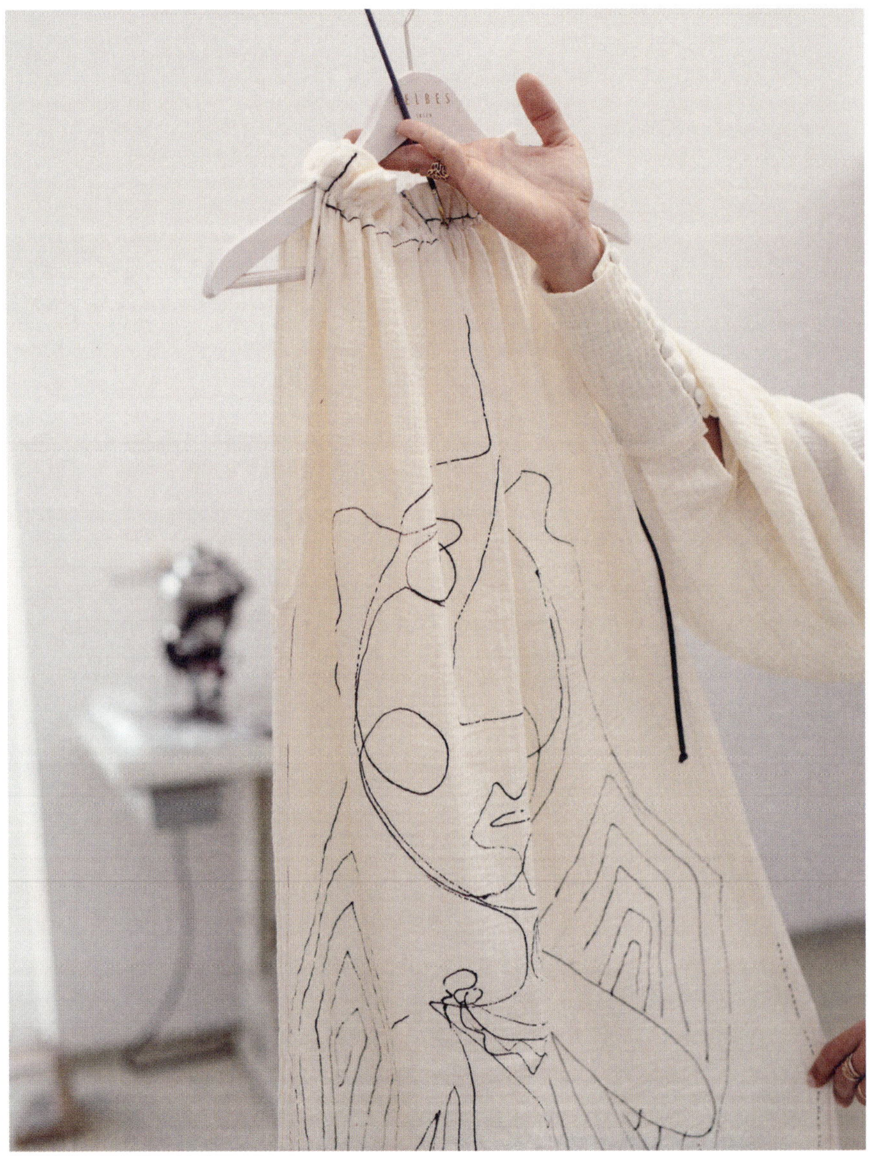

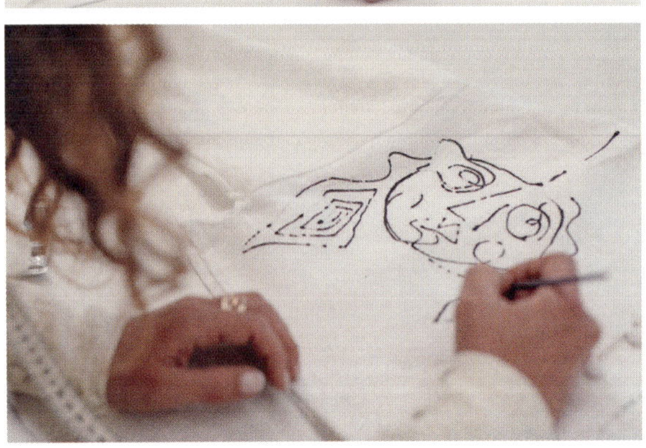

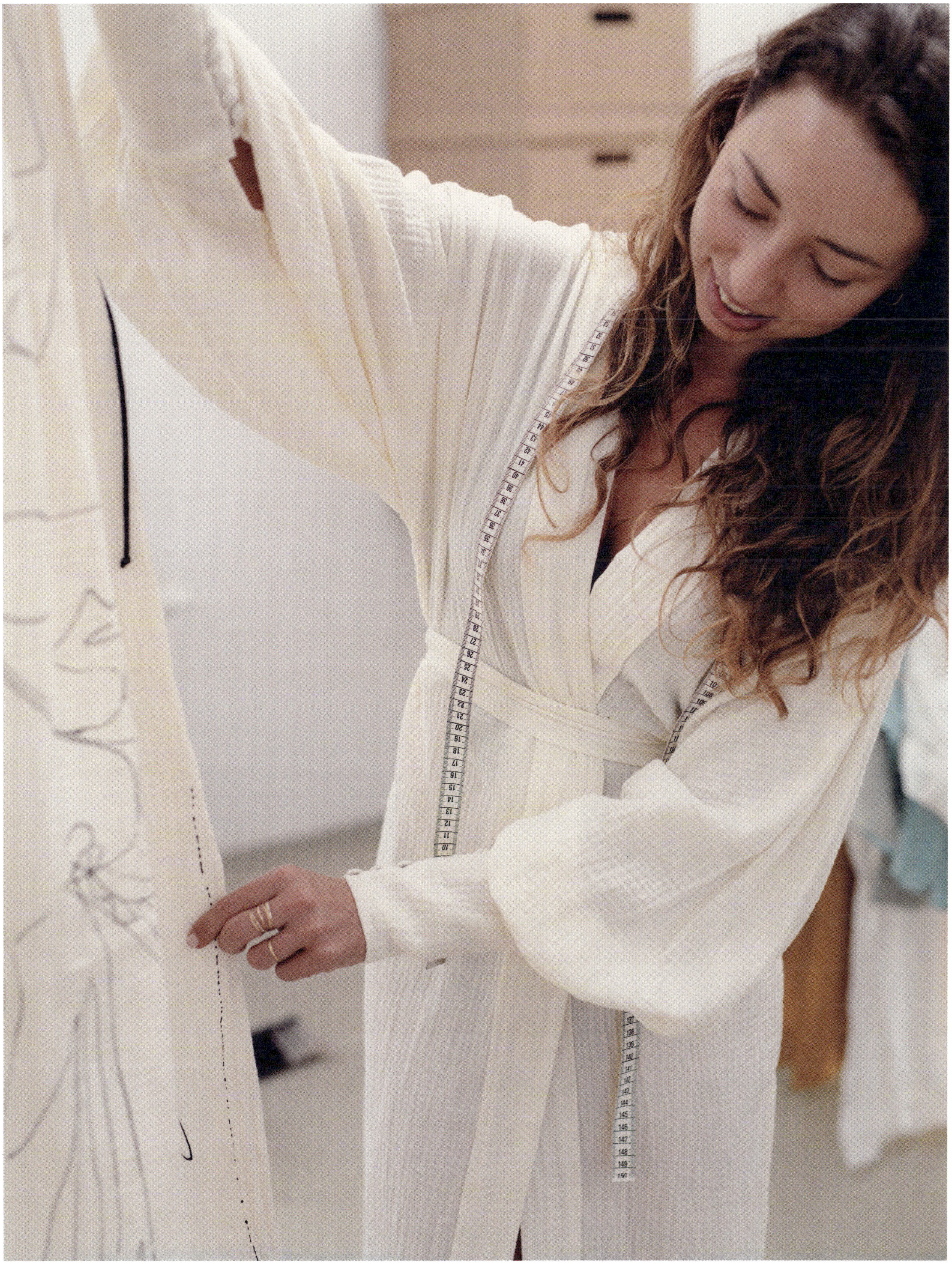

SAN LORENZO
figtree-collection.com

FIGTREE COLLECTION

BOTANICALLY-DYED SILK & NATURE-BASED FASHION

Alba Esteva hand-prints her silk kimonos with dyes that she makes from the natural resources around her. 'I'm self-taught, and have learnt a lot about wildflowers. Through experimentation I've come to know which ones work best.' She also experiments with soil. 'The earth of Ibiza is very colourful', she notes.

First, Alba dyes the silk in a base colour and then overlays a pattern using the bundle-dyeing technique (whereby petals are laid over the silk, which is then rolled tightly into a bundle and steamed, so that the petal pigments stain the material). 'I like playing with abstract forms and textures', she says. 'I don't use the shape of a leaf. I pulverize the leaf and then work with the texture it gives me.' This technique means that each item is unique.

As well as kimonos, Alba makes cushion covers and scarves. Her business, Figtree Collection, started because of Ibiza, she says. Her first visit to the island was in the early 2010s. Airport staff were on strike, so she took the ferry, arriving early one winter's morning. 'I was fascinated by the island's light and beauty', she recalls. She wanted to find a way to stay, and initially commuted regularly from Barcelona, where she worked as an art director in a marketing agency. She explains: 'I already knew that I wanted to do something for myself and that I wanted to change my lifestyle. Ibiza inspired me a lot – its light, nature, this feeling of being free, and finding inspiration in every corner.'

Catalan-born, Alba enjoyed creating art from an early age, and went on to study art (at the Universidad de Barcelona), art direction (Universitat Ramon Llull) and fashion (Escola de la Dona, Barcelona). Even while she was working, she made artworks for herself and her friends. 'Textile art was always my favourite, the best medium with which to express myself.'

Alba sources her silk from factories in Italy that supply big fashion houses, scouring them for remnants and offcuts. She likes the versatility of a kimono, since it can be worn on different occasions and at different times of the day. She also adores the feeling of being embraced by silk and nature.

As well as her dyed-silk collection, Alba designs crocheted and knitted fashion items.

Designing and dyeing take place at home, a small house in the countryside, not far from Santa Gertrudis. 'The owner has "adopted" me, and she's now my Ibiza mother', says Alba. She employs a number of local seamstresses, who work from home.

As well as selling online, Alba has produced a special artichoke-themed collection for Juntos House, a restaurant with an organic farm and concept store in San Mateo (pp. 118–23).

Alba would like to grow Figtree Collection, increase production and eventually work with more materials. But at the same time, she says, 'I want to stay happy with what I do.' ***CD***

Alba Esteva moved from Catalonia to Ibiza in a quest to change her lifestyle. Using her artistic skills and qualifications, she set up Figtree Collection in the country cottage she rents from her 'Ibiza mother'.

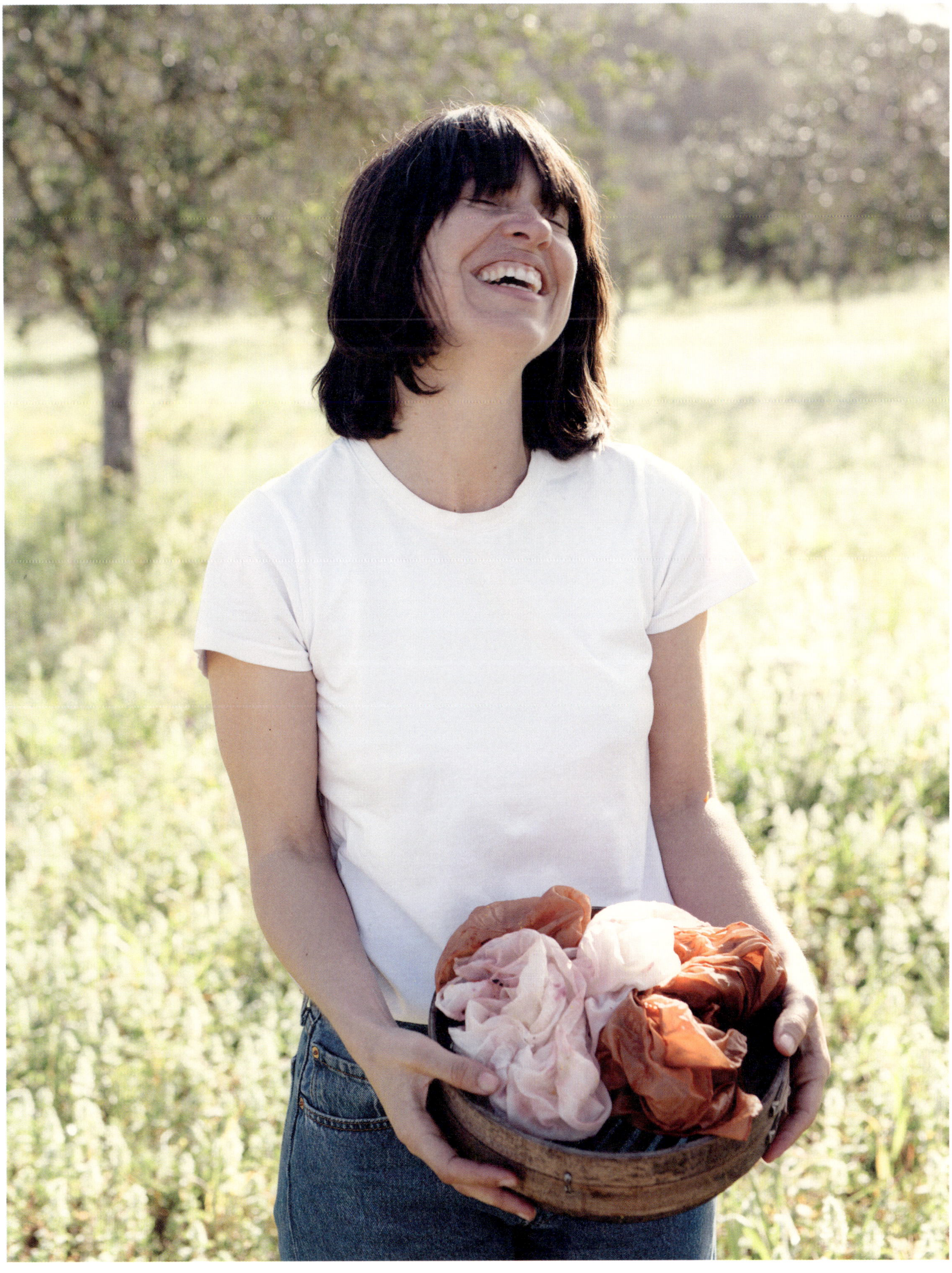

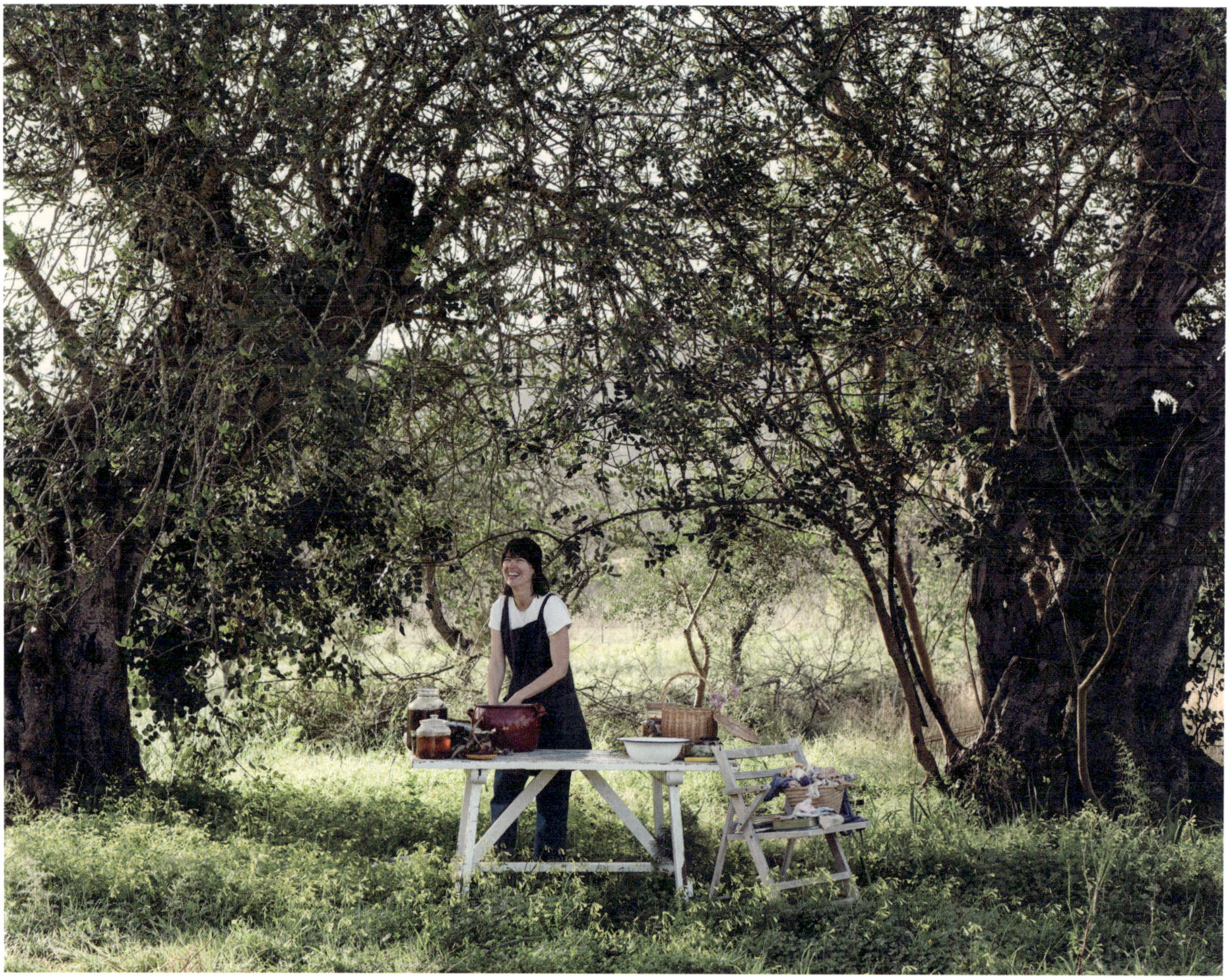

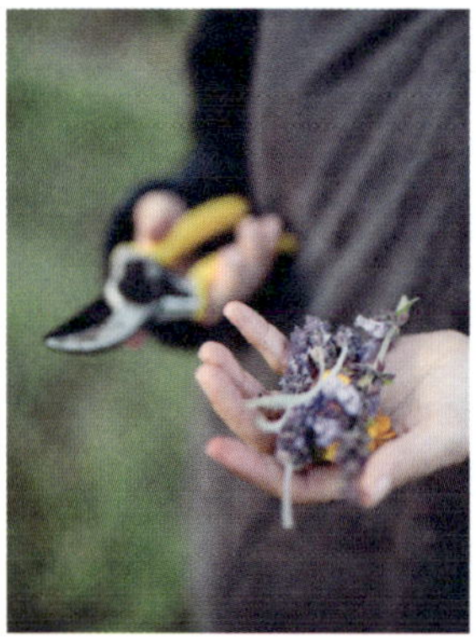

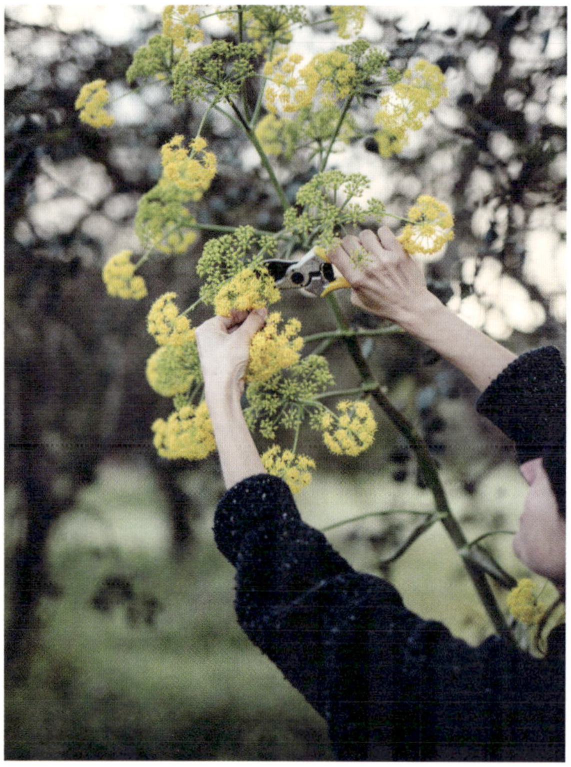

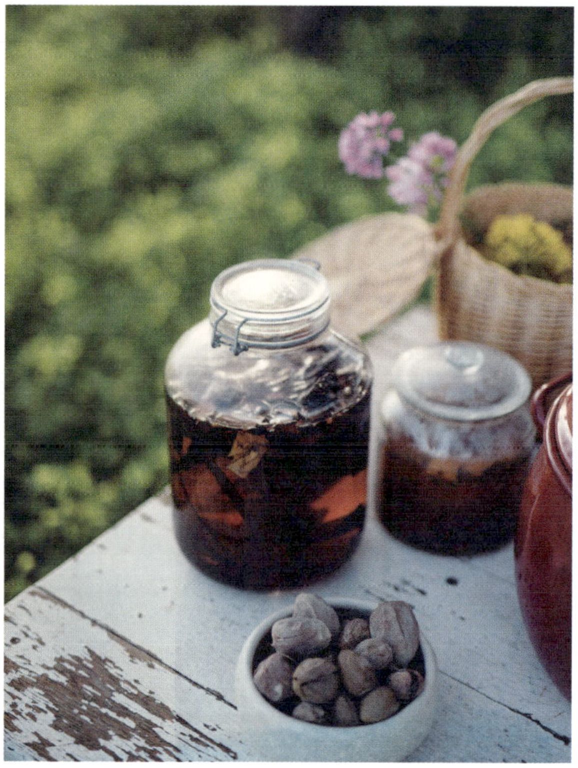

For the bundle-dyeing method, Alba sources wildflowers from her surroundings and from The Floral Studio (pp. 142–49). Her use of this technique means that each item is unique.

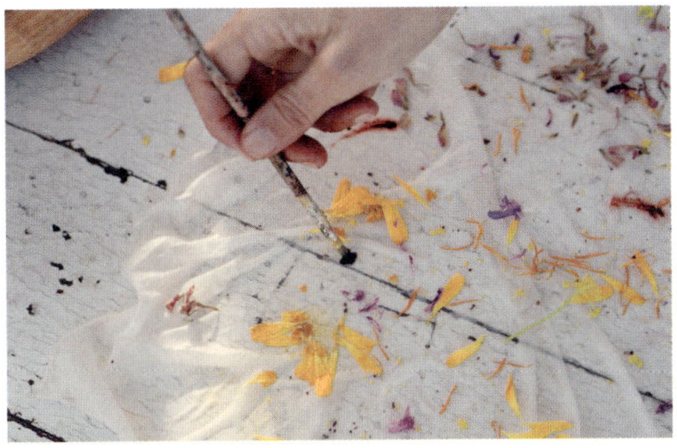

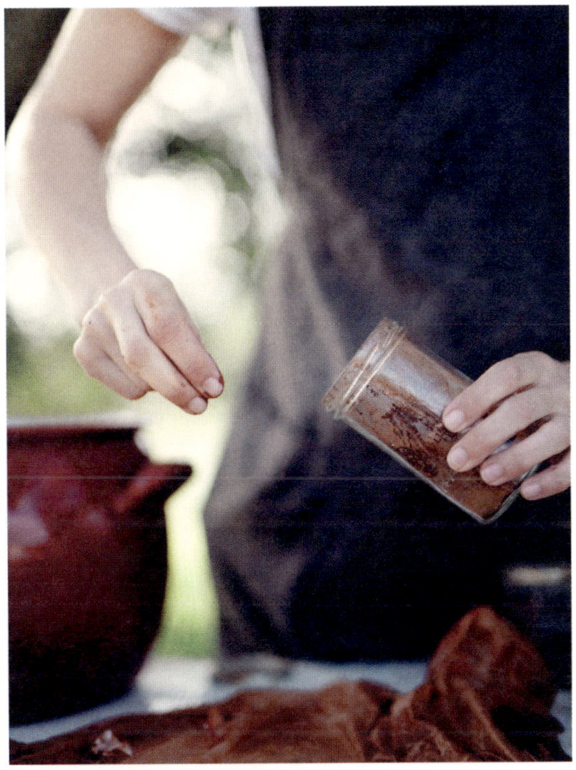

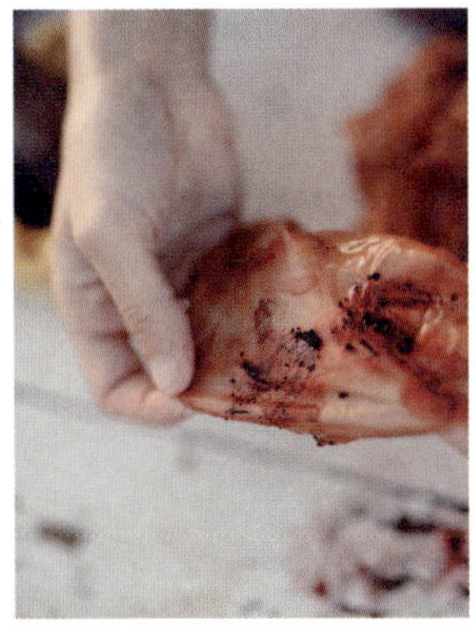

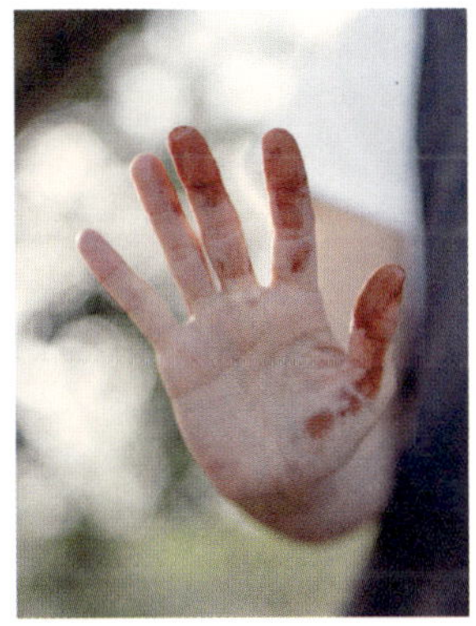

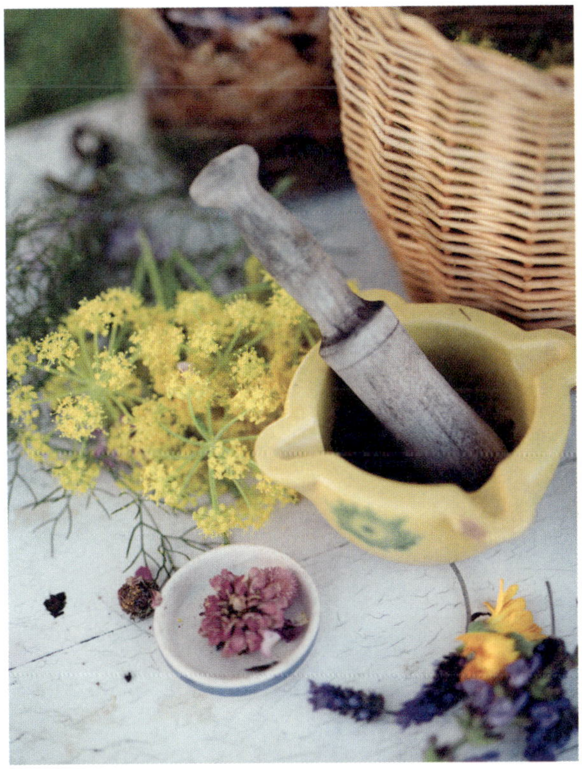

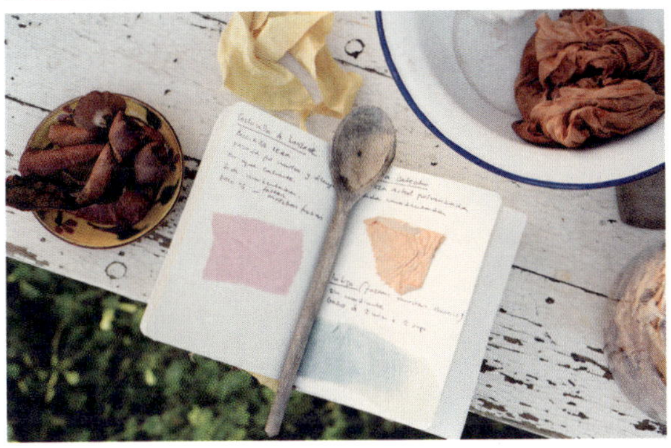

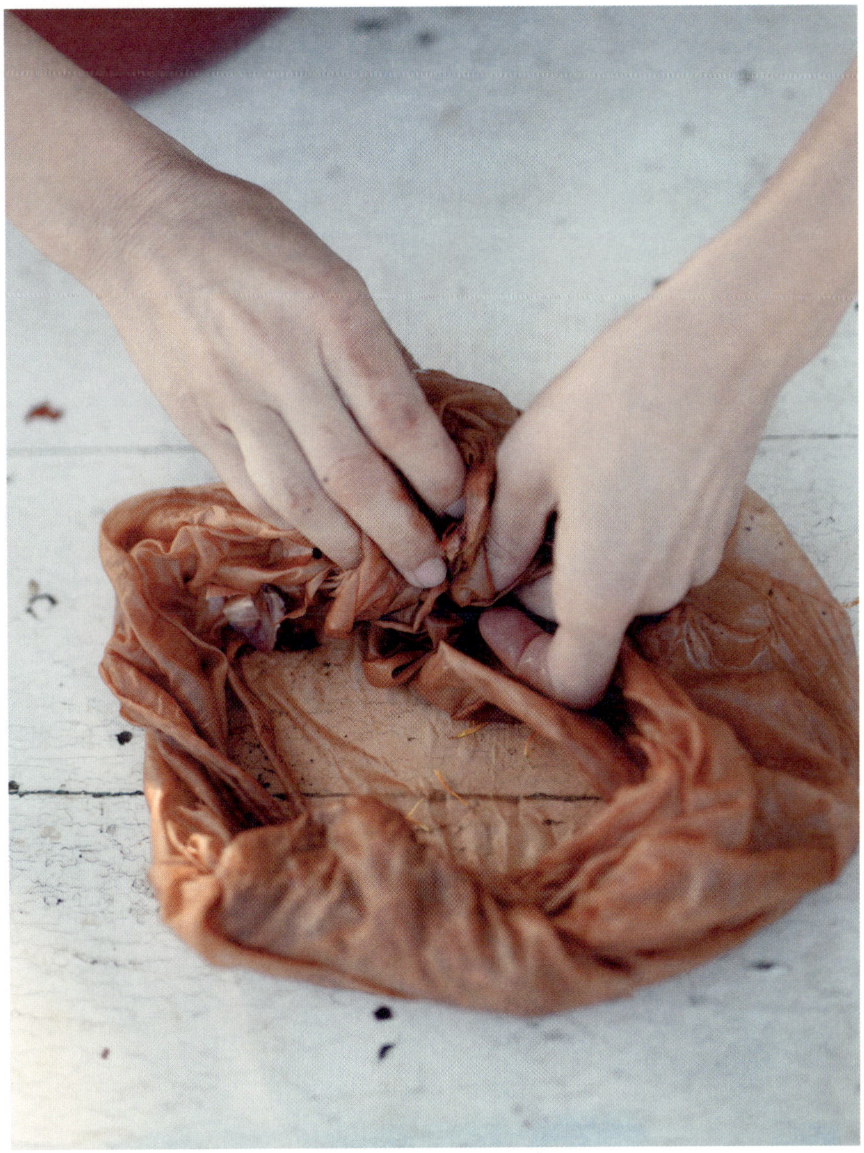

Alba records all her experiments with different natural ingredients in her notebooks. To create the silk kimonos, she starts by applying a base colour and then adds patterns using the petals.

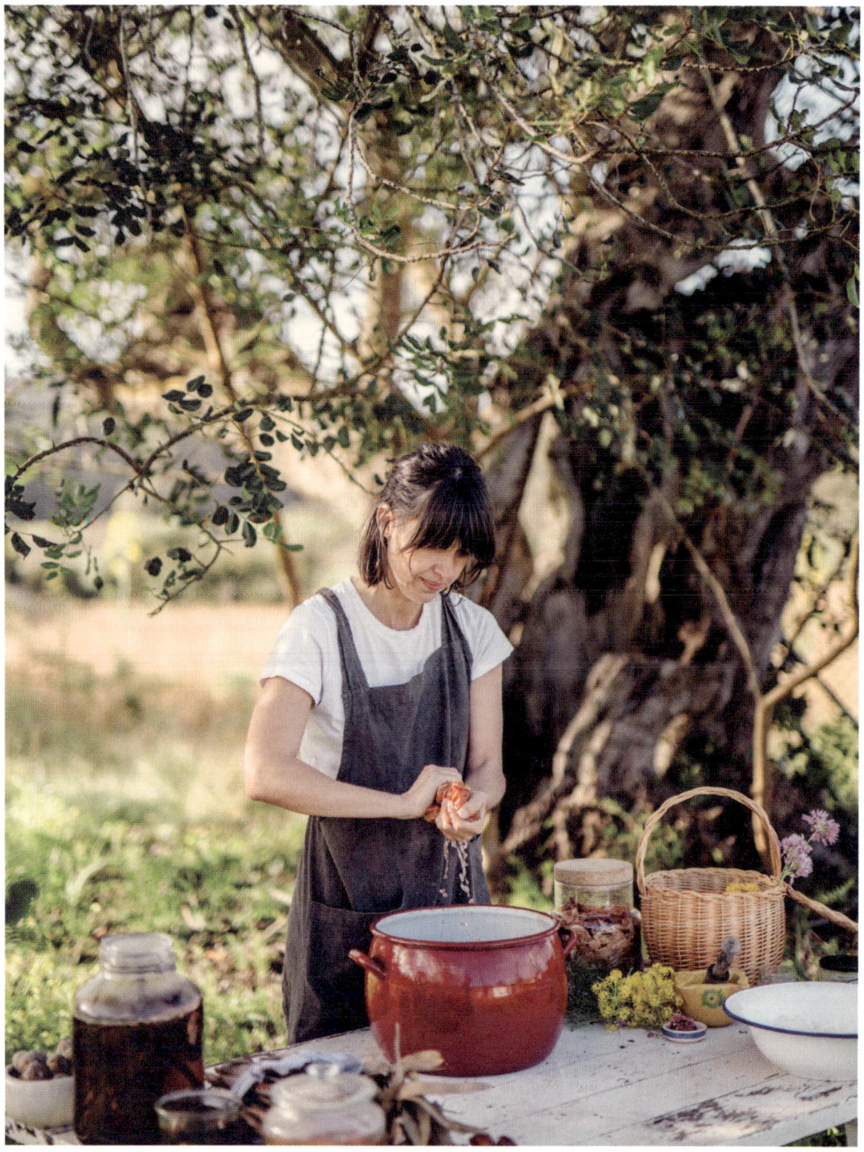

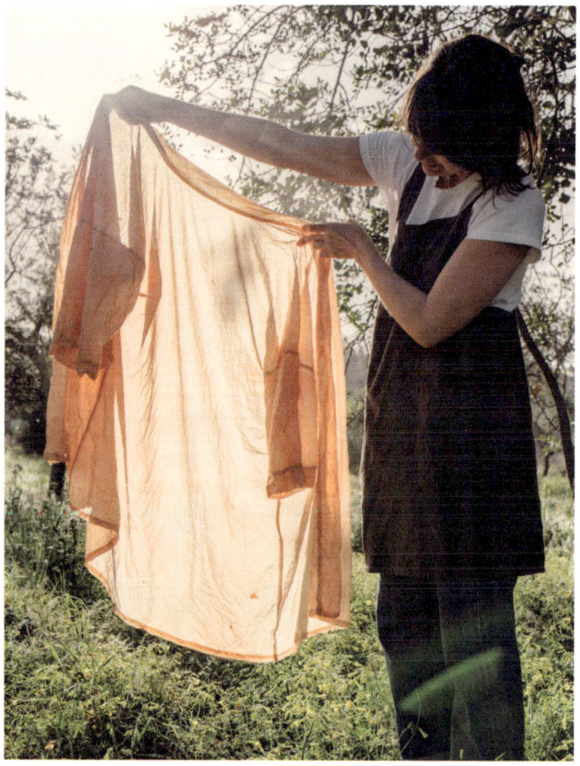

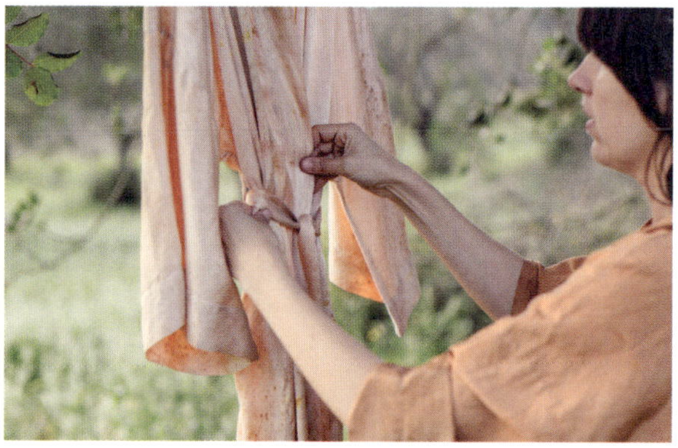

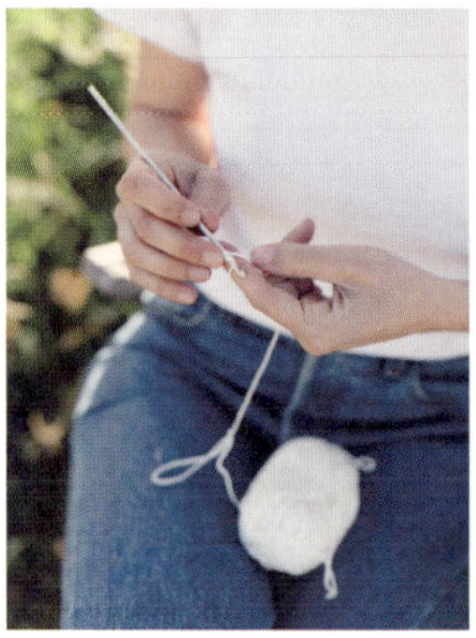

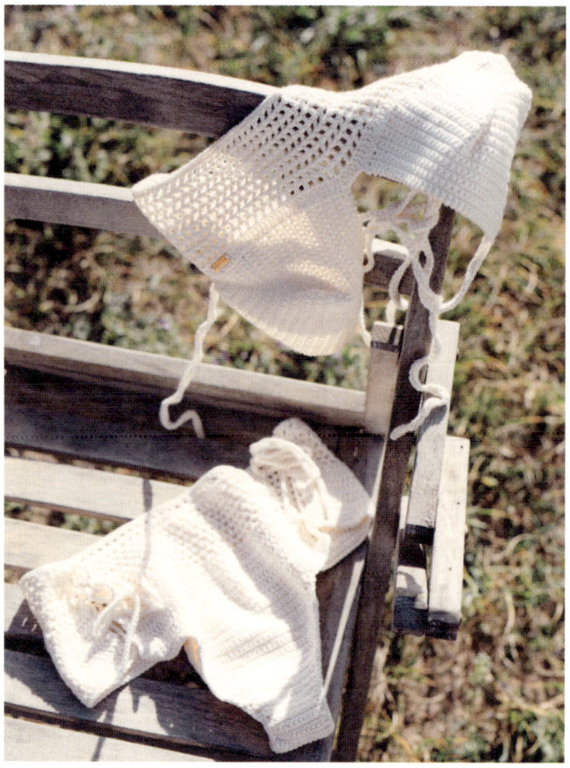

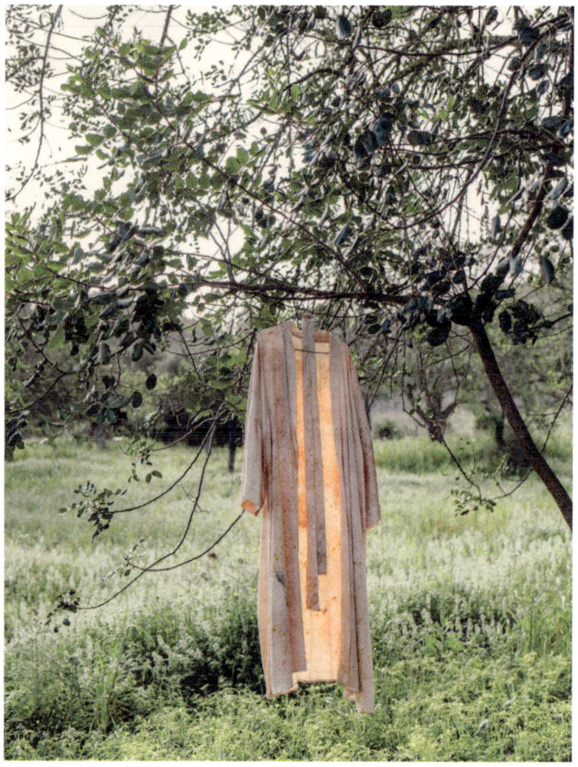

Figtree Collection's range of handmade crochet swimwear is very labour-intensive, so some of the work is carried out by freelance craftswomen in Barcelona.

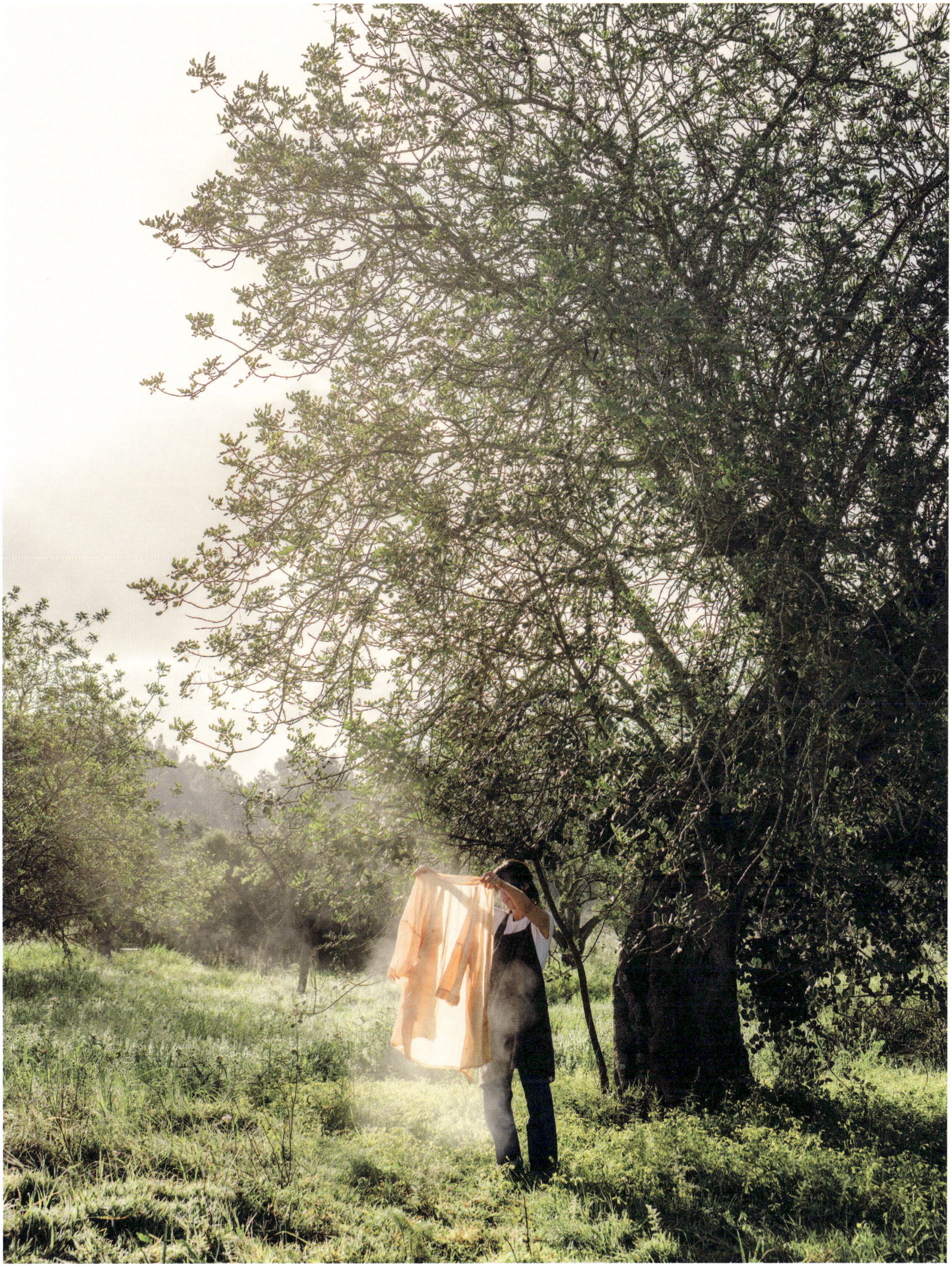

SAN MIGUEL
bomeibiza.com

BOMÉ

LEATHER GOODS

Dario and Valeria Bomé arrived in Ibiza in 1975 after a long overland journey by car from Italy to India and Nepal. In Kathmandu they had been inspired by the quality of the handicrafts on sale and had fallen for the dream of an alternative lifestyle, influenced by the hippy ideals of beauty, freedom and love.

'We wanted to live on an island and we were looking for "our island"', Dario says. 'Ibiza was very special for our generation. Lots of our friends had told us about it. And with its stunning countryside and its welcoming atmosphere, Ibiza had everything.'

A self-taught artisan, Dario made leather goods that the couple sold at Ibiza's first hippy street market, Punta Arabí. When Valeria helped to set up Las Dalias market in the mid-1980s, their stall moved there.

The couple, who were both originally from northern Italy, opened their own boutique in 1991. It is in a beautiful old house in the village of San Miguel, in the north of the island. 'Our shop isn't in a tourist hub, and most of our customers are residents or own a house here, and have known us for years', Dario explains. In addition, many of the celebrities who visit the island come to the shop: 'That's normal in Ibiza.'

Dario draws inspiration from his environment. 'To have time and a simple life is possible in Ibiza, and this allows you to be creative', he says. He is also inspired by the island's natural light.

The couple's daughter, Paloma, was born and raised on the island. When she was seventeen, she left to continue with her studies and spent seventeen years on the mainland. She achieved a degree in fine arts and textiles in Madrid, and then worked in Barcelona in costume design for cinema and theatre. Paloma explains: 'During this period, I realized that I missed nature and that the city was taking more from me than it was giving, and was draining my energy. And I realized that I could add value to my parents' business because it was so related to what I was doing with costumes and textiles.' So she came back to the island to join the family enterprise.

The leather goods are made by father and daughter in their large workshop, which is just 20 metres from the boutique. 'I don't want to make something that sells as a holiday souvenir. I want to create long-lasting products of value', Dario says. He describes his wife as the soul of the retail operation: 'She has very good taste, and styles the shop and advises us on our creative work.'

Bomé's most iconic item is the backpack. Dario has made it in countless different finishes, decorating it with accessories from India. Another popular item is the simple yet functional 'no buckle' belt, which has no metal elements.

The clothing, jewellery and home accessories are designed in and brought from India. 'We've worked with the same families there for decades, and we've helped to promote their work abroad', Valeria explains. 'Many of our producers are now selling worldwide.'

Alongside maintaining Bomé's relationship with its producers in India, Paloma wants to start working with artisans' communities in South America, Africa and Europe.

'Spain has been very generous to us', remarks Dario. The Bomés are members of Ibiza's Asociación de Artesanos, and Dario is a certified *maestro artesano*. 'I feel I've been better supported here than I would have been elsewhere', he claims. ***CD***

Valeria and Dario Bomé founded the family-owned boutique and atelier for fine leather goods in the village of San Miguel. Their daughter, Paloma Bomé, is a skilled artisan and creates the products with Dario.

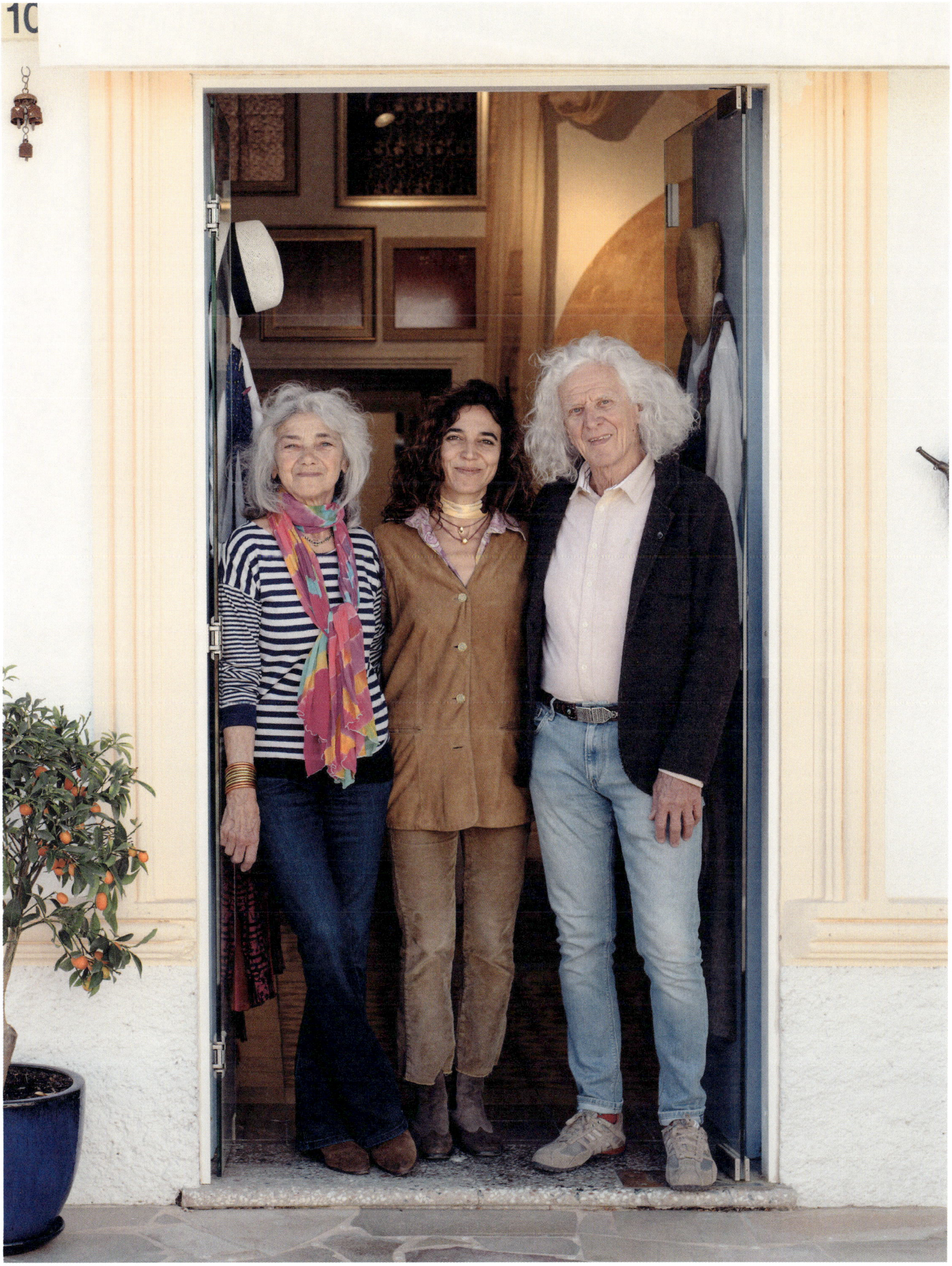
10

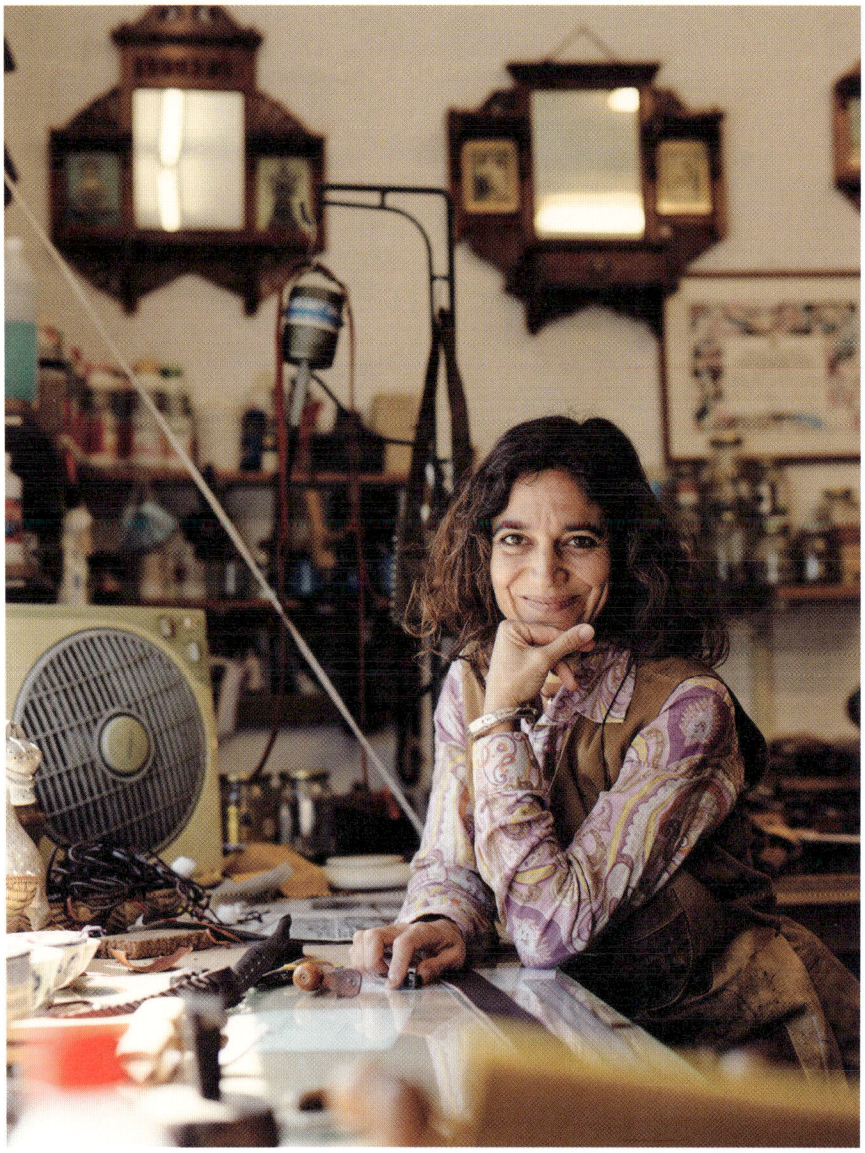

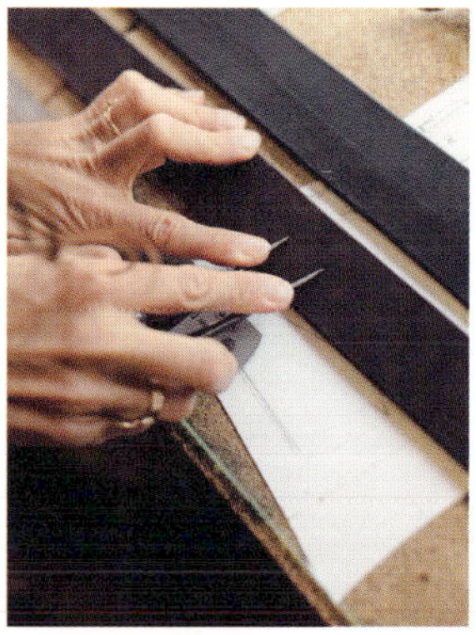

The atelier is full of leather-crafting tools and materials. The artistry and attention to detail that go into each piece are a testament to the family's dedication to the craft.

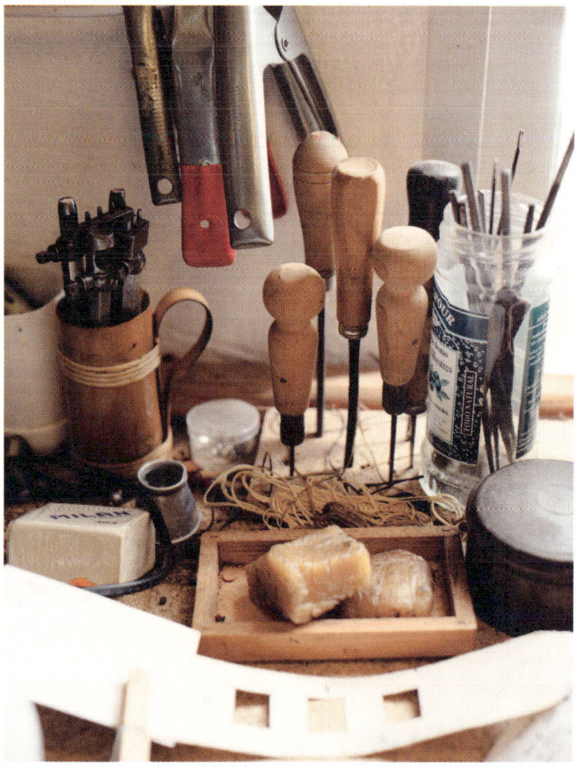

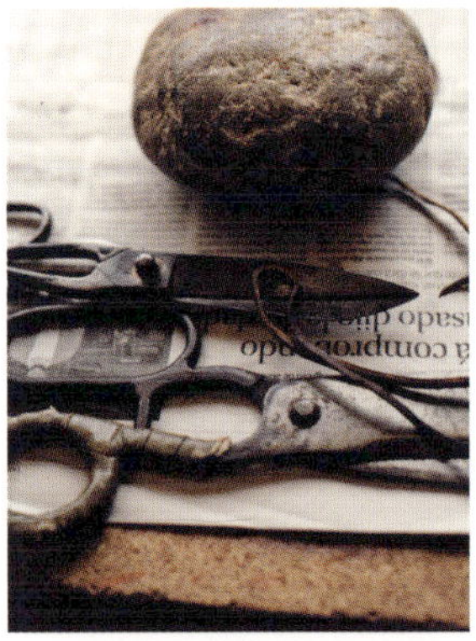

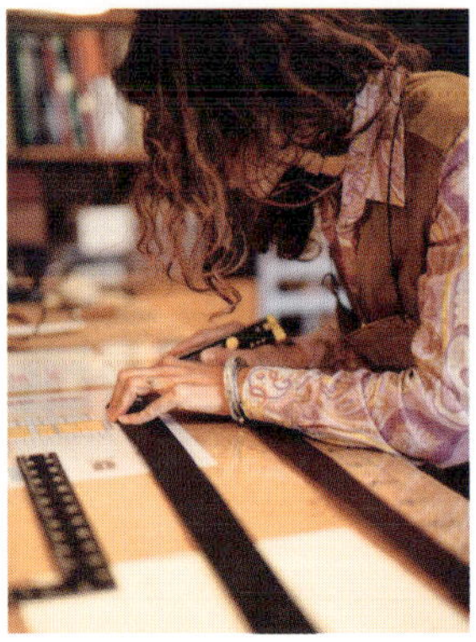

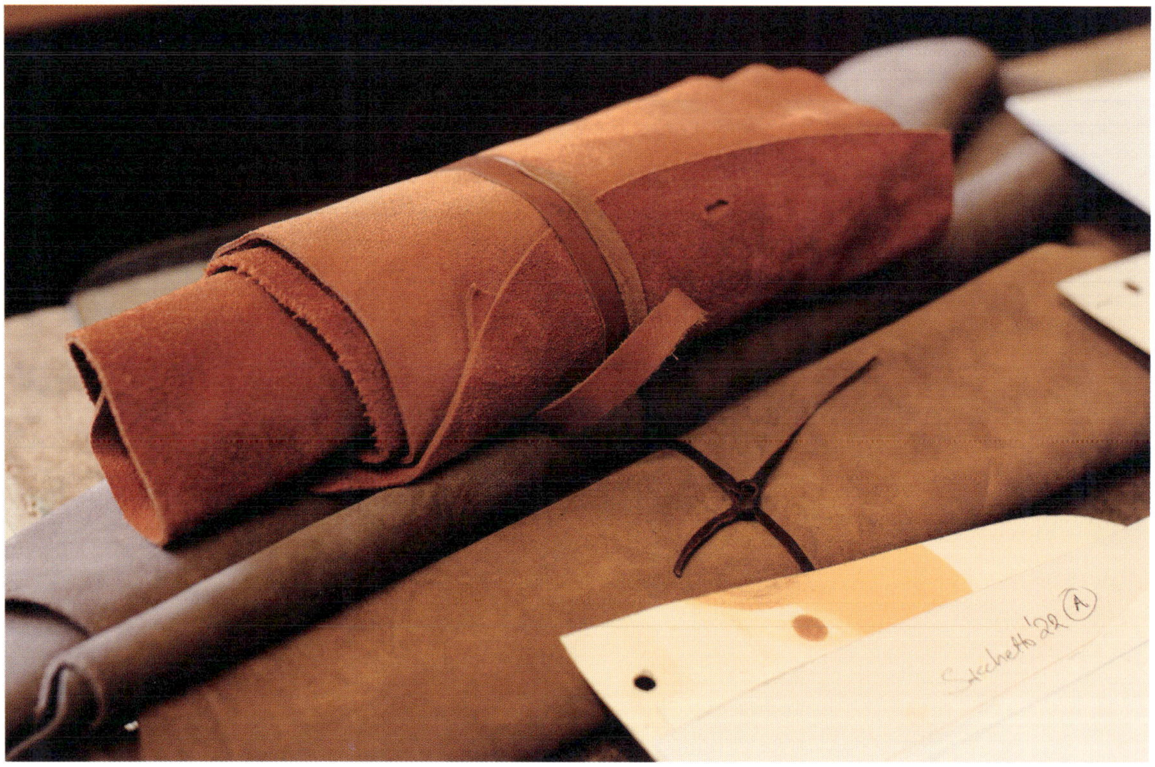

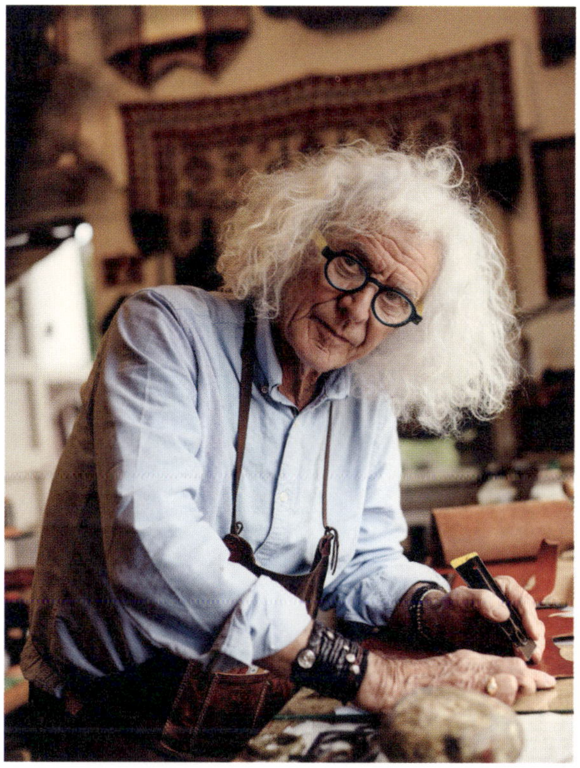

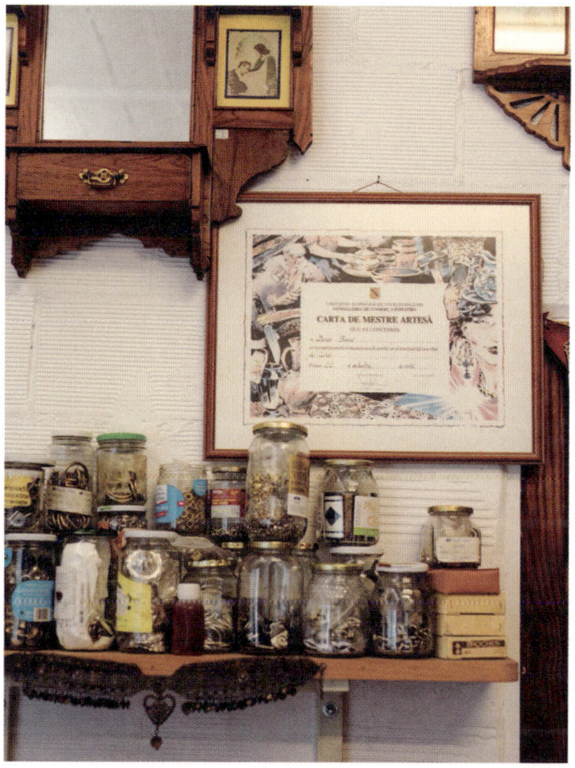

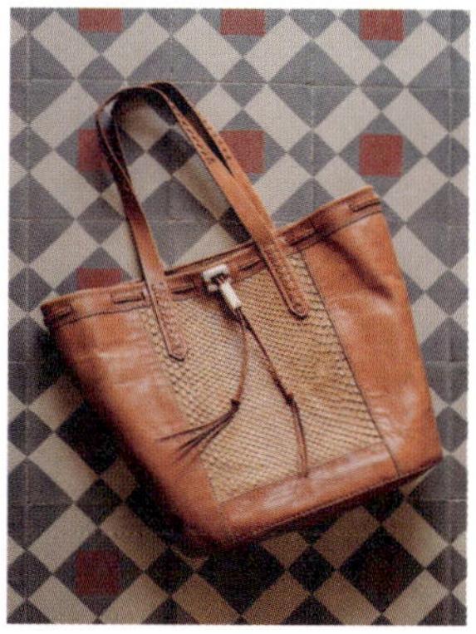

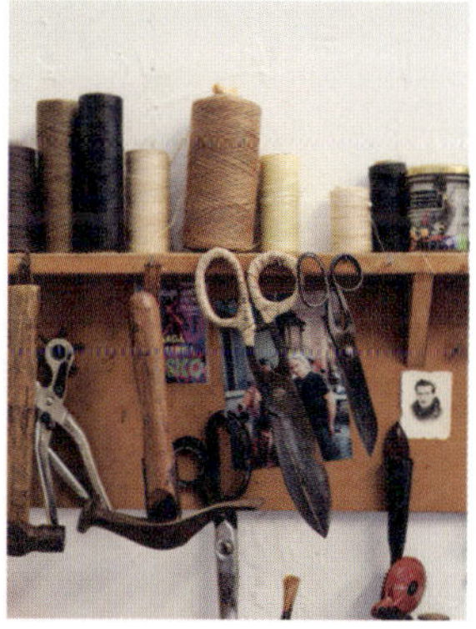

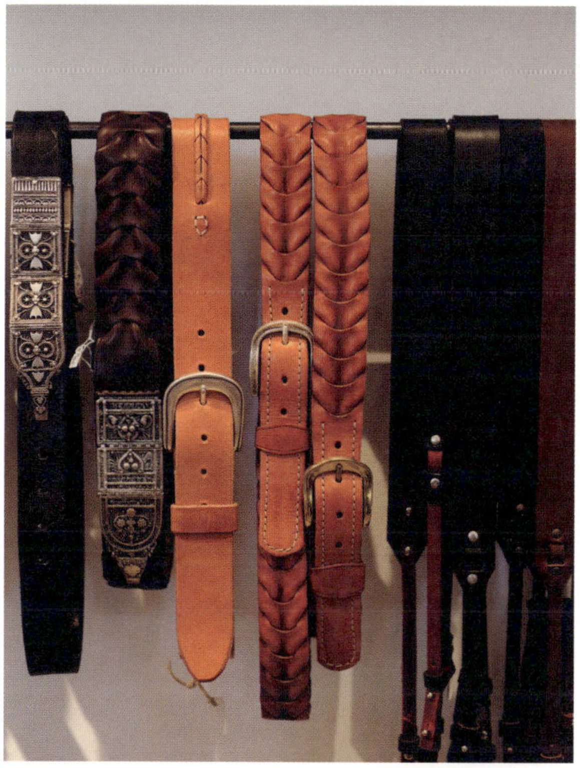

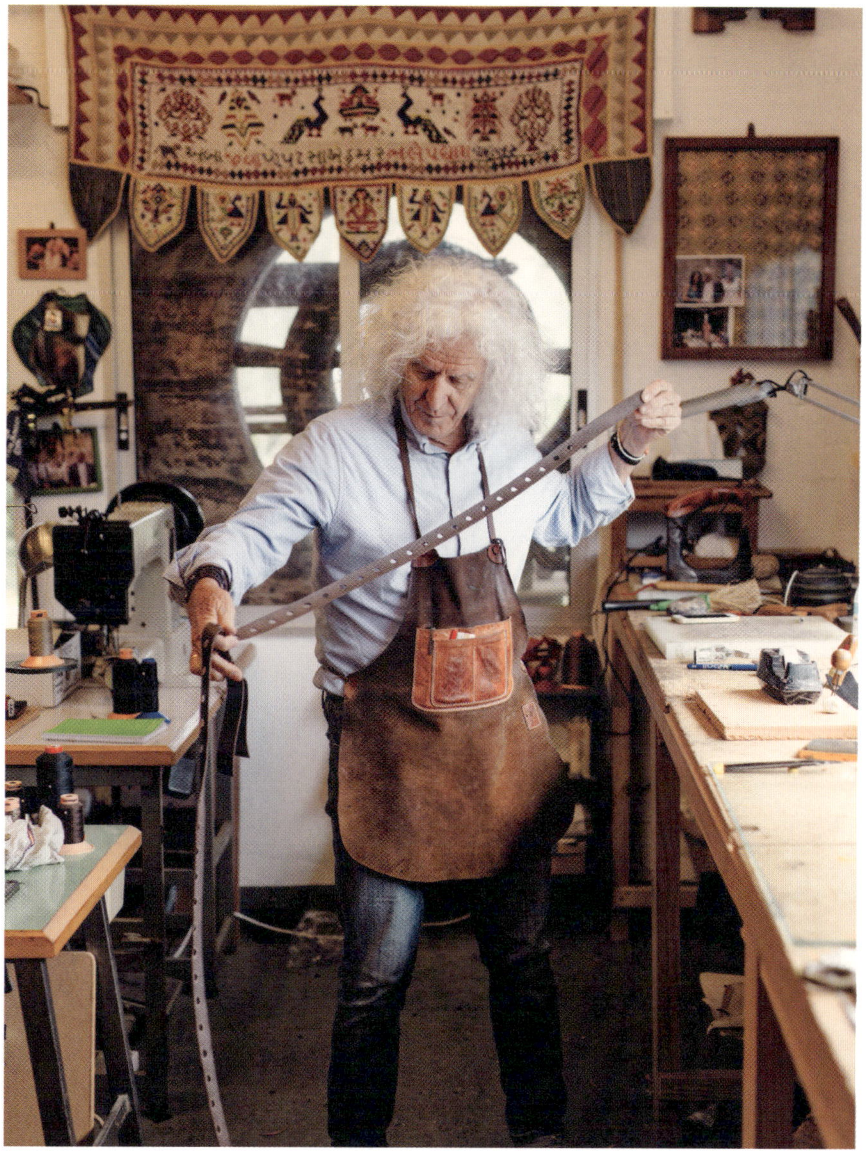

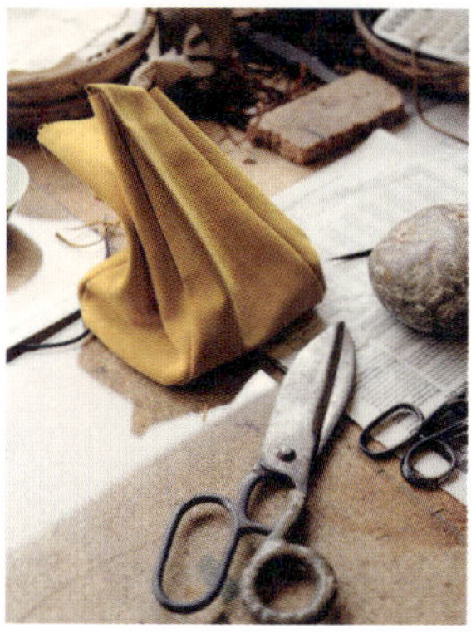

Dario taught himself how to work with leather. Bomé's most popular items are leather belts.

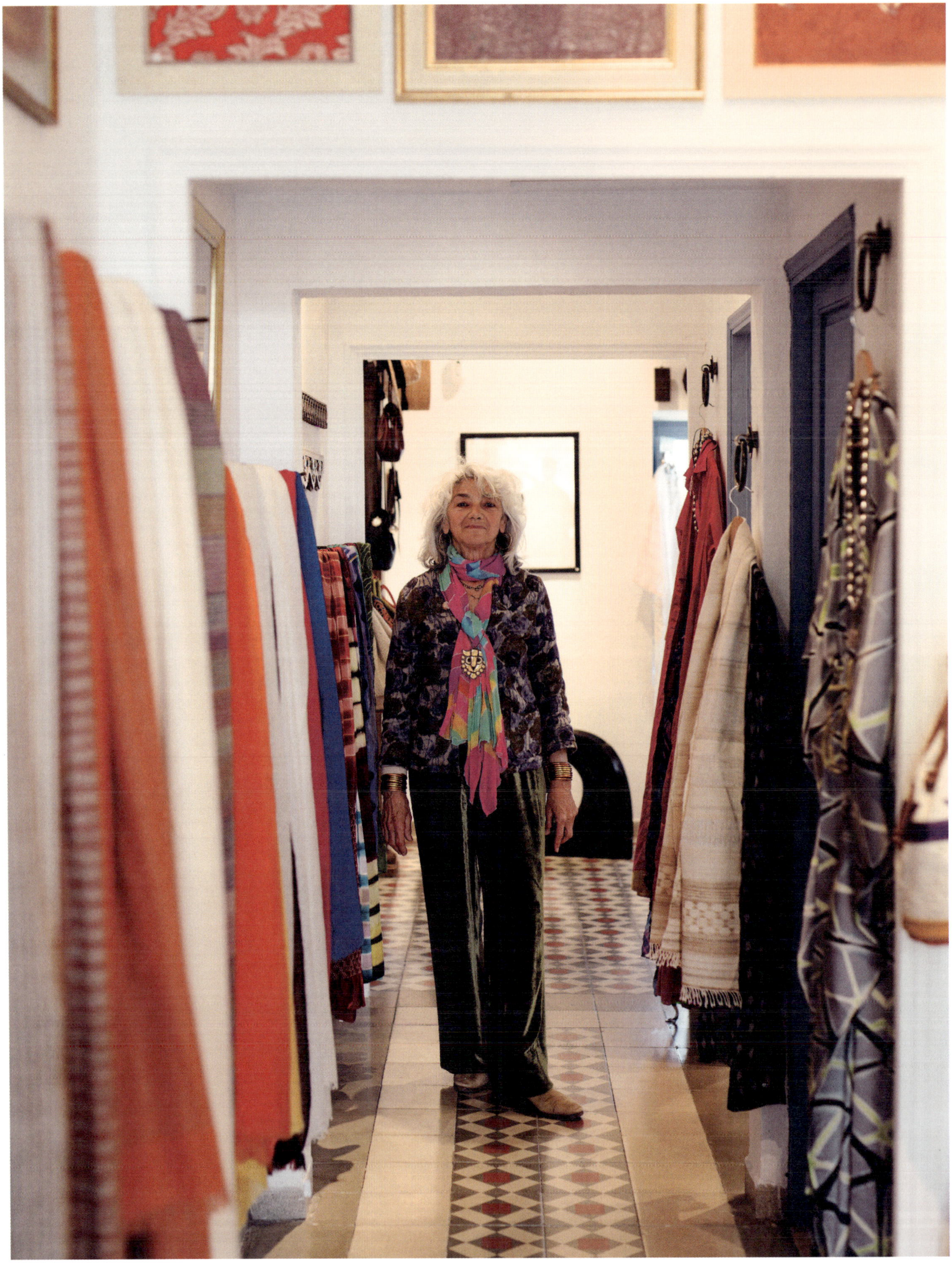

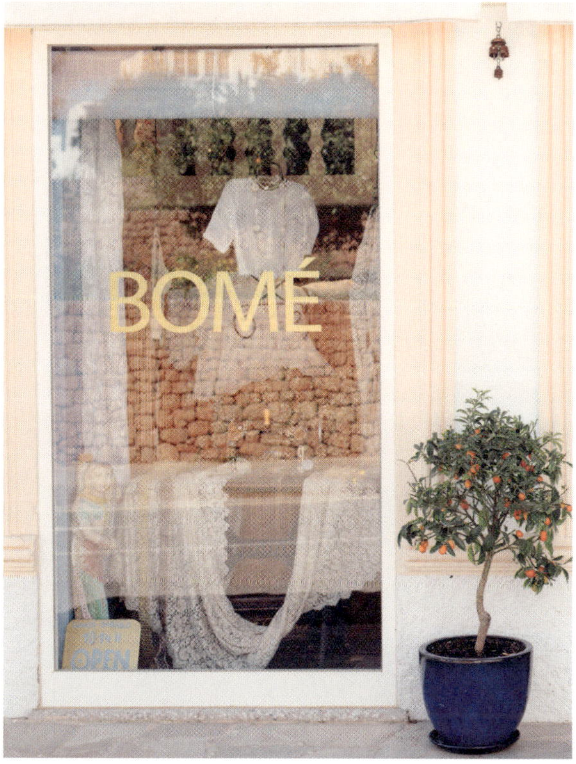

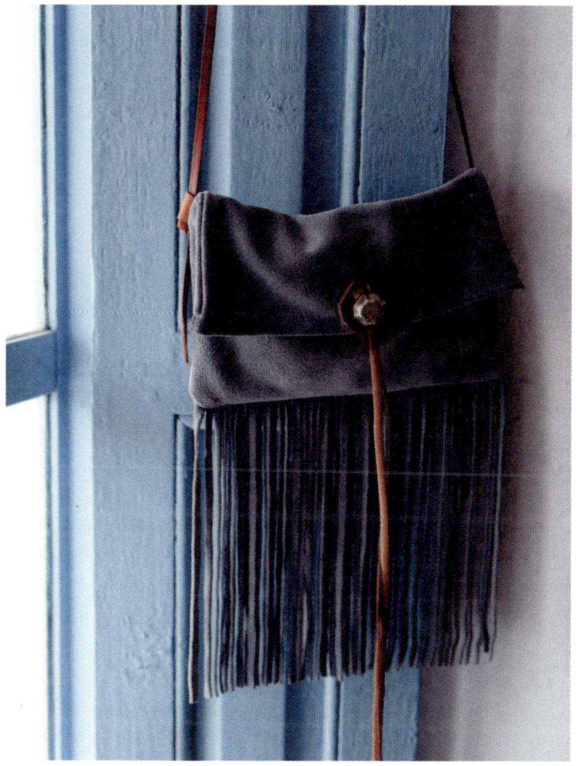

Valeria is responsible for the retail operation, including styling the boutique, which stocks cashmere shawls and other items from India alongside Dario and Paloma's leather goods.

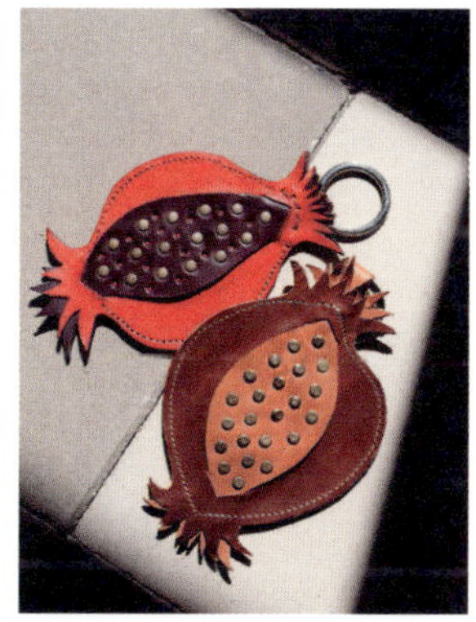

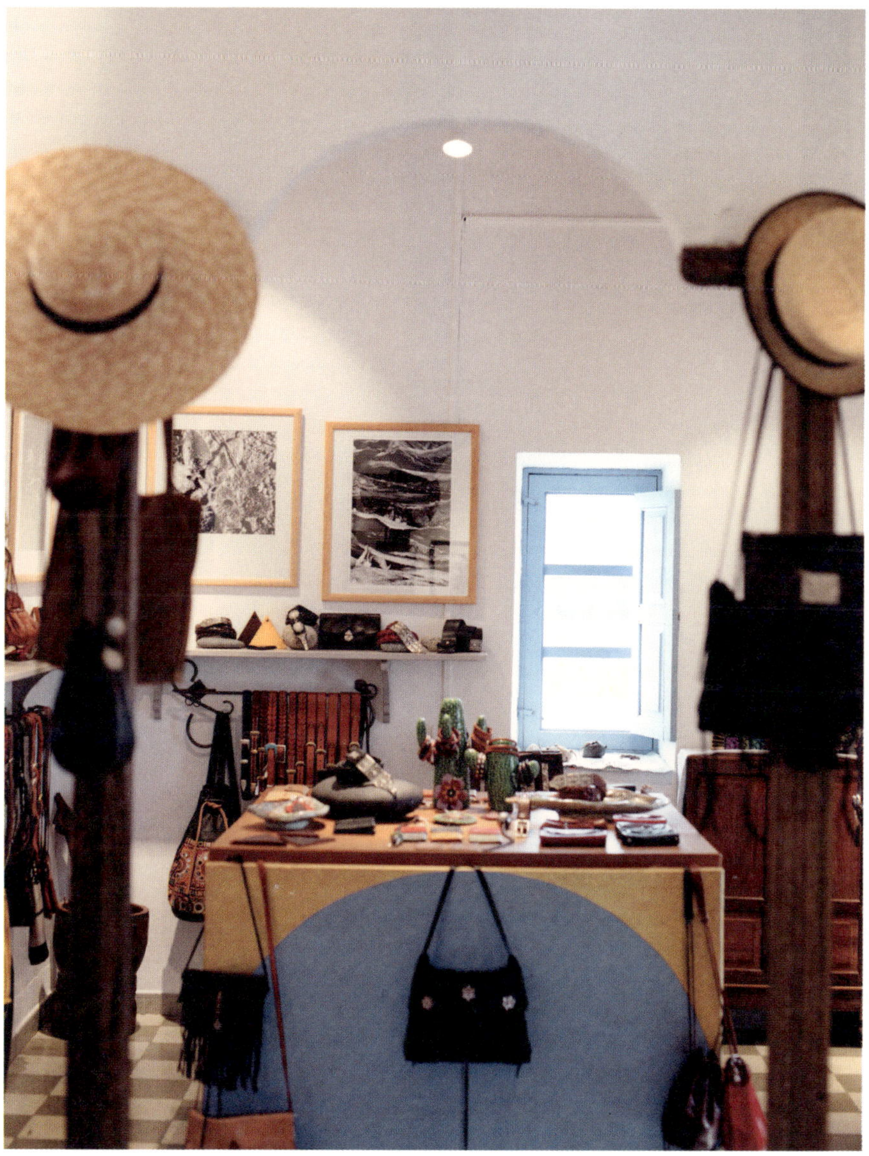

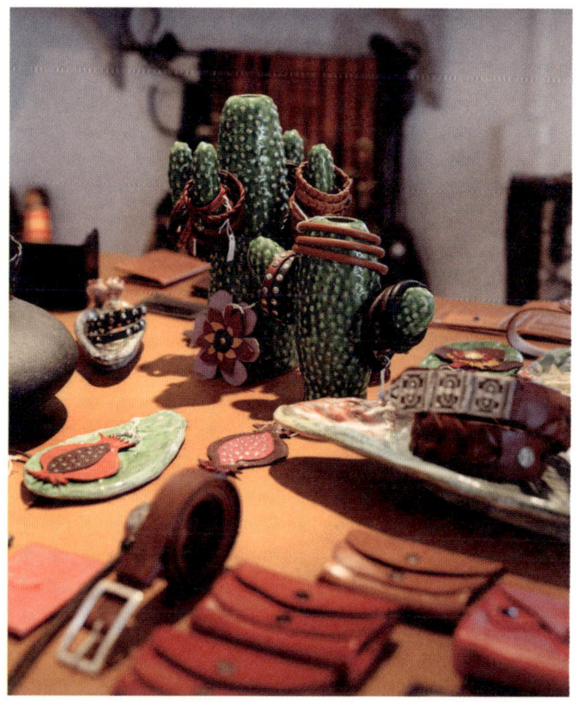

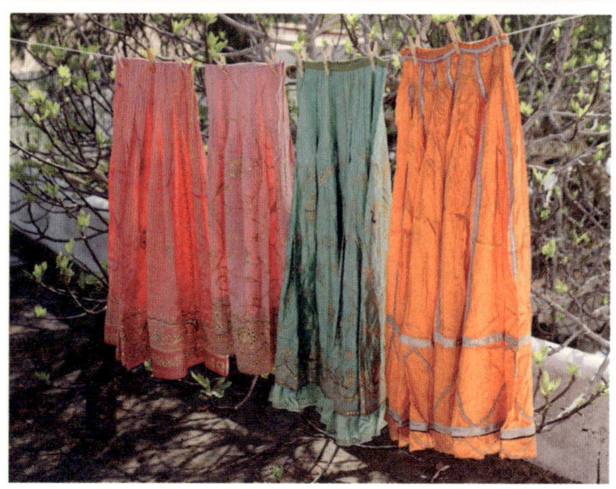

SAN ANTONIO
espardenyesdeibiza.com

ESPARDENYES TORRES

TRADITIONAL HANDMADE SHOES

Before there were machines to make shoes and shops to buy them in, Ibicencos made their own *espardenyes* at home. Ibiza's traditional espadrille-style shoes have uppers of woven yarn rather than canvas, which is more typical elsewhere in Spain.

When the Ibizan government (Consell Insular d'Eivissa) organized classes on making *espardenyes*, Patricia (Patry) Monjo's mother-in-law signed up. She started making the shoes for family and friends, but soon could not cope with the growing demand. She passed the technique on to her daughter-in-law, and in 2016 the Consell d'Eivissa invited them to display their creations at a fair for artisans in Paris. 'We showed the traditional shoe, but also our own version, which featured colourful details like cords and ribbons', Patry recalls.

The feedback was so positive that the duo went into business together, and that same year – 2016 – they were invited to join Adlib Ibiza, an umbrella brand that promotes Ibiza's craftspeople. They first exhibited with Adlib in 2017, in Madrid, and there they presented their debut collection.

Patry, who was born on the island and is now the sole owner of the company, operates from her home in San Antonio, storing her materials in a small warehouse nearby. She has breathed new life into *espardenyes* by incorporating coloured yarn and accessories such as flowers, and by introducing new types of sole, such as wedges.

It takes Patry around four hours to make a pair of *espardenyes*. First she makes the *cordelli*, the yarn that is plaited to form the upper part of the shoe. It is made from pitera, a type of agave that is common on the island. She grates the pitera to extract its fibres – a difficult process on account of the sap being toxic. The sole of the shoe is traditionally formed from a plaited rope made of esparto, a native grass.

Patry works on her own most of the time, but enlists the help of her parents and two local women if there are lots of orders. 'Our main season is the summer', she explains. 'We sell very few pairs in winter.' In total, Espardenyes Torres produces around 200 pairs a year. Patry's goal is to come up with more designs in an effort to further increase sales.

As well as selling around the world – including to South Korea, Australia and Chile – through her website, Patry has a stall at San José arts and crafts market. Some shoes are bought to be displayed in exhibitions or as decoration and will not be worn.

In 2020 and again in 2021, Patry's efforts received a boost when the company's name was mentioned in the press in connection with Spanish royalty: Queen Letizia was photographed wearing Espardenyes Torres.

Nowadays Patry passes on her skills to others by teaching classes in how to make *espardenyes* in the village of San José. ***CD***

Patry Monjo has perfected the traditional, highly labour-intensive skills required to make Ibiza's espadrille-style shoe, the espardenya*, while giving it a contemporary twist.*

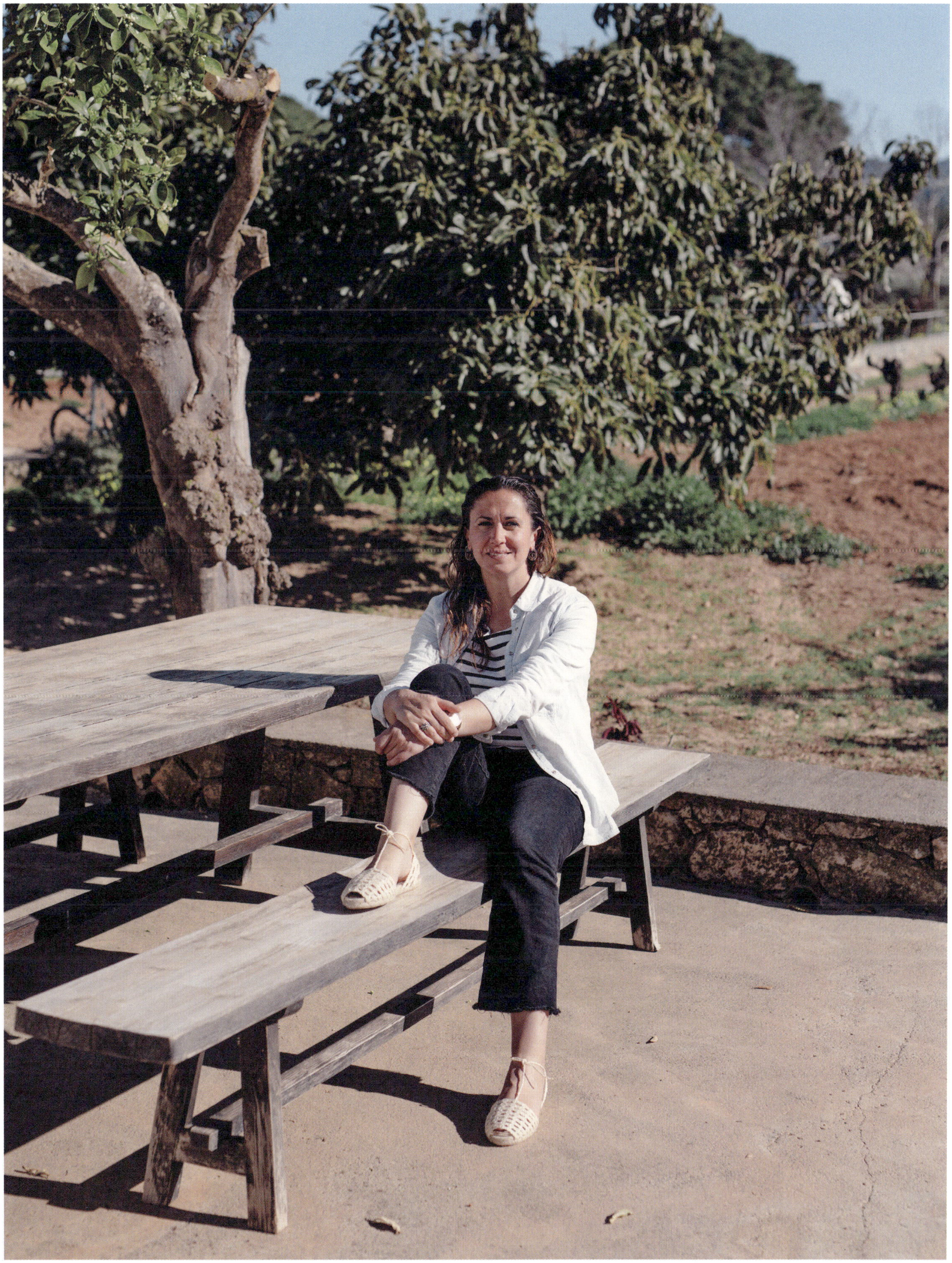

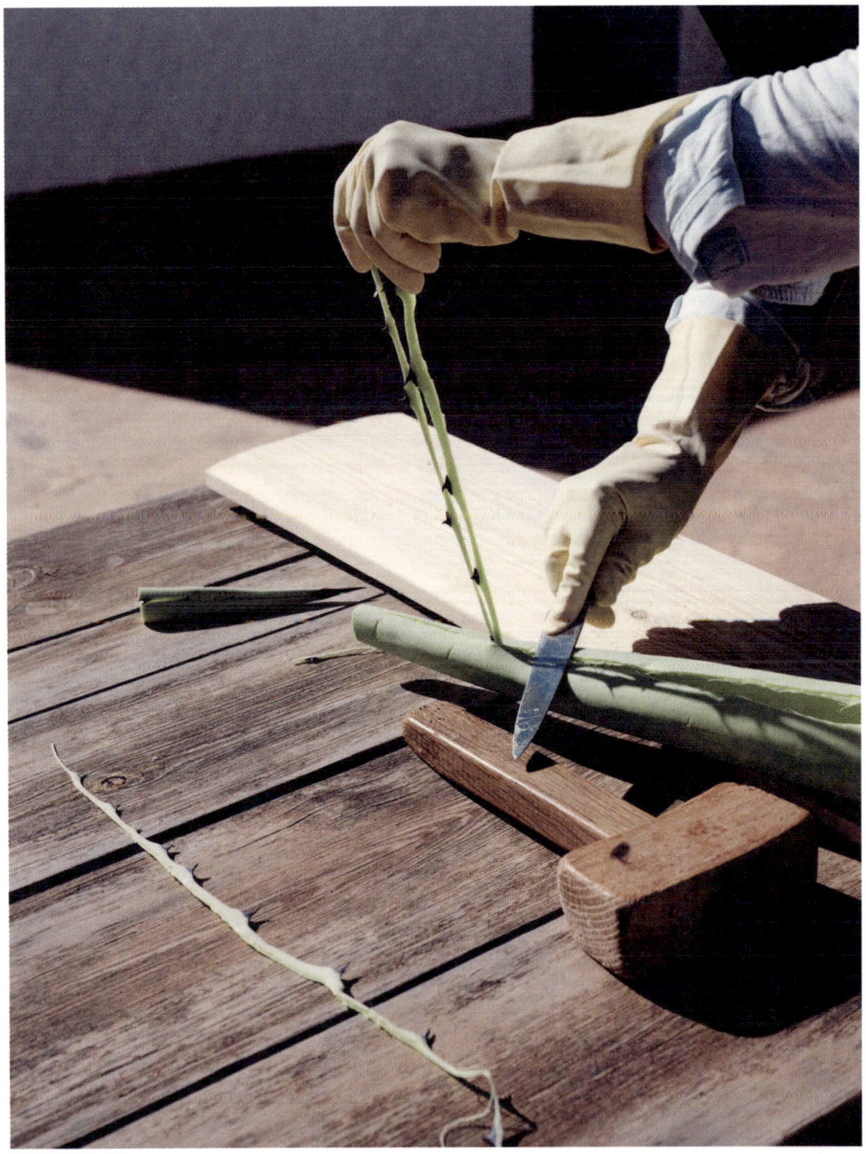

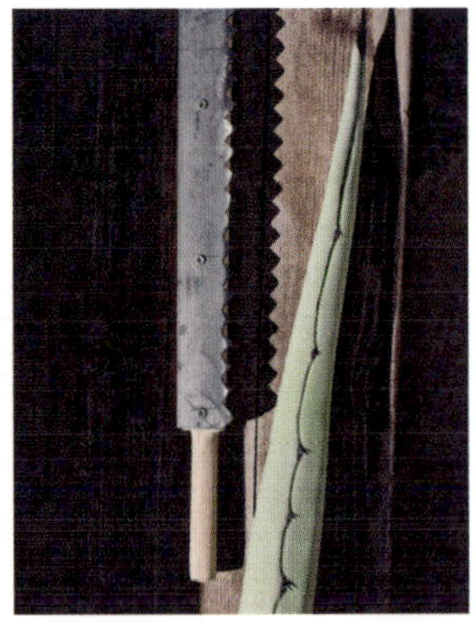

The local agave plant, pitera, is traditionally used for the shoe uppers. It is grated and the fibres dried before being woven. Caution is required because the sap irritates the skin.

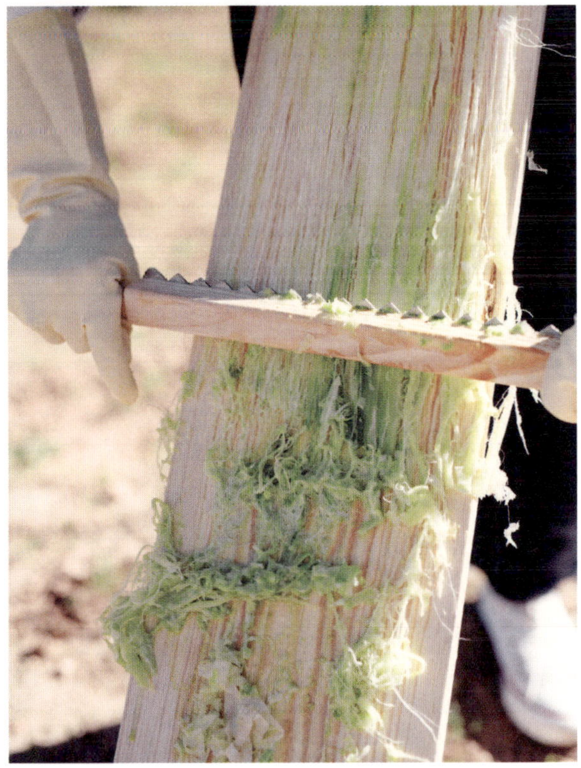

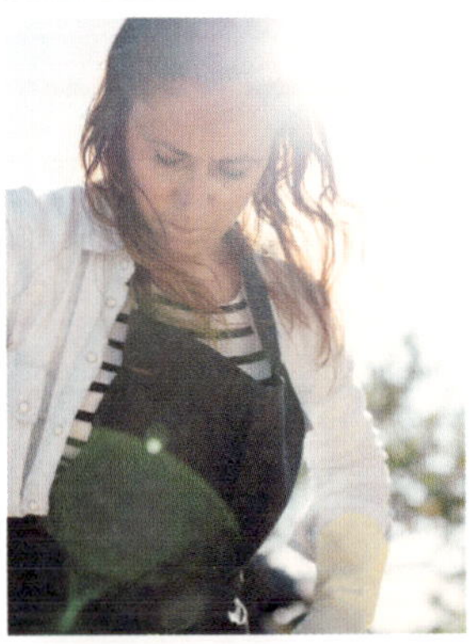

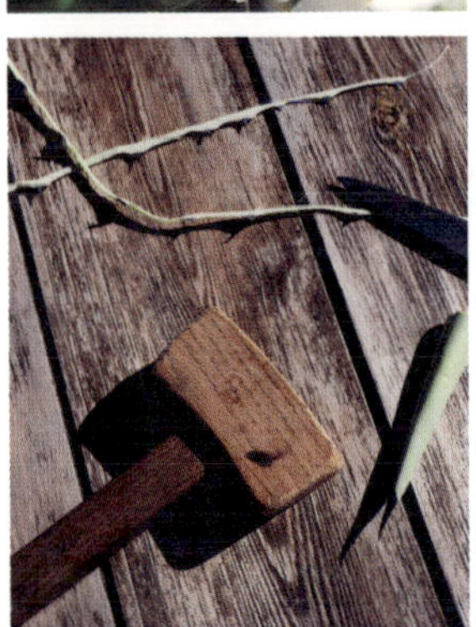

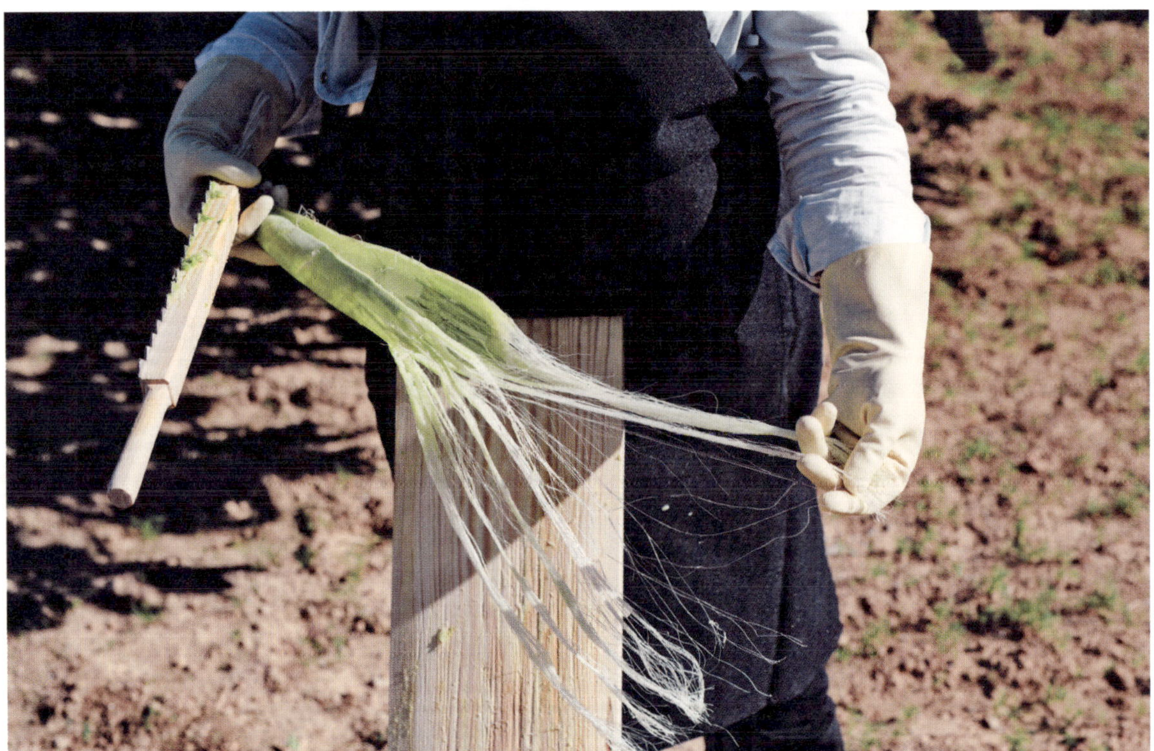

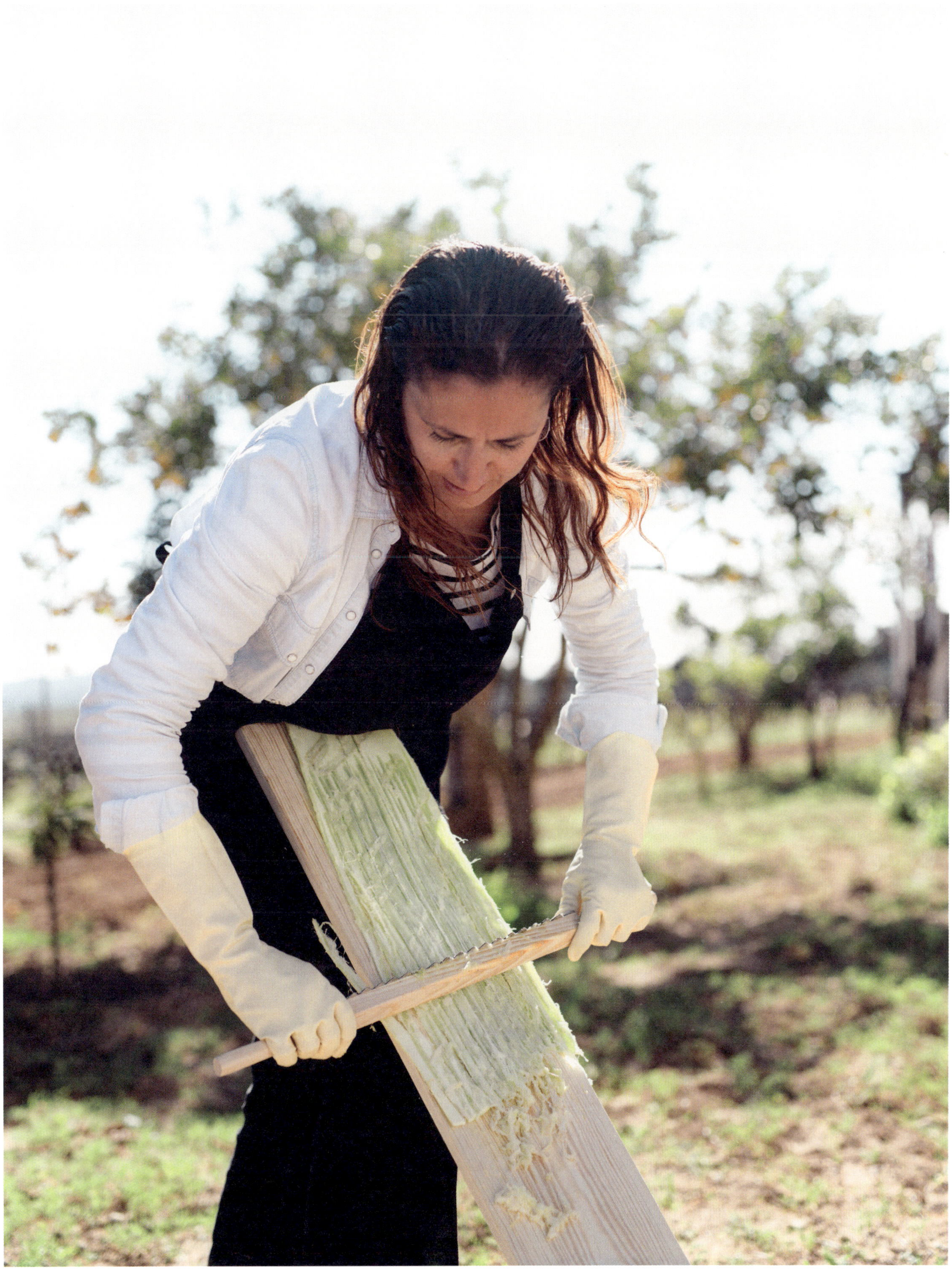

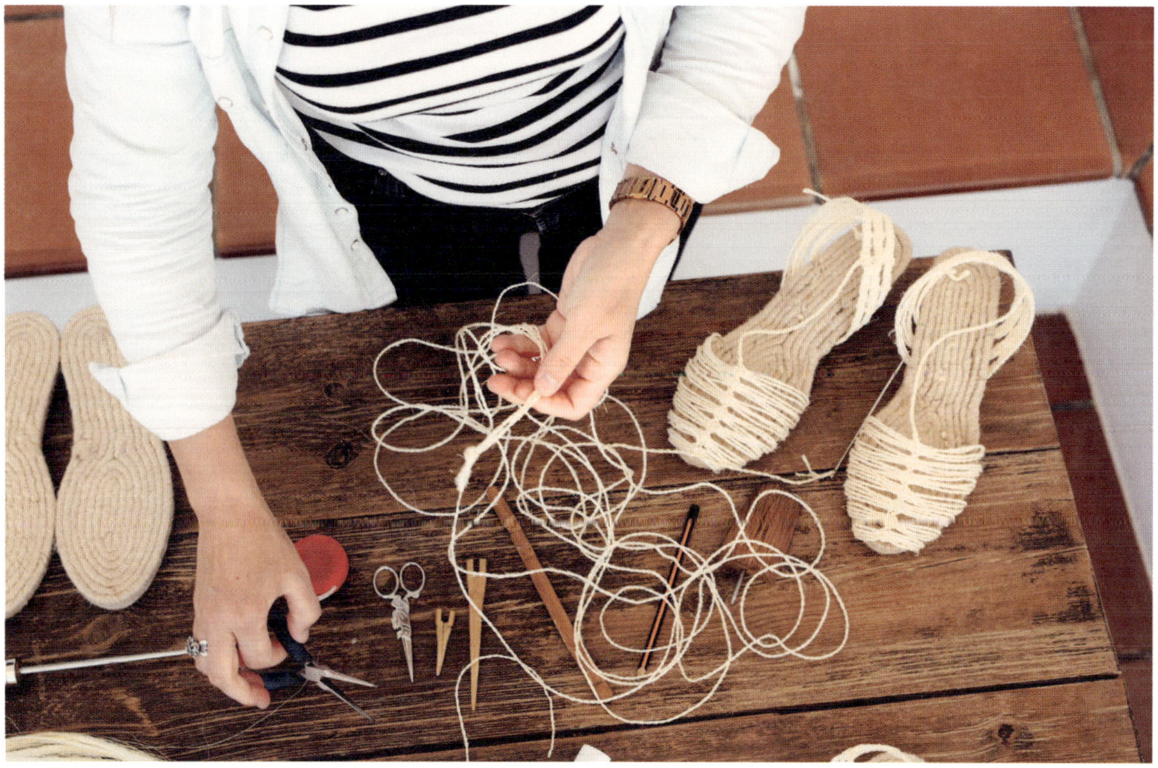

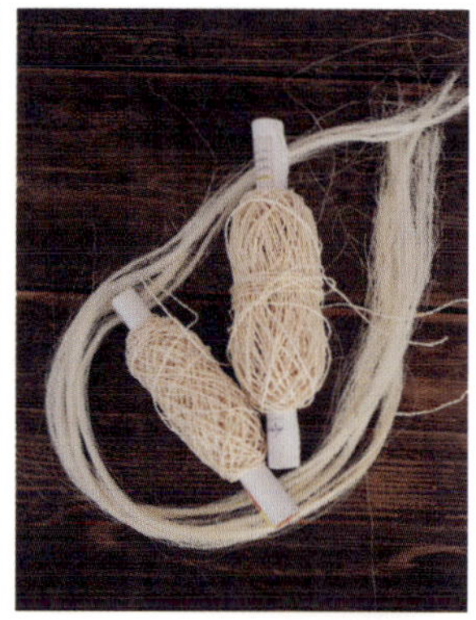

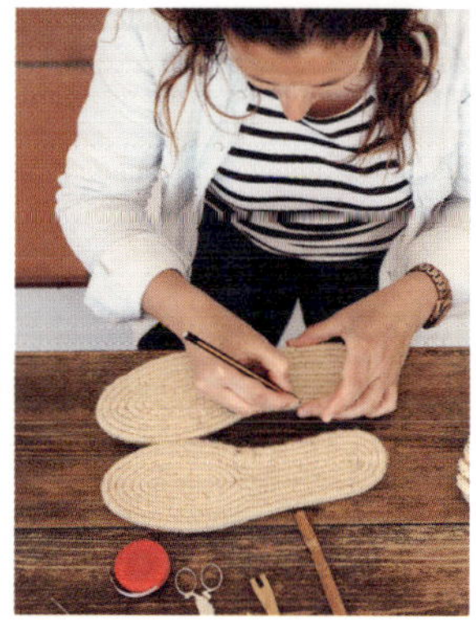

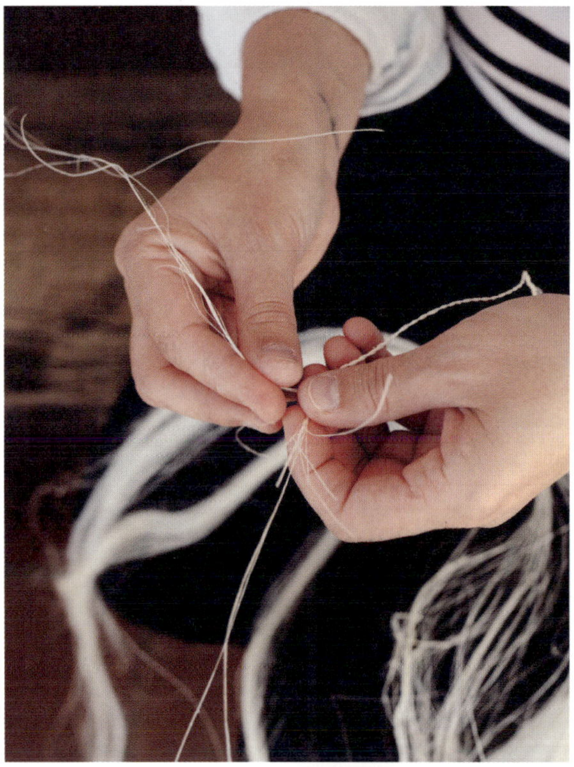

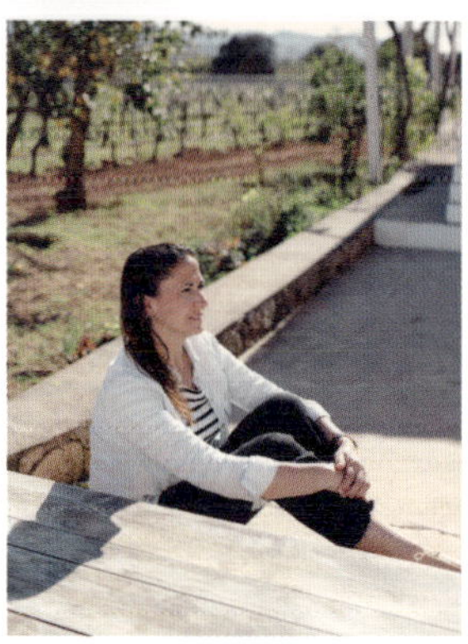

Patry creates different patterns for the uppers as she stitches the yarn on to the soles. The soles are traditionally made from a grass called esparto.

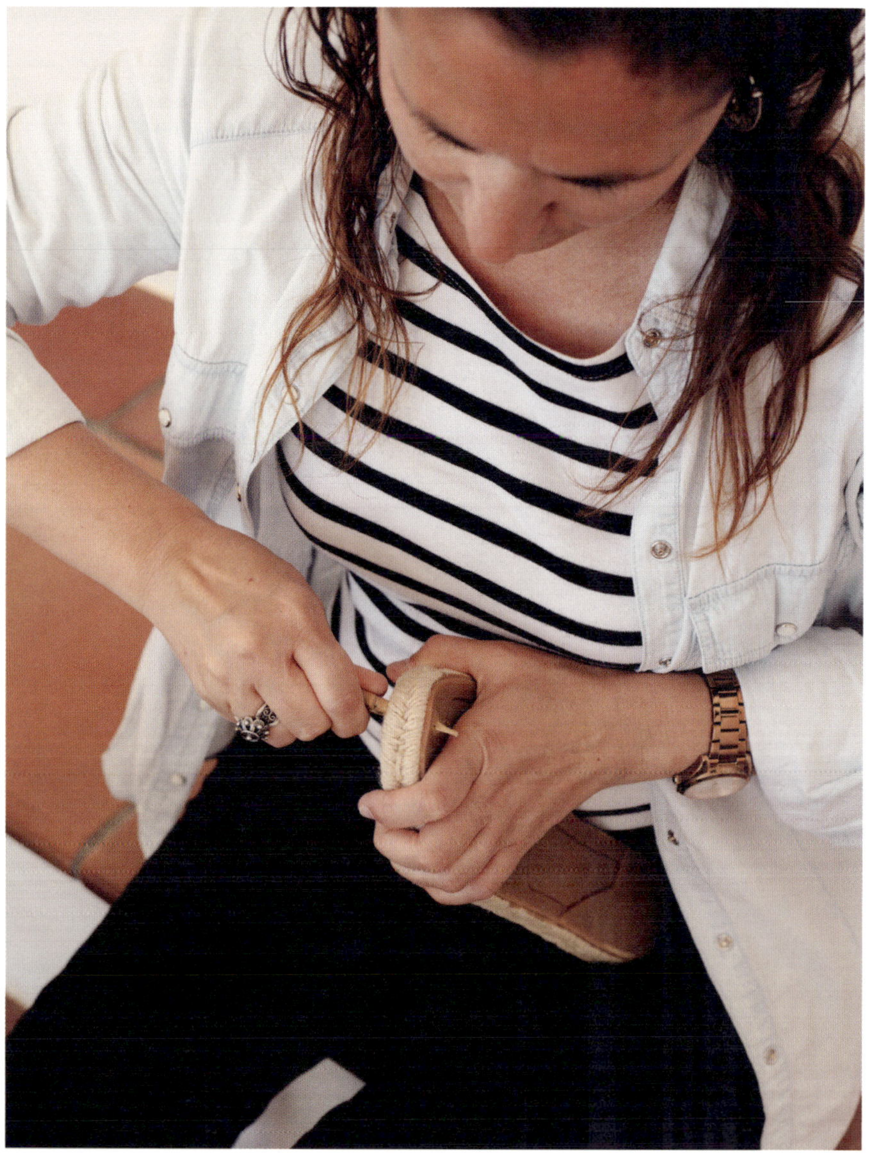

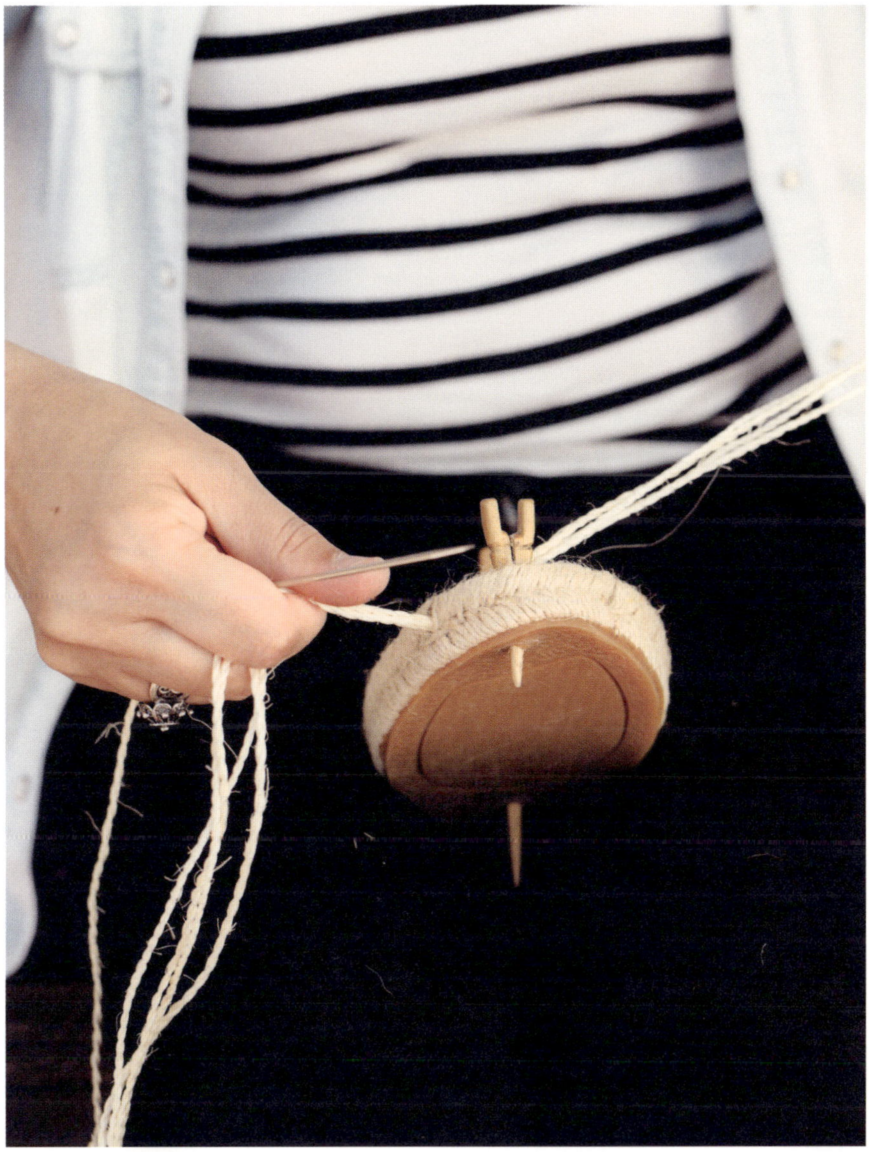
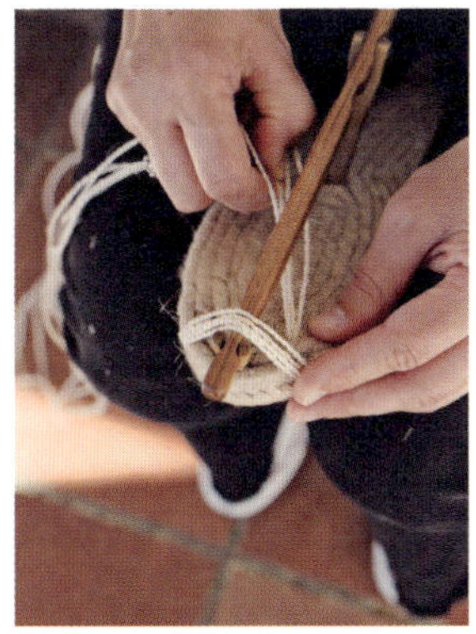
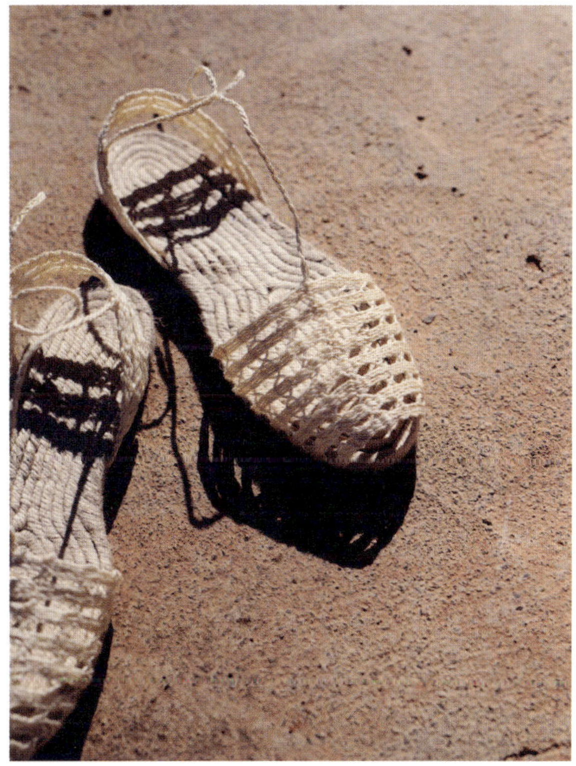
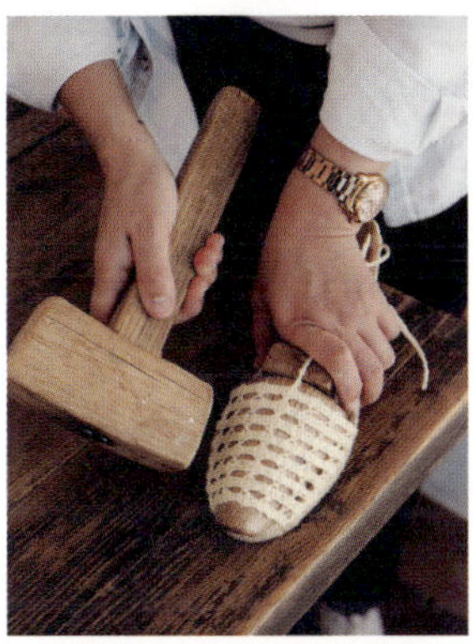
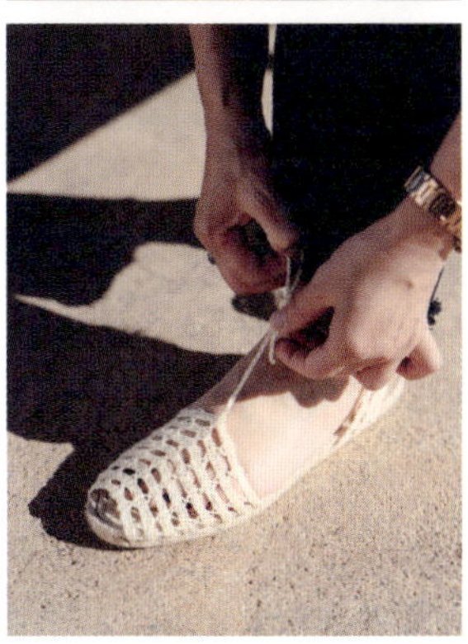
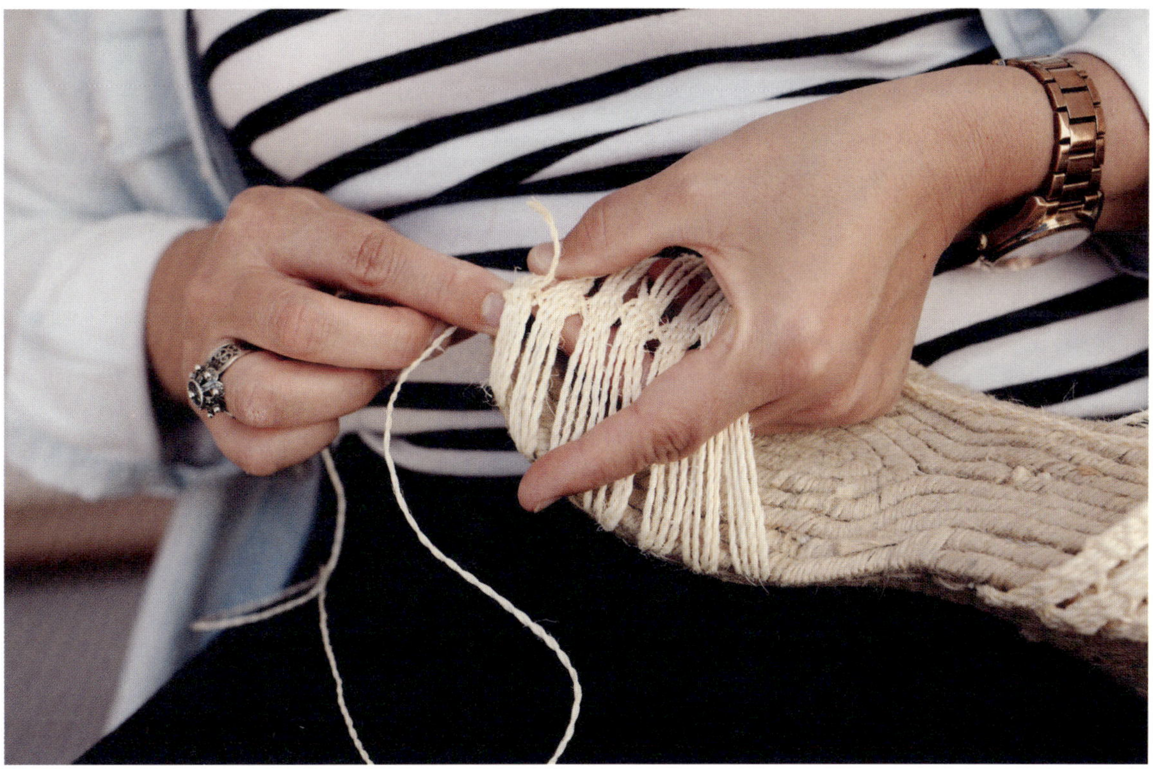

LA MOLA, FORMENTERA
majoral.com

MAJORAL

CONTEMPORARY JEWELLERY

In the permanent collection of the Museum of Arts and Design in New York sit two creations of Enric Majoral Castells.

Barcelona-born Enric fell in love with Ibiza's neighbouring island, Formentera, in 1971. During his compulsory military service he was based in Ibiza and, as he explains, 'One day I "escaped" for a day and went next door.' He rented a bike at the harbour and cycled all over the island. 'It was a paradisal, sleepy backwater.' After his military service, he decided to go back to Formentera for a couple of months, and ended up staying.

Enric had studied civil engineering and got work on the construction of Hotel La Mola. 'I rented a house in La Mola, and soon there were fifteen of us living there. It was a very special atmosphere', he recalls.

Dolors Ballester had also travelled from her home in Barcelona to Formentera, to spend time with friends. She met Enric, and they 'came up with a shared idea about living in Formentera together'.

Enric decided that he did not want to stay in the construction sector. In the late 1960s, 'when Spain was grey and sad because of the Civil War and the Franco regime', he had travelled by van from Barcelona to India. 'I had seen arts and crafts along the way.' He loved creating things, and in Formentera he taught himself to make jewellery after picking up skills from some older French artisans on the island. 'Not having studied jewellery production allowed me to be more open-minded about materials, designs and methods of production', he explains.

In 1974 Enric and Dolors married and set up Majoral, with Dolors looking after the management and marketing. Enric has always created minimal, experimental designs using silver and gold, particularly matt gold and very dark silver. 'I don't use a lot of precious stones, and when I do, they are never the protagonists.'

Initially, the couple sold Enric's pieces from a little roadside stall. Then, in 1984, they helped to establish La Mola's arts and crafts market, and moved their stall there. The island's fledgling tourism industry was growing, and their encouraging customer feedback convinced them that they could make a living from the jewellery.

'When I saw that our business had a future, I realized that I needed the contrast of the city', Enric explains. Since the mid-1980s the couple have spent winters near Barcelona. They set up a workshop in the city and in 1987 opened a shop.

Today both of Enric and Dolors's children are involved in Majoral. Son Roc works on designs in their atelier in Barcelona, while daughter Savina runs the business with her mother.

Majoral has twenty staff in total. They are spread across its workshop and its boutique in Barcelona; its purpose-built atelier-cum-showroom and its boutique in Formentera; and its boutique in Ibiza. Majoral designs are also stocked in boutiques in several other Spanish cities and in Portugal, Italy, Belgium, Germany and the United States.

Enric came up with the original logo: a symbol that represents both the *M* of Majoral and the *E* of his first name when it is turned on its side. 'And if you turn it again, it is reminiscent of the little boathouses found along the coasts of Ibiza and Formentera', he adds. The logo has since been reworked by the designer Martín Azúa.

Enric's accolades include the National Crafts Award, presented by the Spanish Ministry of Industry, Commerce and Tourism; the Professional Career Prize from the Jewellers' Association of Catalonia (JORGC); and the Balearic government's Ramon Llull Award. ***CD***

The designer Enric Majoral Castells established the Majoral jewellery company with his wife, Dolors. Nowadays their son, Roc, also designs jewellery, while their daughter, Savina, runs the business with Dolors.

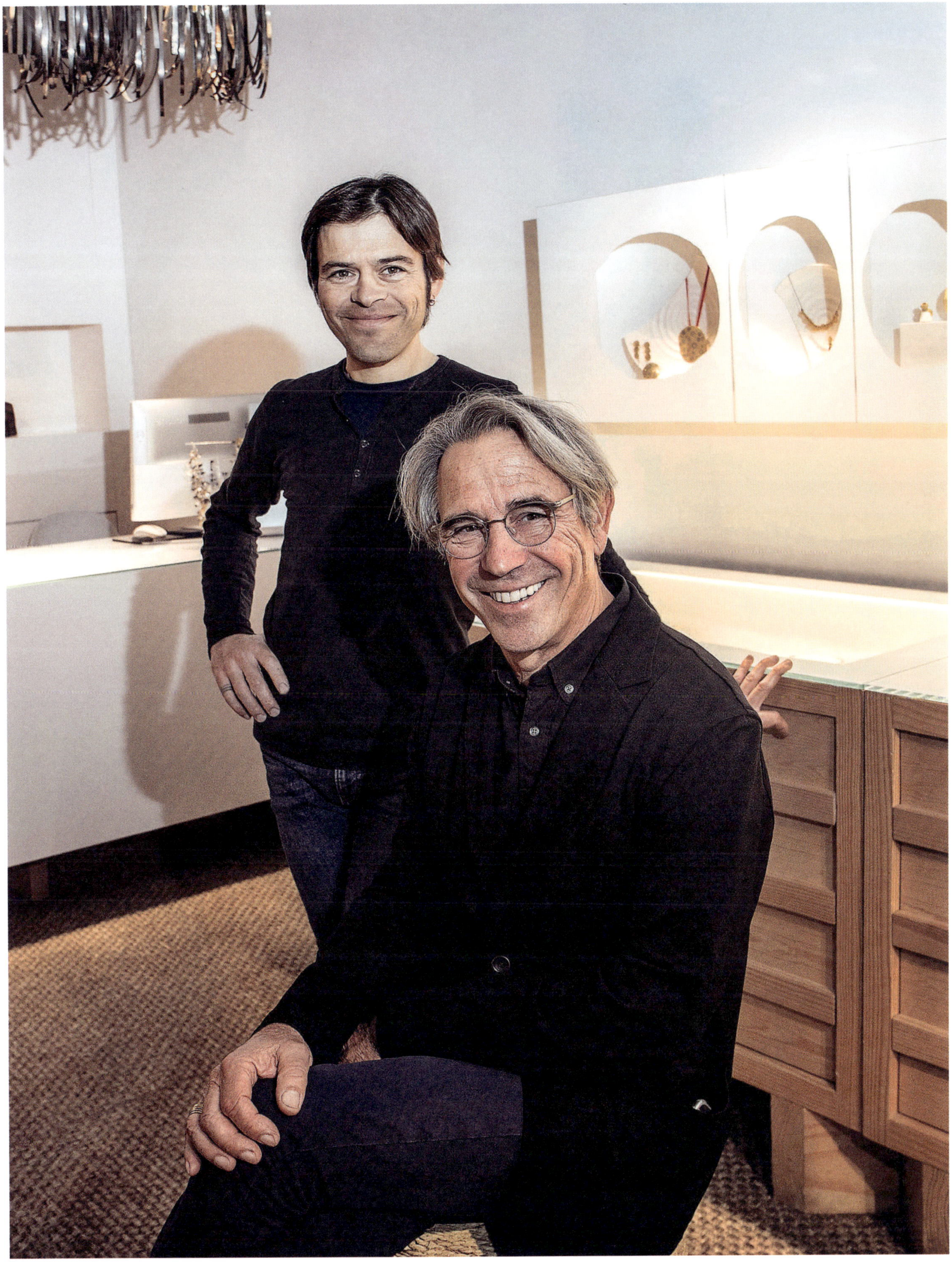

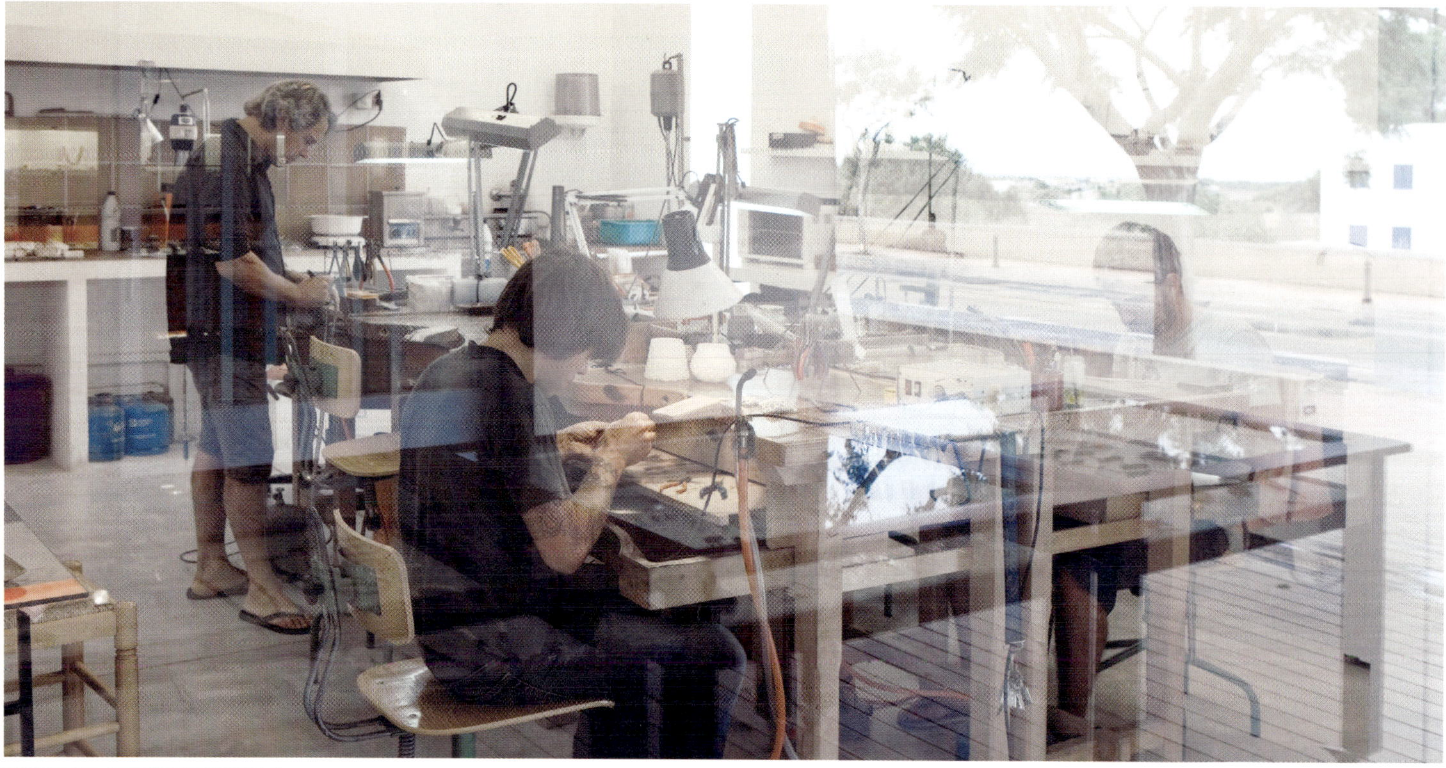

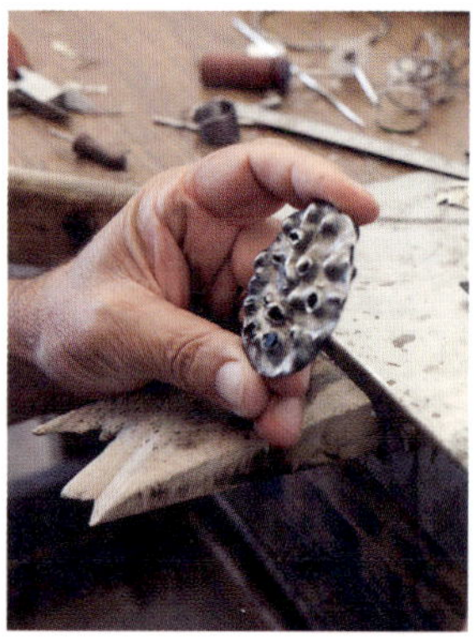

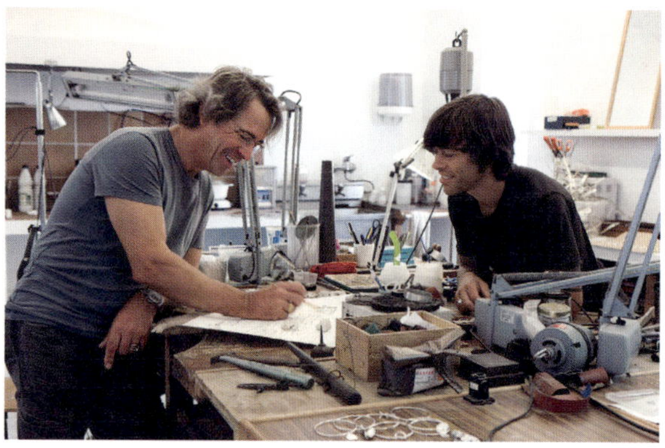

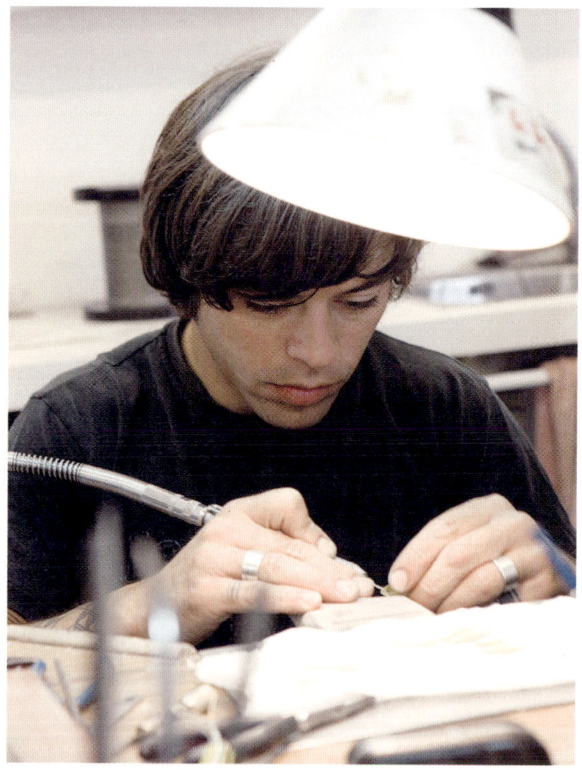

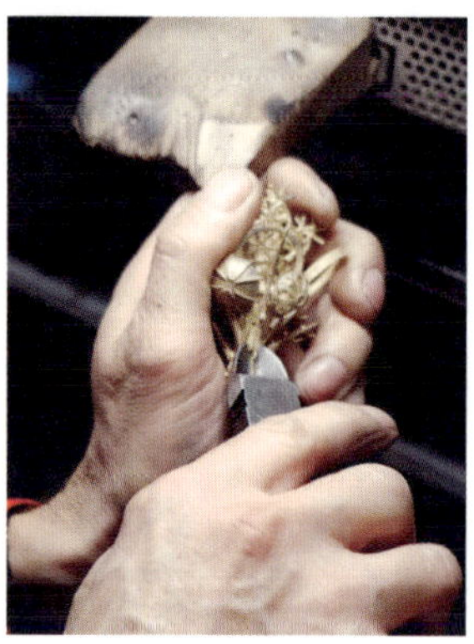

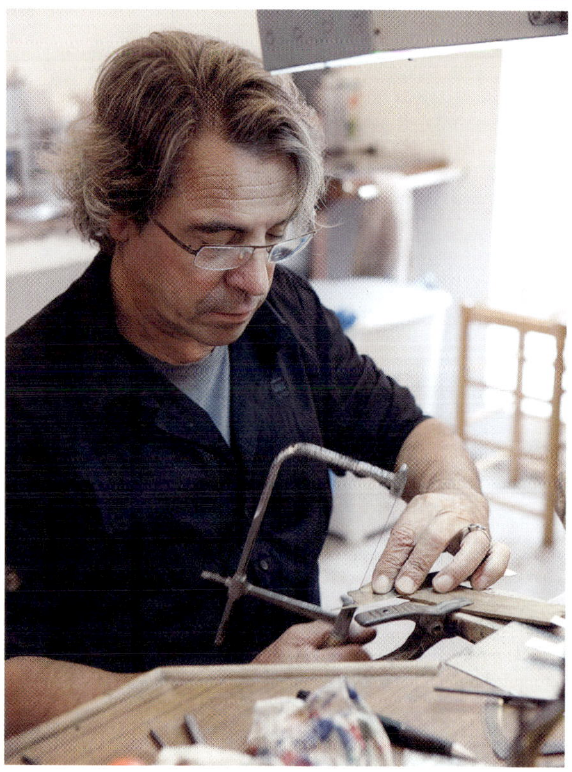

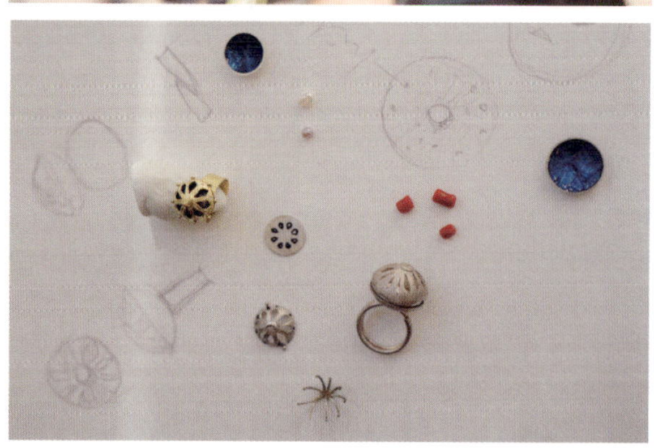

Enric creates pieces in the atelier in Formentera (pictured), while Roc is based mostly in the Barcelona workshop. The special-edition ring (far right) was designed in collaboration with the Ibicenco violinist Lina Tur Bonet.

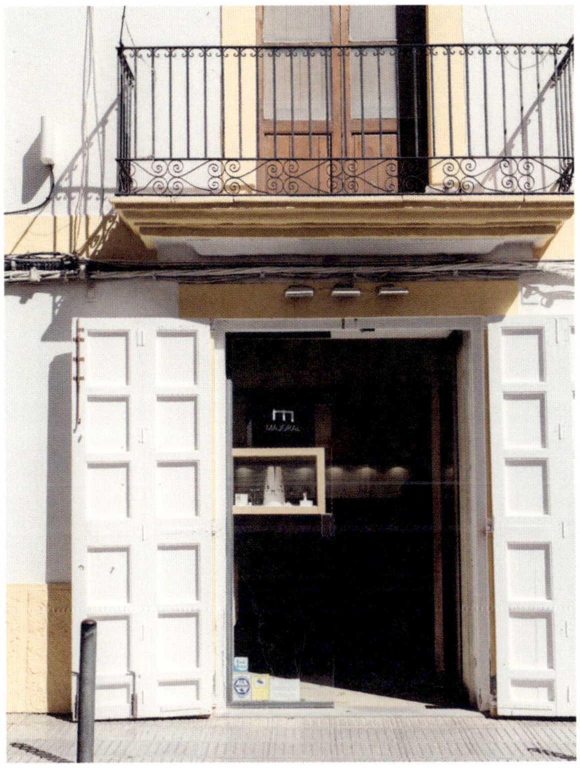

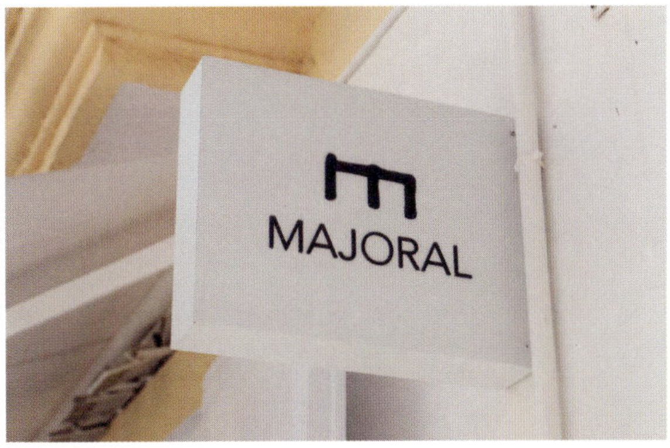

Majoral's boutique in the historic centre of Ibiza Town displays its contemporary, handcrafted jewellery, much of it made of matt gold and dark silver. Enric devised the original design for the brand's logo (left).

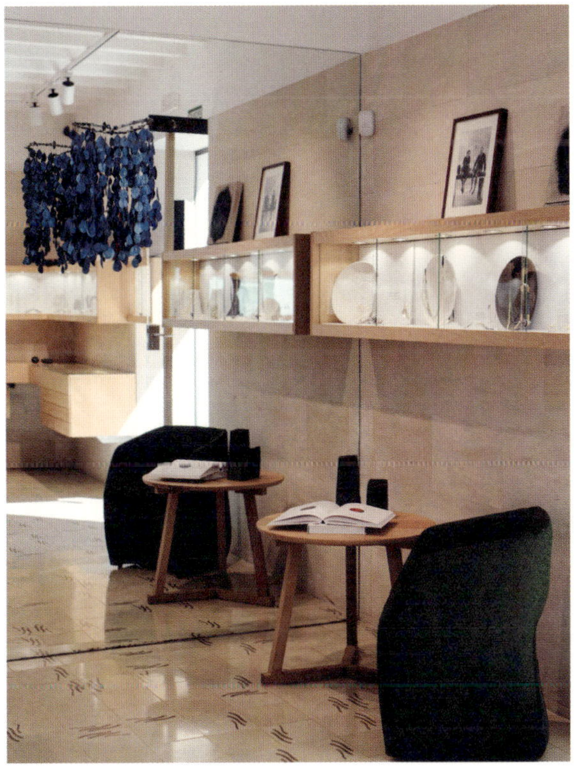

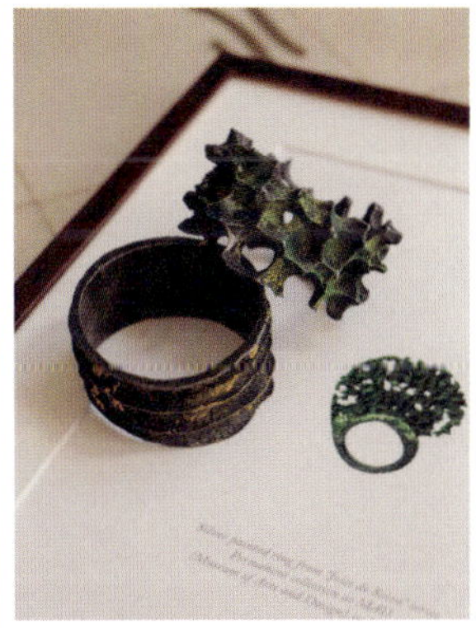

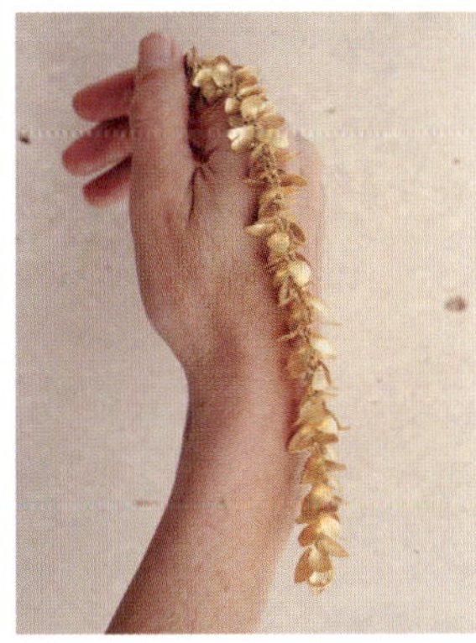

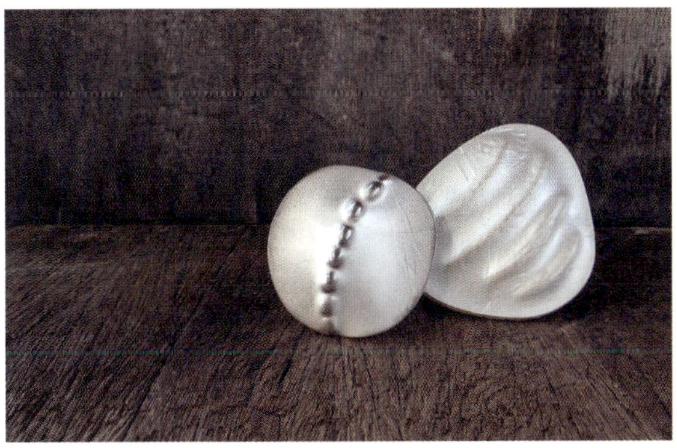

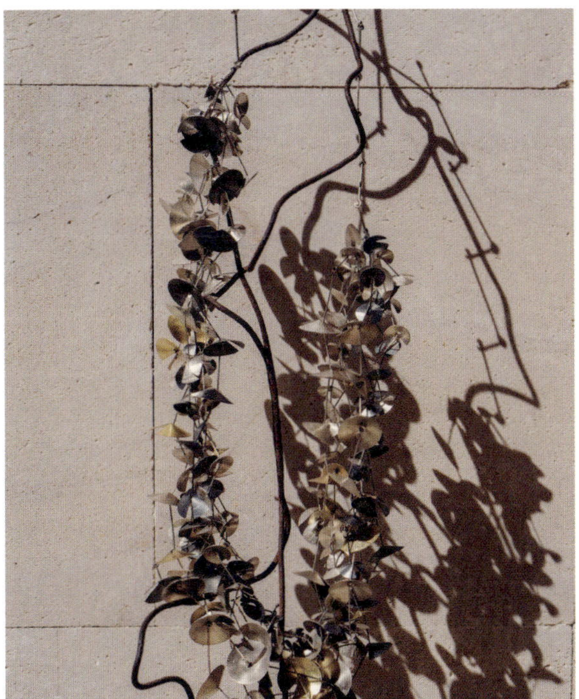

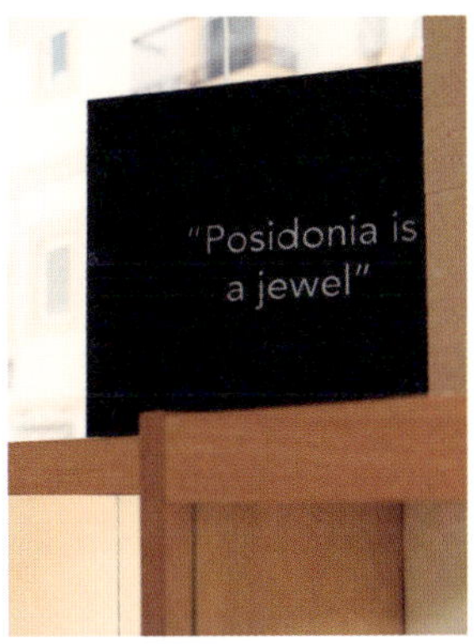

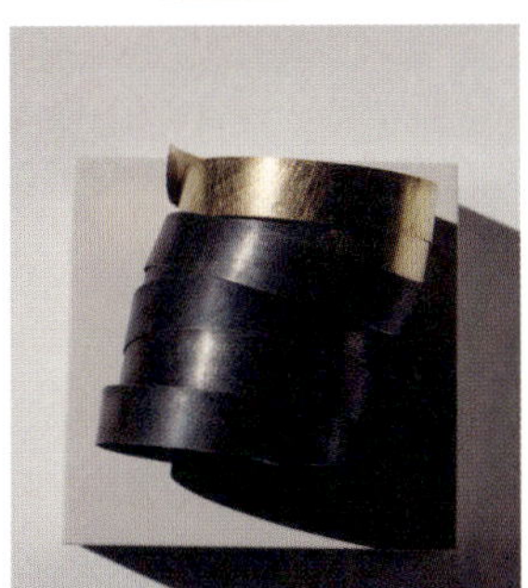

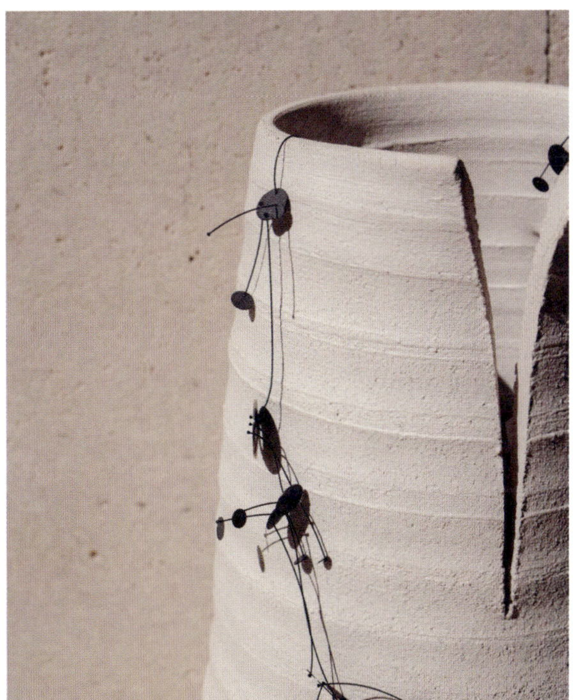

IBIZA TOWN
elisapomar.com

ELISA POMAR IBIZA

JEWELLERY INSPIRED BY TRADITION

Elisa Pomar is the fourth-generation goldsmith in her family. The Pomars have been making traditional Ibizan jewellery since her great-grandfather Joaquín started the business in 1872.

'I founded my company out of a love of tradition', Elisa says. But she has taken the aesthetic of that traditional jewellery and injected it with her own style. Her sometimes provocative creations have been worn by celebrities such as actress Scarlett Johansson and model Bianca Balti, and have featured in advertising campaigns for Dolce & Gabbana.

The island's jewellery has drawn influence from Phoenician, Punic, Arab and Christian cultures, all of which settled here at some point over the centuries. Traditionally, ornate silver and coral jewellery, known as *emprendades*, was given to women as their dowry and was worn on special occasions such as weddings. 'Until recent times, her *emprendades* were the only things that a woman in Ibiza would own', Elisa says.

Elisa's family made this type of jewellery and other pieces in their tiny atelier in the old part of Ibiza Town. 'My great-grandfather was famous. He was known as the king of Spain's jeweller (*es joier del rei*) because, when Alfonso XIII visited Ibiza in 1929, he bought some of the Pomars' pieces to give as presents', she explains.

Elisa recalls how, as a child, she loved watching her father, Josep, or 'Pepín', work and always wanted to copy him. By the time she became a teenager, Ibizan jewellery design had fallen out of fashion. 'I couldn't understand why nobody here – not even my mother – would wear their beautiful jewellery any more.' Only members of traditional dance groups (*las collas*) wore it while performing.

For her eighteenth birthday, Elisa's father gave her a pair of enormous Ibizan-style earrings. 'My friends would ask why I was wearing such old-fashioned designs. I couldn't stand their ignorance.' To increase her own knowledge, she went to Palma de Mallorca to study jewellery design and gemology (precious stones).

Elisa's father died unexpectedly in 2007. 'I decided that my family's beautiful work couldn't end there', she says. She gathered all the information she could find on Ibizan jewellery design, amassing a huge collection of pieces, documents and pictures. Her idea was to create a new brand that would be the culmination of all she had learnt, and she launched it in 2009. 'The brand was born out of the love and respect that I had for my family's work.'

Elisa's main showroom is in the building where she was born. Her four jewellers create her intricate designs – mostly in gold – in several workshops spread across the island. She also has an eight-strong sales and marketing team, and a second showroom, in Ibiza Town's main street, Vara de Rey.

In 2016 Elisa received the prestigious Gold Medal from the Ibizan government, for breathing new life into the island's jewellery crafts.

'What's most important for me is to be happy with what I do and to work with the nice team that I have', Elisa says. 'I like to enjoy my way of life and not be driven by targets. The great thing about Ibiza is that lots of people come to see us anyway, so there is no need to travel to promote what we do.' ***CD***

Elisa Pomar wears several of her rings on each finger, as was common practice among Ibicencas in the past. Typically, a father would instruct a jeweller on the ring designs he wanted for his daughter's dowry.

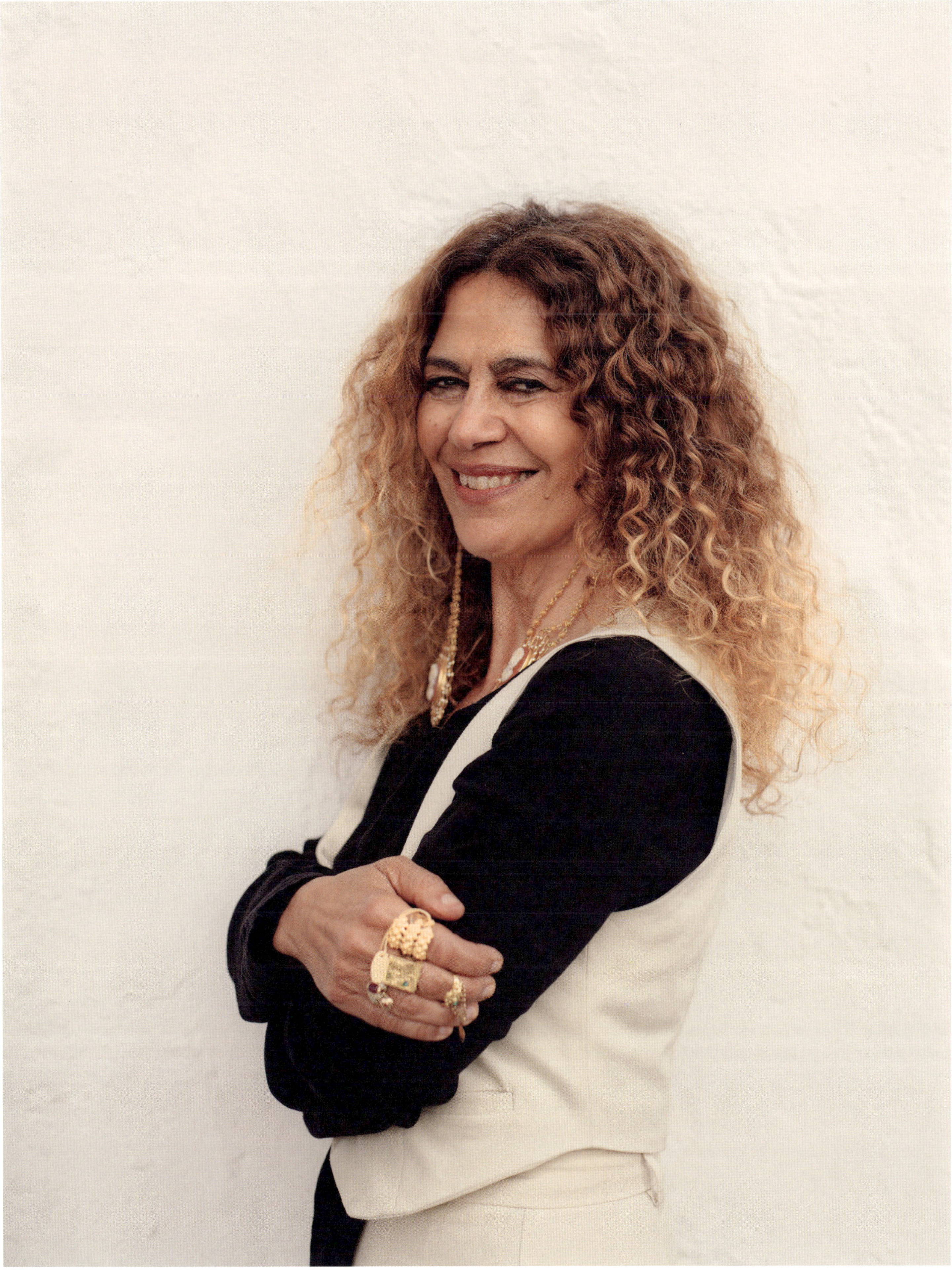

Elisa studied jewellery design and gemology at the S'Estellera Escuela de Joyería in Palma de Mallorca. Her preferred metal is gold, and she combines it with coral, which was said to protect women.

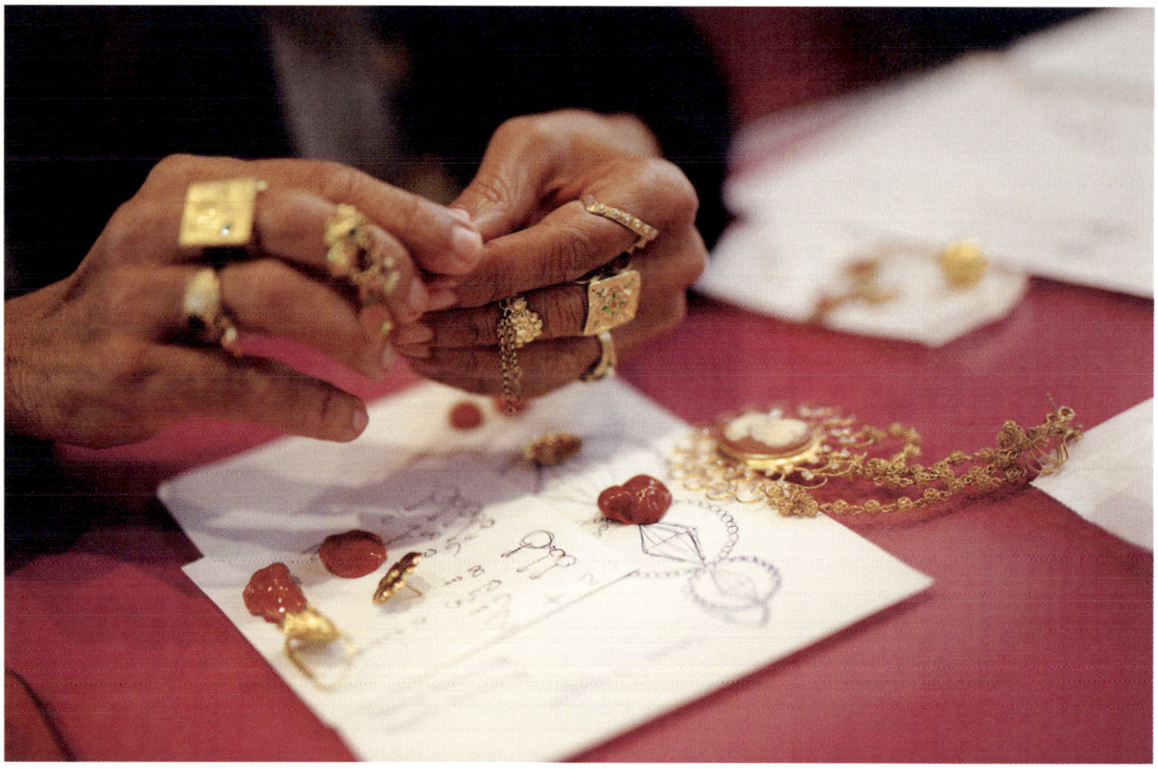

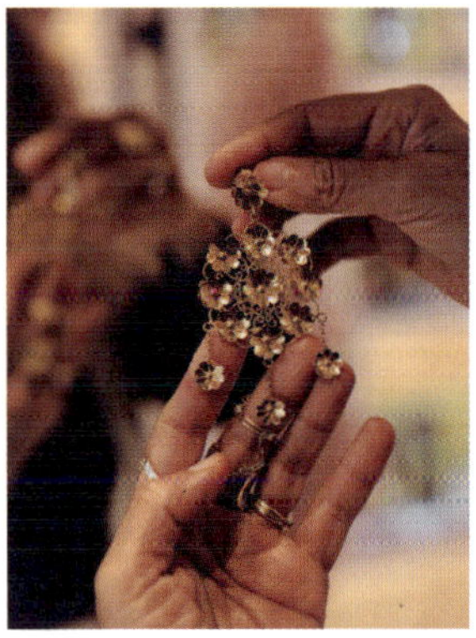

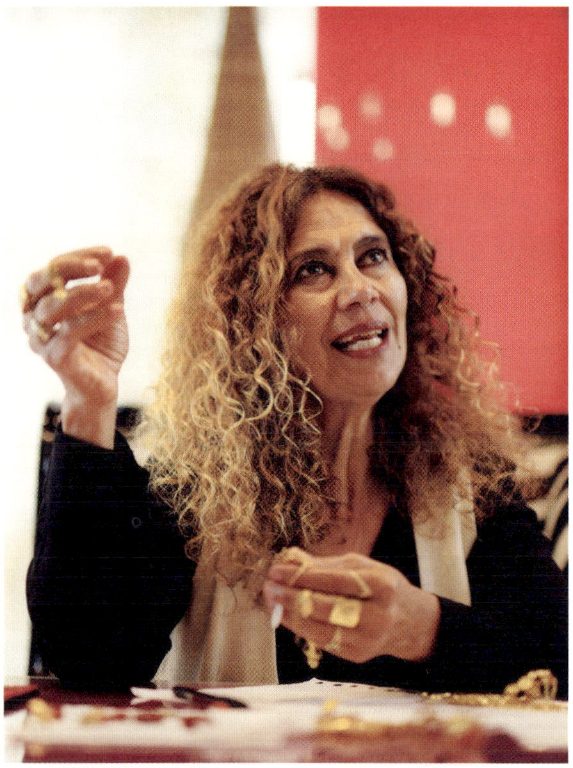

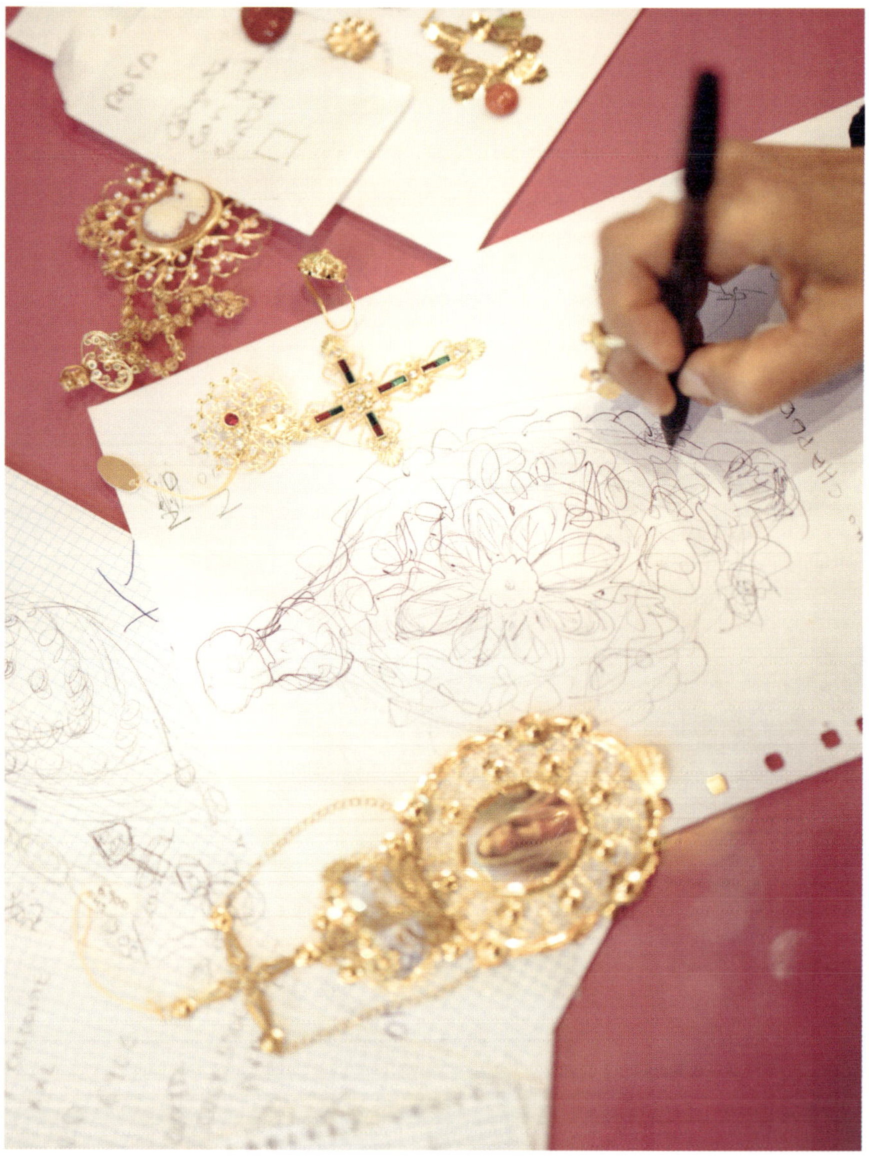

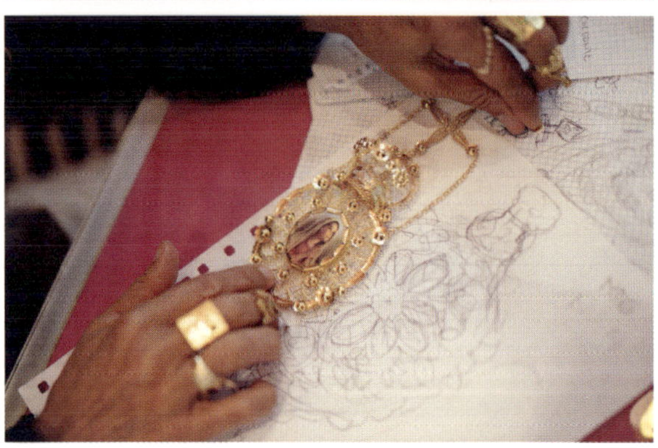

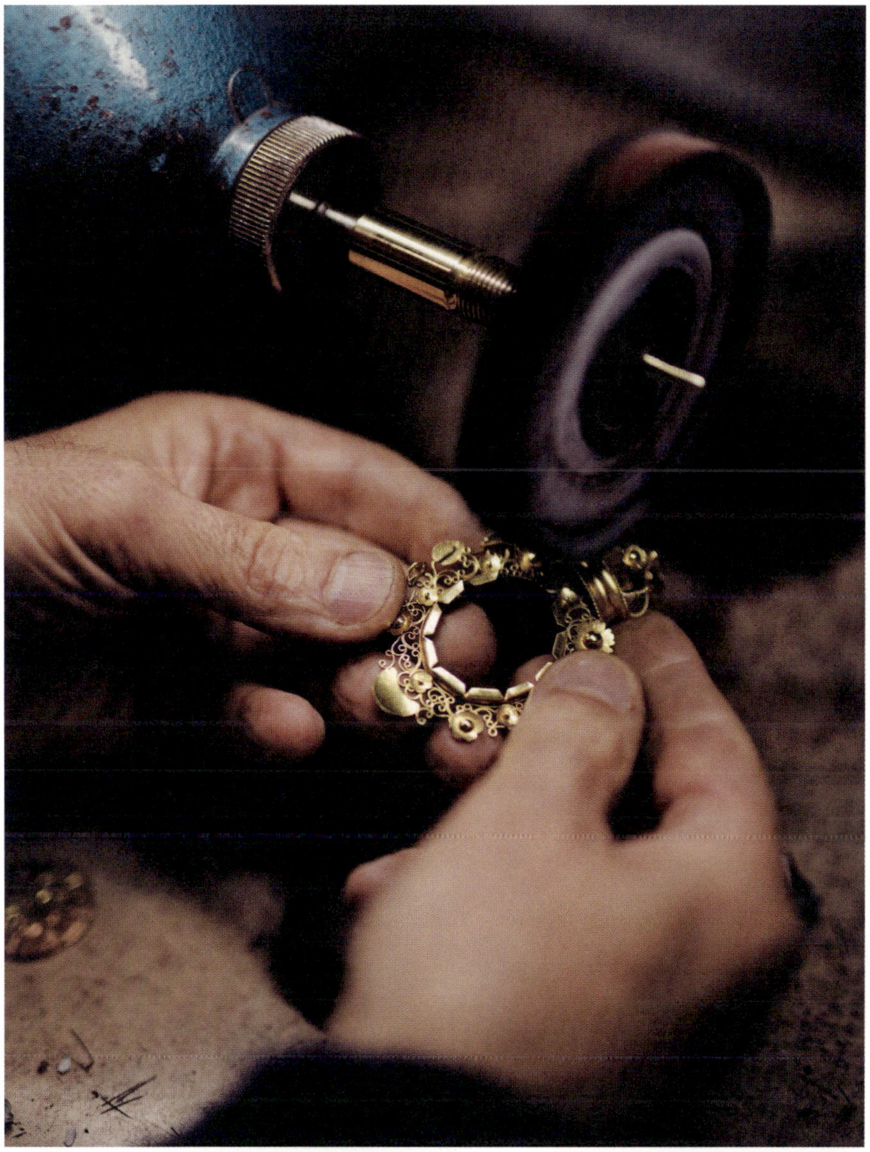

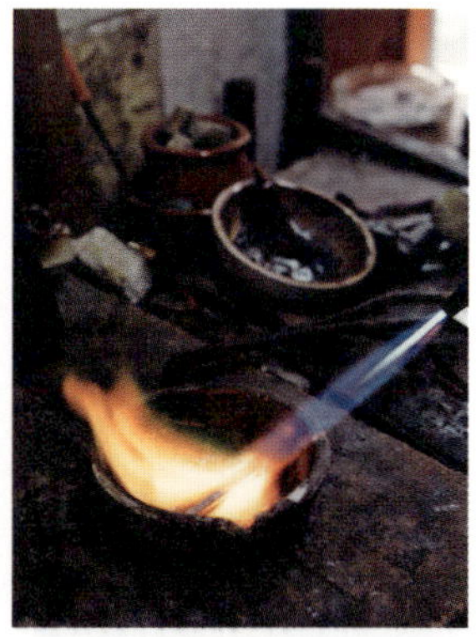

A small team of jewellers create Elisa's designs using traditional methods.

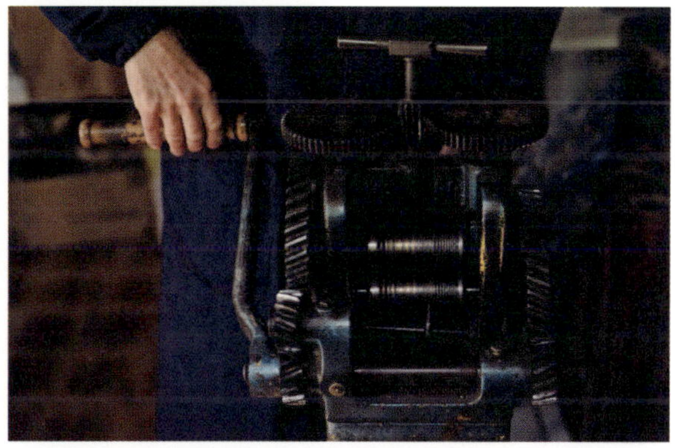

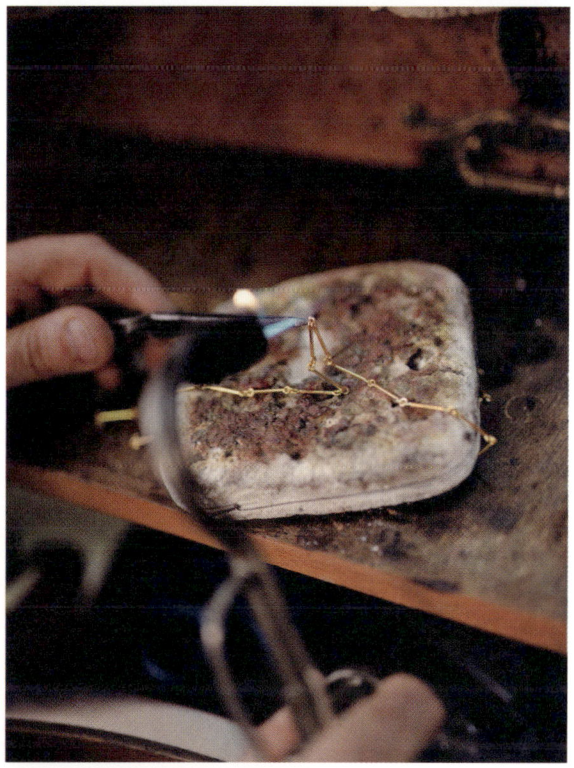

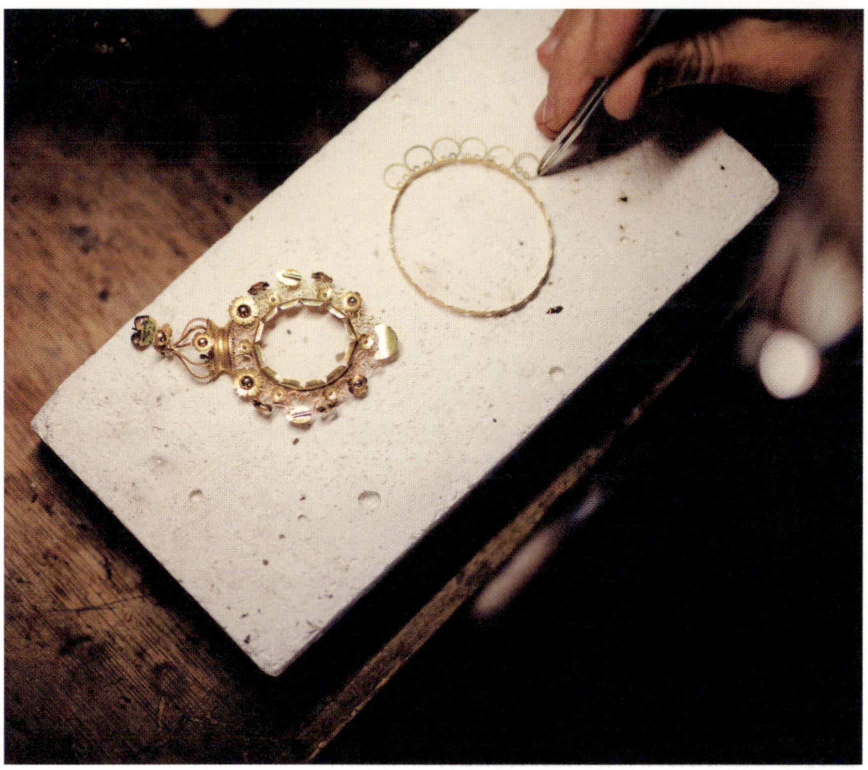

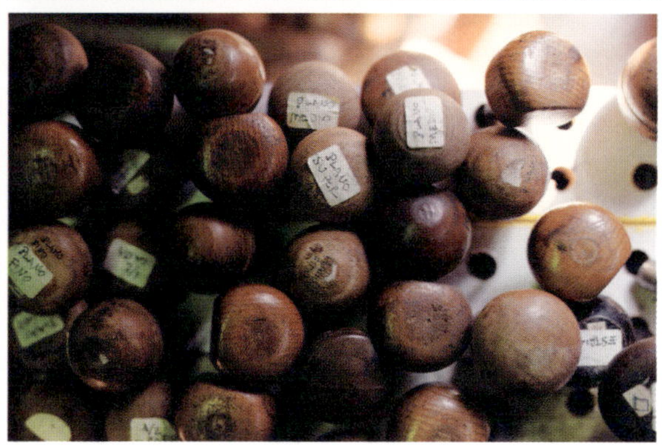

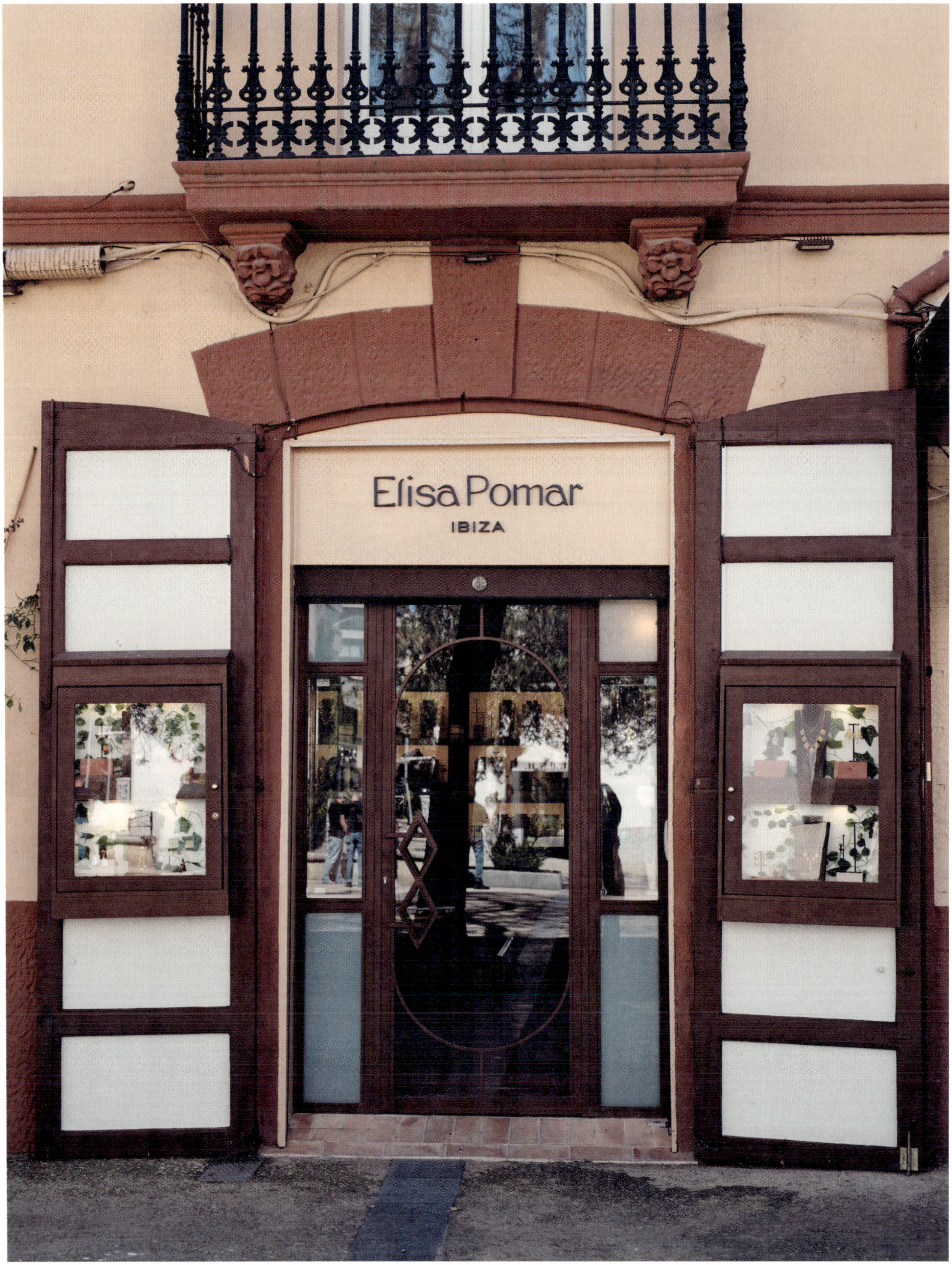
Elisa Pomar
IBIZA

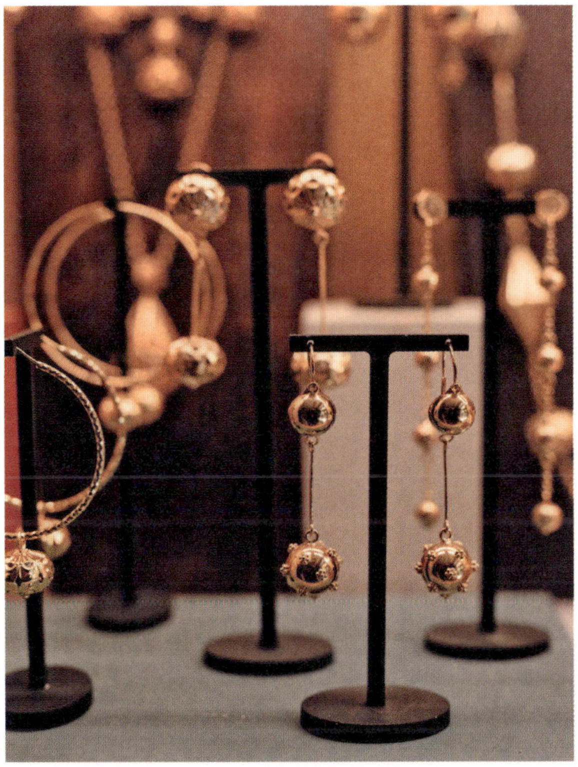

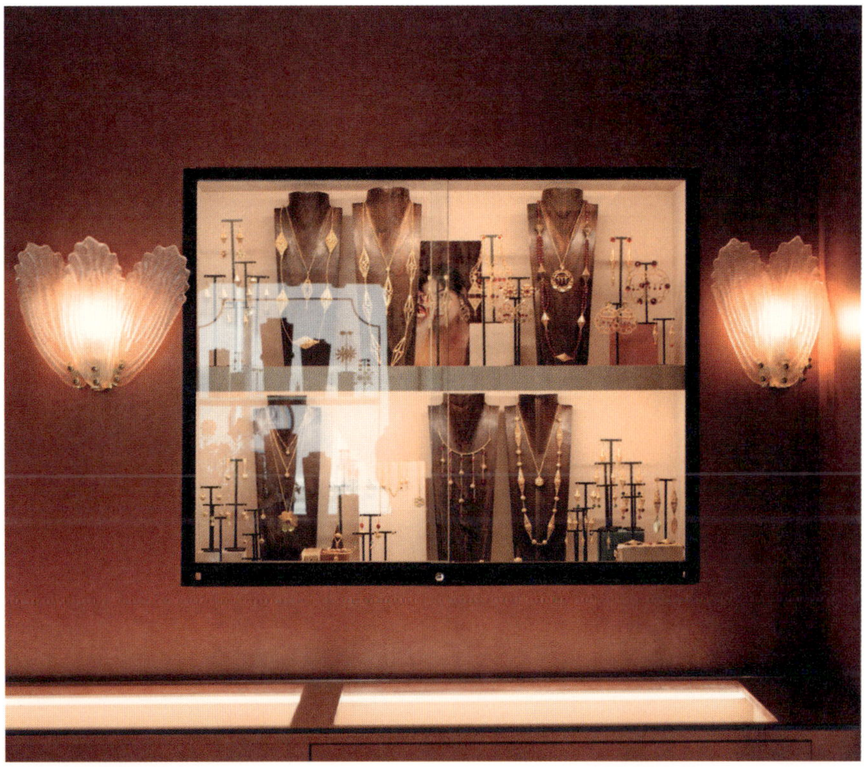

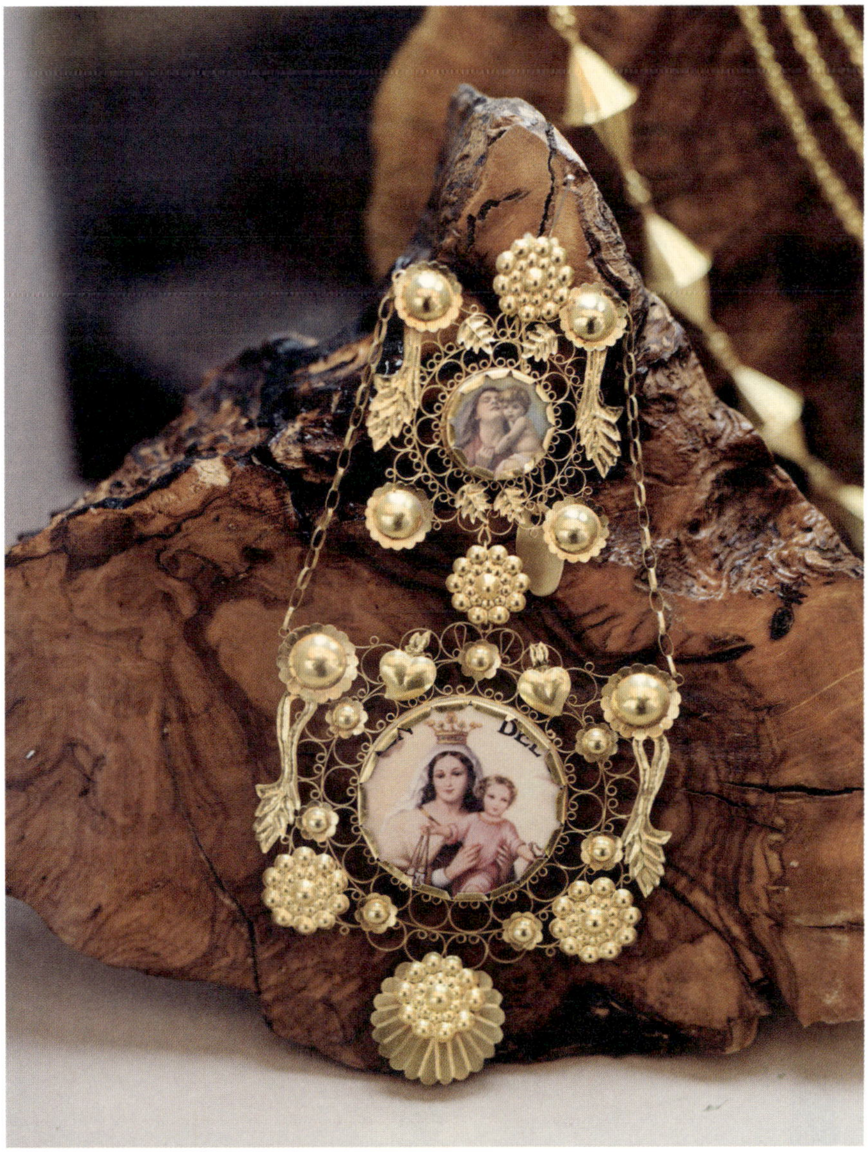

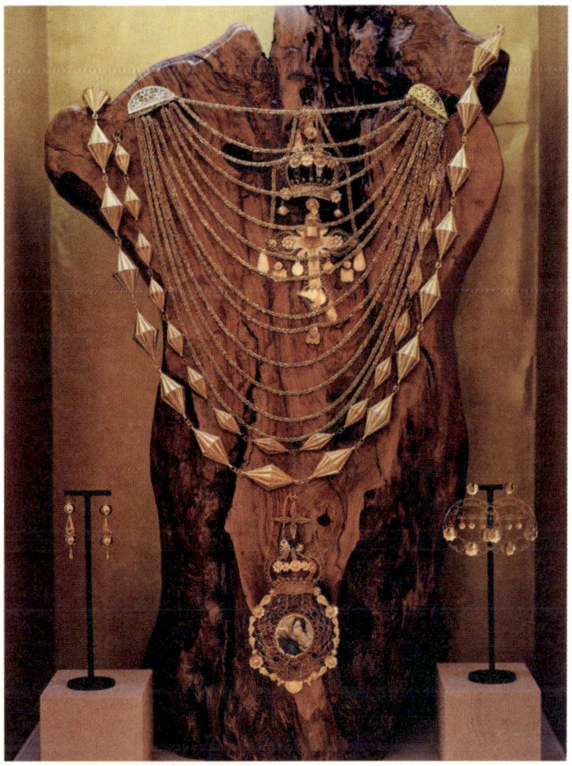

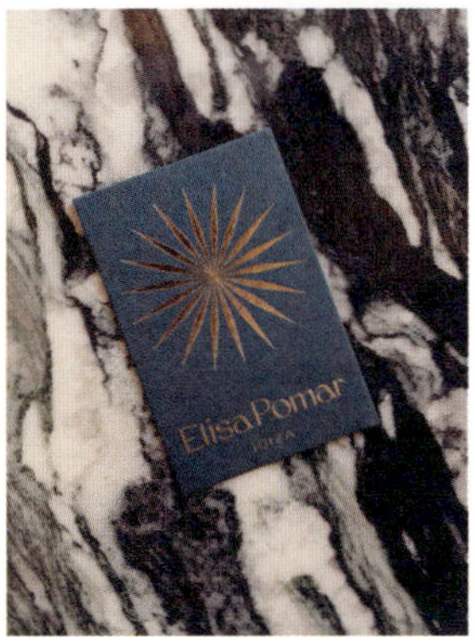

Opposite: Elisa's second showroom is in Vara de Rey, the main boulevard in Ibiza Town.

Far left and above: Much of Elisa's work is inspired by the jewellery, or emprendades, that traditionally formed a young woman's dowry, including a large necklace adorned with a crucifix and images of the Virgin Mary.

SAN JUAN
worldfamilyibiza.com

WORLD FAMILY IBIZA

FASHION COMPANY & CONCEPT STORE

Merel Krielaart and Alok (who prefers not to use his surname) met one summer's evening among the drummers and dancers of Benirràs beach. It was the early 1990s, and their first home together was a camper van. Merel, from The Netherlands, had been a model, and the Barcelonan Alok had worked in real estate on the mainland.

Merel and Alok set up their fashion company, World Family Ibiza, a few years later. It was not planned, rather born out of their lifestyle, interests and talents. 'We just love to travel, to be in contact with other cultures, to taste other cuisines, to see the different ways people dress', Merel says. 'We love markets and collecting things', Alok adds. On their travels, they amassed a wide range of decorative items such as pom-poms from the Pushkar Camel Fair in India. Merel, who had learnt to sew as a child, incorporated them into skirts, jackets, bags and other accessories.

The couple's creations were inspired by Merel's childhood in the hippy Amsterdam of the 1970s and by the indigenous cultures they visited. They began to make a living from their sales, and in 1997 they took a stall at Las Dalias hippy market. This was a turning point. 'By the middle of that summer, we had sold out', says Merel. They then started to produce proper collections, all featuring their 'design signature' – a mixture of different fabrics, patterns, colours, stitching and appliqué techniques, along with the pom-poms that they apply to many products.

World Family Ibiza took off. 'We started appearing a lot in the press', Alok recalls. In the 2000s the brand was stocked in boutiques in seven cities around the world.

But as the brand became more and more successful, work began to take over Merel and Alok's lives. 'So we decided to produce less and to have a better quality of life', says Alok. They stopped exporting and focused on their business in Ibiza. This strategy has allowed the couple to live out their ideal: working eight months a year and travelling for four months – 'in order to have time to be creative', Merel explains. On their travels, they might find, for example, a couple of rolls of fabulous fabric in Thailand or Mexico, and will then use them in future collections.

Most of the collections and one-off bags are made by seamstresses in Ibiza. The company also decorates private events such as wedding ceremonies and birthday parties.

In 2021 Merel and Alok opened a restaurant and concept store between San Lorenzo and San Juan. Five of their six children are involved in the business: sons Asher and Rama run the kitchen and restaurant respectively, and daughter Karuna serves in the restaurant. Meanwhile, Merel and daughter Goldie design the collections, and Alok manages the fashion company with daughter Carlota. (Their daughter Gaya works independently as a DJ.)

Ibiza is not just a base for the business, but also a way of life. 'Here, we can live as we want to', Merel says. 'Our way of dressing, for example, is totally accepted here, and nobody comments on it. In lots of other places, people look at us and think we're a bit weird.'

'Also, the nature and the light are just amazing here.' There are more beautiful and more cost-effective places in the world, Merel admits, 'but here there is an open-minded spirit that allows us to grow our personality'.

'Actually, we don't use the word "work"', Alok points out. 'We create, and that's what we enjoy.' ***CD***

Merel and Alok have perfected their way of life: managing their fashion brand, restaurant and concept store with their children, hosting Namaste parties in Las Dalias, and travelling overseas in their camper van.

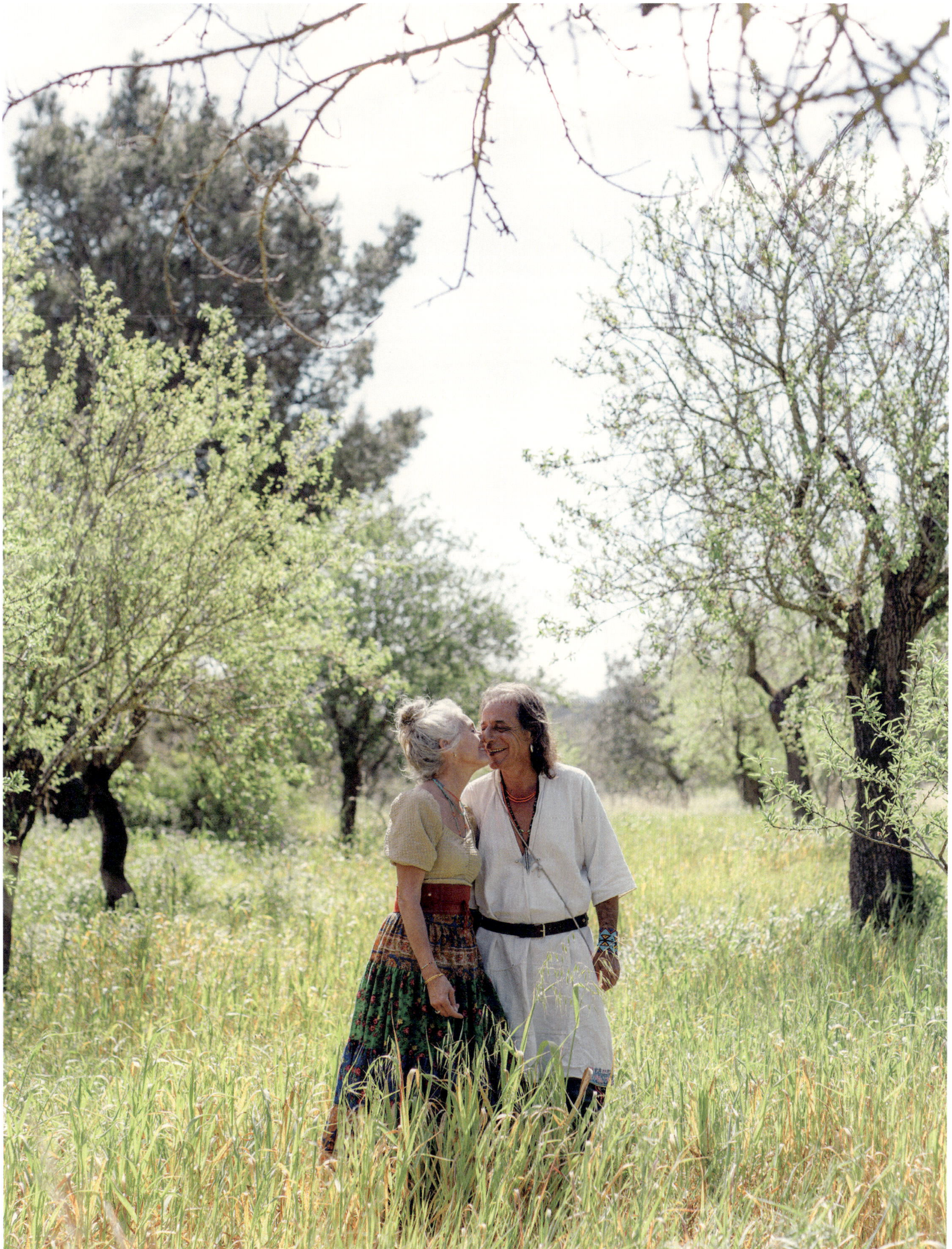

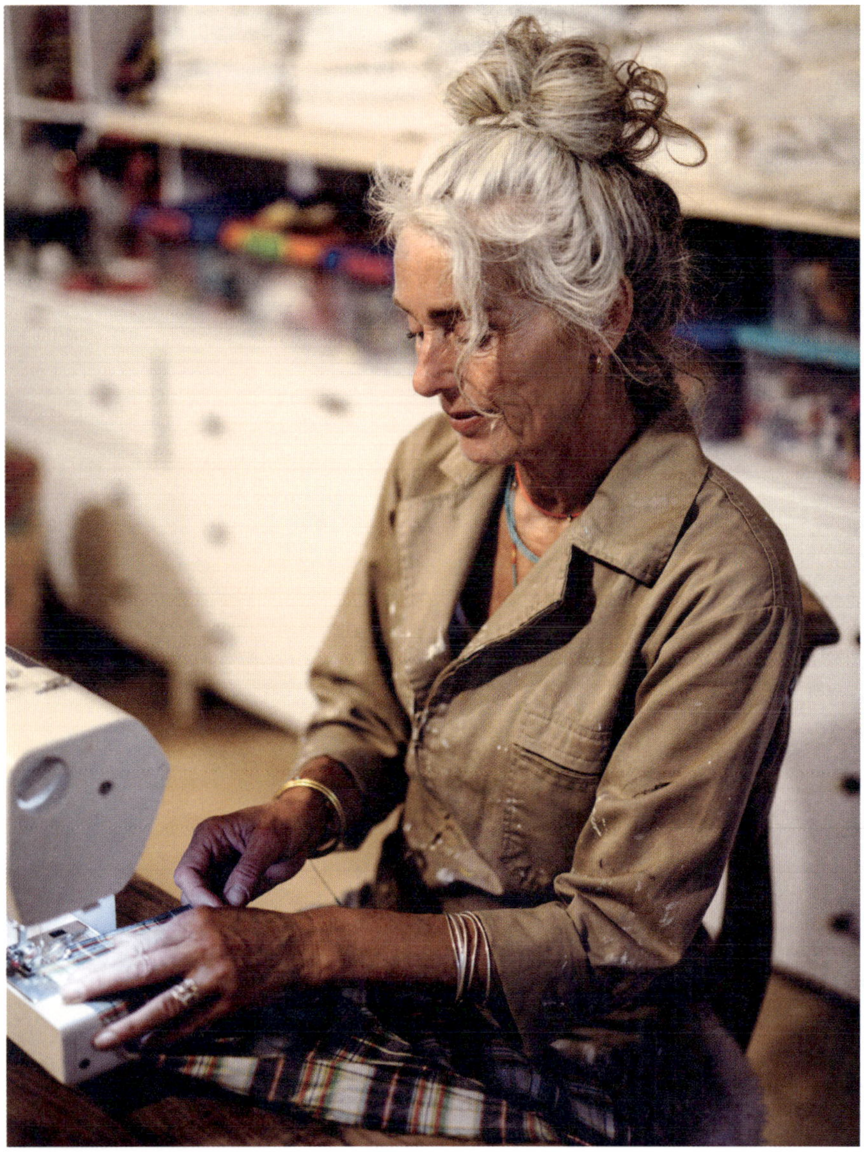

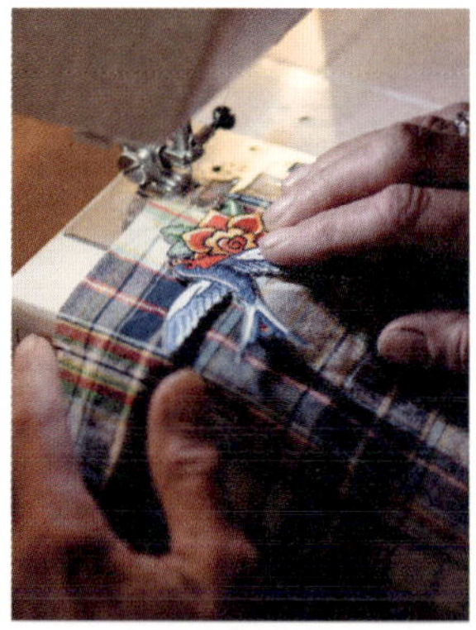

In the atelier, Merel transforms fabrics and accessories – many of them picked up on their travels – into distinctive World Family Ibiza pieces.

Bottom right: Their daughter-in-law Andrea Fernández handles the fashion brand's day-to-day administration.

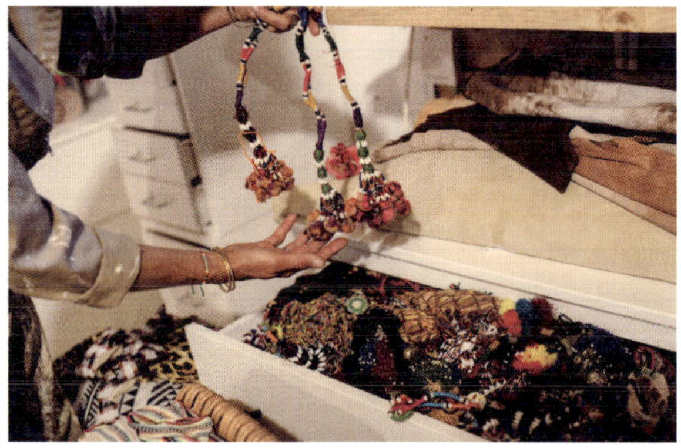

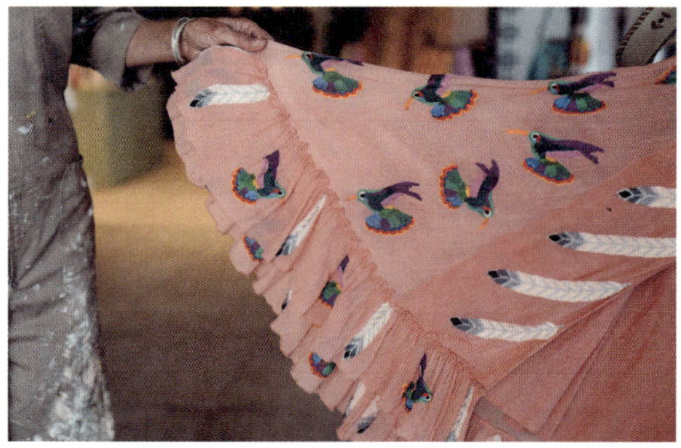

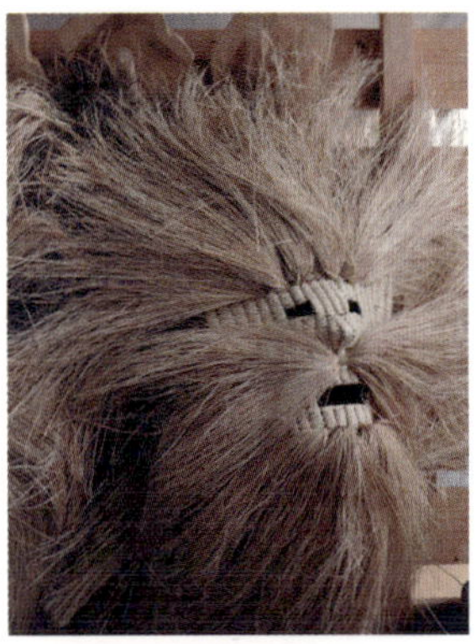

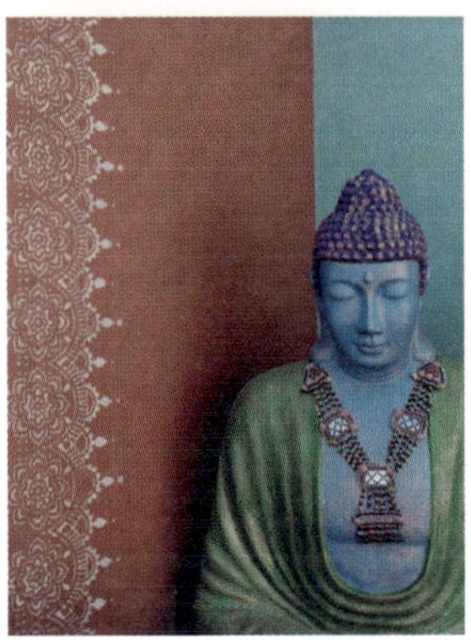

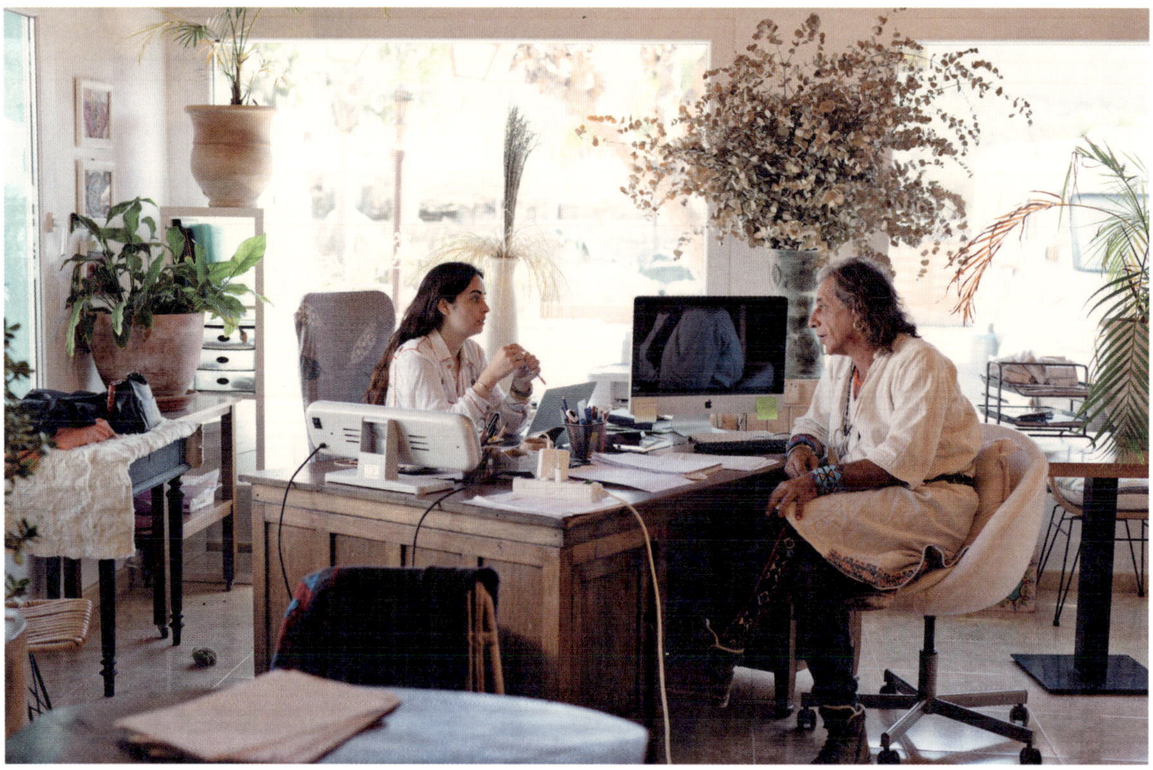

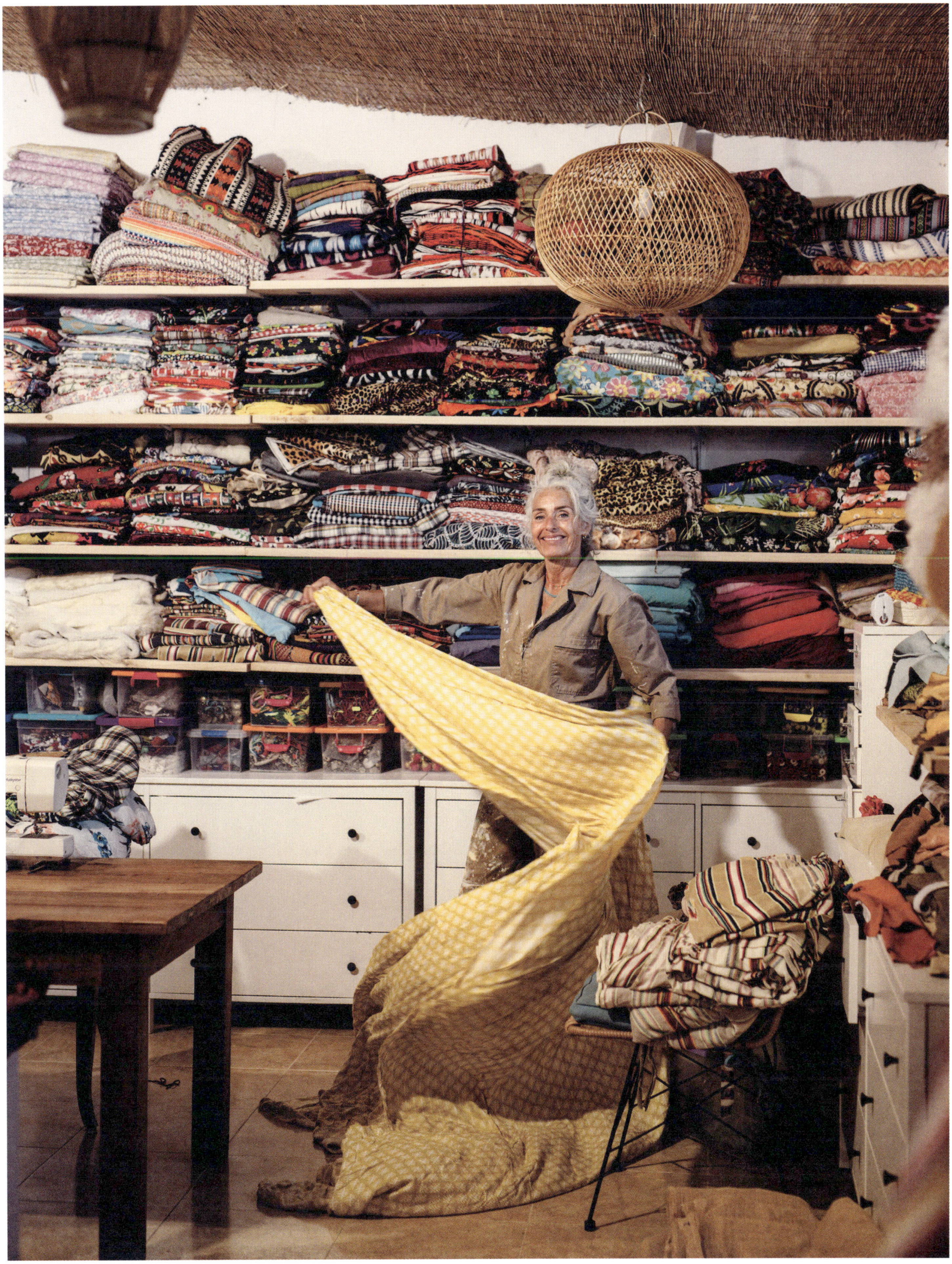

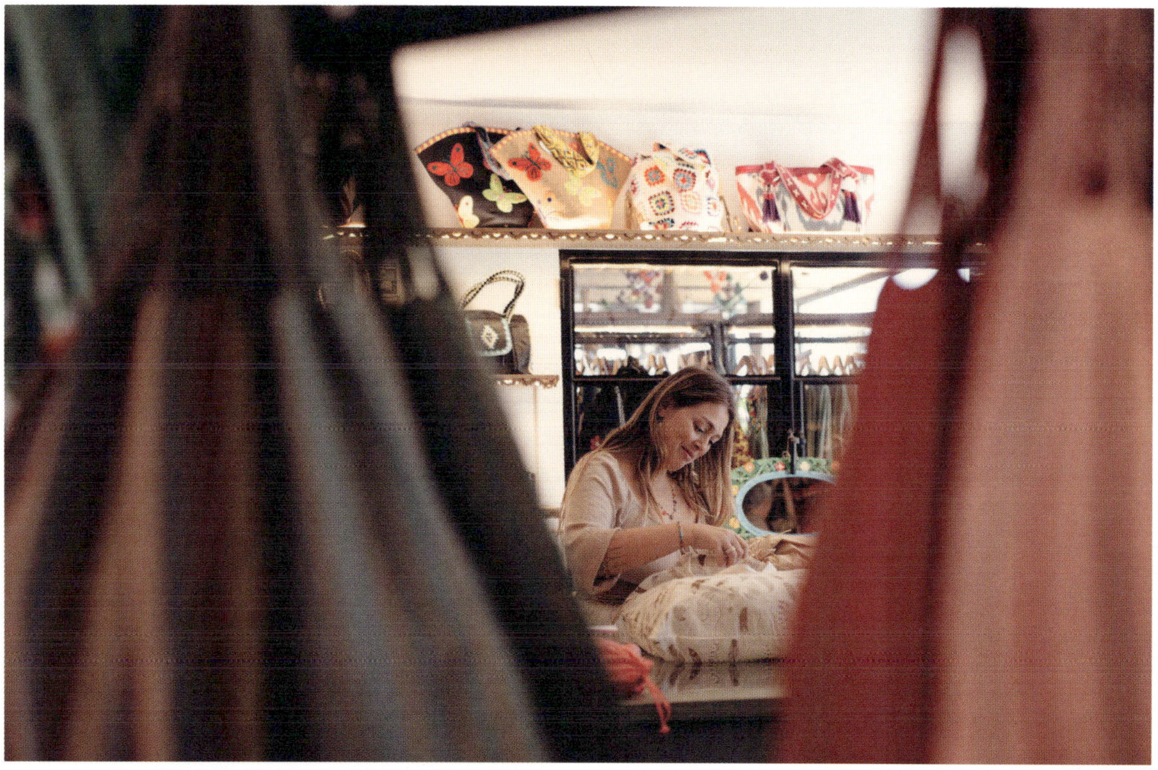

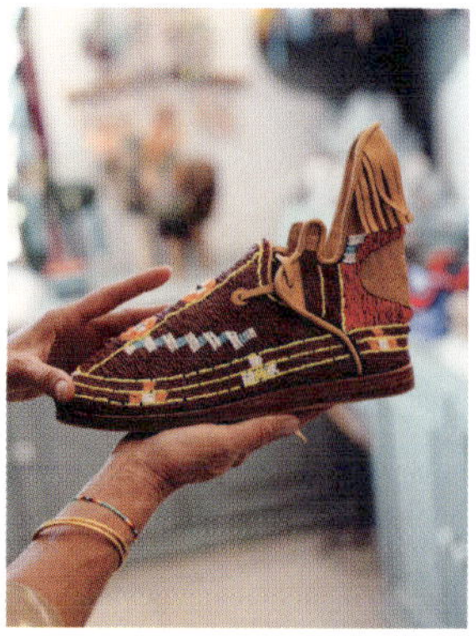

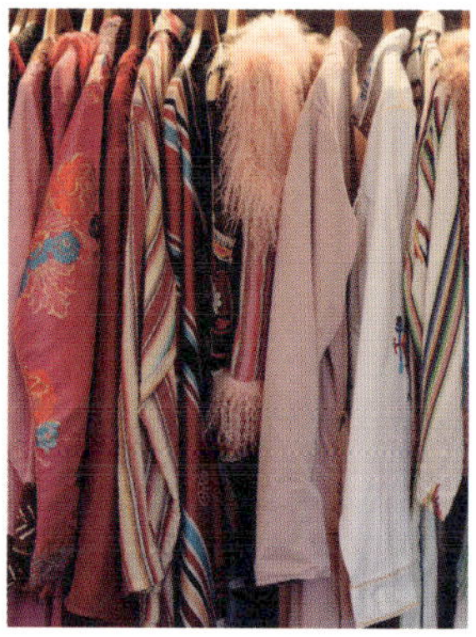

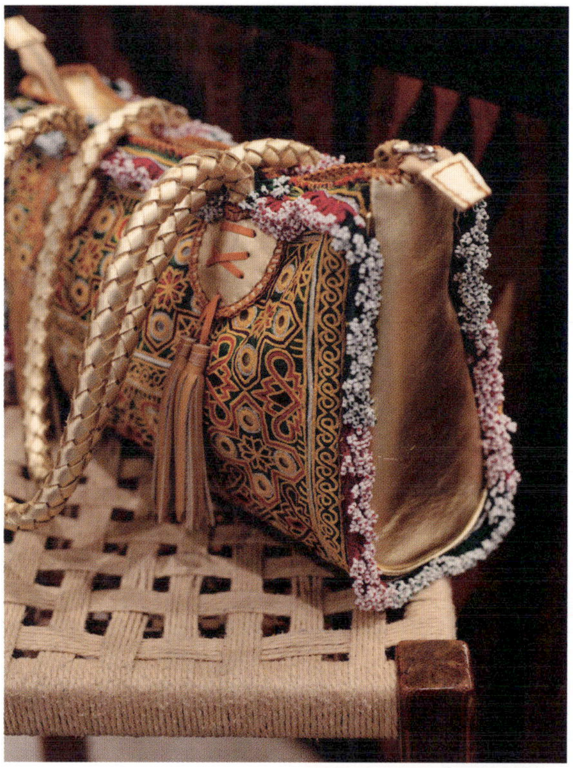

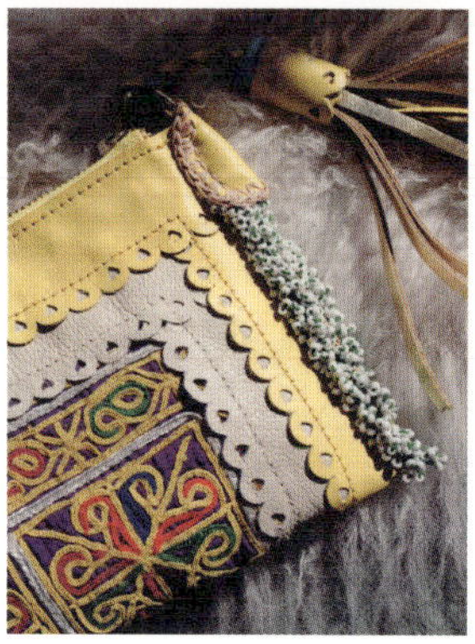

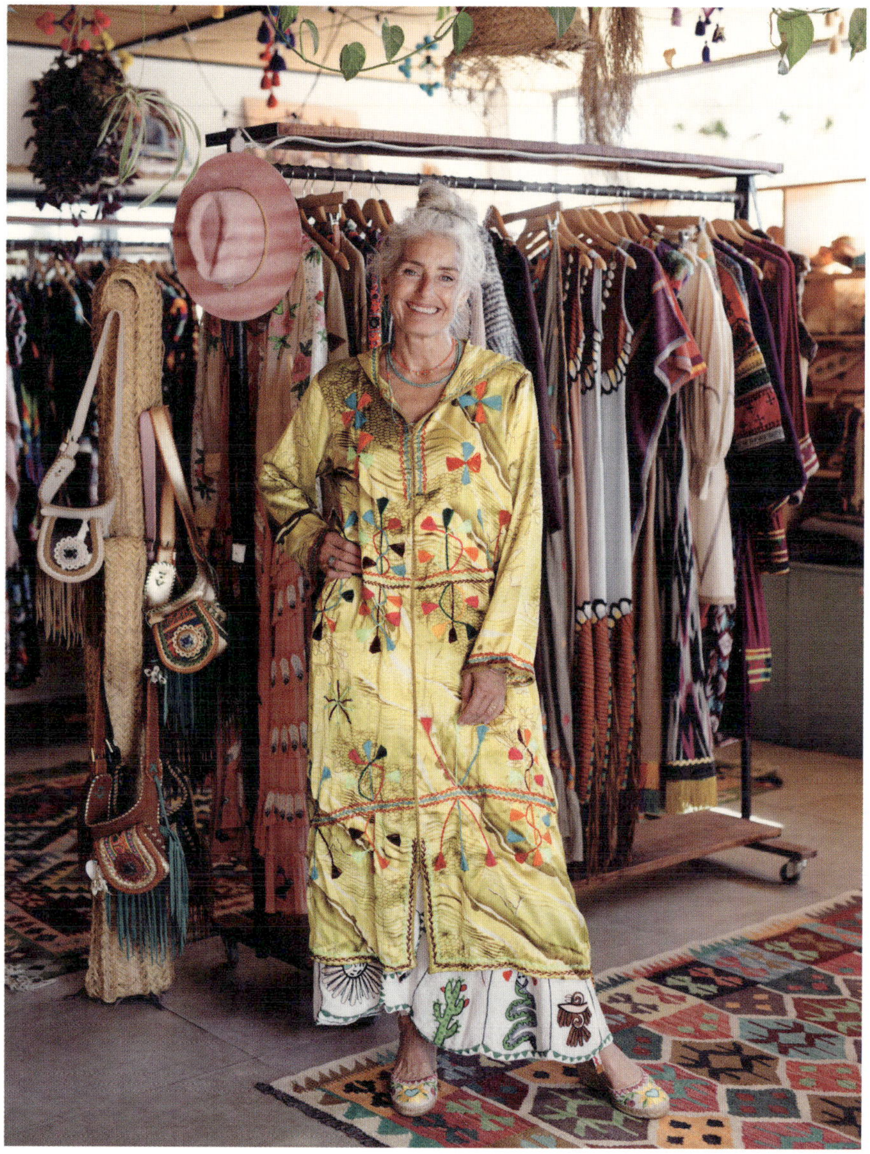

Top left: Daughter Goldie prepares online orders for Dubai and Switzerland.

The highly embellished, eclectic style of the clothes and accessories is a result of Merel's love of mixing techniques, materials and traditions.

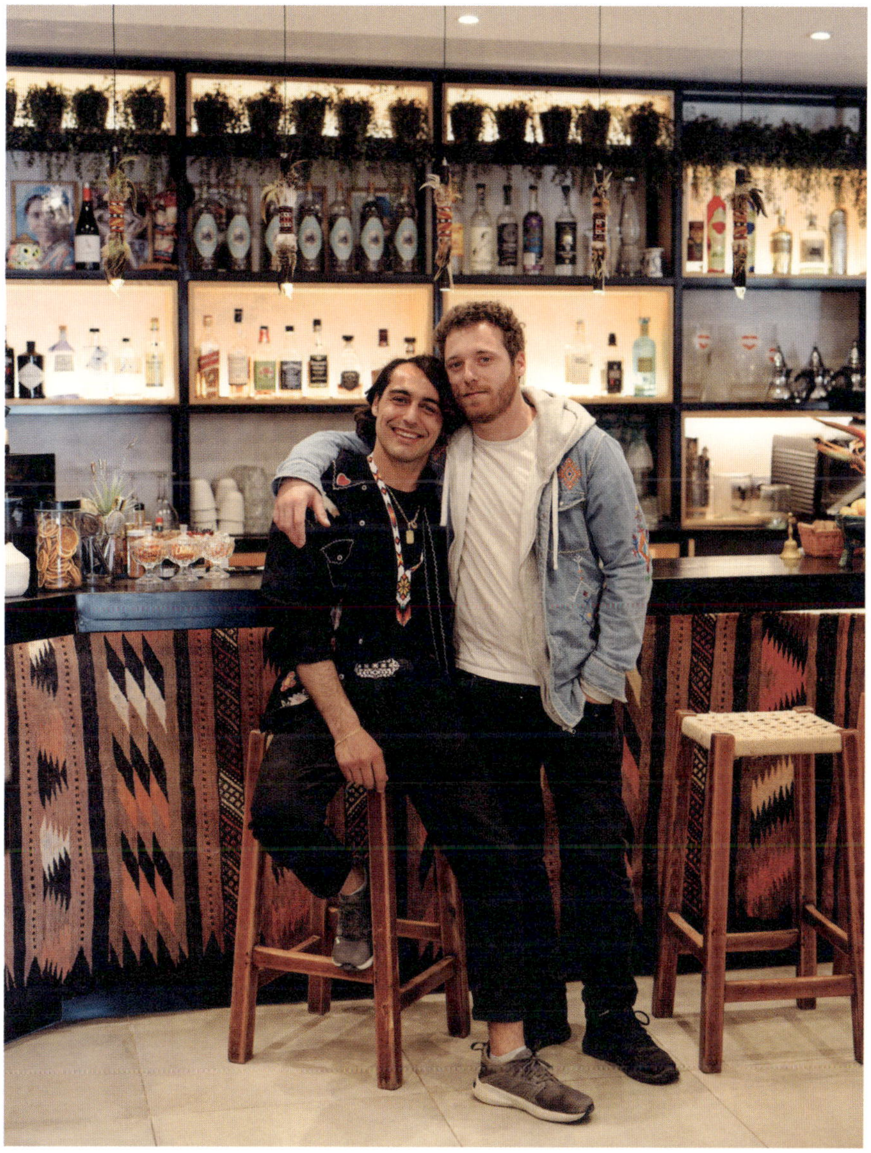

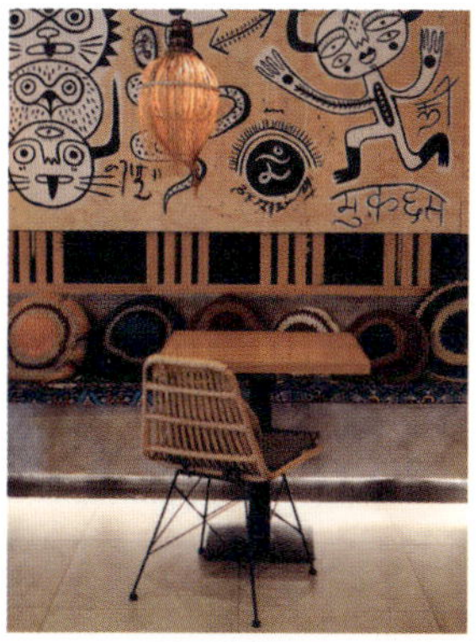

Far left: Sons Asher (on left) and Rama run the restaurant. Its menu features the family's favourite dishes.

Left and bottom left: The striking mural is by the Madrid-born, Ibiza-based artist Violeta Galera.

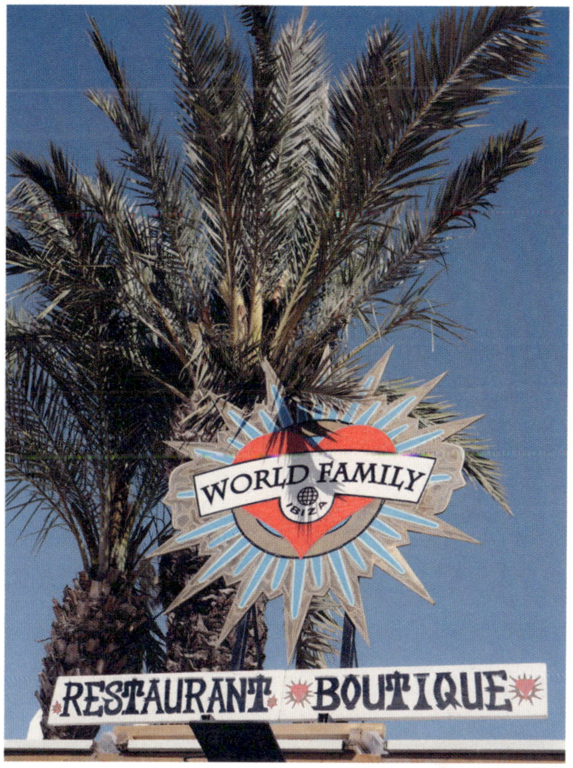

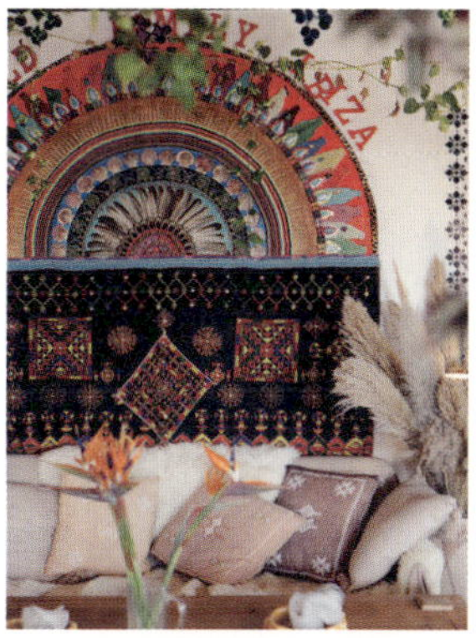

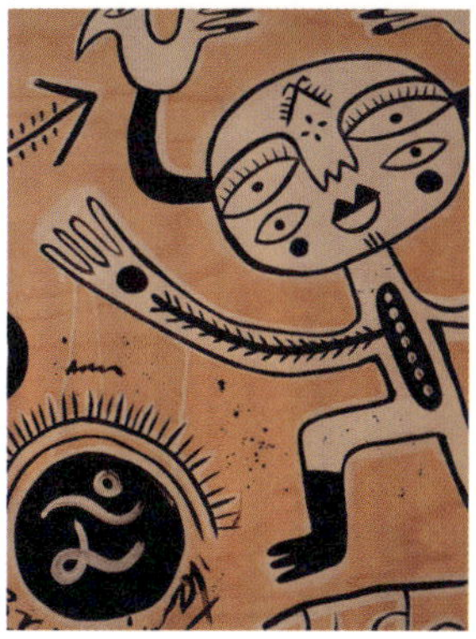

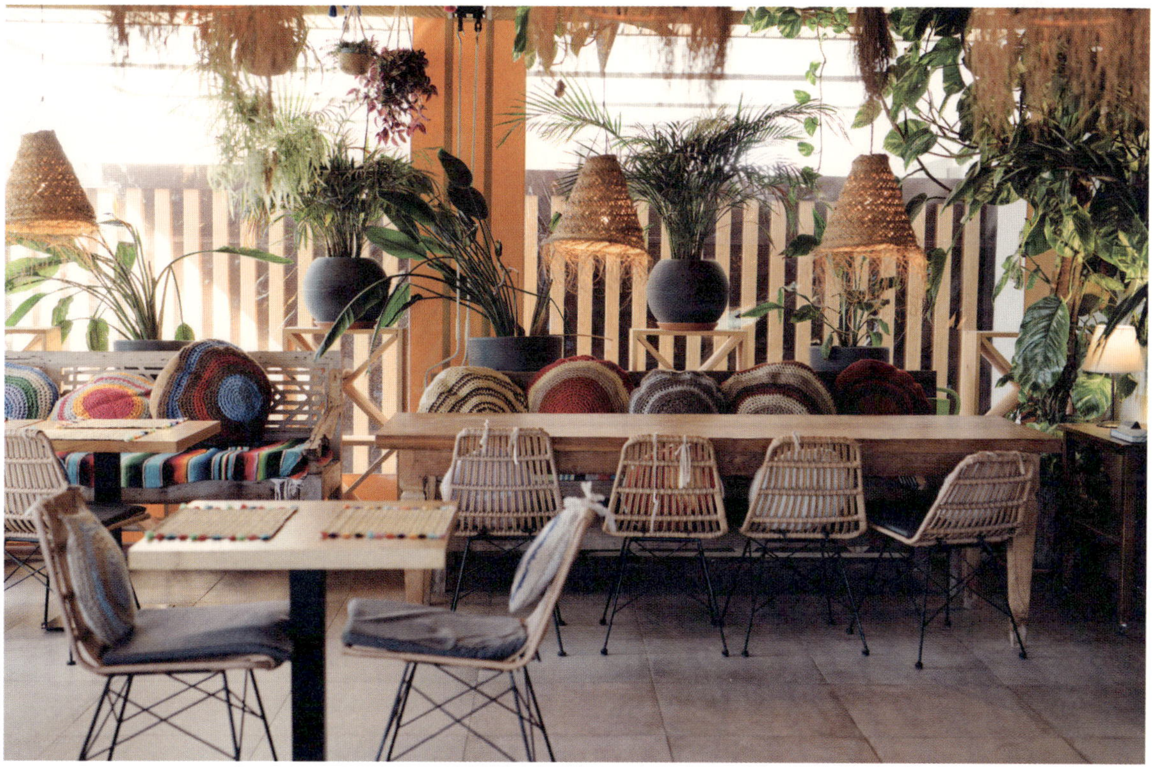

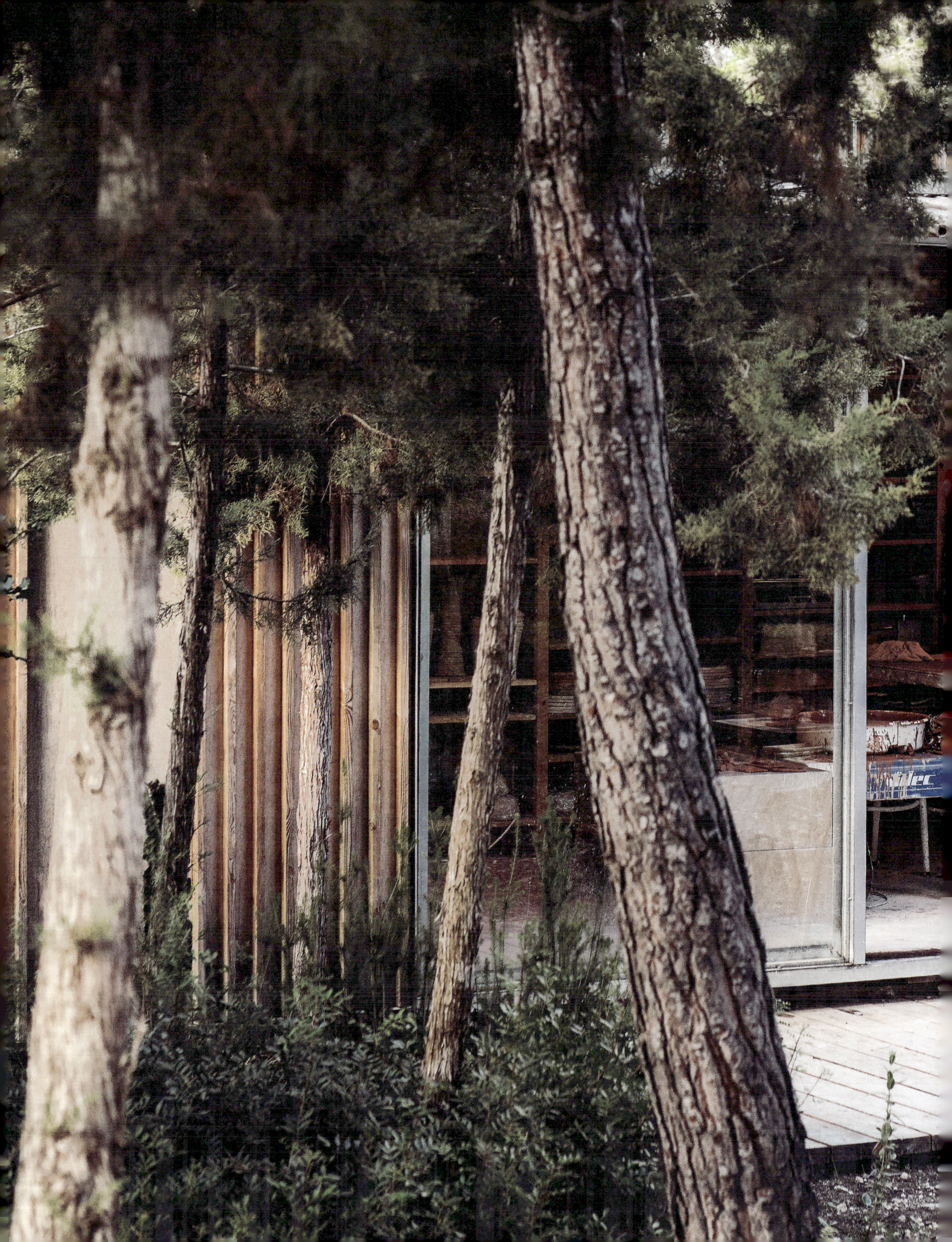

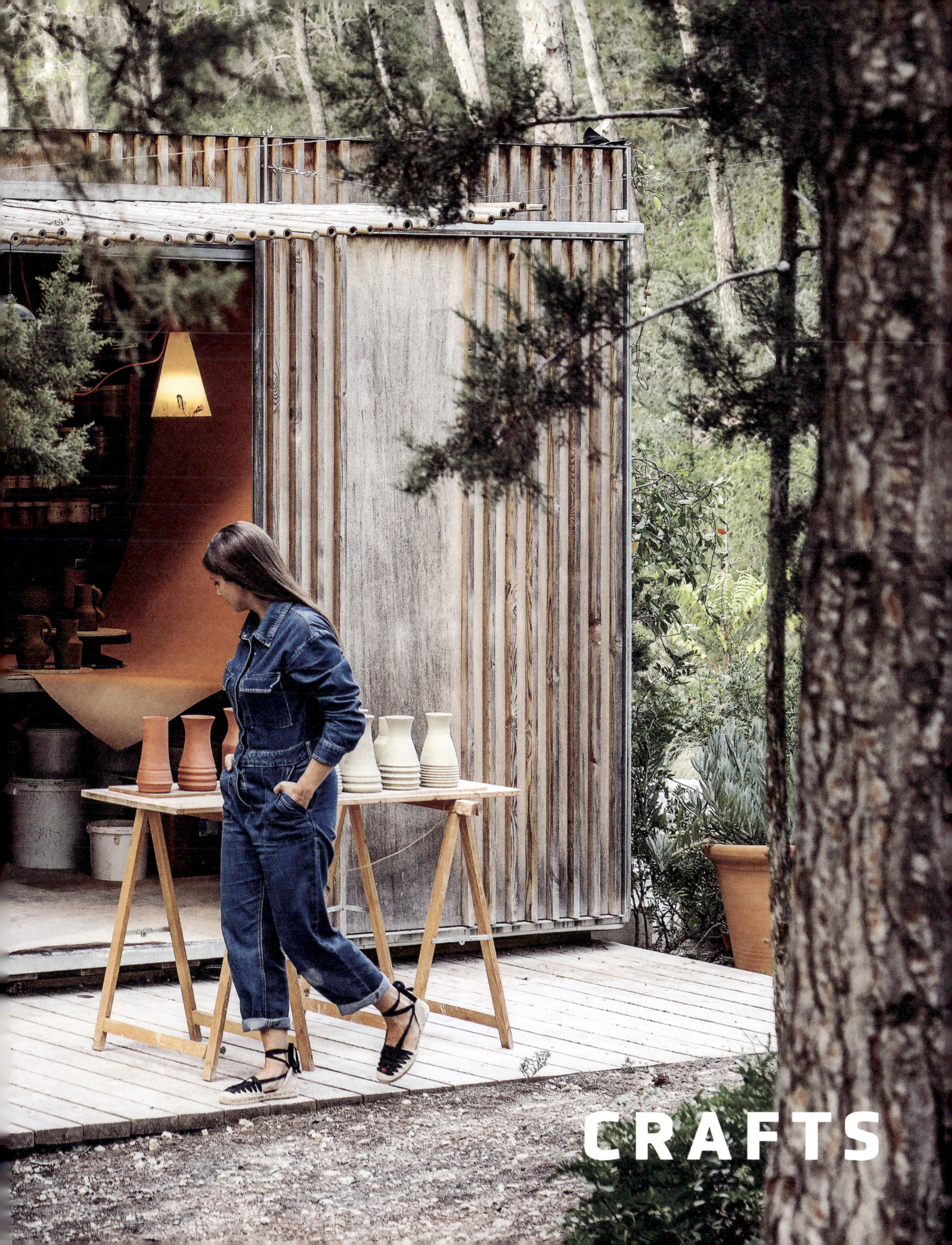

CRAFTS

INÉS VENTÓS

HANDCRAFTED CANDLES

Inés Ventós Soler-Cabot's family has been distilling and distributing essential oils for more than a century. In 1916 her great-grandfather Ernesto Ventós Casadevall bought a two-horsepower electric motor and a copperplate still to distil essences in his workshop at home in the Sants district of Barcelona.

Inés's grandfather Ernesto Ventós Ravetllat carried on the business after his parents died when they were still young. And her father, Ernesto Ventós Omedes, who was born in the same home-cum-workshop, trained as a perfumer from an early age and helped his father. He later went on to train in the cradle of perfumery, Grasse, France, with the Robertet family, and in Geneva, Switzerland, with the Firmenich family. Both are major forces in the fragrance industry.

In 2018 Inés came to live in Ibiza with her husband and children, and it was then that, grateful for her origins, she decided to create a collection of handmade candles. As a child, she had watched her father create olfactory compositions and tell everyone, 'Words are forgotten, but smells are not.'

For Inés, 'Smell is a sense linked to people's feelings, their life and their history.' A spiritual person, she thinks of life as a series of olfactory experiences. Different smells are very evocative for her: 'Young lemongrass reminds me of my childhood. At my grandmother's country house, there was an aromatic herb garden including marjoram, lavender and rosemary. Meanwhile, my great-grandmother's garden had cypress and eucalyptus trees.'

Inés's first two candle collections are 'Earth', which is contained in ceramic pots made by an artisanal workshop; and 'Air', which comes in heat-resistant borosilicate glass made by a traditional glass-blower. The candles are naturally scented, featuring lavender, thyme flowers, cardamom seeds, rosemary, eucalyptus, ginger and young lemongrass. Inés has also developed a fine perfumery range – a blend of natural and synthetic ingredients, comprising Sabina and Parmaqua V.

Inés makes the candles using vegetable wax because she likes the smell and texture, and the way it combines with the perfumes. She explains: 'Today I have the same passion for this work that I saw in my father. I believe a candle is a symbol of well-being and tranquillity. I also see it as a product with a lot of personality that can really help people.'

Inés is determined not to create single-use items, because they are not environmentally friendly. The containers for her candles can be reused, either refilled with wax or repurposed as cups, pots or vases.

As well as selling her own range of candles, Inés is commissioned by companies 'looking for a corporate gift in harmony with their brand values'.

'I like things that are simple and well made, but I'm not looking for perfection', Inés says. 'What I'm looking for is to enjoy every moment in a natural way, without rushing.' ***CD***

Inés Ventós has drawn on her family's legacy as experts in essential oils to create her own range of handmade scented candles. For her, they symbolize well-being and tranquillity.

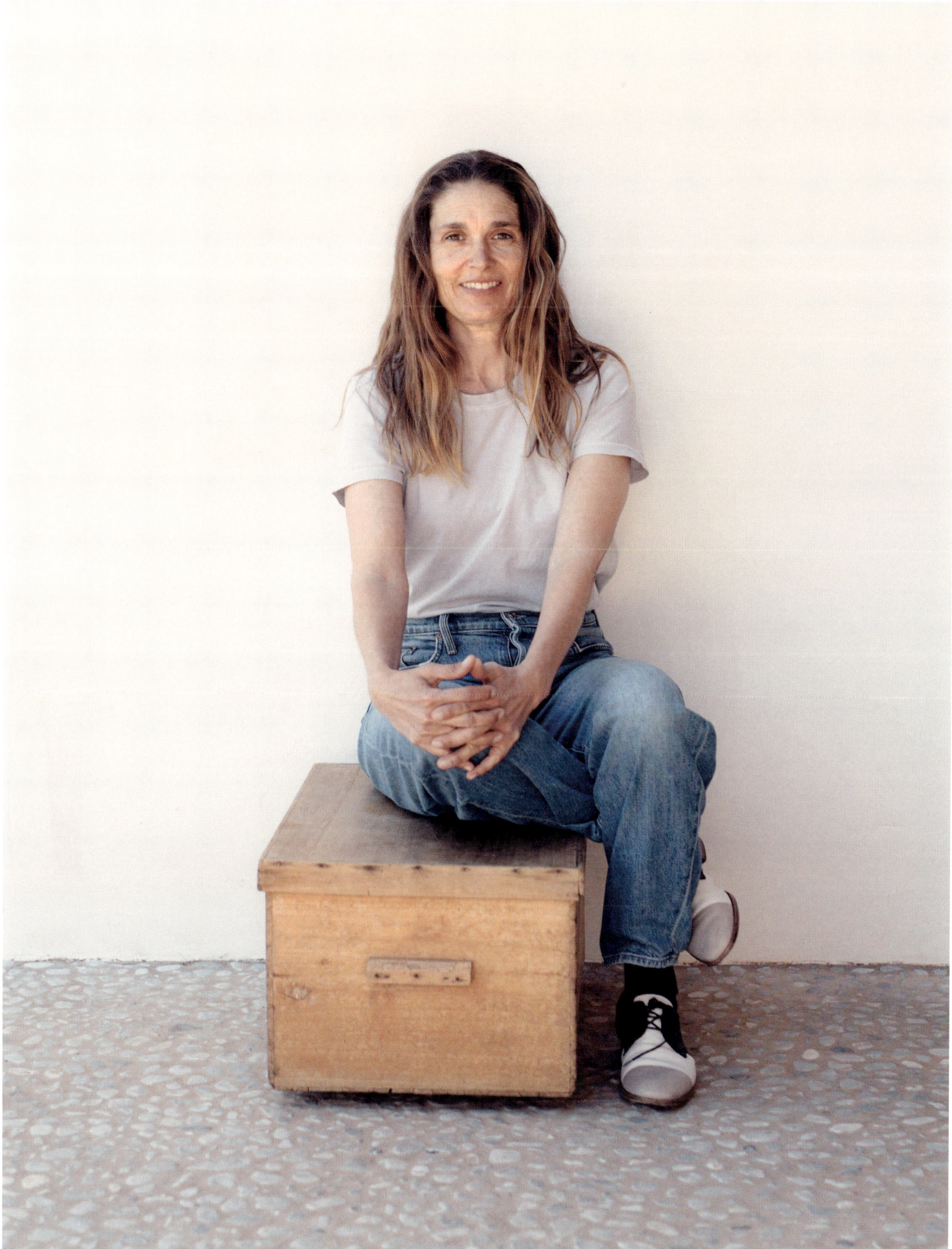

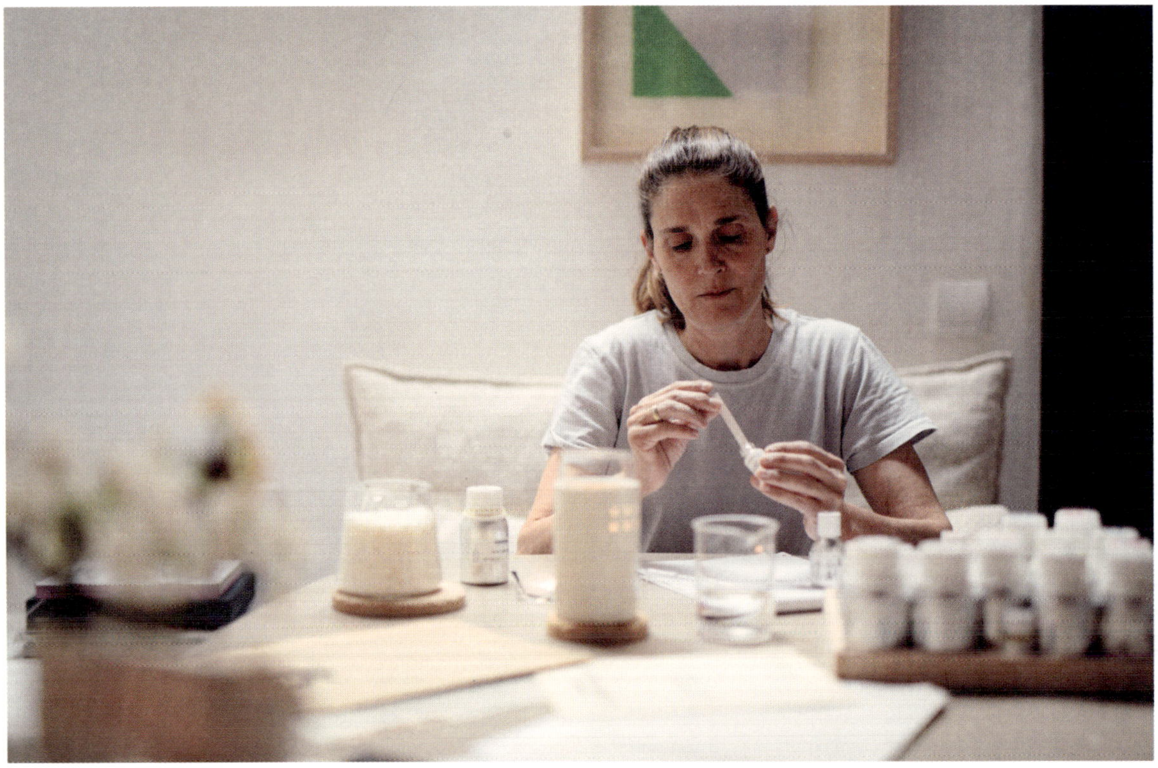

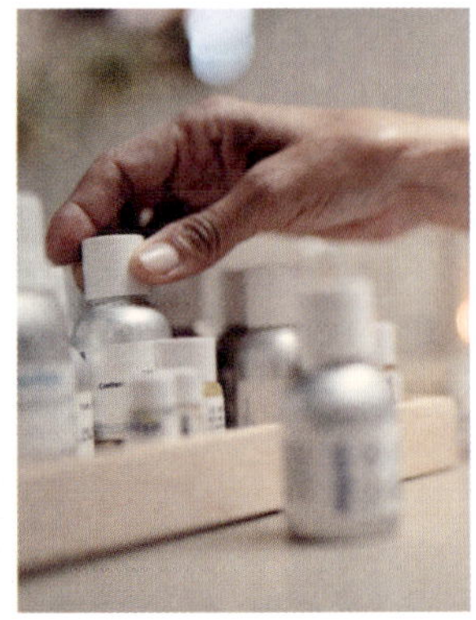

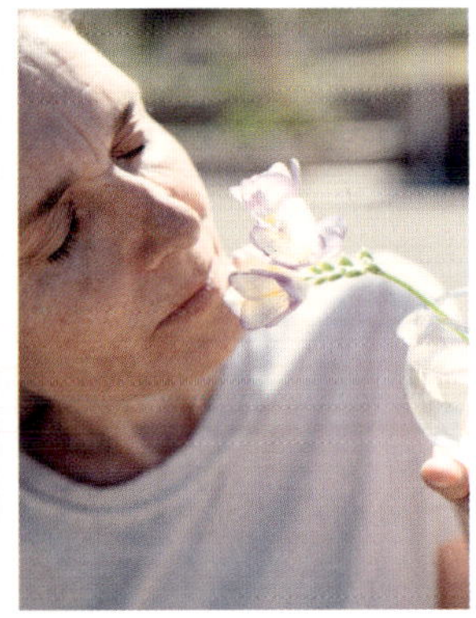

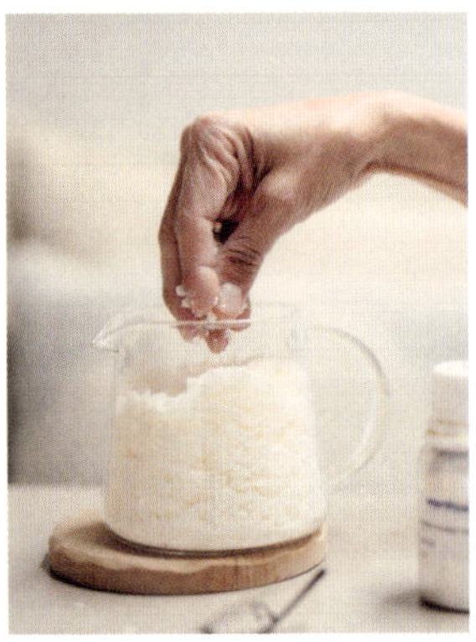

Certain natural aromas are very evocative for Inés, taking her back to her childhood in Barcelona. She draws on these memories to create her own range of scents from plants including rosemary, lavender, cardamom, lemongrass and thyme.

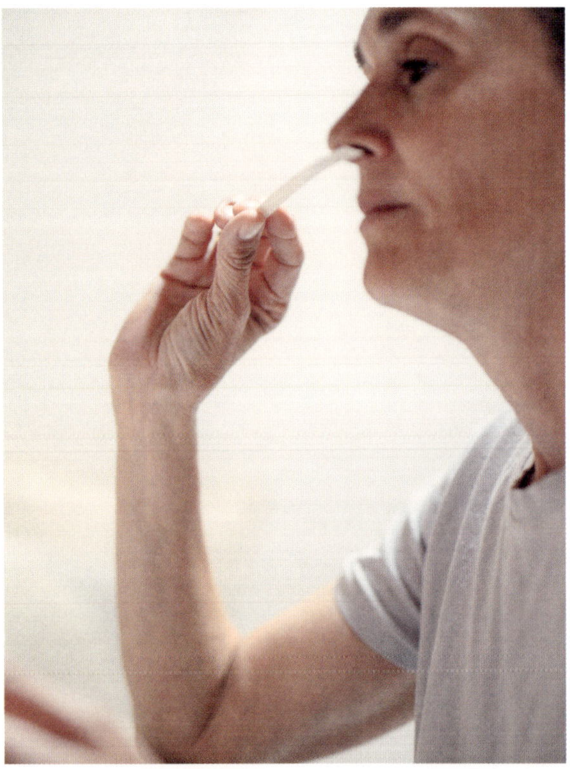

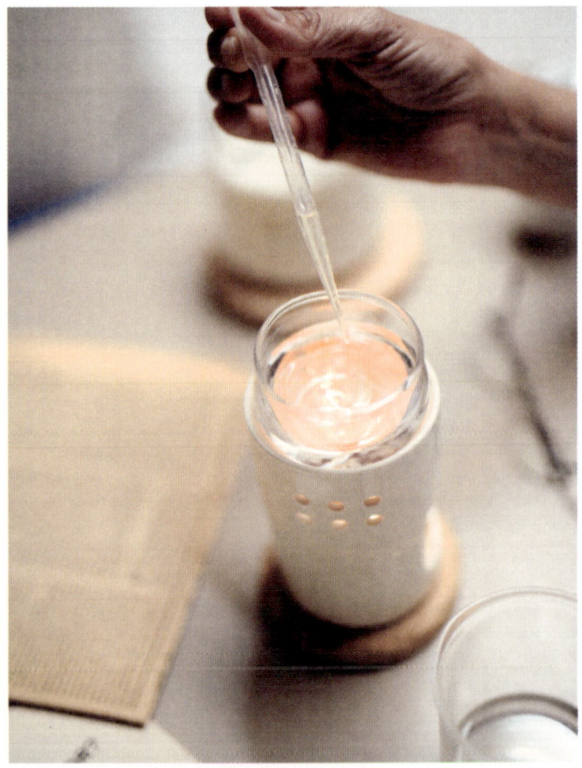

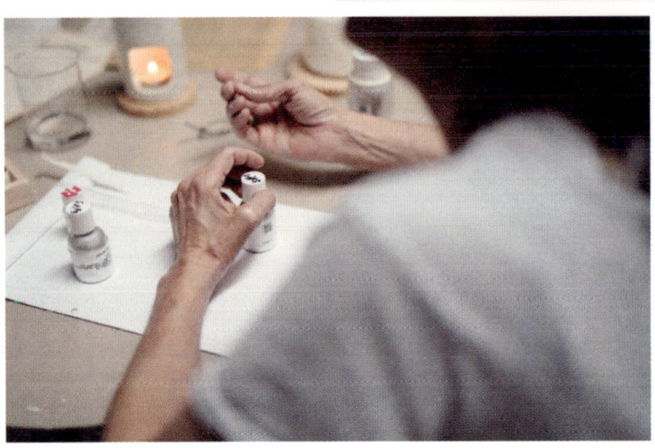

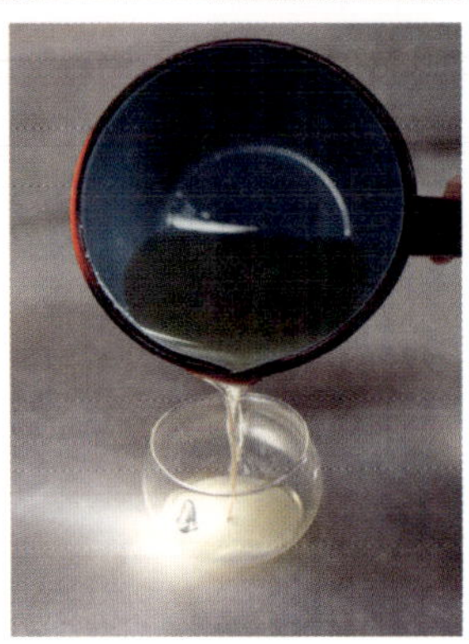

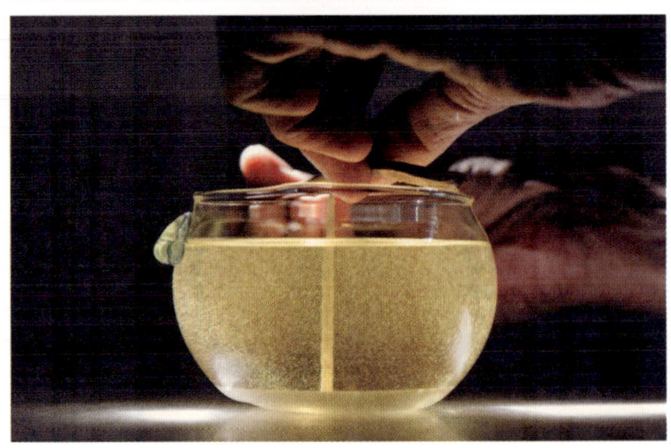

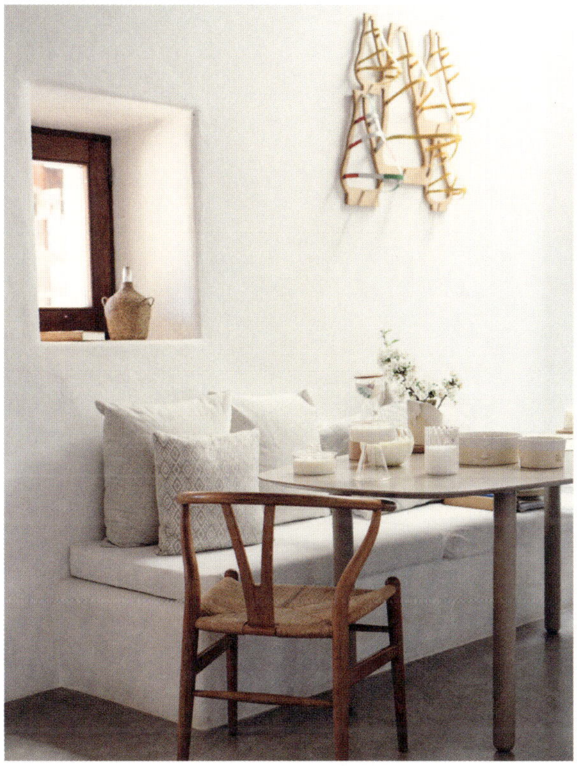

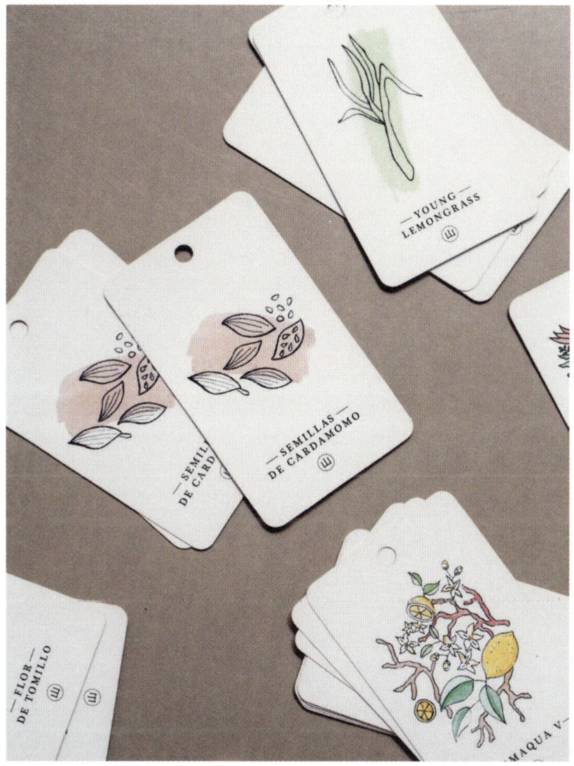

Inés commissions specialist artisans to make glass and ceramic pots, which can have a second life after a candle is finished.

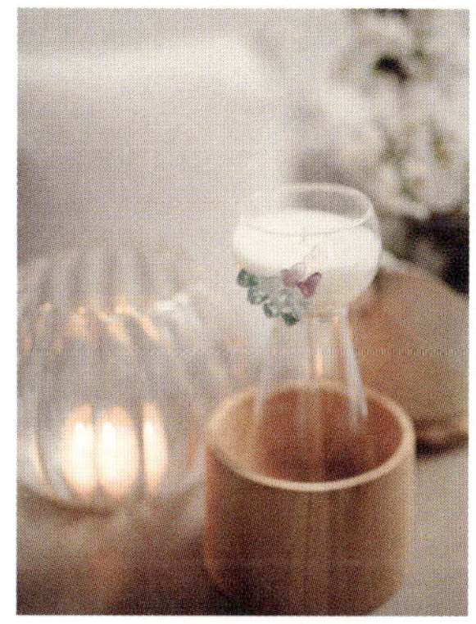

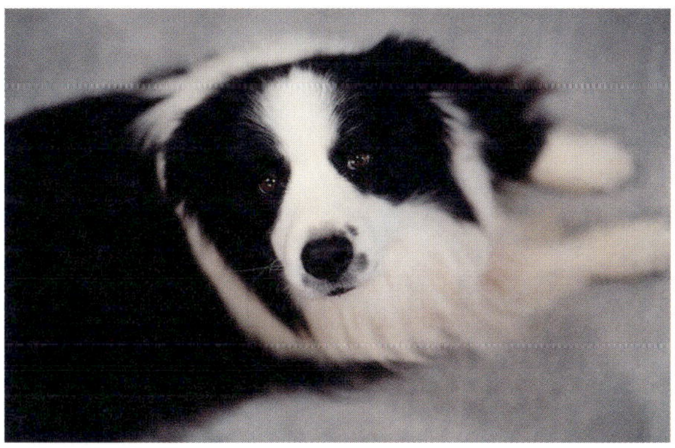

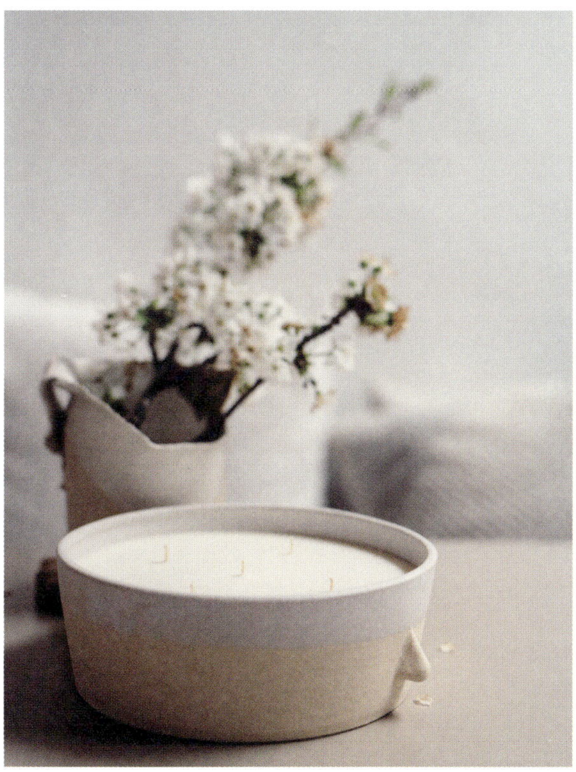

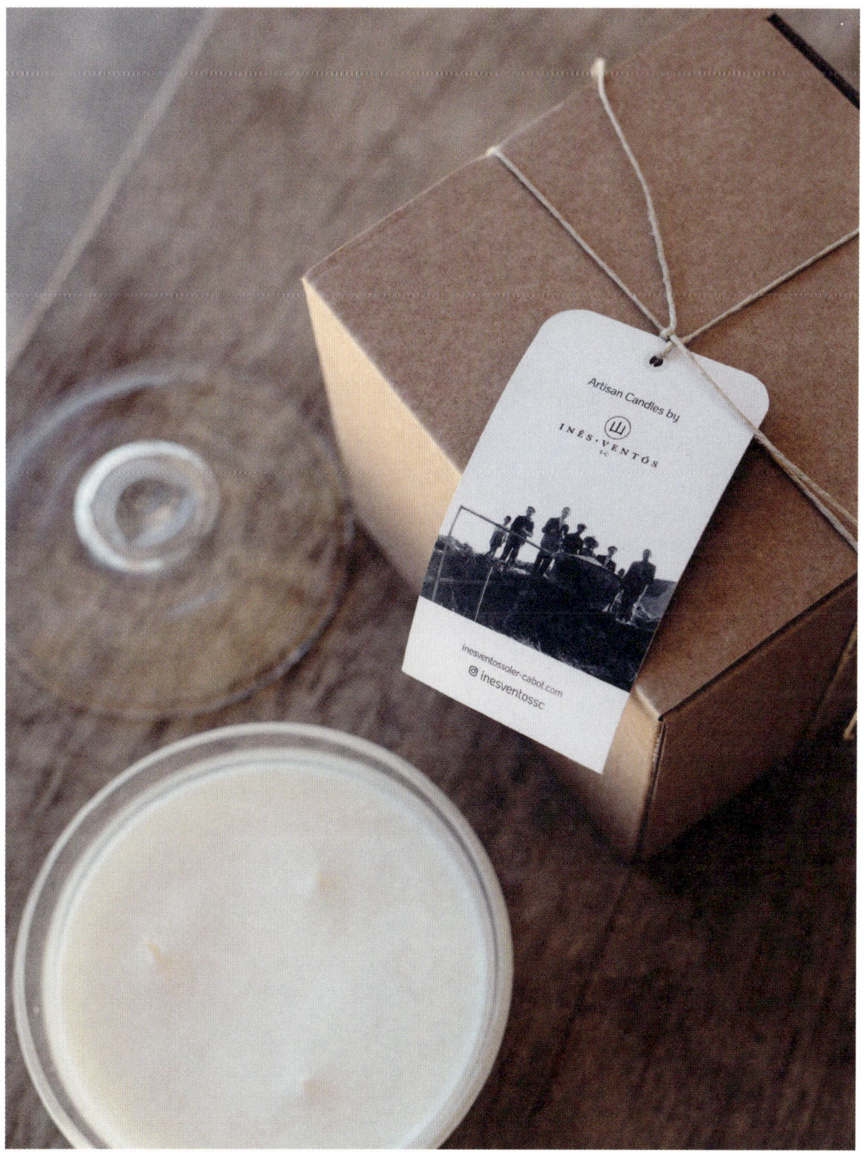

SANTA GERTRUDIS
@yvettespowersceramics

YVETTE SPOWERS

COILED & SCULPTURAL CERAMICS

The Barbadian-born ceramicist Yvette Spowers enjoyed an early artistic epiphany. When she was a child, the famous English fine-china house Wedgwood would visit the main department store in Barbados each year to demonstrate various methods of creating ceramics at the potter's wheel. Although she became instantly enamoured of the process, some time would pass before she was able to take her new-found passion further. Fast-forward nearly twenty years, and a fortuitous series of events brought Yvette to the California studio of the renowned artist Bill Attaway, whose beautiful mosaic column adorns the famous boardwalk in Venice Beach. There, she was finally able to pursue the seed of the dream that had been sown two decades previously. Access to Attaway's studio enabled Yvette to experiment, and she took to the practice quickly, swiftly gaining confidence and honing her own style.

Predominantly self-taught, Yvette uses the ancient techniques of coiling, hand-building and smoke-firing the clay, an approach practised by many primal cultures across the globe. Finishes are achieved by burnishing the pieces with a semi-precious stone – a slow, meditative process resulting in work that is a unique expression of its creator.

Yvette lived for some time in Britain and also in Sri Lanka, where she continued working with ceramics while concurrently managing an art gallery. In 2012 she made the decision to move to Ibiza, enticed by the natural habitat that has drawn artists for decades.

Inspired by the nature that surrounds her – wood, stones, decayed leaves and other vegetation – and by the clay itself, Yvette continues with her own work. She produces an eclectic range of ceramics, the pieces always characterized by her singular style. She now also transfers her knowledge to others, teaching pottery to both adults and children, a gratifying experience that has coincided with an enhanced interest in creative practices on the island, particularly in the realm of ceramics. Several decades ago, Ibiza was home to a prolific ceramics movement and has recently witnessed a resurgence in the art form as an increasing number of people awaken to the infinite possibilities of creating with clay. The concept of craft as a creative process has also seen a renaissance, and the diverse world of ceramics provides the perfect crossover between craft and art. Many people are drawn to the tactile nature of clay and to the ease with which they can express themselves in an immediate fashion. Yvette is widely considered to be at the forefront of this burgeoning island revival.

Never inclined to be bound to one type of practice, Yvette continually seeks to broaden her knowledge and expand her repertoire of skills. She has ventured into the realm of sculpture and also produces bespoke designs for clients, such as the exquisitely crafted lampshades that adorn the living spaces of some of the island's finest homes. ***CE***

From Barbados to Britain and beyond, Yvette Spowers seeks inspiration from the natural world, using ancient techniques gleaned over several decades to produce her ceramic designs.

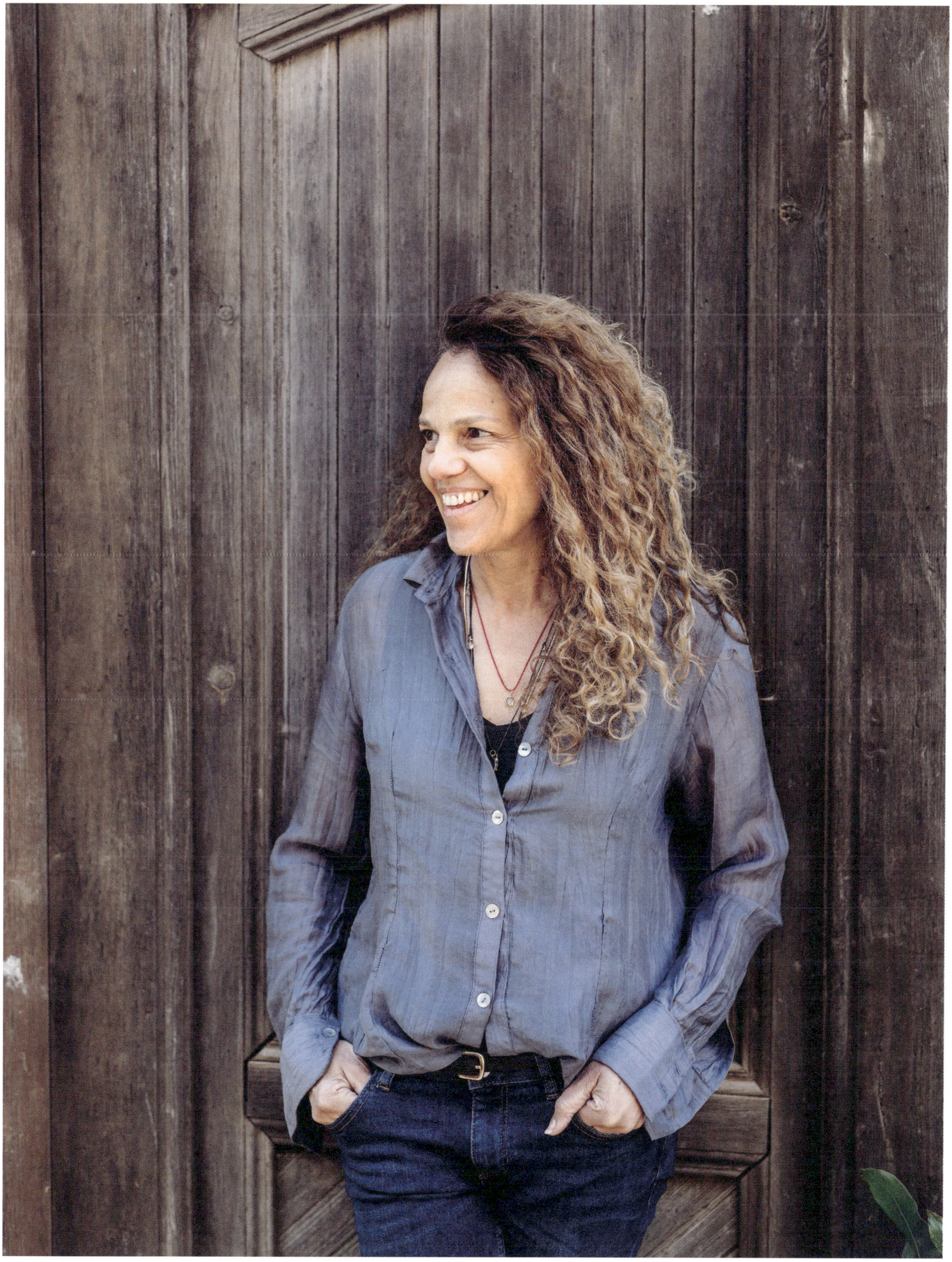

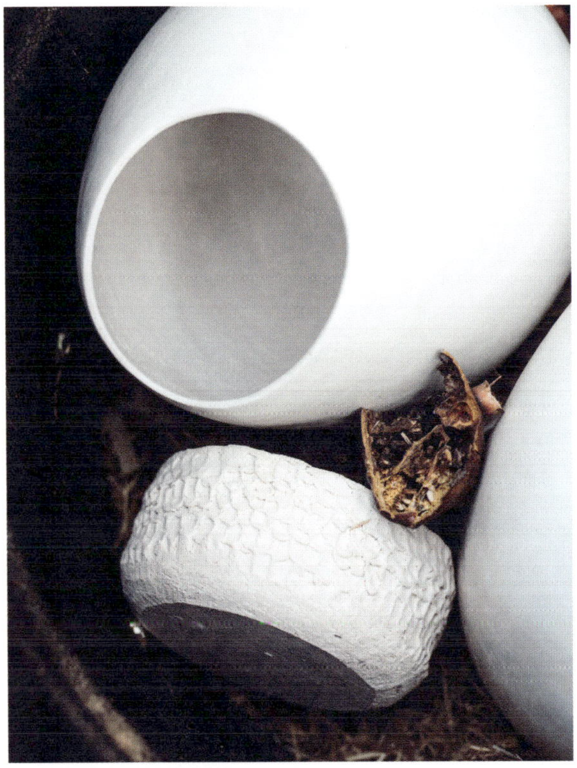

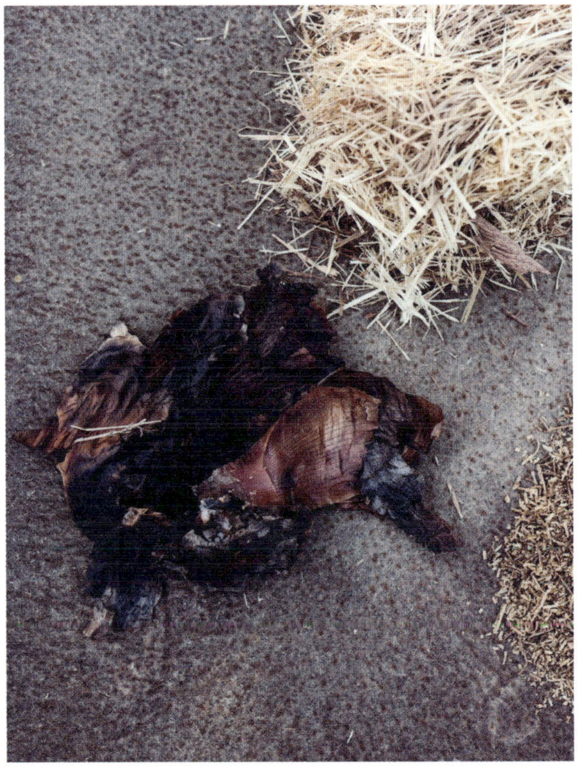

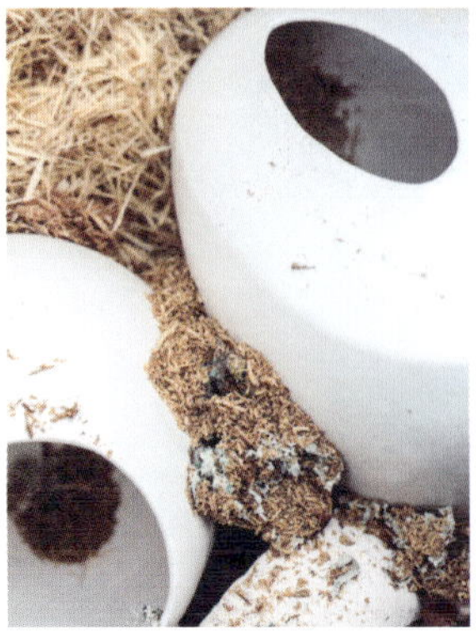

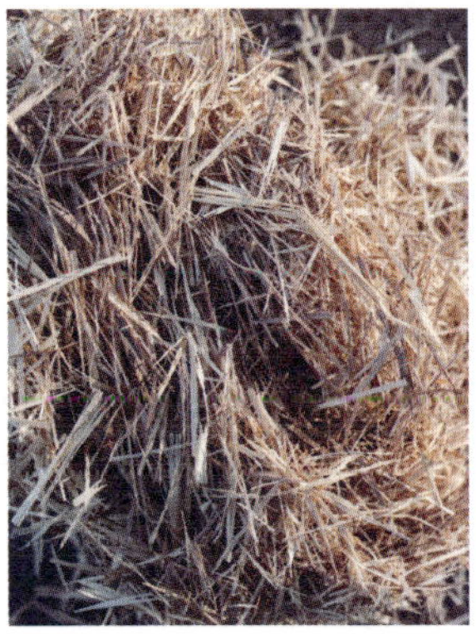

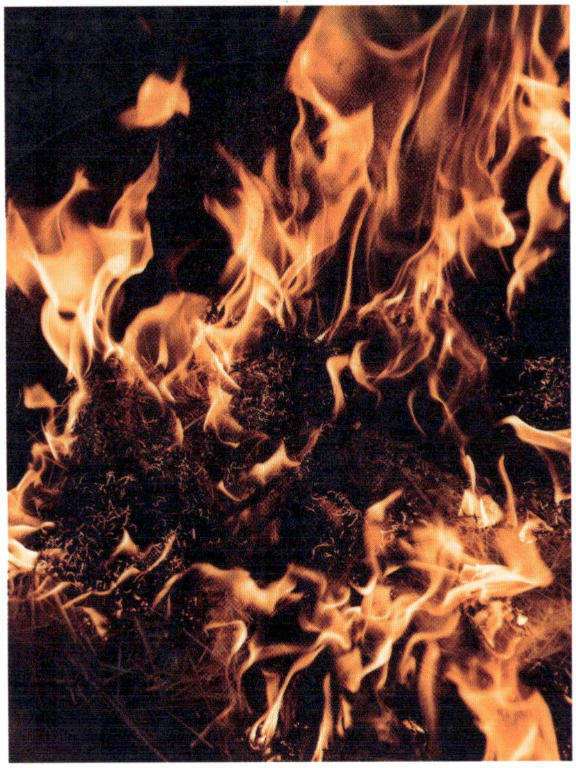

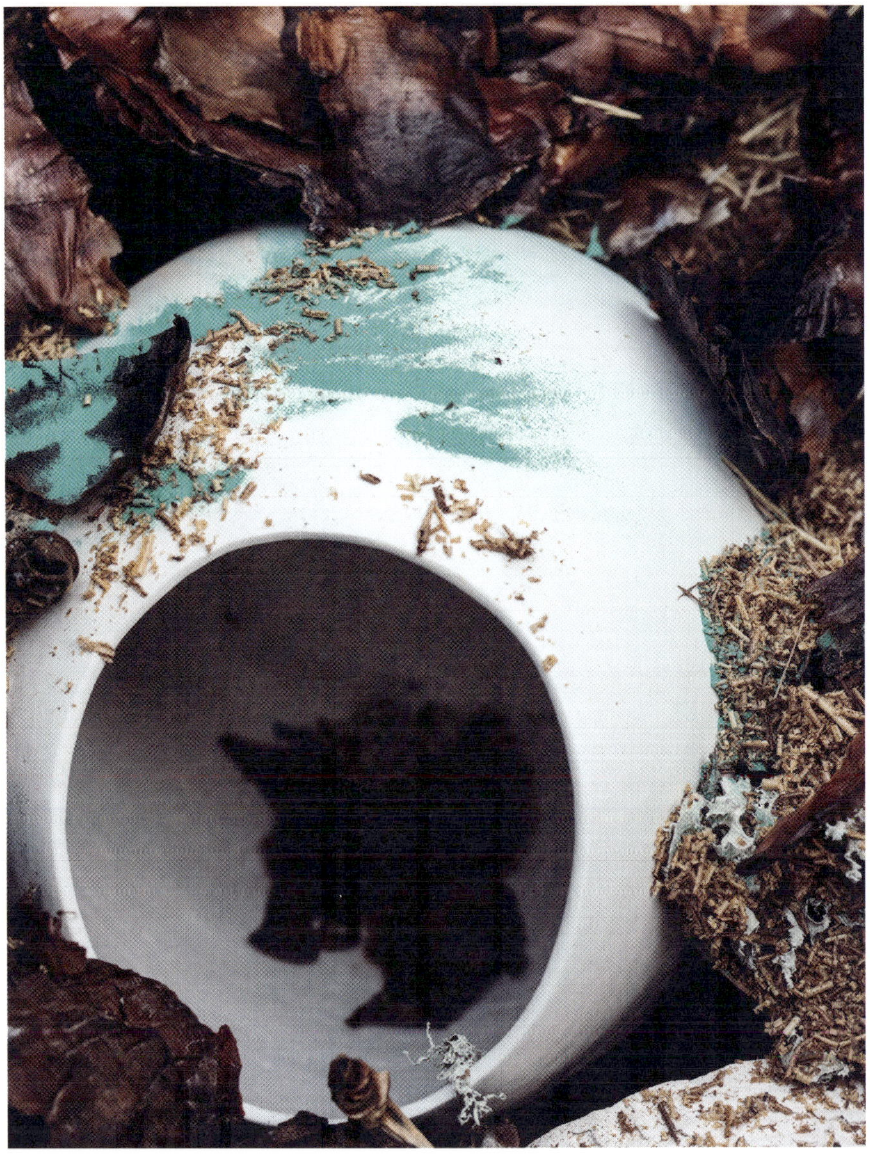

A brick pit is used for the second firing, when materials such as seaweed, sawdust, moss, banana leaves and copper oxide are added to create unique patterns and colours on the surface of the ceramic pieces.

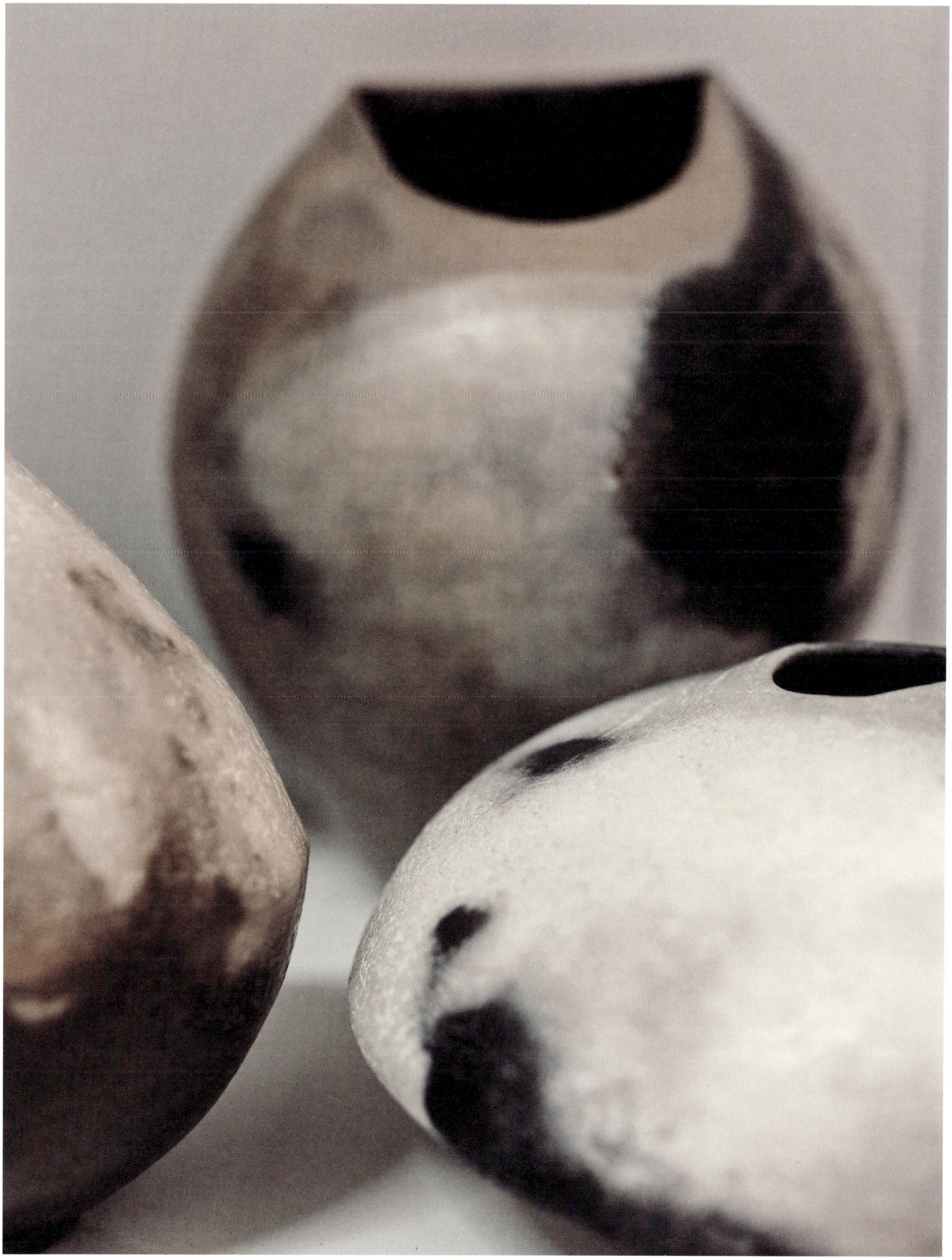

JESÚS
ladio.eu

LADIO CERAMICS

CONTEMPORARY CERAMICS

Like so many children of Ibiza, the urge to escape the island and discover the world presaged a coming of age in the city for Laura de Grinyo. As many children of Ibiza will also attest, such wanderlust eventually comes full circle. After spending six years building her own fashion brand and battling the commotion of Barcelona, Laura returned to the natural refuge of her birth island.

Then a timely gift of a short pottery course ignited an unexpected passion for ceramics. Combining her intrinsic respect for the elements and the fulfilment of a profound yearning for creative expression, the craft guided Laura to learn with Ibiza's artisanal elders, or *maestros de cerámica*. The investment in her own kiln and wheel became a catalyst for the reinvention of her life.

Laura sees the earth as a residue of time; a granulated history that stretches all the way back to the source. In Ibiza, time has been given physical form by the myriad cultures that have sailed through the island. Ladio Ceramics honours these traditions with a sense of playfulness and panache, presenting an ever-growing collection of utilitarian crockery, from plates and cups to bowls and jugs. 'Ceramics have always been the most useful resource for preserving water and food', explains Laura. 'There are different containers designed specifically for milk, water and wine. I study these forms and give them a new twist; it's important to learn about the utility of each item, rather than to focus on the aesthetic.'

Recalling how her mother would often remind her to look beyond the surface of things, Laura strives to lean into her feeling, bringing clear intentions to everything. Artistic collaborations have pushed her craft into more imaginative territory, such as exhibitions in London and Milan and a project with fellow Ibicenco artisans to embellish traditional footwear with ceramic details. She has even developed an experimental underwater show on the seabed. Collaborative projects with artists and the Spanish luxury brand Loewe have led to her work being featured in prestigious galleries and publications.

Part of a new generation paying homage to history while striving to stay grounded in the modern world, Laura is comforted by a belief that, as organic beings, we need nature and connection in order to thrive. 'It's romantic, in a way; a constant fight, in another', she explains. 'I embrace the forces of frustration because things don't always work the way they should. One just needs to learn and to practise more – and every day brings a different lesson.' ***LA***

Laura de Grinyo outside her home studio, which nestles under pine trees. Her work is guided by a belief that the earth is a residue of time and that through her clay pottery she gives renewed life to the earth.

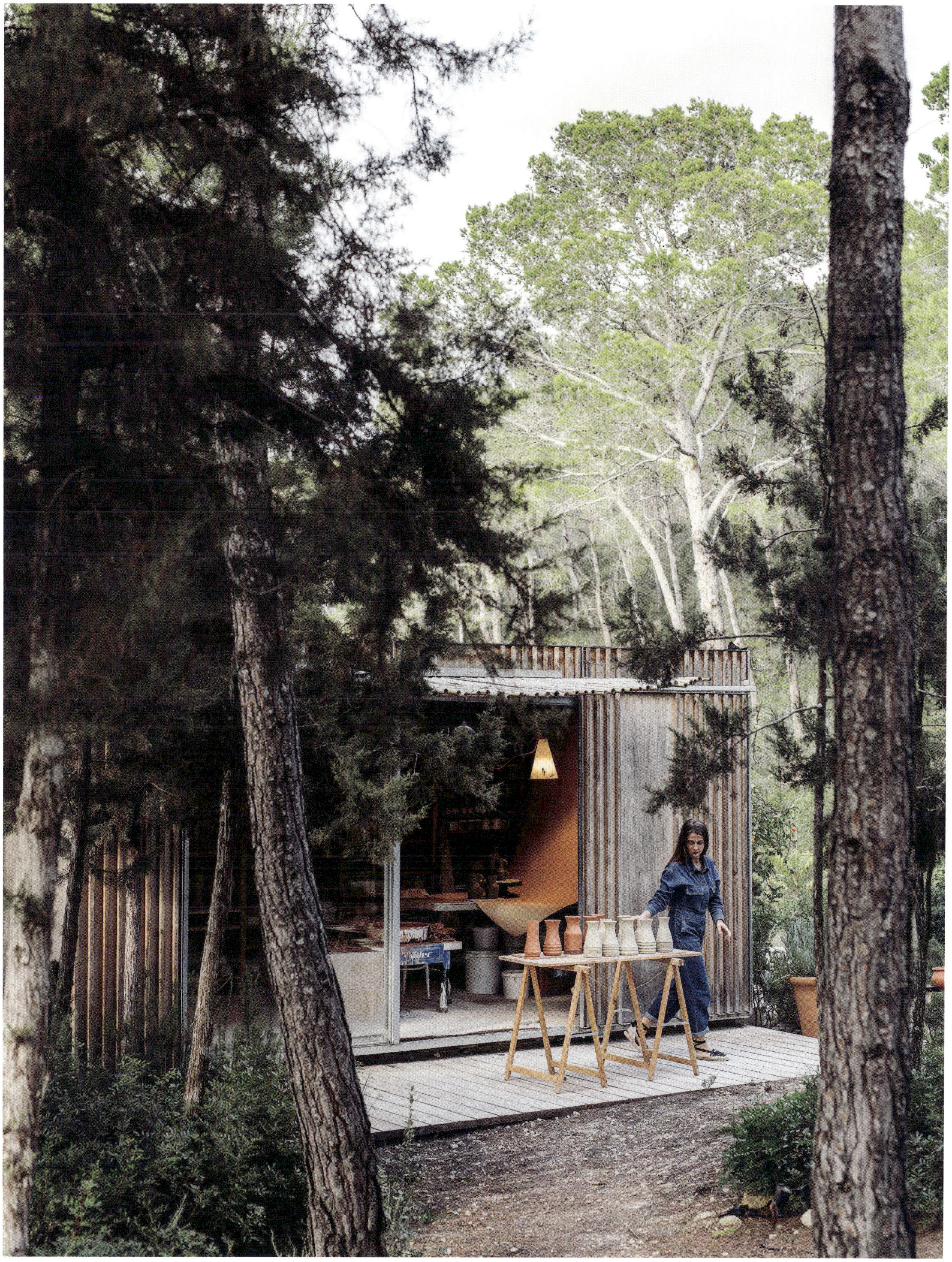

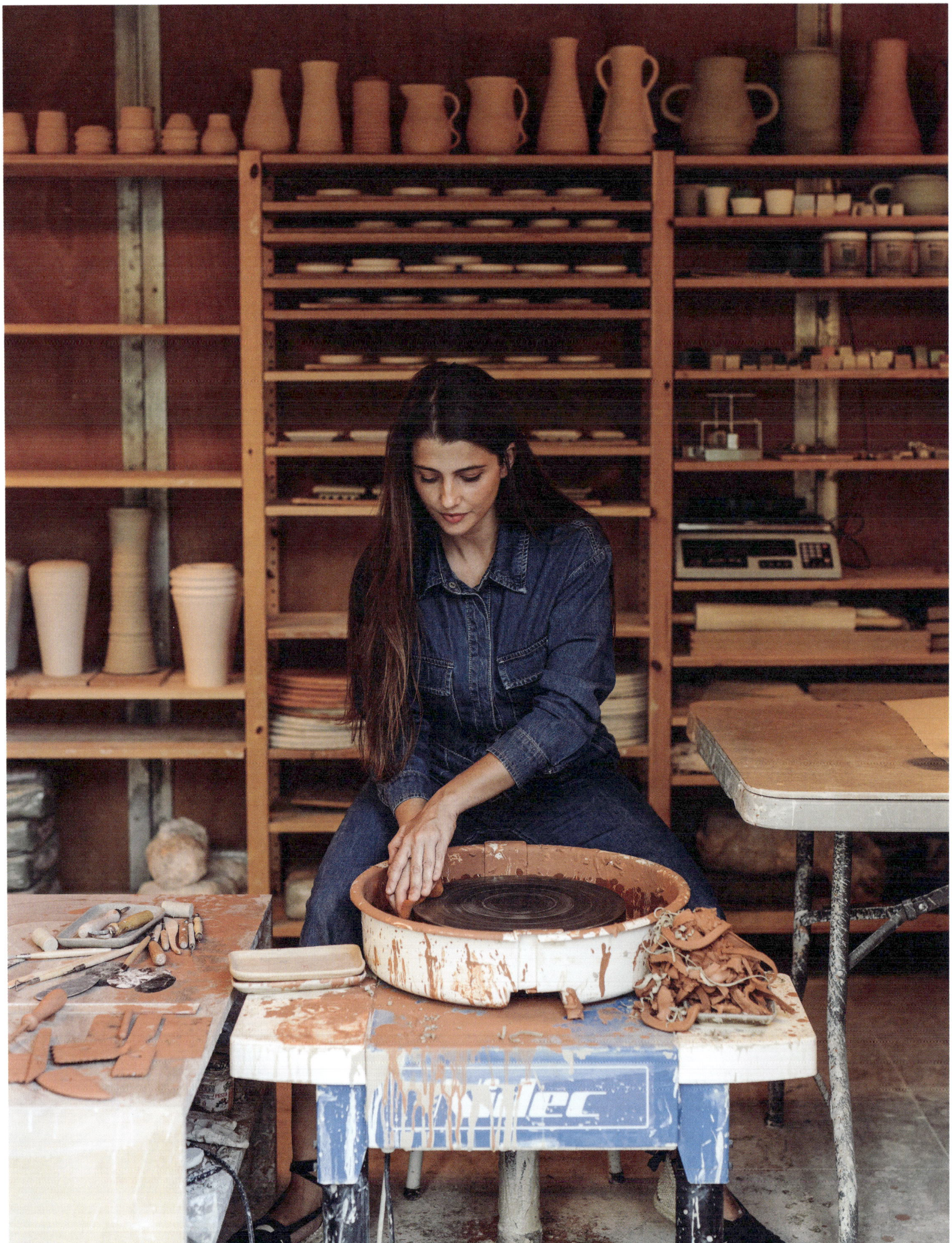

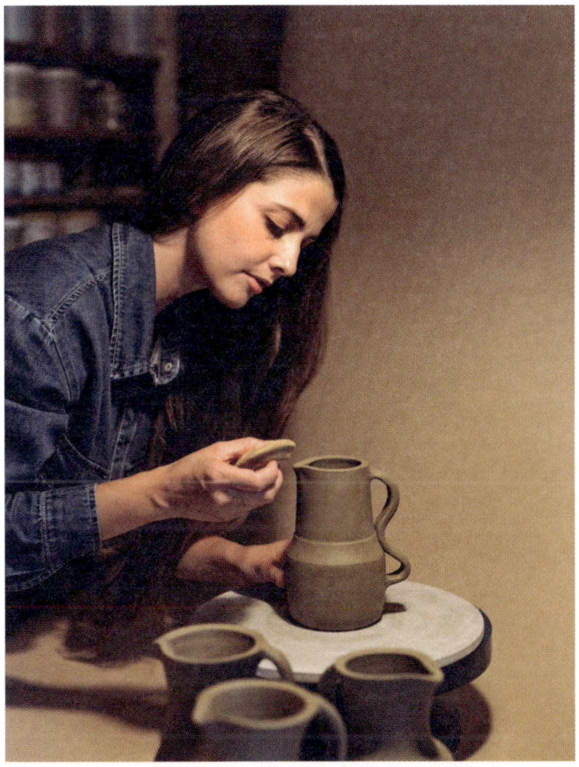

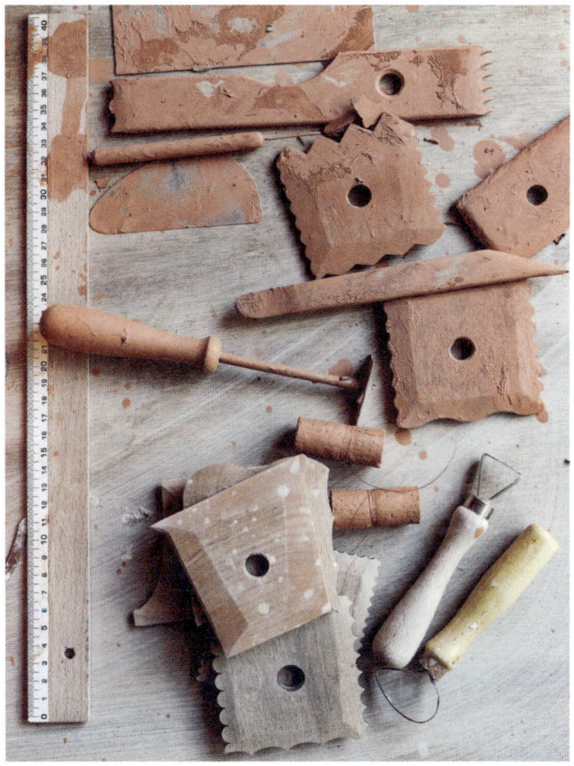

Laura's work table is equipped with a variety of tools that she uses to create her pottery. The new designs showcase her skill and creativity.

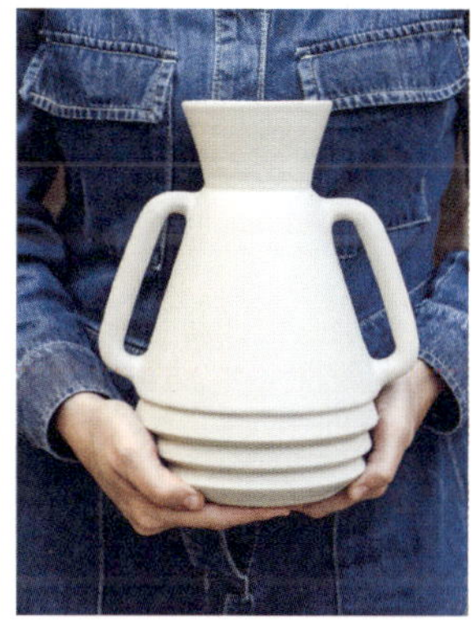

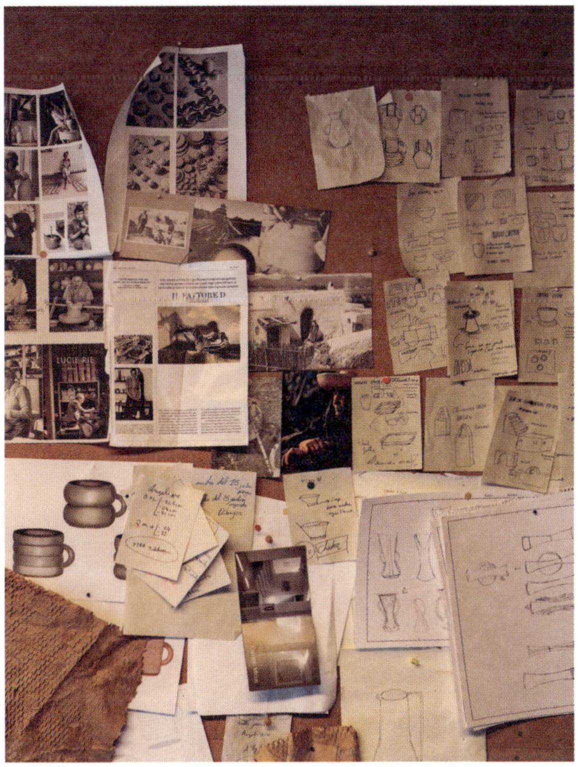

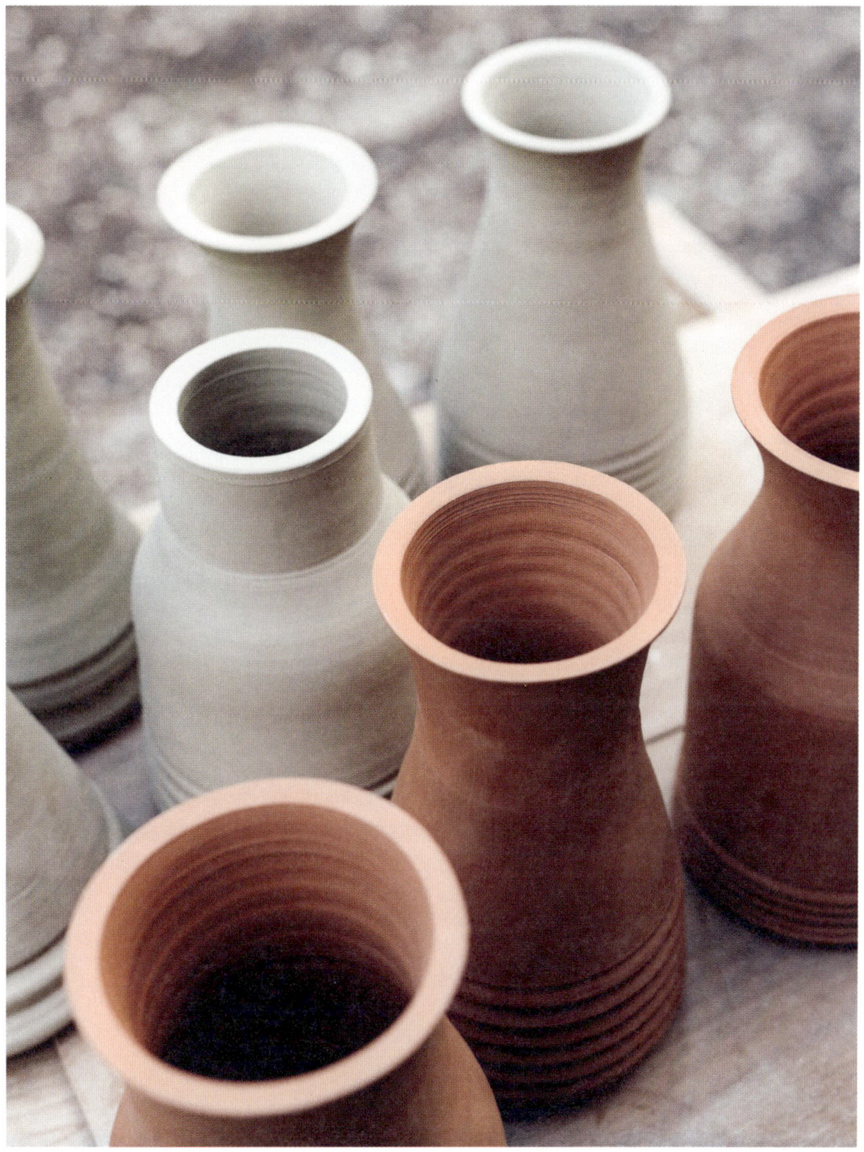

Laura also believes in the importance of honouring her teachers. She trained with the master ceramicist Eric Landon, co-founder of the Tortus studio in Copenhagen. In Ibiza, she learnt with the master potter Adrián Ribas, a nephew of Joan Planells, who was known as Daifa. In 1945 Daifa founded the renowned pottery studio Sa Teulera.

SALINAS

@mariab.ceramics

MARÍA B.

CONTEMPORARY CERAMICS

Although she has been immersed in numerous creative pursuits throughout her life, the Argentinian-born ceramicist María Sejas Balda came to work with clay only relatively recently. Her pieces are so confident and refined that it is difficult to believe she turned to the craft only in 2019.

María's first contact with clay was in the studio of Adrián Ribas from the Sa Teulera workshop, where she learnt the basics of wheeled pottery. She then undertook a few short workshops, reading about, researching and testing out other techniques such as the ancient Japanese method known as *kurinuki*, whereby pottery is carved from a single block of clay. *Kurinuki* is a slow and meditative process that produces truly unique ceramic pieces. The theme of imperfection is one that is evident throughout María's work.

María's reputation spread rapidly through word of mouth, and several of Ibiza's finest restaurants – including the Michelin-starred La Gaia by Óscar Molina, Six Senses Ibiza, the exclusive Japanese bar Omakase by Walt and the Ibiza Food Studio – began to request pieces on which to present their culinary creations. The earthy, organic nature of her vessels makes a fitting match for the food that fills them. Sometimes vessels are created to showcase a specific dish, but always they follow the ethos of the restaurant. It is no surprise that the chefs with whom María predominantly collaborates have a strong leaning towards seasonal, produce-driven cuisine.

After several years of sharing a workshop with another acclaimed island-based ceramicist, Laura de Grinyo (see pp. 68–71), María now has her own space in which to create. Deep in the south of Ibiza, close to the sea and surrounded by nature, it is one of many diverse elements that she cites as sources of inspiration for her work.

While the strong demand for her tableware shows no signs of easing, the artist is now turning her hand to lamps and other items of homeware, all characterized by her signature style. ***CE***

A relative newcomer to the world of clay, the ceramicist María Sejas Balda has swiftly gained a loyal following among some of the island's finest dining destinations.

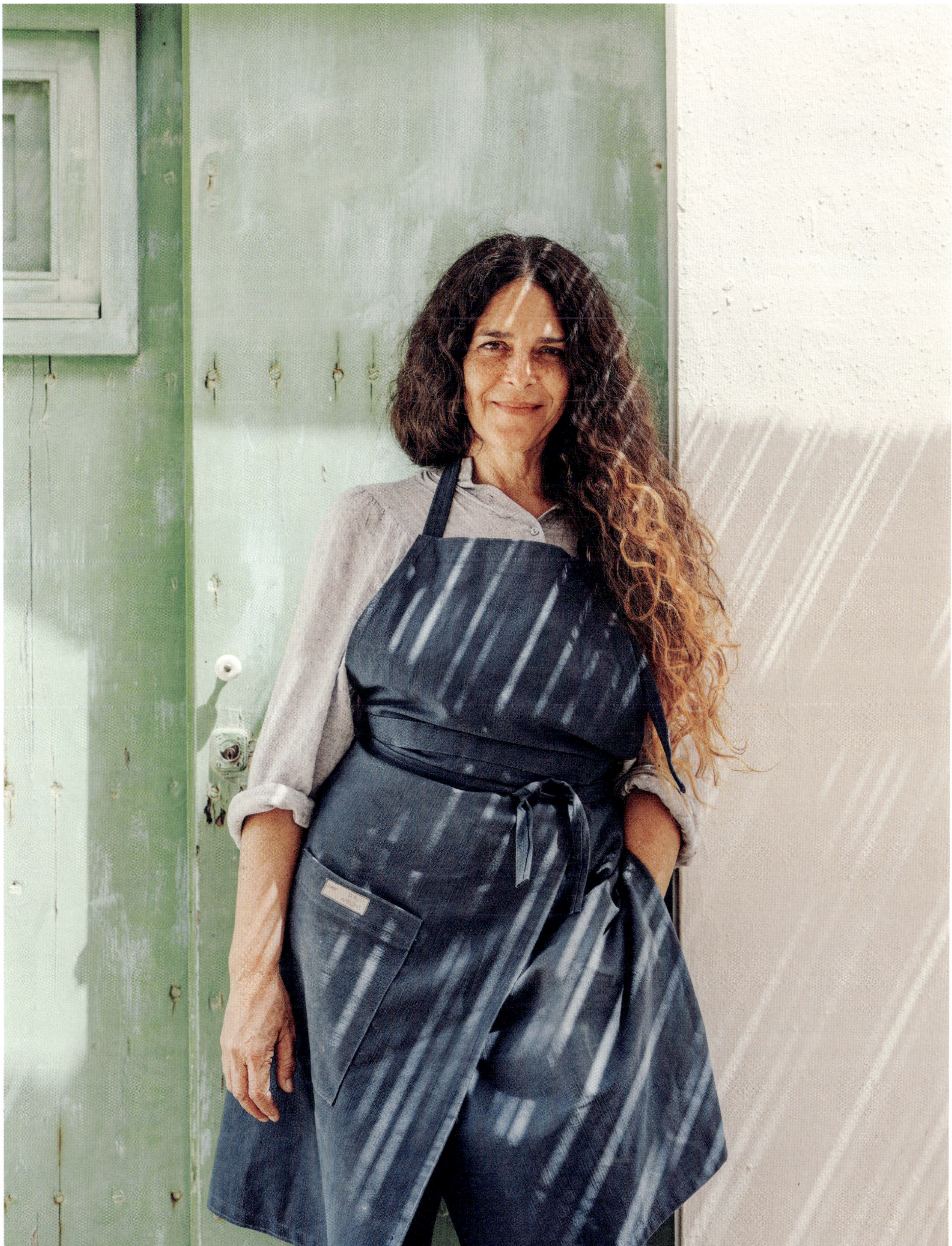

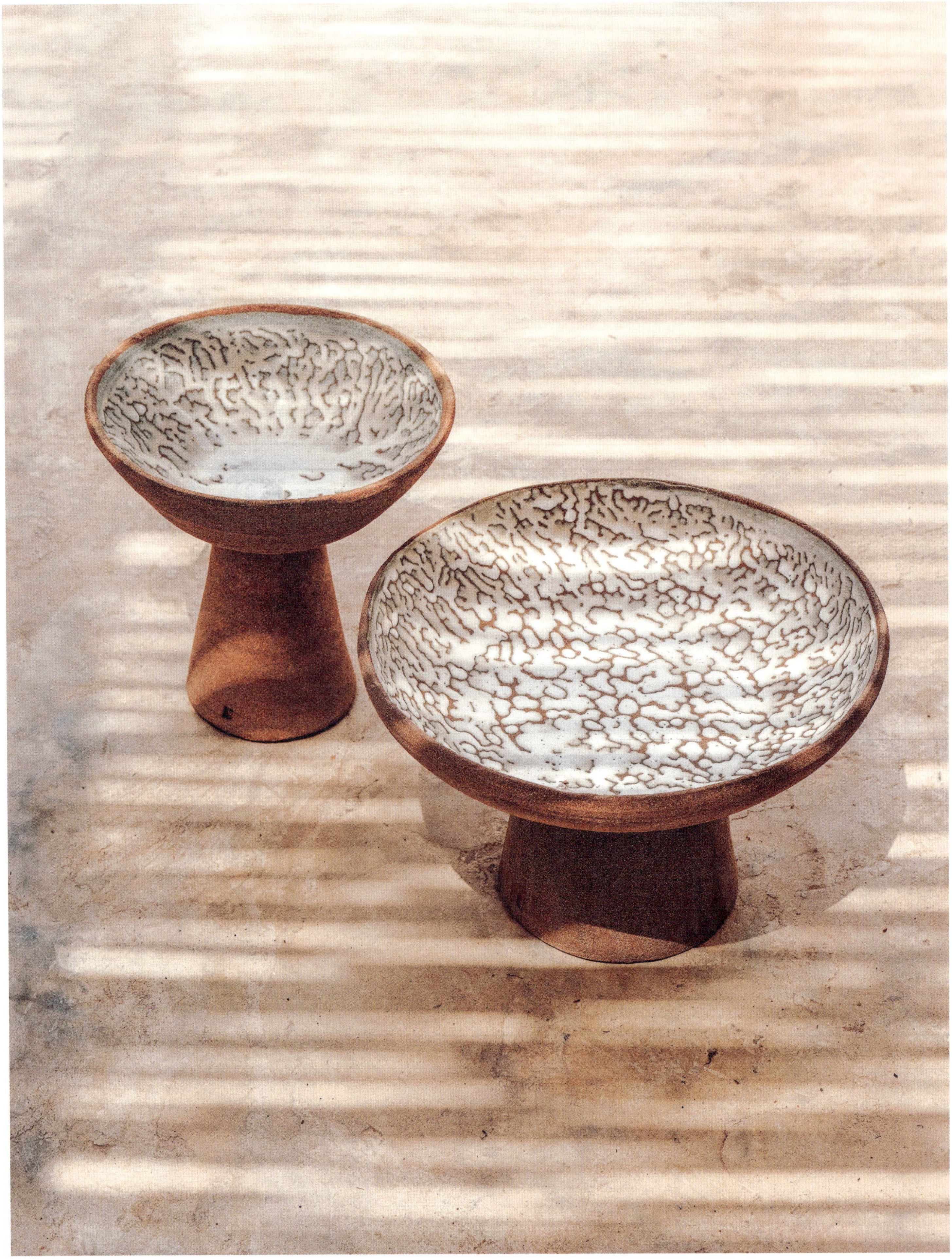

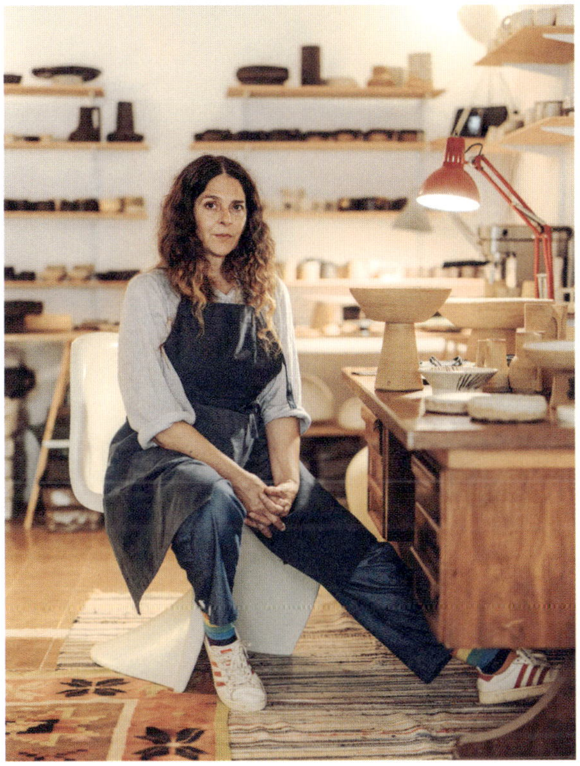

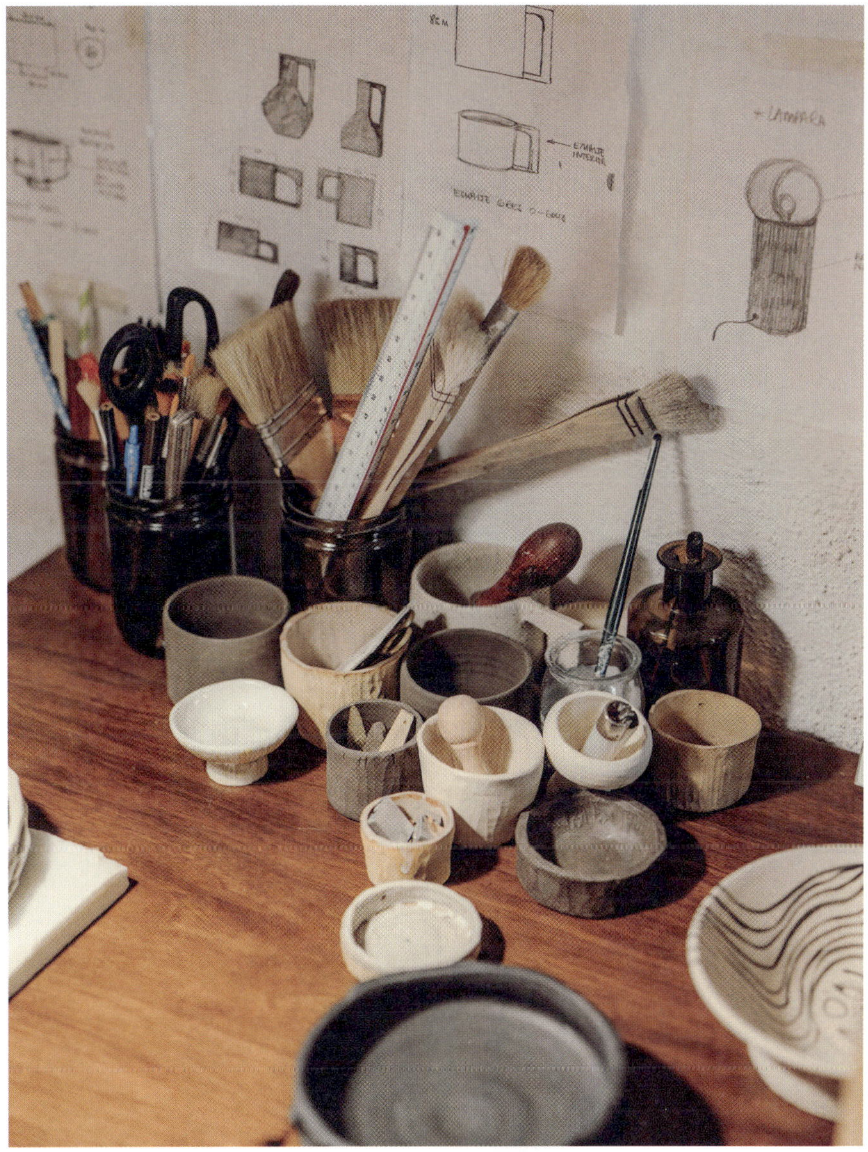

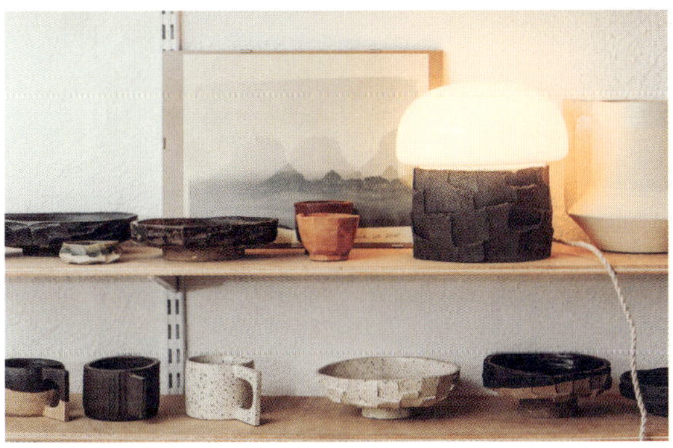

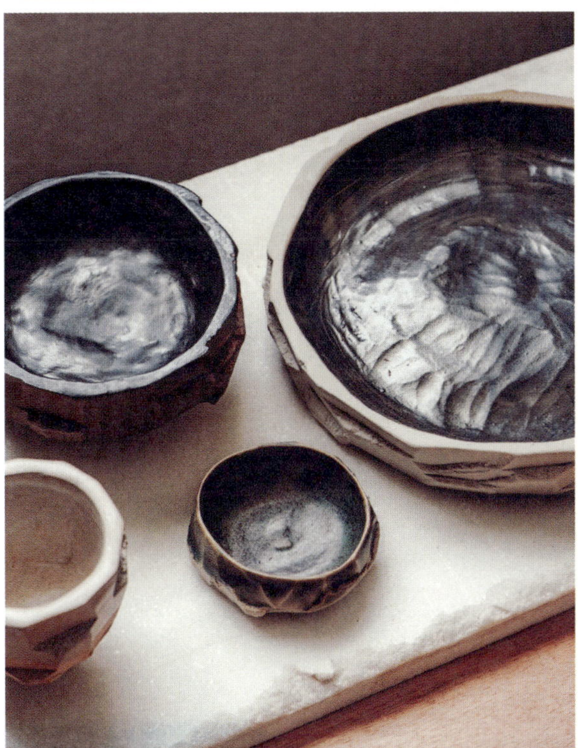

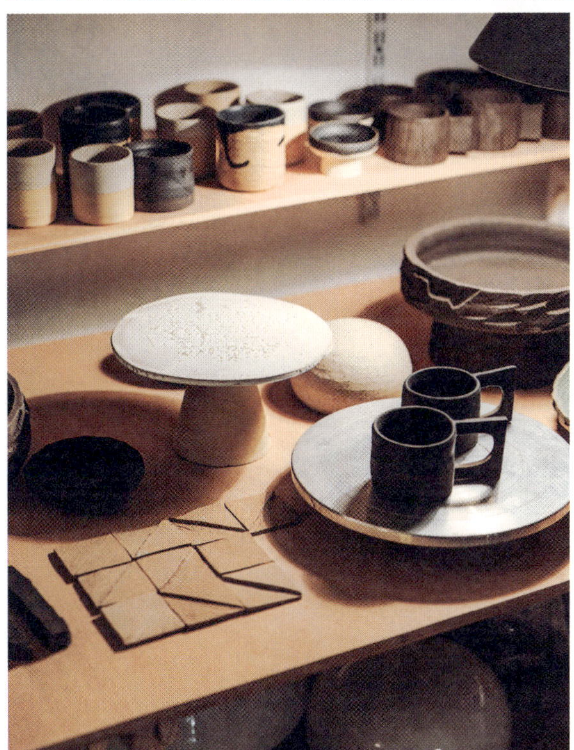

María's background as a graphic designer inspired her to explore new creative outlets, leading her to study pottery and the various techniques used to mould and shape clay.

ART & CULTURE

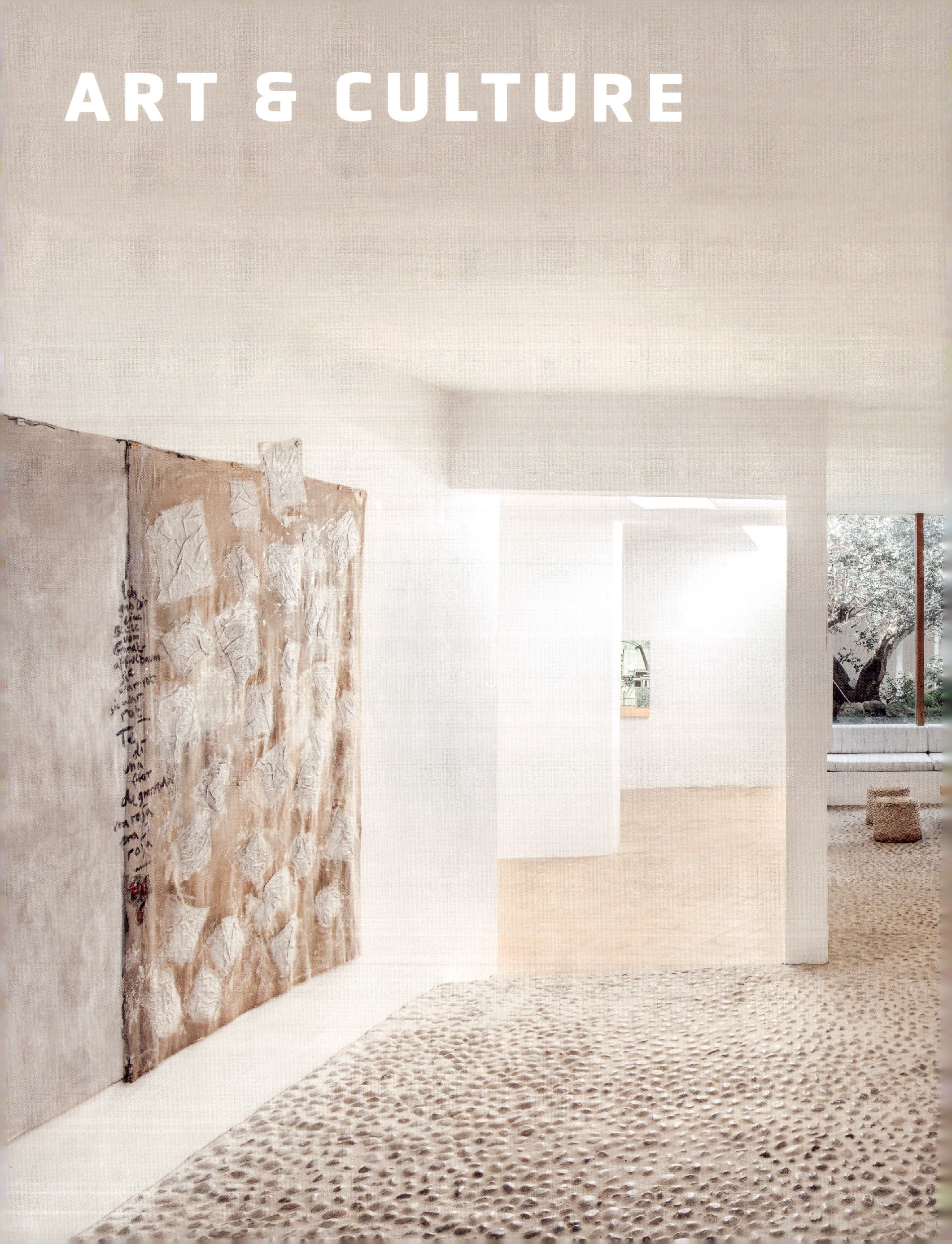

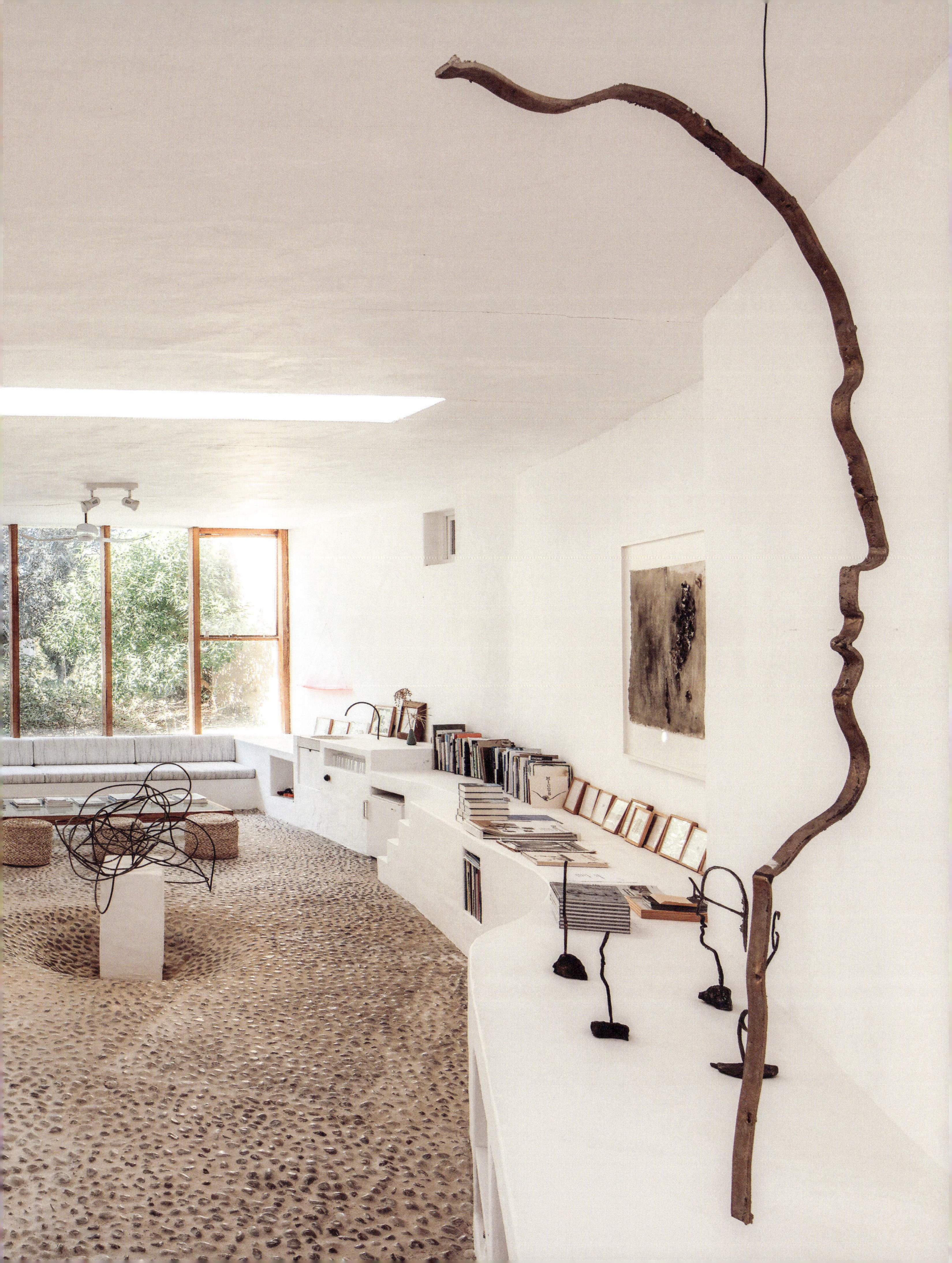

IBIZA TOWN
antoniovillanueva.com

ANTONIO VILLANUEVA

MULTIDISCIPLINARY ART

The multidisciplinary artist Antonio Villanueva was born in the ancient city of Toledo, above the plains of Castilla-La Mancha. It was there that he began his painting journey, working as an apprentice to the local artist Enrique Vera.

Antonio moved to Madrid to complete a degree in engineering and later embarked on a career in the industry, driven by his dream of saving enough money to move to Paris to paint full-time. This ambition came to fruition in 1962, when he quickly fell in with a group of bohemians in Saint-Germain-des-Prés, in the city's 6th arrondissement, an area renowned for attracting artists, musicians and writers. He worked for a time as a cartoonist, illustrator and actor, and then settled in Lanzarote for several years, before returning to Madrid, where he gained prominence for producing satirical comic strips for several newspapers.

Following an invitation from friends, Antonio first visited Ibiza in 1968, residing in Santa Eulalia and spending much of his time in the legendary Sandy's Bar, a popular meeting place for a host of artists and actors. He continued with his painting practice alongside other acclaimed Ibiza-based artists, including Peter Unsworth and Manolo Monpo. In 1993 he moved to Ibiza permanently, painting in his studio in the Morna Valley and exhibiting his work around the world.

In 2004 Antonio moved his studio to a semi-abandoned industrial warehouse that he transformed into an artistic centre where numerous fellow artists take up temporary residences to produce a series of exhibitions, video art, experimental theatre, music and design.

Antonio continues to work on a wide range of concepts, largely inspired by daily events and by the island itself, including the *Posidonia* series, his ode to the Mediterranean. His plan is to feature more of his abstract and figurative sculptures and paintings in a forthcoming book, a follow-up to a monograph published in 2006.

Spurred on by an increased sense of urgency following a health scare, Antonio is, as ever, embracing new opportunities. Recently he delved into the world of NFTs, and he remains busy exploring further innovative ways in which to share his work with a wider audience. ***CE***

Working in a range of media and with a career spanning more than sixty years, the Toledo-born artist Antonio Villanueva continues to draw inspiration from his varied life experiences.

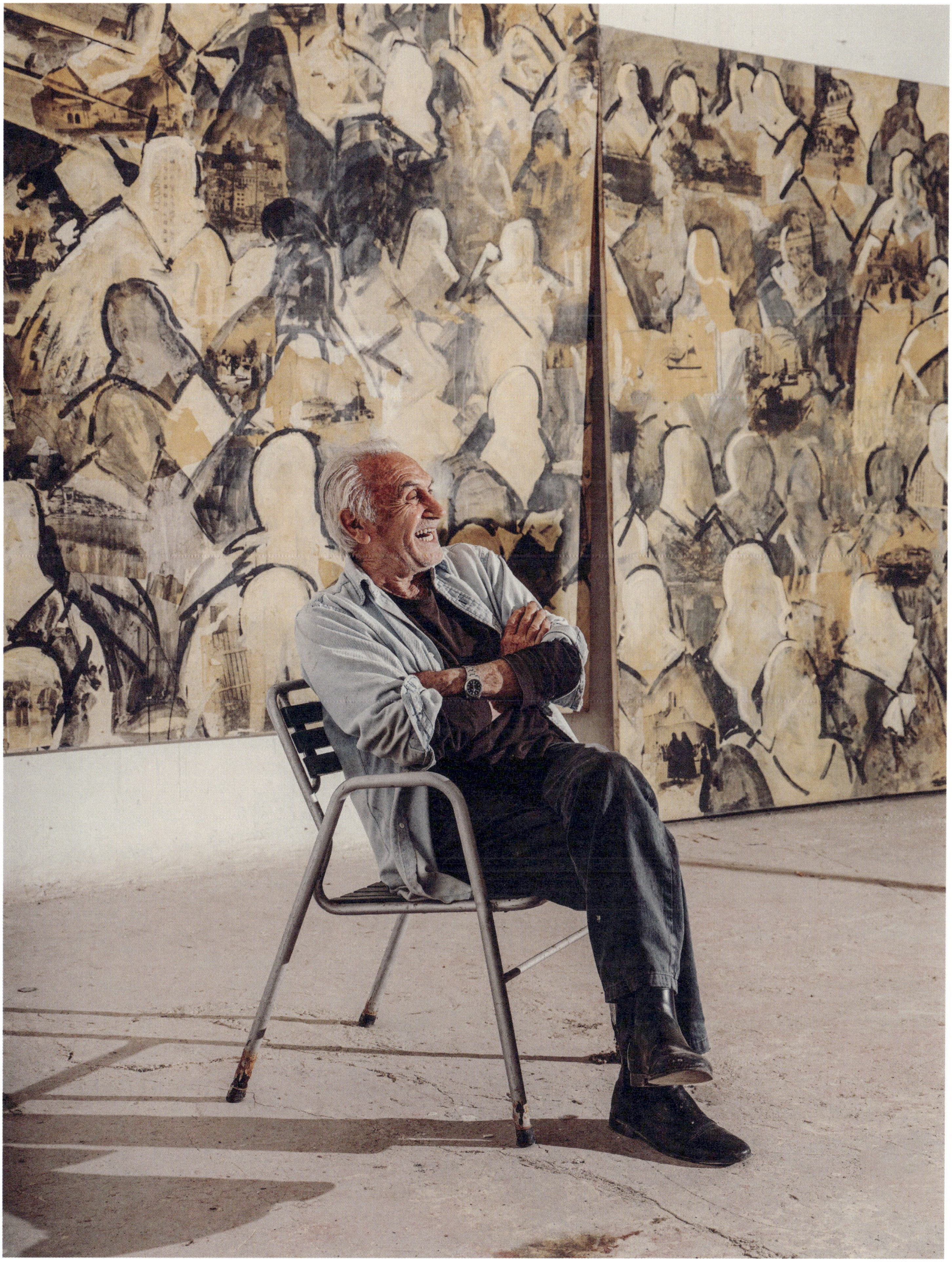

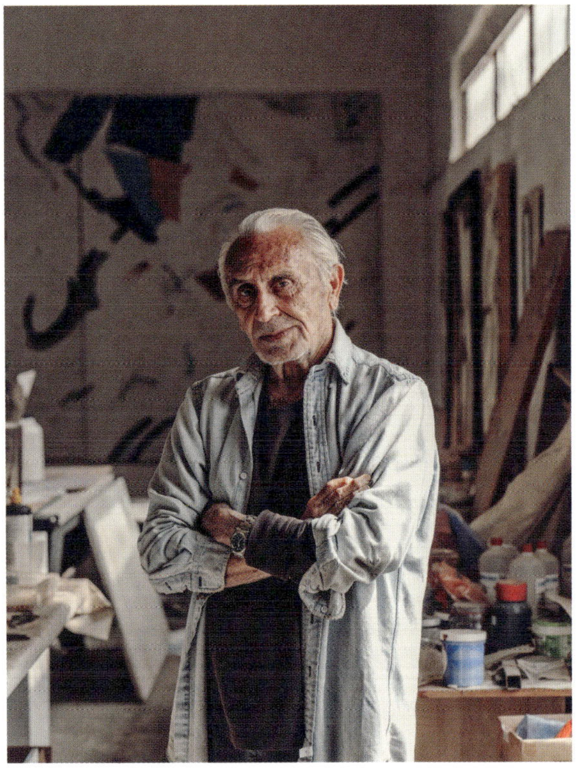

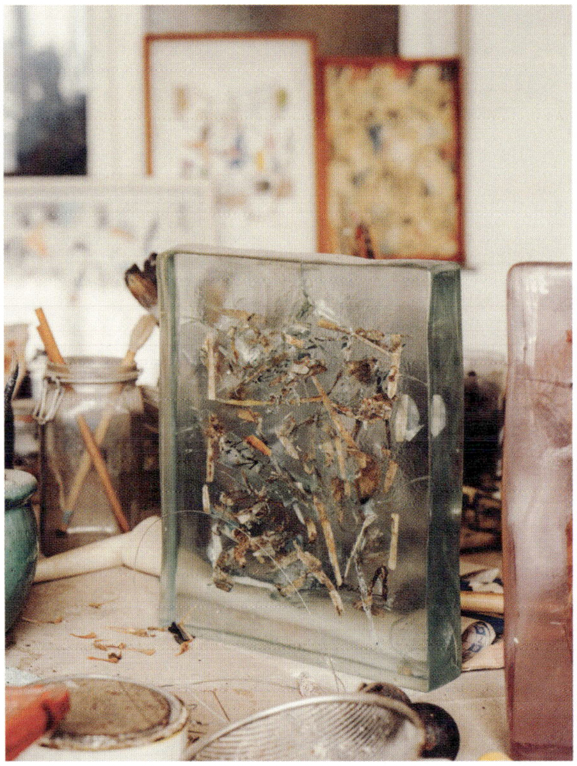

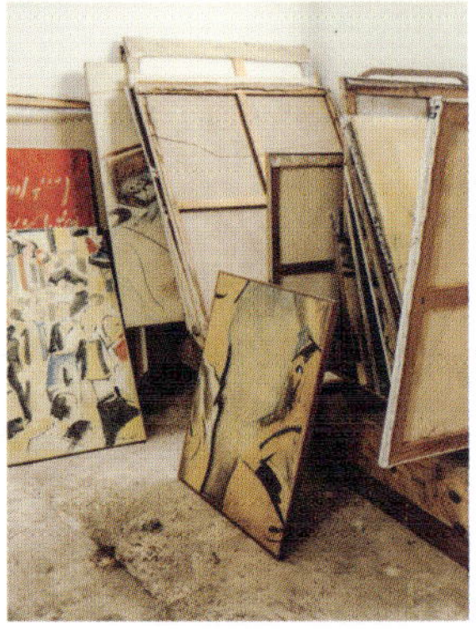

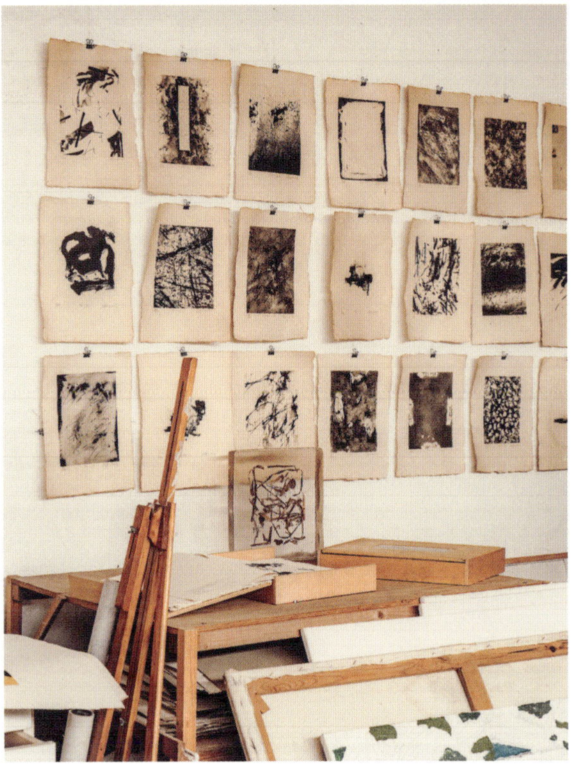

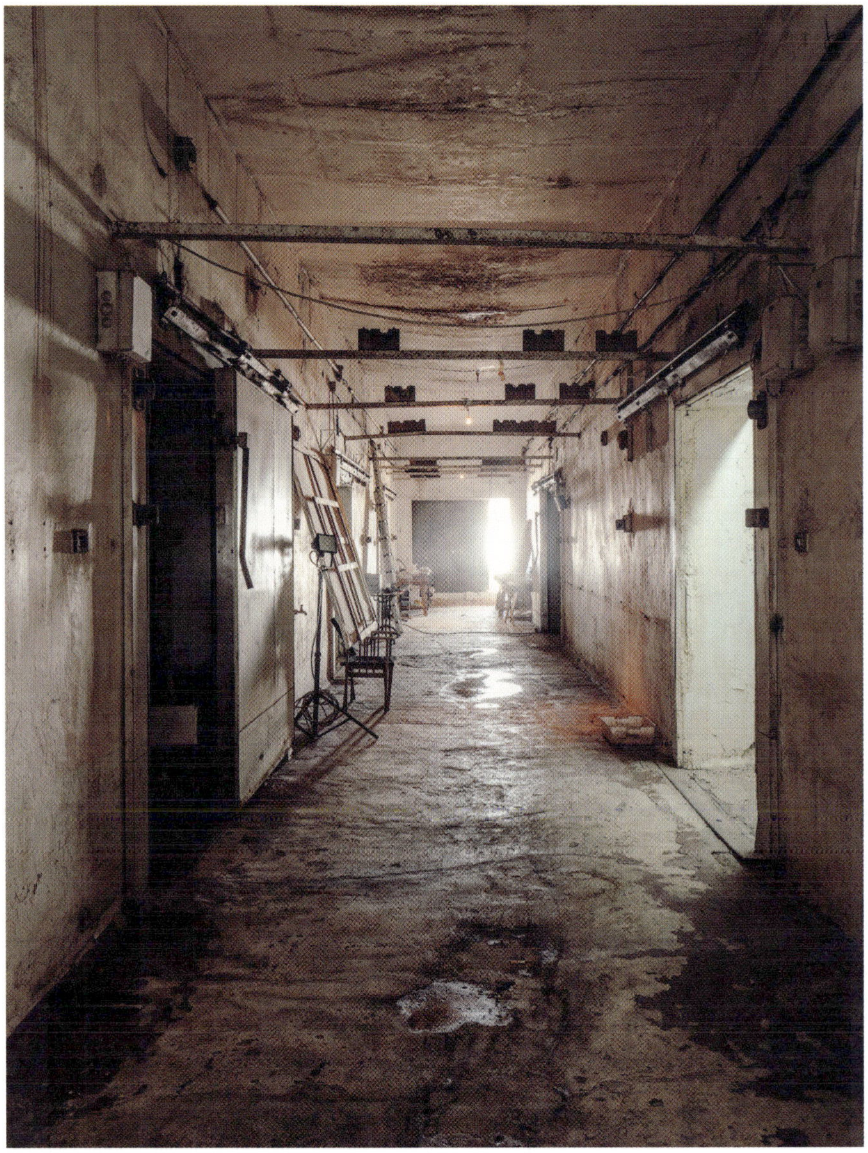

Antonio's atelier showcases pieces from his entire œuvre. He integrates Posidonia oceanica, *precious seagrass found around Ibiza, into his works in resin to draw attention to its importance to the Mediterranean ecosystem (top centre).*

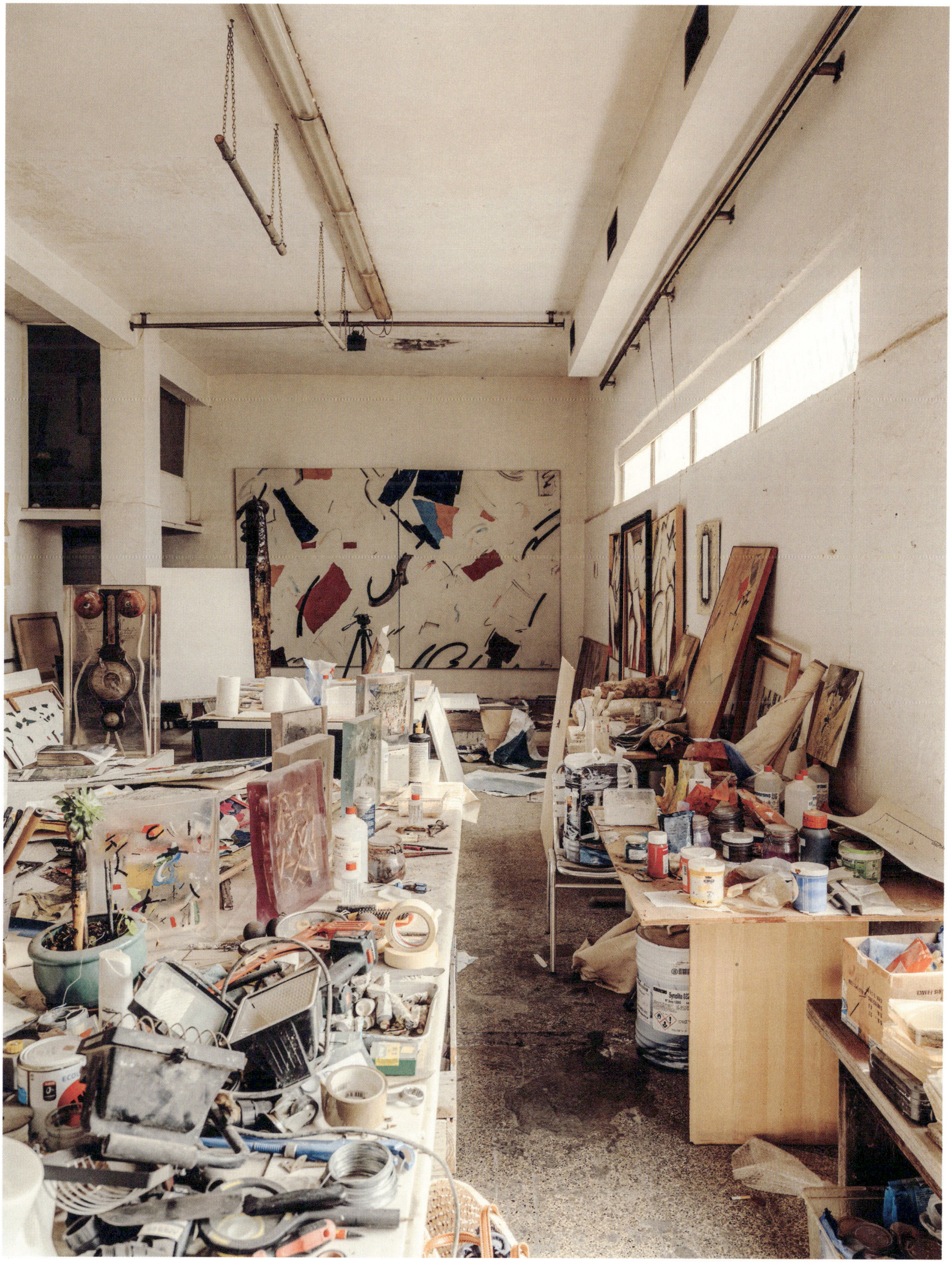

SANTA EULALIA
@sandradekeller

SANDRA DE KELLER

PHOTOGRAPHY

Sandra de Keller's signature portraiture is hung on the walls of homes and hotels all around Ibiza. The Swiss-Spanish-Austrian artist and conceptual photographer has lived on the island, on and off, throughout her whole life. Her most recognizable projects, such as her Renault 4 car-door portraits, marry local iconography with a sense of fun and contemporary flair.

For six decades, the Renault 4 has been the workhorse of Ibicenco farmers. Its reliable engine and ability to traverse bumpy country roads have led to the car becoming a familiar sight across the island. This ubiquity came to Sandra's attention as she drove around in her first car, a 1972 R4. Years later, as she started photographing Ibiza's landscape and eccentric characters, she began collecting the rear doors from abandoned Renault 4s. Her idea was to use them as frames for a fun new concept of portrait photography.

The *Renault 4 Life* series – which has involved shooting friends, families and even podenco dogs inside Sandra's own classic car – was first shown at the Photo 14 photography fair in Zurich, then at MAK (Museum of Applied Arts) in Vienna and the Leica Gallery in Los Angeles. The ever-evolving project survives in the form of the successful *Studio on Wheels* series, and remains particularly popular with art collectors seeking a personalized statement wall piece.

'I need to be by myself a lot', Sandra confides. 'Mainly to recharge my batteries. This is possible in Ibiza, and it's why I live here. To be happy on this island, you need to know how to be alone.'

Since 2019 Sandra has spent much time slowly yet determinedly transforming the former home of Rolf Bischel into her own residence and studio space. The eccentric former owner – also an artist and photographer – moved to Ibiza in the 1970s. 'He left behind a sort of fantasy village', Sandra explains. 'People come here and don't know where up and down are any more. It feels like a sort of playground for adults, and remains as a house for art and creativity.' She adds: 'Rolf's example of how to coexist so peacefully with nature and animals also endures.'

A person of unabashed integrity, Sandra possesses an open heart, inquisitive mind and ever-roaming lens that are forever fixed on the island's multiple layers. It is almost as if the Ibizan terrain – like a perpetually changing, living artefact – were a canvas where the myriad happenings come into sharper focus. Just like her interminably demanding house, Sandra's photography keeps Ibiza's ever-developing story alive. ***LA***

Sandra de Keller outside her house with Bubu the donkey. A chance encounter between Sandra, a Swiss-Spanish-Austrian artist, and Rolf Bischel, an eccentric fashion photographer and the house's former owner, became a story that swirls together themes of stewardship, legacy and the ebb and flow of creativity.

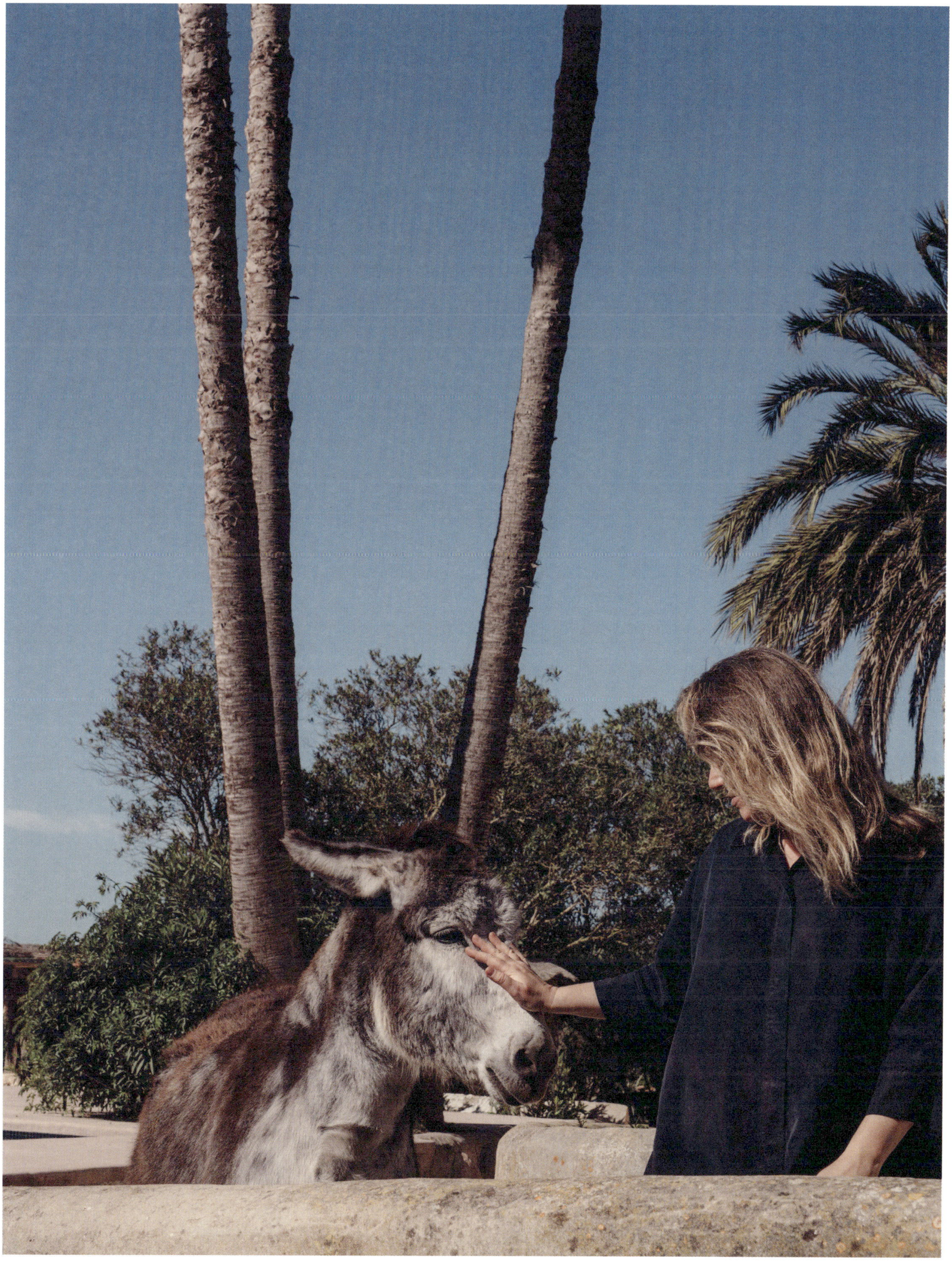

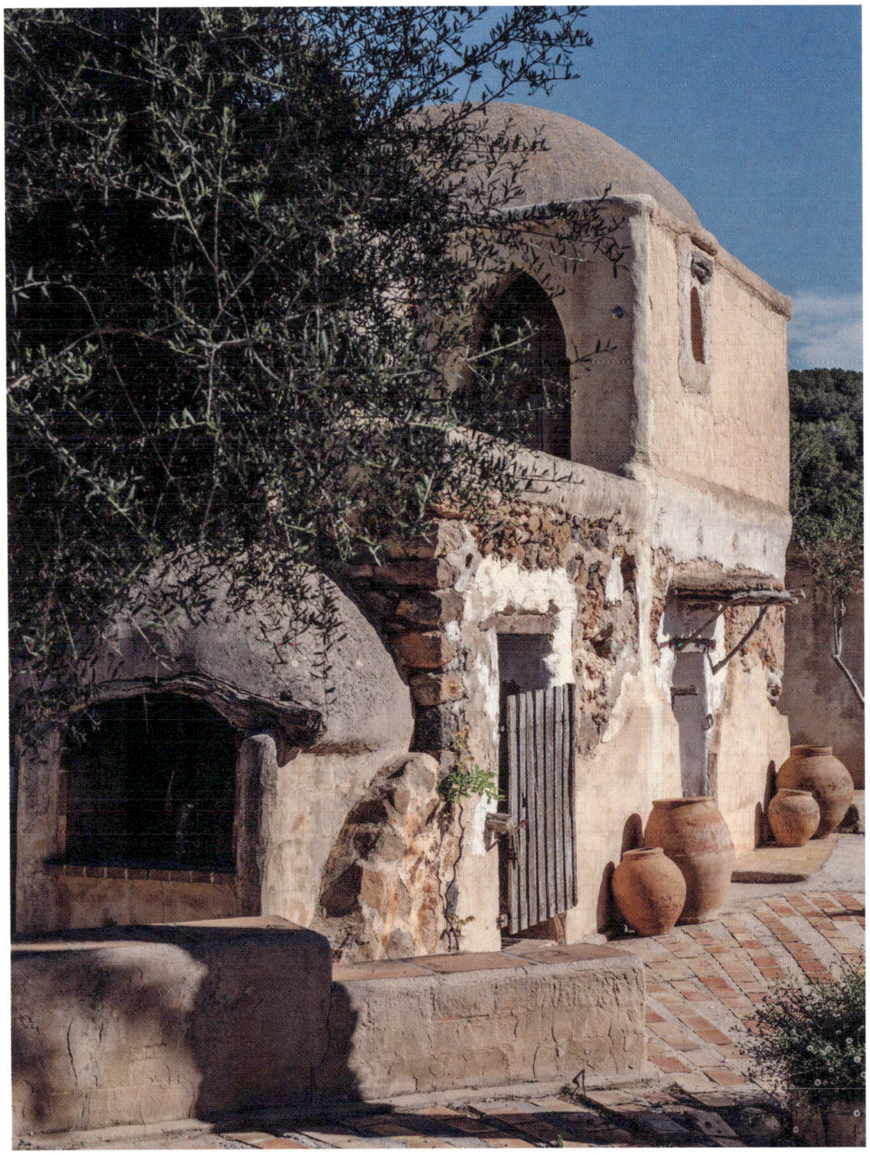

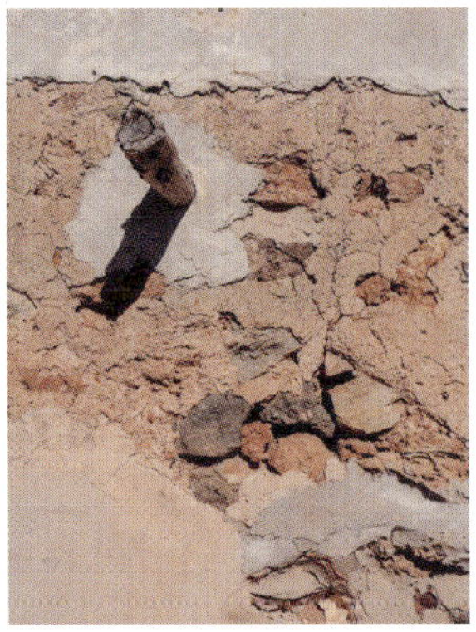

Preserving the half-finished, time-textured character of the buildings was important for Sandra as a way of safeguarding Rolf's memory.

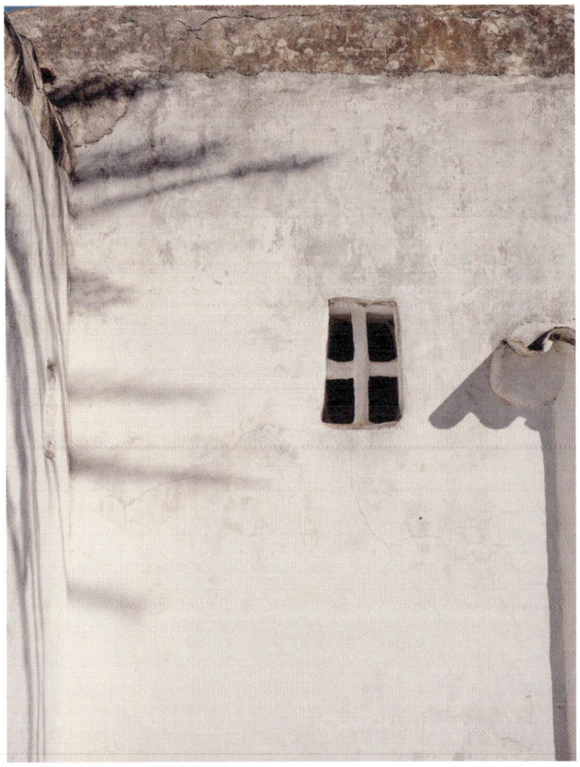

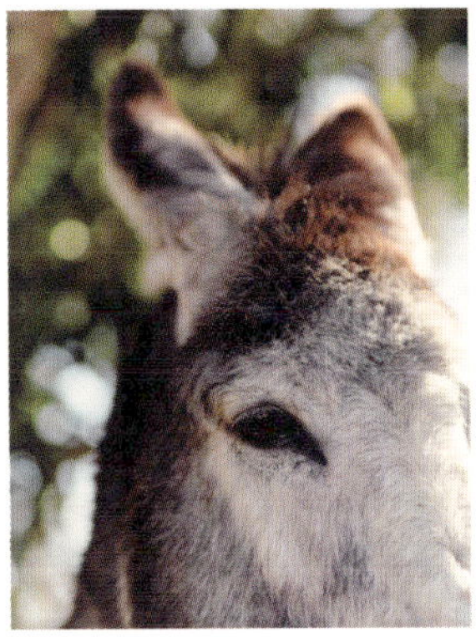

Right: Sandra outside her house with her mobile photographic studio, her Renault 4.

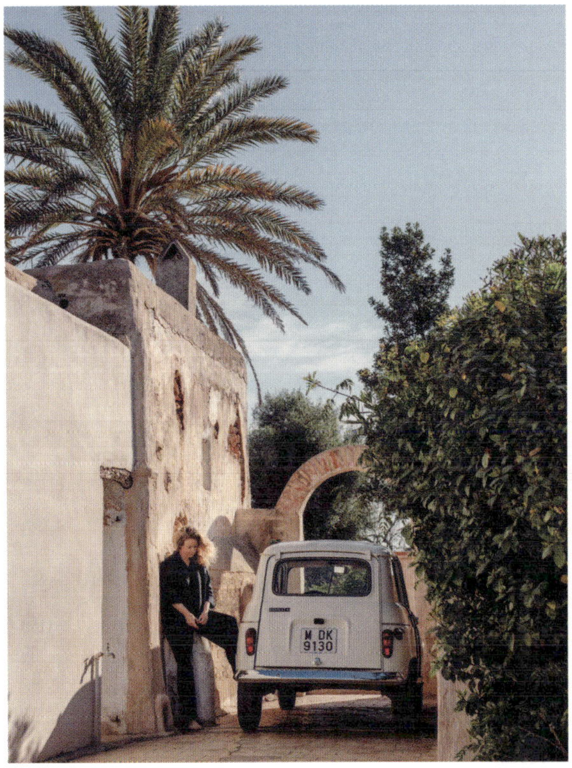

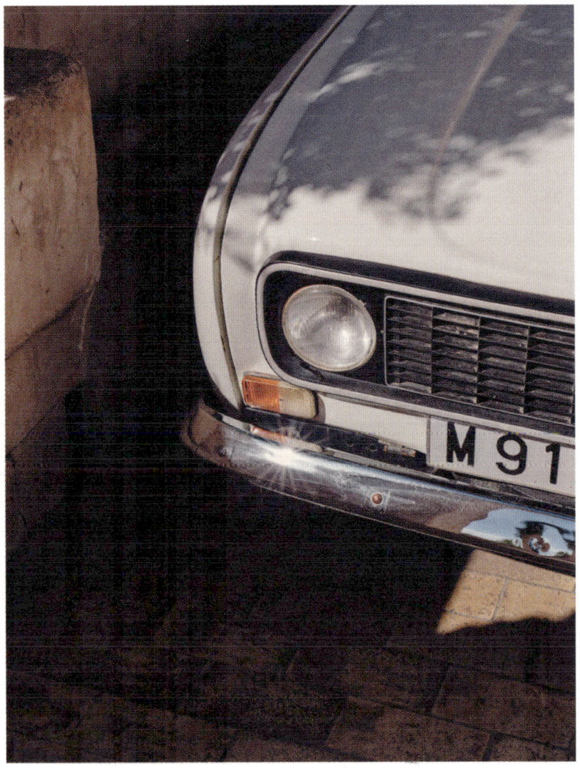

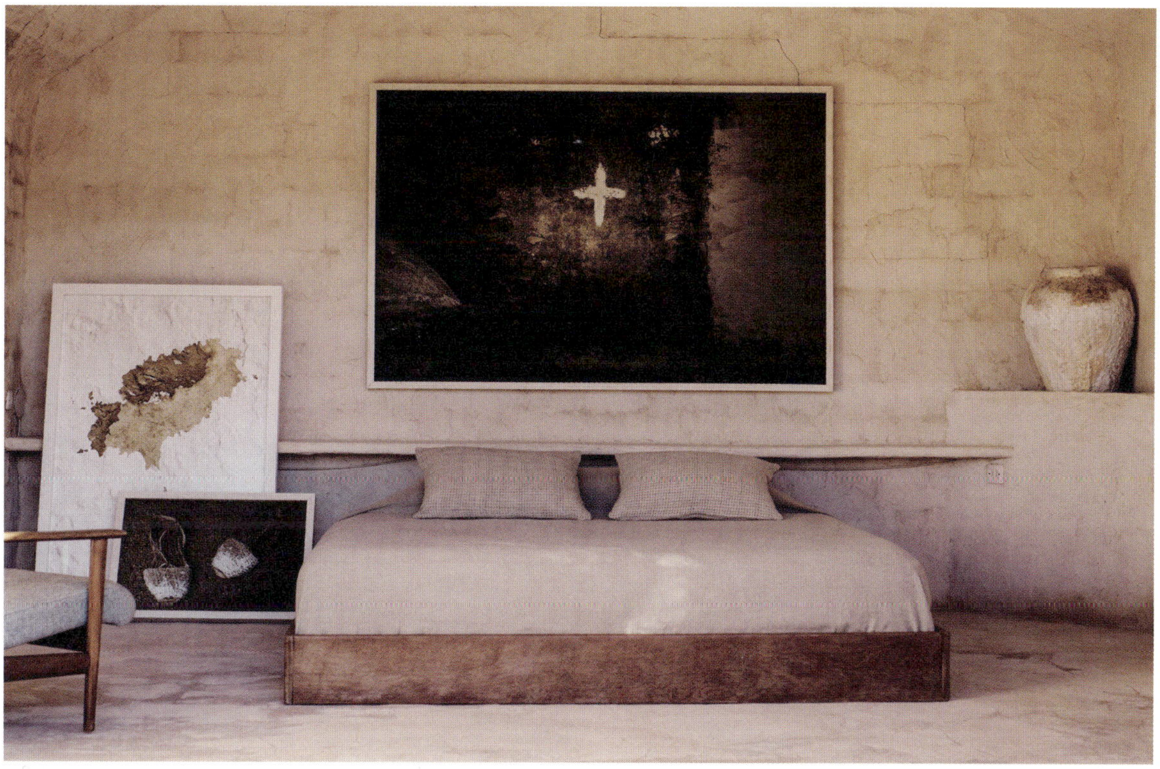

Below, left: A portrait of a traditional Ibicenca, or payesa, reflects Sandra's knack for subverting the island's iconography.

Bottom: Sandra's Renault 4 Life *series features photographs taken through the rear window of her car, then framed in the back door of an old, abandoned Renault 4.*

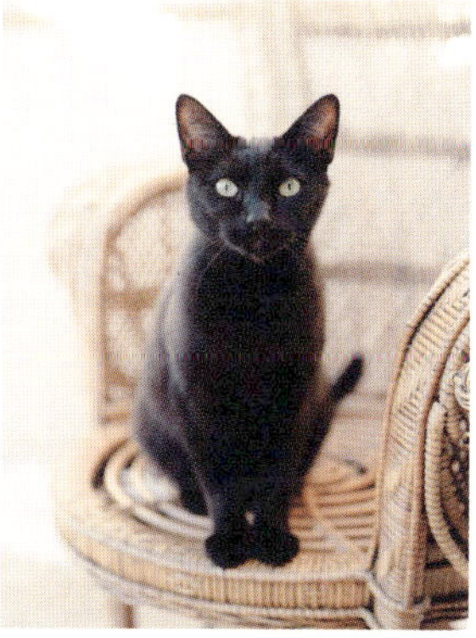

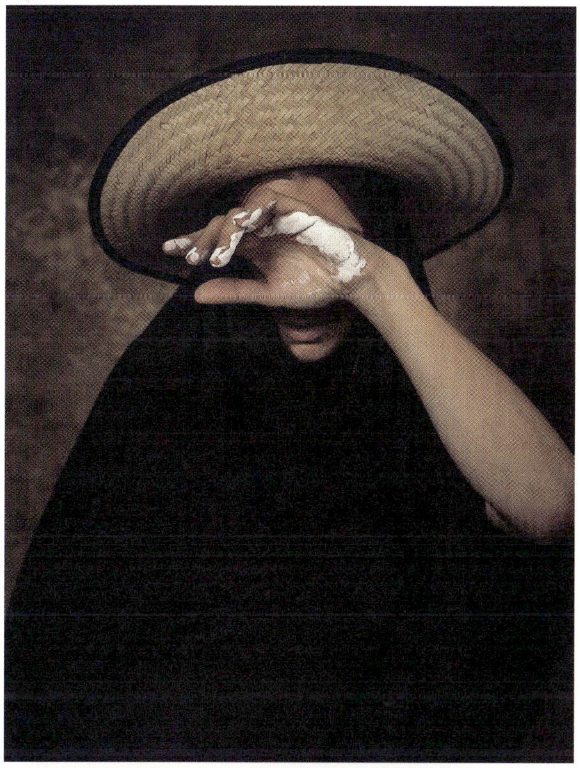

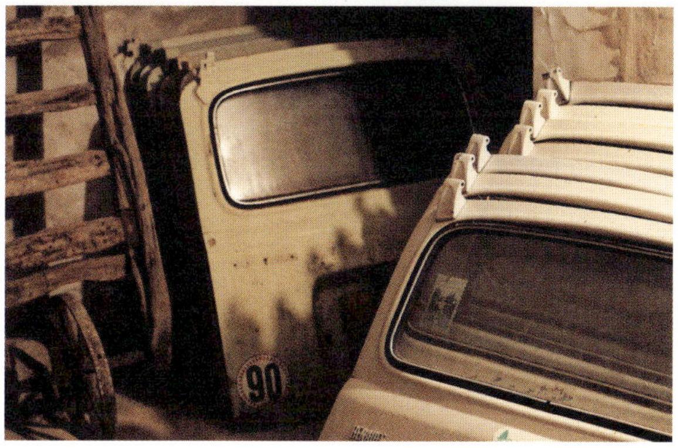

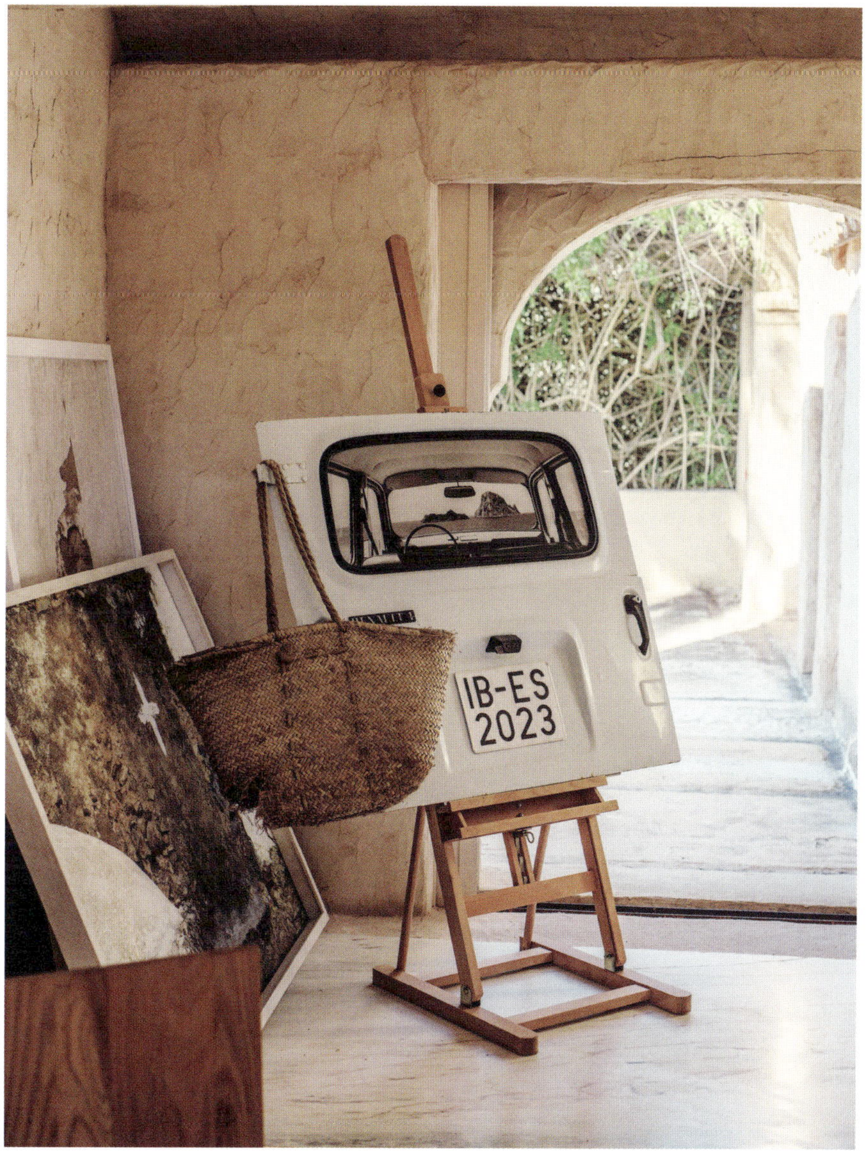

SAN MATEO
alinedelaforcade.com

ALINE DE LAFORCADE

WOVEN ART

The fibre artist and global gypsy Aline de Laforcade spent time in an assortment of countries before settling in her adopted home of Ibiza in 2016. Born in Beirut, she lived and worked in Saudi Arabia, Australia, Paris, London, Brussels, Monaco and also New York, where she worked for the artist James Rizzi for over a decade.

Although Aline had never before lived in such tranquil surroundings, the sense of freedom and the diversity prevalent in Ibiza was not dissimilar to the environment that she had experienced in New York, and she felt an instant sense of belonging on her arrival on the island. Inspiration was plentiful and found predominantly in the native architecture and natural landscapes – raw, rough and textured, much like her work.

Aline's fascination with woven tapestries, coupled with her innate sense of curiosity, led her to learn more. Her weaving journey truly began when she came to Ibiza, and has flourished ever since. The language of textiles is particularly meaningful to her, because it has been the silent dialect of women for millennia.

Aline's weaving skills are self-taught, and she painstakingly builds the looms herself. She perceives this process as being integral to maintaining ancient techniques, the primitive methods being a timely reminder of where we come from and a return to our origins. In a world where machines do everything for us, the value of an item handcrafted in such a traditional fashion is representative of our desire to return to our most essential human needs; a possibility to reconnect with primal instincts, to feel without thought.

Aline's creations take their cue from the textures and colours in front of her, and from this starting point stems the impulse to find them a form – an intuitive and primal process that is both slow and meditative and allows time for adjustments along the way. When seeking colour combinations, Aline turns to nature, inspired by the terrain that surrounds her and by the animal and vegetal textures common in the ancient folkloric costumes of Eastern Europe.

As our lives become digitalized, increasingly bereft of visceral pleasure, Aline's creations bring into the home an element of the natural world and with it an opportunity to own something that not only is aesthetically impressive but also has a tactile quality that invites us to touch as well as see. ***CE***

A dedicated nomad before succumbing to Ibiza's charms, Aline de Laforcade has been inspired to create vibrant and evocative textiles using ancient techniques.

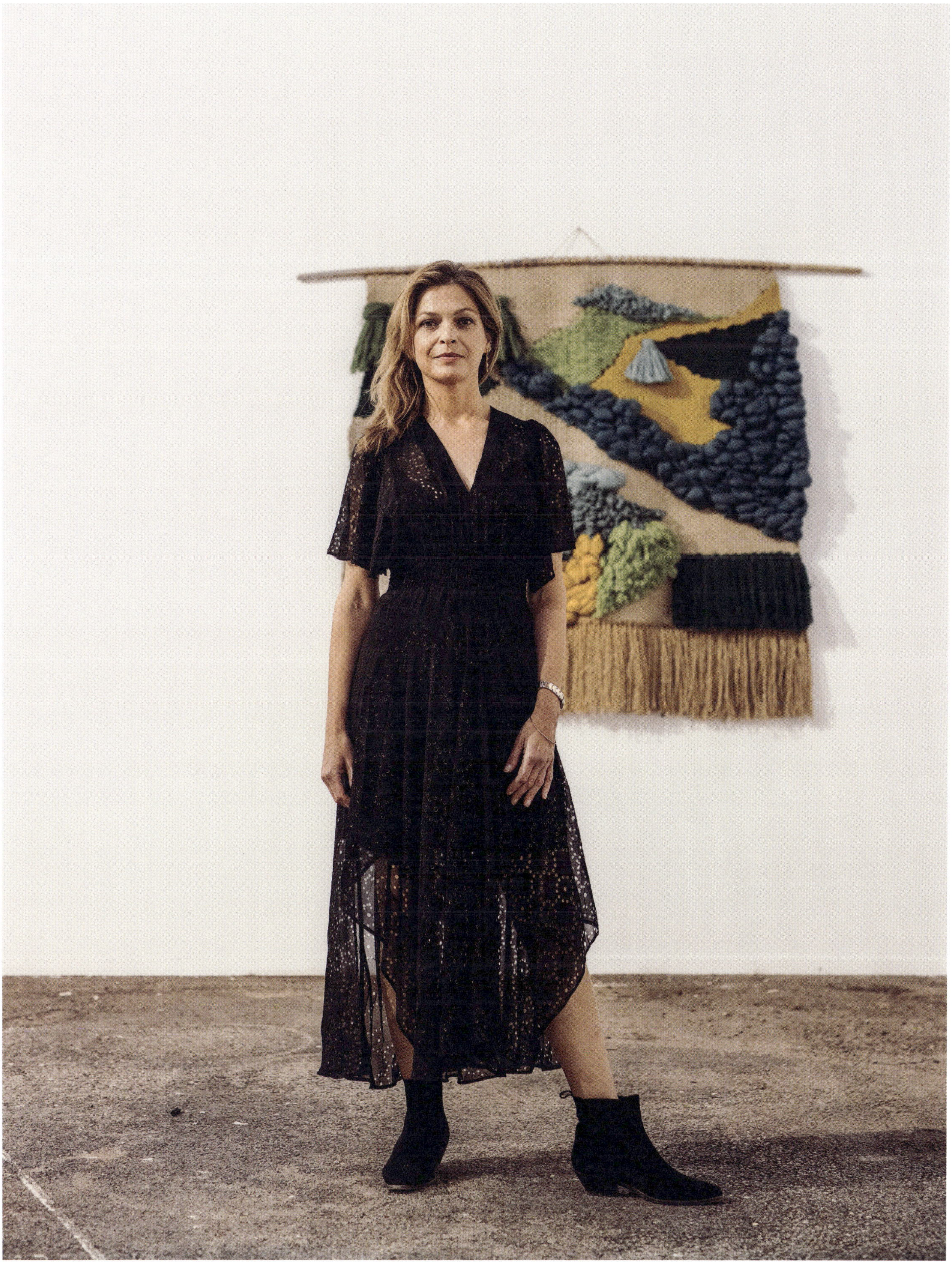

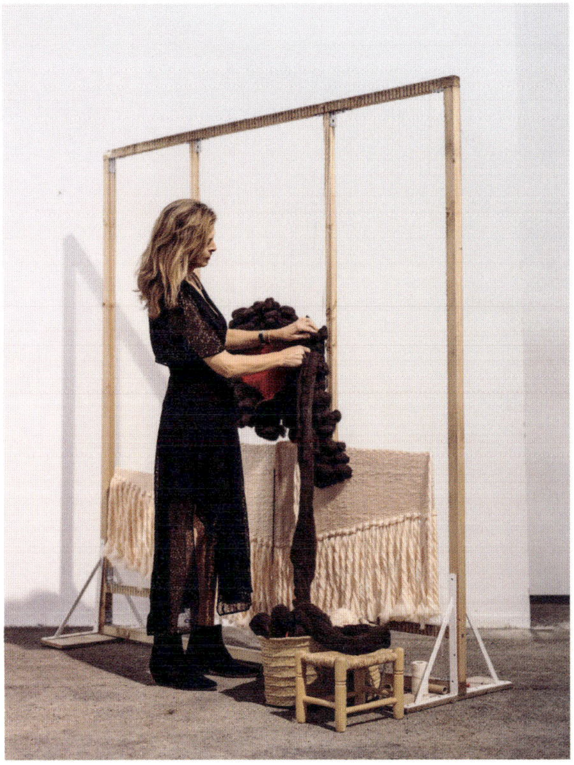

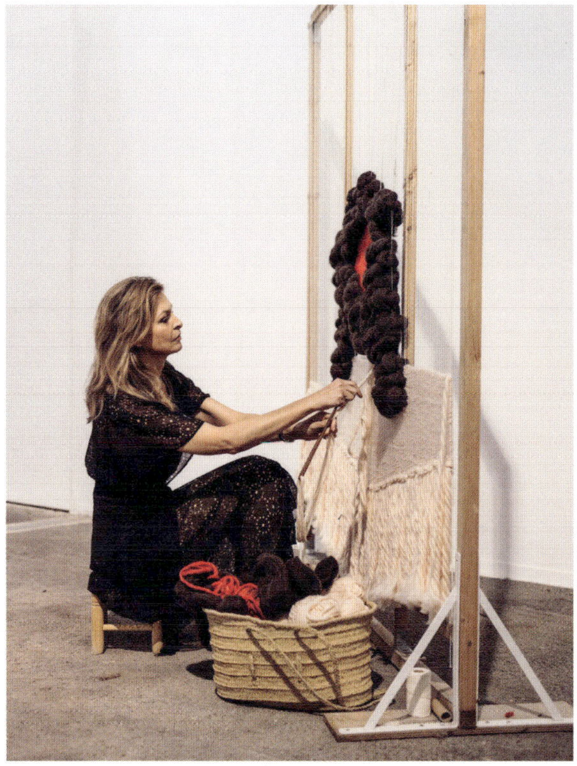

Aline draws inspiration from Eastern European folkloric costumes that blend animal and vegetal textures, such as those worn by the Kukeri of Bulgaria and those sported at the annual Busójárás celebration in Hungary.

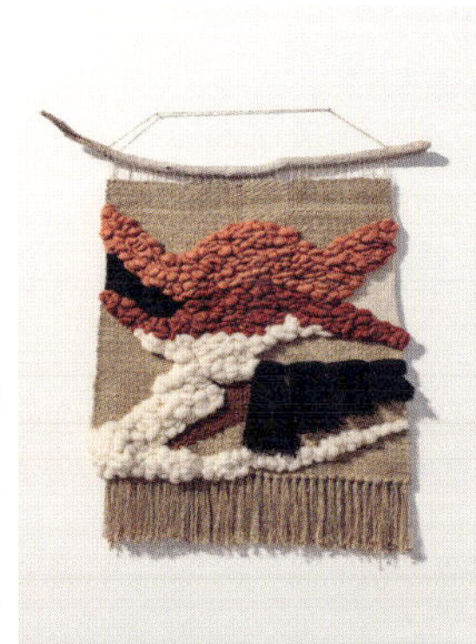

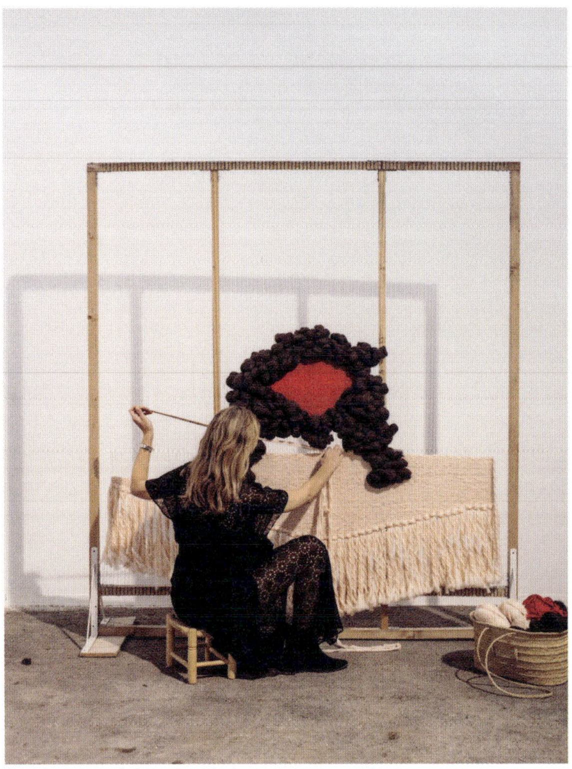

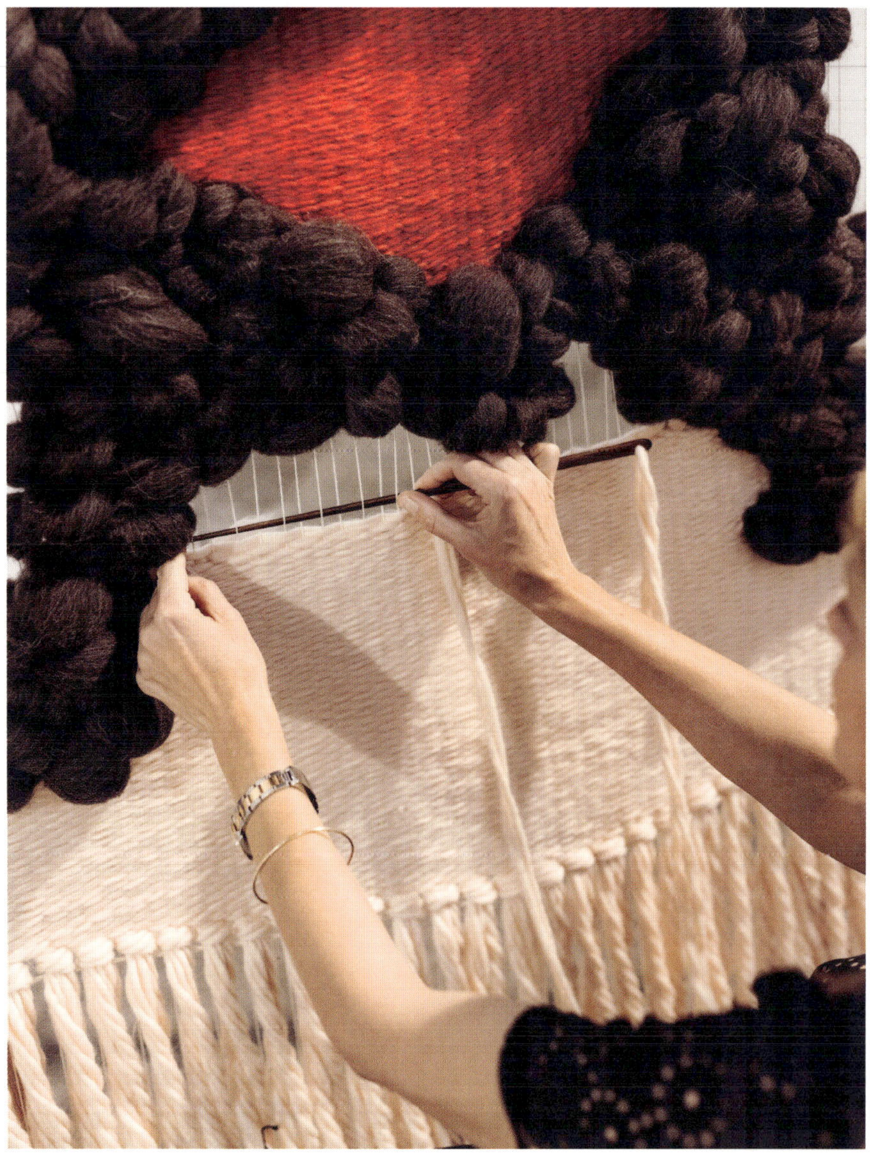

Weaving requires balancing a linear technique and multiple elements at once to produce harmony. Attention to detail and an understanding of how elements work together are essential in this creative process.

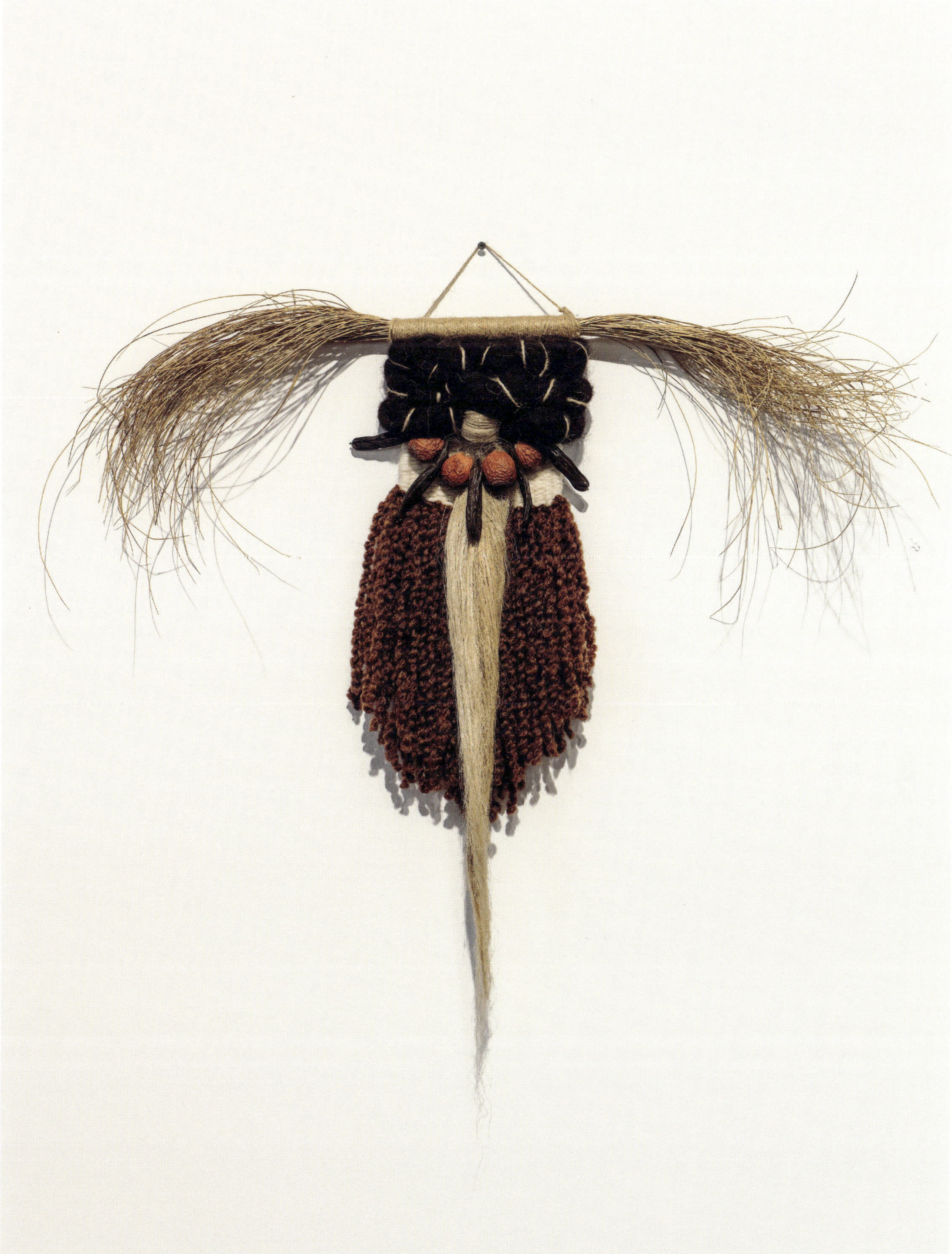

TALAMANCA
@prudencedudan

PRUDENCE DUDAN

MIXED-MEDIA ART

Prudence Dudan's studio is an inspiration. The French-born artist works from the high-ceilinged, light-filled top floor of a heritage-listed villa on a hilltop. The Can Pep Simó enclave near Talamanca was designed in the late 1960s by the architect Josep Lluís Sert (see pp. 239–41).

Many major figures of the mid-century avant-garde movement lived around or visited this hilltop, including Joan Miró and his wife, the patron Pilar Juncosa; photographer Joaquim Gomis; and architects Albert Illescas de la Morena and Erwin Broner.

'The architecture of Can Pep Simó is very radical, pure and brutal in some way', Prudence says. 'It has been preserved, and you feel as if time has stopped. You could be in a Jacques Tati movie.'

For her work, Prudence finds this environment and its connections with a bygone world of creativity very inspiring. 'It has opened up new fields of creative investigation for me.' For one project, she used photographs by Gomis (who was a great friend of Sert's). She mixed painting, textiles and collages with images from his series *Artesanía*, which was an inventory of vernacular Spanish objects. Her project was exhibited at Galería También in Santa Gertrudis (pp. 100–103) in 2022. And she has completed several art residencies at the Fundació Pilar i Joan Miró in Mallorca. Some of the work she started there was shown in Brussels in spring 2023 by Amélie, Maison d'Art, the gallery in Paris that represents her.

Rather than creating one-off pieces, Prudence's method is to make a series. She thinks of the process as 'a kind of gymnastics'. The starting point is often ephemera that she has collected and that have meaning for her: paintings, drawings and pieces of photographs from books, and fabrics. 'There is already a story behind how I came across this material. I rework these images to give them another life', she explains, adding that she sometimes uses collage techniques. 'It's an exercise in appropriation.'

Before starting to show her art in 2021, Prudence had a career in the design world. She studied graphic design at the École Nationale Supérieure des Arts Décoratifs (EnsAD) and at Sciences Po, both in Paris. She followed her studies with a one-year residency at New York's Center for Book Arts, which promotes the exploration of books as an art form. 'This was a very important experience', she says. Her work involved graphic experimentation on artists' books – 'a beautiful opportunity for me because the centre has all the craftsmanship of books together in one space'. There she began to investigate books and images conceptually as medium or material.

'In an increasingly digitalized world, where images are infinitely multiplying, I try to activate other ways of dealing with them', Prudence explains. 'Through the manipulation of images and raw material, my practice explores the different ways of reading – whether texts, images, gestures, situations, light or landscapes – and always seeking metaphorical meaning.' ***CD***

Paris-born Prudence Dudan's artistic practice is centred on carefully selecting existing materials and manipulating them to give them new meaning.

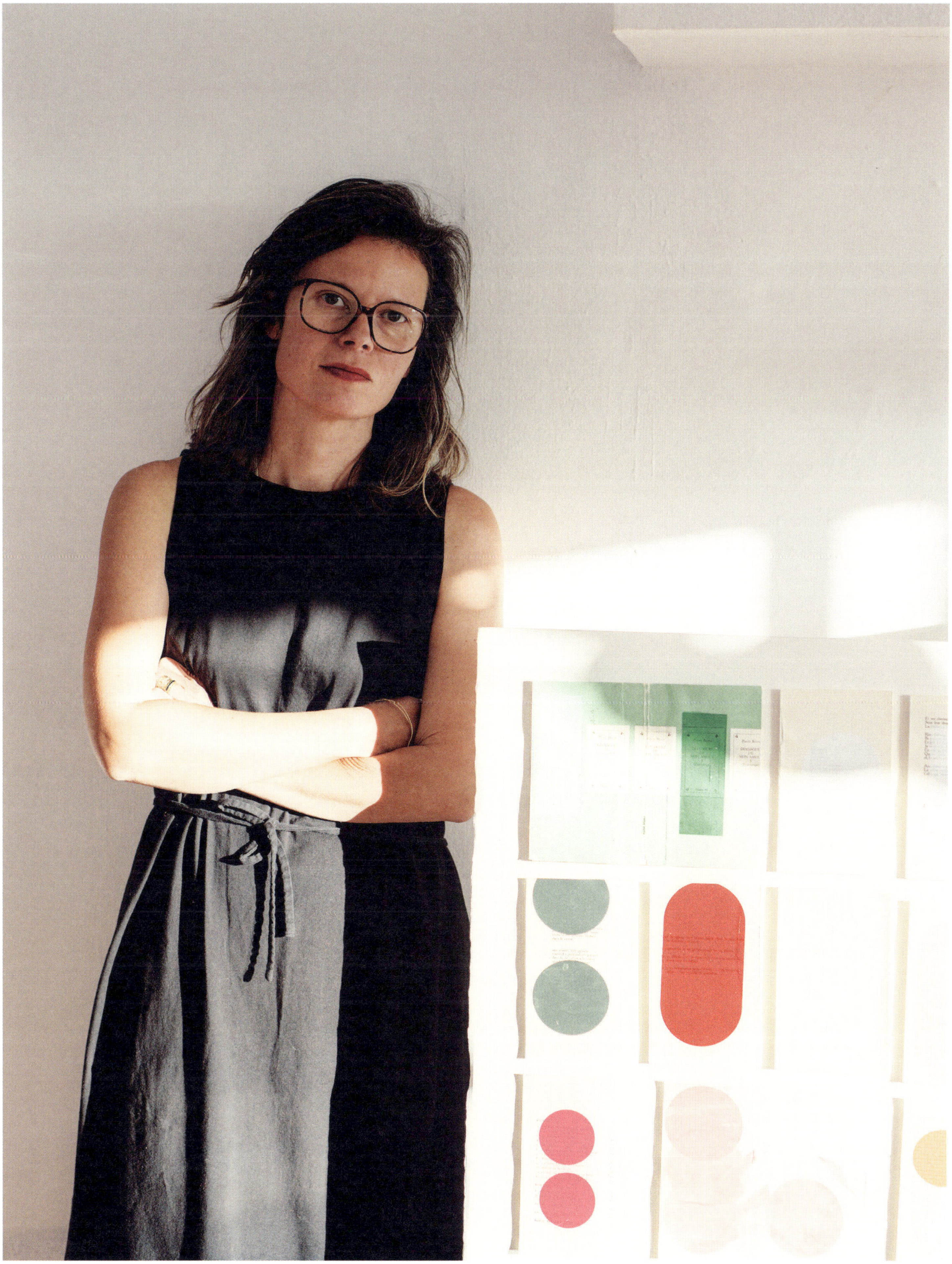

Prudence's studio, on the top floor of a 1960s house by the architect Josep Lluís Sert, benefits from abundant natural light. Rather than making one-off artworks, she creates series.

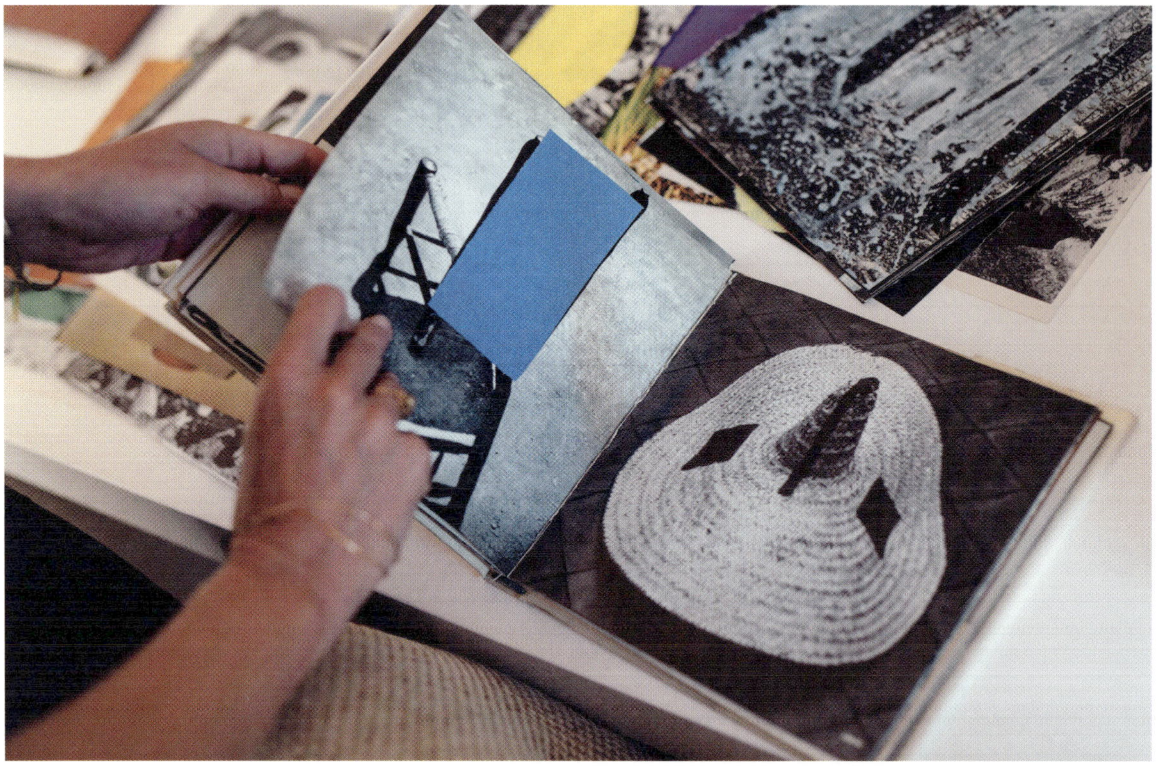

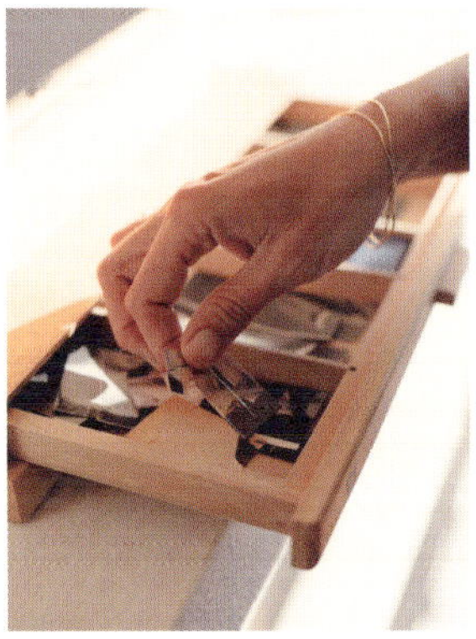

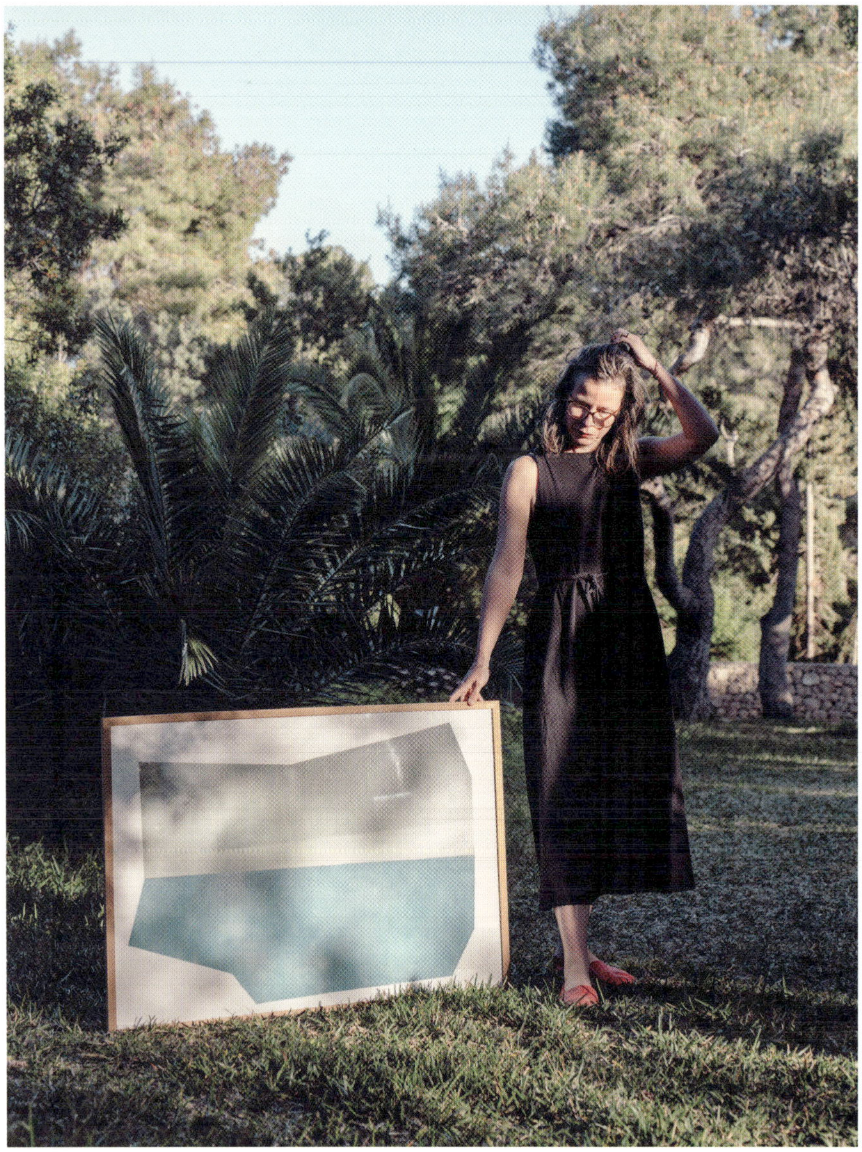

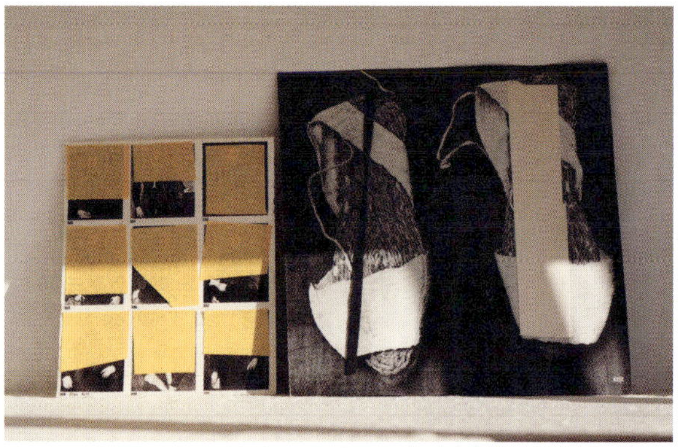

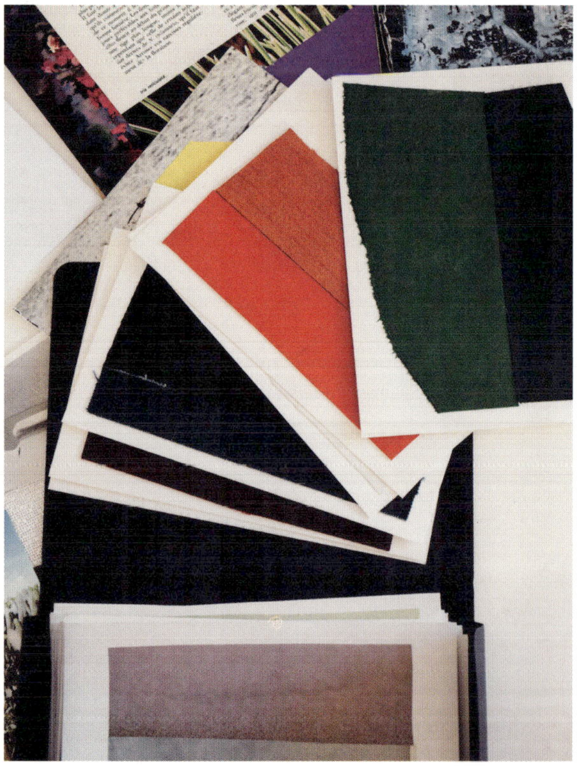

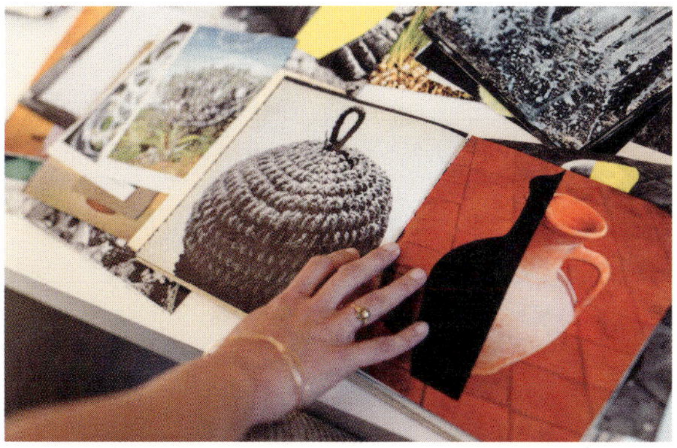

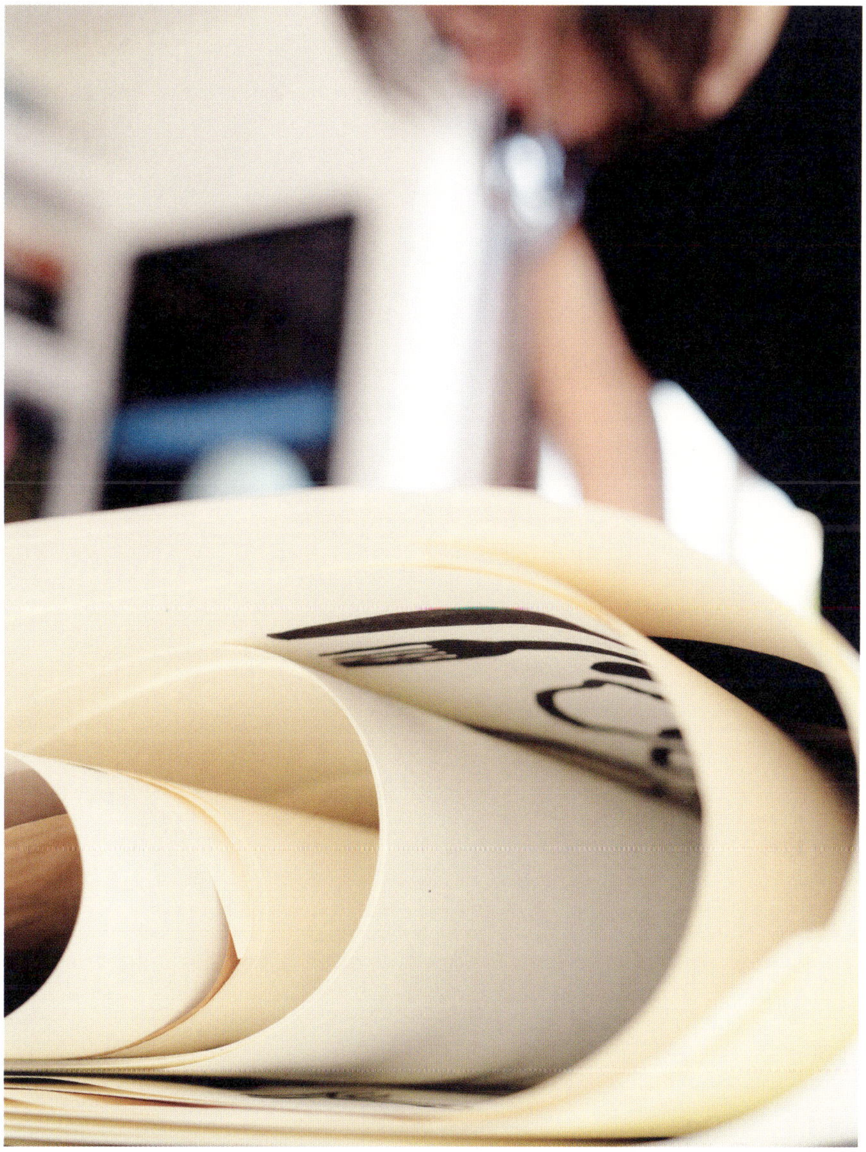

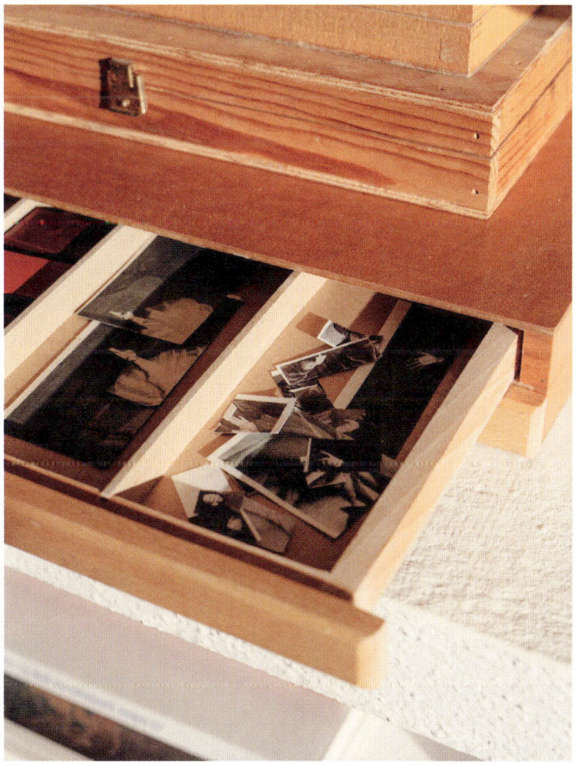

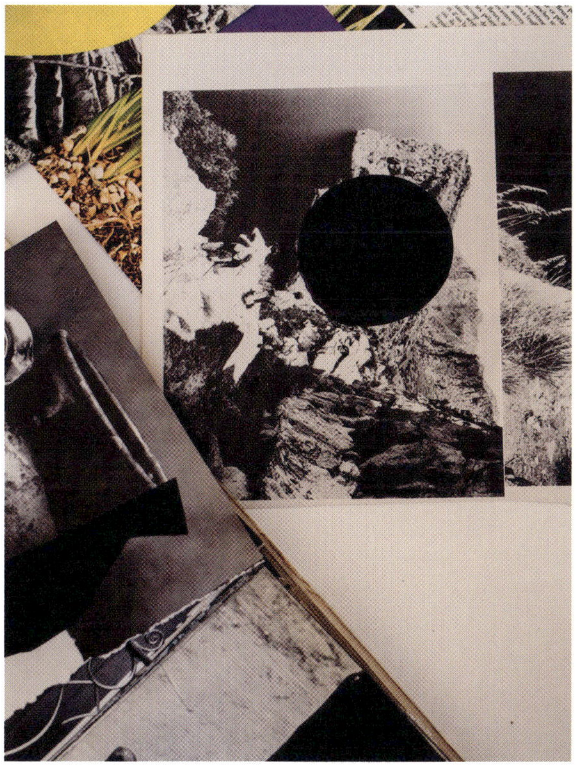

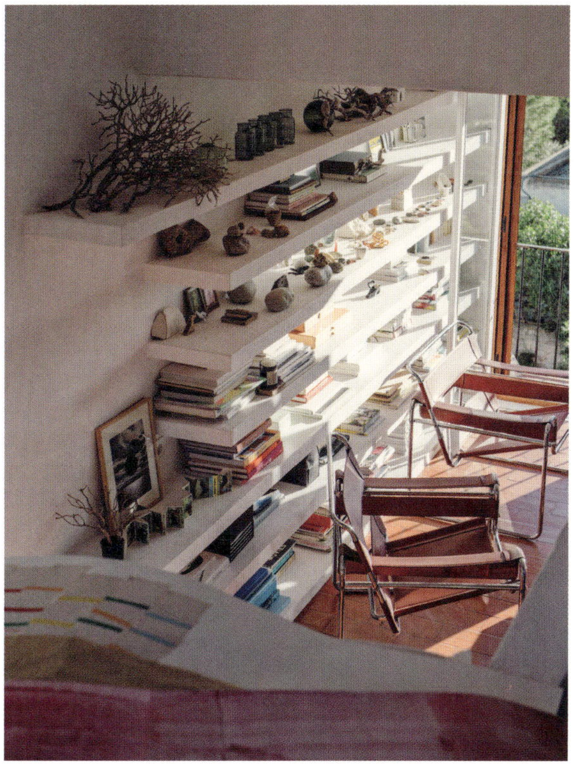

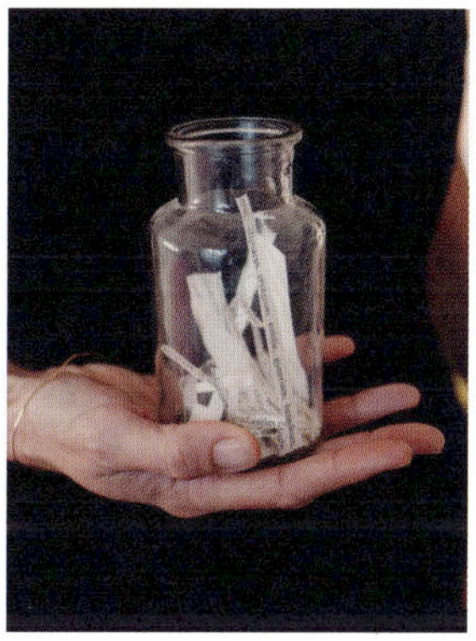

Prudence works with mixed media, so she collects various materials, such as photographic prints and books. She takes several months to create a piece, and her studio is filled with sketches and works in progress.

JESÚS
espacio-micus.com

ESPACIO MICUS

ART SPACE

Artists often describe Ibiza as a natural temple illuminated by a sublime white light. The artist and aspiring architect Eduard Micus unwittingly magnified this idea, enshrining the island's unique luminescence in his own studio-gallery, which stands out on account of its almost windowless walls.

Micus's initial plan was not quite as lofty. Motivated more by the need to find extra space for his art – and to secure some peace and quiet away from the family home – he built a sort of 'living monument'. Decades later, it survives as a celebration of art, architecture and creative freedom.

'The first time my father said he wanted to build something, the whole family responded, "Oh no! Not more buildings!"' recalls Eduard's daughter, Katja Micus. 'He'd always baulked at modern museums with too many windows, saying they look nice from the outside but aren't very practical as a gallery.' Intent on exhibiting his growing collection of artworks, he designed a multi-room, near-windowless space with skylights that let the light shine down from above. 'Making your own place is like drawing a picture', says Katja. 'It's a form of self-expression.'

Like many artistic émigrés settling on the island, Micus was looking to replace the cacophony of urban life with a sense of freedom found in greener pastures. Born in Germany in 1925, he had begun abstract painting at a young age and lived in a cabin he built in a woodland district of Höxter. At the Staatliche Akademie der Bildenden Künste Stuttgart he rubbed shoulders with architects and artisans, sparking his propensity for experimentation with materials and a fondness for contrasts. By the time he arrived in Ibiza in 1972 and started building the family home, he was well versed in transversal design, an expertise that allowed him to make such a valuable contribution to the island's cultural patrimony.

A polymath who played with textures, colours, light and shadow, Micus could switch from creating canvases adorned with wood carvings to designing steel staircases and abstract metal sculptures that hint at the human form. His studio building is likewise marked by contrasts. Almost cave-like, the series of split-level rooms contain ever-shifting slivers of light that accentuate the passing of the hours, months and seasons. The space is also an example of Micus's much-loved *coudrage* technique, which stitched together different materials like a three-dimensional collage writ large.

After Eduard's passing in 2000, Katja, a trained goldsmith, decided to open the studio to the public as a gallery. 'I started with four annual exhibitions', she explains. 'It was life-changing.' Twenty years later, she is still going, and people are still coming. 'I do it for the artists. Helping them makes me happy.' ***LA***

Katja Micus curates a programme of exhibitions in her father's former studio, which now showcases contemporary artists alongside original works by Eduard Micus. It remains one of the island's preferred gathering places to see and appreciate culture and art.

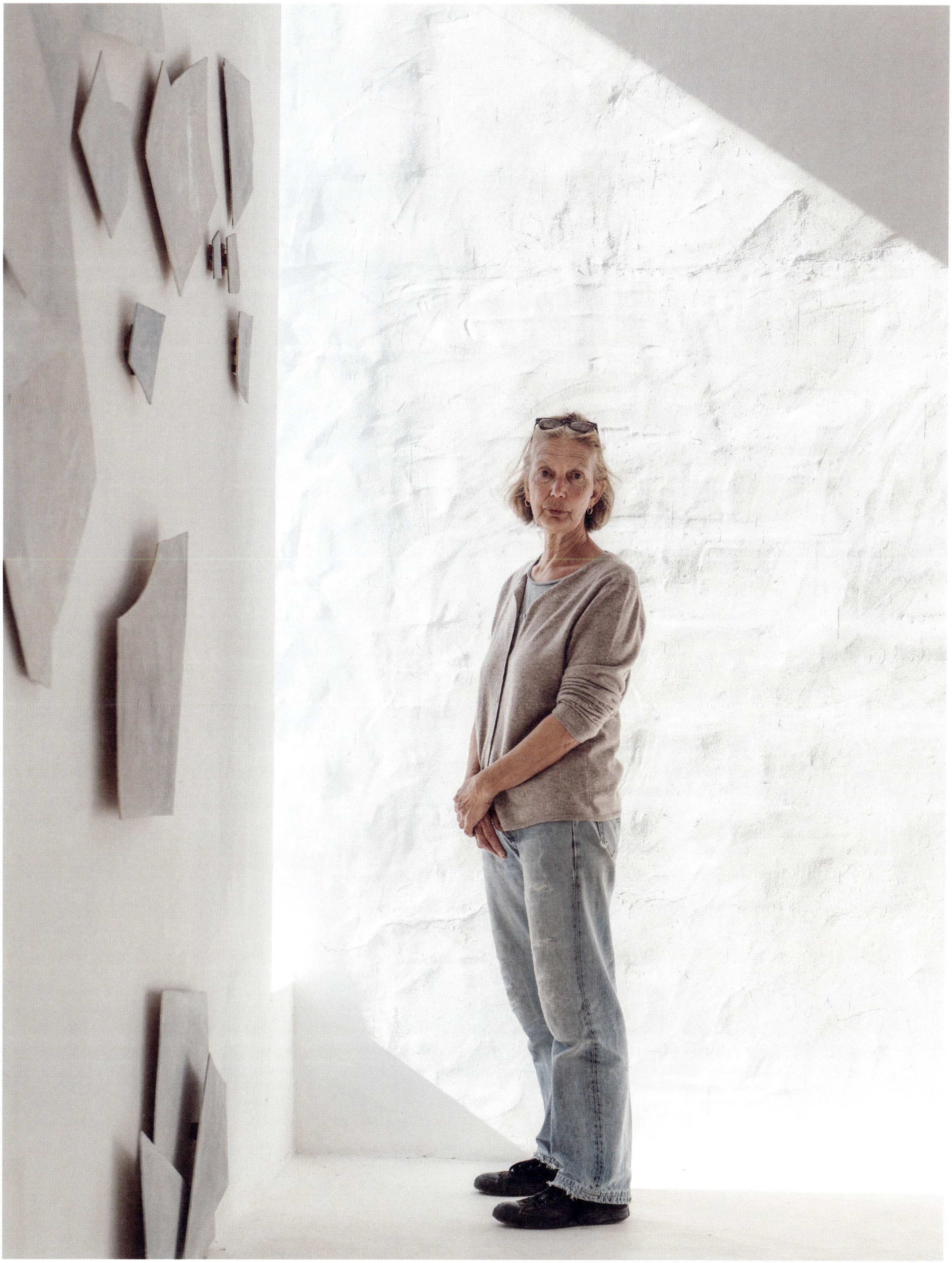

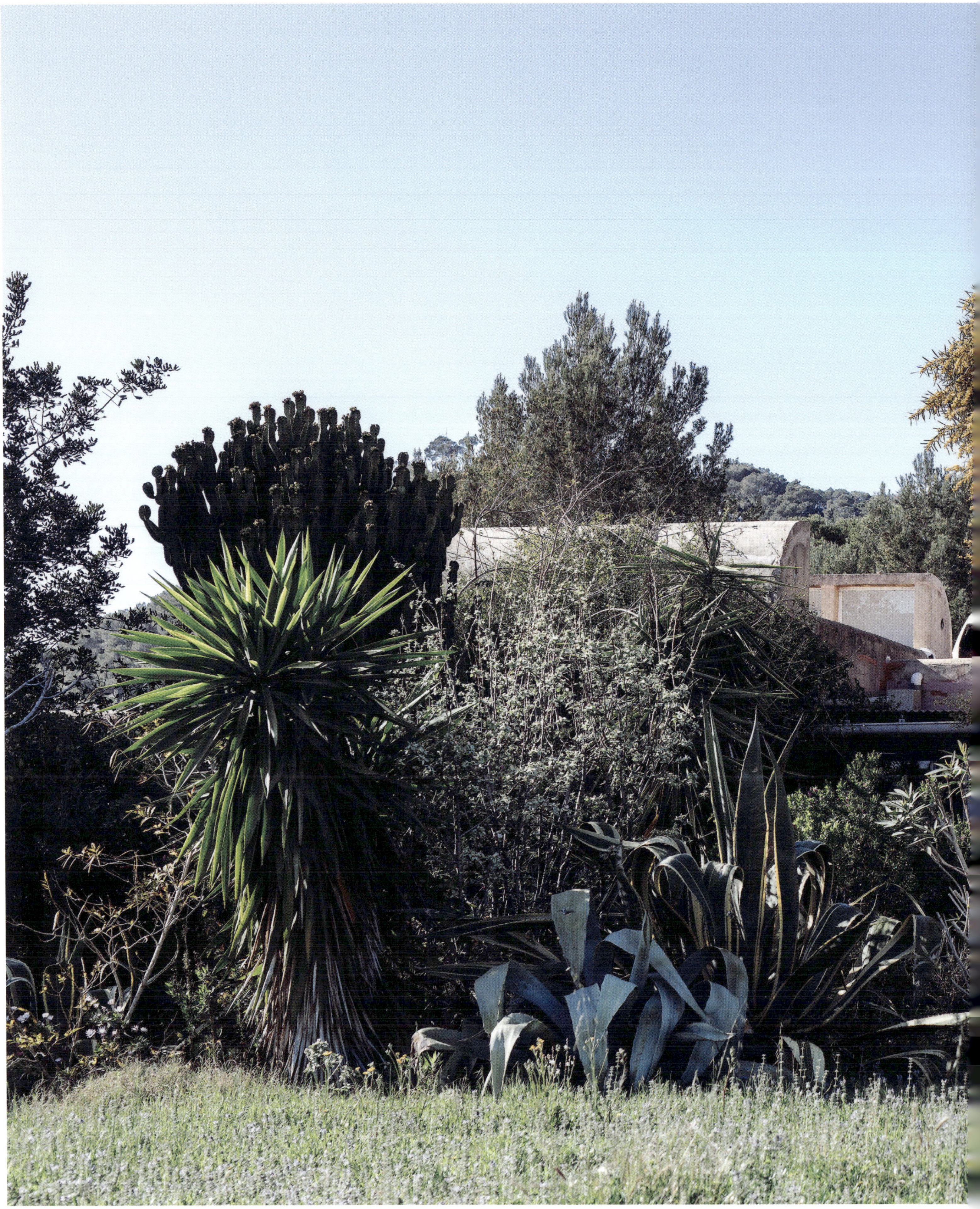

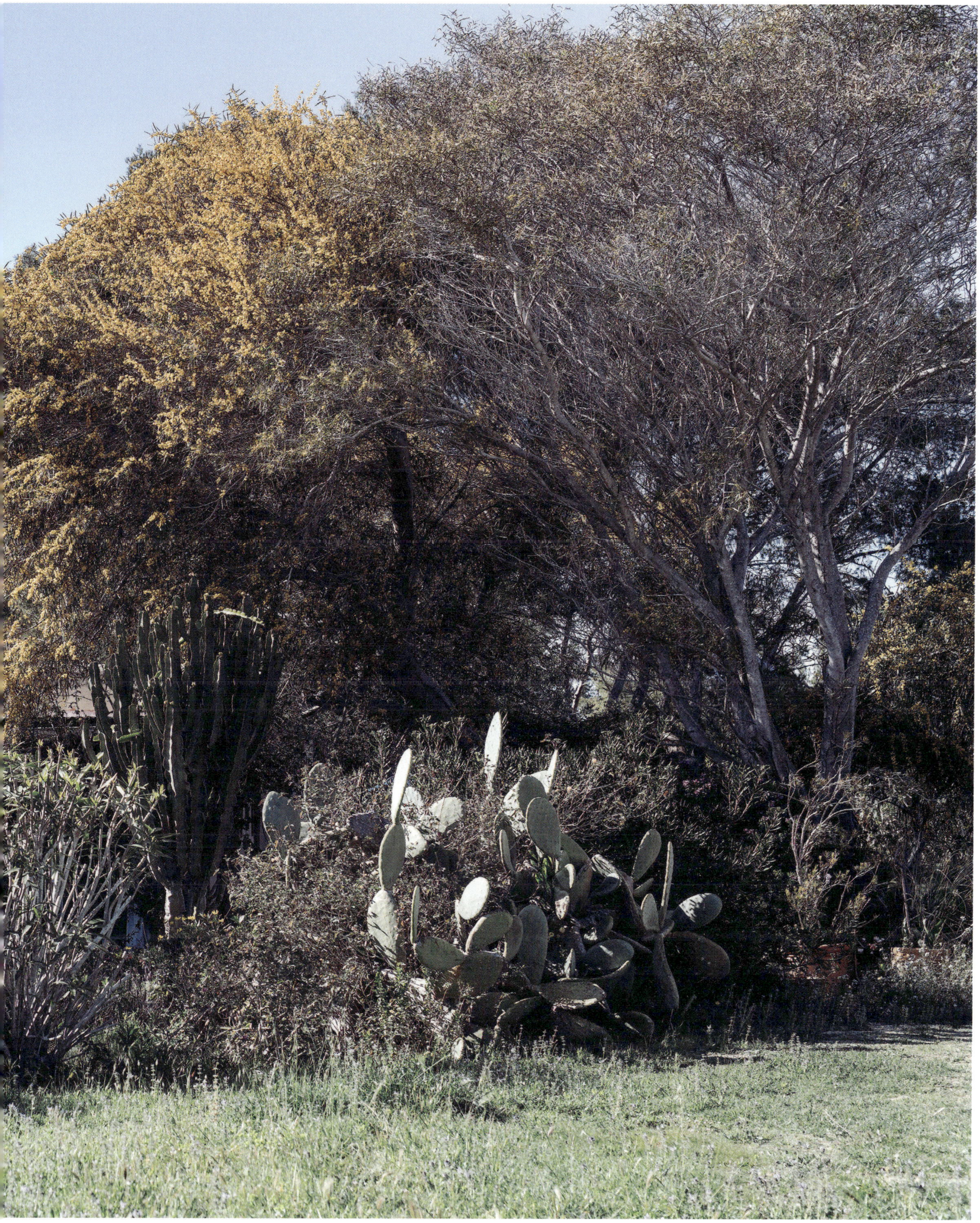

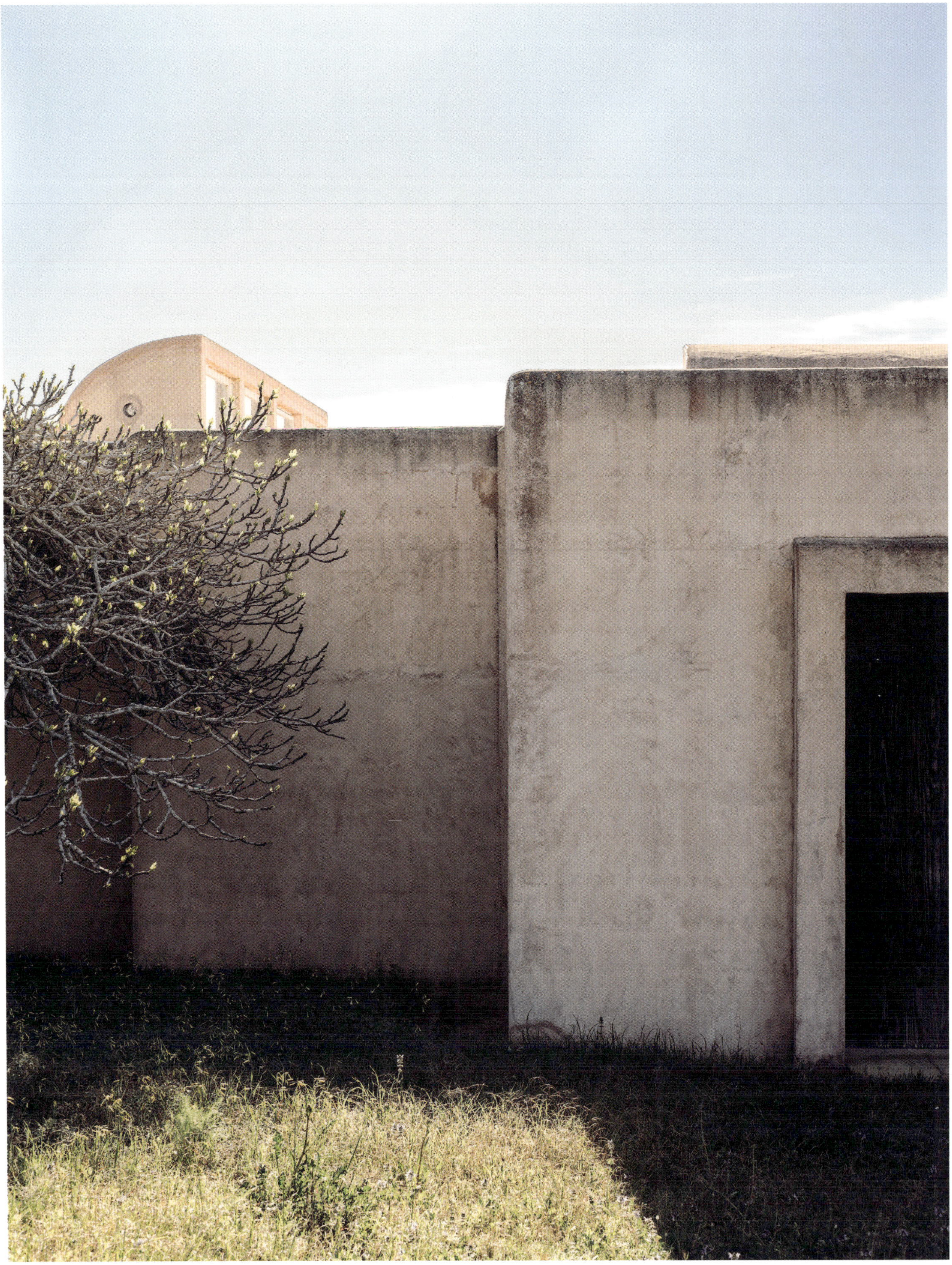

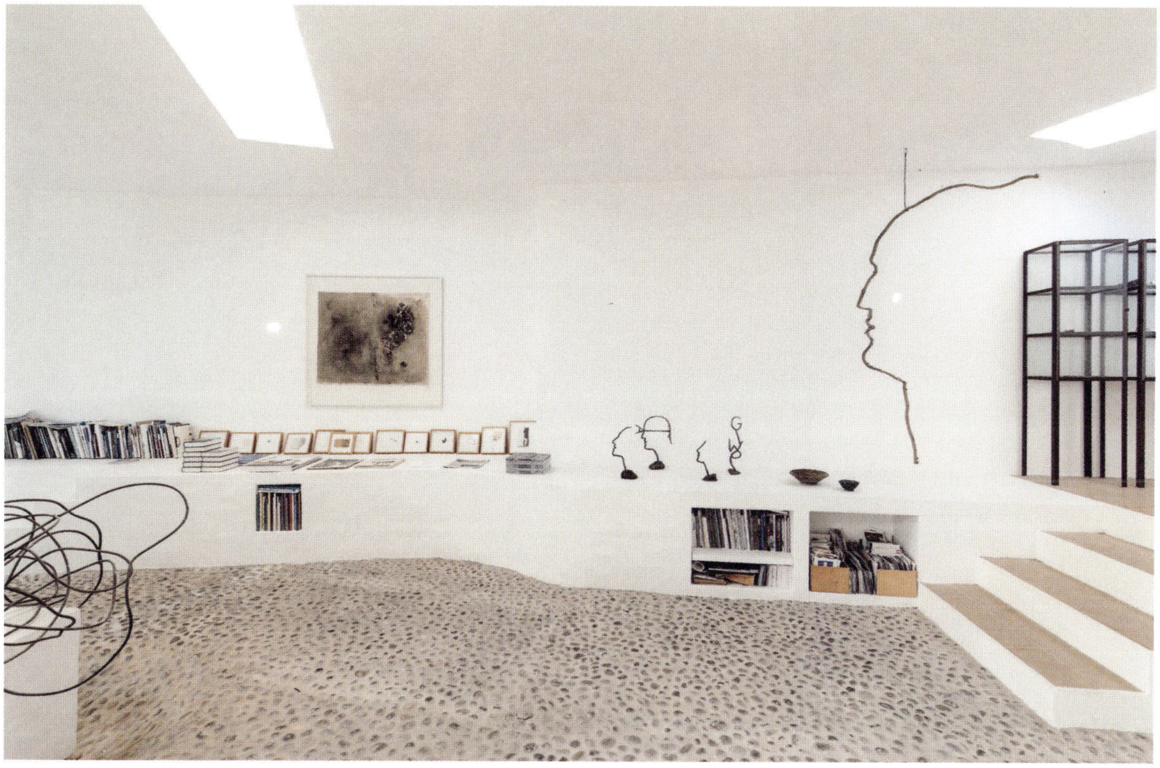

The building's signature skylights bathe the almost windowless space in a distinctive light. Artworks by the late Eduard Micus (below, left) are spread around different areas of the gallery. Metal sculptures by Maria Catalán and Martin Bialas are permanent fixtures of the central room (left).

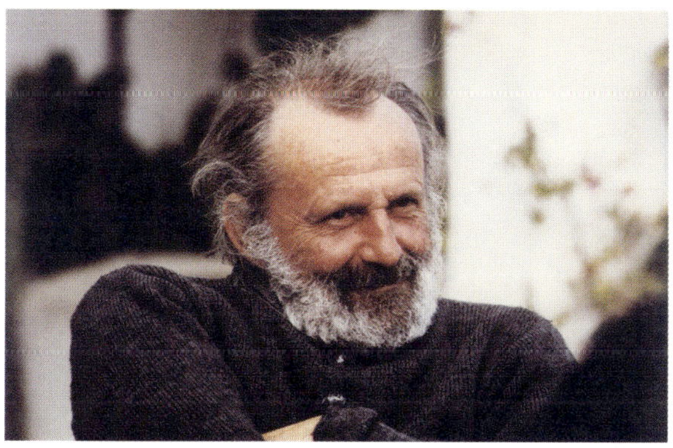

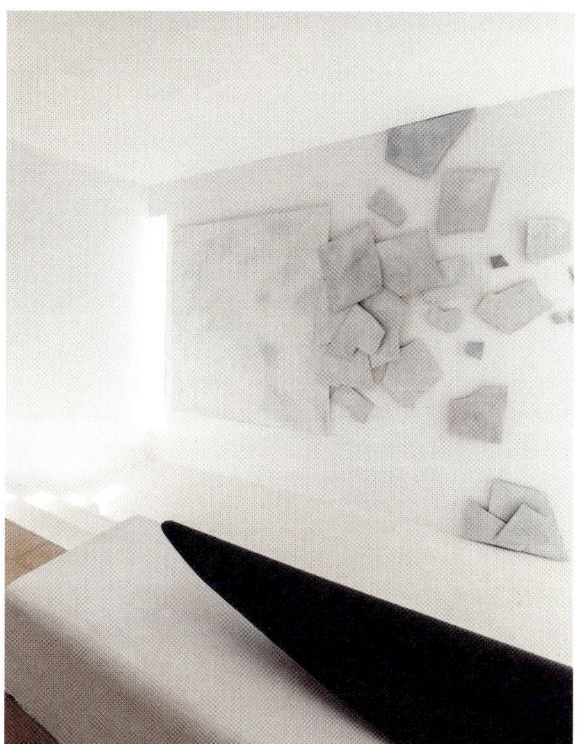

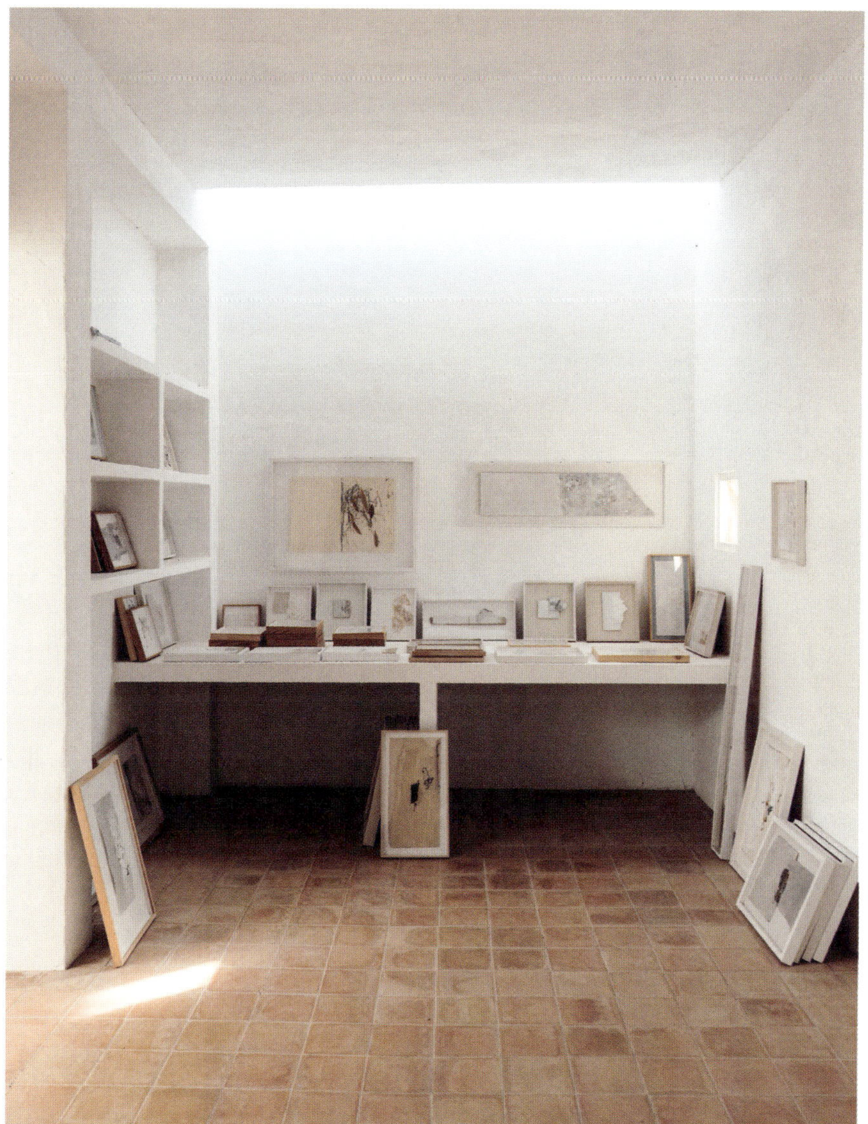

SANTA GERTRUDIS
@galeriatambien | @natalierichtambien

GALERÍA TAMBIÉN

ART SPACE

Inanimate objects have souls. This wonderful, bold, whimsical idea gives life to Galería También, a joint venture by Jorge Fernández López and Natalie Rich Fernández.

A cabinet of curiosities in the heart of Santa Gertrudis de Fruitera, their space serves as a showroom, shop, exhibition hall and quasi-museum all rolled into one. Putting twentieth-century design on a pedestal, every exquisitely curated object sits like a story waiting to be told.

'People are very curious', explains Jorge. 'When they step inside our space, there's always a hunger to know more.' Gesturing towards a cabinet caressed by the light fingerprint of time, he continues: 'I call this patina the soul. The surface carries a lot of information; people can see it has lived many lives.' Natalie agrees. 'People seem to fall more in love with objects that have souls', she says.

The French couple's Ibiza reset began in 2018, after a period of change prompted some soul-searching and a decision to move permanently to an island they previously enjoyed purely as a summer escape. Jorge bid farewell to the high-intensity music industry. Natalie, an artist, was eager to embrace new sources of inspiration and to find more space in which to create. They inaugurated Galería También that same year.

'We've narrowed the focus of the project little by little, but our aesthetic has stayed true to ourselves', says Jorge. 'All the pieces here could be in our own home. We don't follow market trends, nor matters of supply and demand. Our strength is our love of what we do.'

The couple's home near San Lorenzo is a half-century-old traditional residence that sits alongside a smaller, cubiform construction featuring vast windows and design cues plucked straight from Santa Fe or Palm Springs. The juxtaposition is a reminder of a time when houses in Ibiza were experimental playgrounds for design and farms became unlikely hotbeds of the avant-garde. Just like the gallery, the house is furnished with the dignity of doing things well and a promise to safeguard the legacy of well-made objects for future generations.

Several years on, the couple's shared vision continues to grow, manifested through multifarious forms of functional design – and a tendency to finish each other's sentences. Their newly adopted surname – También – underlines their commitment to this fresh chapter even further. From stories about India's post-independence design renaissance to those on the origin of *payés* chairs popularly used on Ibizan farms, their passion for well-made things is palpable at every turn.

Natalie's sculpture art is part of the ever-changing narrative. 'What I try to do is channel everything into a story', she explains. 'You can see this in the painted designs on my ceramic pieces, which are also lamps or vases or something else entirely.' Pointing to several wall pieces that look like tools but are actually sculptures, she adds, 'I like to keep everything open to interpretation.'

At the heart of Jorge and Natalie's eclectic vision is the joy of the unexpected. And, just like Natalie's own work, which spans the spectrum of painting, illustration, sculpture and ceramics, Galería También feels like a perpetually evolving exhibition – inspirational, encyclopedic, one that refuses to be defined within narrow terms. ***LA***

At Galería También, Jorge Fernández fuses the island's distinctive artisanal legacy with the world's most prestigious design pieces. Natalie Rich Fernández is an artist who explores the ever-changing line between the functional and the fanciful, the useful and the timeless.

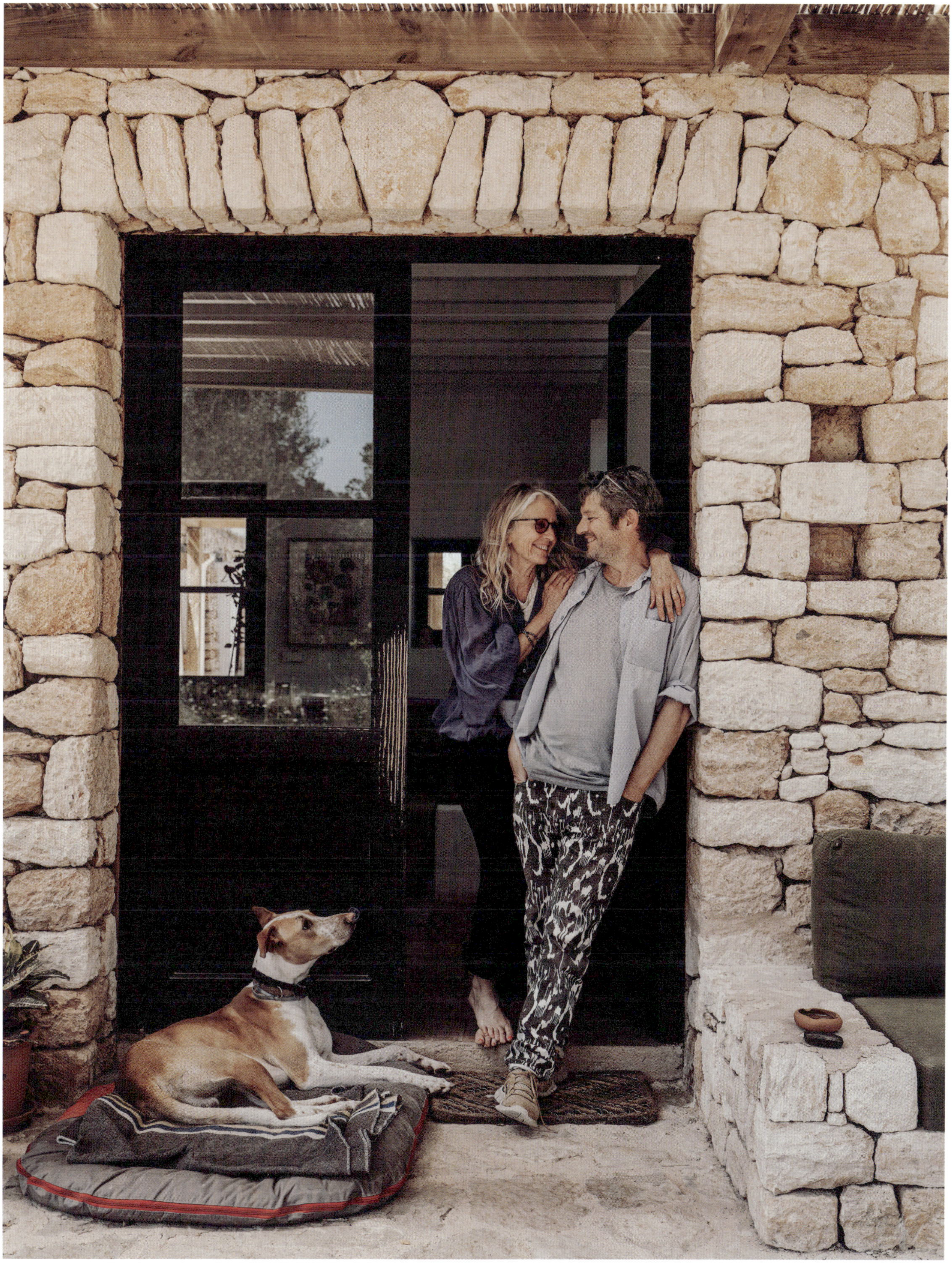

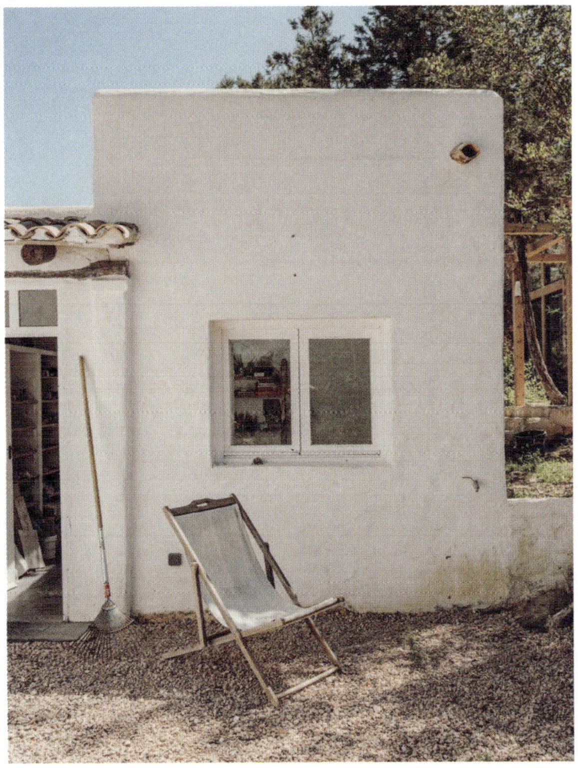

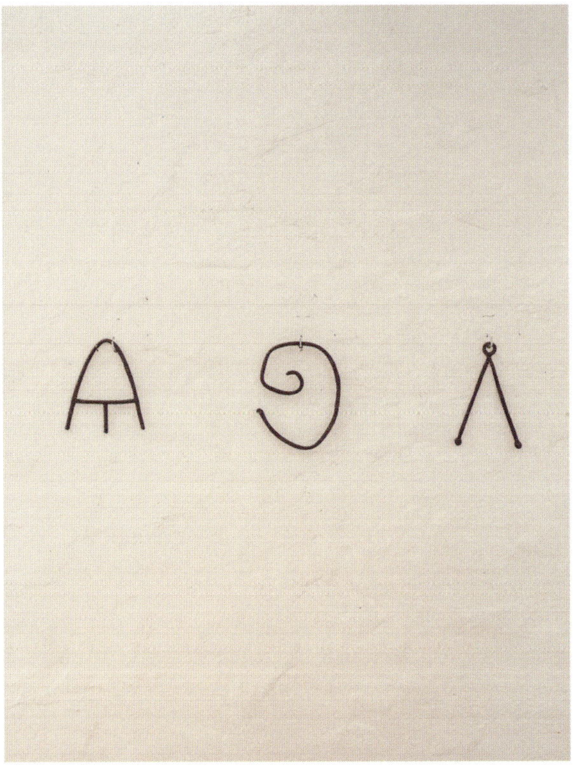

Filled with materials, tools and miscellanea, Natalie's atelier in San Lorenzo reflects her multidisciplinary approach to art and craft.

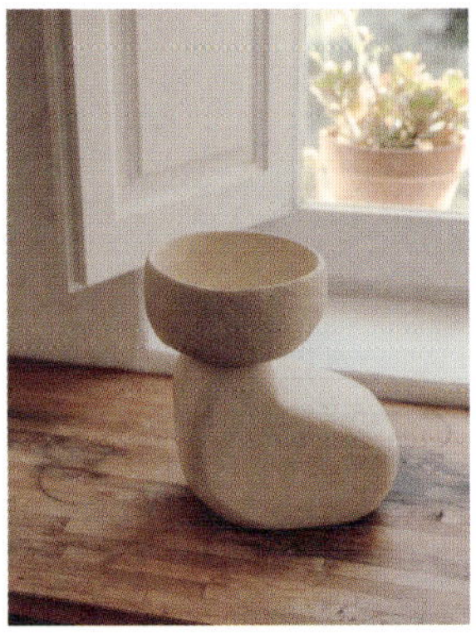

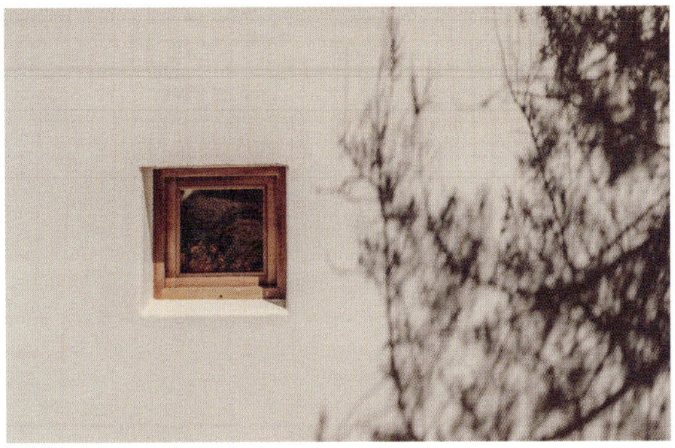

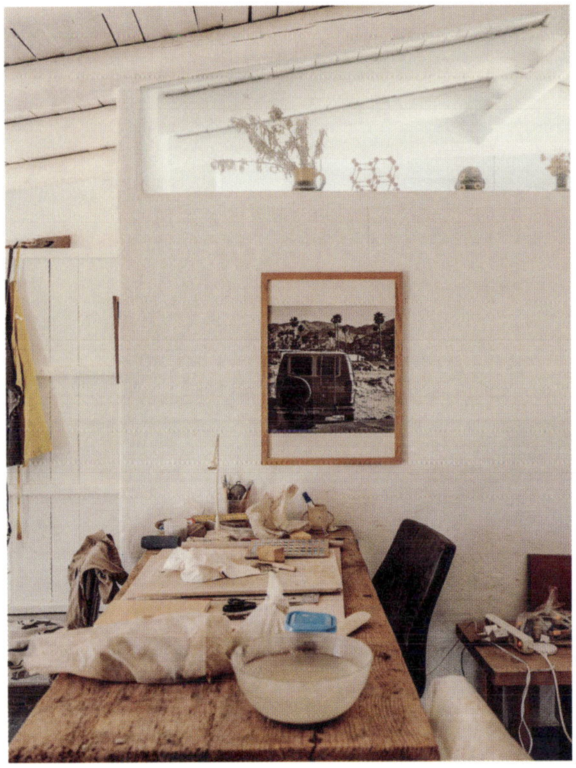

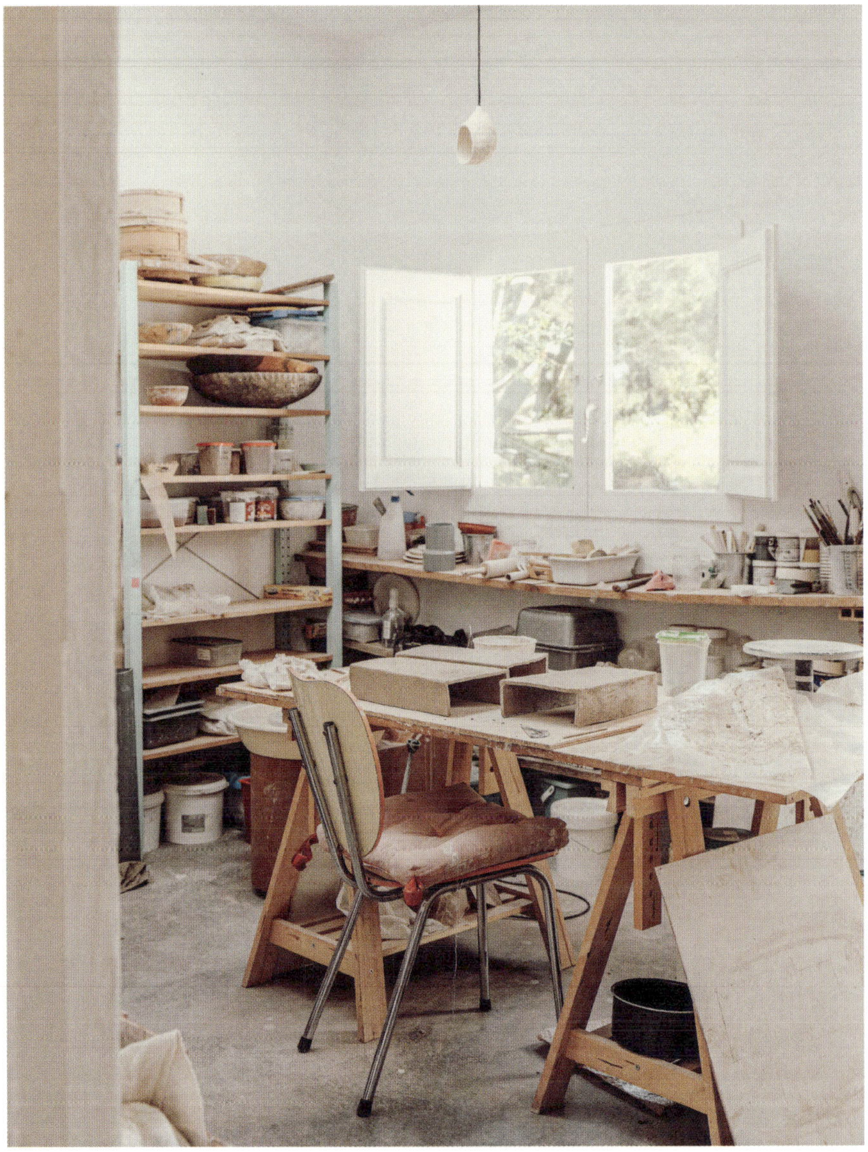

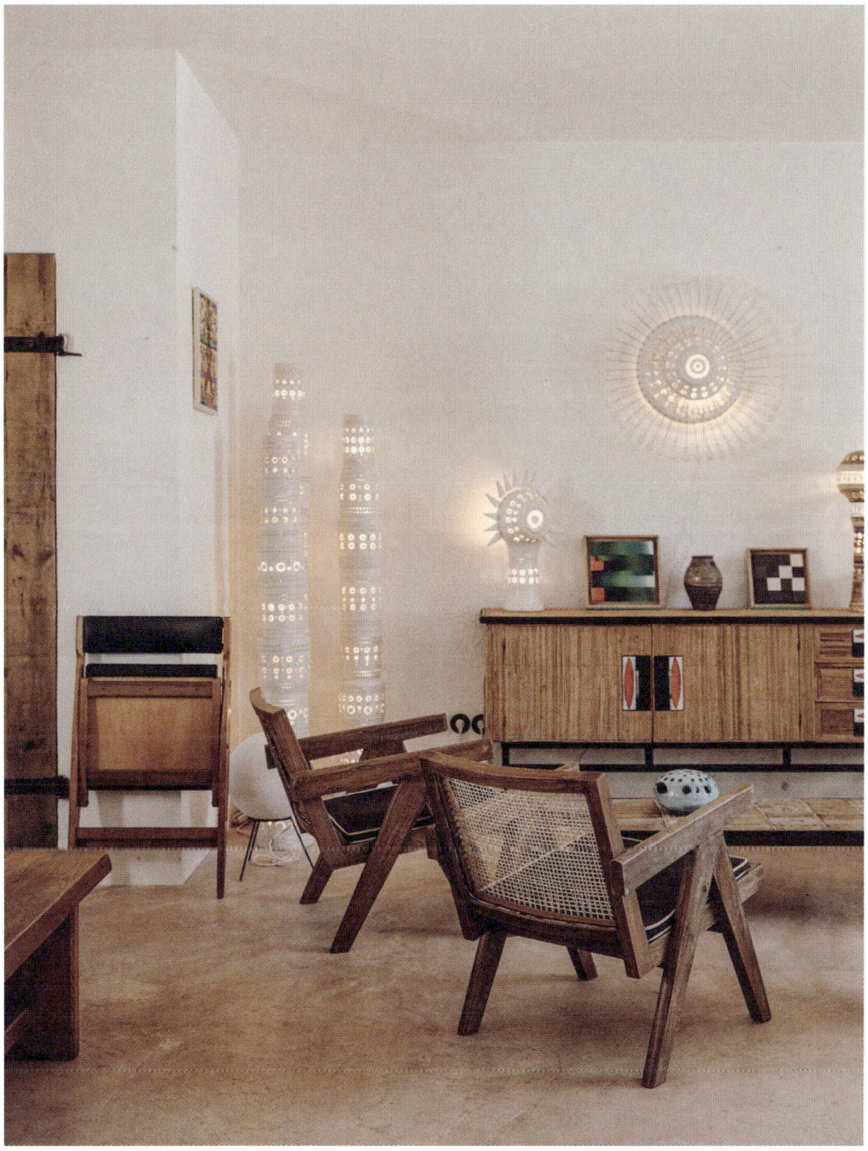

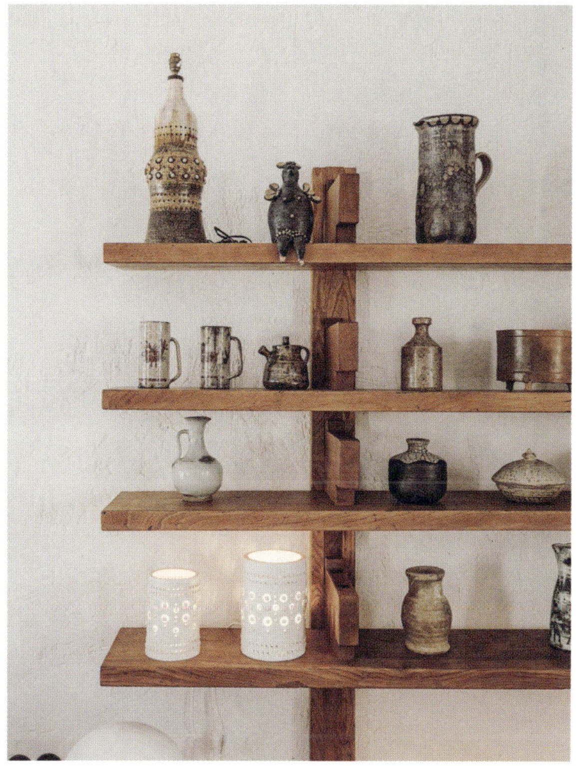

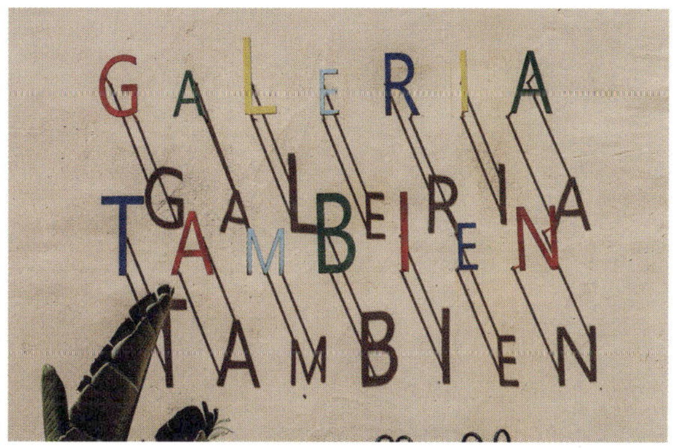

Inside Galería También is an eclectic range of objects, such as white ceramic sculptures by Georges Pelletier and chairs by Pierre Jeanneret (above, left).

Right: Natalie's own creations also have pride of place, including these ceramic wall pieces, which resemble metal tools.

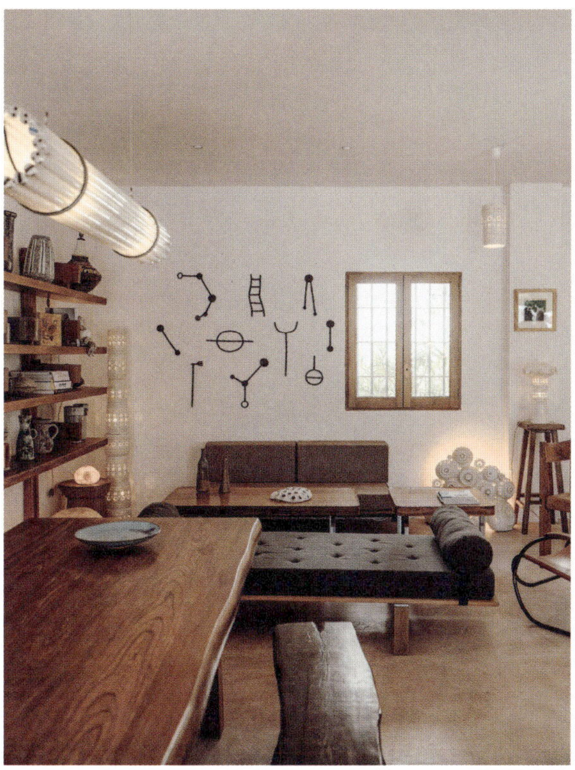

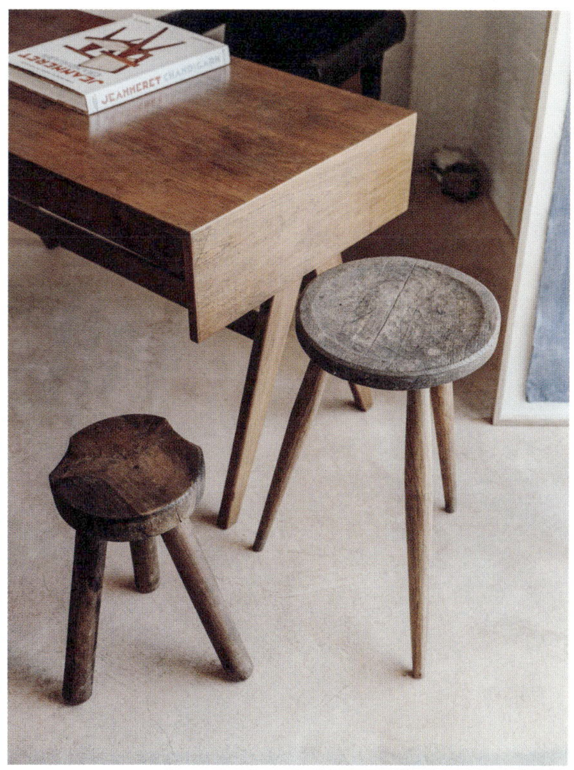

SANTA GERTRUDIS
@el__domo

CLOVIS NEYMO

SCULPTURE & DESIGN

Like many young creatives who wind up in Ibiza, Clovis 'El Domo' Neymo landed here at the tail end of a journey in search of purpose, vision and identity. He had waved goodbye to a job in film and advertising, lured by a thirst for change that only adventures in travel promised to quench. Along the way, he discovered an inspirational creative community on Isla Holbox, an island just north of Mexico's Yucatán Peninsula. 'I saw how these creatives – young and old – coexisted. It ignited my curiosity about the importance of creating small, visually artistic spaces', he recalls. 'I departed with an idea to create my own small, collaborative village – this is still my ideal.'

After a stint in southern Spain learning eco-friendly building techniques, Clovis became increasingly fascinated by the domed structures typical of parts of North Africa. He began searching for somewhere to experiment with his own domes, and then, just one week before the first lockdown of the Covid pandemic, his parents (Jorge Fernández López and Natalie Rich Fernández of Galería También; pp. 100–103) offered up their garden in Ibiza. The global shutdown pressed pause on his wanderlust, forcing a sense of focus. 'This was how I honed my own building method', he explains. 'During this time, I built two types of dome with a mix of different techniques: the traditional adobe method, building around a metallic structure, and a more ecological approach, where I used natural elements as much as possible instead of chemical products.'

However, only a few years later, Clovis does not want to be restricted by the label of dome-maker. He has expanded, turning his skills to creating embedded shelving units, desks and al fresco bathrooms, as well as sculpted furniture and lamps. Swapping the family home for one of the satellite residences inside the infamous Es Polvorí compound (a former Franco-era military bunker on the outskirts of Santa Gertrudis), he seems more determined than ever to realize his dream.

An unabashed sense of experimentation manifests the vision. 'In Africa they use only earth. Here in Ibiza, I add limestone (*cal* in Spanish) to protect against strong seasonal rains', Clovis explains, before adding with a hushed laugh, 'Of course, there are a few more details, but let's call them "secret ingredients".' Recent projects have included a large-scale wall installation of shelves, and corner benches and bedside tables made from such diverse materials as wood, metal and glass. The objective is always the same: to give each space a seamless flow of function, storage, display and decoration.

Popular both in Ibiza and around the Mediterranean in the 1960s and '70s, this more permanent and sustainable solution to home furnishing is undergoing a small renaissance thanks to self-taught artisans like Clovis. 'Mixing classic fixtures of the old fincas with a more modern touch is ideal for Ibiza', he says, going on to describe the island as naturally conducive to creativity. 'I'm grateful I landed here because I have plenty of time and space to keep exploring my craft without constraints.' ***LA***

The French artist Clovis Neymo blends traditional techniques with innovative methods to construct unique living spaces, furniture and sculptures that bridge the gap between past and present.

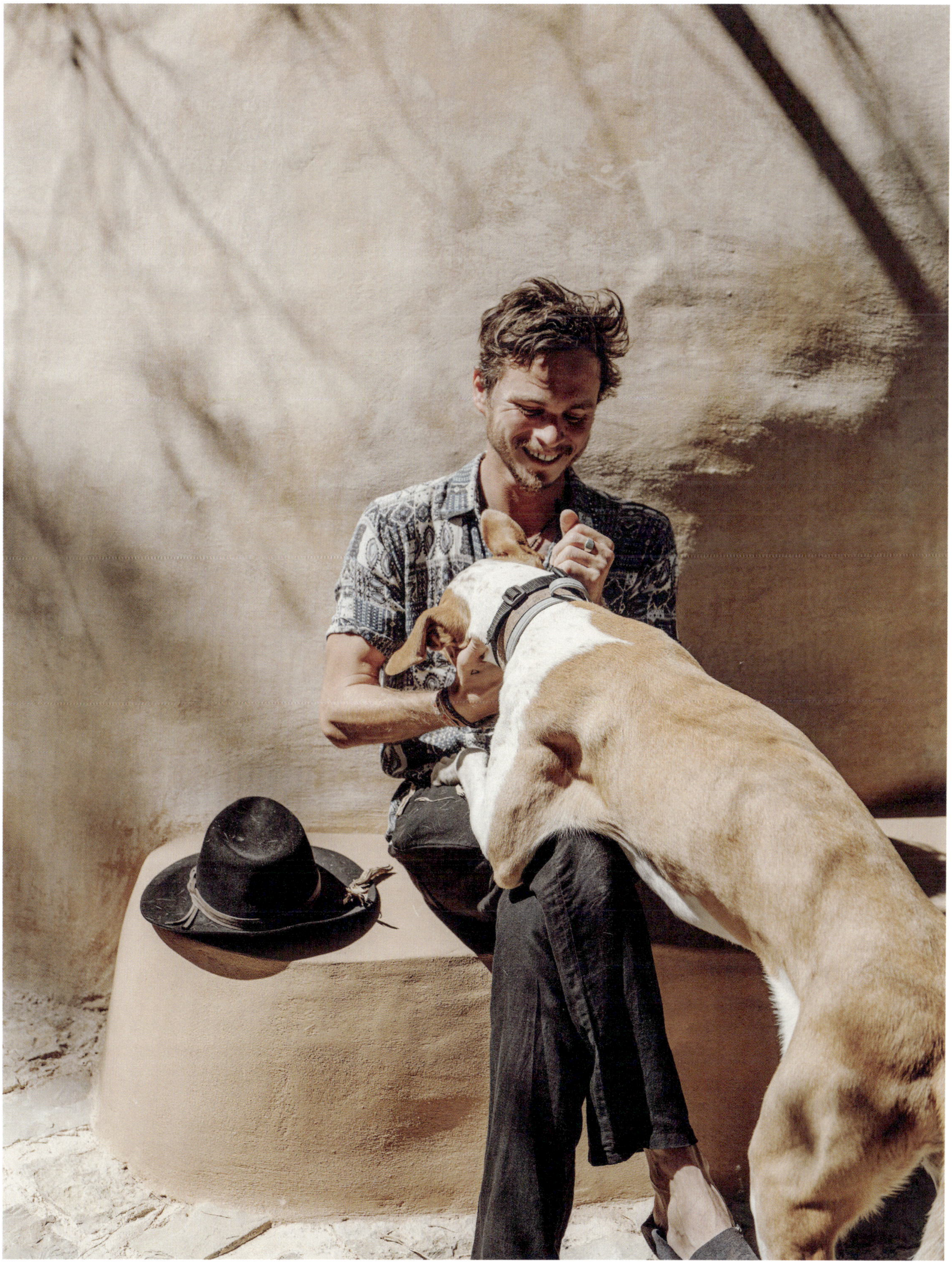

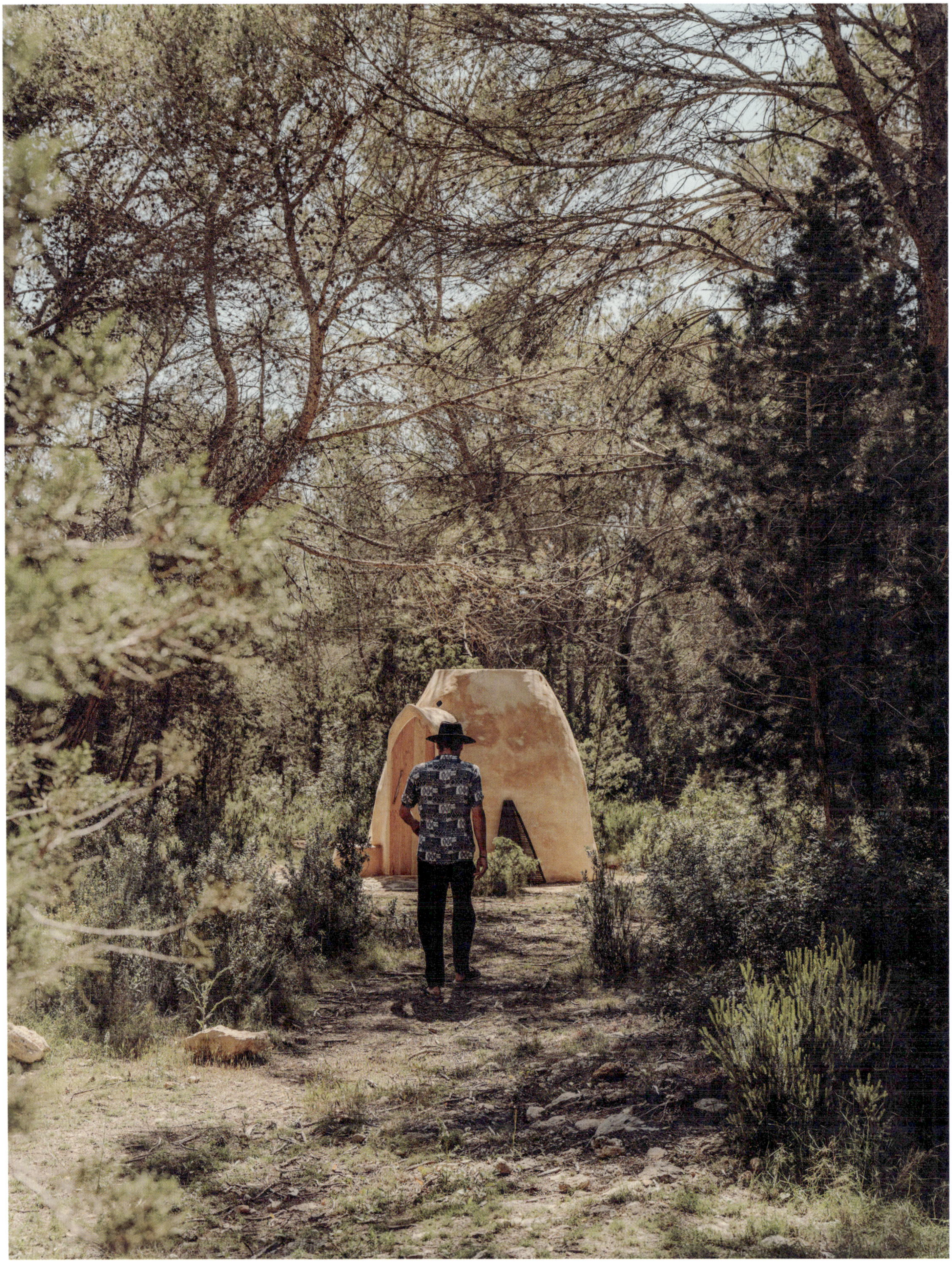

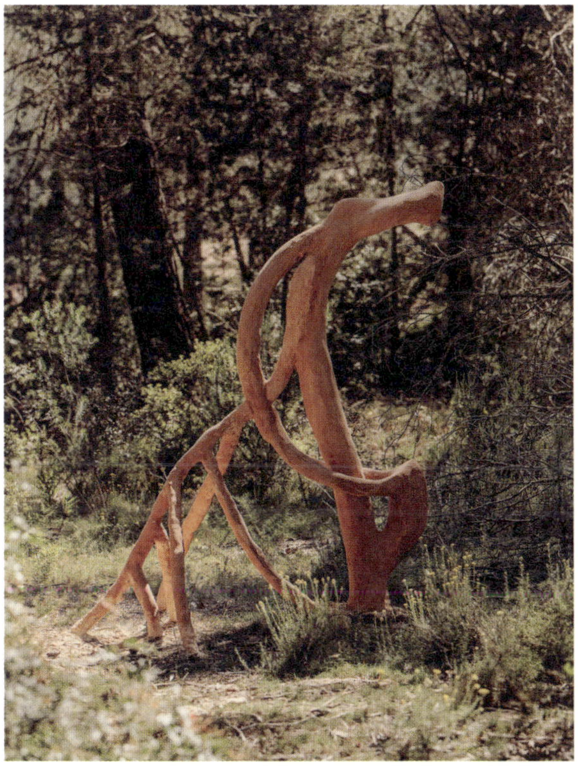

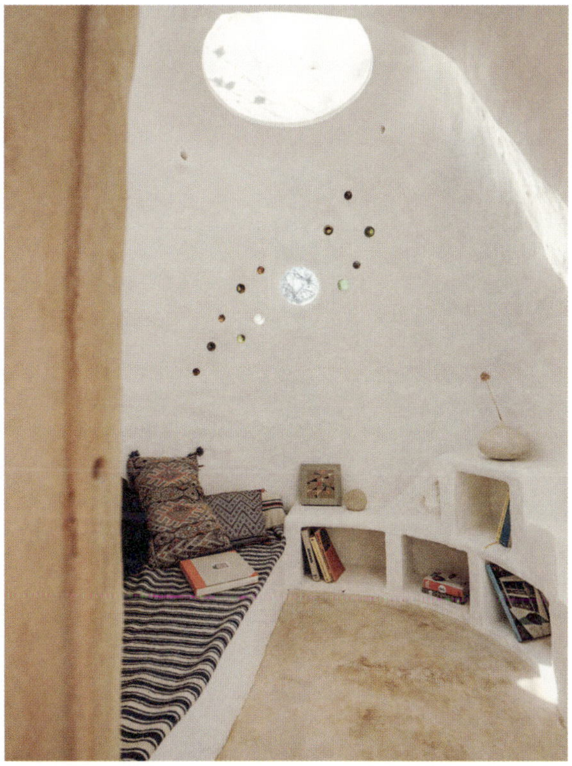

The artist's early works focused on the creation of shelters and retreats, a concept that incorporates various light sources into inviting interiors designed for relaxation and rest.

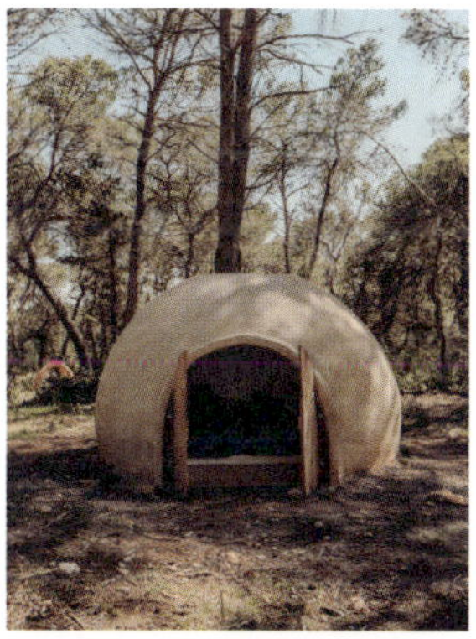

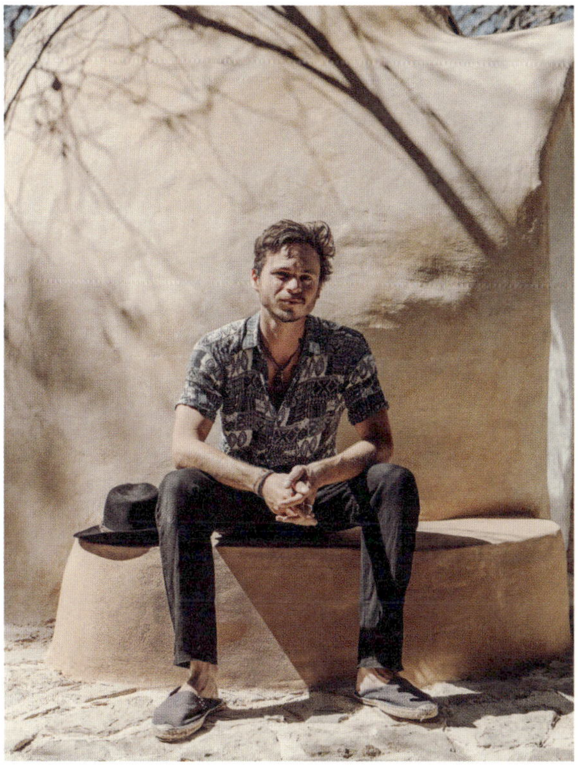

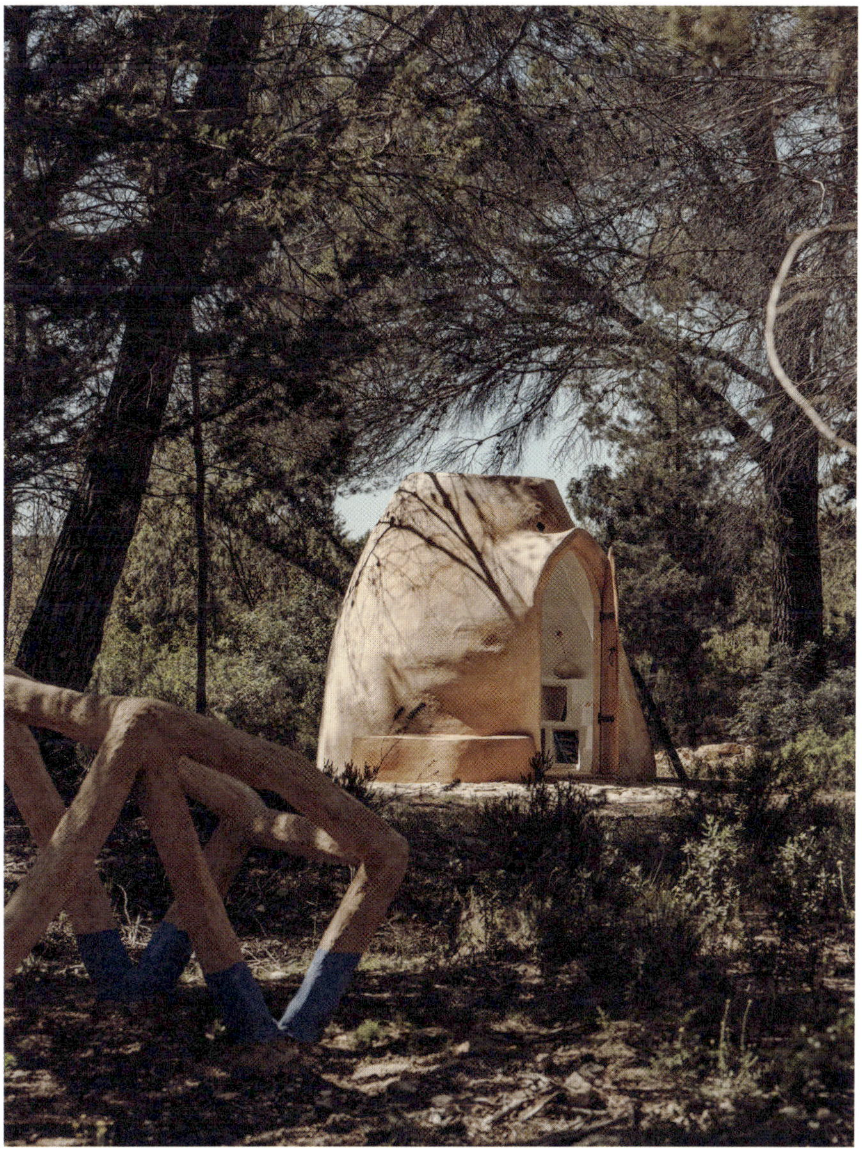

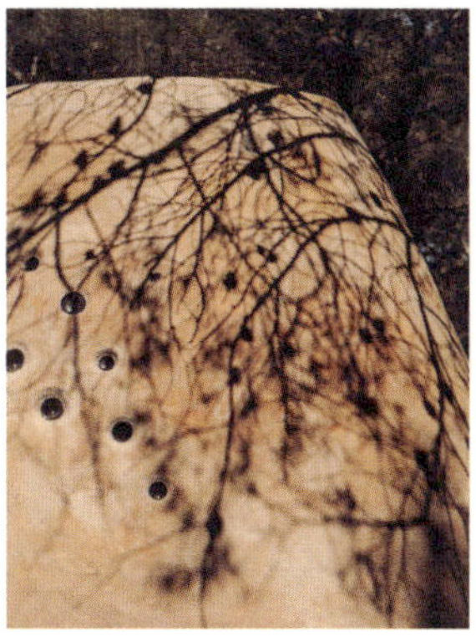

SANTA EULALIA
canjayrecordingstudio.com

CAN JAY

RECORDING STUDIO

'Ibiza reminds me where I came from. I really feel at home here.' Like many free-minded creatives during the Covid pandemic, Cumhur Jay was both pushed and pulled on to the island by an instinct to survive and thrive. Escaping Paris via a hastily signed lease agreement sealed by video call, he first set foot on the long-neglected property on moving day in May 2020. A music producer and sound engineer, Turkish-born Jay (as he is always known) arrived armed with an idea that evolved into a vision and gradually took shape through a mix of vintage colour and modern tech.

Jay's ambition – to create a live-in sound studio – was backed up by intuition, finely tuned over the course of twenty years in the music industry as an artist, DJ, producer and sound engineer. He was convinced that some musical artists were yearning for a more peaceful place to create and record, and his plan was that Can Jay's immersion in nature and its eschewal of the rules and timetables of conventional urban recording studios would cater to such artists and anyone experiencing a sudden burst of creativity.

The first obstacle, however, was the jungle-like foliage engulfing the property. 'My friends dubbed the place "Can Okupa" [squat house] because it looked so impossibly overgrown', recalls Jay with a smirk. Bit by bit, the wilderness was tamed and the characterful, 600-year-old *casa payesa* cleared, cleaned and appointed with playful artworks and vintage furniture. The cosy vibe, transmitted through a surfeit of rugs and sofas, was honed jointly with Jay's business partner, Leila Arató, whose sense of style was nurtured by her upbringing on the island. The house's former olive mill was transformed from a ruinous state into a state-of-the-art recording studio. The old stable is now a sleekly designed vinyl library.

This duality between the traditional and the contemporary – from weathered fixtures and retro-future furniture to hi-tech switchboards softened by time-worn textiles – creates an unexpected energetic interplay, imbuing the house with a sense of unbridled possibility. 'Having people stay here shapes a new outlook for the future', explains Jay. 'Ibiza is not just a place to consume music, but also to make music.' Leila agrees, calling the house 'purpose-built for the creative process, somewhere to stay, let things flow, where the "inspo" comes naturally'.

Jay's penchant for perfectionism has brought regular upgrades to the recording equipment. What started as a small collection of vintage synthesizers and modern keyboards has grown to include an iconic (and Acid House favourite) Roland 808 drum machine, an Octave Cat synth and a Moog modular system. Jay, who has been DJing in such Ibizan clubs as Space and DC10 since 2011, has also recorded a couple of solo albums. His encyclopedic industry knowledge and appreciation of quality rhythms and beats helped to realize a vision that blends lifestyle with a professional sensibility for service.

'It's a complicated endeavour because recording studios are quickly becoming the dinosaurs of the music business, especially as budgets are tightened and because so many artists and labels work remotely', says Jay. 'This remains a passion project, though. Instead of just extracting what they want from the island when they come to Ibiza, it's important that people also leave something behind – especially those who come here to create.' ***LA***

Cumhur Jay converted his finca's old olive mill into a state-of-the-art recording studio. Conveniently, the 3-foot-thick walls provide in-built sound insulation.

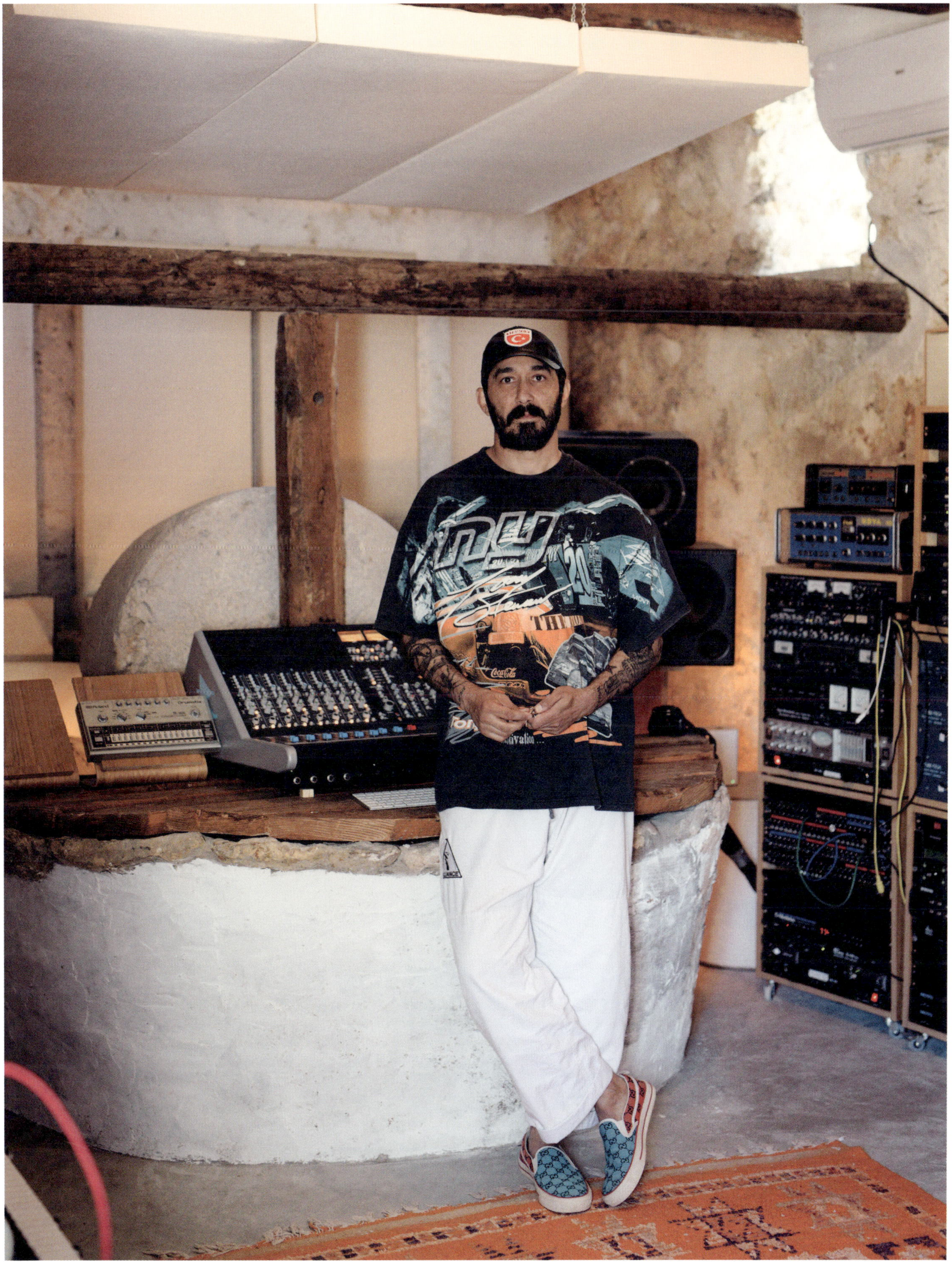

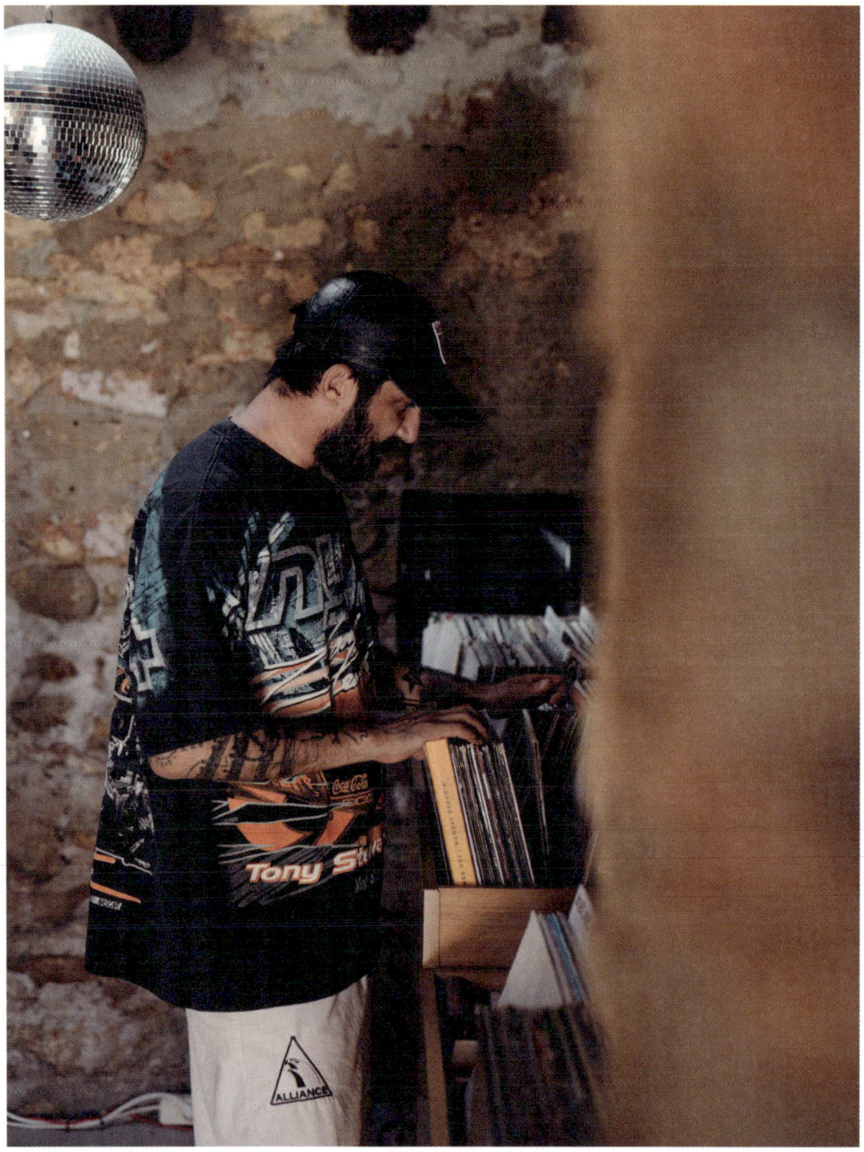

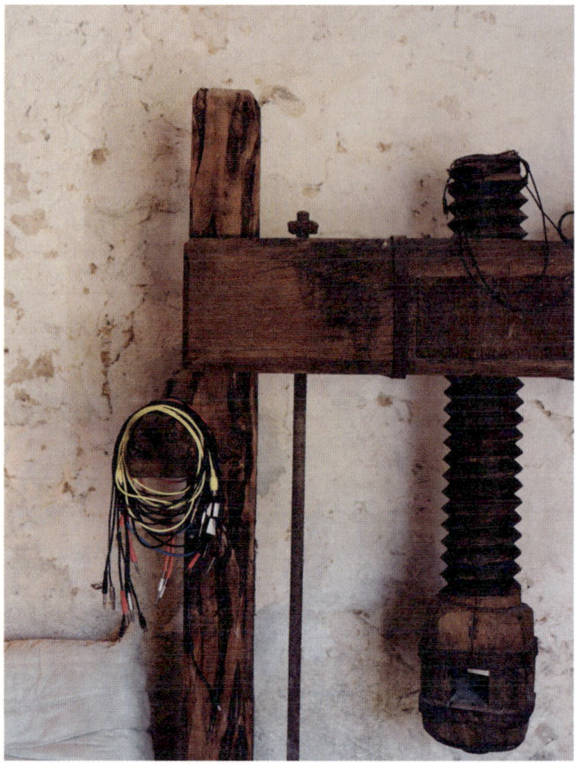

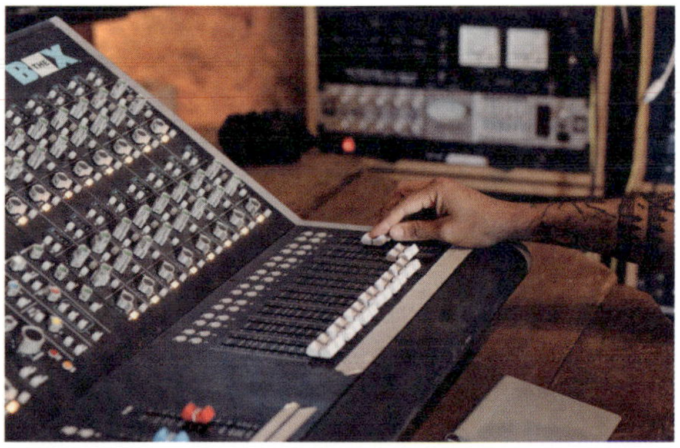

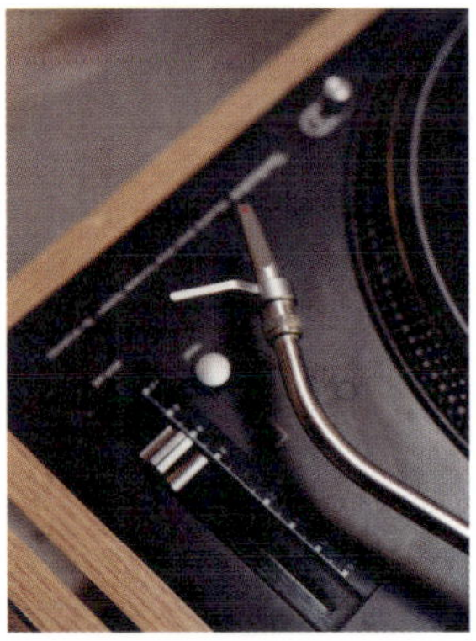

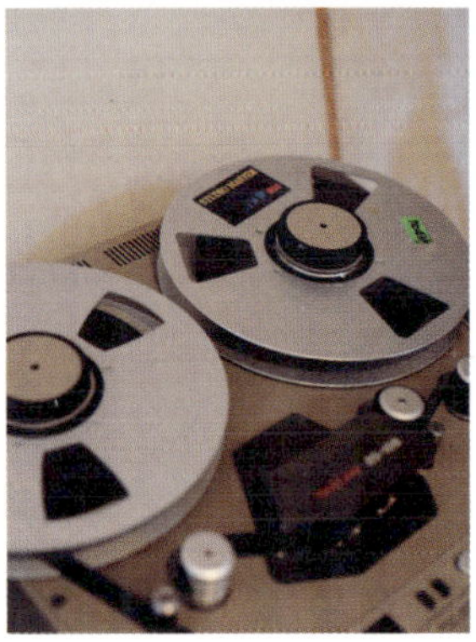

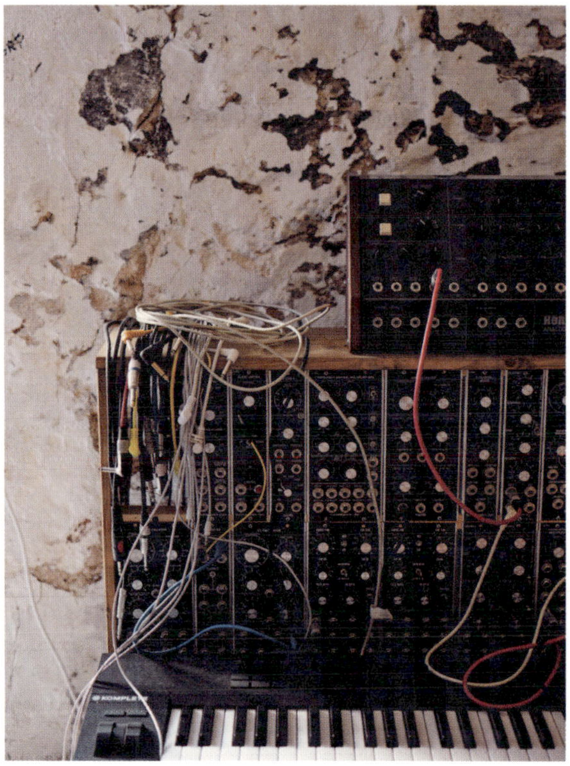

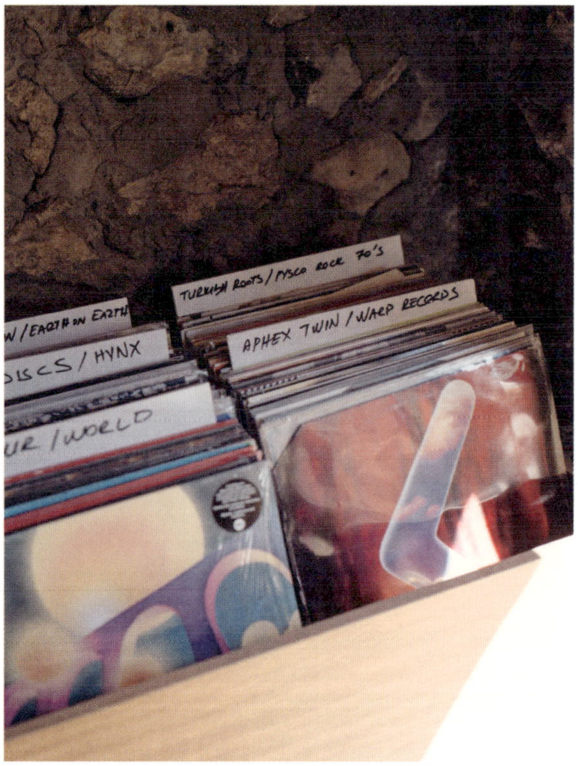
TURKISH ROOTS / PYSCO ROCK 70's
APHEX TWIN / WARP RECORDS

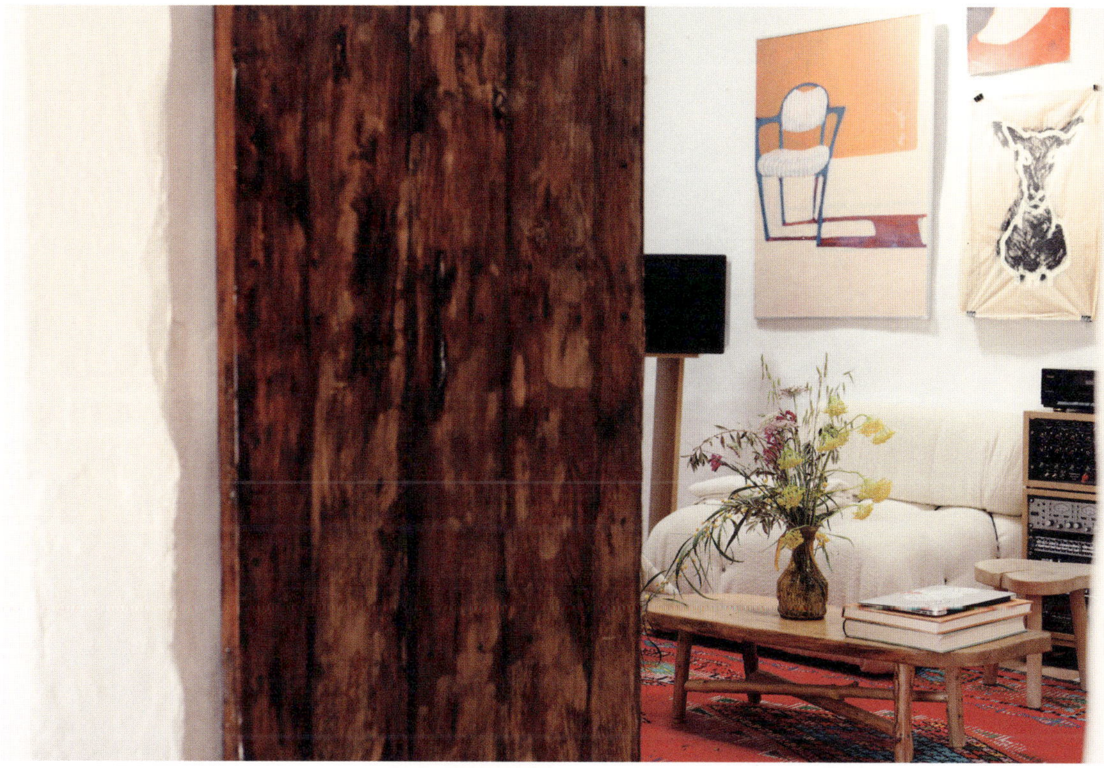

Can Jay is more than a recording studio. Jay and his business partner, Leila Arató, transformed the house into a creative hub designed to 'help music come to life'. Works by artists such as Pepo Moreno colour the walls (below, left), rooms are warmed by vintage furniture, and the former stable has been turned into a vinyl library.

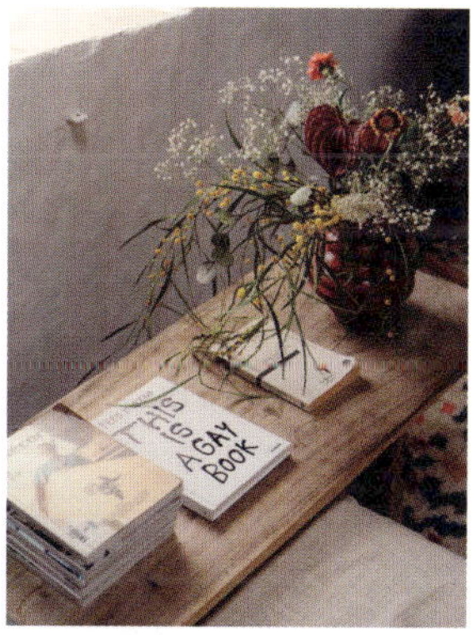

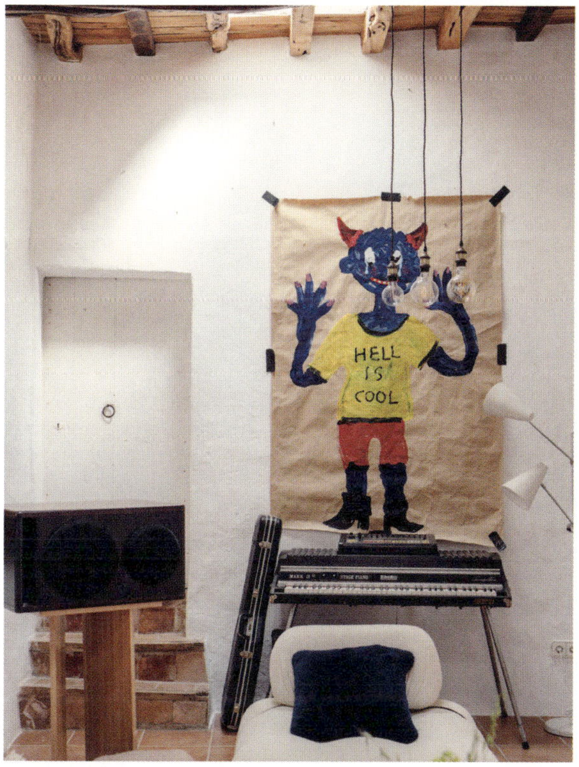

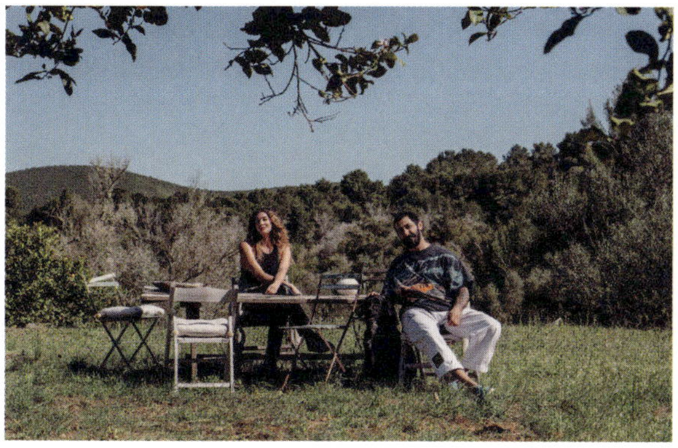

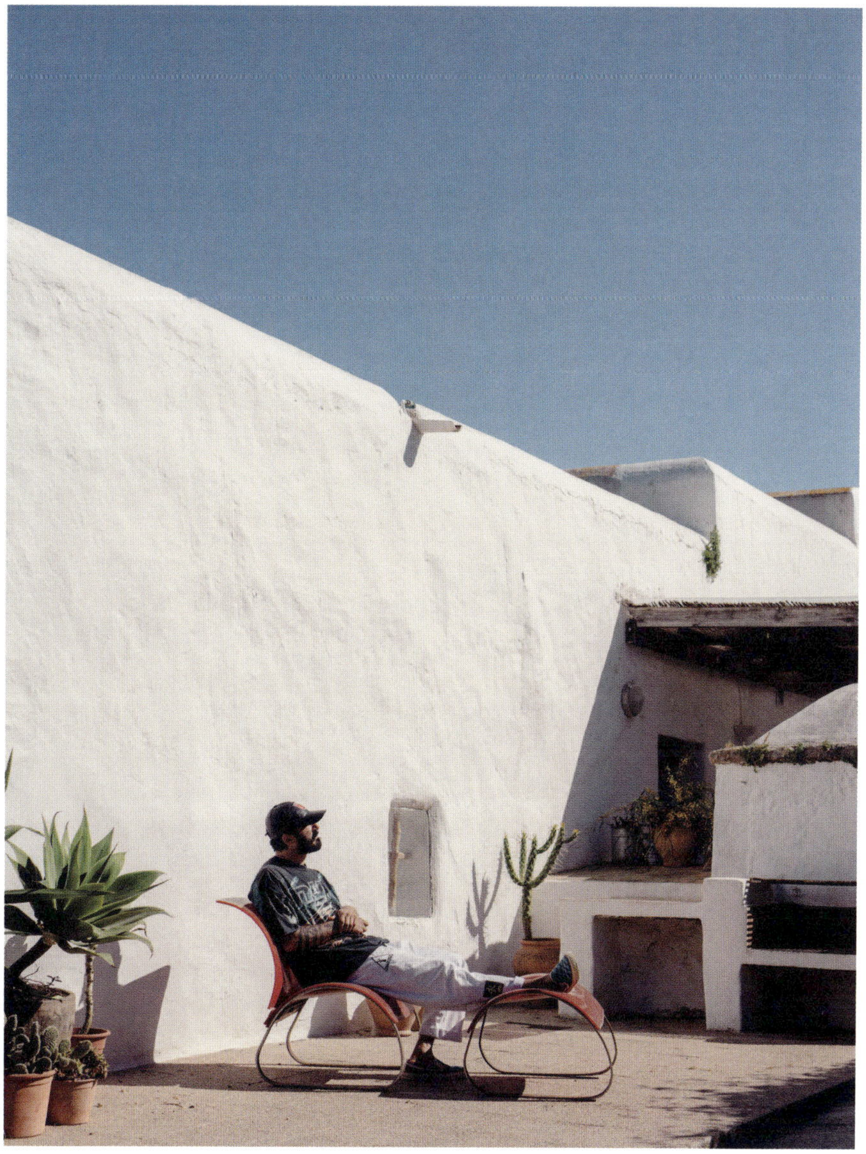

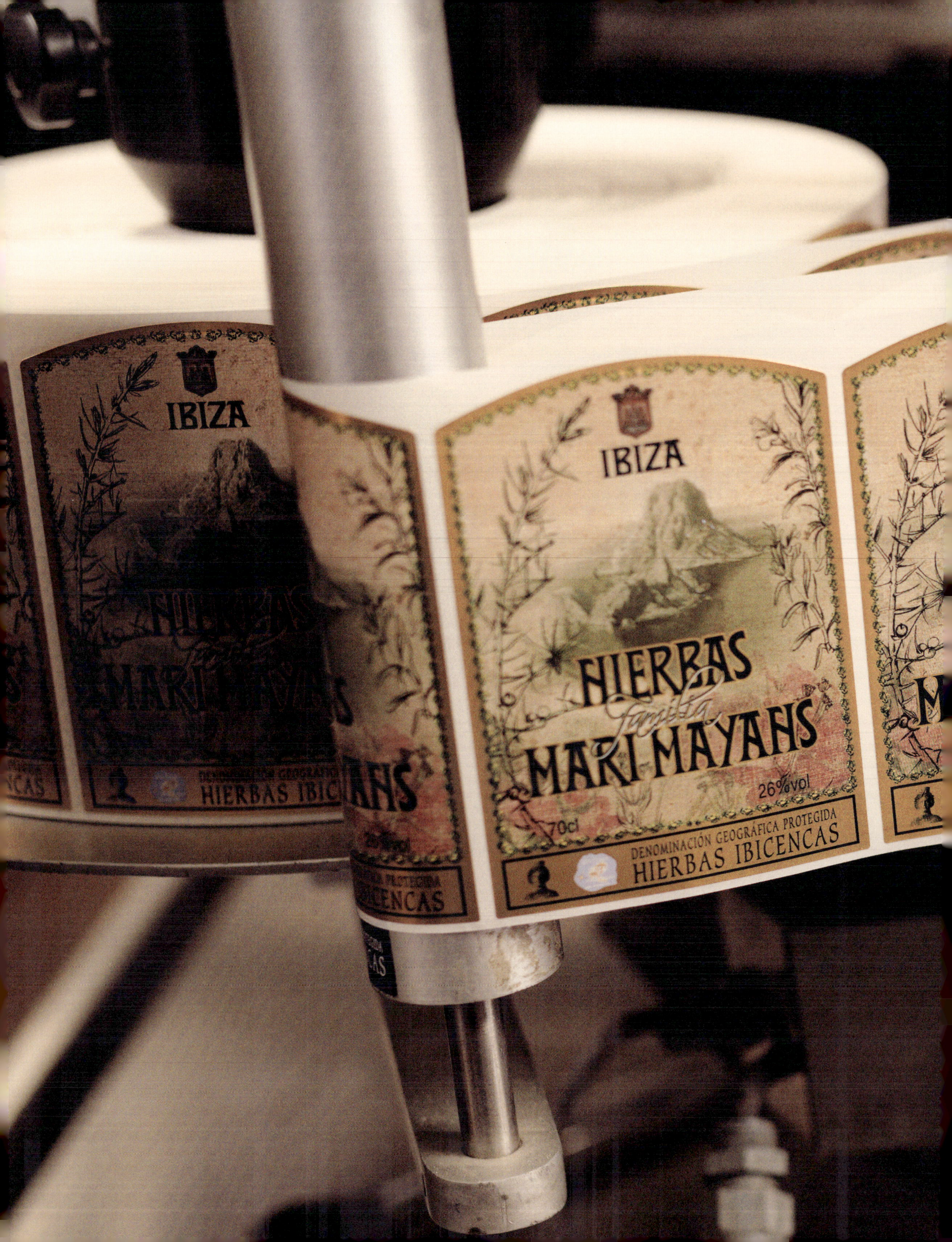
IBIZA
HIERBAS
familia
MARI MAYANS
26%vol
70cl
DENOMINACIÓN GEOGRÁFICA PROTEGIDA
HIERBAS IBICENCAS

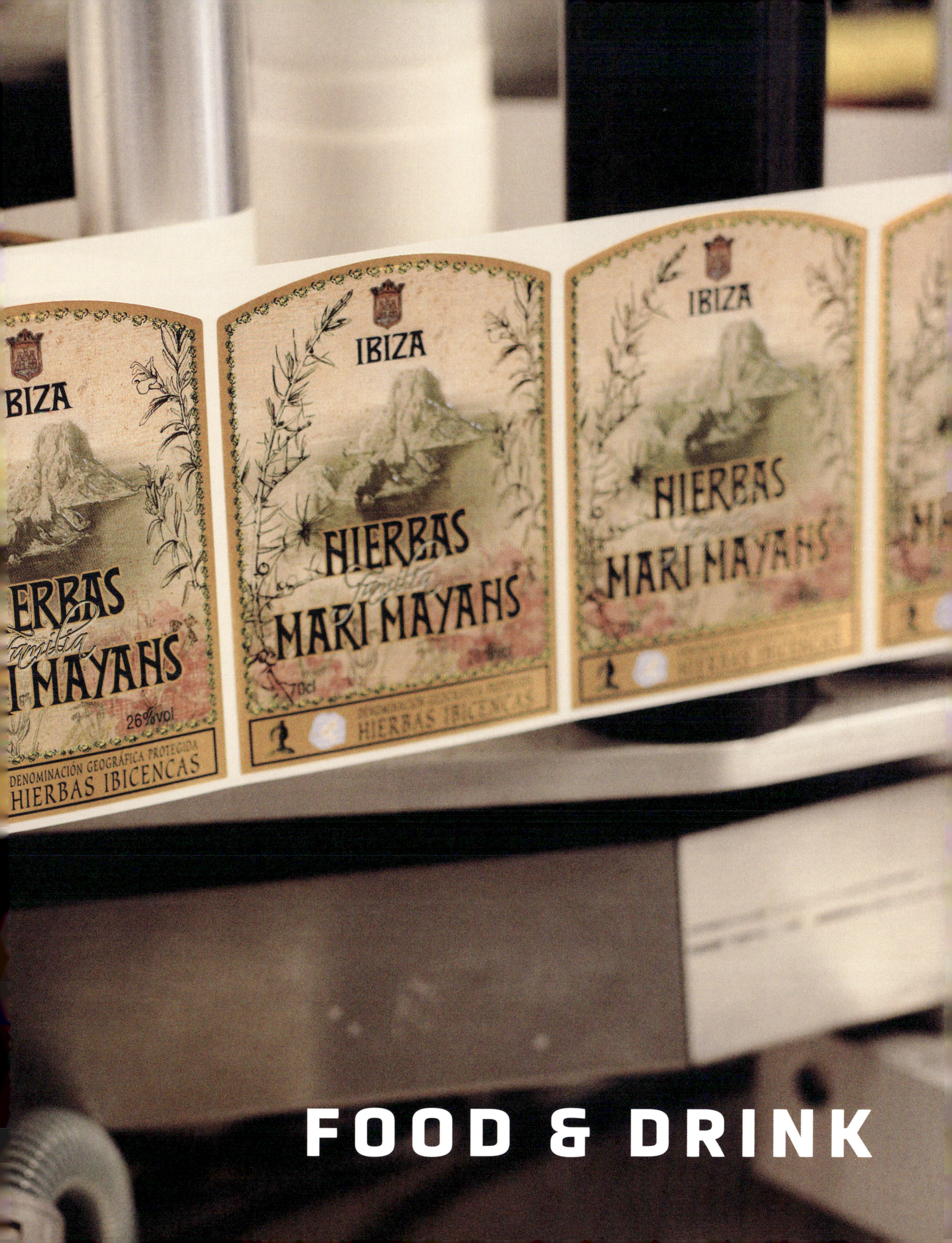
IBIZA
HIERBAS
Familia
MARI MAYANS
26% vol
70cl
DENOMINACIÓN GEOGRÁFICA PROTEGIDA
HIERBAS IBICENCAS

FOOD & DRINK

MARÍ MAYANS

IBIZAN LIQUEURS

Juan Marí Mayans was a kind of druid, according to his great-great-grandson Carlos Marí Mayans. 'He was always working with herbs and plants, and people consulted him on herbal cures for their ailments', Carlos says.

Juan was also an entrepreneur, taking his *llaüt* (small fishing boat) from his home in Formentera to Barcelona to buy such goods as sewing thread and tinned food and selling them back home. He then found work in a Barcelona distillery and learnt about the process of making spirits. Back in Formentera, he set up his own distillery in 1880.

The first liqueur Juan made was Frígola, whose main ingredients grew on his land: thyme (*farigola* in Catalan) and oranges. But the market in Formentera was not sufficiently big, so Juan moved production – and his family – to Ibiza. There he started making more liqueurs, including *hierbas ibicencas* (Ibiza's best-known liqueur). Juan's version, Hierbas Ibicencas Familia Marí Mayans, in its distinctive bottle shaped to suggest the silhouette of a traditional woman peasant farmer, accounts for 92 per cent of all *hierbas ibicencas* sold on the island. The company also makes *palo* (a type of vermouth), absinthe and three different gins.

The factory is located in a large industrial area, Polígono Industrial Montecristo, between Ibiza Town and San Antonio. It uses traditional techniques to produce about 500,000 litres in total a year, 70 per cent of which is sold in Ibiza and Formentera. The rest goes to mainland Spain and beyond, including Japan.

The family-owned company is now in the hands of directors Carlos and his brother, Bartolomé, who both left Ibiza to study business, administration and management in Mallorca. In 2009 they quit their jobs there – Carlos at the private bank GE Finance (General Electrics) and Bartolomé at the construction company Dragados – to return to Ibiza and take over Familia Marí Mayans. Today they have twenty-five staff employed across production, administration, warehousing and distribution.

Hierbas Ibicencas Familia Marí Mayans contains eighteen different herbs and flavours, including lemon verbena, orange, lemon, aniseed, rosemary and thyme. 'We use only natural ingredients for all our drinks', Carlos explains. 'All the herbs are grown here and in Formentera.' The plants are gathered by hand by local farmers, who bring them to the factory, where they are selected, weighed and added to the alcohol. The recipe remains the same as the original and is a family secret.

Their particular topography means that Ibiza and Formentera have a wide variety of microclimates. This enables their fields to have certain levels of minerals in the soil and humidity in the air, which become infused in the aromatic plants, giving them their specific flavours.

However, the supply of herbs is drying up. 'Some farmers are no longer growing them', Carlos says. So the company – which has never owned a building in its long history – has bought a 4-hectare (10-acre) farm close to San Miguel, where it grows its own herbs. The brothers intend to move production there and to build an exhibition space and tasting facility. ***CD***

Brothers Carlos (opposite) and Bartolomé Marí Mayans run the drinks company founded by their great-great-grandfather Juan in 1880 in neighbouring Formentera, after he had learnt the trade in a distillery in Barcelona.

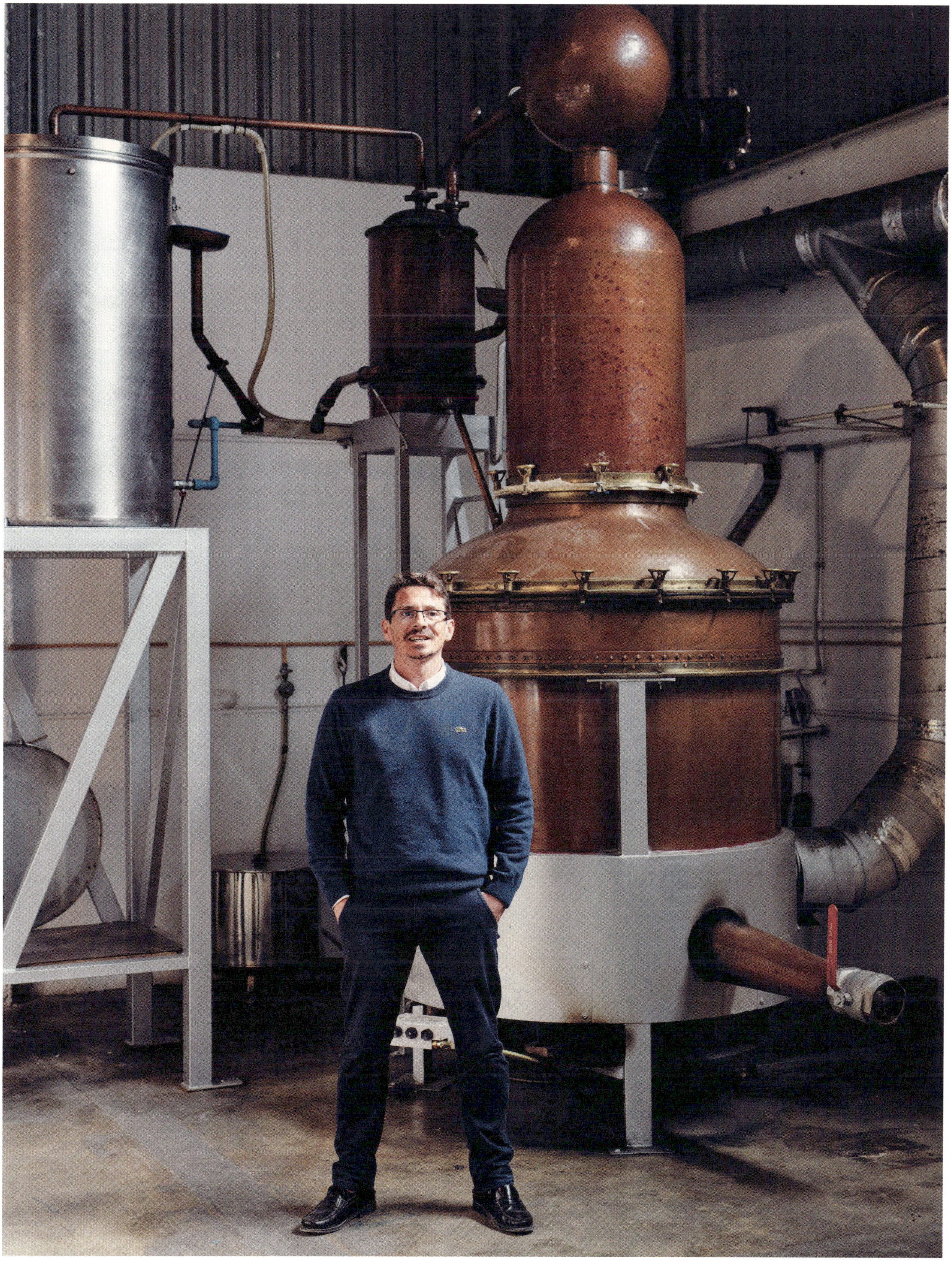

The family's liqueurs, including Hierbas Marí Mayans – their version of the island's famous hierbas ibicencas *– are flavoured with aromatic herbs and fruits, which are picked and prepared by hand.*

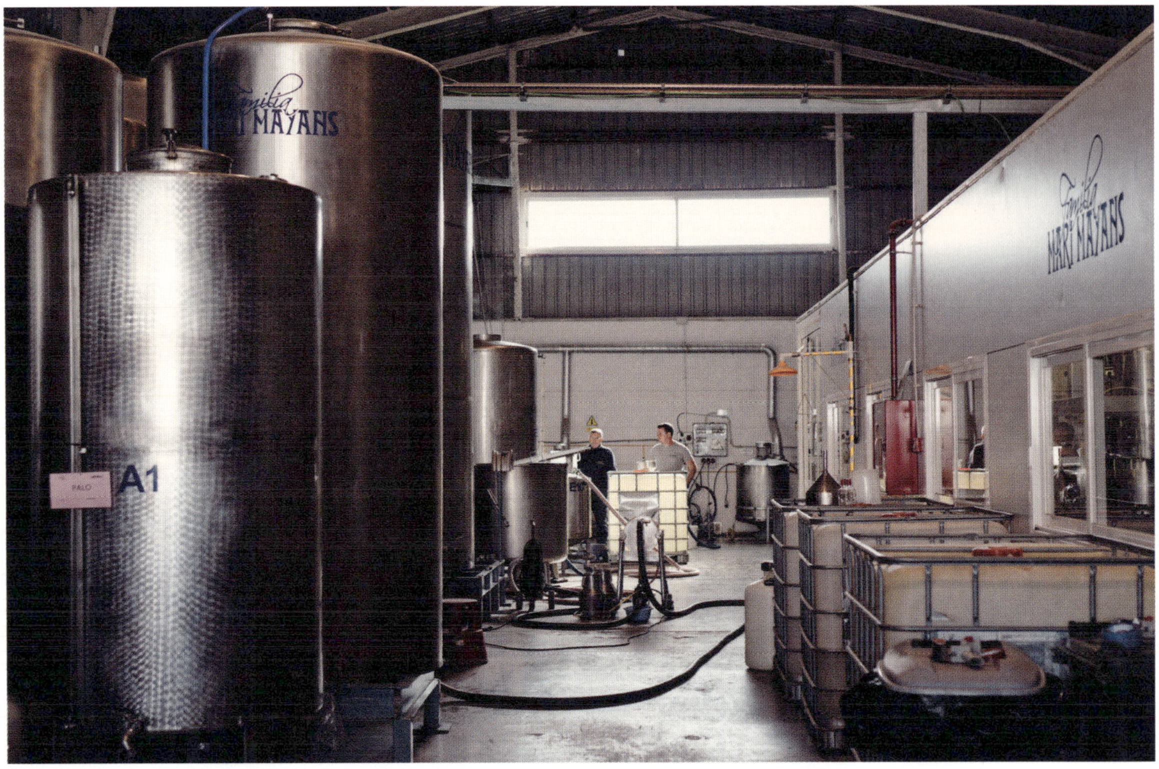

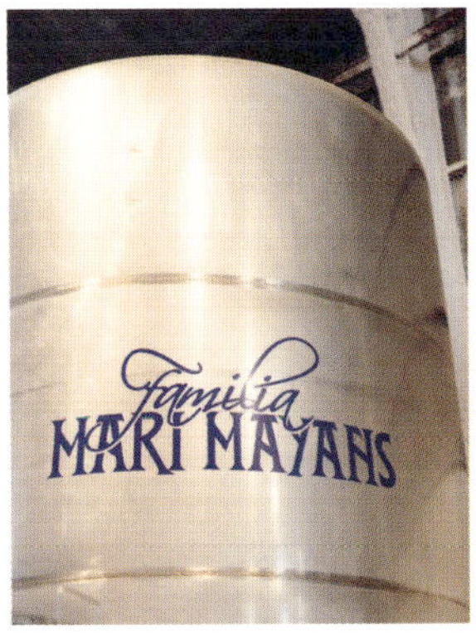

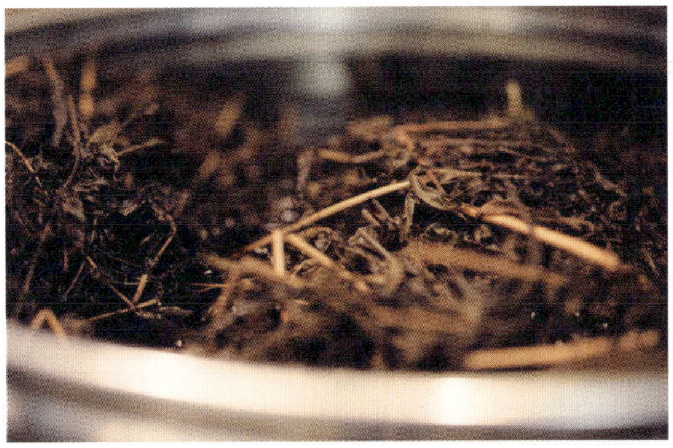

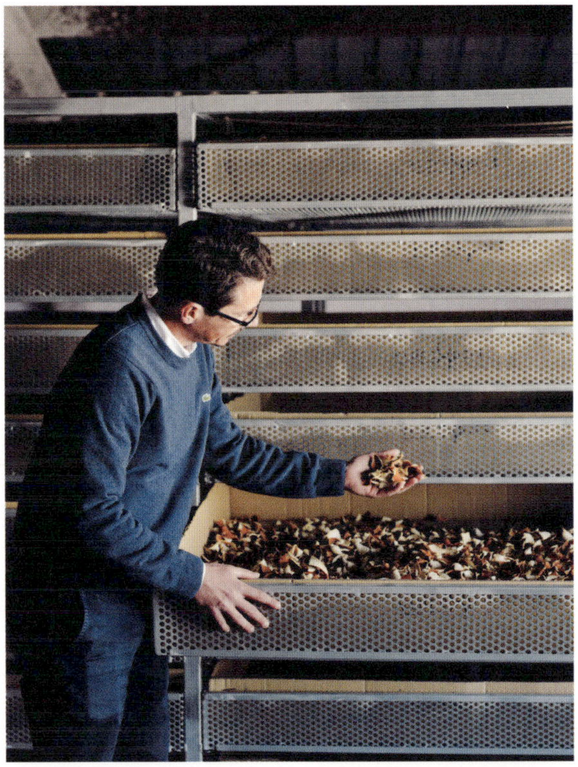

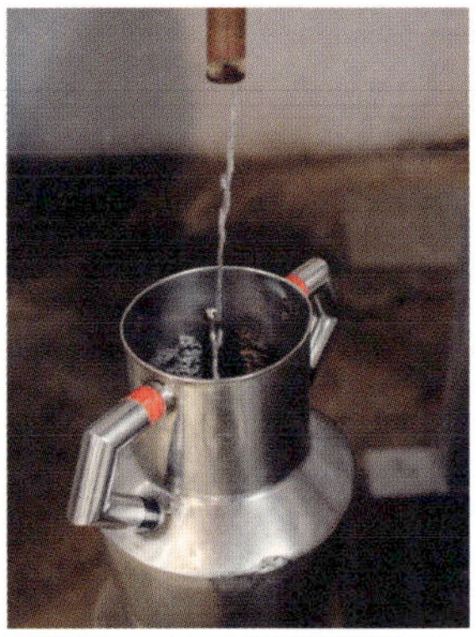

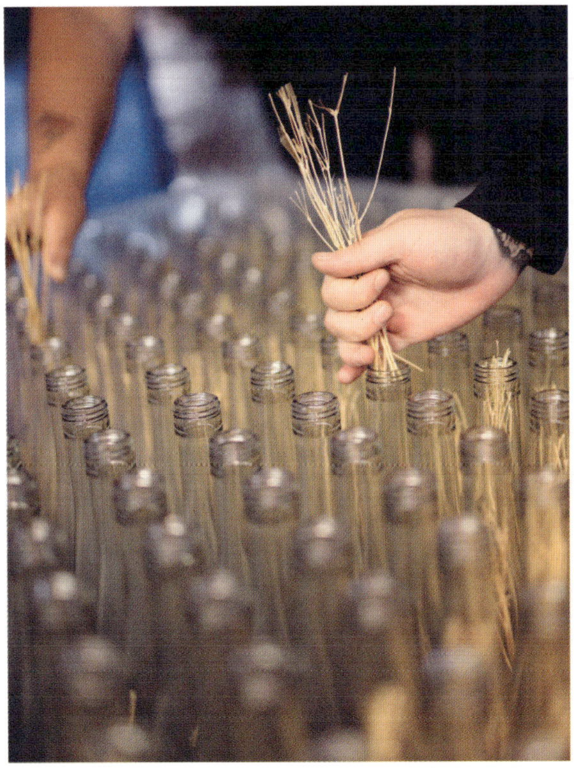

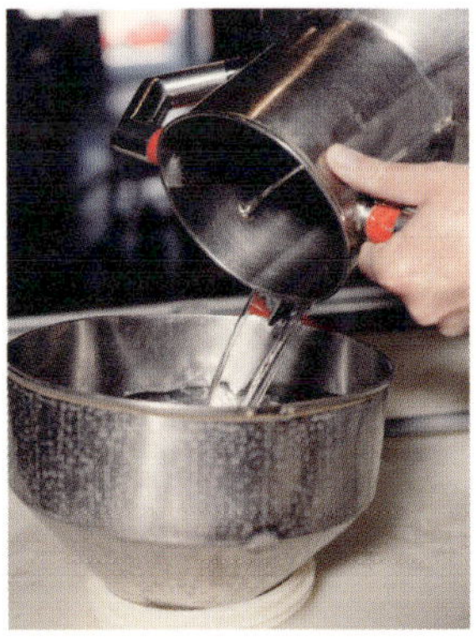

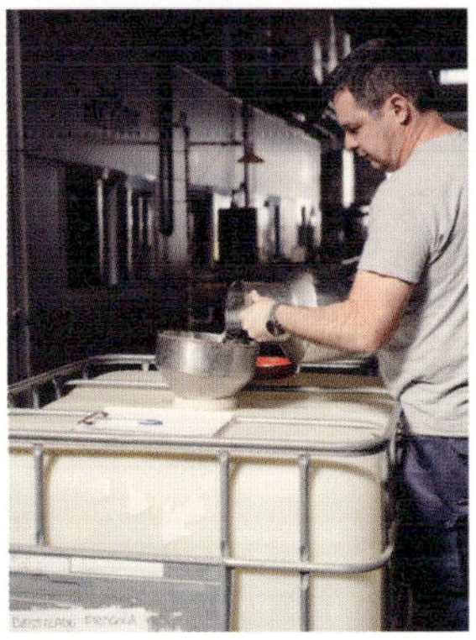

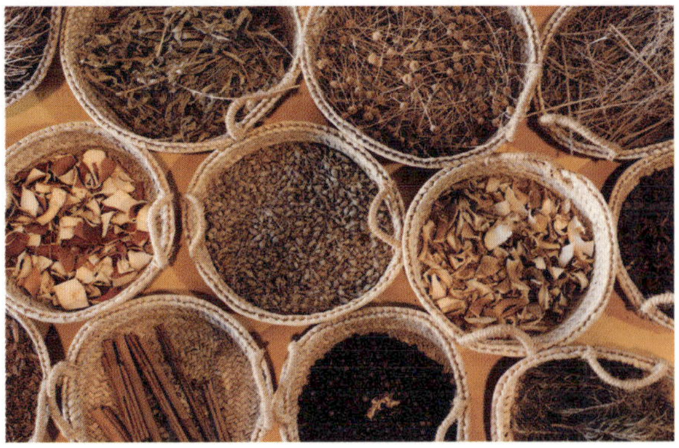

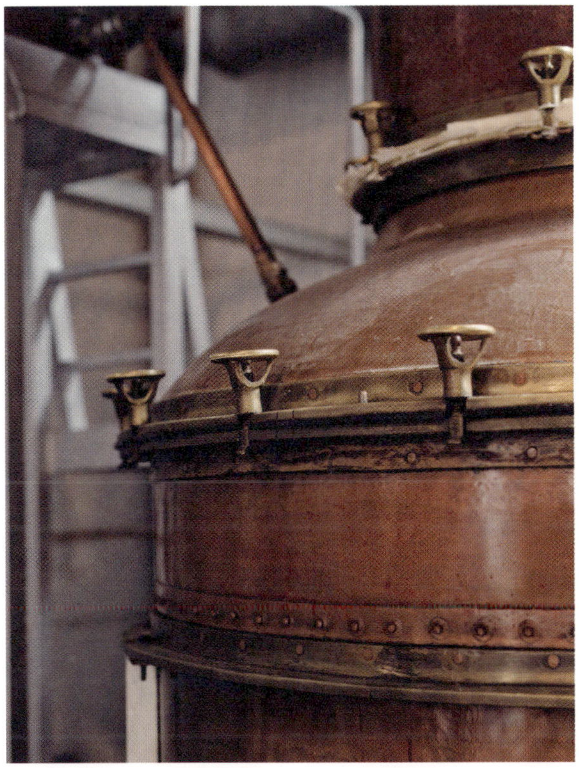

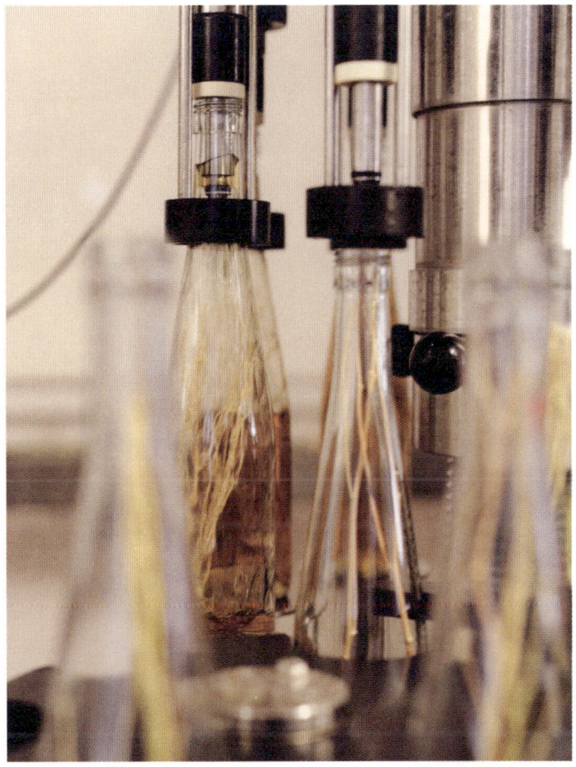

The factory in Polígono Industrial Montecristo bottles around 500,000 litres a year. The recipe for Hierbas Ibicencas Familia Marí Mayans features eighteen different natural ingredients, including lemon verbena, aniseed and thyme. The bottling of the con rama version of the liqueur is shown here.

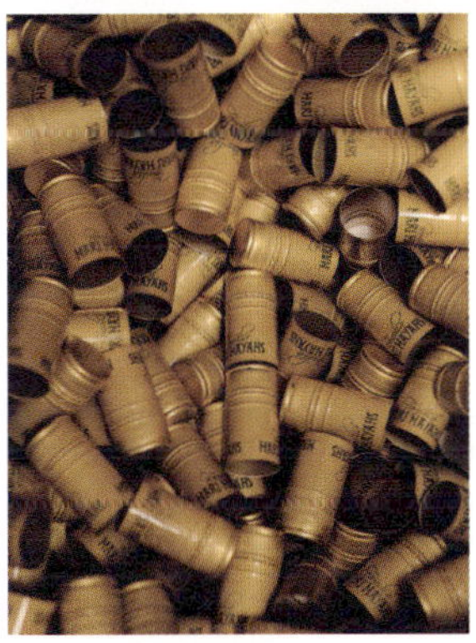

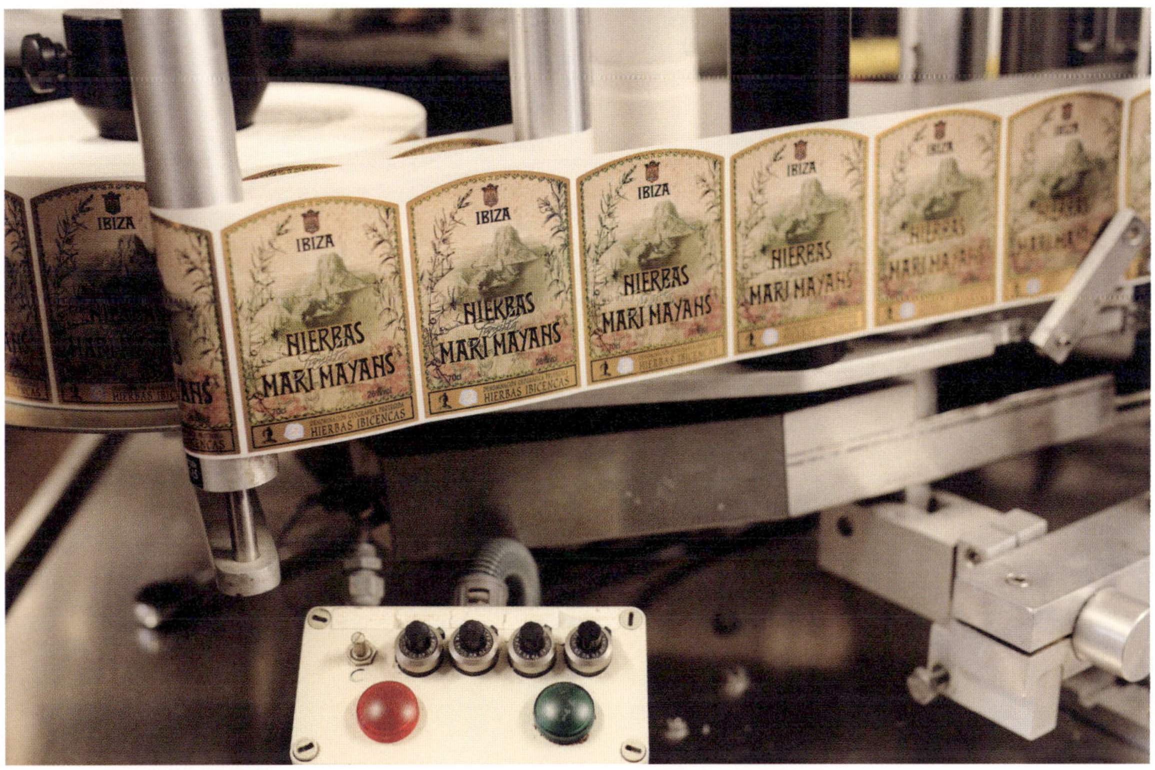

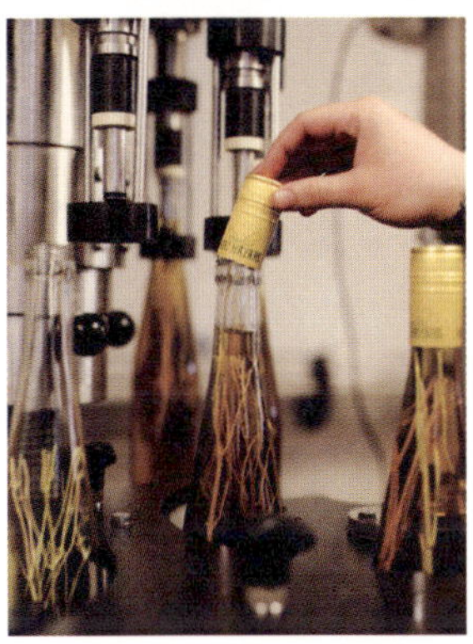

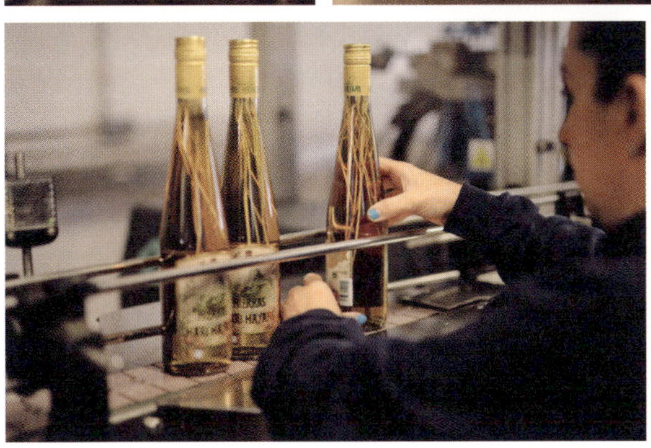

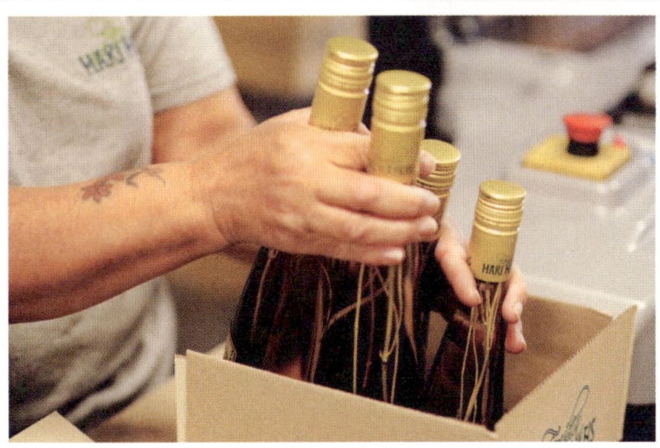

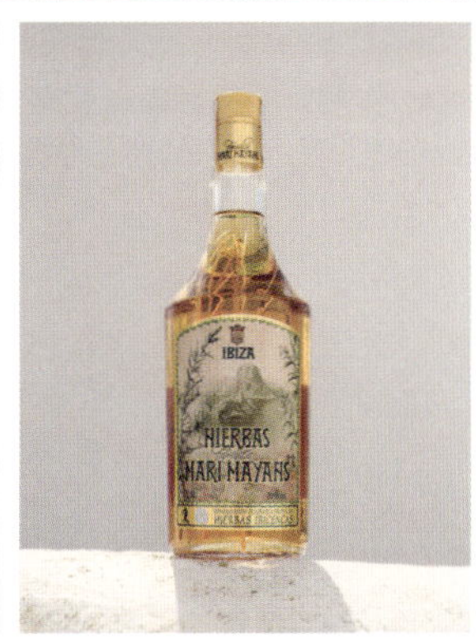

SAN MATEO
juntoshouse.com | juntosfarm.com

JUNTOS IBIZA

RESTAURANT, BOUTIQUE & REGENERATIVE FARM

Sophie Daunais (Canadian) and Christian af Jochnick (Swedish) gave up their London life and relocated to Ibiza, their favourite holiday destination, in 2018. At that time, they had two small children, and Sophie did not want to return to her job in education. 'We liked the idea of raising our children close to nature', she recalls. 'But I was a bit worried that we wouldn't be able to find anything interesting to do here, workwise.'

The couple decided to combine Christian's interest in regenerative farming with Sophie's love of interior design and hospitality. Regenerative agriculture means going organic but also farming in a way that gives back to the land – an approach that attracts the right insects and that does not use too much water or deplete the soil of resources.

Sophie and Christian bought farmland and later a building containing a restaurant in the village of San Mateo, in the north of the island. They spent the first eighteen months picking rocks out of the soil so that they could start planting. Renovating the building and adding a shop took another year and a half. They opened Juntos House (*juntos* means 'together') for business in spring 2022, and Sophie now has a sixteen-strong team there.

Sophie operates a 'farm-to-table' kitchen restaurant, where the menu depends on what fresh produce has been harvested. 'This is a major challenge for a restaurant, because we must change the menu all the time', she says. 'It also involves adapting the recipes and pricing.'

For the boutique, Sophie drew inspiration from her mother: 'When I was a child, I saw my mother being creative, making beautiful table decorations, painting and cooking. She never sold any of it, but I somehow had the vision for myself, for my kids to see me crafting. Now I don't craft in the same way my mum did, but more by assembling teams of people who deliver my vision.'

The boutique stocks the farm's produce, including Juntos honey. The pair introduced bees when they first moved in, as part of their regeneration plans. But, as Sophie explains, to begin with, 'the land was so dead that the bees couldn't find enough flowers. I could see swarms of bees going to our neighbours' orange orchard. When our land improved, the bees started to stay. They got the pollen from our plants, and the taste of our honey changed. Today all our bees stay on our land, and the honey is the best we've ever had.'

The boutique also sells locally sourced homewares and other items, including kimonos from Figtree Collection (pp. 24–29). Sophie has ambitions to expand the range to include more products from the farm, such as essential oils, sauces and fermented foods. She also plans to stage art exhibitions and other events, and to run workshops at Juntos. 'Now I'm very happy here', she says. 'It's possible to live authentically. You get to be yourself and to live your truest life.' ***CD***

Sophie Daunais set up Juntos Ibiza with Christian af Jochnick. She runs the Juntos House restaurant and boutique, while Christian is responsible for Juntos Farm.

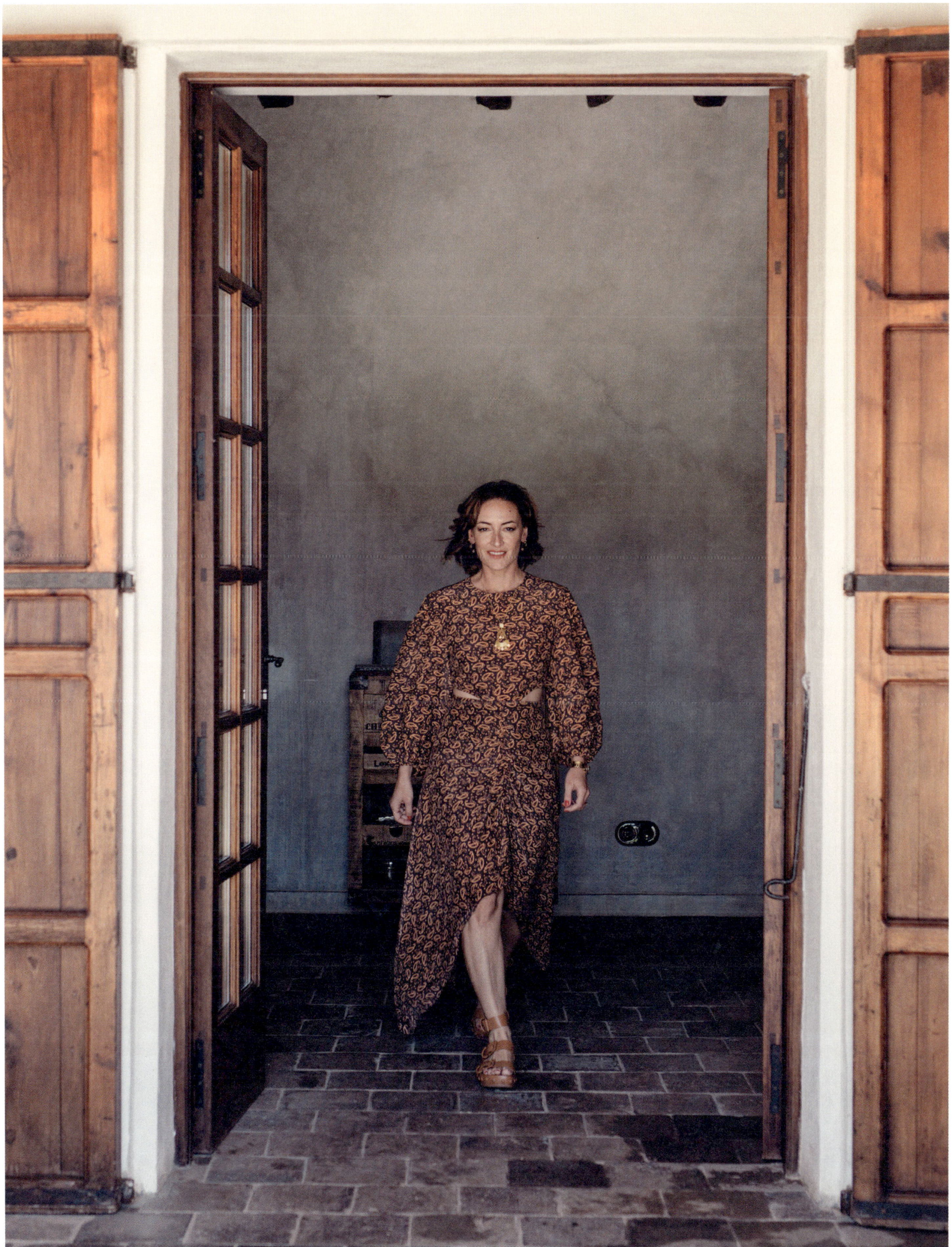

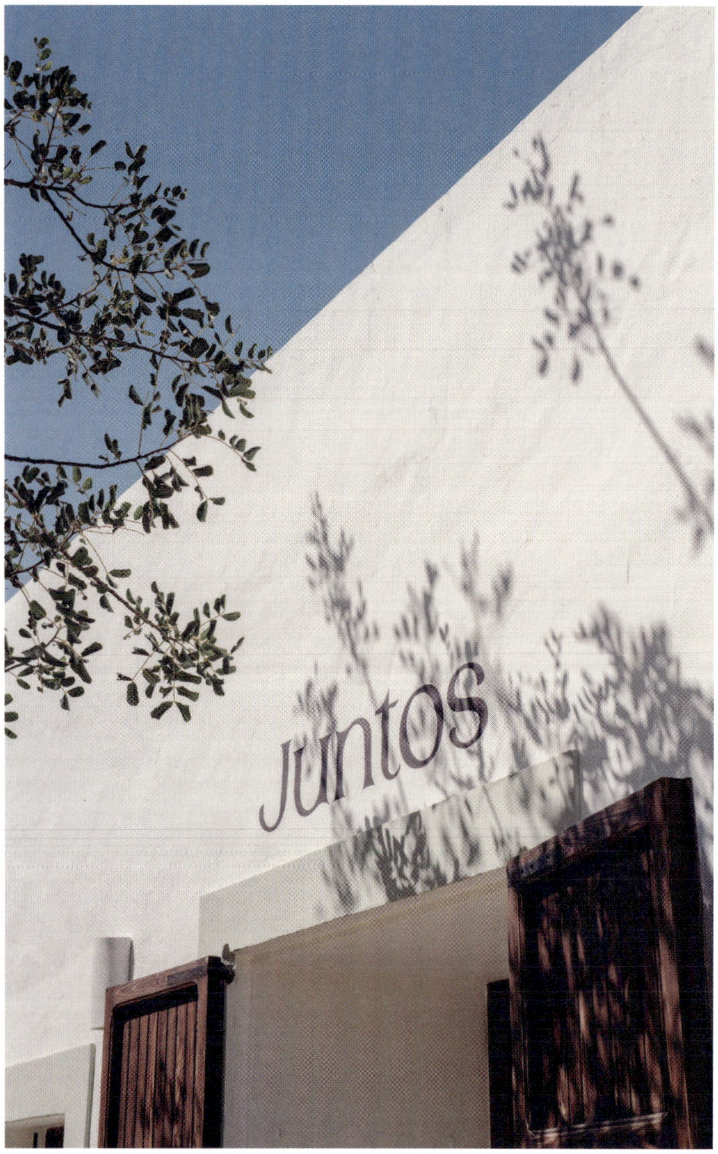

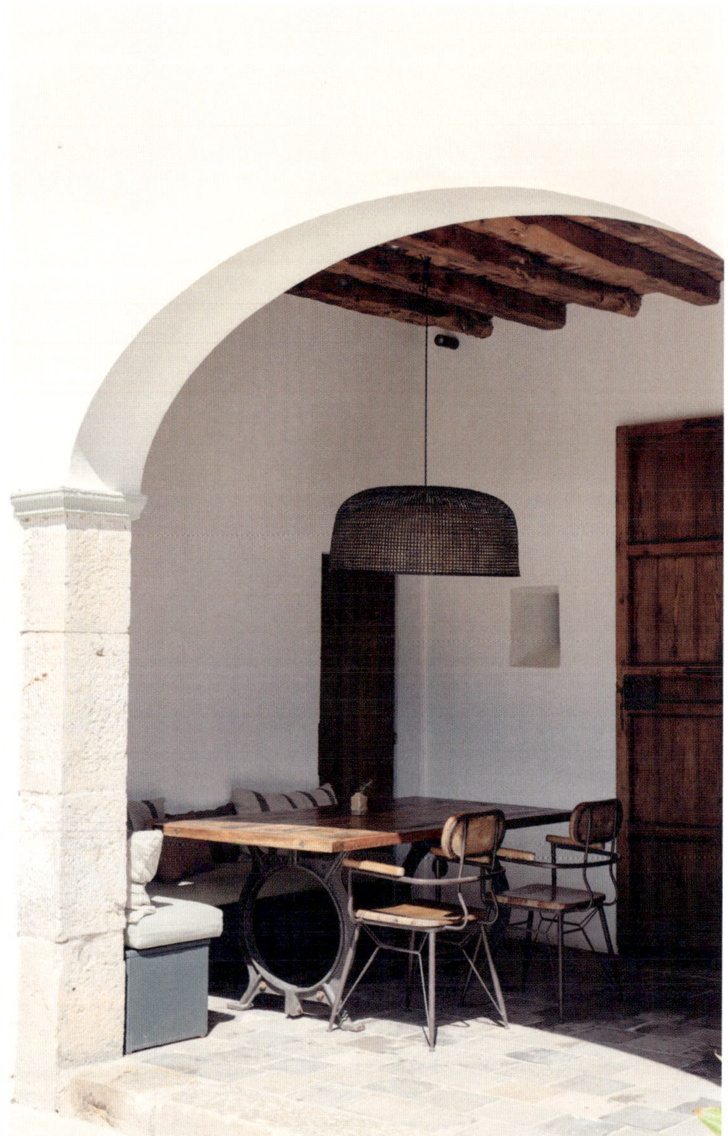

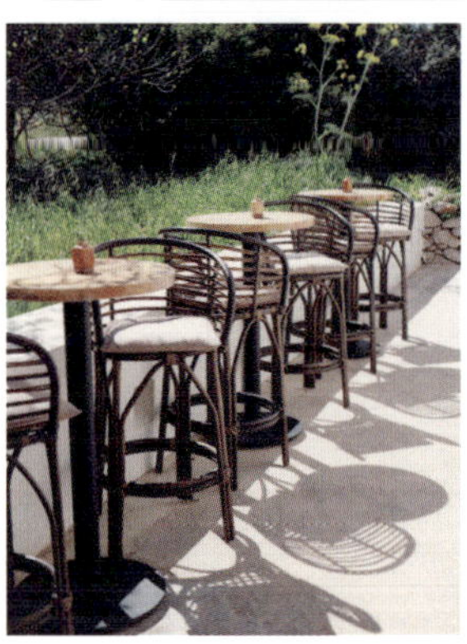

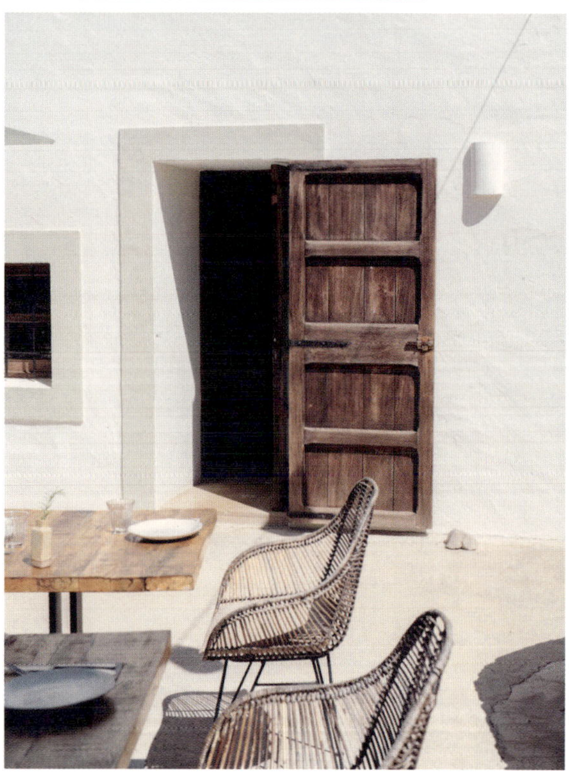

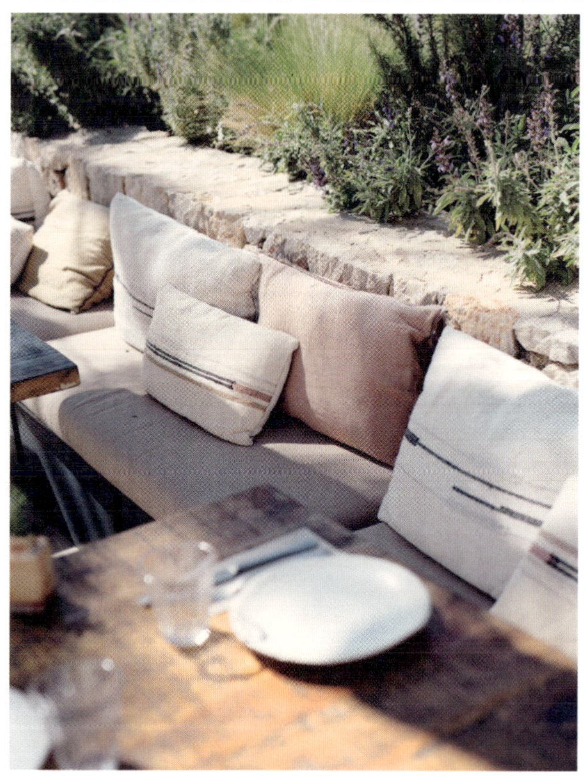

Juntos House is based in an old building in the village of San Mateo. Working with her sixteen-strong team, Sophie combines her love of interior design and hospitality.

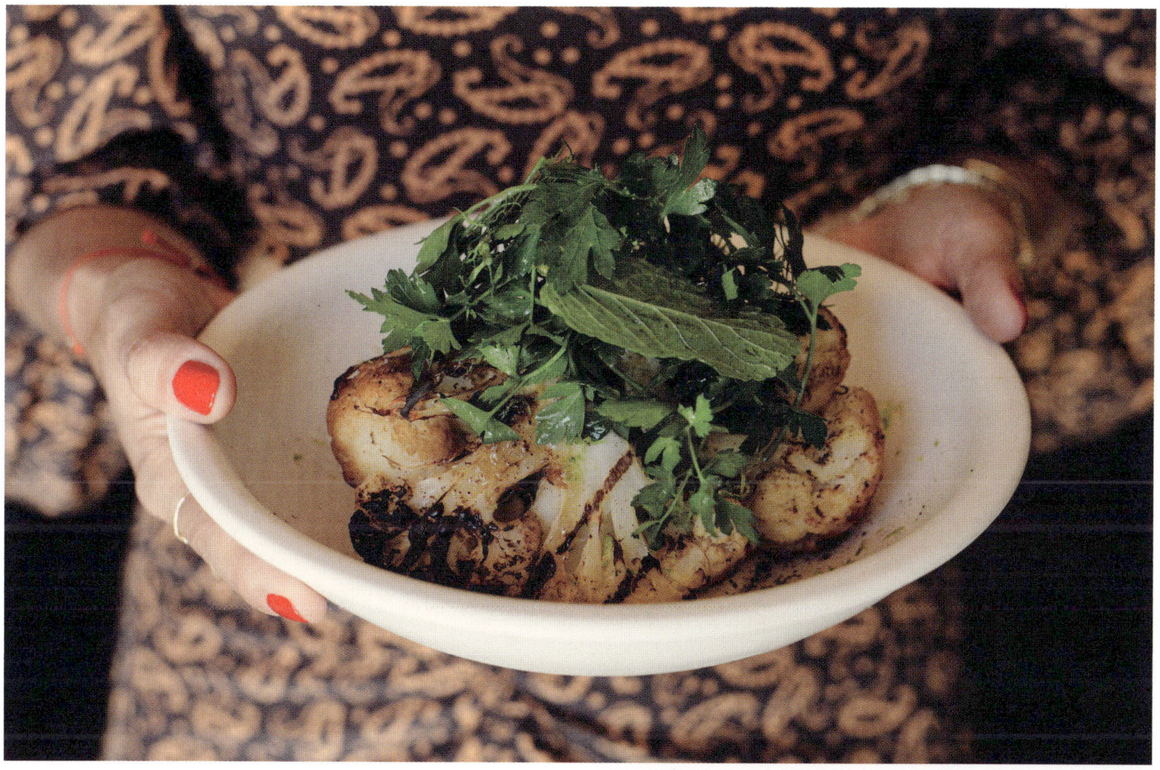

The restaurant operates a 'farm-to-table' kitchen, with Christian supplying much of the fresh produce. Local artists contributed to the interior design, including The Floral Studio (pp. 142–49), which created the flower display suspended over the bar (bottom right).

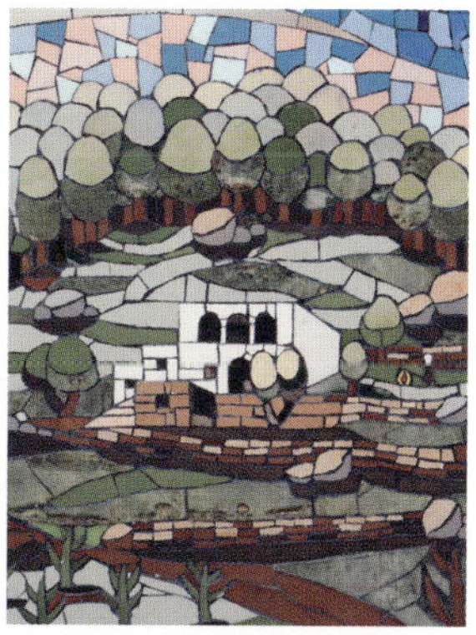

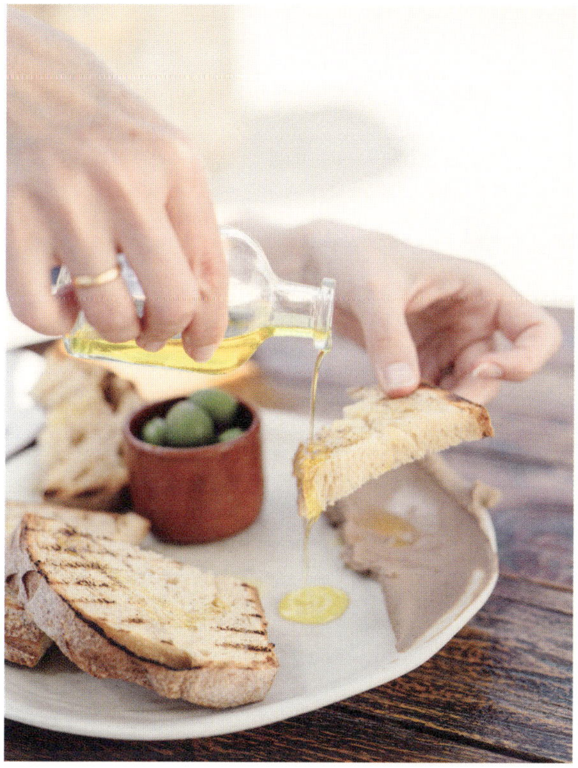

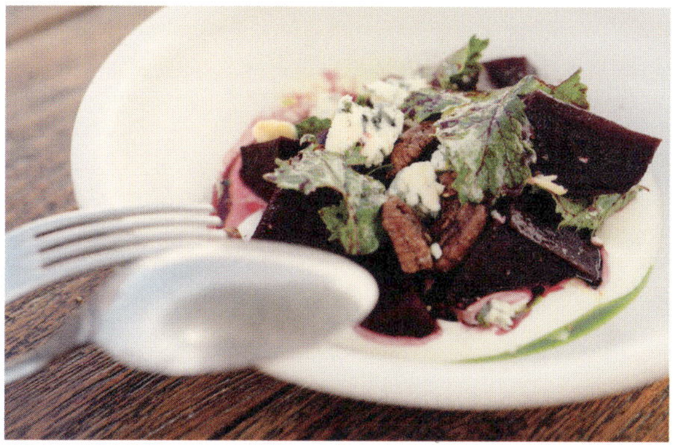

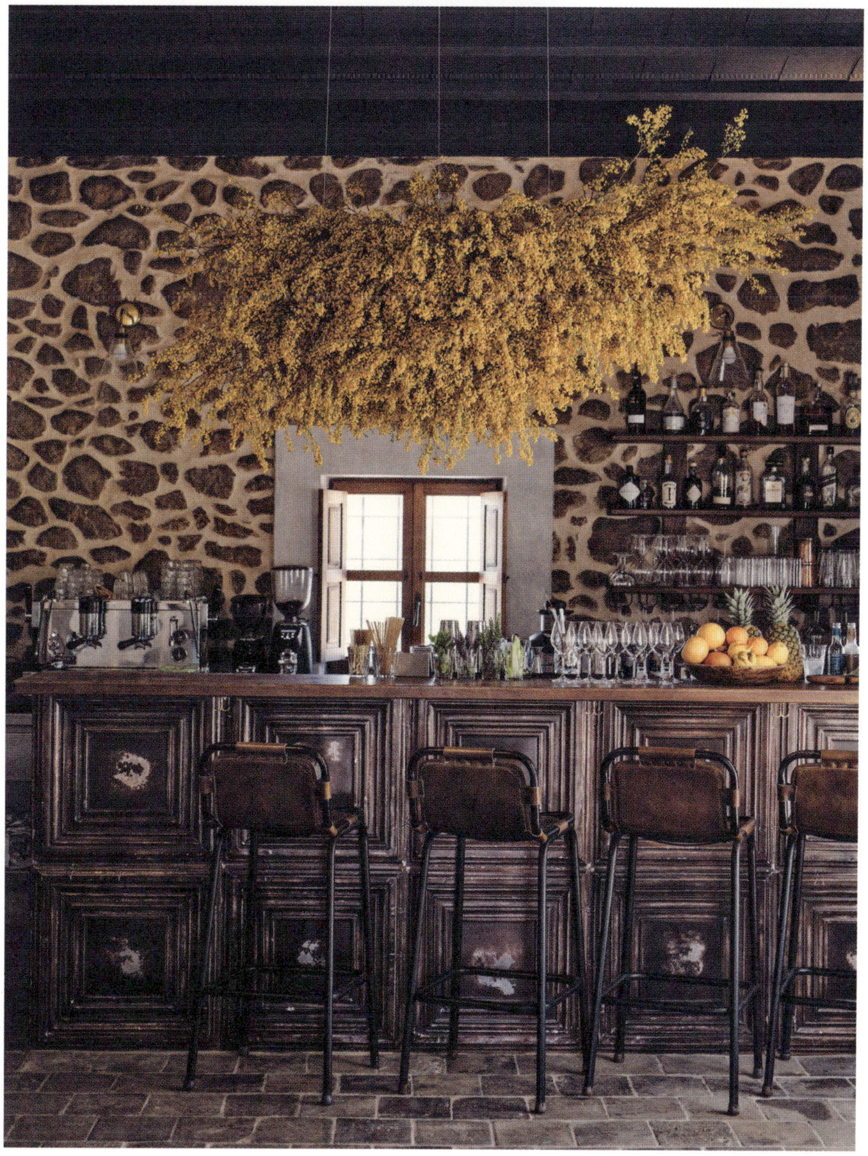

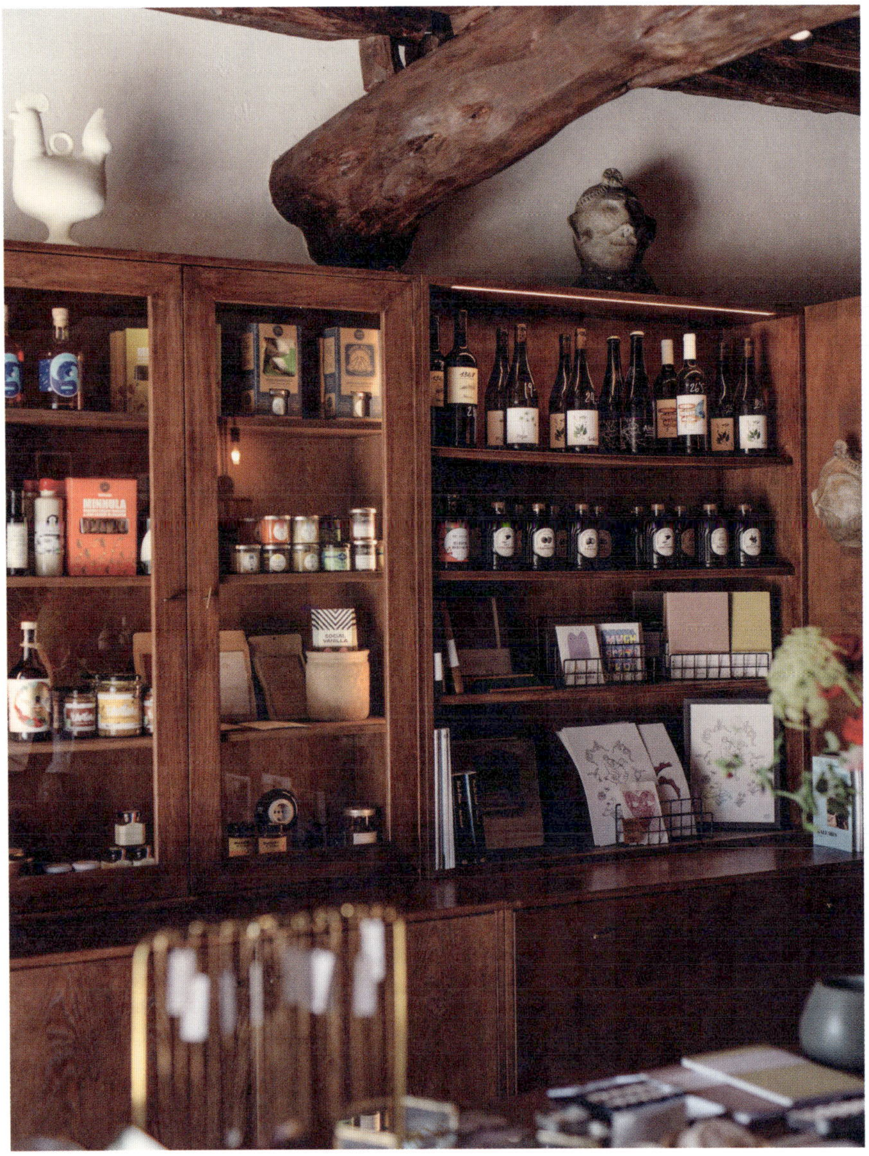

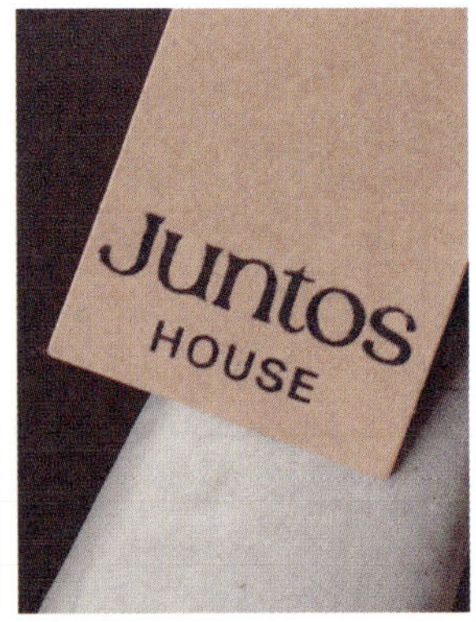

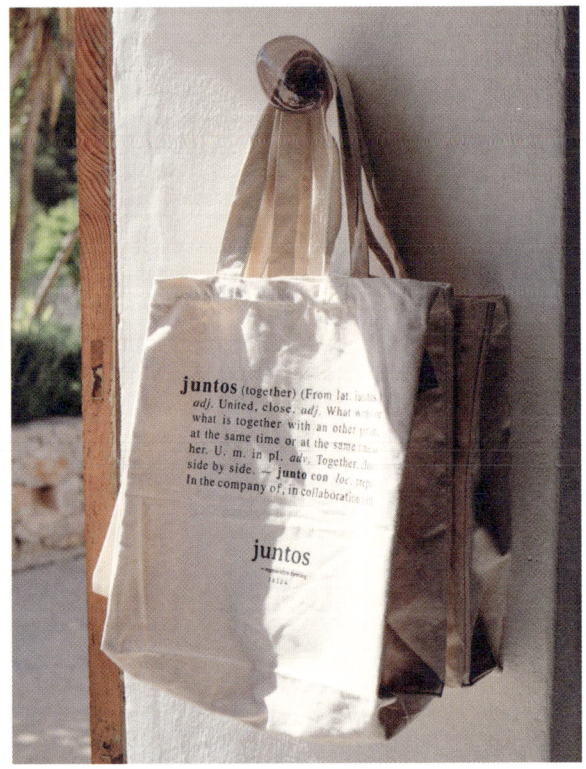

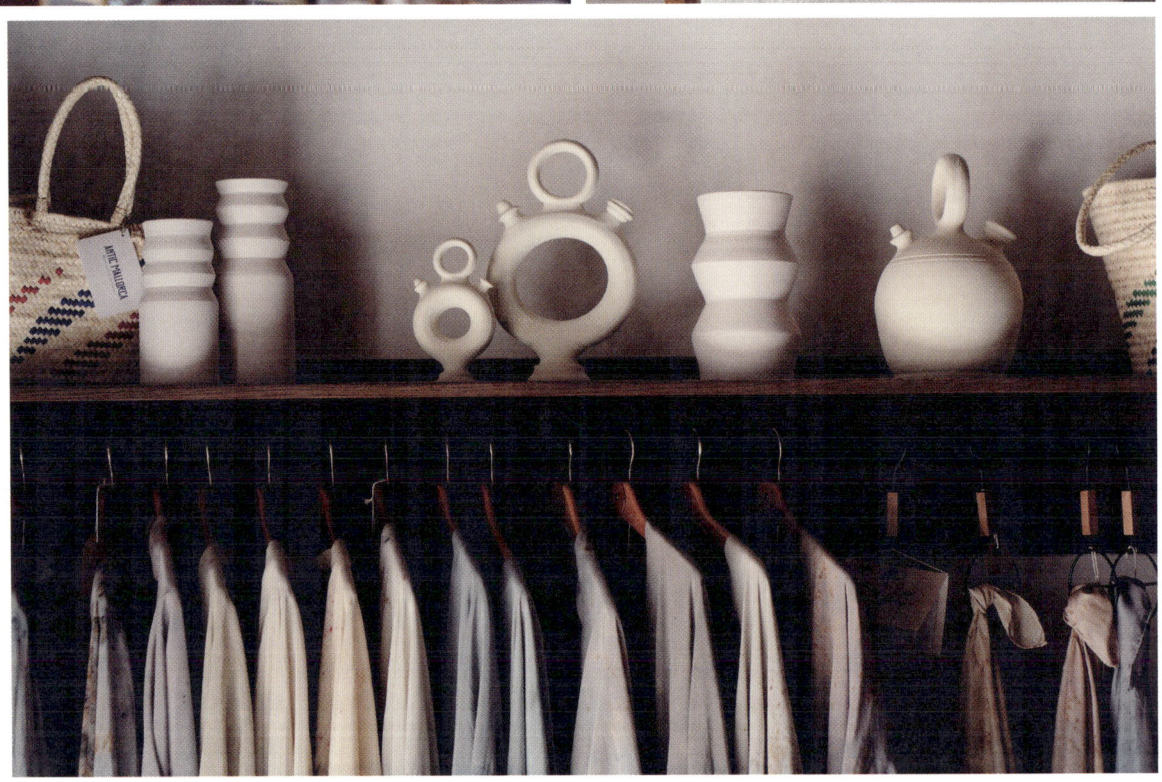

The boutique is next door to the restaurant, and stocks produce from the farm, items created by local makers and a number of European labels.

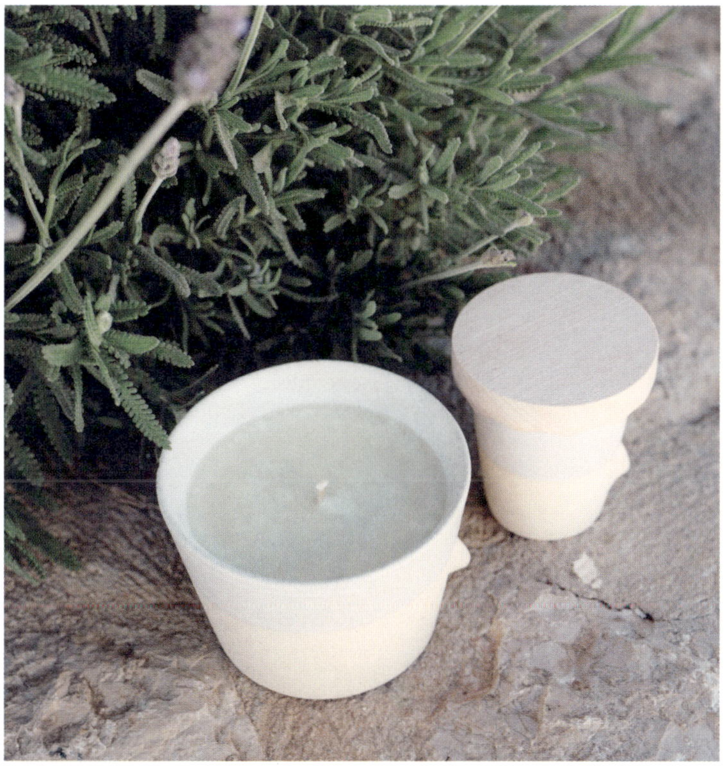

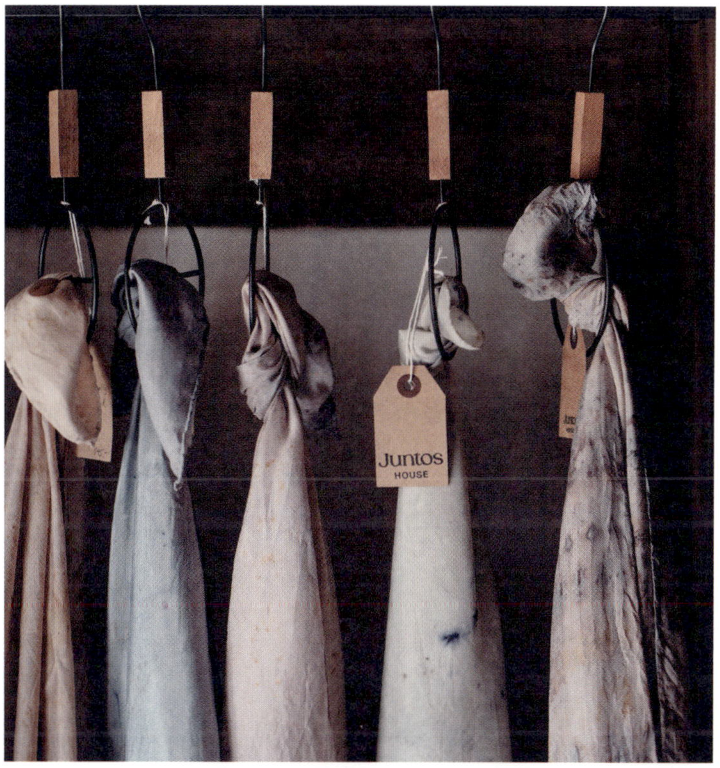

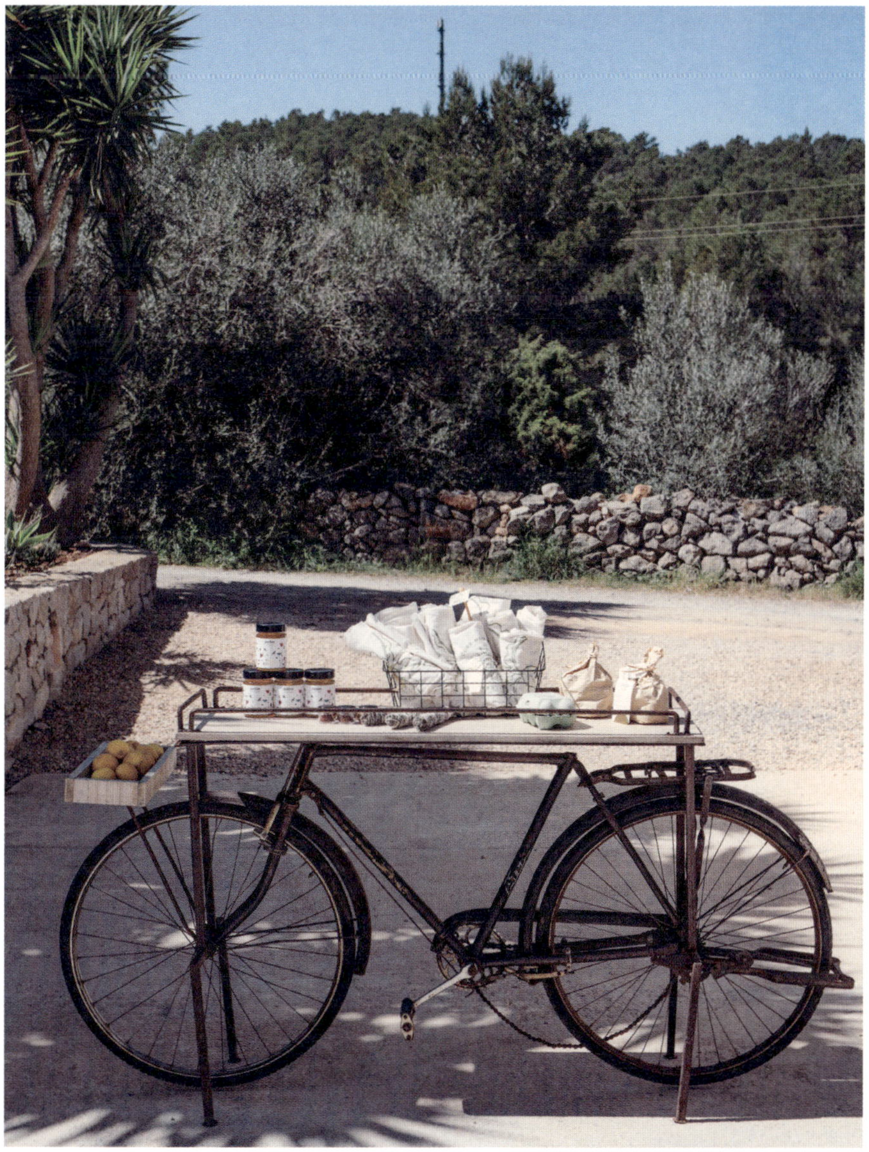

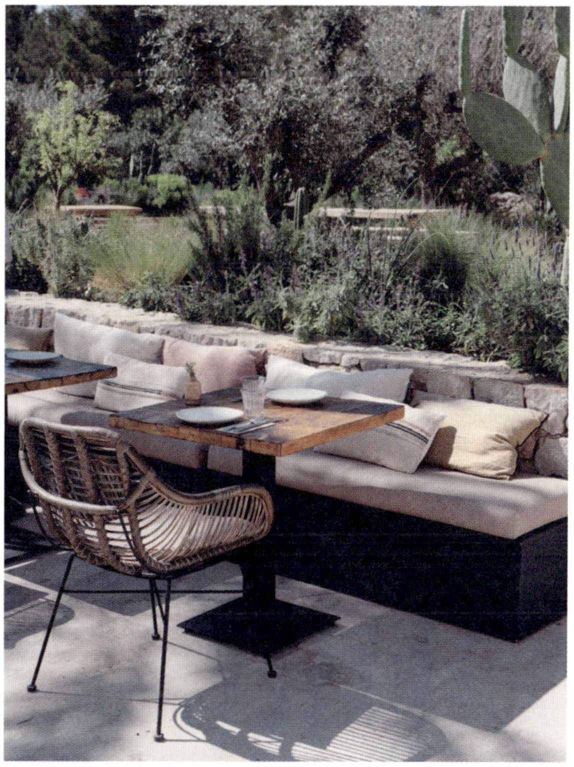

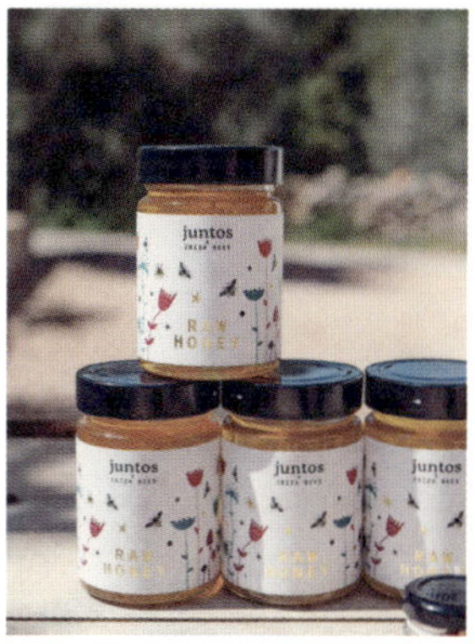

Also on display in the boutique are scented candles by Inés Ventós (pp. 60–63), honey from the farm, and kimonos and silk scarves from Figtree Collection (pp. 24–29).

SAN ANTONIO
bodegascanrich.com

CAN RICH

WINE, OLIVE OIL & VERMOUTH

Until recent decades, wine in Ibiza was made only by farmers for their own consumption. The Ibicenco Vicente Riera decided to produce quality wines that would put Ibiza on the oenophiles' map. In 1990 he bought the 20-hectare (49-acre) arable farm Can Rich – *can* meaning 'house of' in Catalan – on the west of the island, between San Antonio and San Rafael. He started planting grape vines in 1997, and four years later the first bottles of Can Rich were produced.

Today the business is run by Vicente's son Juan Riera and daughter-in-law Stella González. From local and foreign grape varieties, they make each year about 60,000 litres in total of white, rosé, red and sparkling wine. They also produce around 10,000 litres of *hierbas ibicencas*, the island's traditional liqueur, along with vermouth and extra virgin olive oil. Their second farm, within Las Salinas nature park in the south, has 17 hectares (42 acres) of olive trees.

Viniculture has a long history in Ibiza. 'The Phoenicians came to the island on ships from Syria and Lebanon in the seventh century BCE', Stella explains. 'They settled here and started making wine and olive oil, storing them in slender earthenware jars known as amphorae.'

The couple wanted the farms to operate on an organic basis. 'My father-in-law asked us what this meant, and when we explained it to him, he said that this is exactly how Ibicenco farmers have always operated', Stella says. But, she adds, of the handful of vineyards on the island, 'We are the only one that is certified organic.'

After the harvest, the winemaking process begins with fermentation. Then the wine is aged in Can Rich's cellar, in either barrels or amphorae.

All this work is carried out by Stella, Juan and members of their five-strong team. They bring in help to prune the vines, and they often need more workers in summer for the harvest. 'By then everybody is busy working in the tourist industry', Stella explains. 'So we all must work harder during that period.'

There is a story behind the name of each of Can Rich's wines, some of them reflecting the island's history. The name of Ereso, a white wine, derives from a medieval misreading of the Greek name for Ibiza, Ebesos. And a rosé called Bes is named after the Egyptian god who may also have given Ibiza its name. Can Rich's logo features a Phoenician boat, the shape of which was informed by the hippocampus, a mythological creature with the upper body of a horse and the lower body of a fish.

The company's main market comprises Ibiza's restaurants and individual customers. Some wine is exported to the Spanish mainland, Germany, Switzerland, The Netherlands and Belgium.

Can Rich's wines draw their taste from their setting. 'The proximity of the sea gives the wines a special note,' Stella says, 'so they have a strong personality and taste different from wines from Rioja or other large wine-producing regions.'

Can Rich has won Vinum Nature, EcoRacimo and Ecovino awards for a number of its wines, including Blanc de Blancs Extra Brut, Blanc d'Àmfora, Blanco Ereso and Tinto Lausos. ***CD***

Can Rich farm and winery was established in 1990 by Vicente Riera, and spans about 40 hectares (99 acres). Today it is managed by Vicente's son and daughter-in-law, Juan Riera and Stella González.

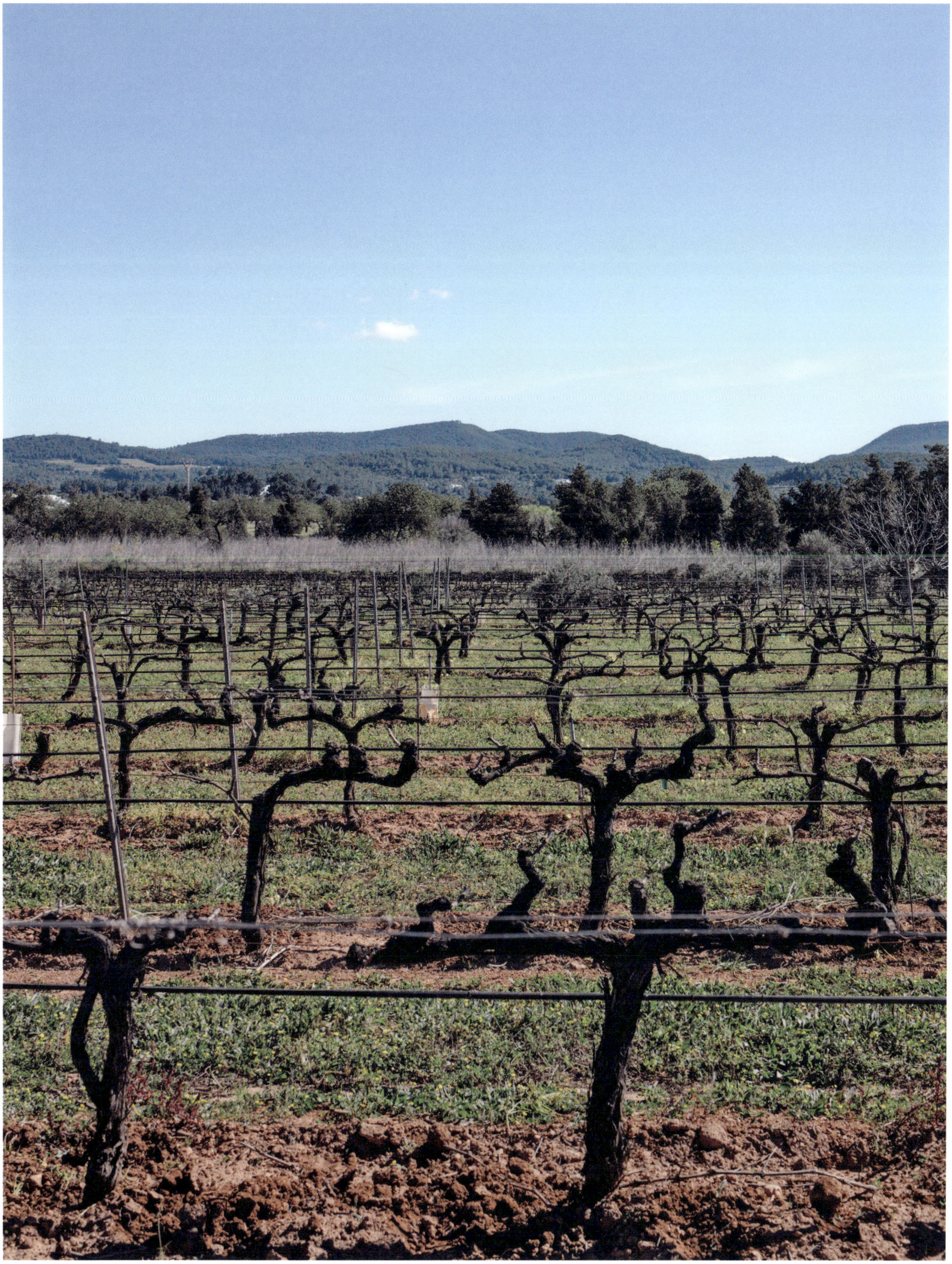

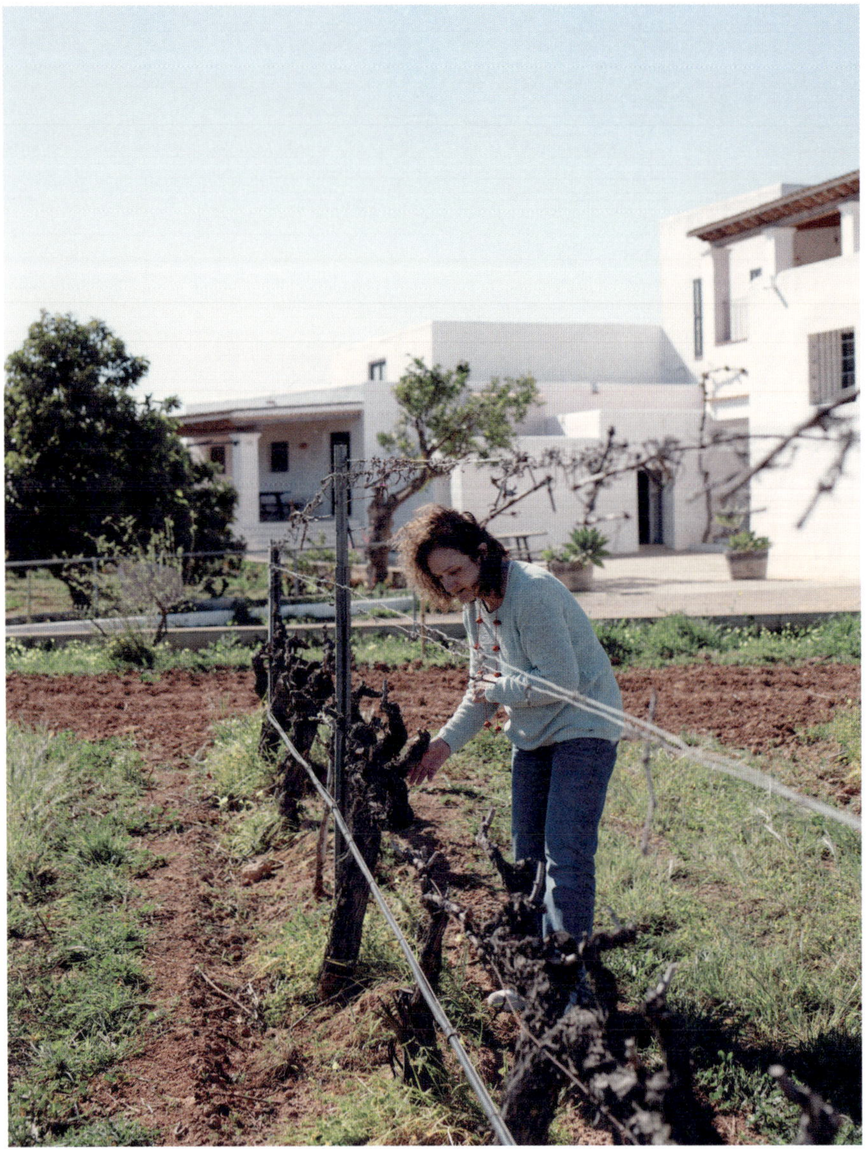

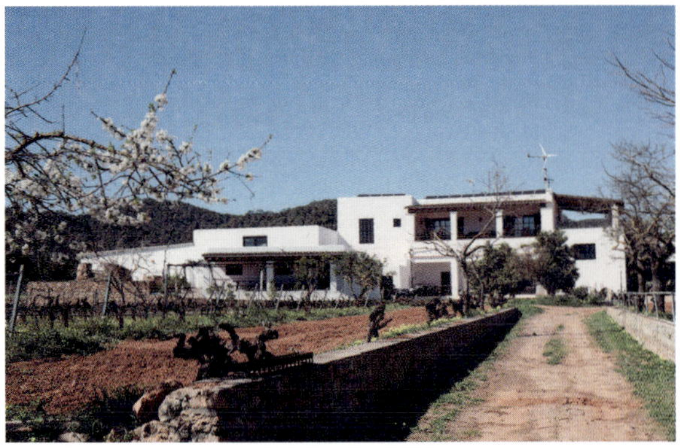

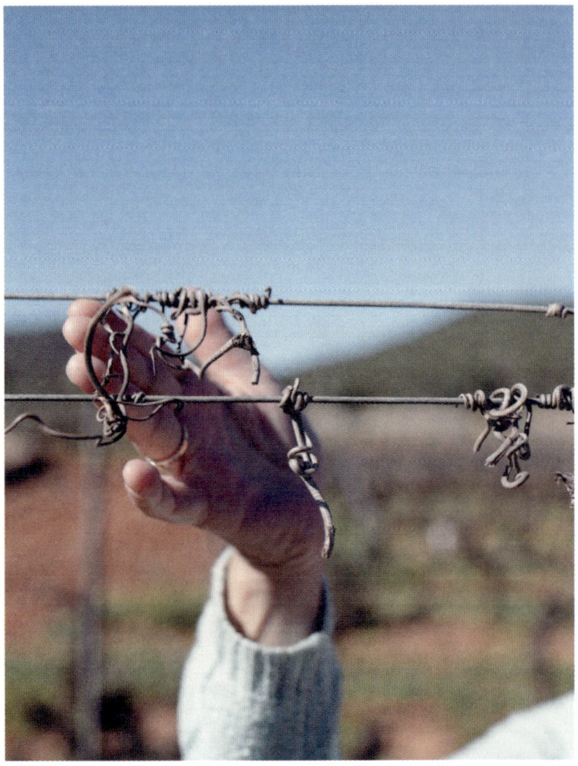

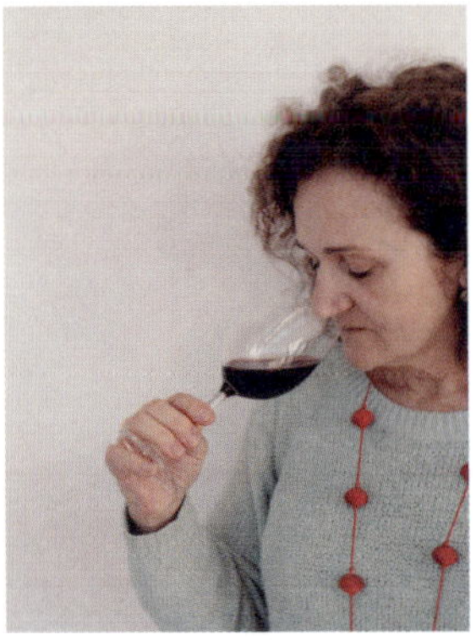

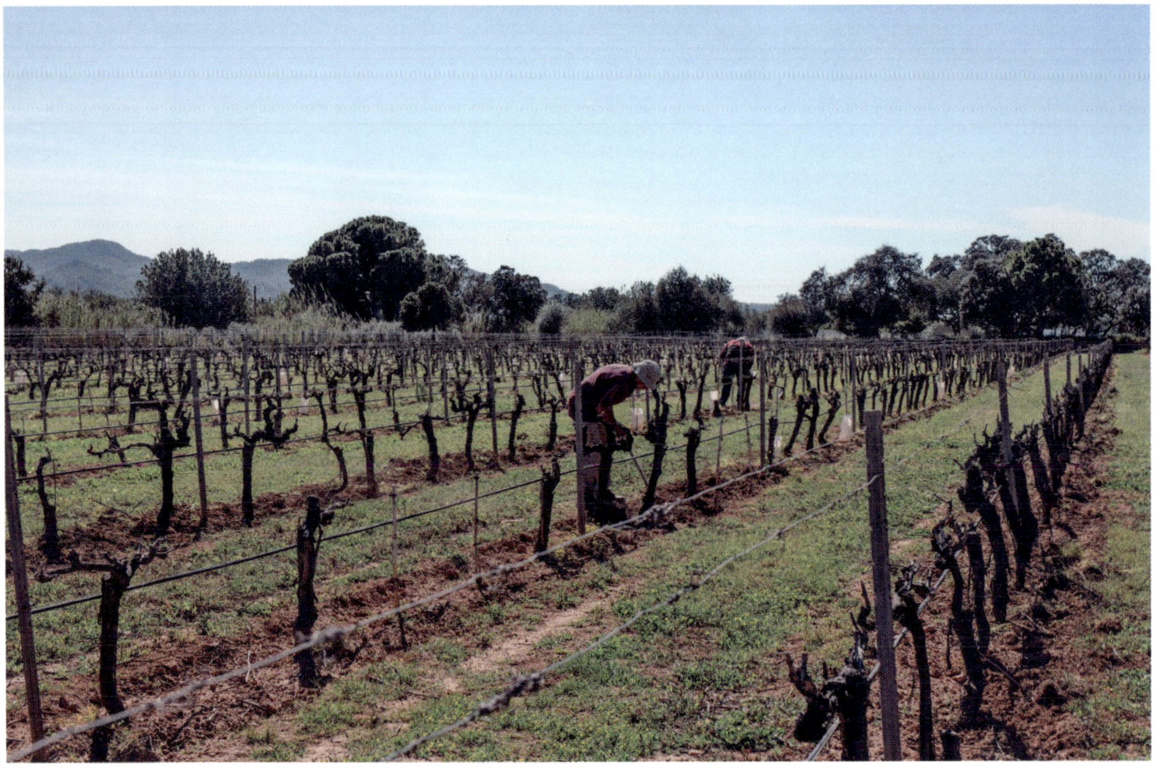

Can Rich follows traditional farming methods and is certified organic. Stella (above) and Juan employ a team of five, and bring in extra workers to help with pruning and harvesting tasks.

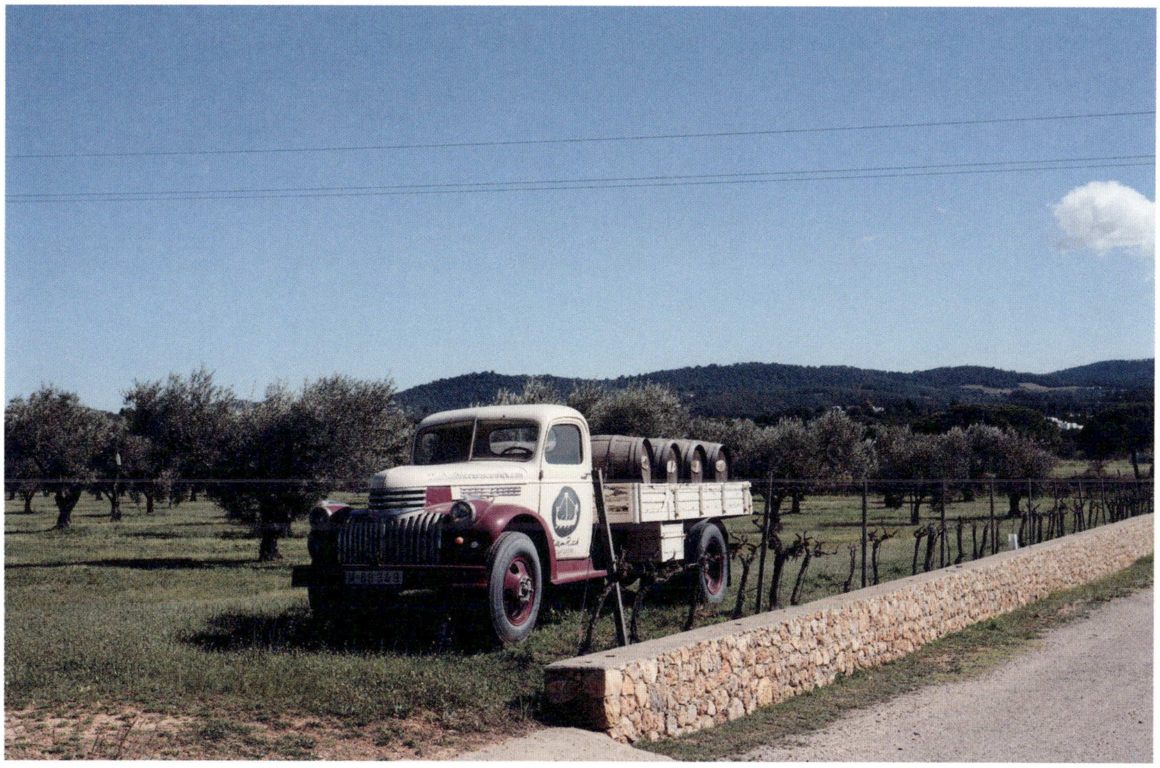

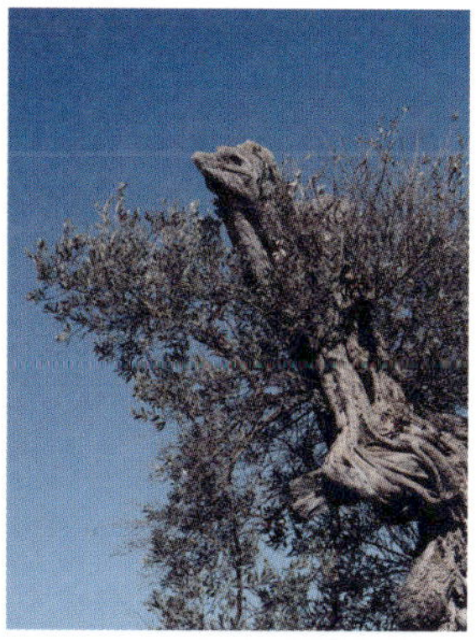

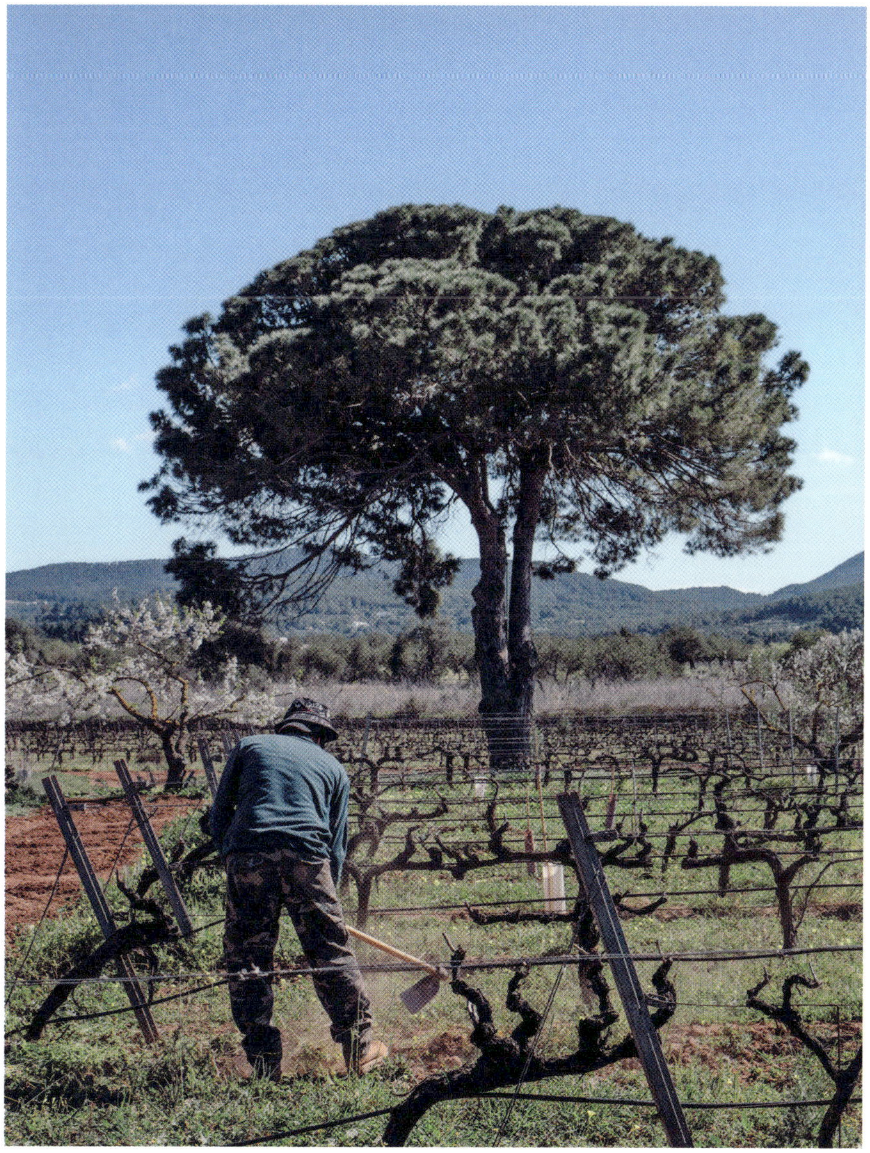

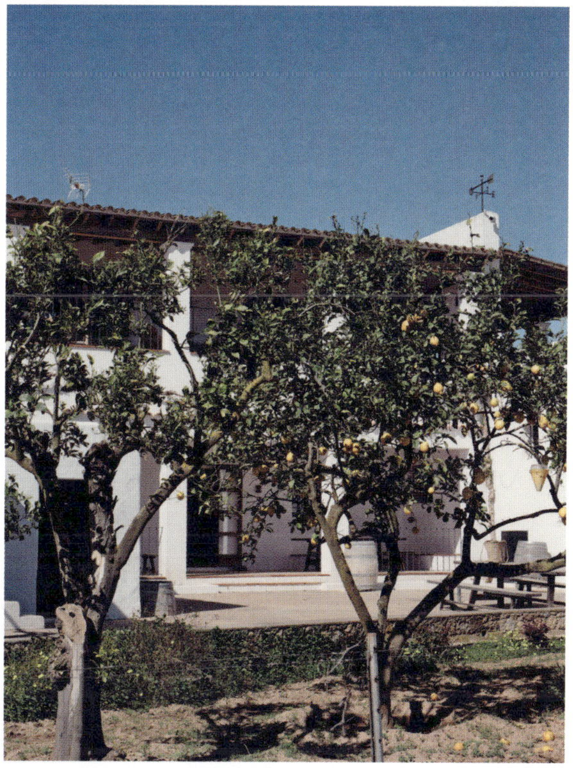

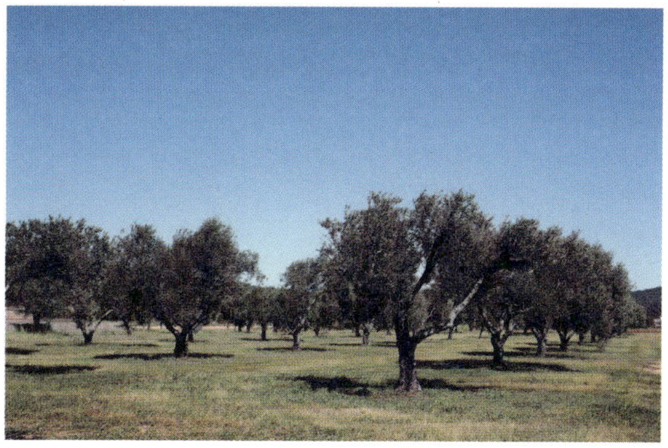

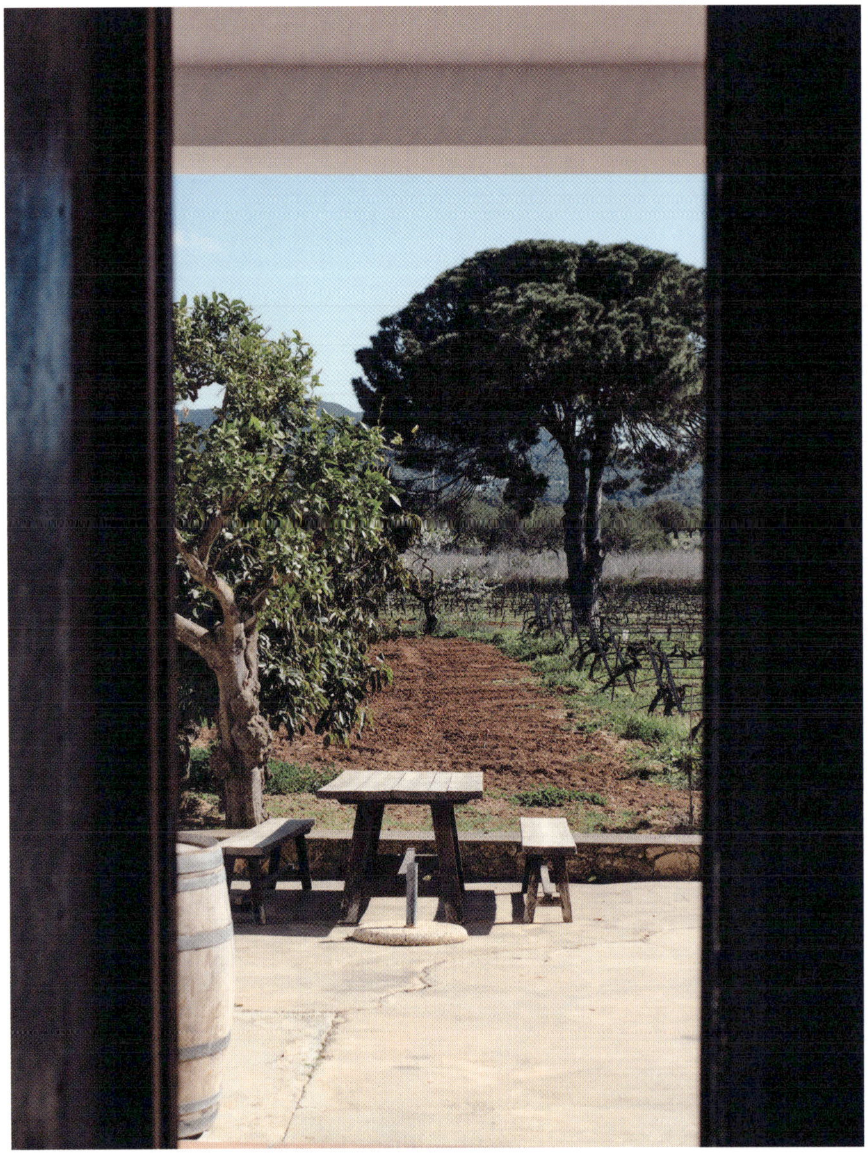

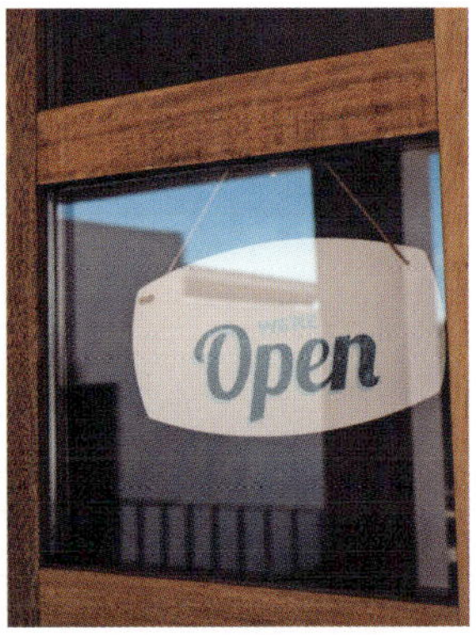

Can Rich's wines are aged in barrels or amphorae after fermentation. The winery has won awards for its high-quality wines, which can be sampled and bought at the farm near San Antonio.

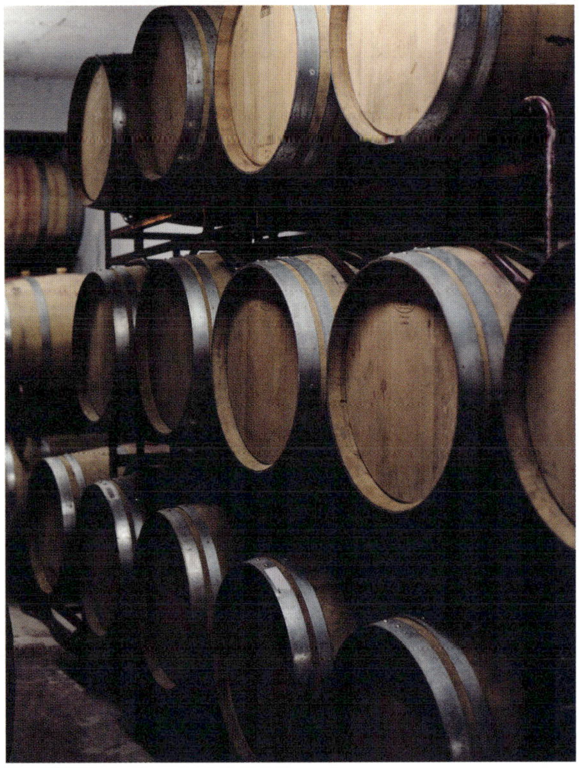

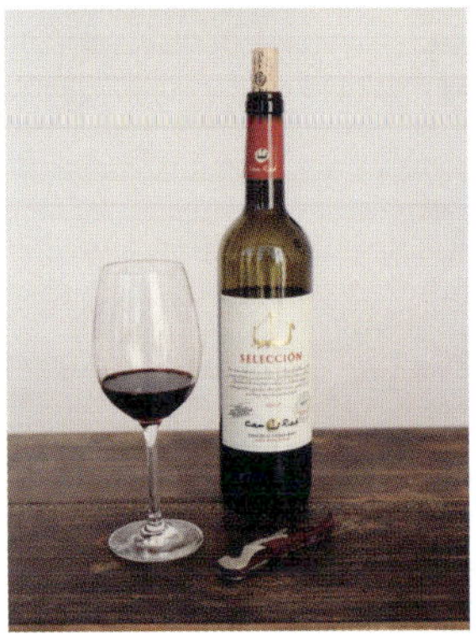

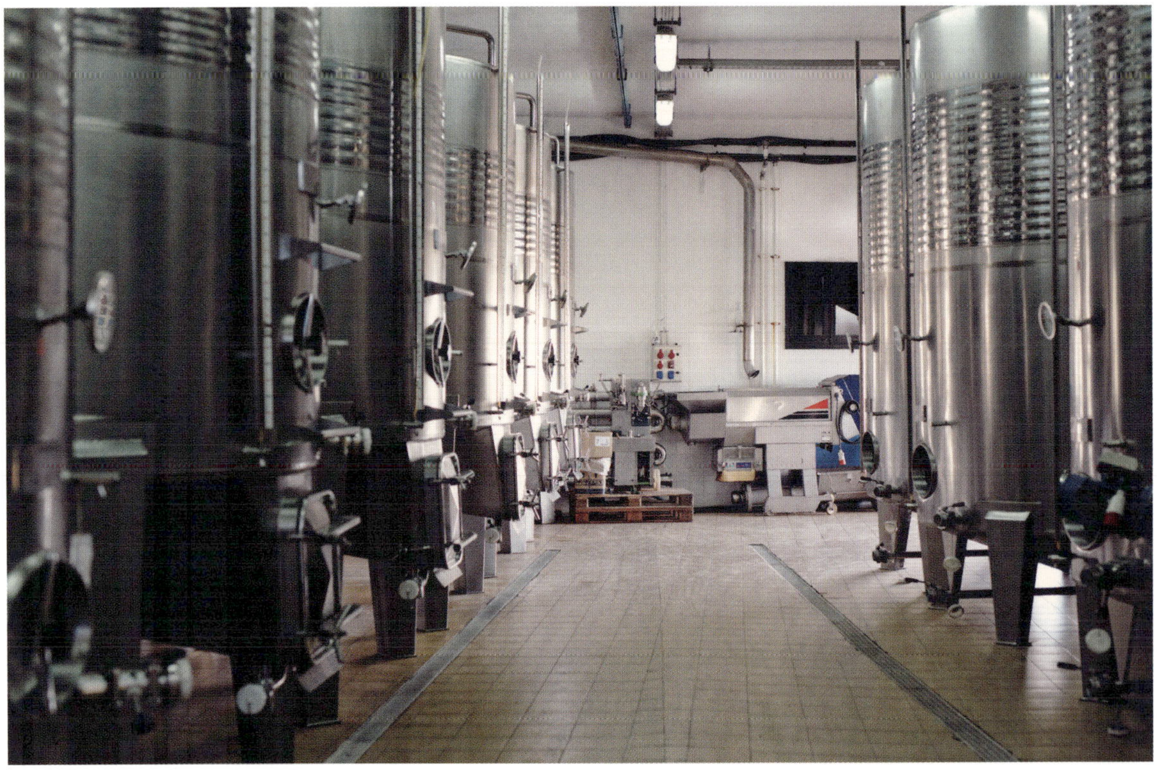

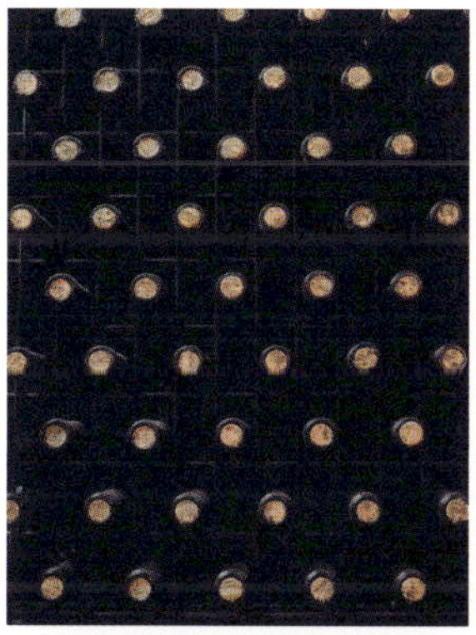

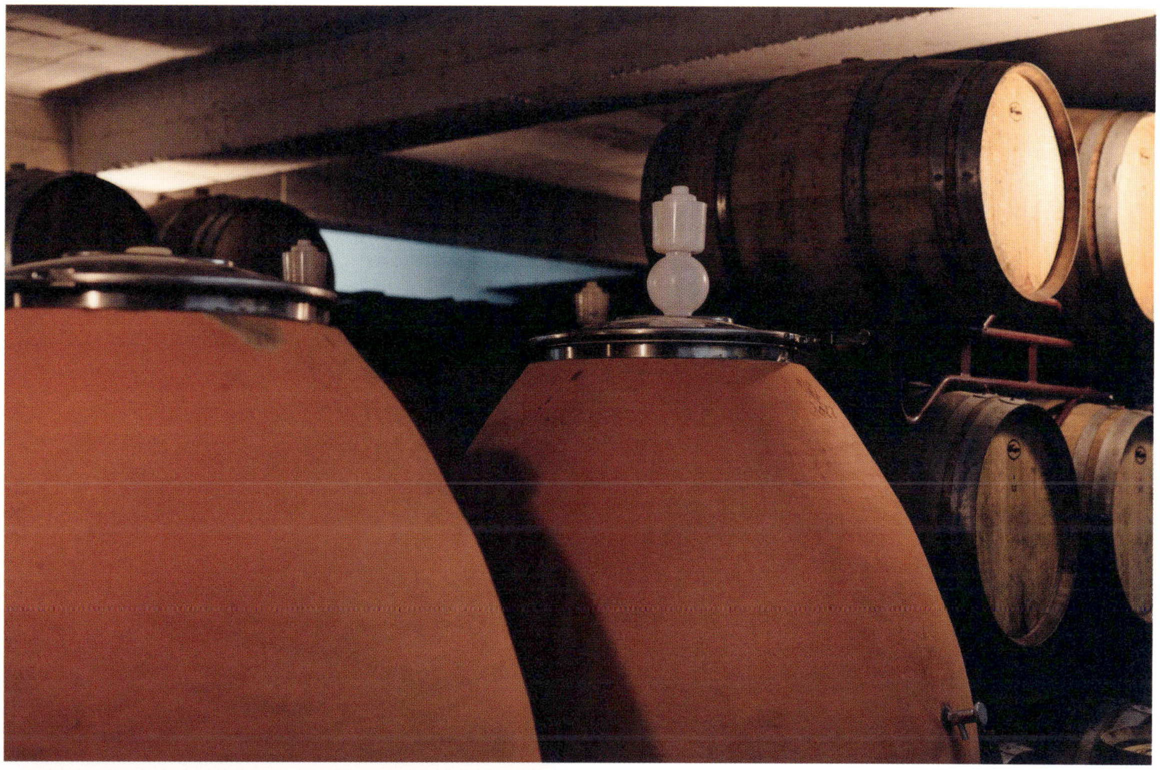

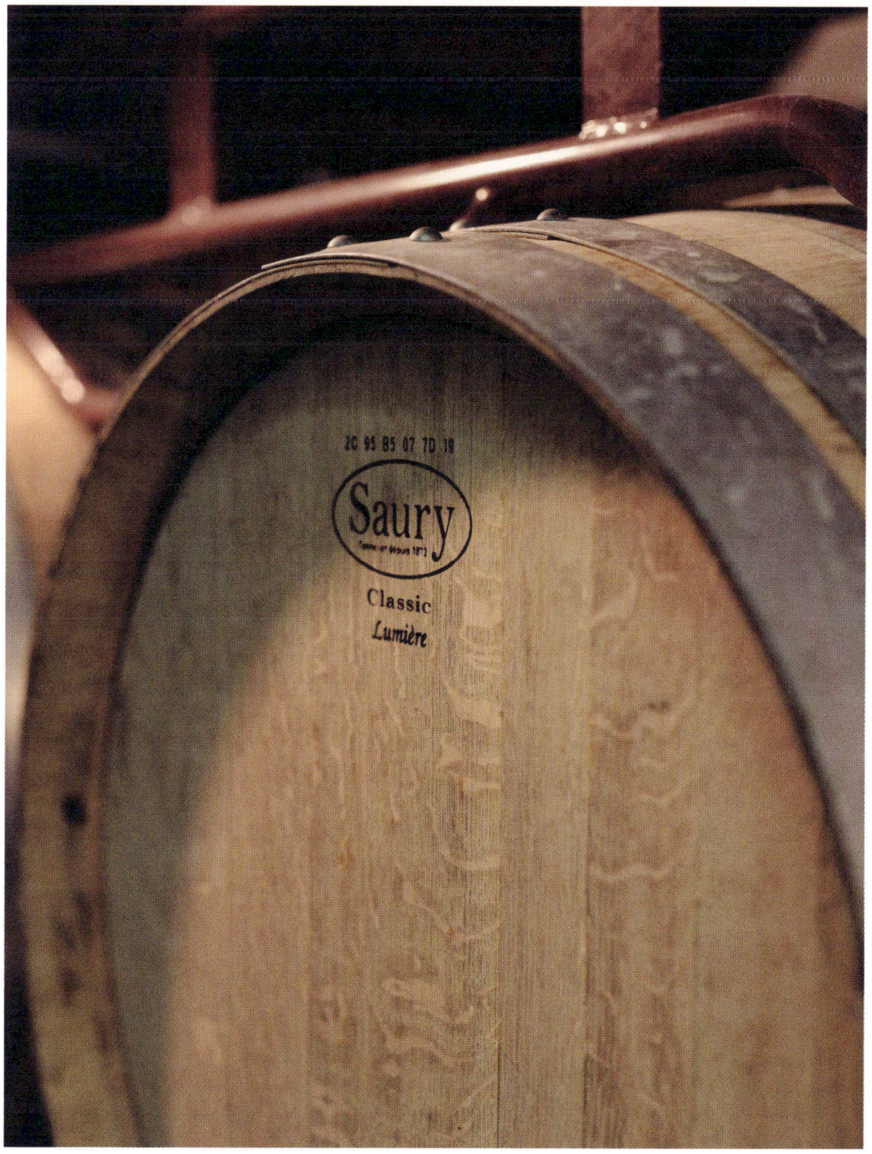
Saury
Classic
Lumière

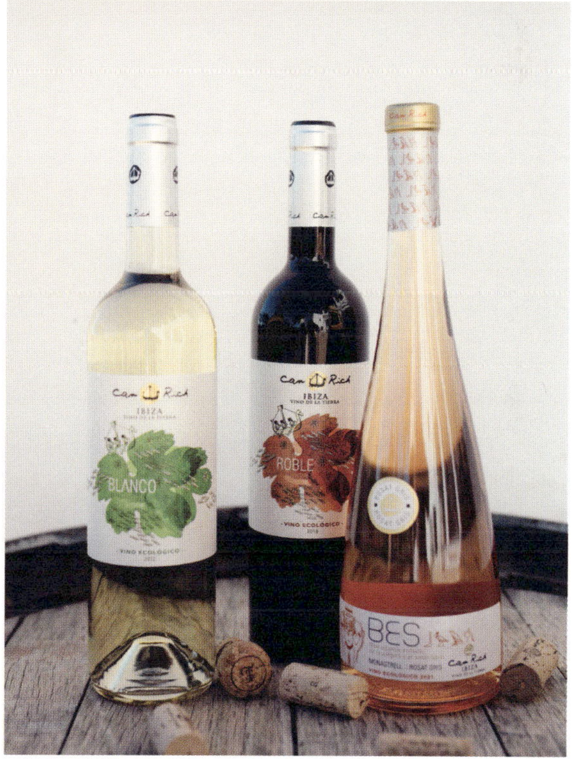
IBIZA
BLANCO
VINO ECOLÓGICO
IBIZA
ROBLE
VINO ECOLÓGICO
BES

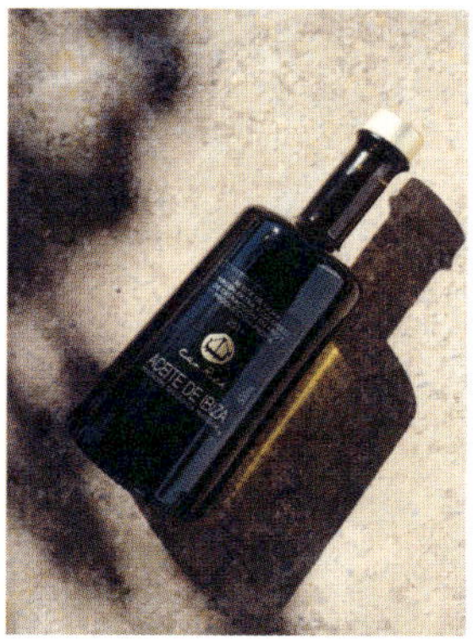

SANTA GERTRUDIS
@can___rei

CAN REI

TRADITIONAL BAKERY

Nieves Torres Cardona was born in the house from which she runs her bakery. Can Rei – the name of the house and her business – is in the countryside outside the village of Santa Gertrudis.

Back in the late 1990s, Nieves wanted a job that she could do from home because she needed to look after her elderly parents. So she asked her mother and aunt for their recipes for three of the island's specialities. She built a bakery to one side of the house and started making *buñuelos*, *orelletes* and *flaó*, the last of which was filled with cheese from her aunt's sheep and goats.

Flaó is a classic Ibizan dessert, and references to it date back to the thirteenth century. Its crust is filled with cream cheese made from cow's, sheep's or goat's milk, and it is flavoured with a special mint that is found only in Ibiza and which Nieves grows herself. Some *flaó* includes aniseed, but not that of Can Rei, because it is not the family tradition.

Nieves explains that the flavour of *flaó* depends on the season: 'In winter the cheese is greasier than in summer, because the animals drink less in the colder months. That means we must adapt the recipe.'

Nowadays Can Rei buys its cheese locally, purchasing its cow's cheese from one of the last dairy farmers left on the island. Whenever supplies are running low in Ibiza, Nieves buys extra cheese from the other Balearic Islands and from the mainland.

Orelletes (named on account of their ear-like shape) are sweet, fluffy pastries flavoured with grated lemon peel and aniseed liqueur. They are deep-fried in olive oil and sprinkled with sugar. *Buñuelos* are dough fritters flavoured with grated lemon peel, apple and aniseed.

Historically, each of these three sweet treats was associated with a particular season or occasion. *Flaó* was made at Easter, because by that time of year the animals had had their calves, lambs or kids, and their milk could be used for cheese production. *Orelletes* were eaten at special events such as weddings and baptisms, and are still handed out as gifts on those occasions. *Buñuelos* were made for All Saints' Day, on 1 November, and for the *matanza* (*matança* in Catalan). An important event across rural Spain, the *matanza* was the winter's day when the household pig was slaughtered. Friends and family were invited to lend a hand with the slaughtering and butchering, and in Ibiza these helpers were given *buñuelos* as a thank you.

From her three signature pastries, Nieves's output has expanded to include a large range of cakes and some savoury products. As well as supplying Ibiza's restaurants and shops (its *flaó* is even stocked by other bakeries), Can Rei sometimes ships products to the Spanish mainland and elsewhere. 'Those orders mostly come from Ibicencos living abroad and from visitors who got to know our products here in Ibiza', Nieves explains.

In the early days of the bakery, Nieves, her mother and her aunt were the only staff. Now the team has seven members in total, working the three ovens all year round. 'We don't have much space in the bakery, so we're trying not to grow the business', Nieves remarks. And anyway, it is a challenge to find workers – a problem faced by many companies, she adds. When the island's numbers swell with summer visitors, there is more business; 'Then we work harder', she says. ***CD***

Nieves Torres Cardona built a bakery on the side of the family home and started with her mother's and aunt's recipes for three island specialities: buñuelos, orelletes *and* flaó.

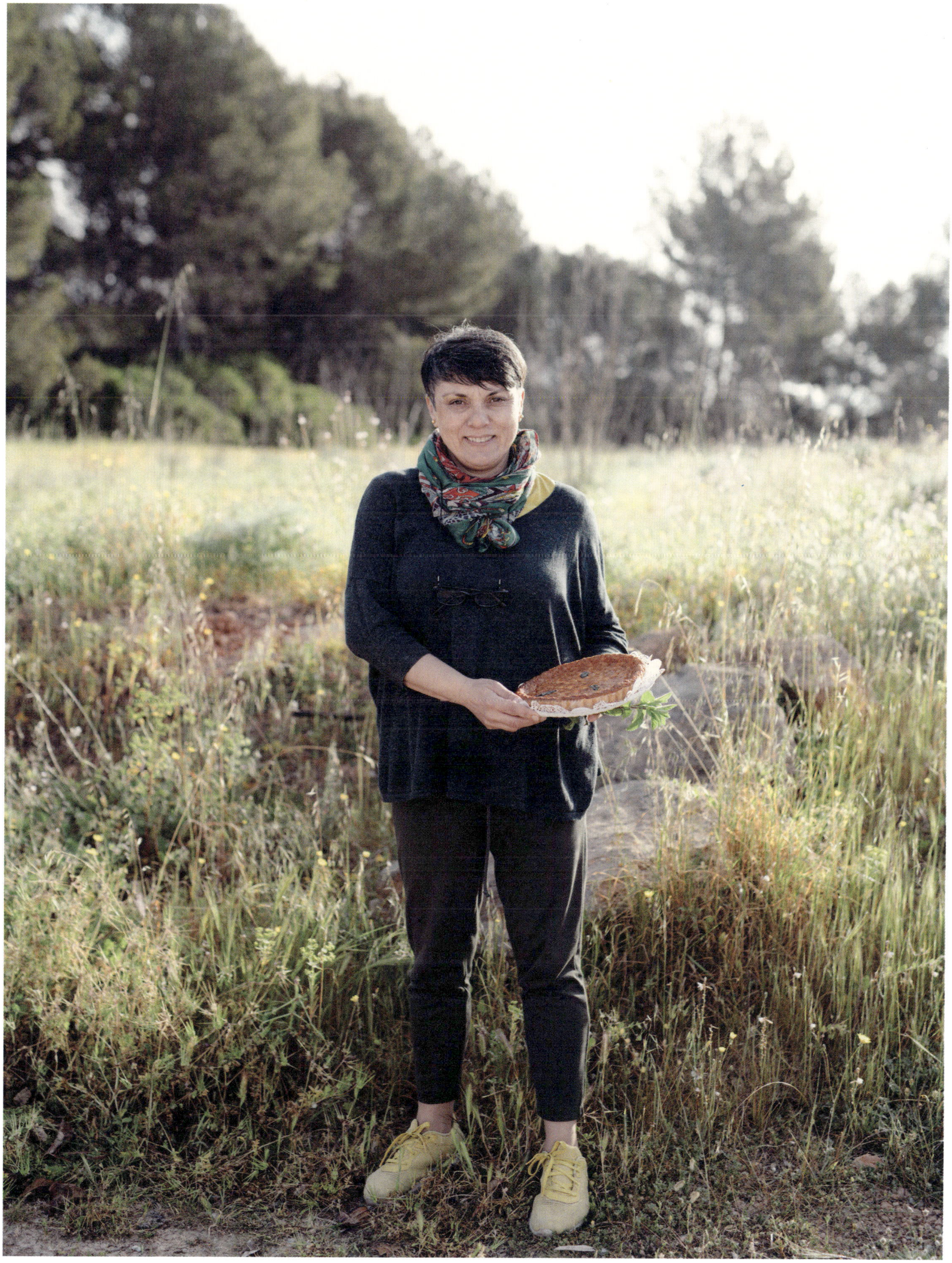

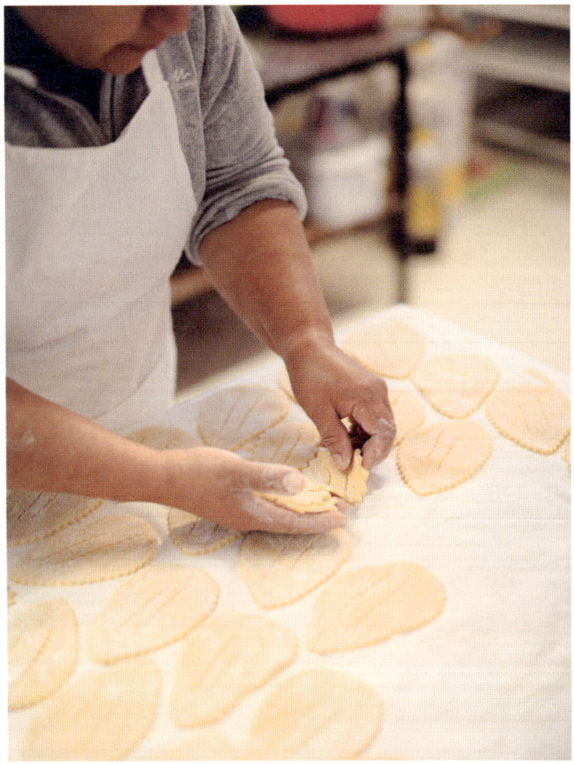

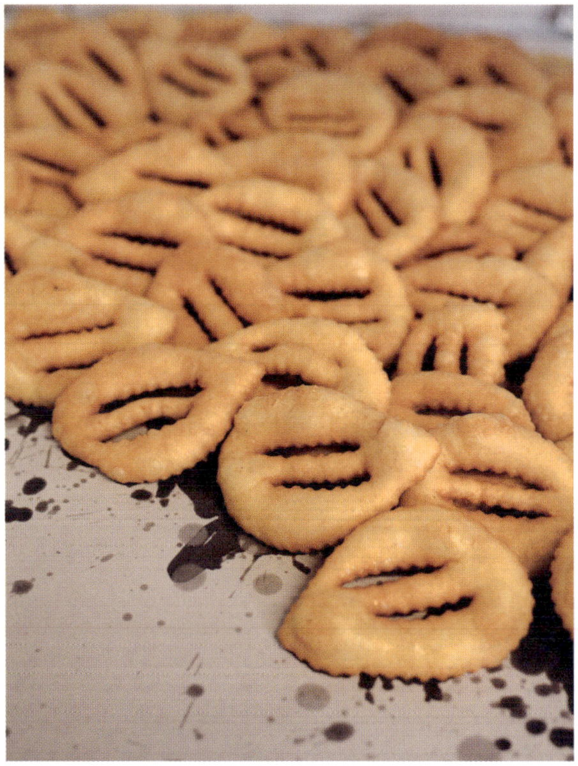

Orelletes *(left and below)* are ear-shaped sweet pastries typically handed out at important family events. Savoury empanadas *(centre and bottom left)* are filled with calamari, sausage, chicken, veal or tuna and peppers.

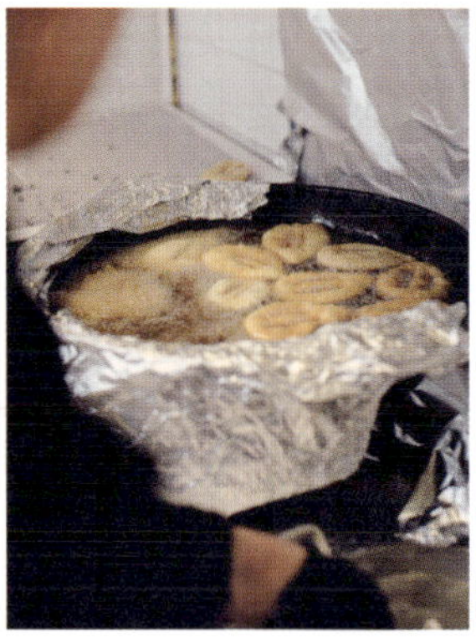

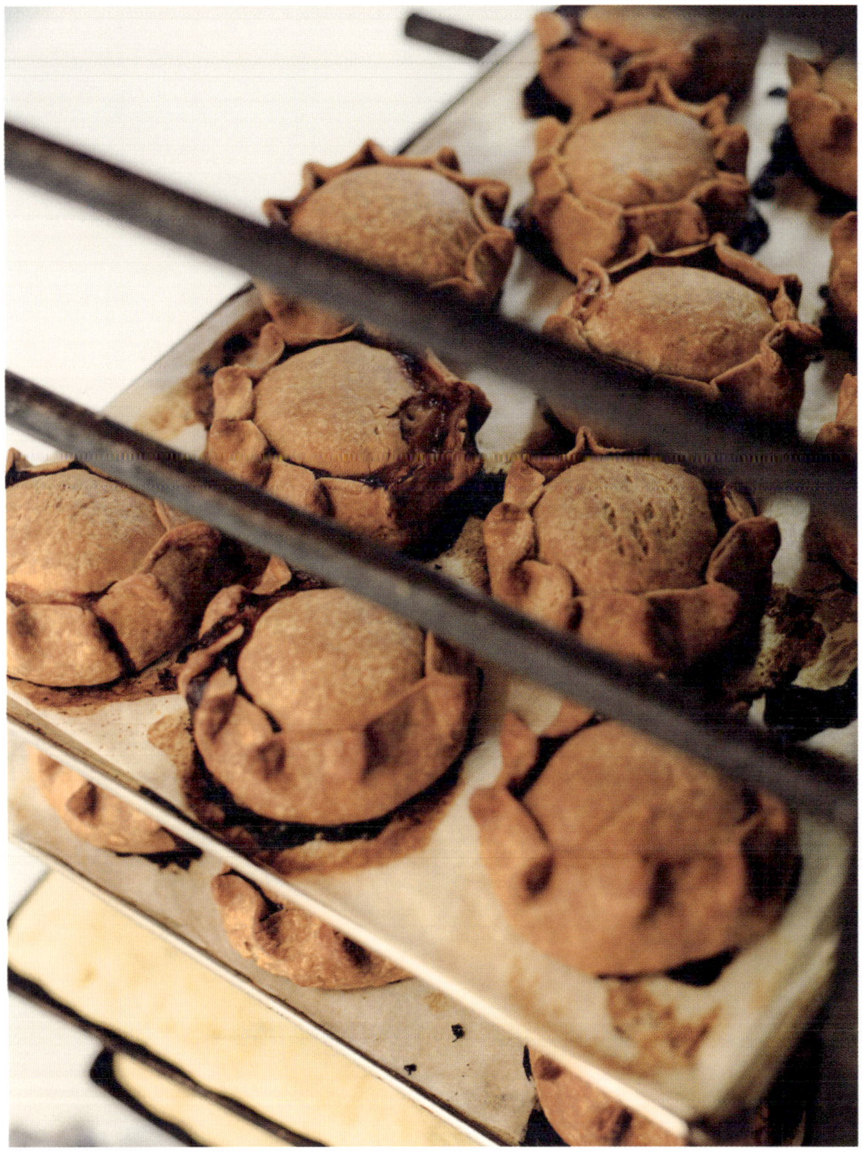

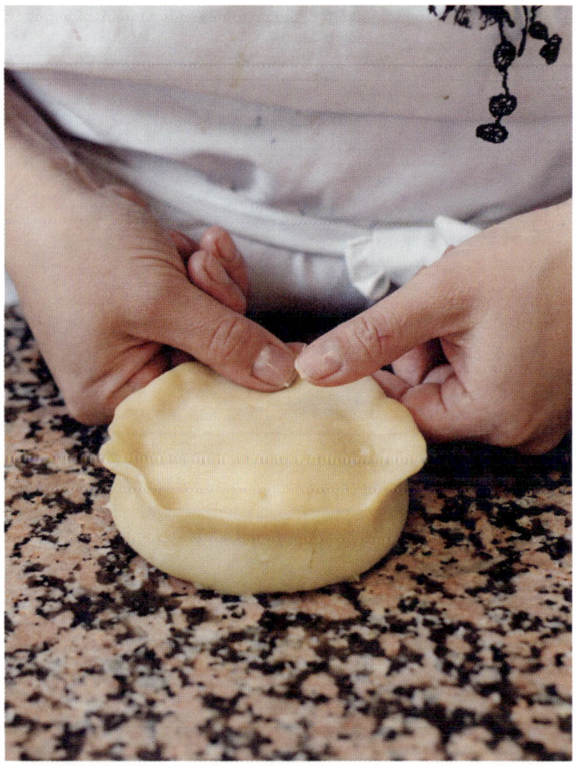

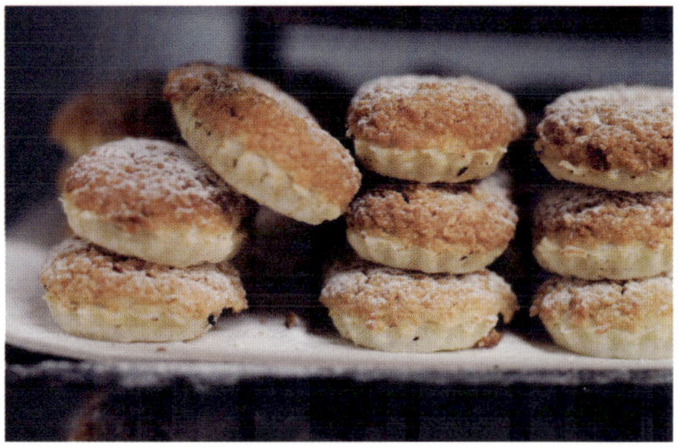

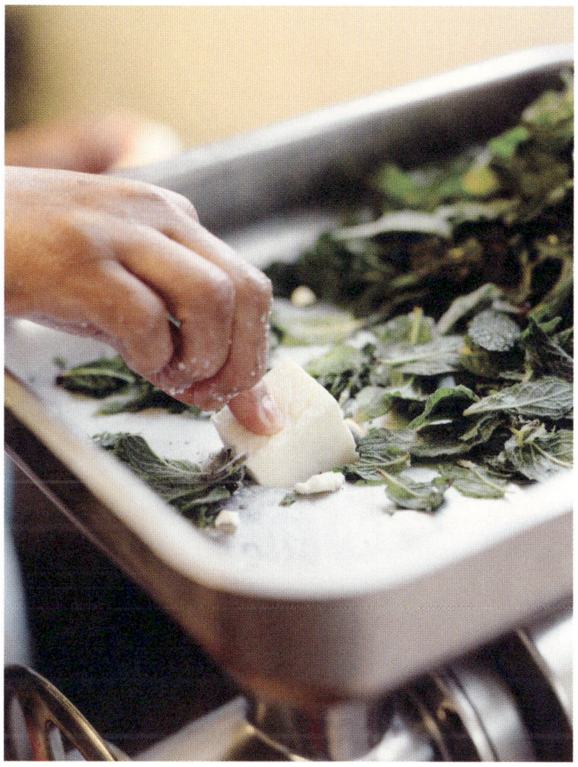

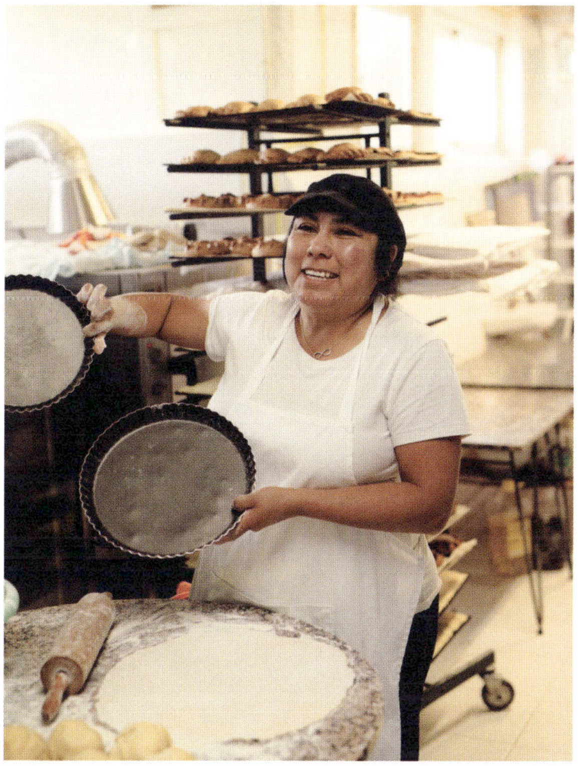

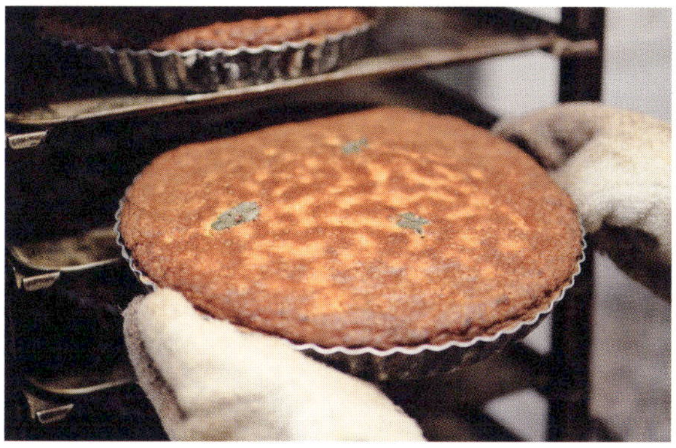

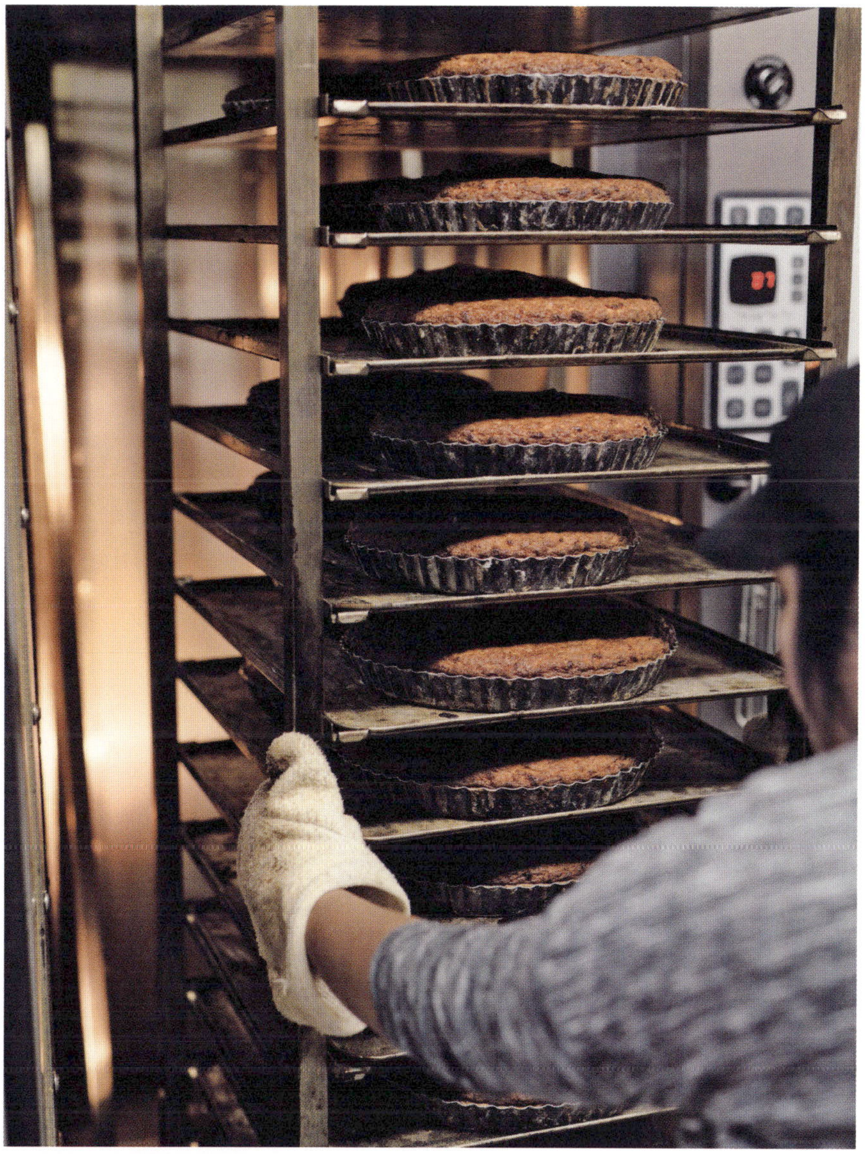

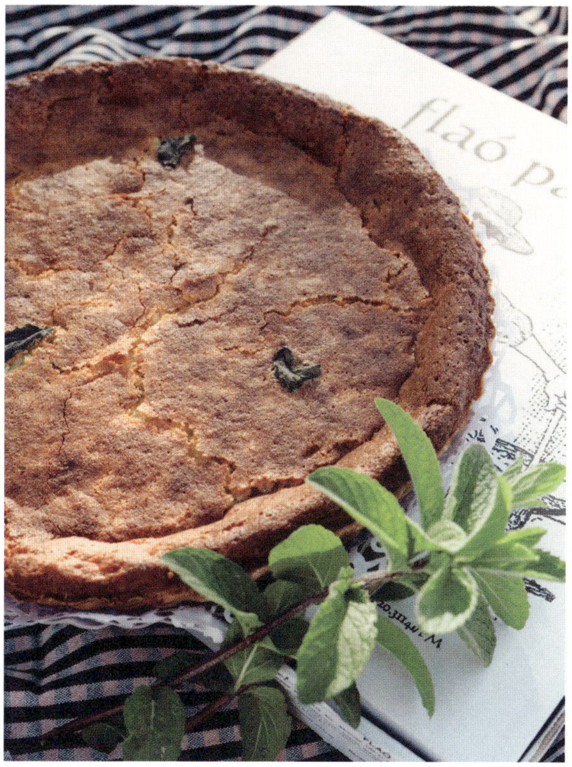

An Ibizan dessert that dates back 700 years, flaó is made with cow's, sheep's or goat's cheese, and includes a type of mint specific to the island.

SAL DE IBIZA

GOURMET SALT PRODUCTS

'Ever since I was a little kid, I have dreamt of bottling and selling Ibiza's salt.' Daniel C. Witte's dream came true after his film-production company became insolvent during the financial crisis of 2001.

Daniel was born and brought up in Germany and still lives there, but his parents belonged to the first wave of foreigners who bought property in Ibiza in the 1950s. 'I've spent all my holidays on the island since I was a baby', he explains. 'The German poet and art dealer Ernesto Ehrenfeld was a family friend, and through him we met the island's early celebrities, such as the architect Erwin Broner.'

During those holidays, Daniel's family often had lunch at the restaurant Can Salinas, near the salt lakes. 'From there I would look at the salt mountains and dream of creating a brand for Ibiza's salt', says Daniel. He established Sal de Ibiza in 2004. His supplier is Salinera Española, which has been owned by the same Mallorca-based family since 1878. The salt marshes of Ibiza, Las Salinas, are a UNESCO World Heritage site and are classified as a nature reserve by the government of the Balearic Islands. They also produce top-quality salt.

Daniel's brainwave was to ask Salinera Española to harvest *fleur de sel* – something the company had never done before. When the natural salt in the marshes' evaporation ponds crystallizes on the water's surface, it forms salt 'flowers'. Since the fine crystals form only in strong sun and in certain natural conditions, *fleur de sel* is impossible to produce at an industrial scale and has to be collected by hand: the delicate flakes are carefully skimmed off the surface with special wooden rakes.

Because it retains more natural moisture than other salts, this gourmet product has a particularly mild and delicate taste. 'The crystalline salt structure of these grains allows them to melt in the mouth', Daniel explains. '*Fleur de sel* shares little more than its name with common table salt.'

To begin with, Daniel did everything himself, learning pottery in order to make the ceramic jars that contain the salt, and hand-cutting the corks and labels. The branding created by Daniel shows a pictogram of the sun in reference to Tanit, the Carthaginian goddess of fertility who is Ibiza's patron saint. He explains that he chose turquoise for the packaging 'because through the colour's association with a world-famous jewellery brand, I felt it underlined how precious the salt is. It suggests something fine and noble.'

Daniel's first customers were the famous delicatessen Feinkost Käfer in Munich and the department store KaDeWe in Berlin. 'The *fleur de sel* type of salt wasn't very well known at this time, so my product was a novelty', he recalls. Today Ibiza and the Spanish mainland are his biggest markets. The three Sal de Ibiza shops on the island are run by the company's distributor.

The business has twelve members of staff and is headquartered in Berlin, where Daniel lives. Annually, around 80 tonnes of salt – half of it *fleur de sel* – are transported to northern Germany and to Catalonia. There, it is packaged in workshops staffed by disabled people. As well as *fleur de sel*, they package pure sea salt; salt with flavourings such as green pepper, lemon and hibiscus; and special editions that support charities, including Pink Ribbon Deutschland and the Ibiza Preservation Foundation.

As for Salinera Española, 'The owners were pleased that someone wanted to develop a brand for their Ibiza salt', Daniel says. 'I still get fond messages from them when they see it in hotels and shops around the world.' ***CD***

German-born Daniel C. Witte, who has been visiting Ibiza since he was a baby, set up the Sal de Ibiza brand to promote the product of the island's natural salt marshes.

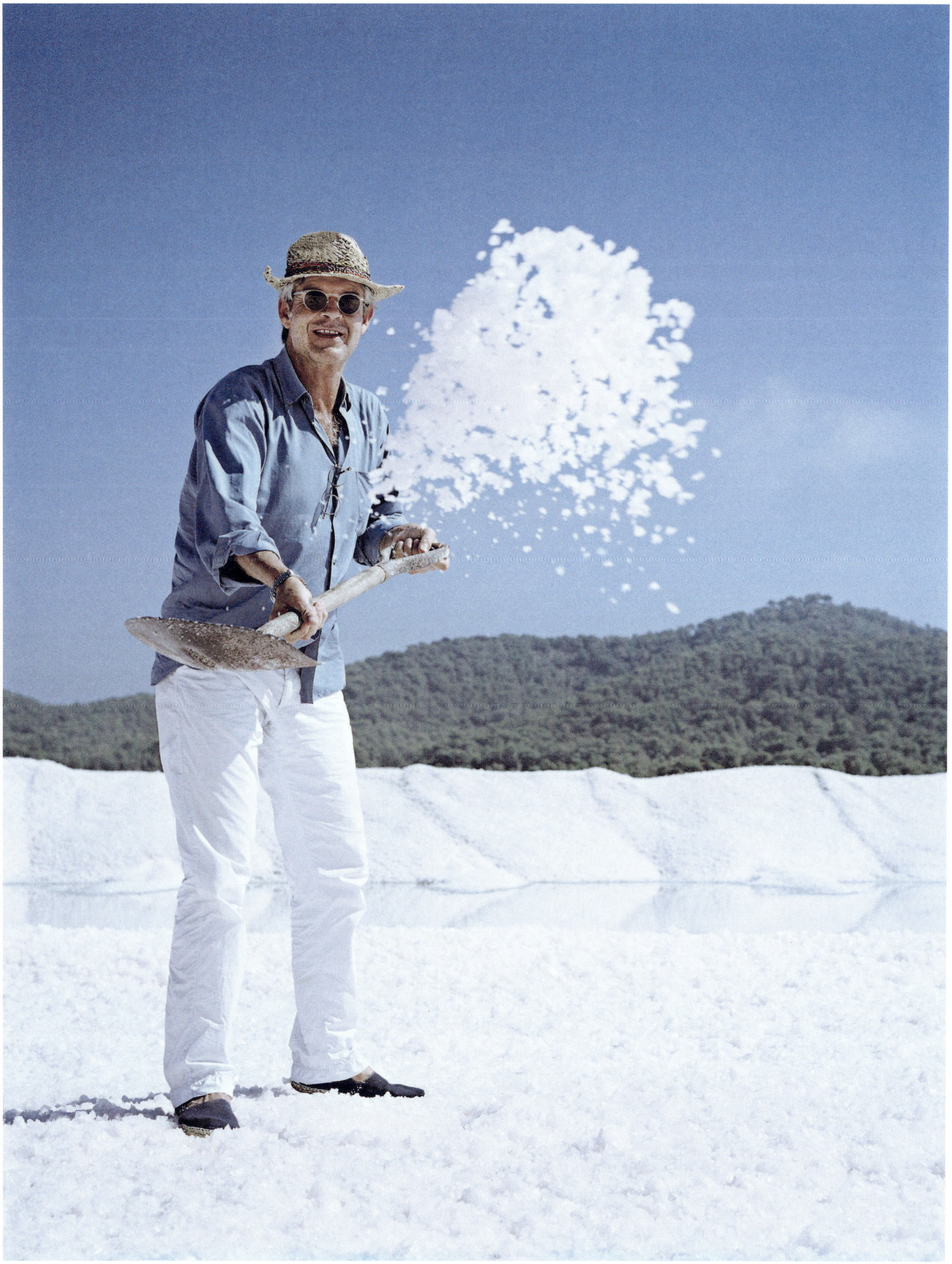

Daniel checks out the product with José María Ramos of Salinera Española, which owns the salt marshes. Micro-organisms give the evaporation ponds their bright-purple colour.

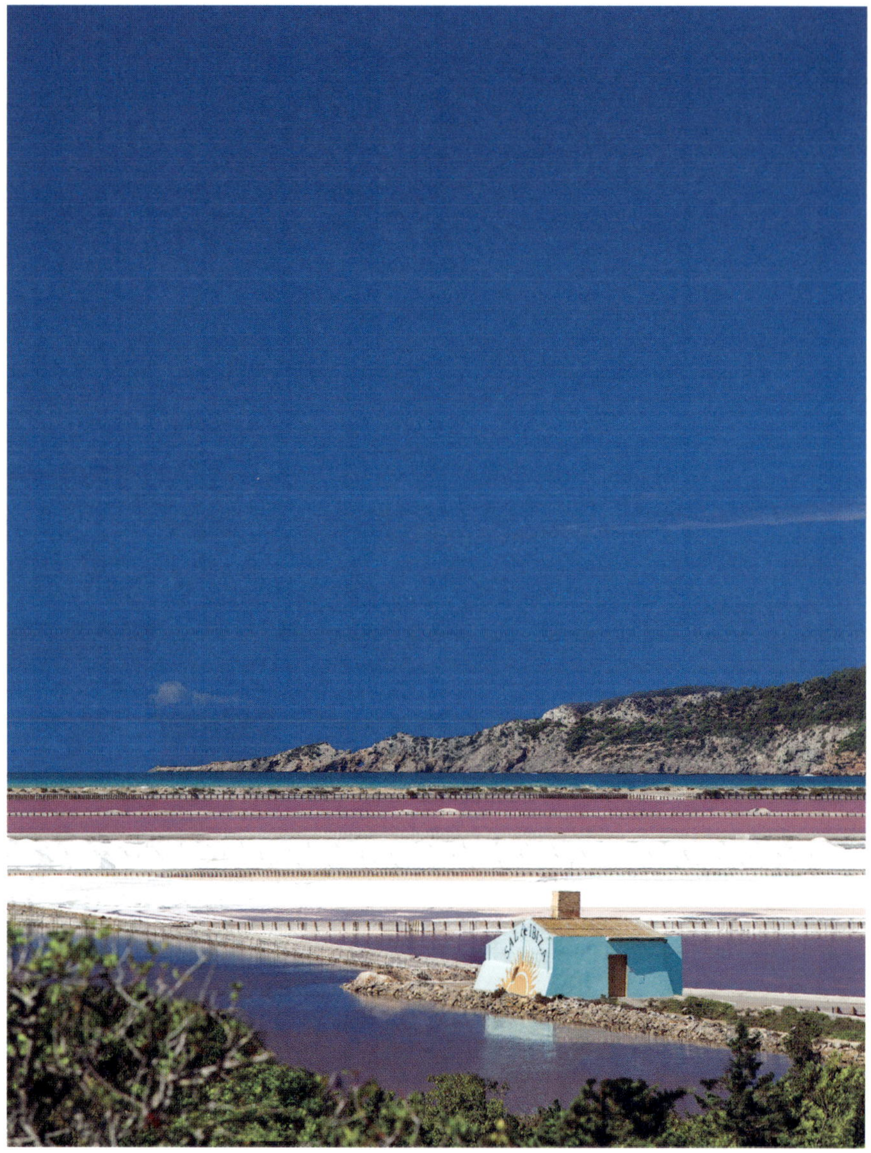

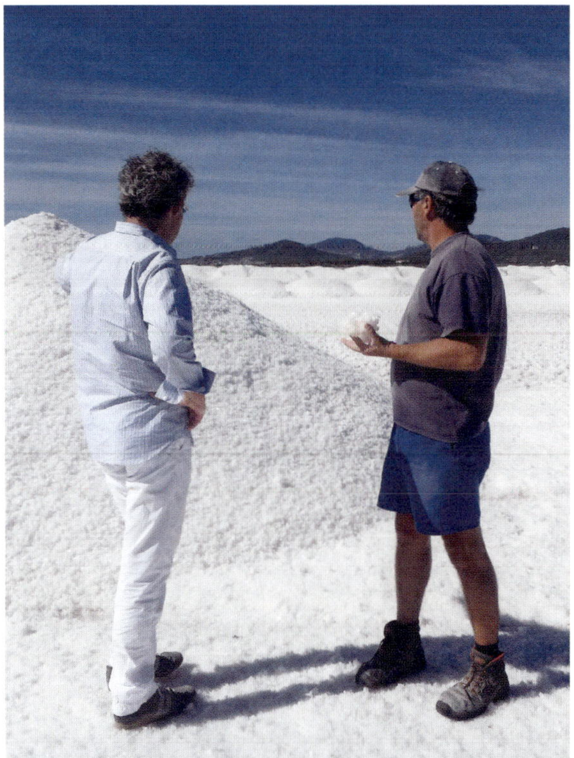

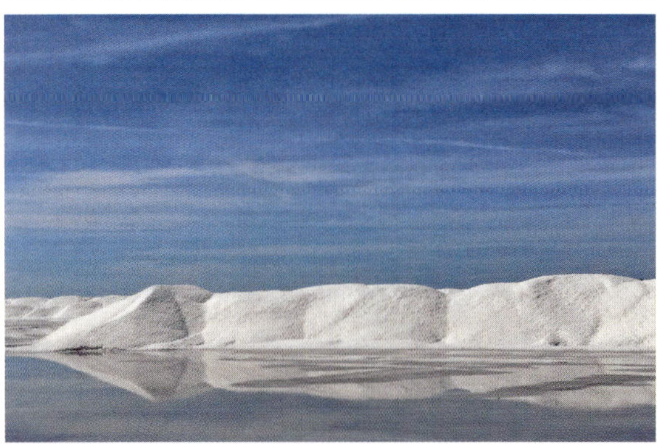

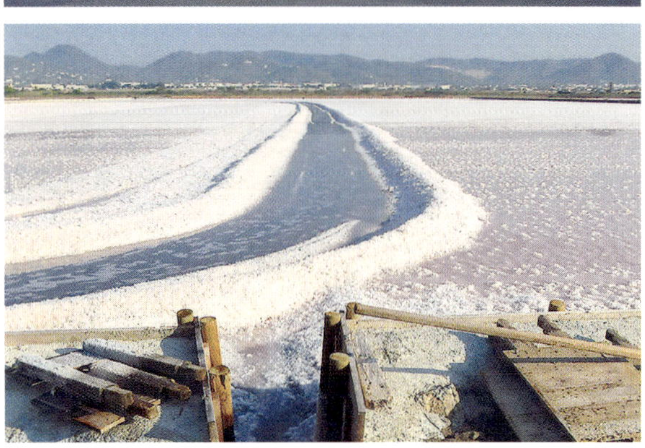

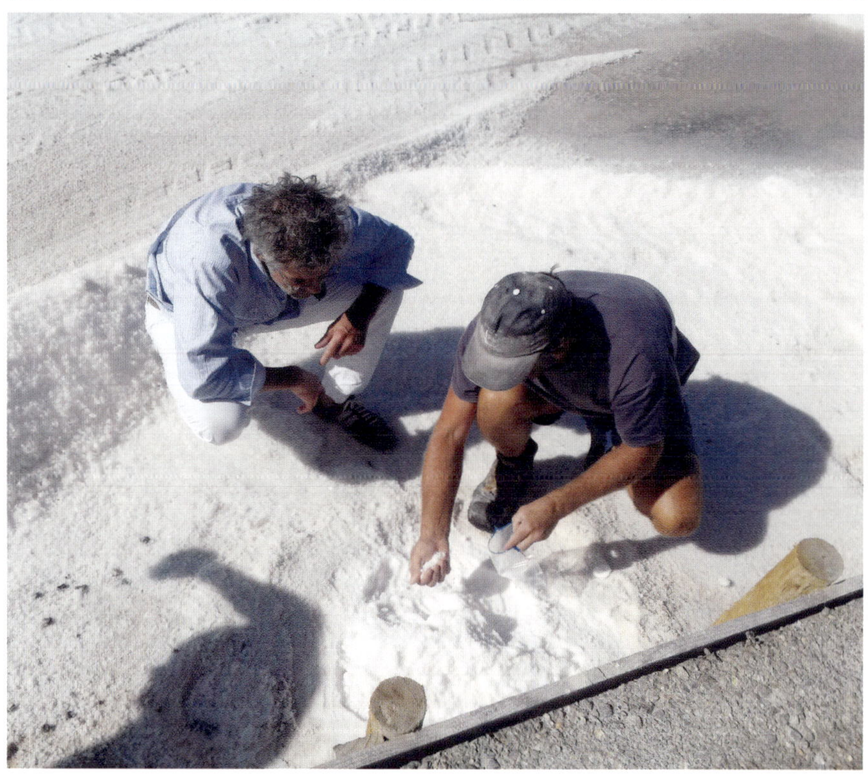

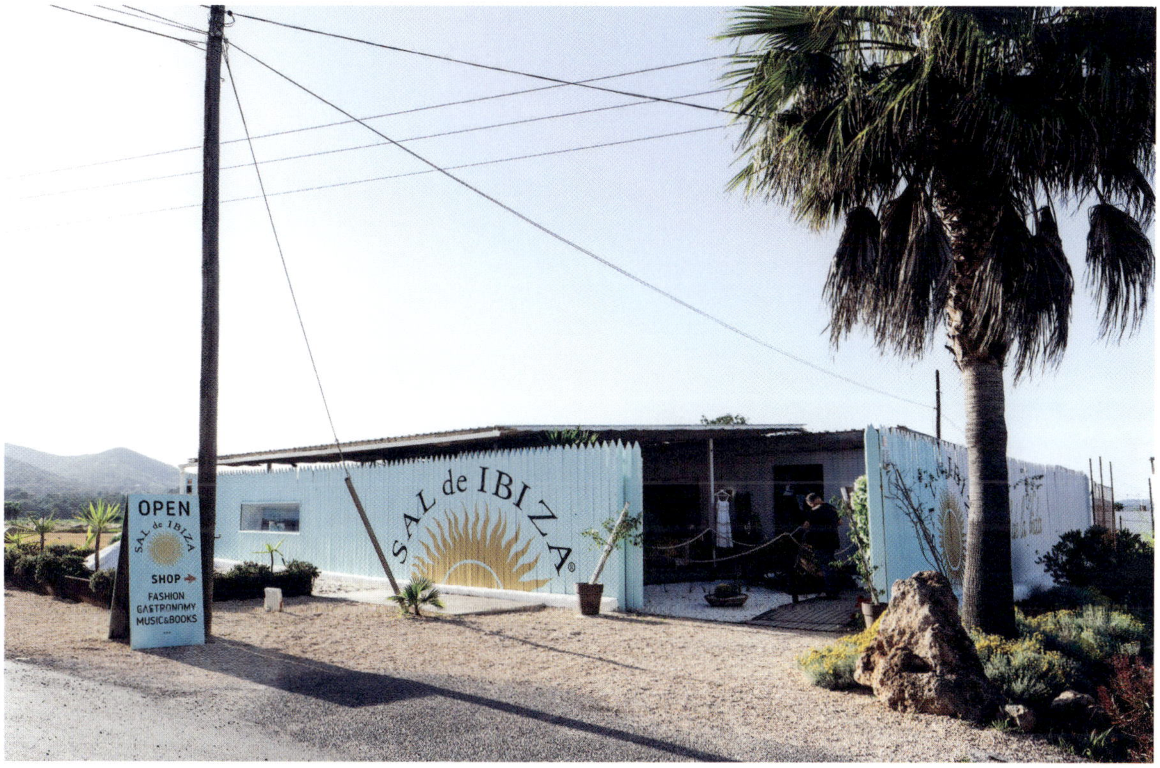

Left and below: A Sal de Ibiza store stands on the road between Ibiza Town and Santa Eulalia.

Below, left: The white, blue and pink jars contain flavoured fleur de sel, and a portion of the profit from these special editions is donated to charities such as the Ibiza Preservation Foundation.

Bottom right: Salted nuts and crisps are also part of the product range.

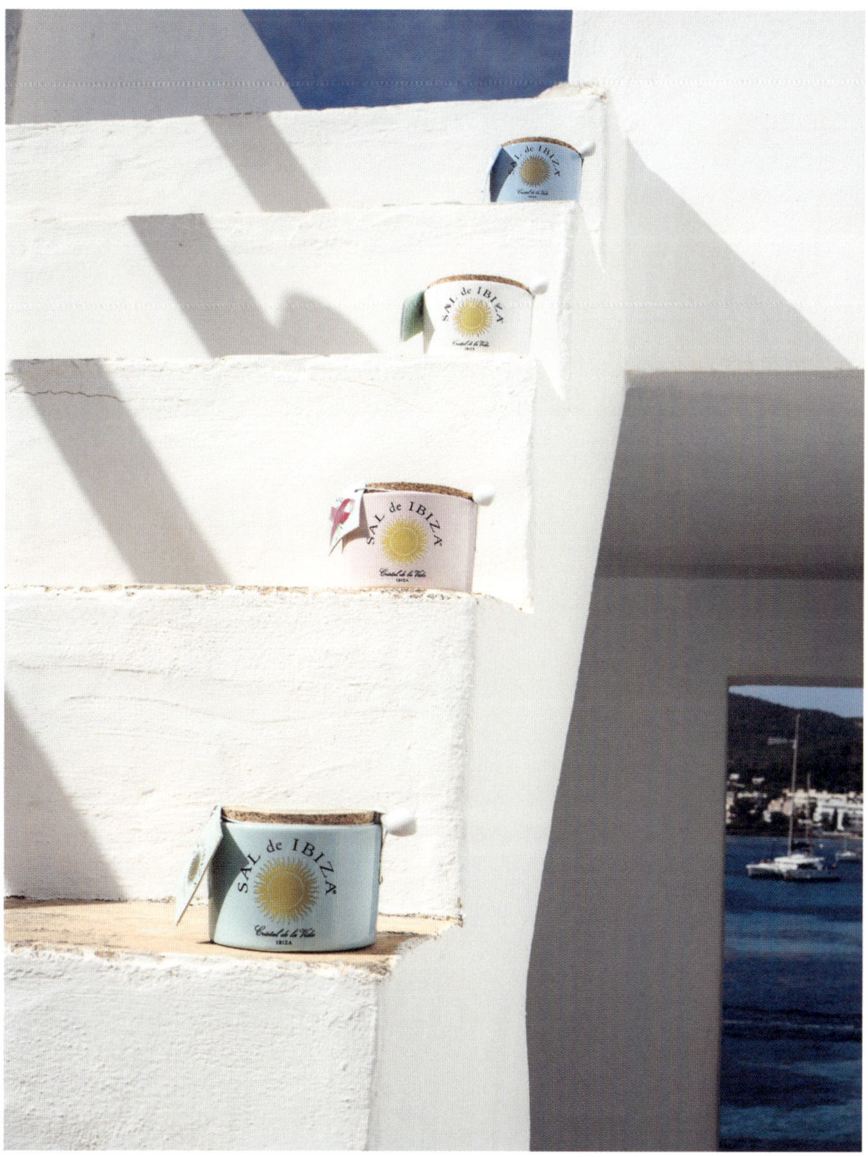

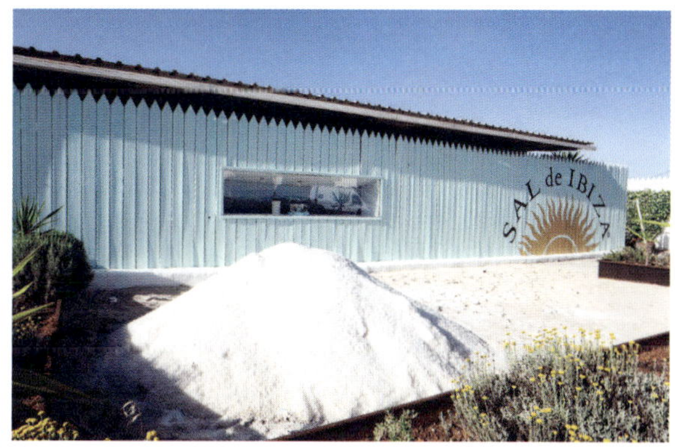

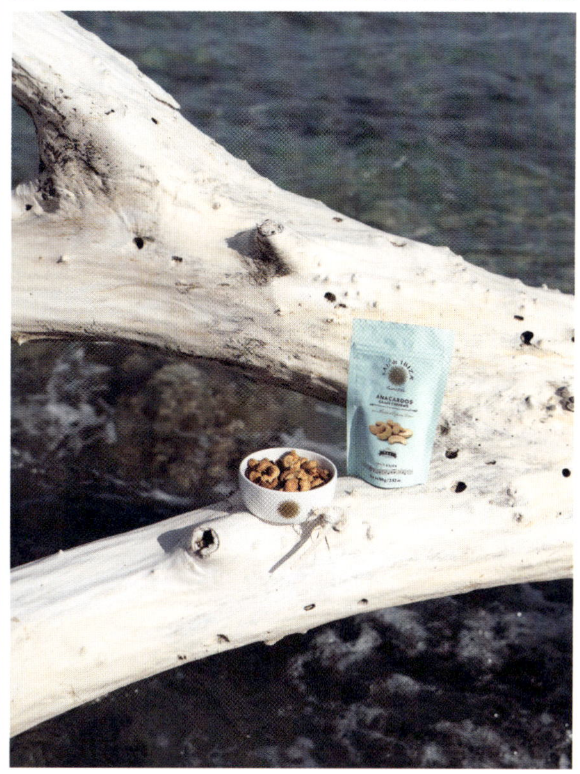

CA NA NEGRETA
cafesibiza.com

CAFÉS IBIZA

ROASTED COFFEE

After the Spanish Civil War, which ended in 1939, Ibiza was so poor that many people left the island to seek work elsewhere. Vicente Tur did just that, and went to Venezuela. Despite arriving with no Spanish (only Ibicenco), he obtained work dredging the port, made some money and got the idea for his own business.

Vicente was inspired by the coffee-drinking scene in South America, and – an entrepreneur at heart – decided to roast coffee beans back home for locals and for the fledgling tourist industry. In 1958 he set up Cafés Ibiza in a cave in the Barrio de la Marina neighbourhood of Ibiza Town.

While demand was good, supply was tricky. At that time, the Franco regime controlled imports, and Vicente was unable to buy enough green (unroasted) beans through legitimate channels. So he resorted to the black market, going out in a rowing boat at night to collect the beans from smugglers' ships. This went on until Franco's death in 1975.

Since 1986 the coffee-roasting facility and the warehouse have been located on the main road between Ibiza Town and Santa Eulalia, in Ca na Negreta, an industrial zone that is also home to a carpenter, an architect's office (Estudio Vila 13; see pp. 216–21) and other warehouses.

After Vicente died in 2003, his daughter Rosario Tur Planells took over the business. She had grown up on the island and studied economics at the University of Valencia. Nowadays, Cafés Ibiza has twenty staff. They work in the roasting area and the warehouse, deliver the roasted beans and ground coffee, and service the coffee machines that the company sells to local restaurants and hotels. As an additional service, Cafés Ibiza sells coffee-related items: sugar, milk, napkins and coffee cups. 'In the summer, we need a few more people because there is much more work', Rosario says.

While the main market is Ibiza, some coffee is exported to Switzerland, Germany, the UK, France, Austria, The Netherlands and mainland Spain. 'We feel like ambassadors for the island', says Rosario. 'It's very important for us to deliver top quality.'

The company's Italian roasting machine roasts 120 tonnes of coffee a year, using beans from long-standing suppliers in Brazil, Colombia and India. Its organic beans come from Honduras.

At the time of interview, Rosario was awaiting the arrival of a new roasting machine from Italy. 'With two machines, we'll be able to guarantee our output, even when demand is high.'

The firm's logo (coffee beans arranged in the shape of a flower) and packaging were designed in the 1960s by one of Vicente's friends, an artist. 'The branding is very original,' Rosario adds, 'and I like the way its bright colours stand out on supermarket shelves.' ***CD***

Rosario Tur Planells's father, Vicente Tur, established the Cafés Ibiza coffee-roasting company in 1958, on his return from working in Venezuela. Rosario has run the business since 2003.

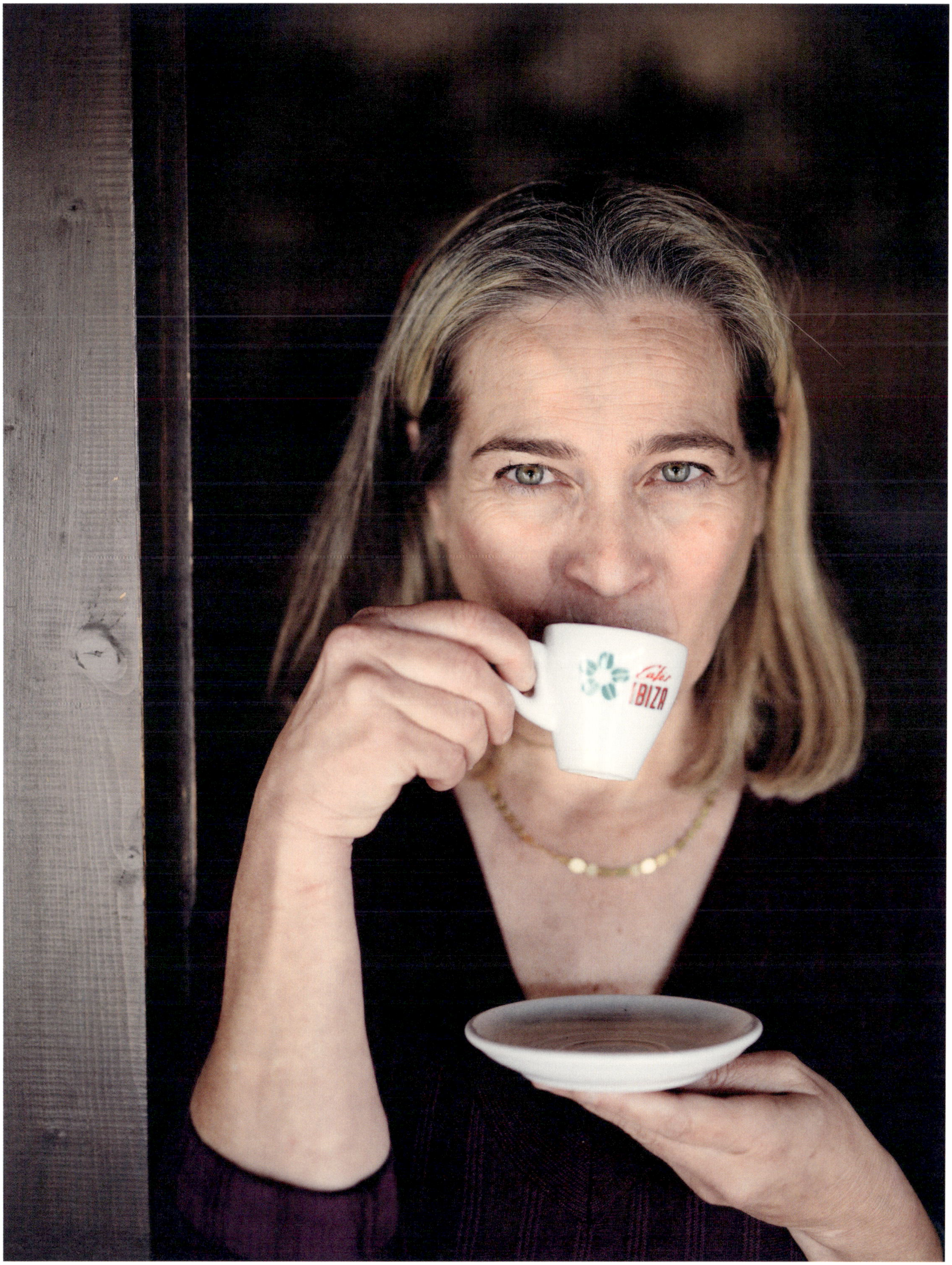

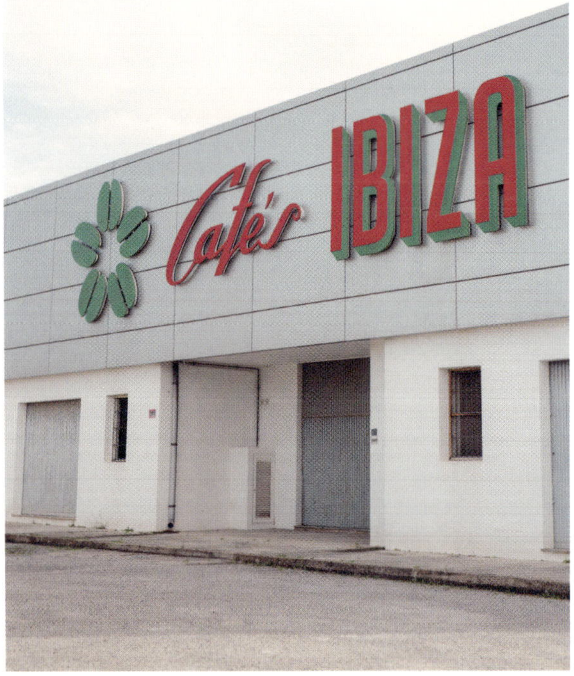

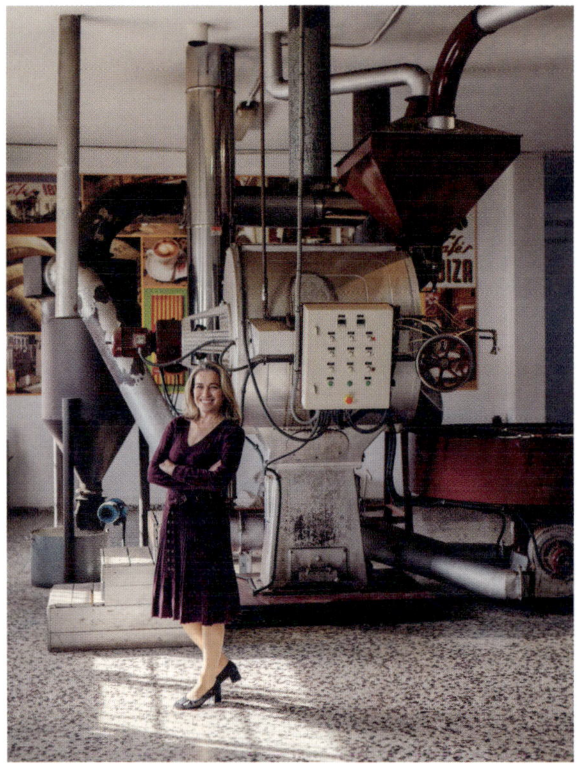

At the warehouse, in Ca na Negreta, the beans are roasted and packaged, then delivered to the island's shops, cafés, hotels and restaurants; some coffee is exported.

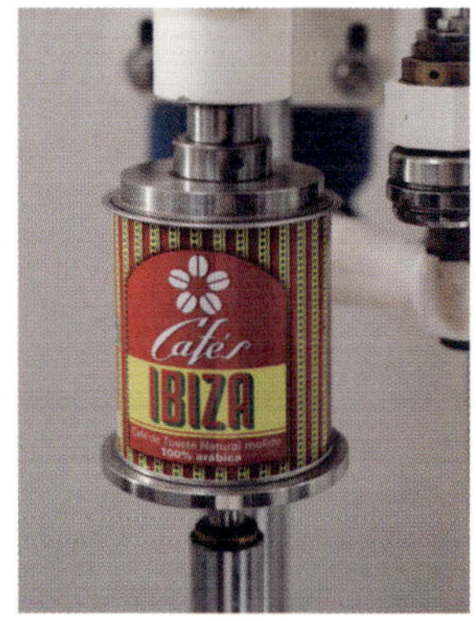

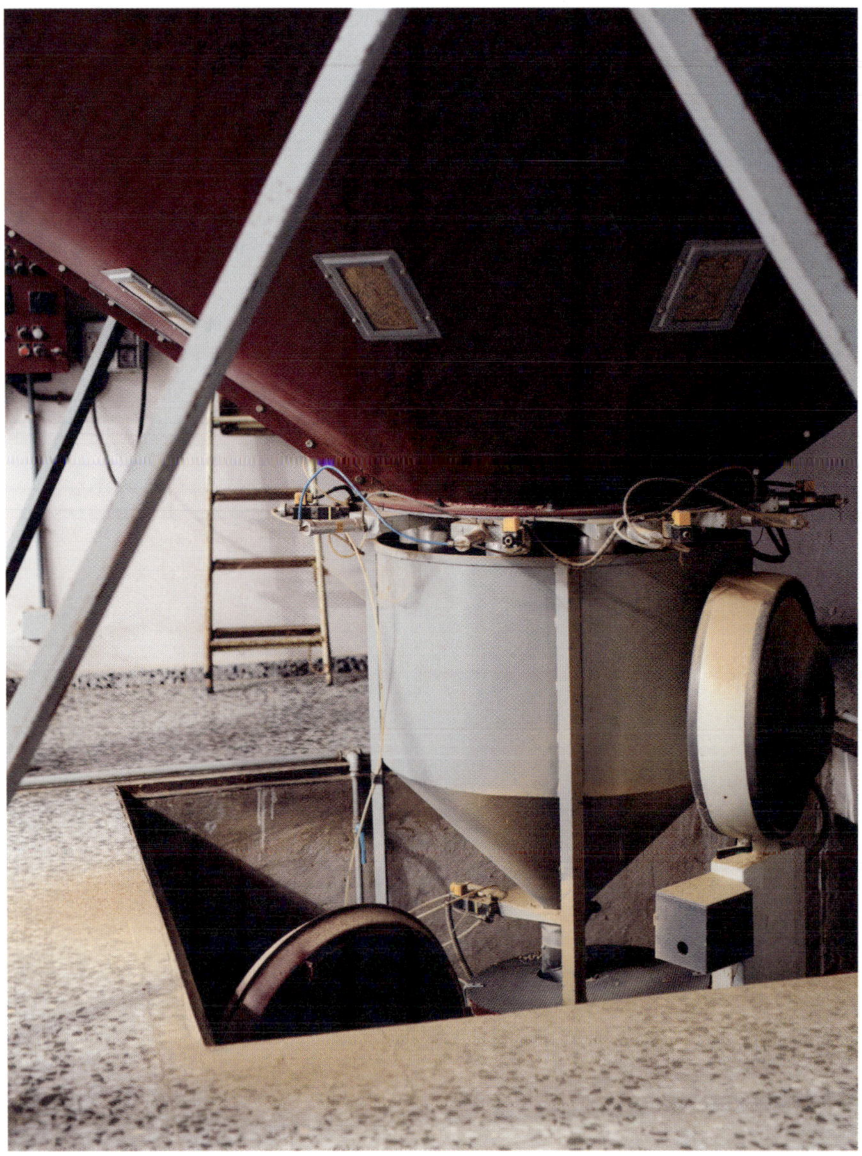

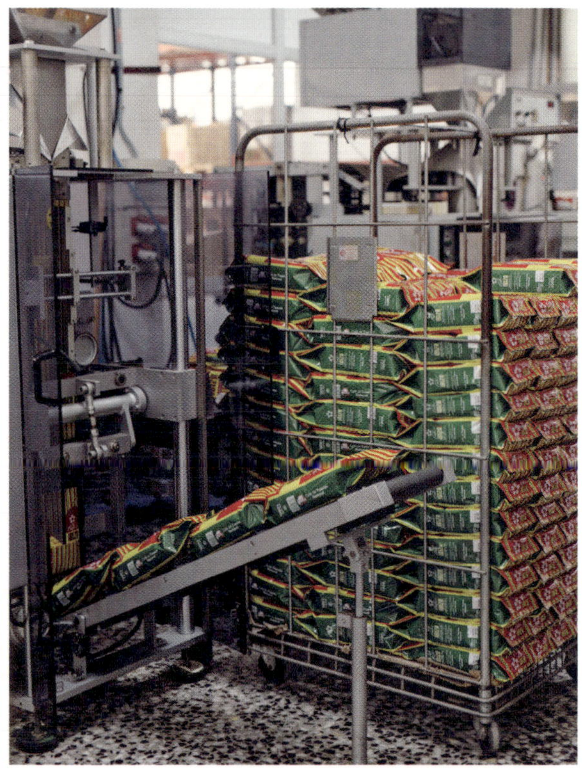

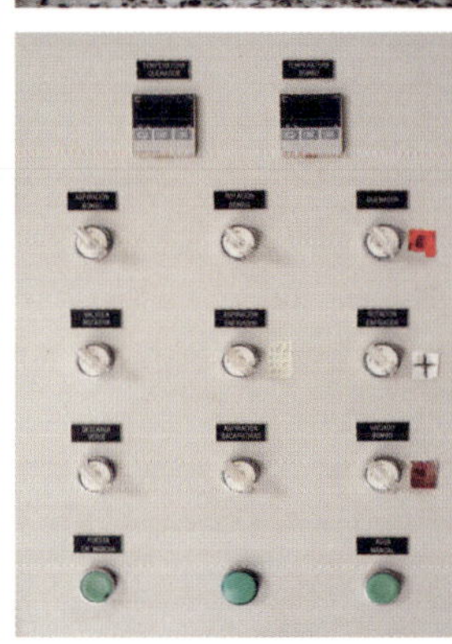

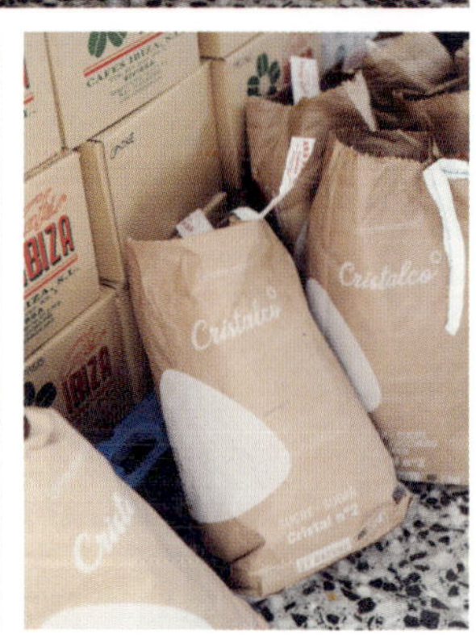

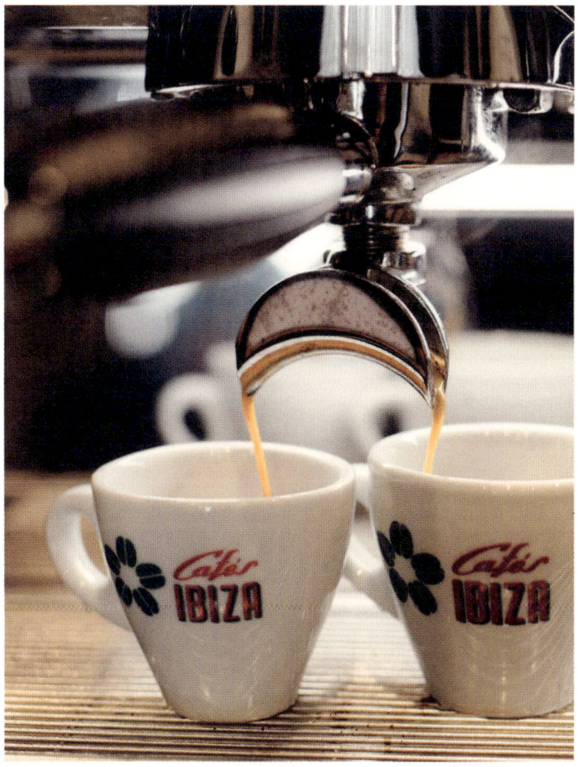

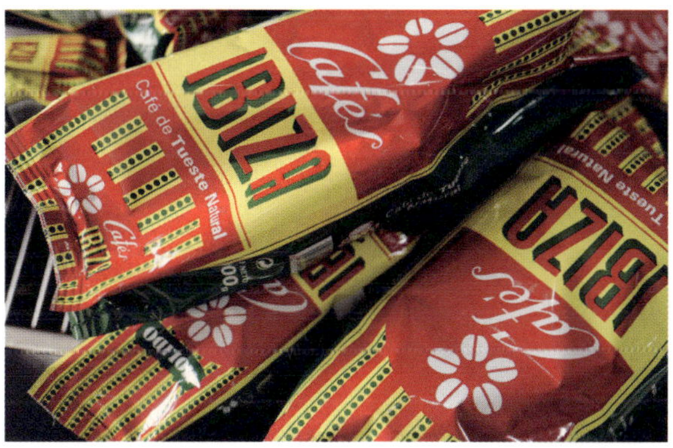

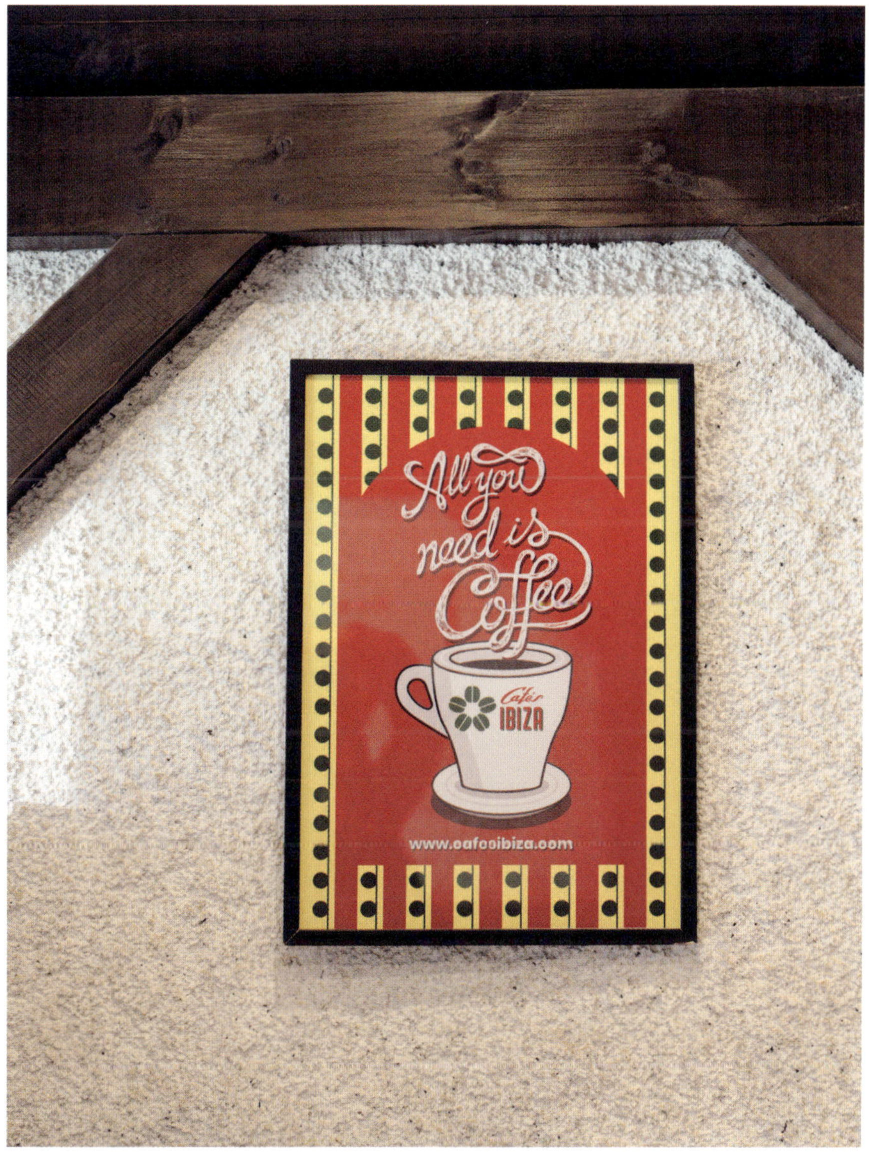

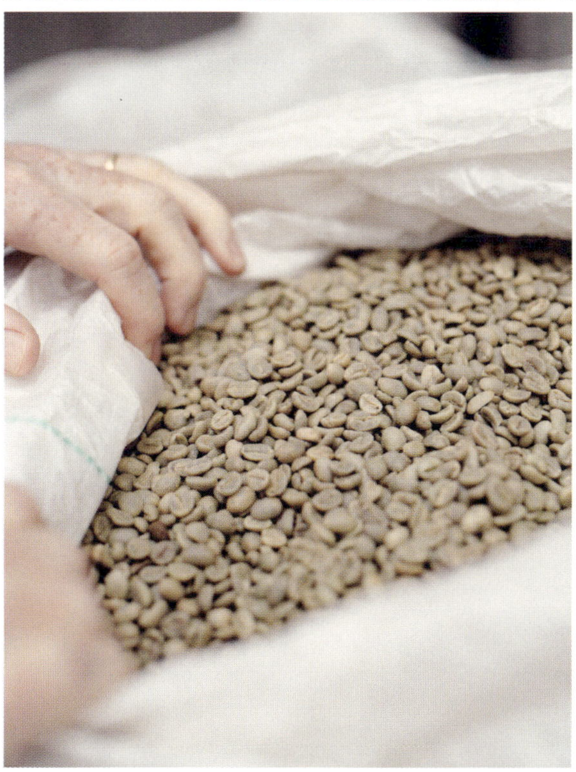

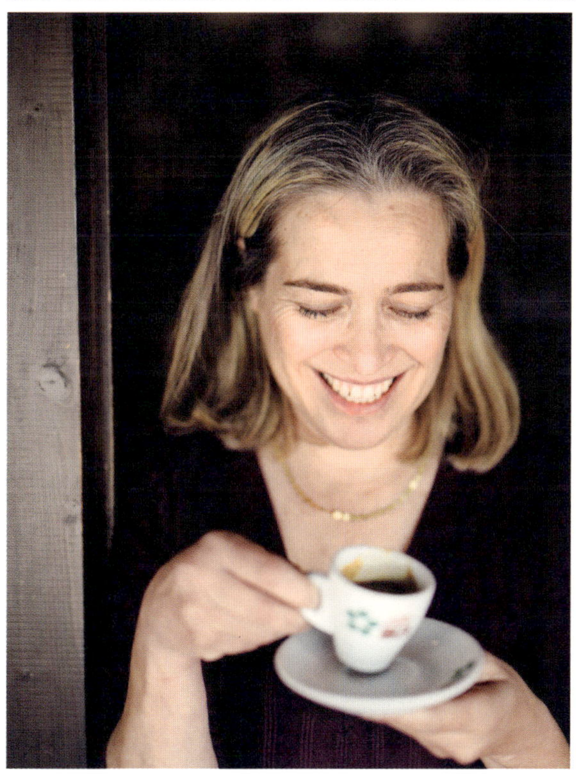

The Cafés Ibiza logo has remained the same since the 1960s. Its design – a simple flower formed by five coffee beans – was by an artist friend of Vicente's.

SAN MIGUEL

@thefarmibiza | @thefloralstudioibiza

THE FARM/ THE FLORAL STUDIO

SUSTAINABLE AGRICULTURE & FLOWER FARM

Staked into the side of a road between the villages of San Miguel and San Mateo, a small sign points to 'flowers and vegetables'. Follow the dirt path a little further and you will find both types of crop in abundance at The Farm. It is also home to the ever-budding love story between Alonso Colmenares and Francesca Munizaga.

'We came here first, then the farm appeared', says Alonso, a Madrileño who took his first trip to Ibiza in 1997, when he was working as a broker in London. 'I used to have a lot of fun partying, but then I bought a ruin in San Agustín for only €25,000. I fixed it up and immediately got a sense of what Ibiza is really like.' Francesca had also landed on the island, after zigzagging across the globe during a frenetic stint in the music industry. 'I was all over the place,' she recalls, 'constantly travelling, but never enjoying places.'

Everything changed when the two met. Love led to the birth of twins. A nineteenth-century colonial-style farmhouse became the family home, then the hybrid headquarters of a spirited vision for regenerative agriculture. 'Living here made us see our connection points with nature more clearly', explains Alonso. 'We see the sunrise and the sunset every day. When I'm in Madrid, the buildings obscure the view.'

Larger aspirations have taken root. The couple's project The Farmers Club is striving to improve the way islanders consume fresh produce as well as their most precious resource, water. Freshly grown herbs and vegetables are delivered to some of Ibiza's best restaurants. An ambitious, 500-strong pomegranate grove is now bearing fruit. This is all part of a 'big-picture' vision for permaculture, pushed into action by a consulting service for other farms. The aim is to regenerate 3 per cent of the island's 'zero-arable' land by 2030. 'I don't particularly like the "look at me", show-off part,' admits Alonso, 'but communicating milestones is important, especially when you're trying to transform a place.'

While Alonso continues to divide his time between island farming and an advertising consultancy in Madrid, Francesca has been perfecting her own home-grown art form with her floristry business The Floral Studio. Cultivating flowers and creating exquisite arrangements has been a grounding experience, one that Francesca describes with an almost transcendental allure. 'I always say that you must be able to root before you can bloom. It's a sort of therapy when you touch the soil. You put your hands on the soil to disconnect from all your worries and stresses. Touching the soil also enables us to connect with who we truly are – part of the earth – even though sometimes we're led to believe that we are separate from the plants and animals.'

The couple are true believers in the persuasive power of nature to quell the relentless urges of urban life. 'Nature slows you down', says Alonso. 'You see how the garden grows, how the seasons change, how the rain brings joy. But stopping isn't about relaxing', he adds with a loud laugh, admitting that he rarely relaxes. 'Stopping is more about keeping your head down and your vision clear. It's this sort of connection that fuels real preservation efforts.'

While the land has a way of bowing people to its will, this couple meet these natural forces halfway, leaving the scions of a more sustainable future in their wake. ***LA***

Alonso Colmenares and Francesca Munizaga made the transition from metropolitans to ambitious eco-farmers, and soil care has become the central pillar of their regenerative vision.

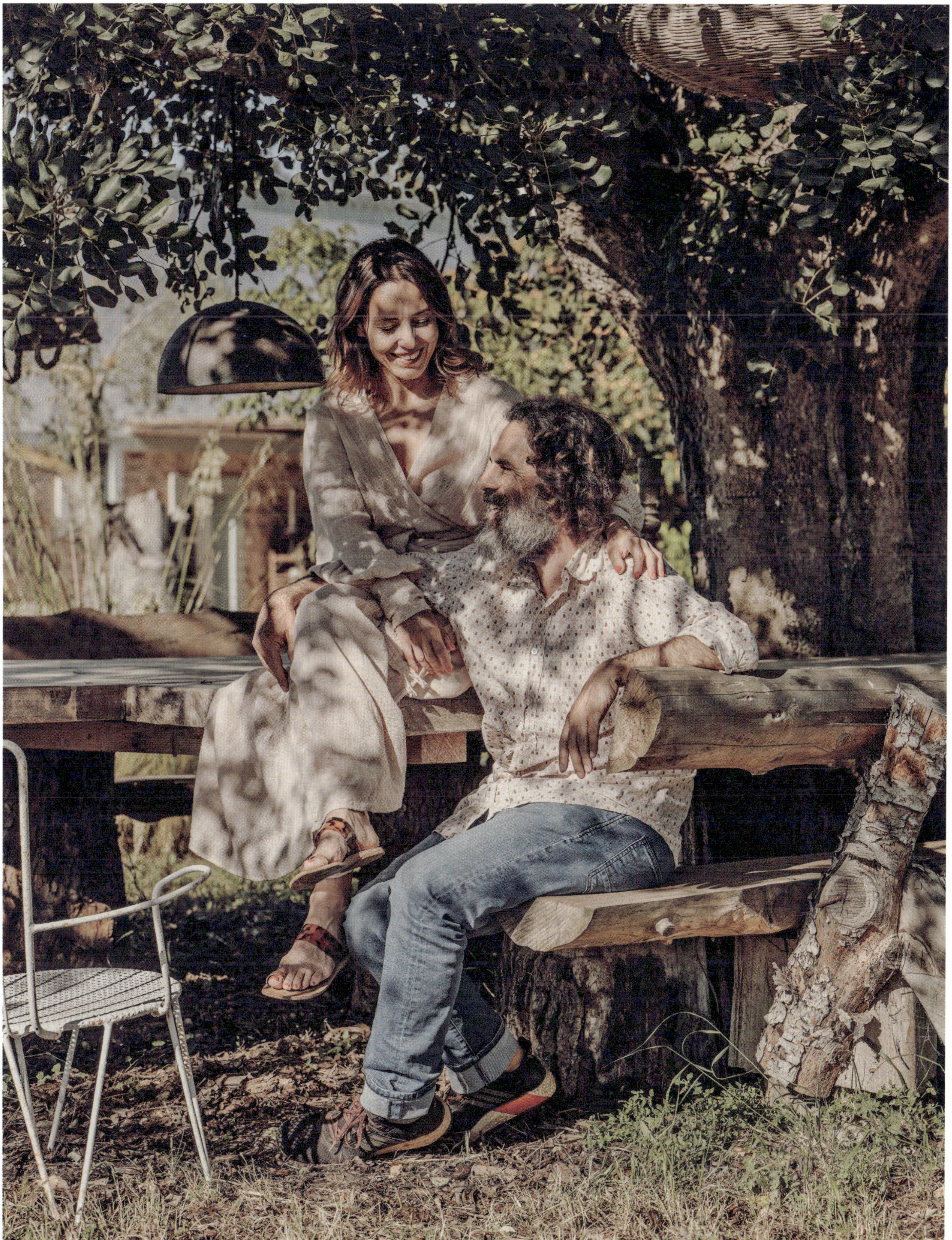

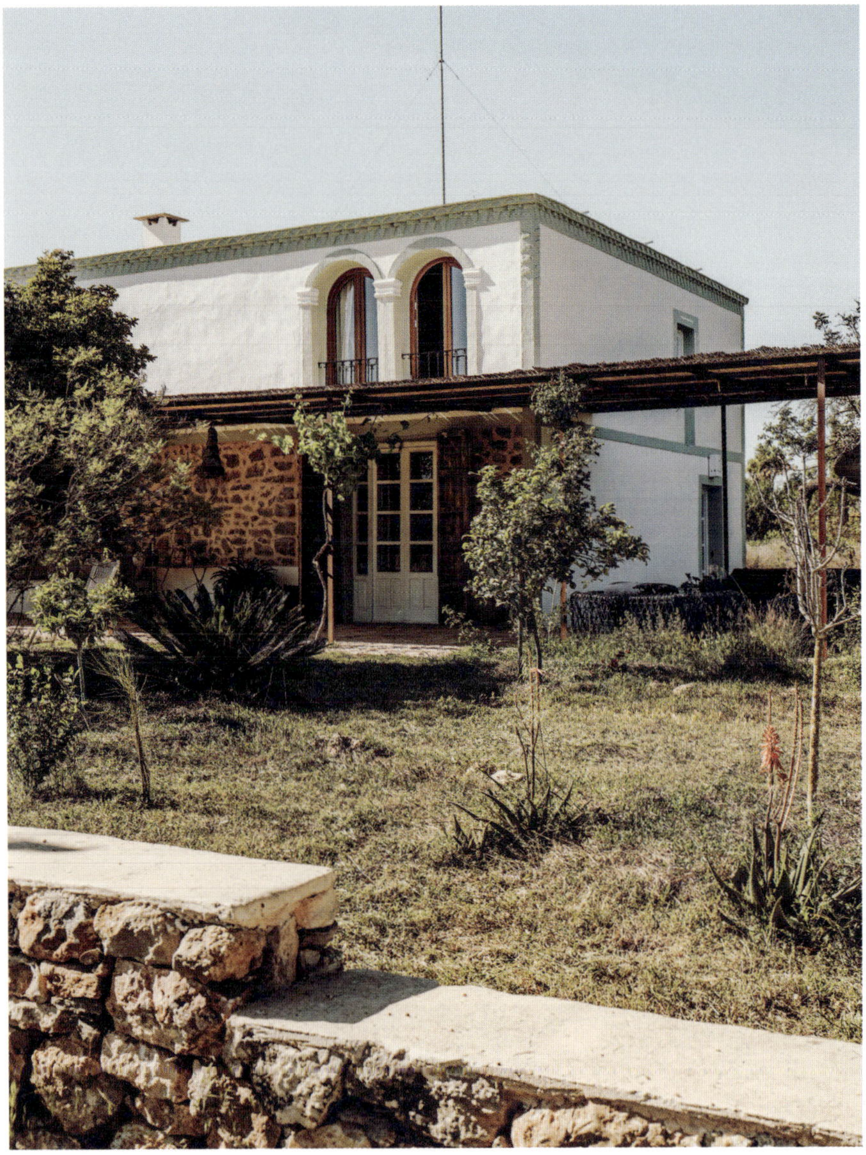

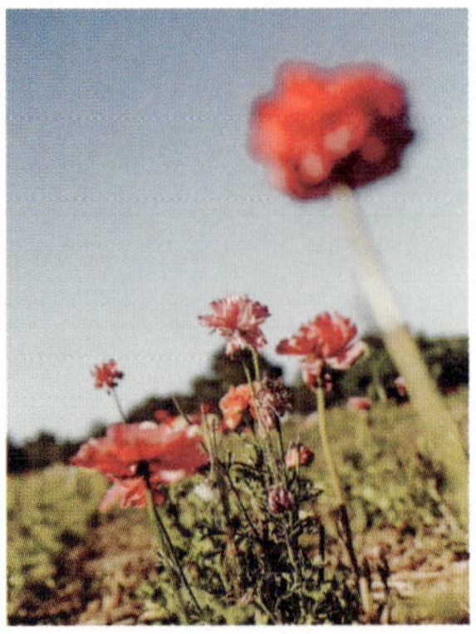

Far left: The nineteenth-century house features smooth white stucco and round-arched windows, a vernacular popularized by colonists returning from Latin America.

Bottom right: A portrait of Alonso dressed as Che Guevara, from Sandra de Keller's Renault 4 Life series (see pp. 82–85).

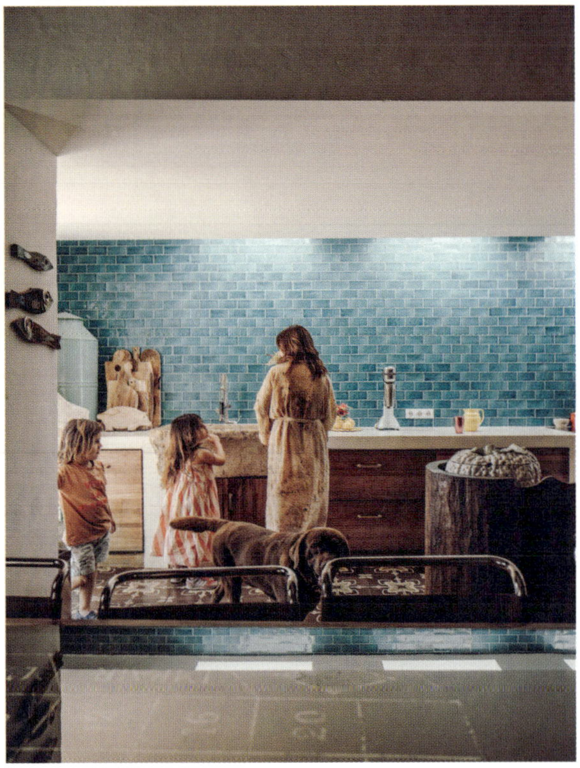

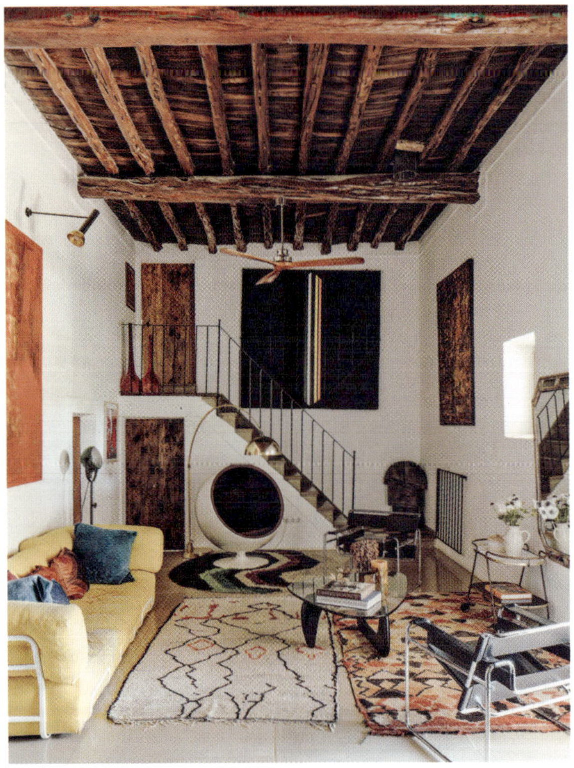

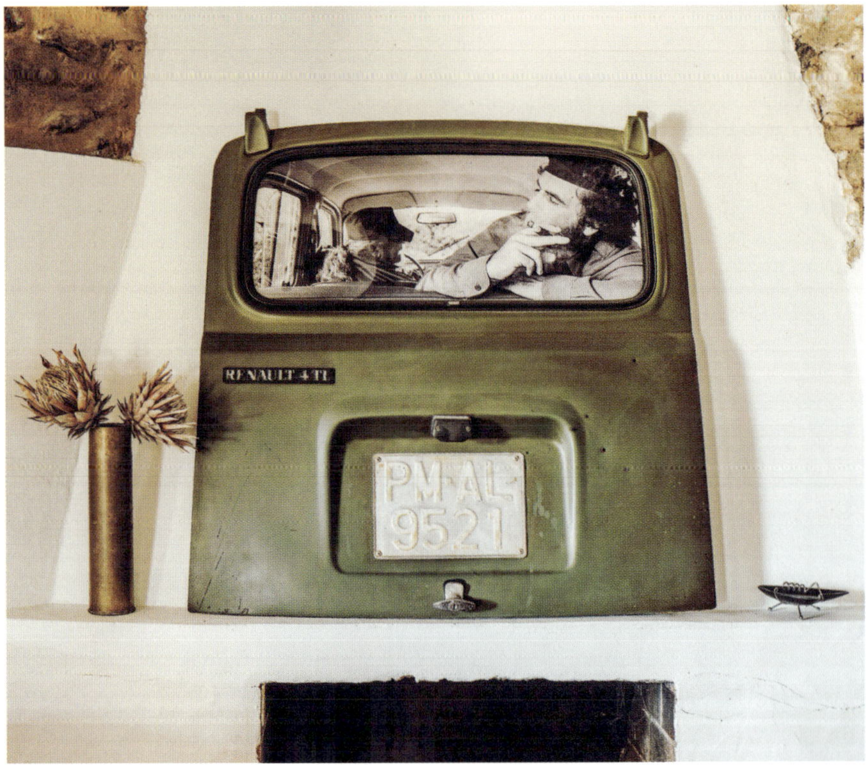

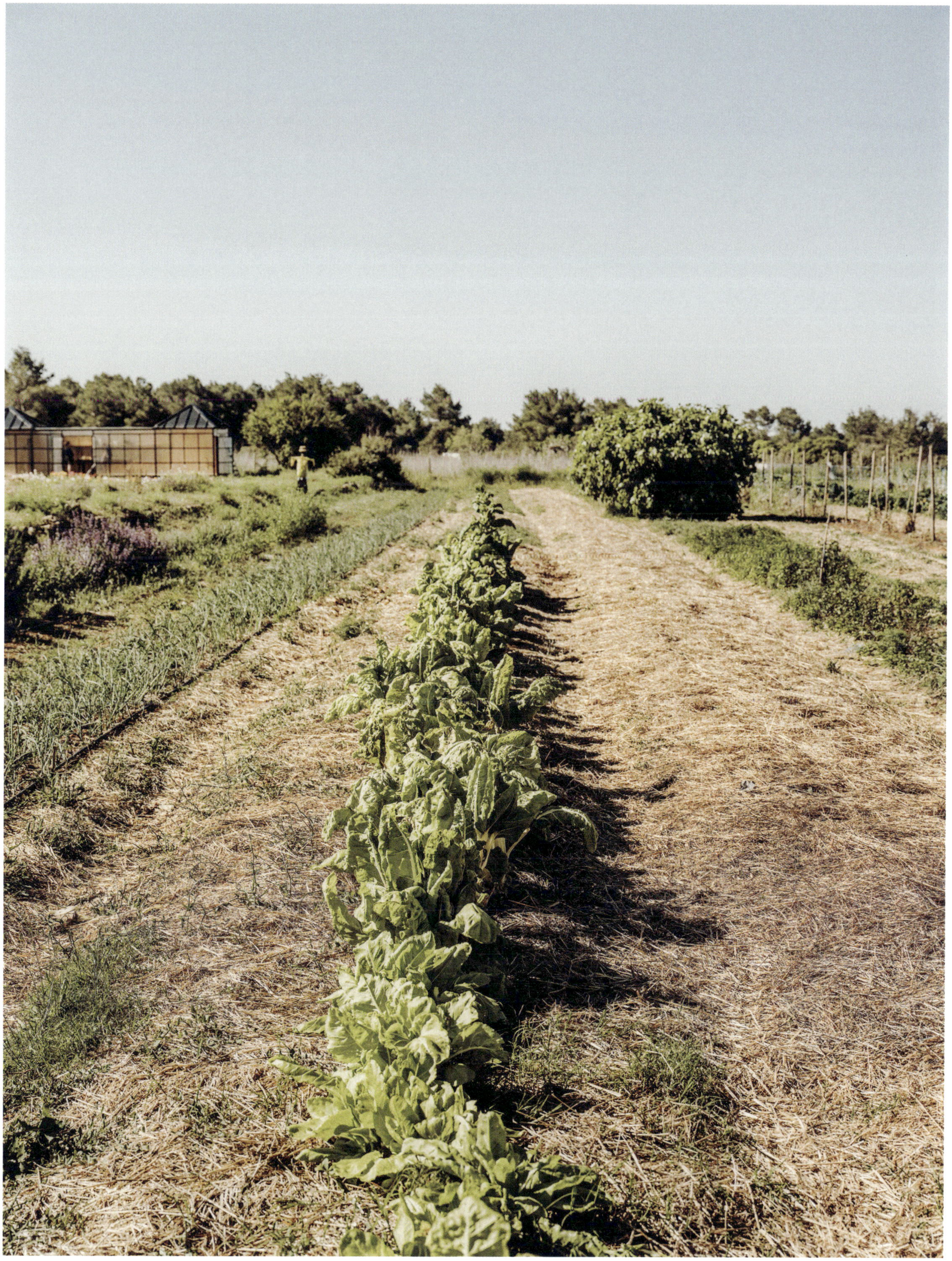

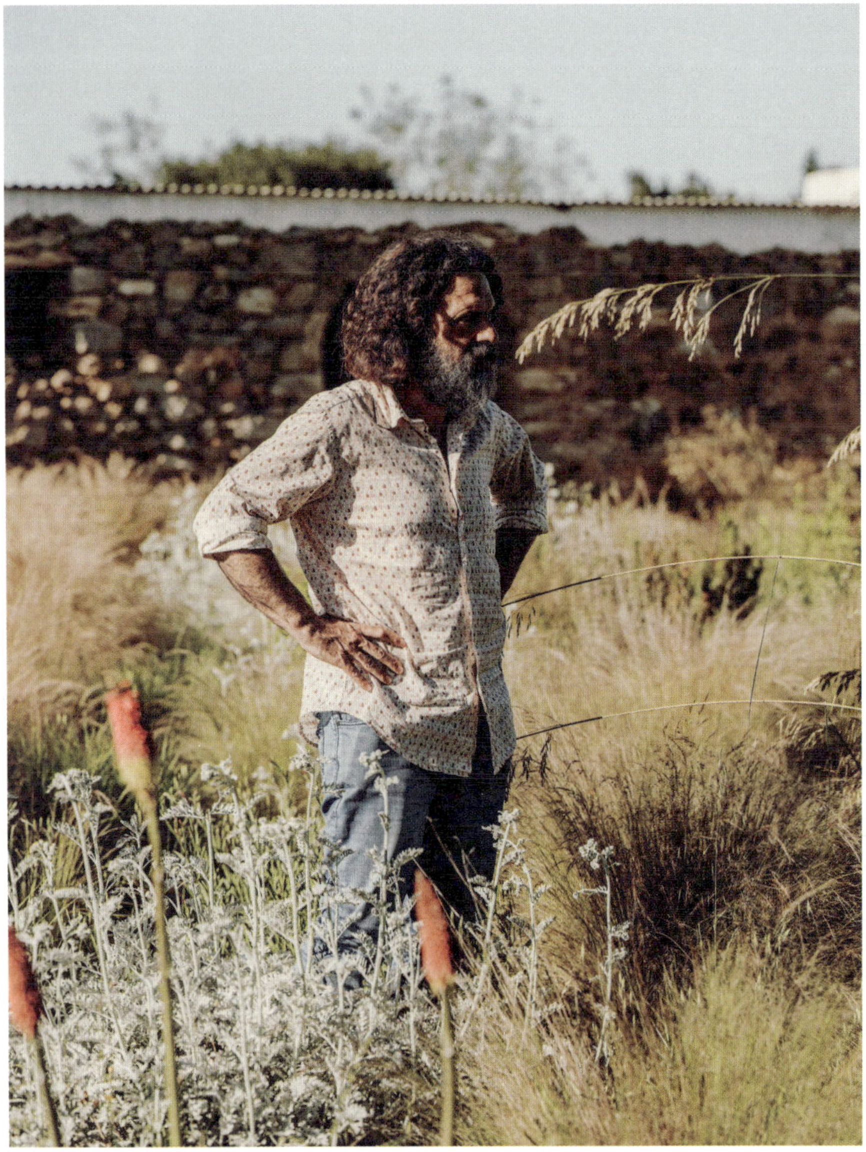

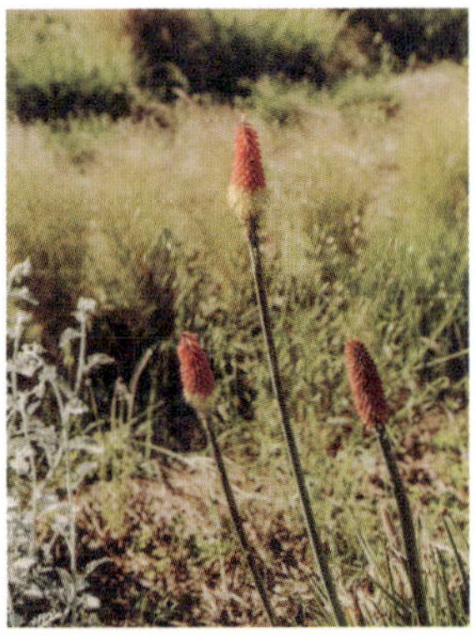

Alonso grows and sells high-quality farm produce while actively promoting a 'buy local' culture. He planted over 500 pomegranate trees as part of an effort to revive the island's agricultural ecosystem.

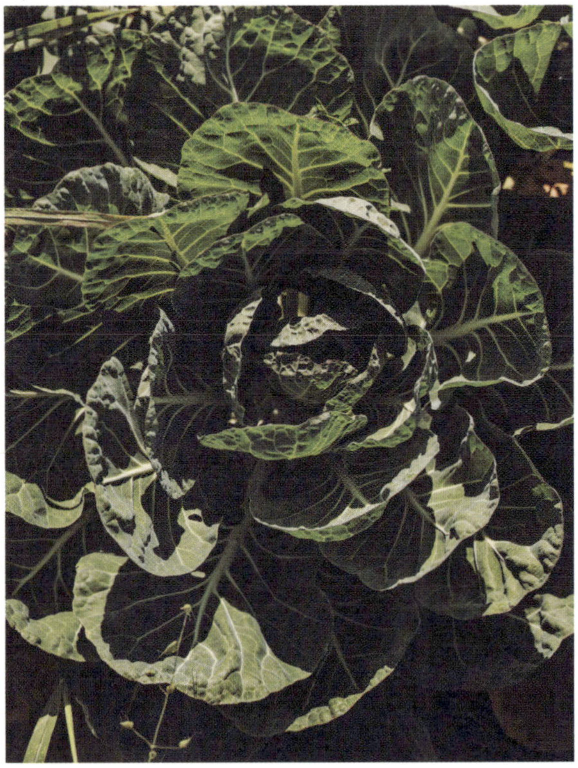

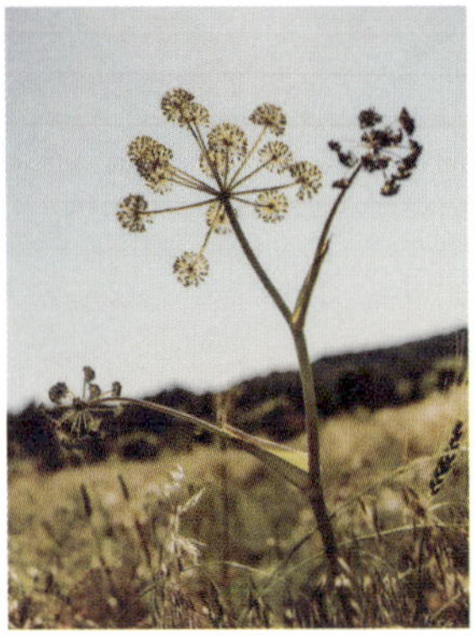

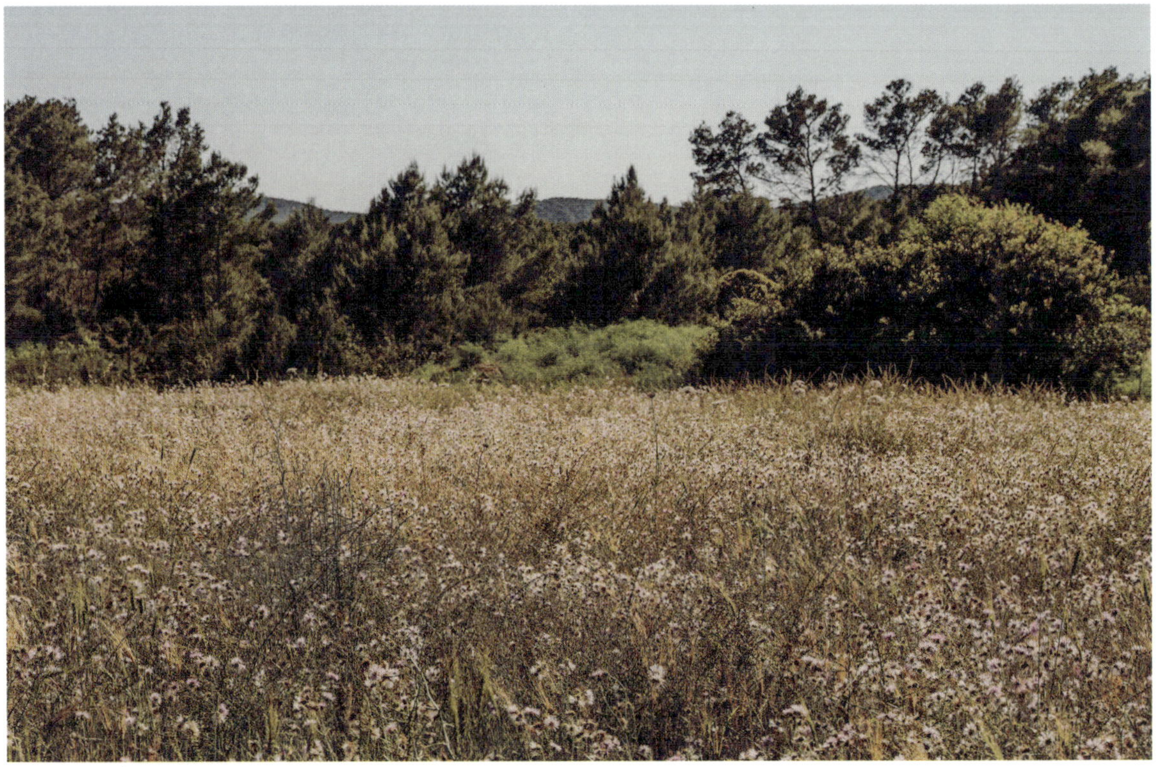

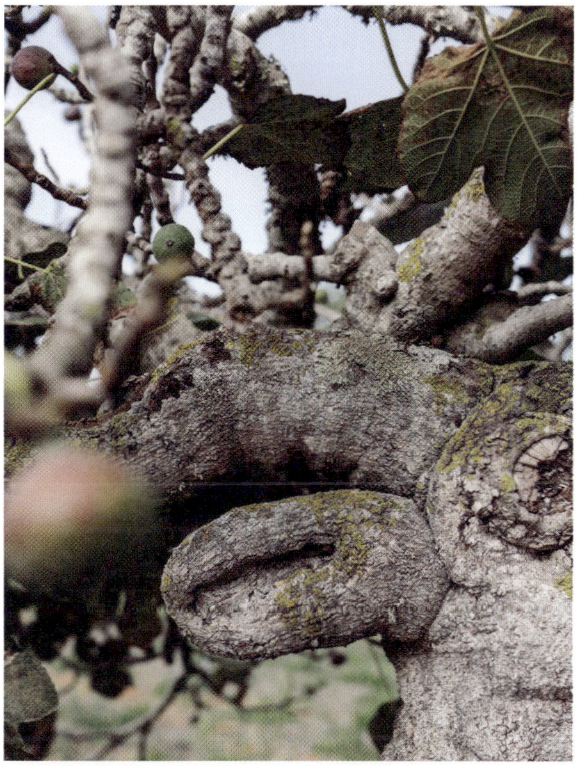

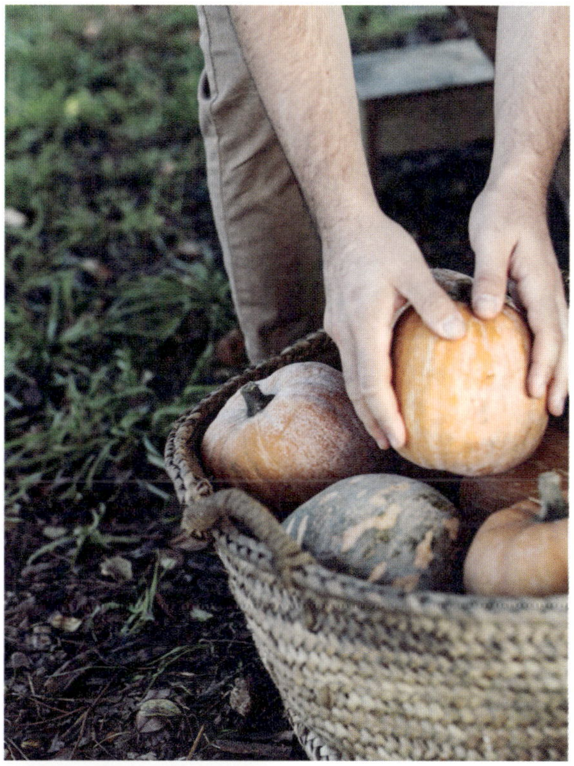

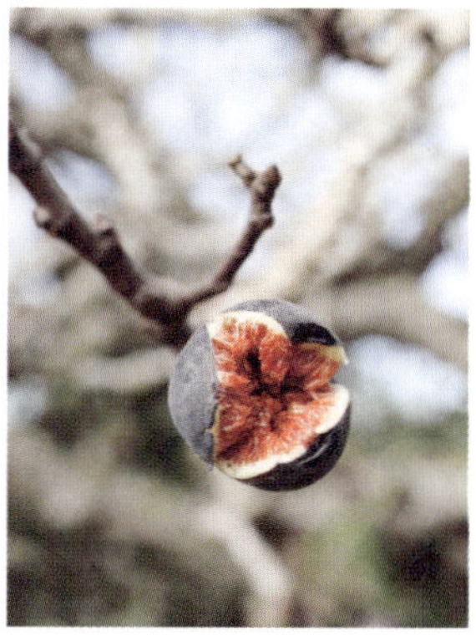

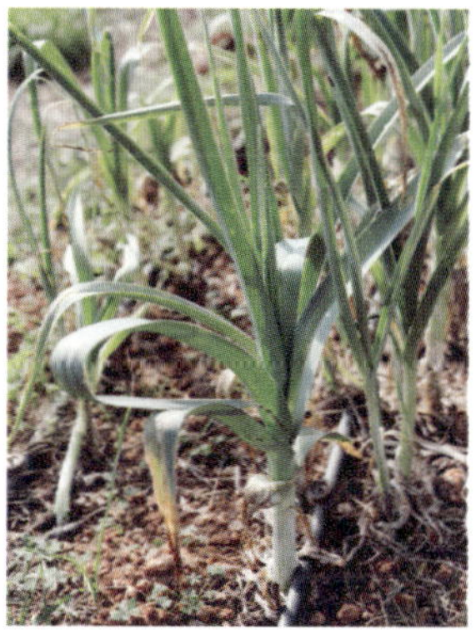

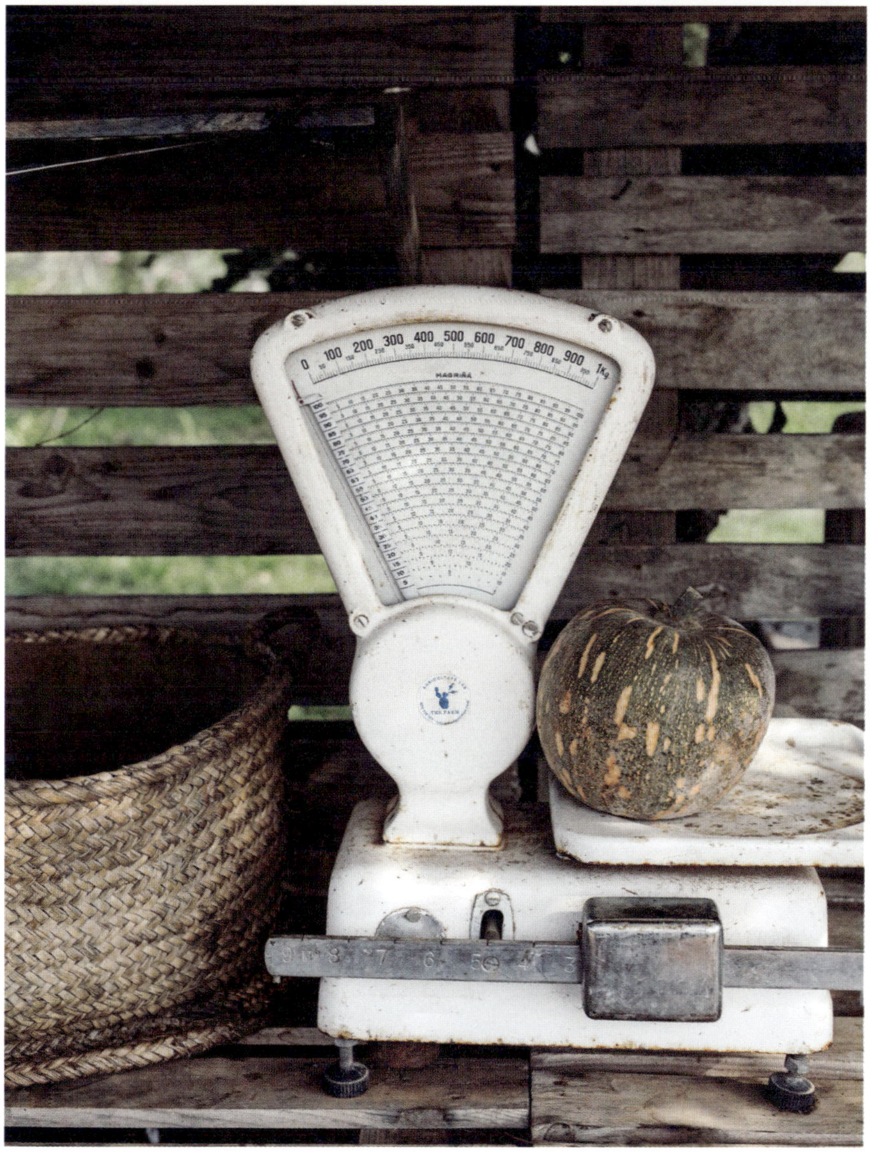
0 100 200 300 400 500 600 700 800 900 1kg

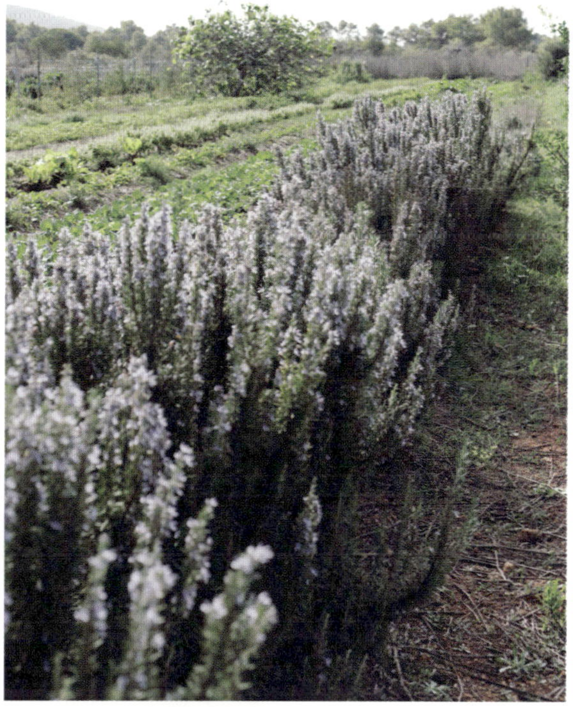

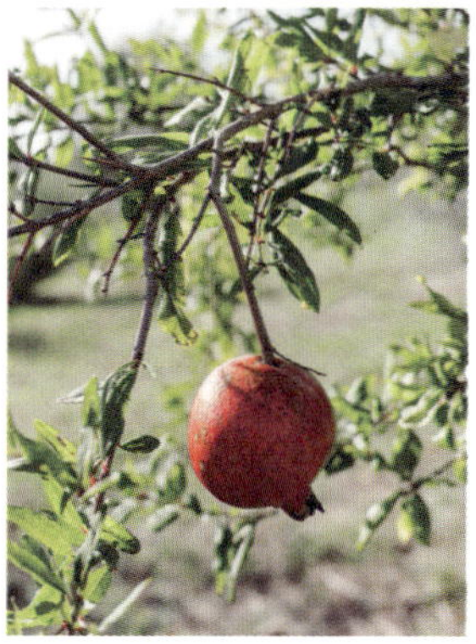

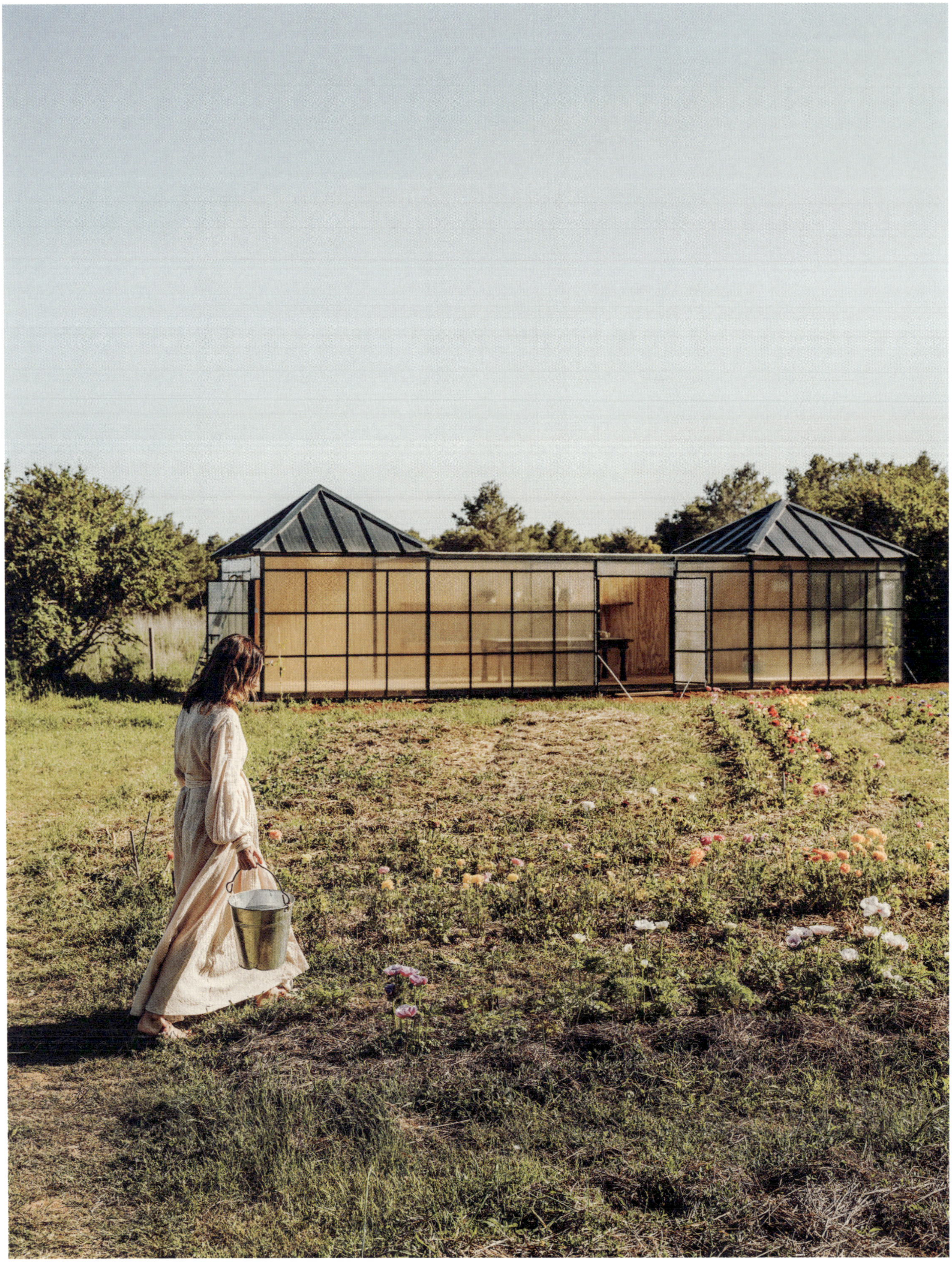

Francesca creates bespoke floral arrangements for restaurants and for events such as weddings. All flowers are grown on the farm. In the middle of the colourful, abundant flower beds, the greenhouse doubles as an atelier.

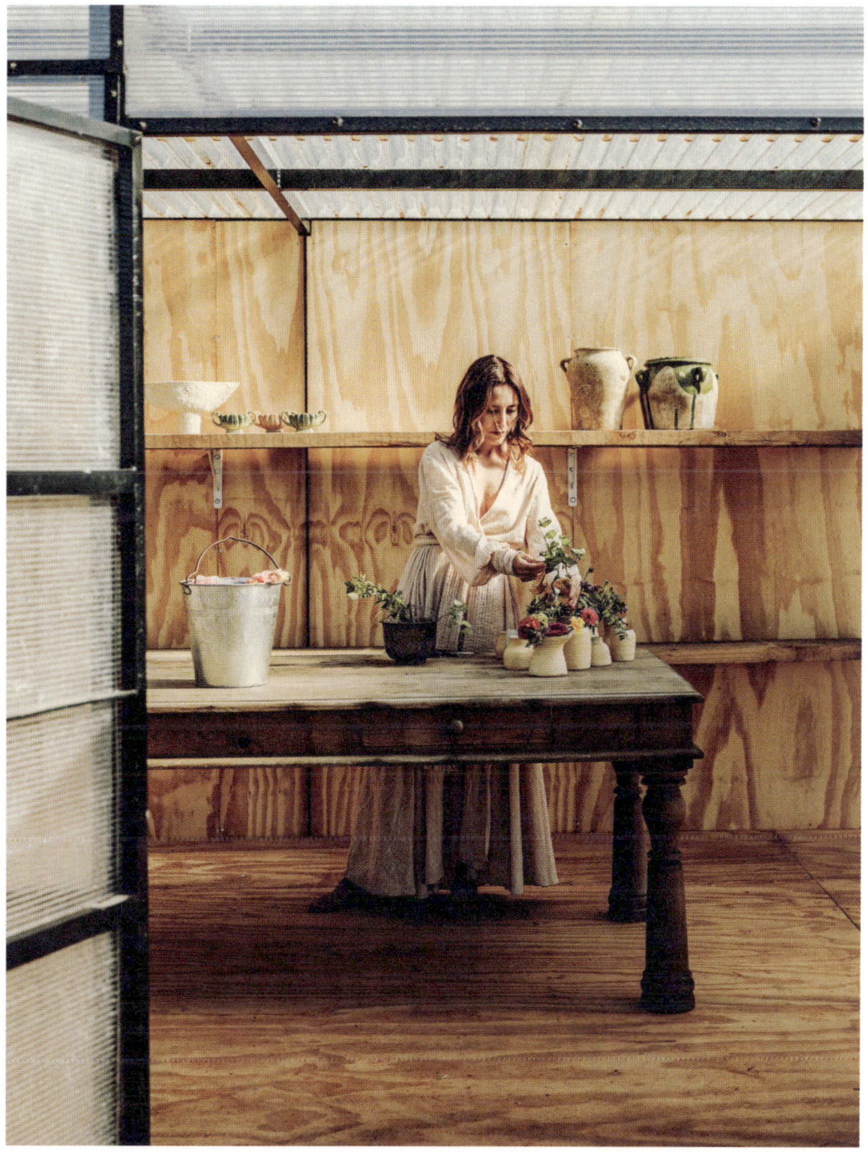

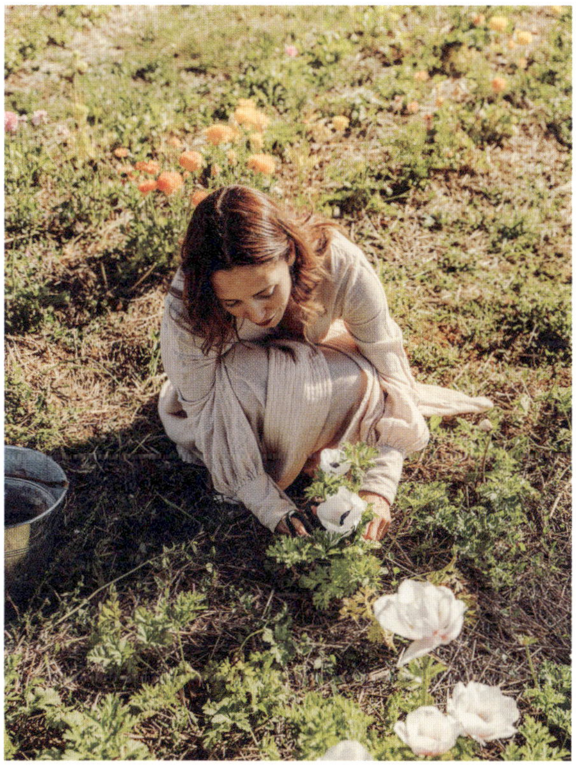

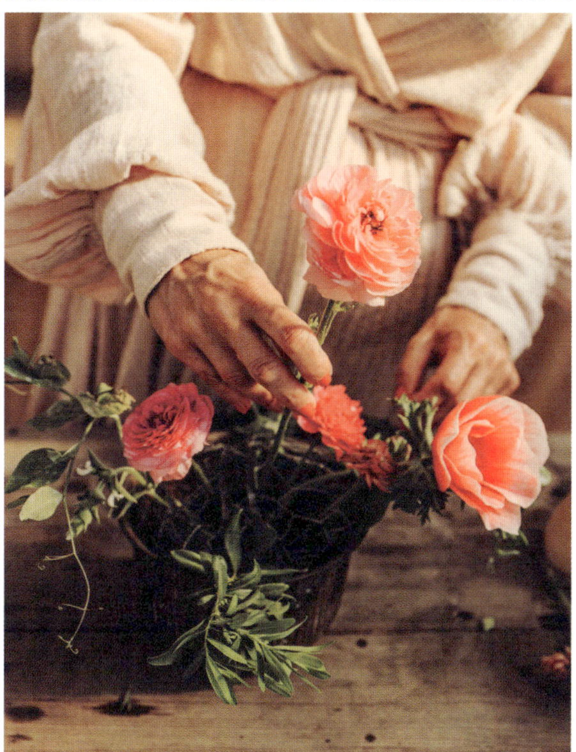

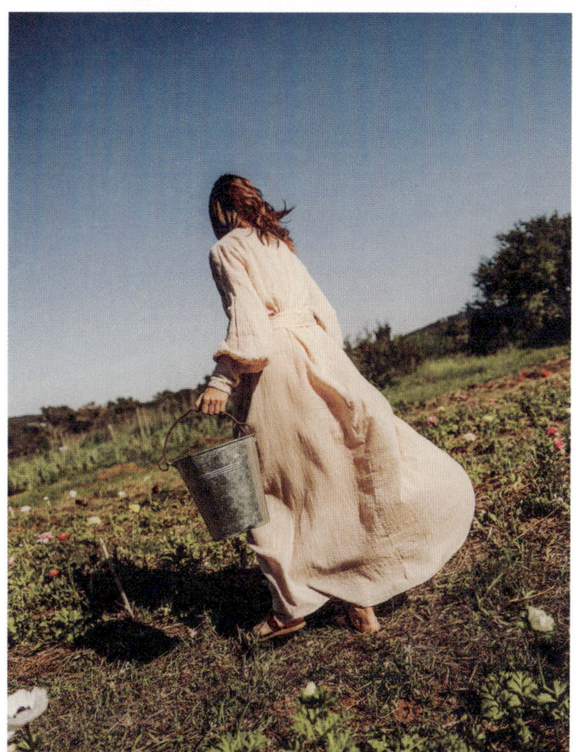

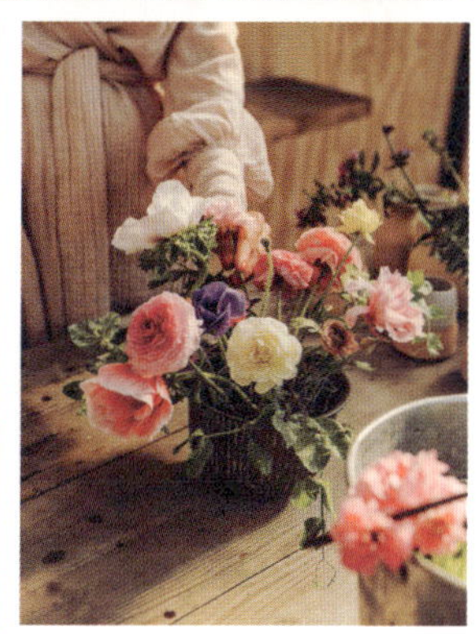

SAN ANTONIO
@sescabretes

SES CABRETES

GOAT FARM & CHEESE PRODUCTION

The pastures of Ses Cabretes are scattered with benches and wooden platforms – climbing equipment for the 120 goats owned by Pilar González and Fina Prats.

From their goats' milk, the two women make *queso payés* (farmhouse cheese), which they sell to the island's shops and restaurants, including the renowned Es Ventall in San Antonio. Some meat is also sold to restaurants.

Pilar, a vet from Cordoba, came to Ibiza with her husband when he got a job here after the 2008 economic crisis. Ibizan-born Fina returned to the island after studying environmental sciences in Gerona, Catalonia.

In 2012 the Ibizan government, the Consell Insular d'Eivissa, launched an initiative with the European Union to support rural development. Part of the initiative was focused on the island's many small goat farms, with the aim of commercializing both the farms and cheese production. Pilar and Fina met through the initiative, having been employed as vet and livestock-keeper respectively. They decided to set up their own goat farm and cheese production, Ses Cabretes (meaning 'little goats'), to make cheese in the traditional Ibizan way.

Four years later, the pair moved to their current address – a bigger farm in the countryside near San Antonio – and quadrupled their number of goats to 120.

The goats are milked by machine every day. 'They've got used to it, and they make their own way to the machine when they see us arrive in the morning', Pilar says. The output of milk varies widely, but on good days it is around 140 litres.

Initially, Pilar and Fina sent their milk to local cheesemakers based in farmhouses, 'but the batches varied too much', Pilar says. So now they make their cheese in a production facility that they set up with help from the Consell d'Eivissa in the industrial zone Blanca Dona, near Ibiza Town. 'The cheese is still made using artisanal techniques, but with a more standardized production, which means basically that the humidity and temperature are stable', explains Fina.

After the milk has been pasteurized, fermenting agents and then plant-based rennet are added. The rennet is made in the traditional Ibizan way, from water and the dried flowers of wild artichokes. This gives the cheese its distinct aroma. Cheesemaking is a process with many steps, ending with maturation, which takes 10 to 20 days for the semi-soft (*tierno*) variety, 20 to 40 days for medium-hard (*semi-curado*) and more than 40 days for matured (*curado*). Six litres of milk result in around 1 kilogram of cheese.

To learn how to improve the production process, Pilar attended courses in Santander and Cordoba. The two women have also been on a course in France to learn how to make blue cheese, with a view to expanding their product list in the future. They also plan to teach cheesemaking classes. ***CD***

Using artisanal techniques, Fina Prats (opposite) and Pilar González produce a range of cheeses from the milk of their Murciana goats, which live on their farm near San Antonio.

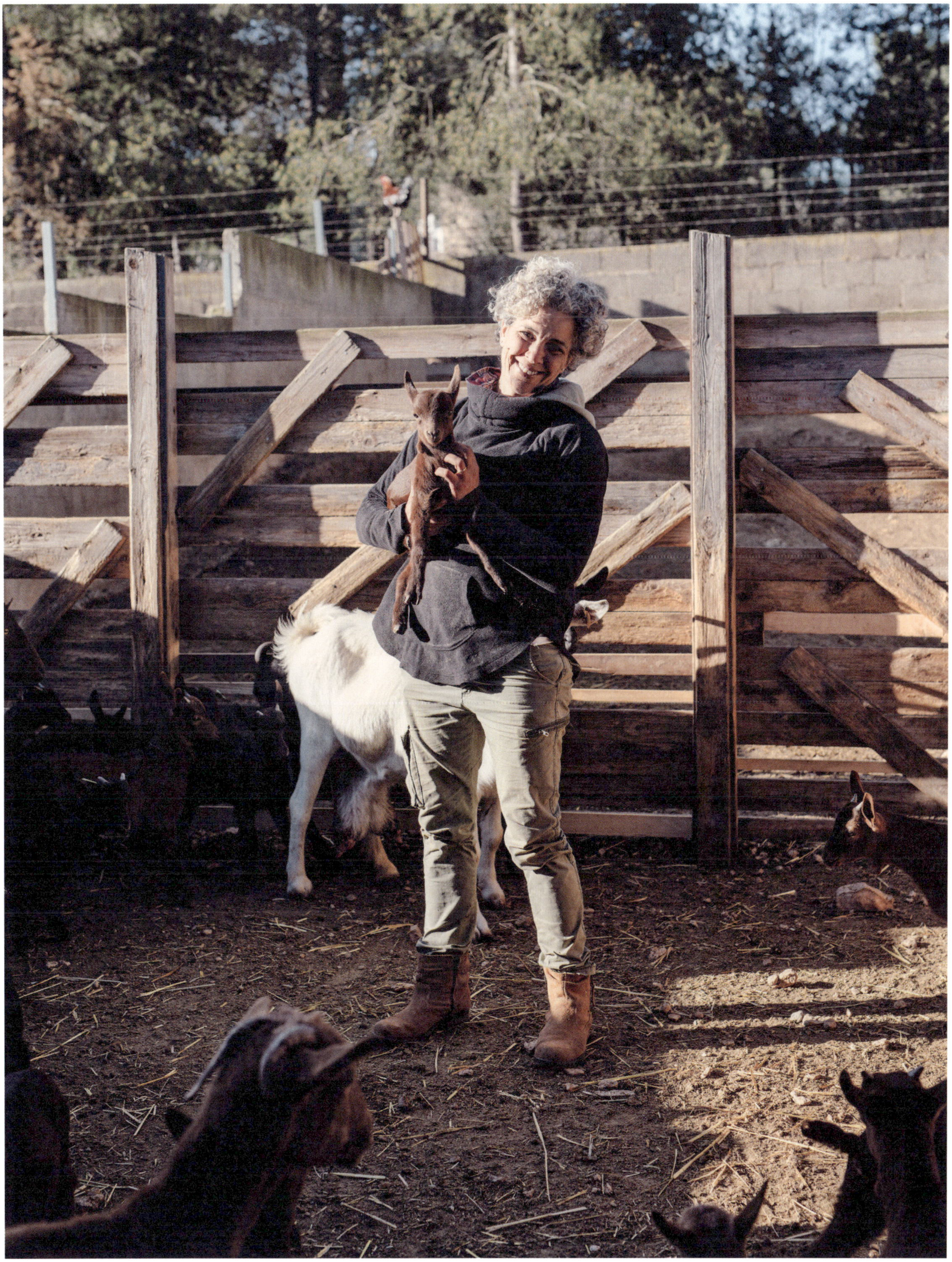

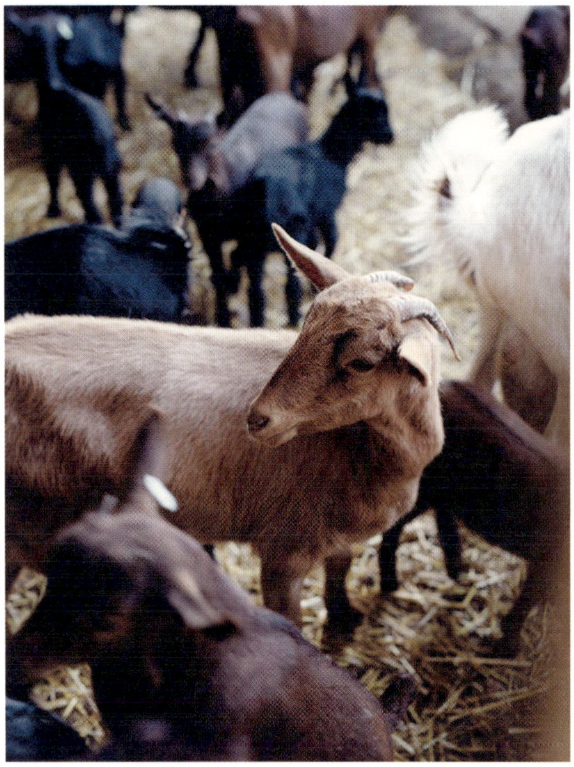

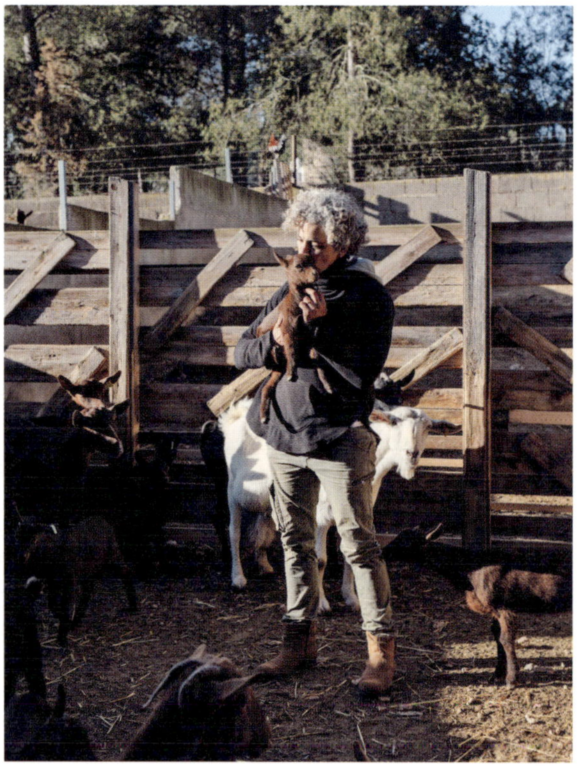

The goats spend ten to fifteen minutes a day at the milking machine. On a good day, they can produce up to 140 litres of milk, and it takes 6 litres to make 1 kilogram of cheese.

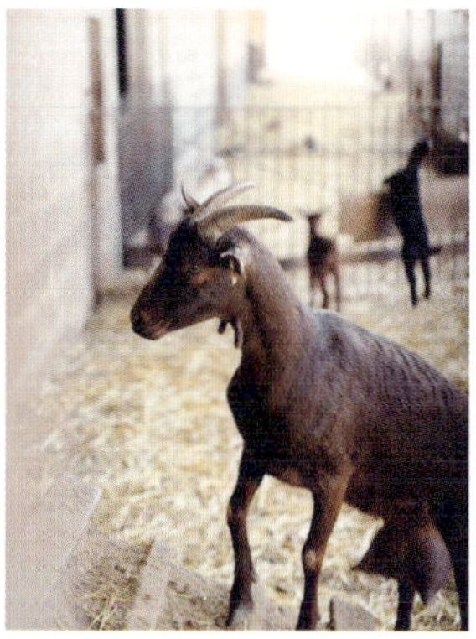

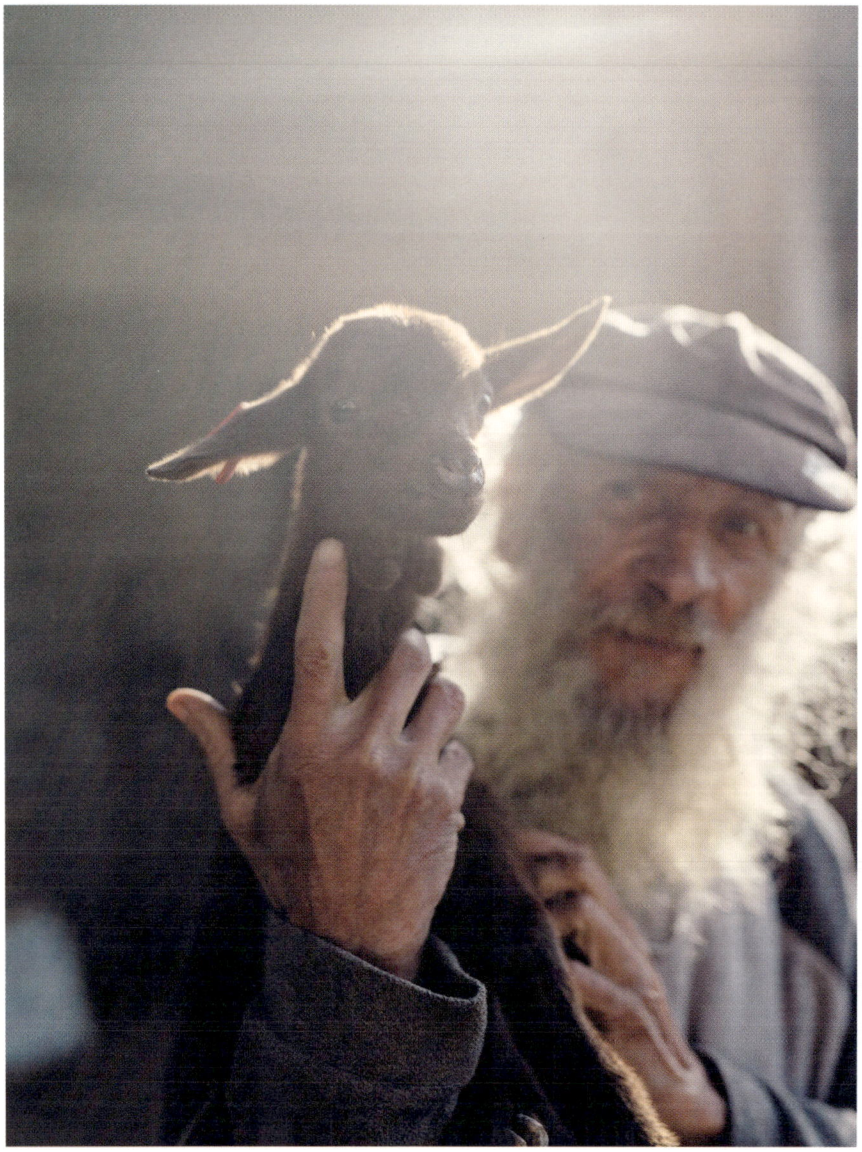

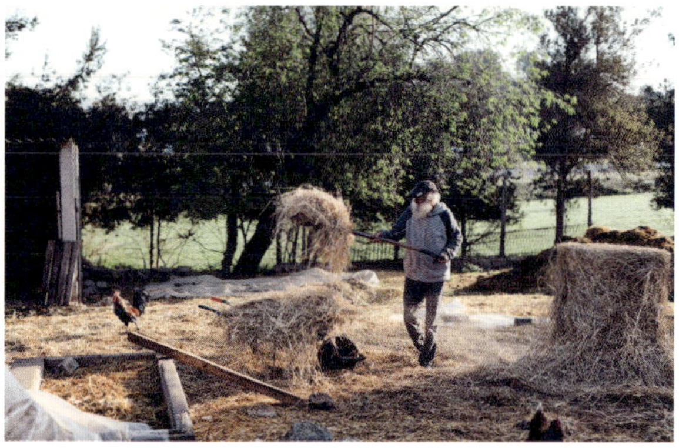

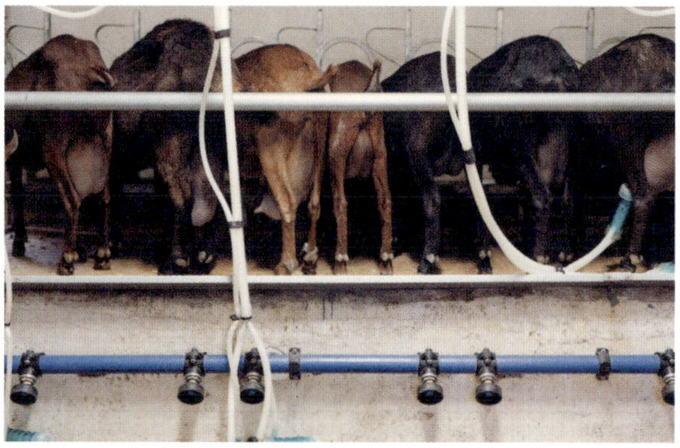

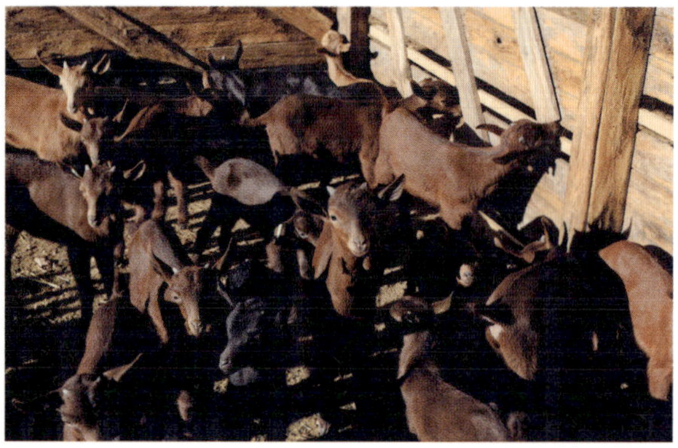

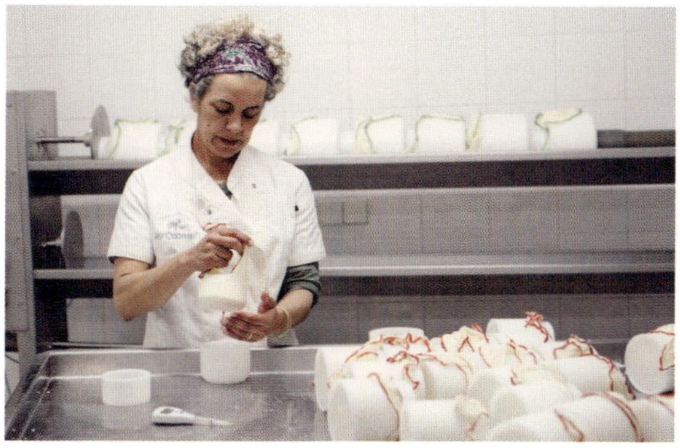

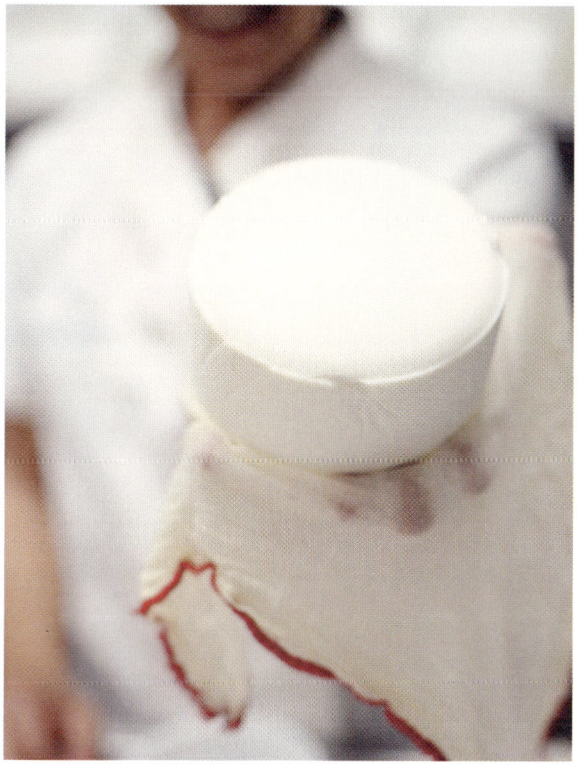

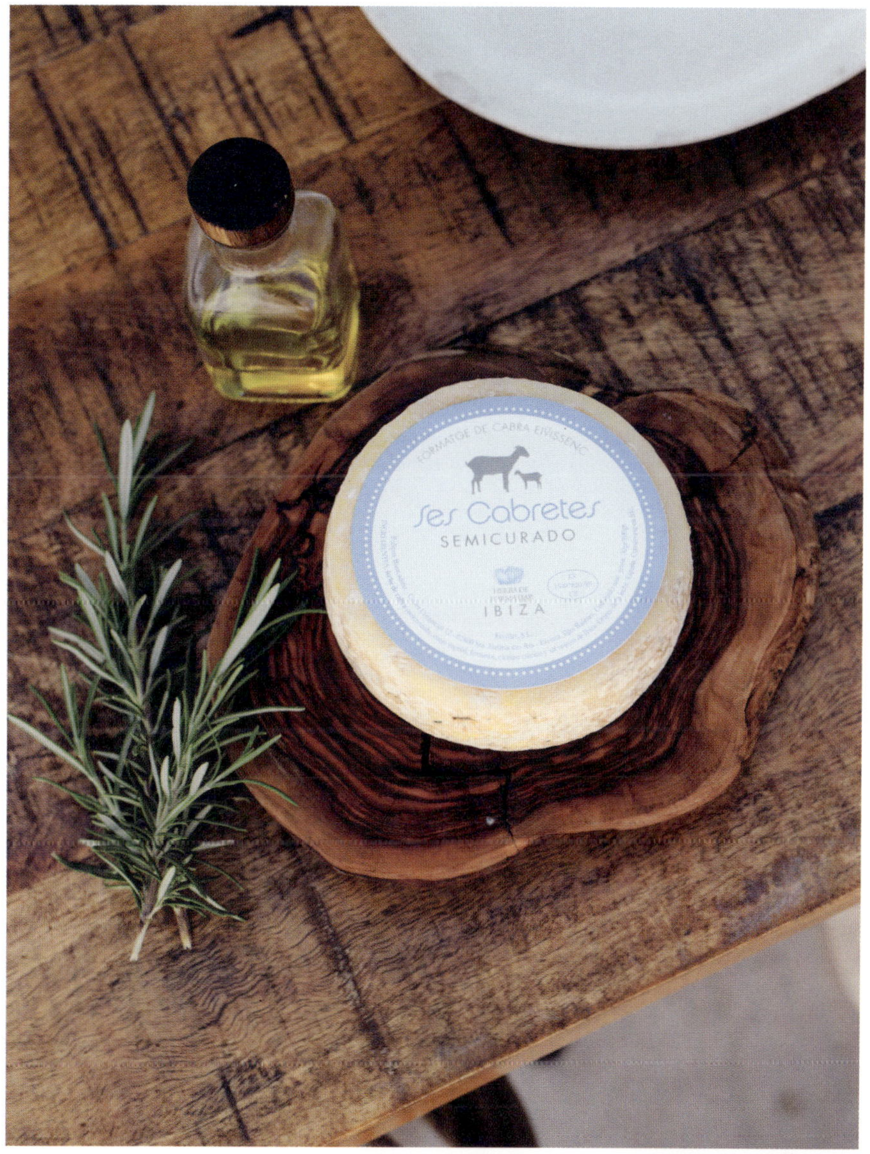

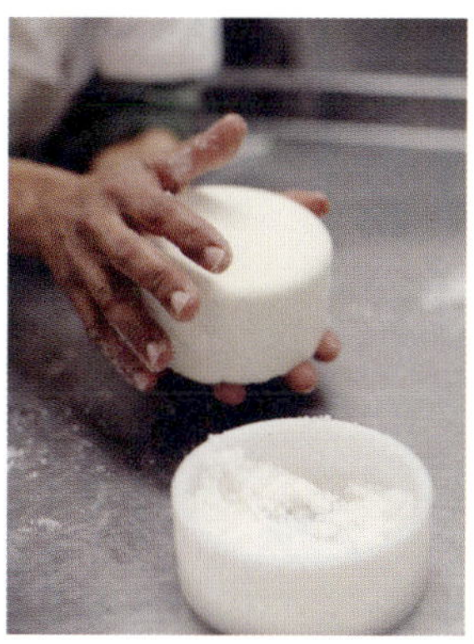

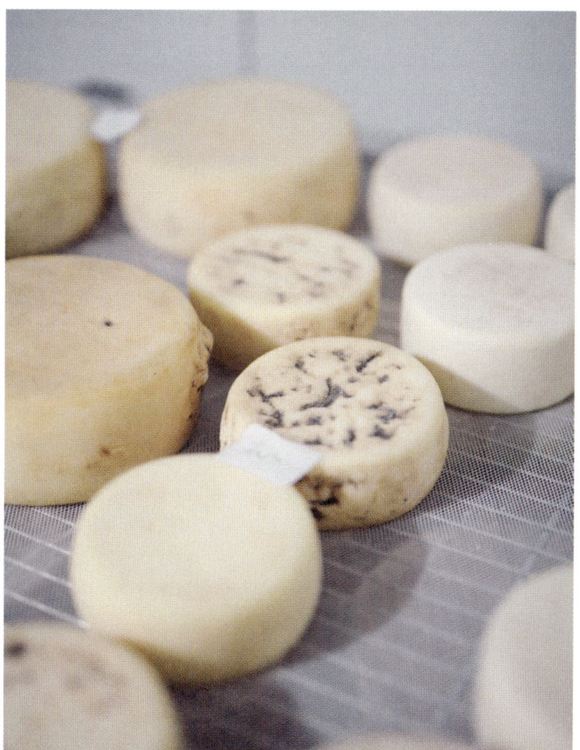

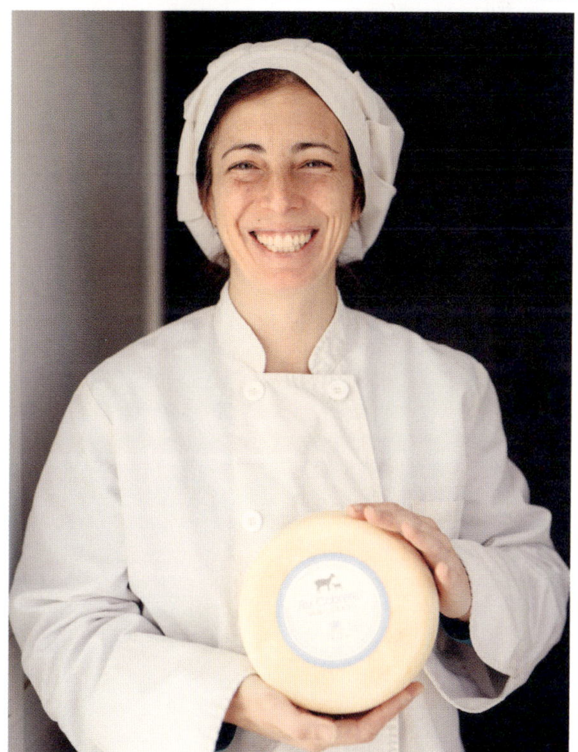

When the whey is drained, the curds are pressed by hand and put into moulds, which are placed in a press. When it has achieved the right pH level, the cheese is moved to the cooling chamber to mature.

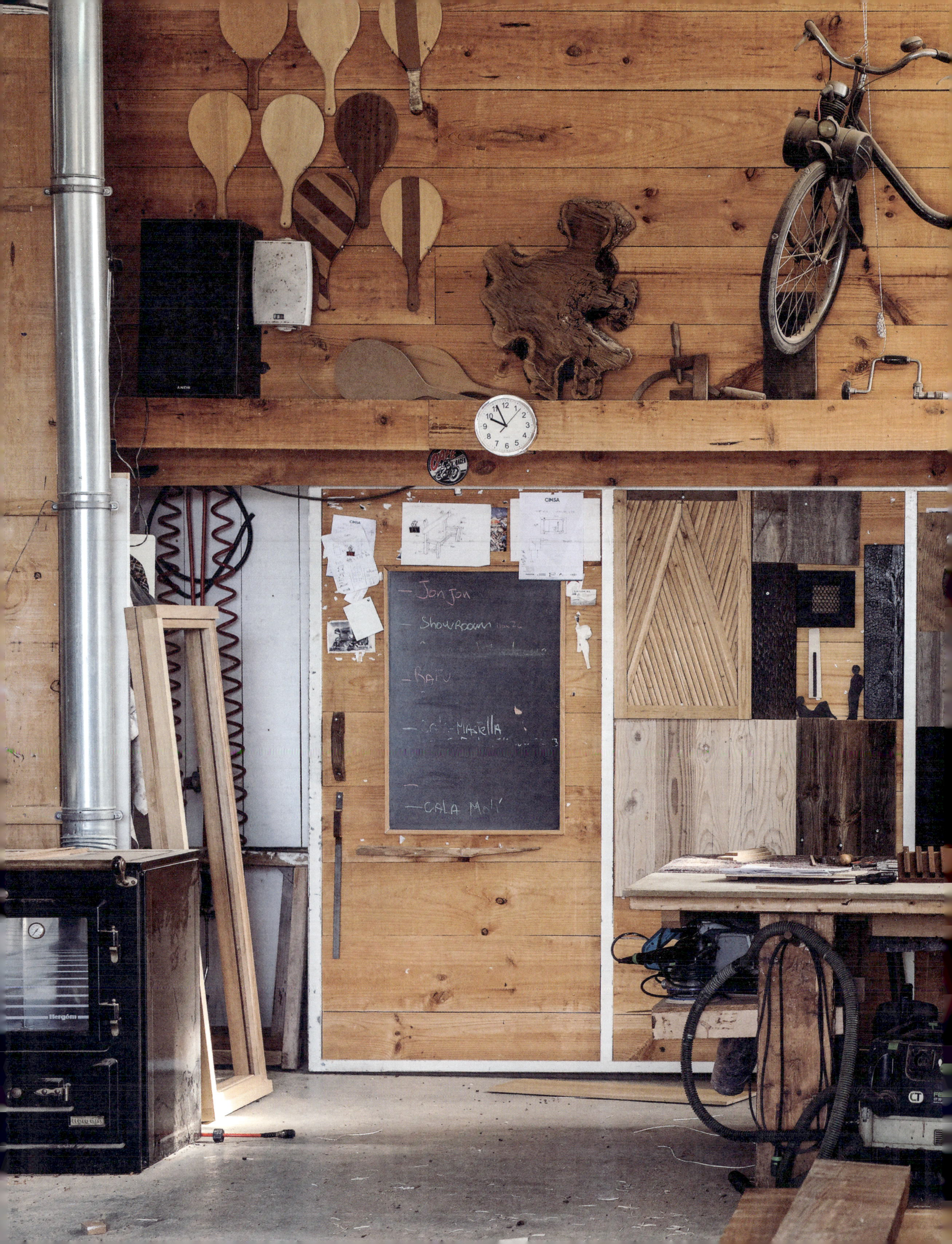
CIMSA
Jon Jon
Showroom

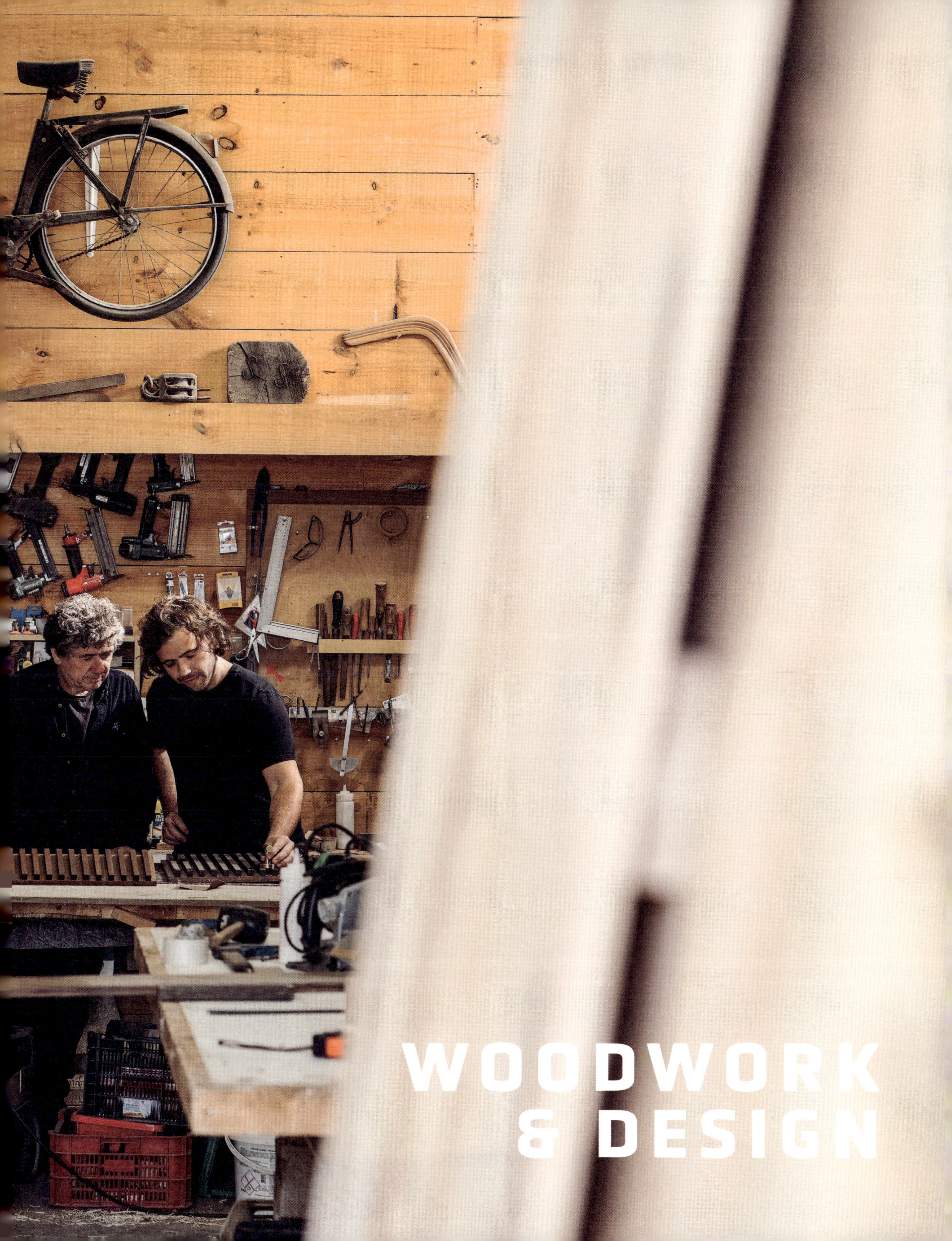

WOODWORK & DESIGN

SAN CARLOS
indigoartchitecture.com

INDIGO ARTCHITECTURE

BESPOKE CARPENTRY & INTERIOR DESIGN

This Italian couple's creative bond was born from a festive place. They met in Ibiza on the eve of the new millennium, and their romance bloomed into a collaboration that has coloured more than two decades. Davide Chianese studied fashion design and tailoring in Switzerland and Florence, and was drawn to decor and interior design while working in the world-building department of set design at Shakespeare's Globe theatre in London. The artist and multidisciplinary designer Anna Tassini holds a degree in contemporary art from the Accademia di Belle Arti di Brera in Milan and relocated from the Spanish city of Granada to Formentera before finally finding her place in Ibiza. Today the pair design some of the island's most dynamic kitchens – and the occasional wooden nightclub.

Honing their creative vision while art-directing some free-spirited parties in Ibiza Town, the couple expanded their business into restaurant design and ultimately into the home. Their finesse for spatial design is derived from a sensibility to serve and respond to the manifold needs, desires and imaginations of the people using their interiors. At the core of their approach is the kitchen, which both describe as the true heart of every home. 'The positioning of ingredients, plates, pots and pans, and your interaction with them – everything becomes a ritual', says Anna. 'We transmit to our clients the importance of these small feelings, and explain why the kitchen is one of the most complex structures of the house – almost like a compact world in itself.'

The couple's own home and workshop, on the outskirts of San Carlos, formerly belonged to a family of carpenters and farmers. A secluded spot providing both comfort and space to immerse themselves in the creative process, this is where they conceptualize, carve and build bespoke interiors for anyone looking to layer their home with sentiments that transcend surface-level aesthetics.

Much time is spent matching the right wood to specific parts of a house. 'Never underestimate a project', says Davide. 'Consider the Japanese method of building a north door only with a north-facing wood, which we don't tend to do in Europe. If you apply a south-facing lumber to a north-facing door, the wood reacts in a different way and starts to contort.' Davide always investigates the provenance of a tree by going to the source and choosing how it is cut. Anna agrees, indicating the woodwork in their house, angled to catch the evening sunshine. 'Detailed considerations today affect how things move in the future', she explains.

Nuanced preferences for earthy tones and textures result in lengthy conversations about almost every fixture. The couple often finish each other's sentences, but they do not always agree – a fact that ultimately enriches final choices.

Describing creativity as a mixture between medicine and integrity, Davide and Anna are on a quest to build spaces that are seamless, synergetic and special to all those inhabiting them. Their approach has led to the careful repurposing of *casa payesa* kitchens for contemporary use and to more soulful fit-outs of modern villas. Indigo Artchitecture even revamped Akasha nightclub in Las Dalias with bold wooden interiors and chandeliers. This is a couple whose artistic vision is intent on reimagining ritualistic space – but always at their own considered pace. ***LA***

Davide Chianese and Anna Tassini are passionate about creating spaces that are inviting, stylish and ambient. For each interior, they take into consideration individual elements such as light, evolution of materials and behavioural factors, in order to build a balanced, cohesive whole.

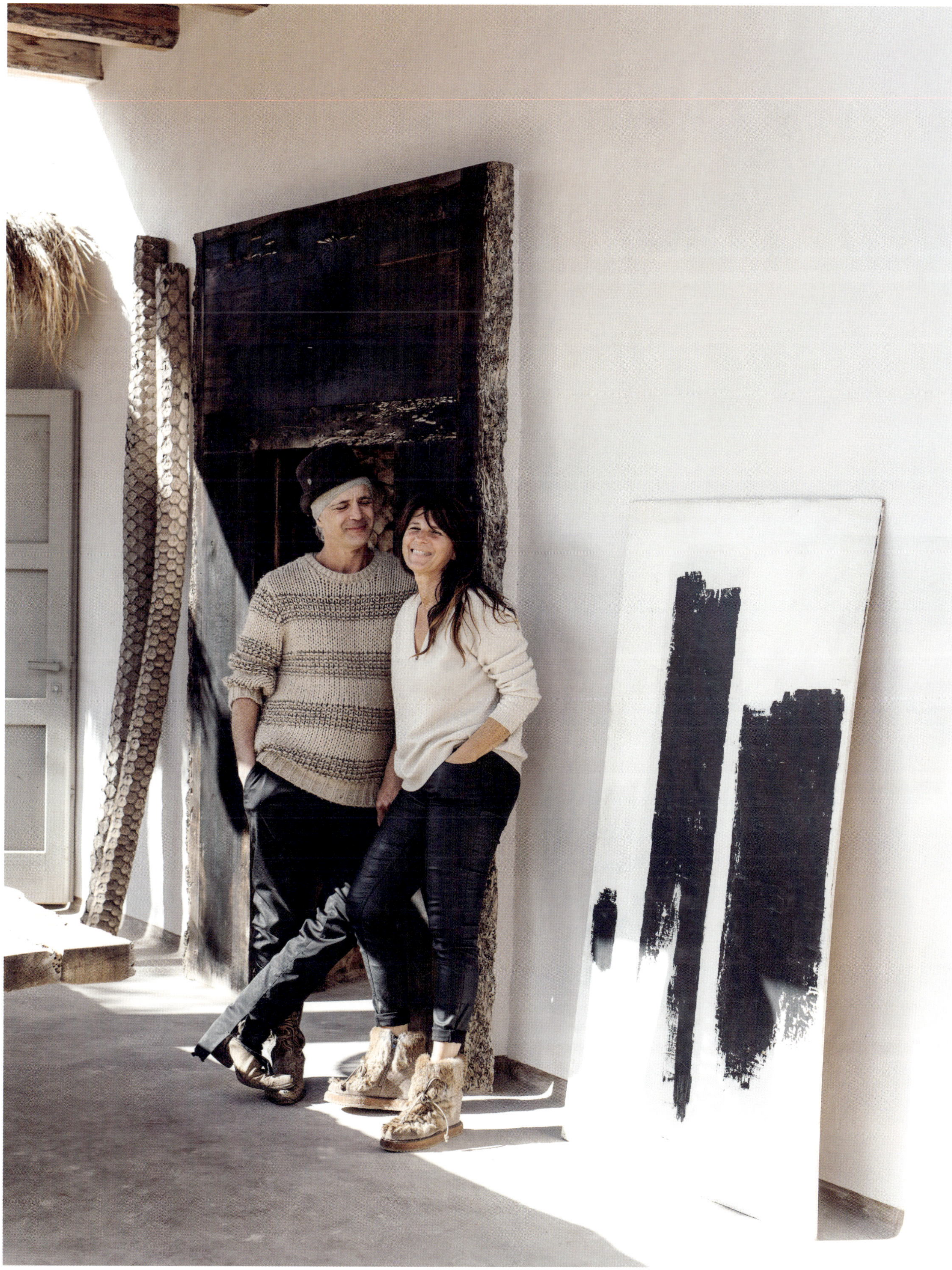

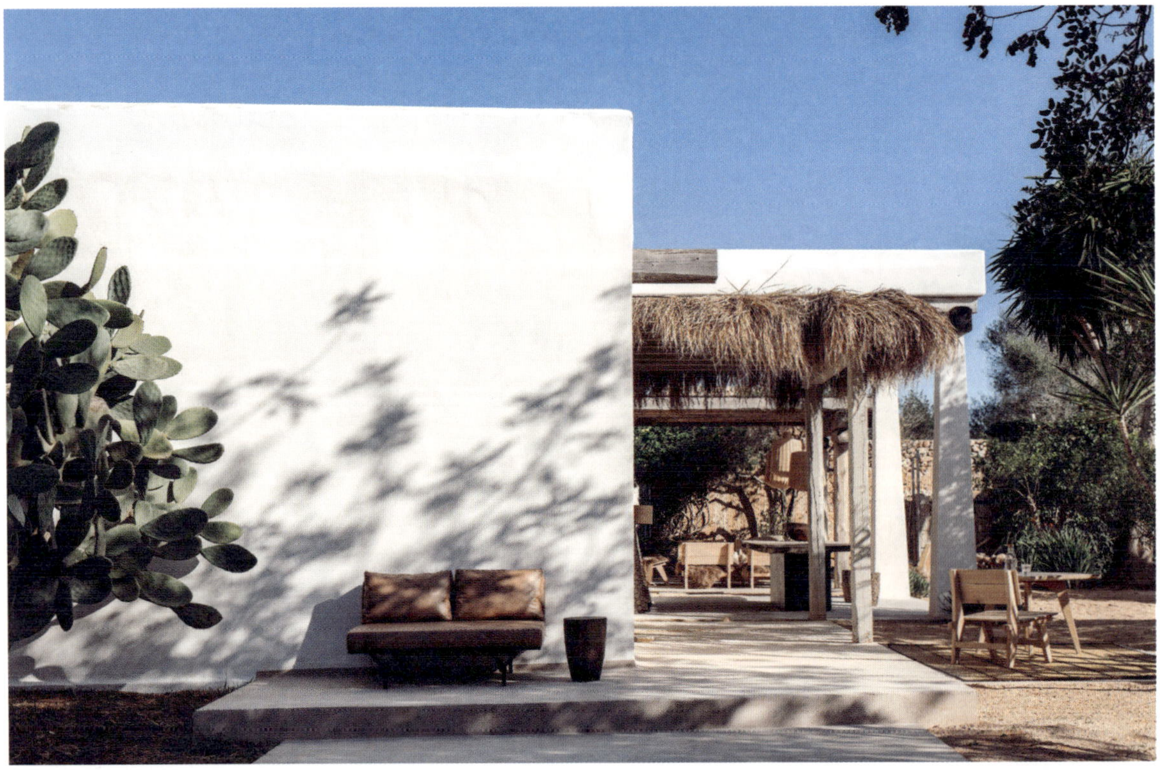

The idyllic former farm now serves as the artistic couple's home, office and workshop.

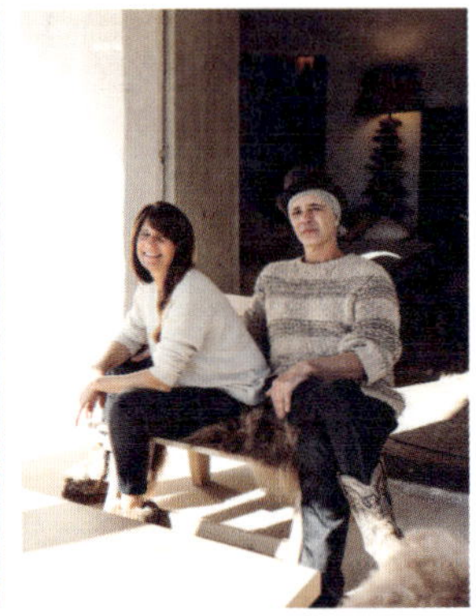

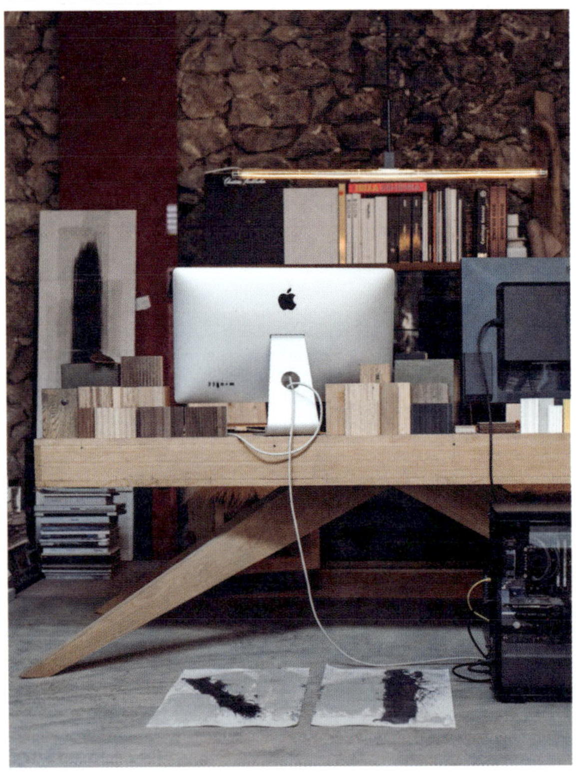

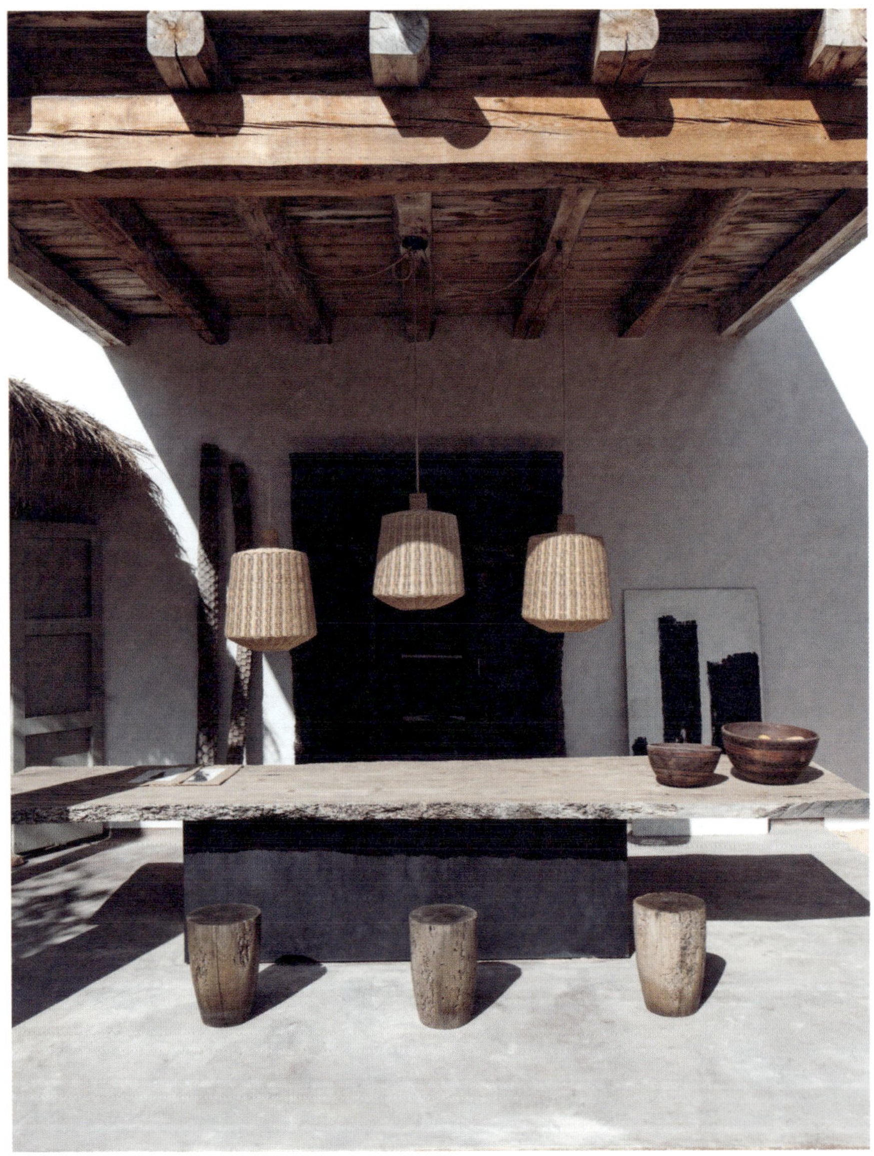

The living areas are characteristic expressions of texture and warmth. The living room (opposite) features light fittings made by Davide, while soft furnishings and natural textiles bring cosiness to the concrete floor and limestone walls. The patio (right) functions as the main dining area, where the couple enjoy their first espresso of the morning.

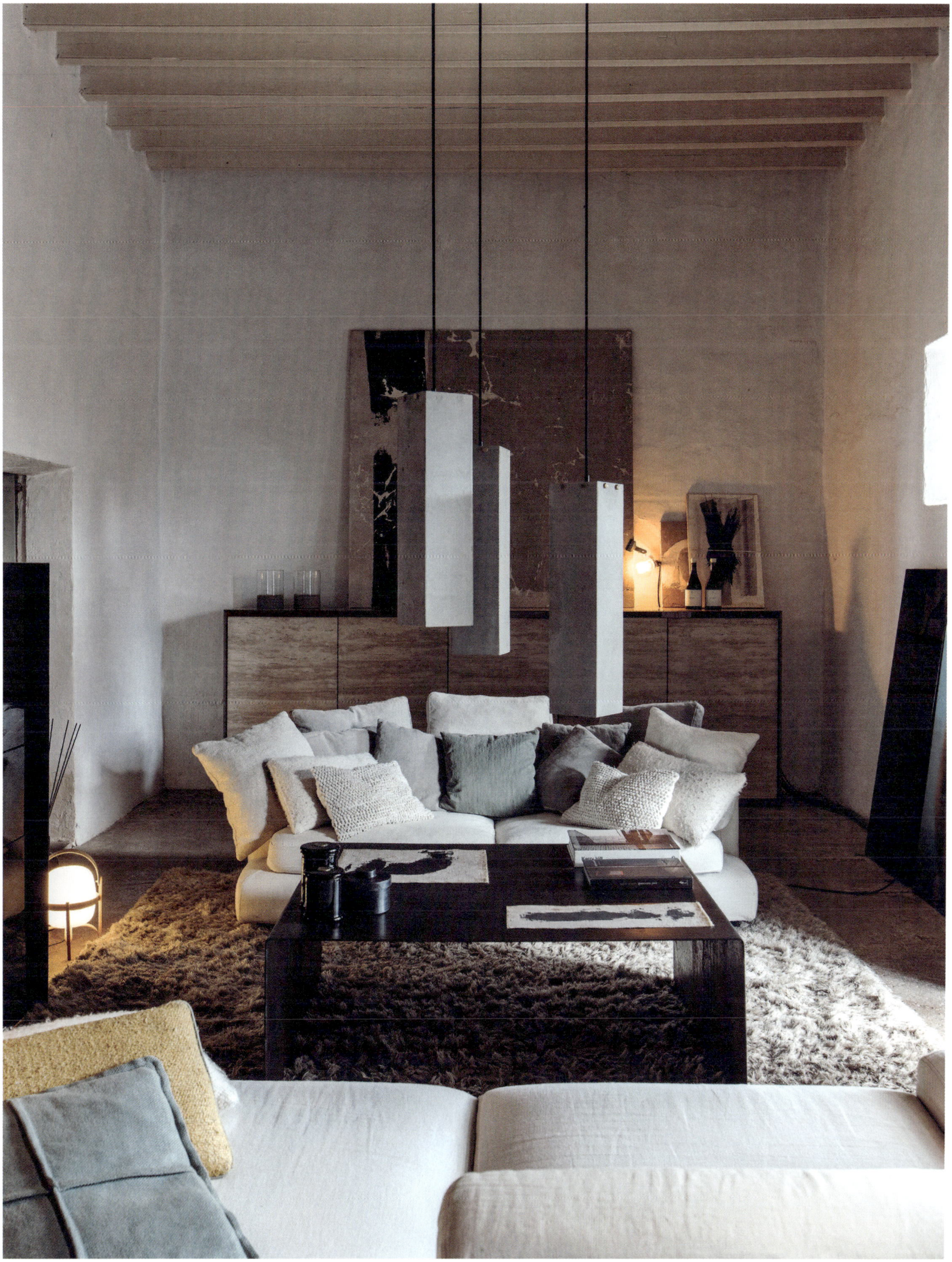

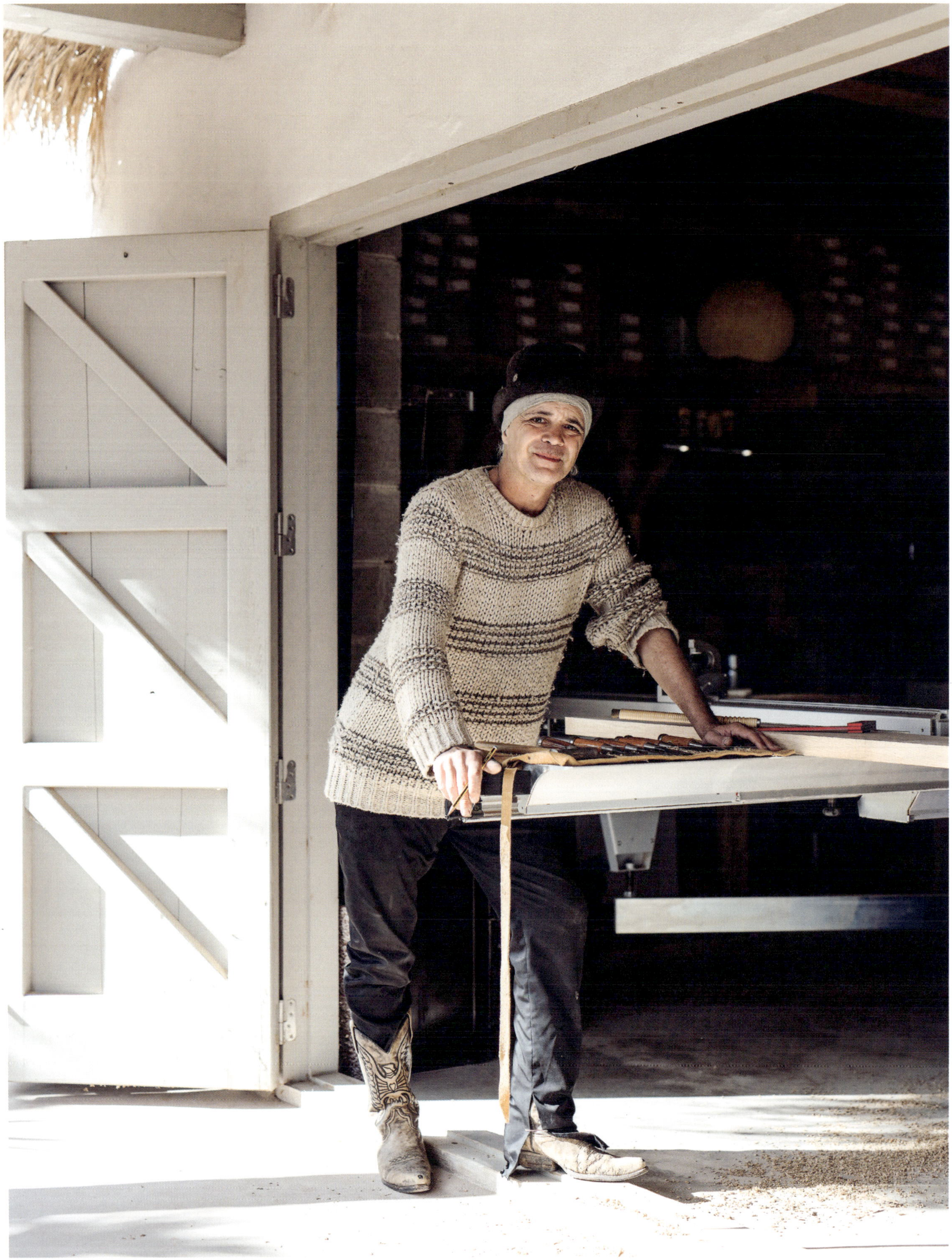

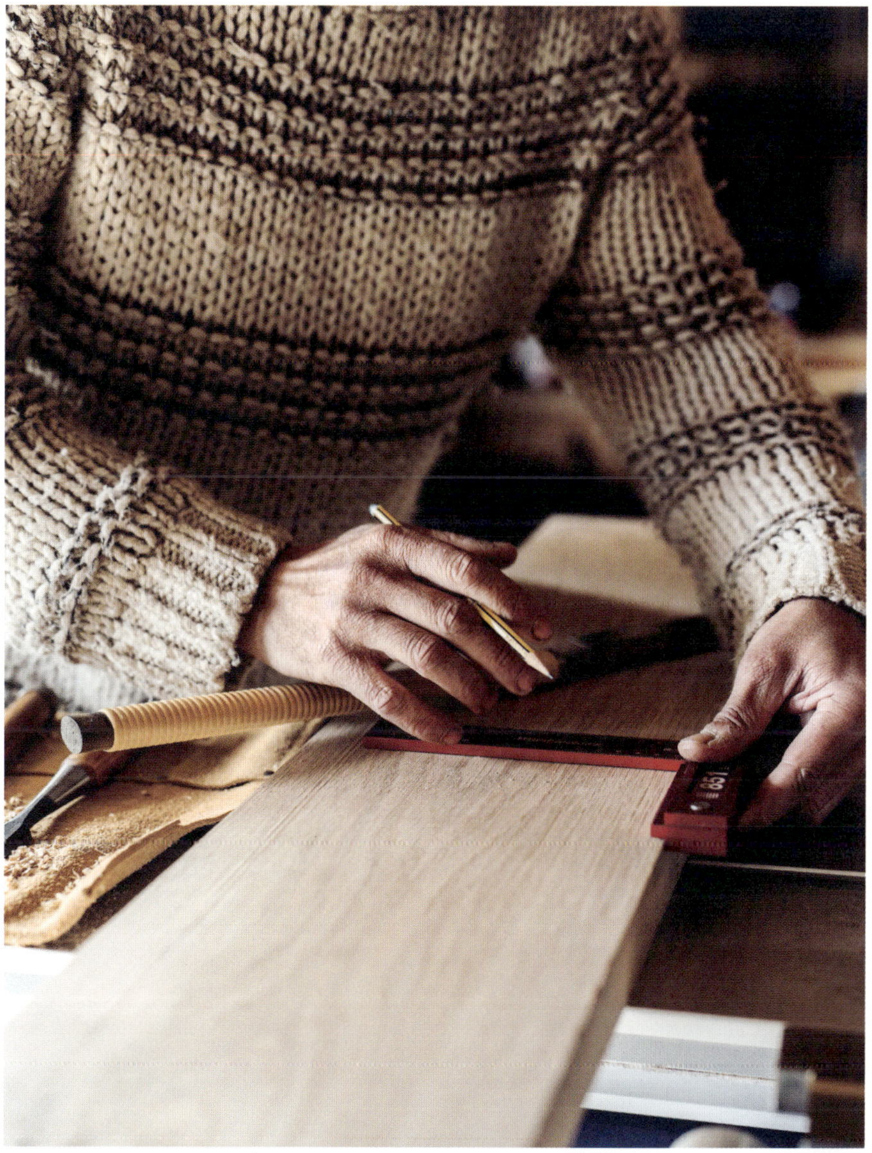

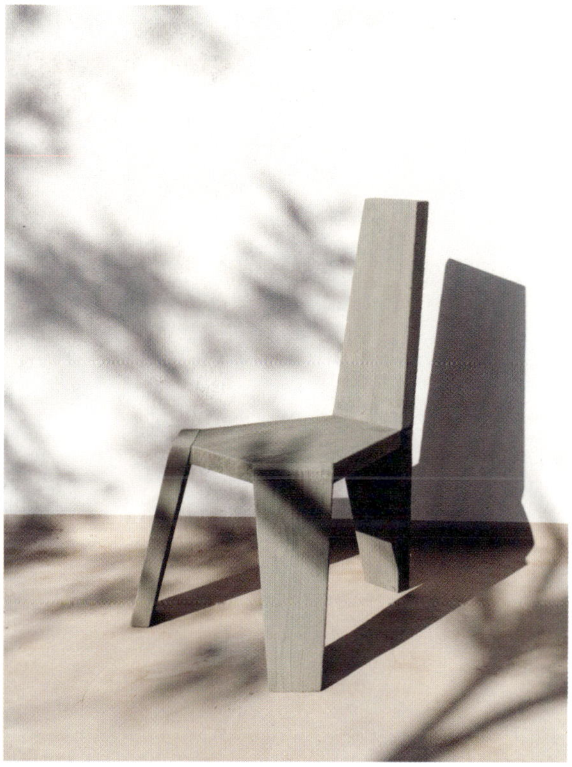

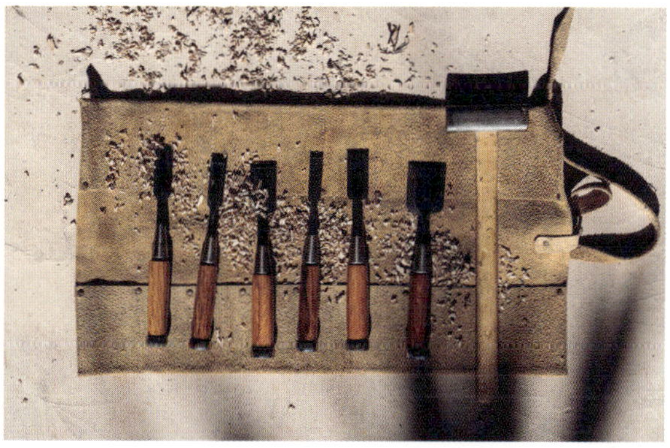

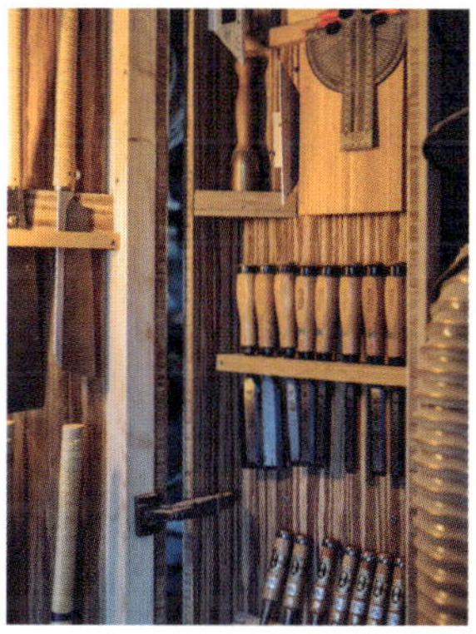

Davide's workshop is where he brings the design concepts to life, utilizing a diverse range of specialized tools and materials.

Overleaf: Two kitchens by Indigo Architecture. On p. 162, a private commission with travertine stone and black metal. On p. 163, a compact counter design of black glass sits solidly inside the couple's own home.

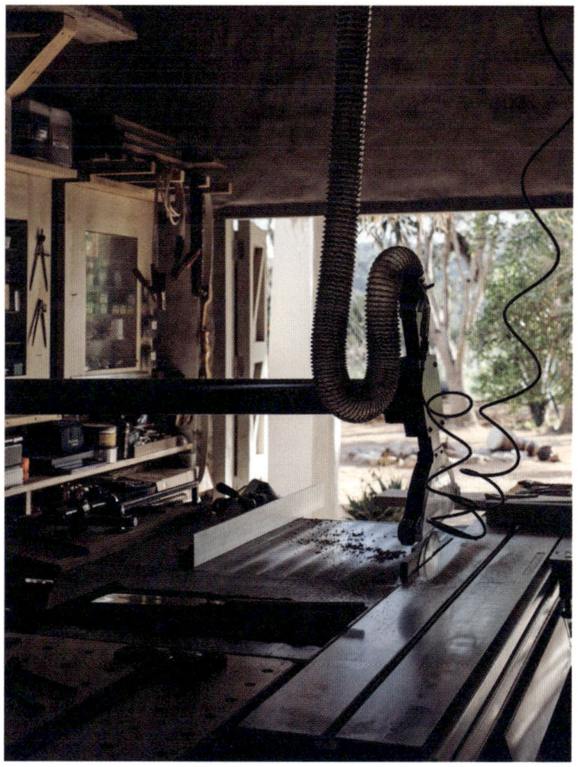

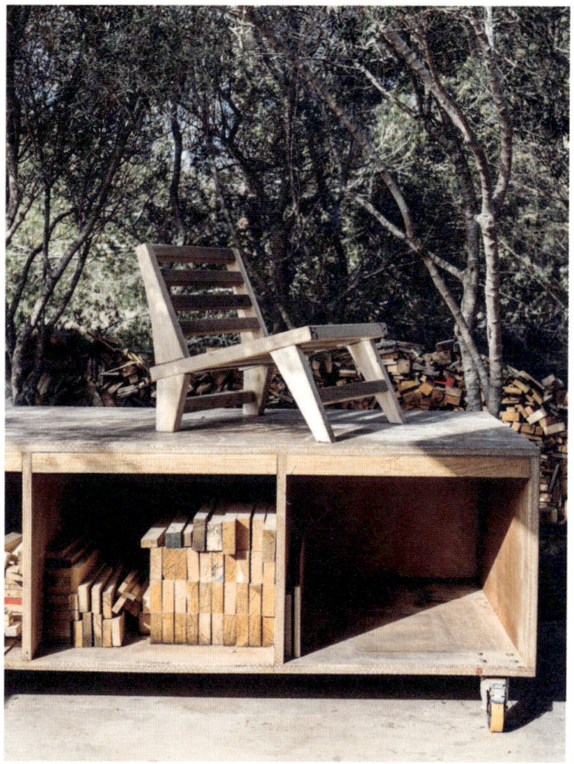

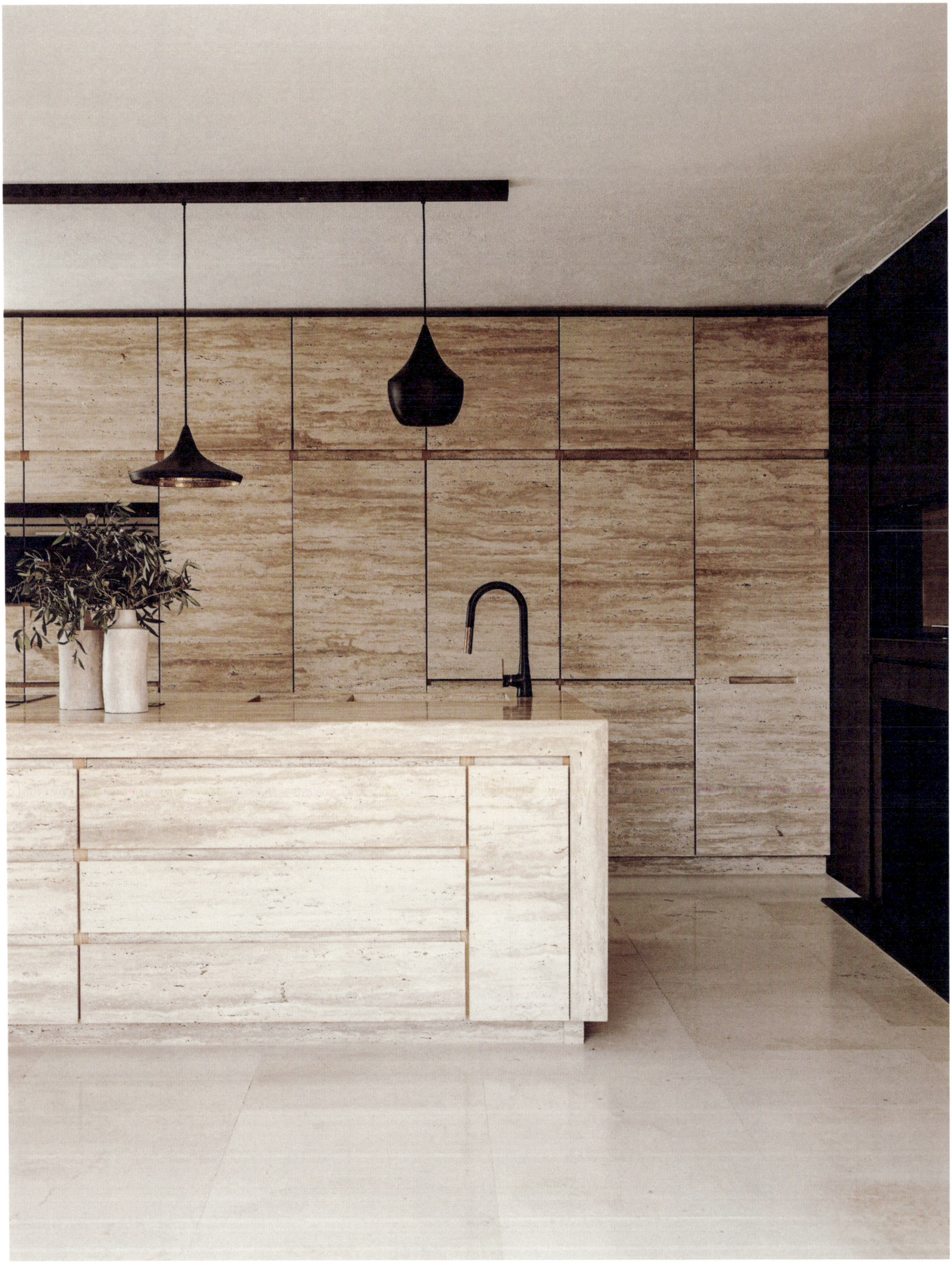

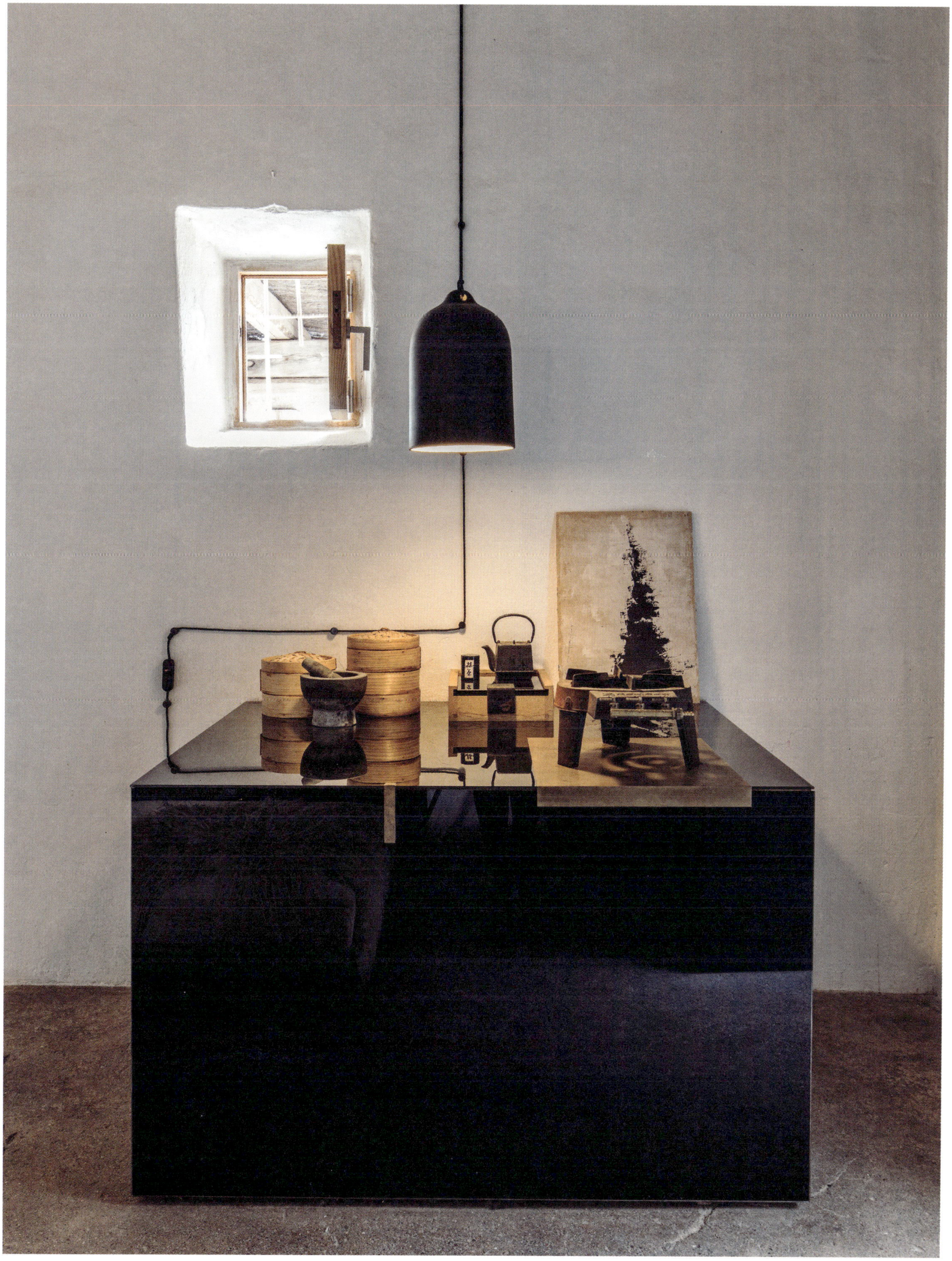

SANTA EULALIA
@carpinteria_thierry

CARPINTERÍA THIERRY

BESPOKE CARPENTRY

A carpenter who sculpted himself into the realm of artistry, this Frenchman has crafted a legacy that is being followed by his three sons, whose own woodworking skills prove that talent does not fall far from the family tree.

'I don't like doing anything boring.' Thierry Billaud does not speak in long-winded sentences. He pauses pensively before adding, 'This means, I'm always on the lookout for more complicated jobs.' Humble and mild-mannered, he is a man of few words, one who prefers to let his masterful messages come out in his woodwork.

Inside his spacious workshop on the old *camino* to Santa Eulalia, Thierry strides purposefully between each room, surveying the stacked timber, sawdust-sprinkled machinery, and several pieces of furniture that are gradually being sculpted into life. He immigrated to Ibiza in 1986 and found an immediate demand for his specialized craftsmanship as a ship's carpenter. 'The idea was to spend a year or two on the island', he recalls. 'That was more than thirty-five years ago.'

It took Thierry just two years to open his own workshop, a space that has steadily swollen to accommodate bigger tree trunks for more ambitious creations, such as outdoor tables and a large canoe hanging like a trophy on the wall outside his cosy wood-panelled office.

If woodwork is Thierry's language, he inflects his craft with a mixture of artistic and pragmatic aplomb. 'A piece of custom furniture has to work with the energy of the house, the room, the people', he explains. 'I always visit the space first, then we draw up the initial idea, and the search for the right wood begins.'

Today Thierry's sons continue to carry the torch, carving their names in a family tradition that takes its cue from nature. Synonymous with a sense of organicism, the workshop creates cabinets, doors, statement furniture and sculpted ornaments that all groove to the contours and cues of their source material.

'As my sons have grown up, there has been an evolution of the work', explains Thierry. 'Our output is very different today from when I first started. Just like a tree, everything evolves – but you must always learn to make do with what you have.'

While the workshop has a reputation for specializing in utilitarian woodwork, a passion for wooden sculpture means that plenty of unique pieces end up complementing the more customary creations. 'Our clients are frequently surprised by the level of detail when we deliver finished pieces', Thierry says.

Pondering the possibility of retirement, Thierry seems less excited about the prospect of rest and more enthused about having extra time to create simply for creation's sake. 'That's true freedom', he notes with a smile. ***LA***

Thierry Billaud, an accomplished carpenter originally from France, has been running his studio in Ibiza for more than three decades and now works alongside his three sons. The family's flair for woodworking is evident in the skilful repurposing of salvaged timber, often sourced from antique suppliers in France.

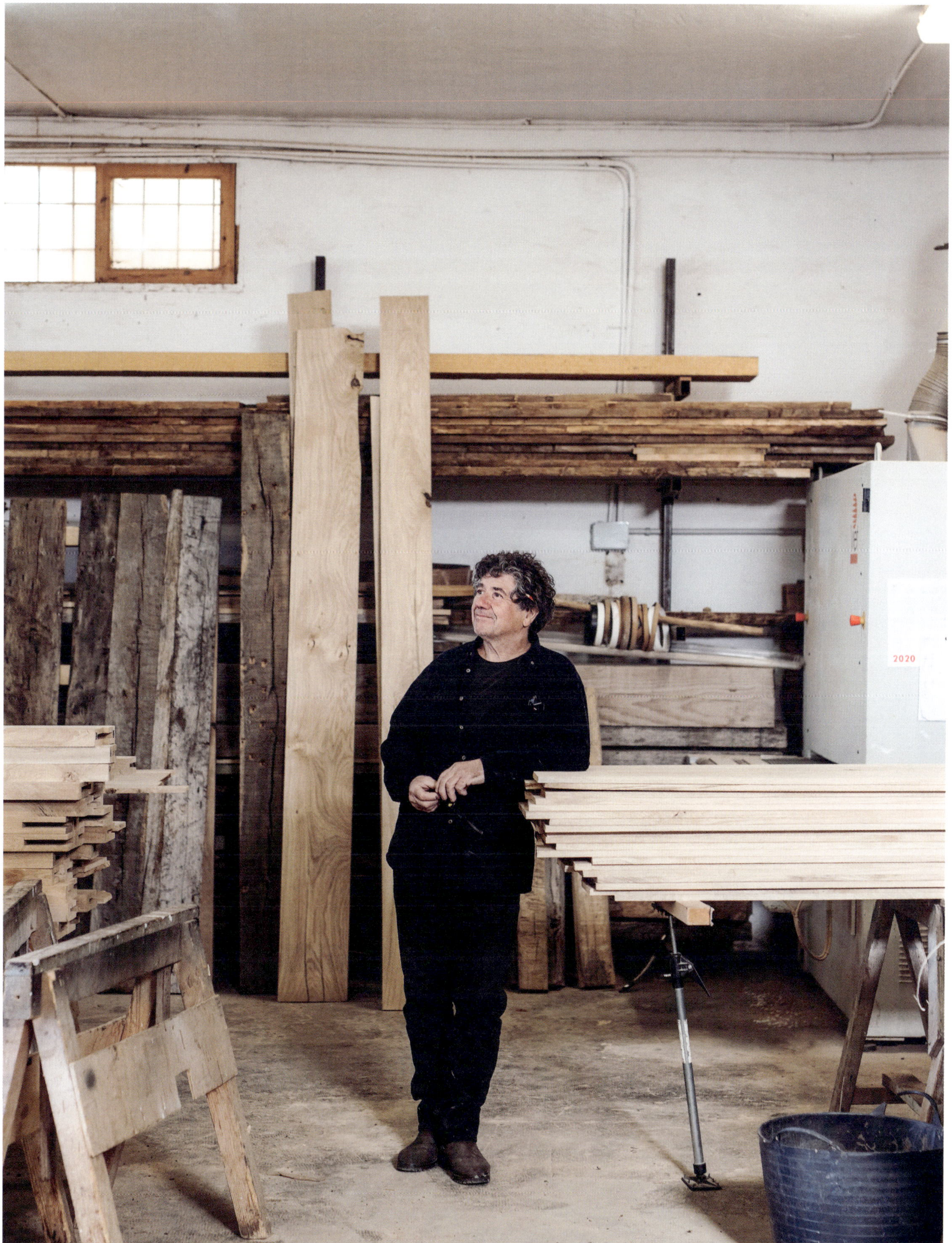

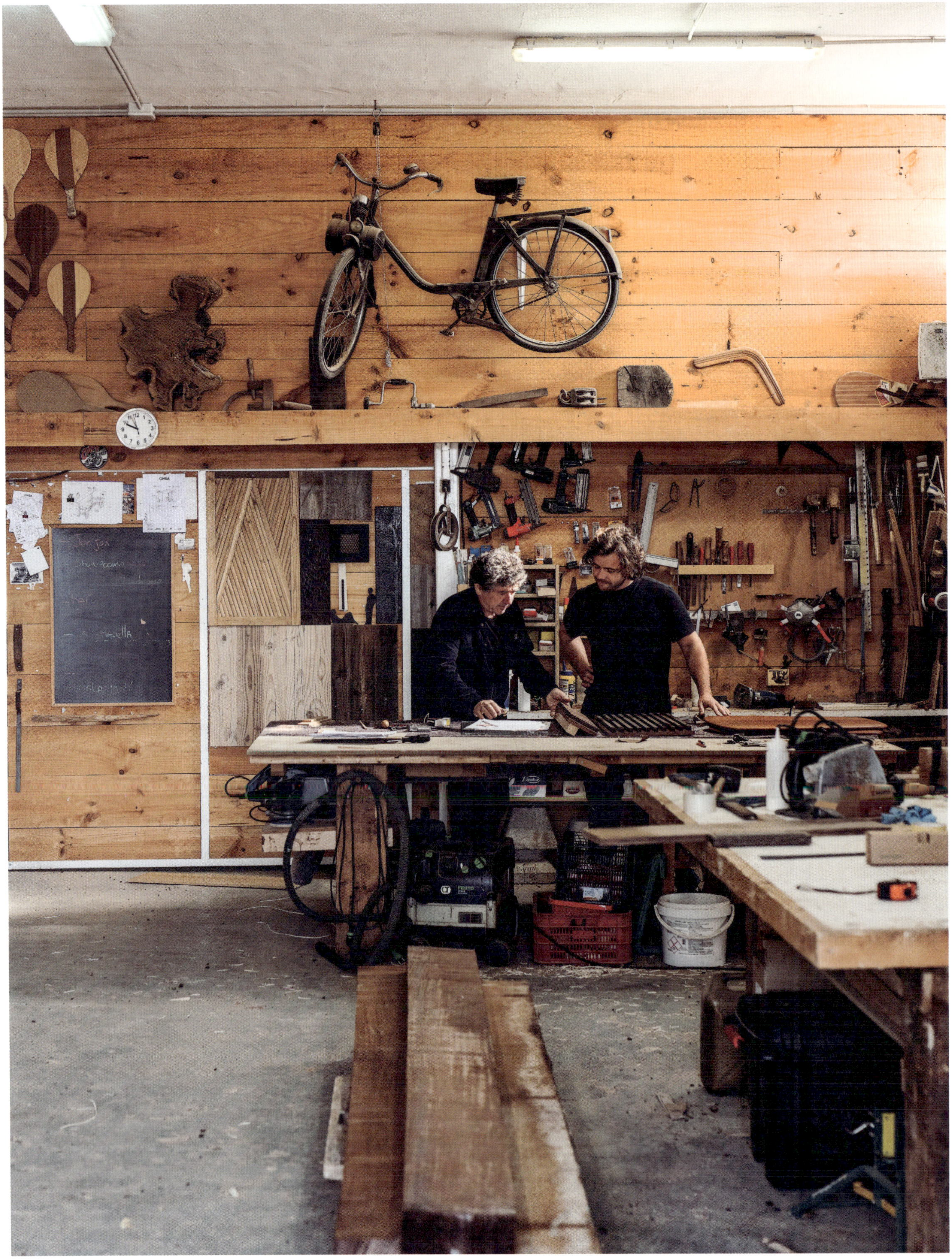

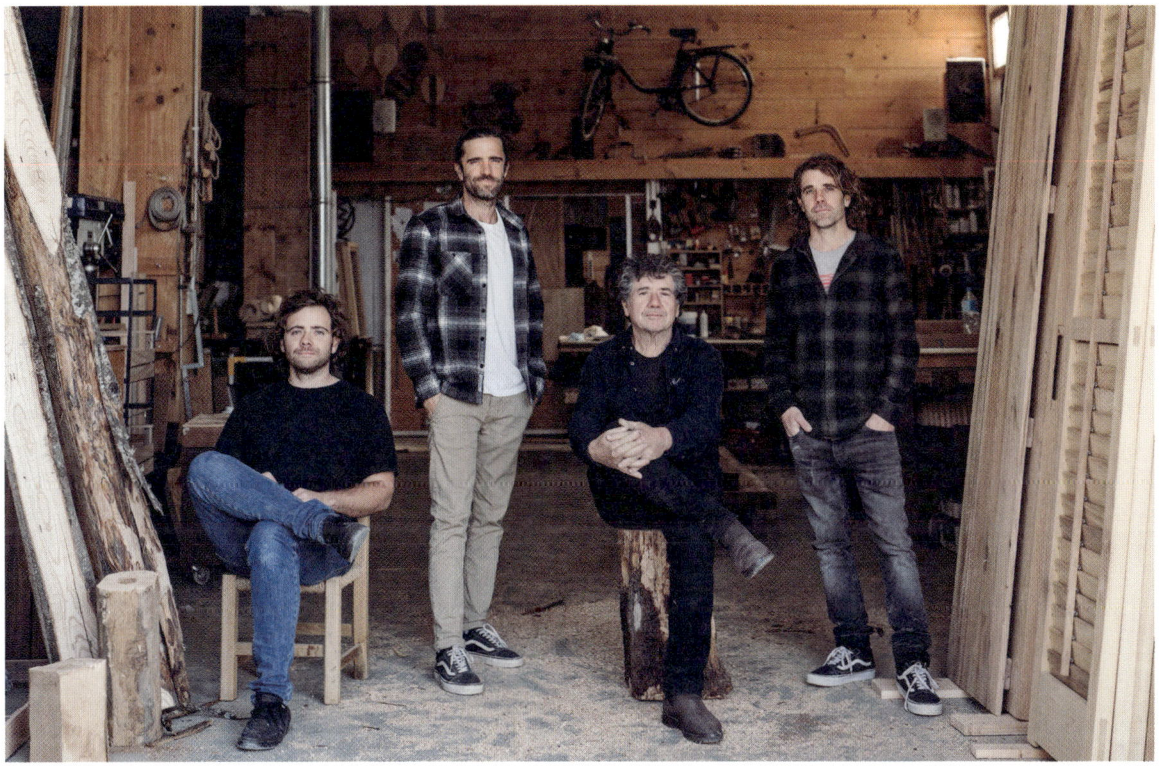

Opposite: Thierry inspects progress on a project with his youngest son, Enzo.

Left: A family portrait of (from left to right) Enzo, Romain, Thierry and Morgan.

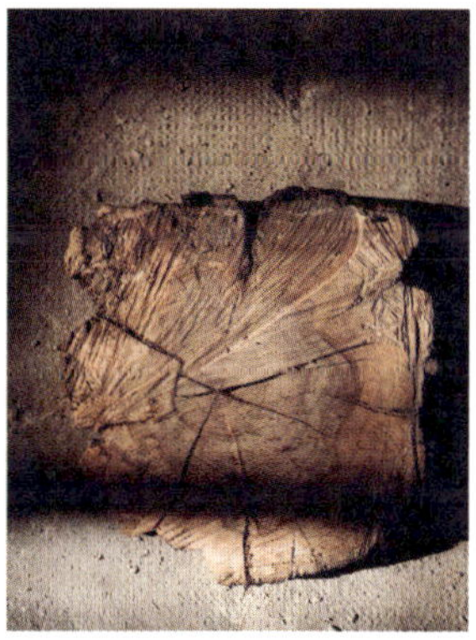

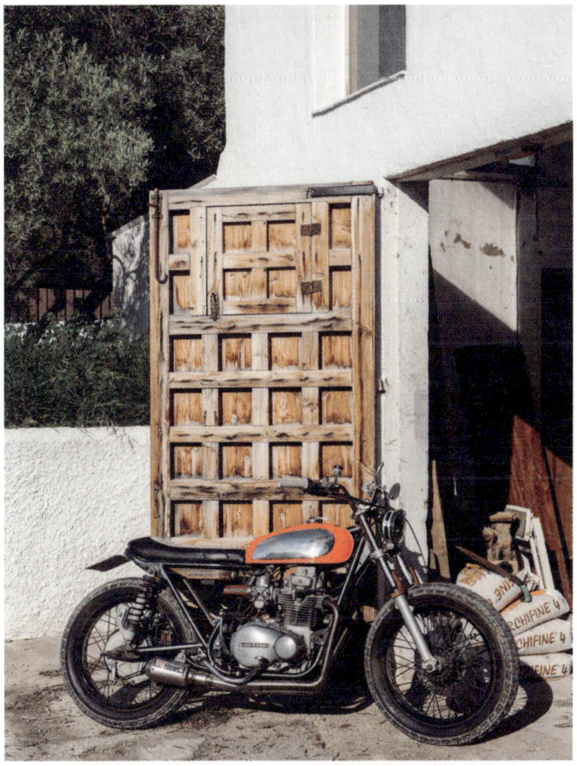

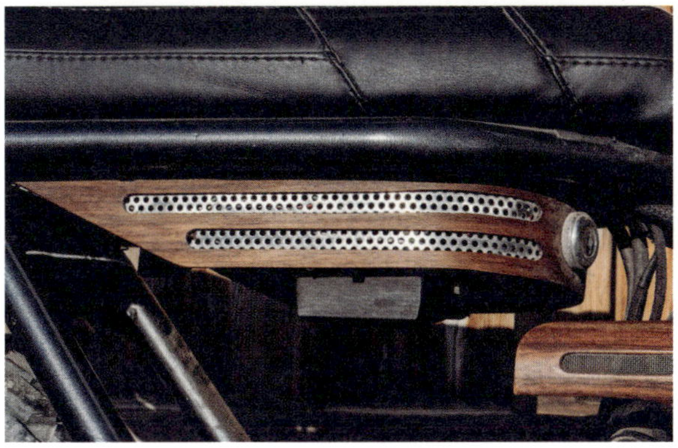

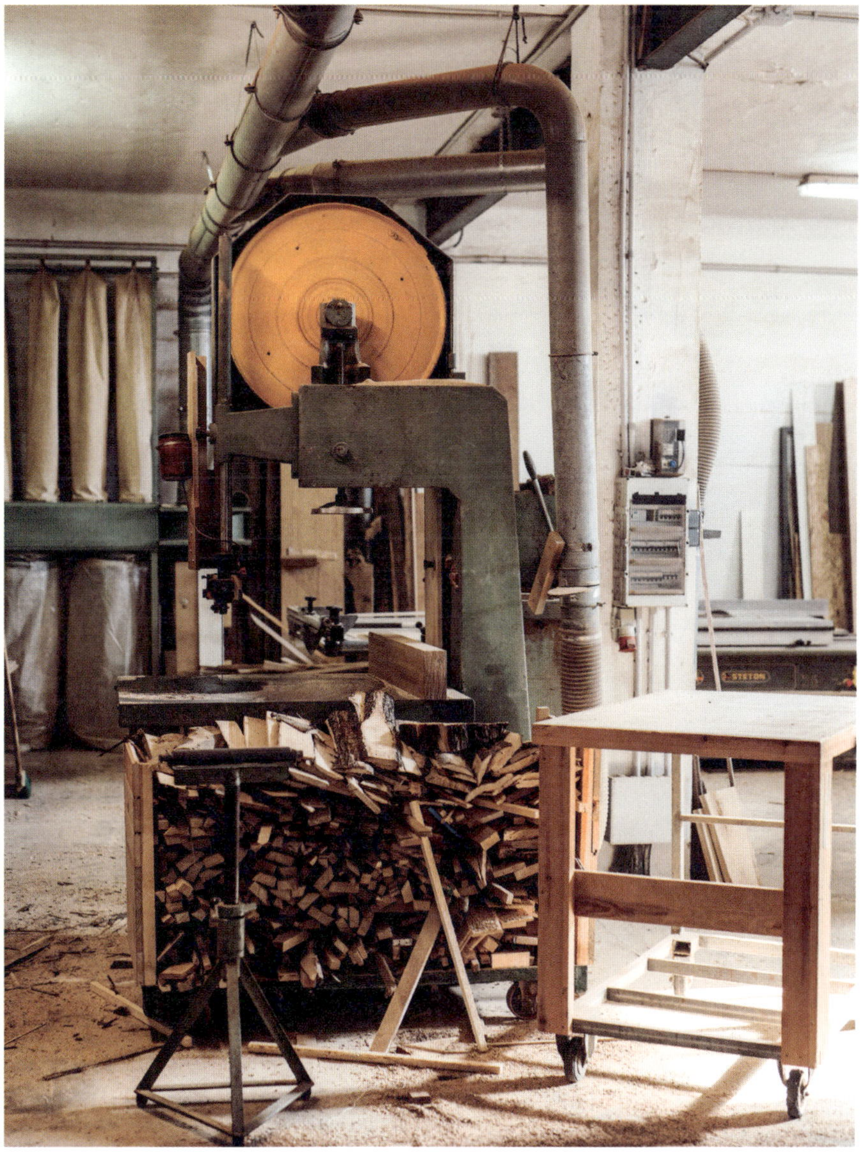

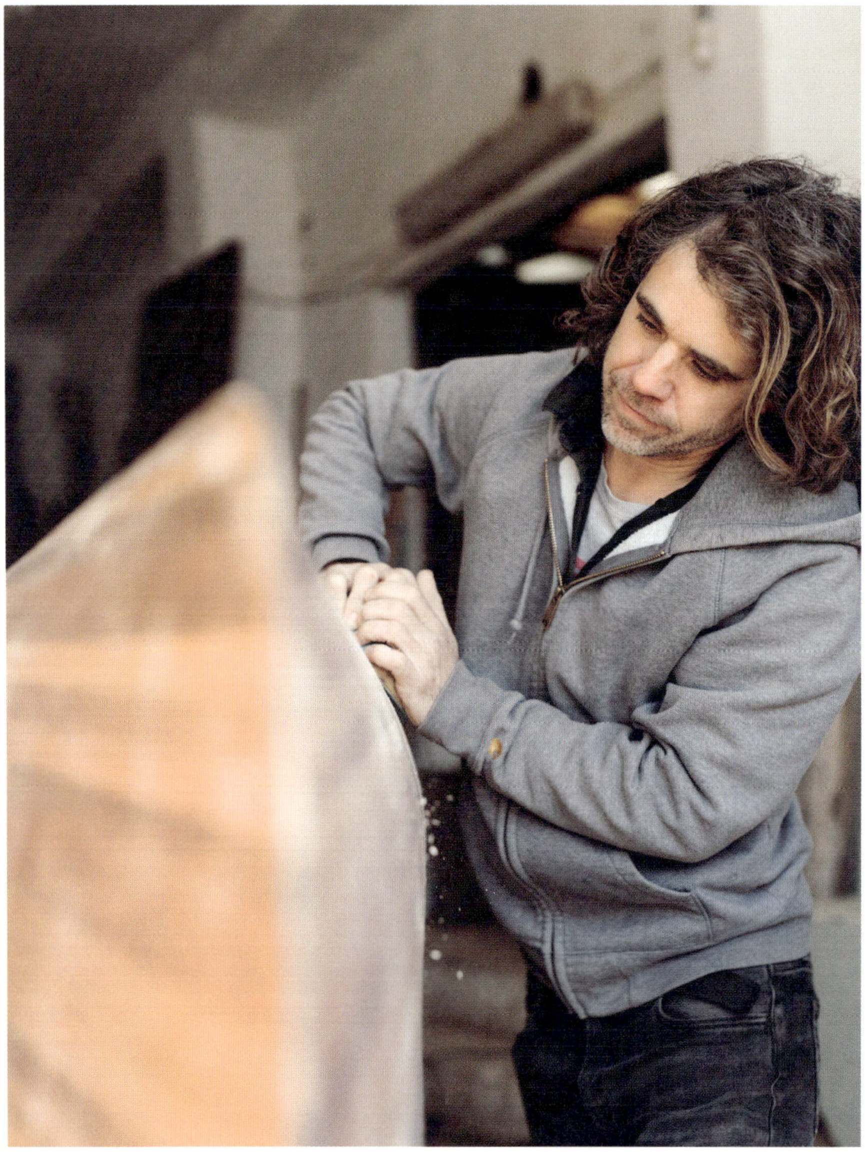

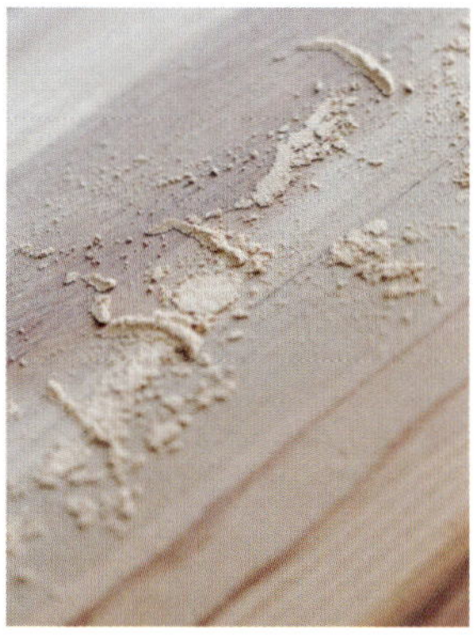

Crafting a dream: Enzo's skill in boatbuilding is a testament to the family's unwavering passion for unique projects.

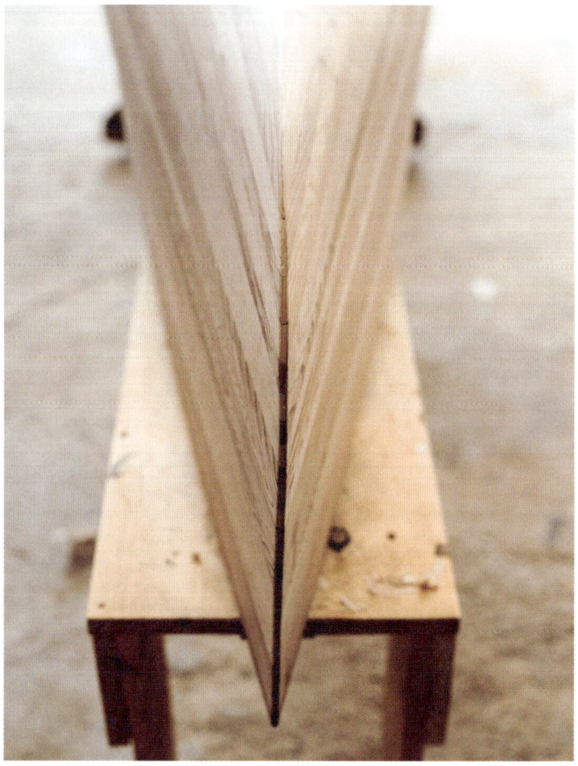

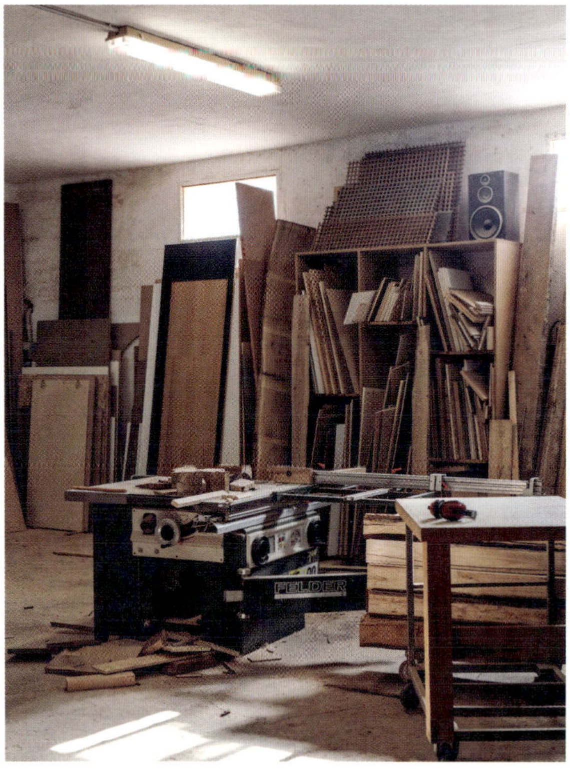

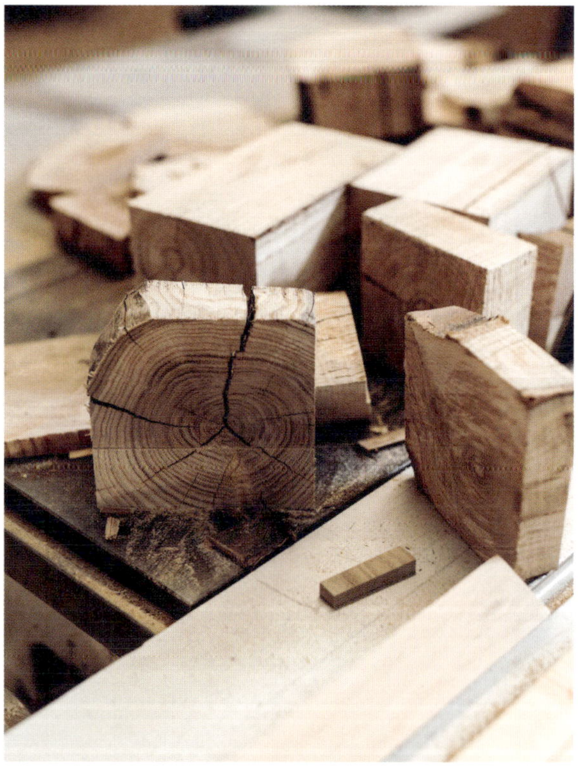

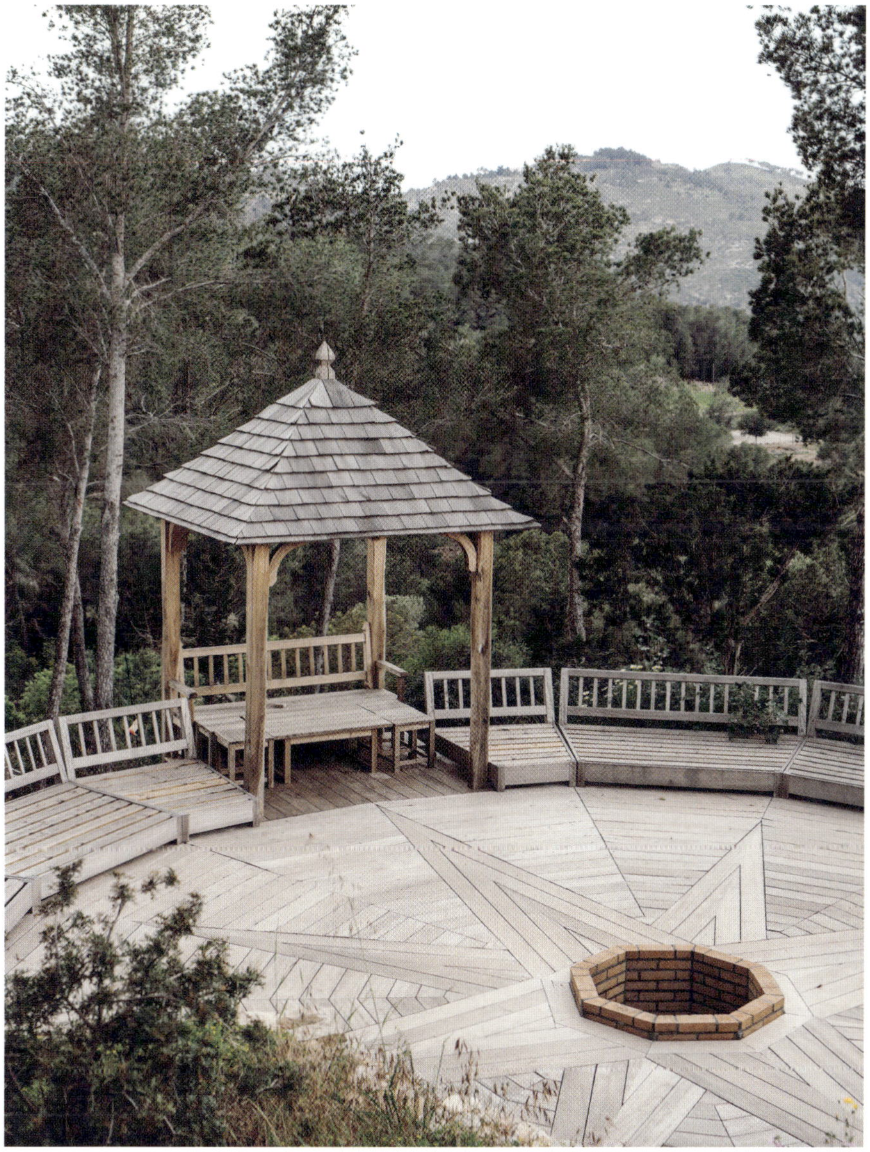

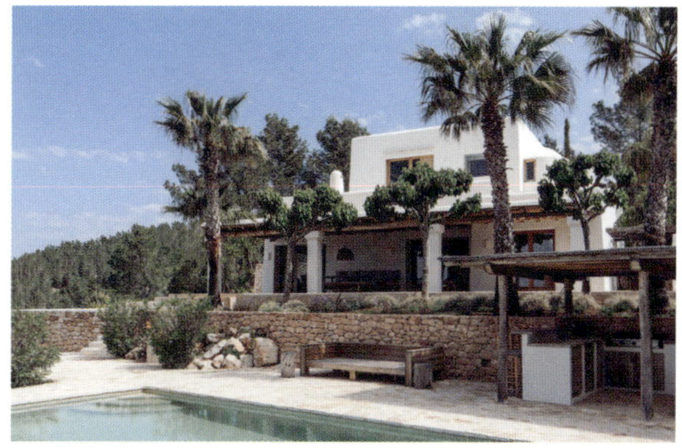

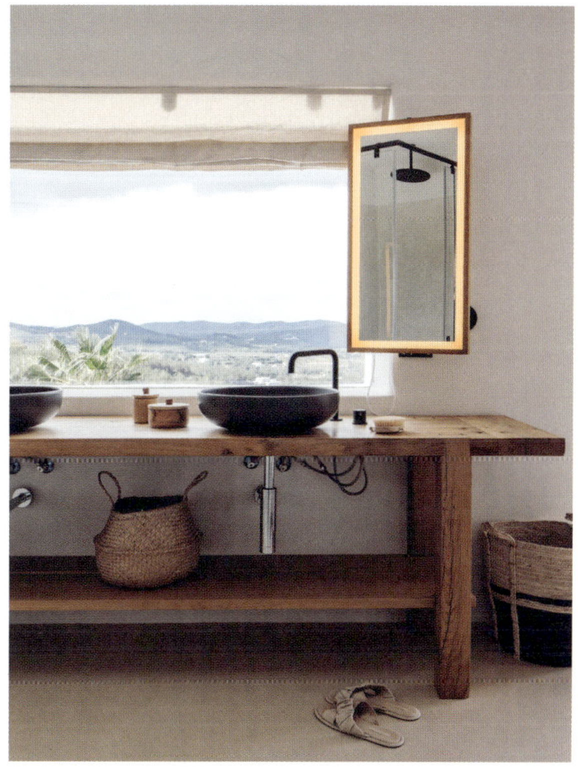

Above: The decking for an outdoor cinema, designed and constructed for a private client at a property near Benirràs, includes a central fire pit for the colder months.

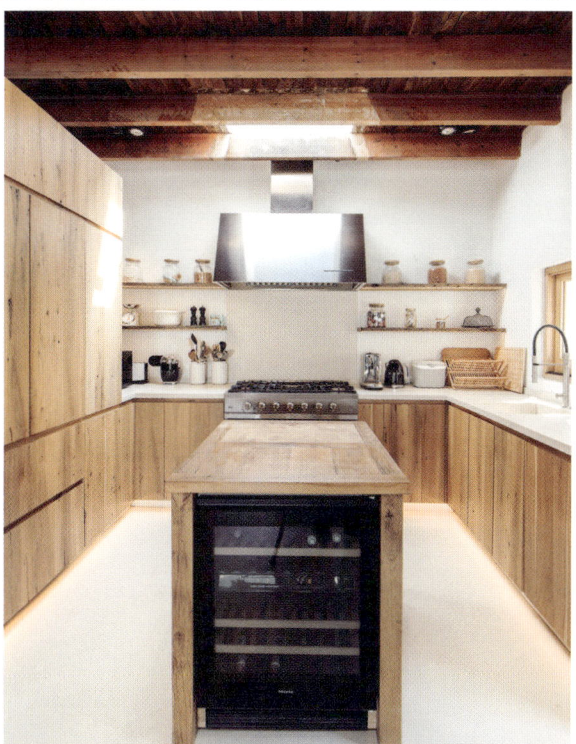

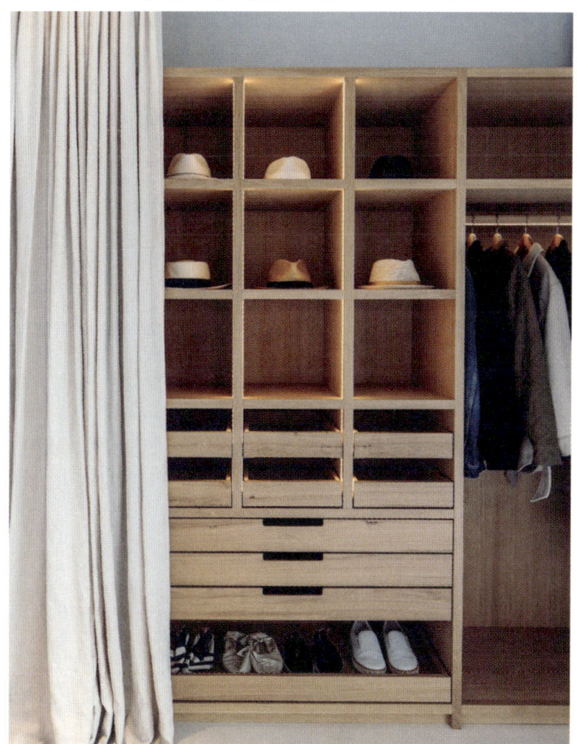

This page (except above): Commissioned to renew the heart of this private home in San Juan, the workshop artfully designed new wooden fittings and furniture to transform the bathroom, kitchen and wardrobe.

SANTA GERTRUDIS
@cancastelloibiza

CAN CASTELLO

RESTORATION & INTERIOR DESIGN

Early in the summer of 1987, a young Pura and José washed up on the shores of Ibiza from mainland Spain. José knew the island well, and the free-spirited pair had a loose plan to stay and work for the season before leaving to travel the world. 'Then José came up with the idea of staying for a while', smiles Pura. 'And that was that.'

More than thirty-five years later, and the Spanish couple are deeply rooted in Ibiza's soil, helming Can Castello, an interior-design and architectural practice near Santa Gertrudis that specializes in custom carpentry and the restoration of historic buildings. 'We're both passionate about old houses and about conserving their original materials and their sense of history', says Pura. 'In historic island houses we work with noble elements: stone floors, wooden doors and traditional lime walls. These elements have a soul, and they have the natural patina of the passage of time. It is this patina that sets historic properties apart and gives them the sense of authenticity that we are trying to preserve.'

José is a master carpenter, and the pair are extremely capable: shortly after arriving in Ibiza, they spent time living on a wooden schooner. The boat required constant upkeep and restoration. It was a steep learning curve and became, according to Pura, 'the perfect school'. Wood has become the common thread in all of Can Castello's projects, and the couple are renowned for their re-creation of Ibiza's authentic doors and windows using antique timber. José is lyrical about the material's qualities: 'Wood is a dignified material, and it retains a lot of energy. With salvaged pieces, there is a clear sense that the wood holds memories.'

This passion translates into custom-made doors and windows, such as those created for Can Pep Simó (see pp. 239–41), and into furniture adapted to suit the needs of clients, but it is not without its challenges. 'Wood can be unpredictable', explains José. 'It's crucial to work these older pieces with great care, usually manually, to preserve their integrity. Our goal is to create one-off, timeless pieces, ensuring that tradition combines with innovation.'

Pura and José collaborate with the finest names in art and architecture, and are at the forefront of the movement to revive and restore Ibiza's historic houses, creating luxurious, liveable homes that maintain deep aesthetic links with the past. In nearby Formentera, the pair worked closely with the owner of a historic rural home to bring the house's inherent beauty into the twenty-first century. Formentera's vernacular architecture is distinct from that of Ibiza on account of its pitched roofs and exposed stone walls. Can Castello's use of rough, earthy textures at Casa Formentera complements this style, as does the studio's commissioning of artisans such as the *maestra* weaver who re-created the Balearic heritage jute-woven chair seats.

Over the course of the decades, Pura and José have become deeply entrenched in what it means to live and breathe the islands. They are as inseparable from Ibiza as they are from each other. 'The island herself is the thing that we keep coming back to', says Pura. 'The light, the nature, the antiquity and the creative essence of the people here. Ibiza will always be the backdrop to which we dedicate our lives.' ***MB***

Pura and José have spent more than thirty-five years guarding Ibiza's noble treasures as part of their restoration and interior-design business.

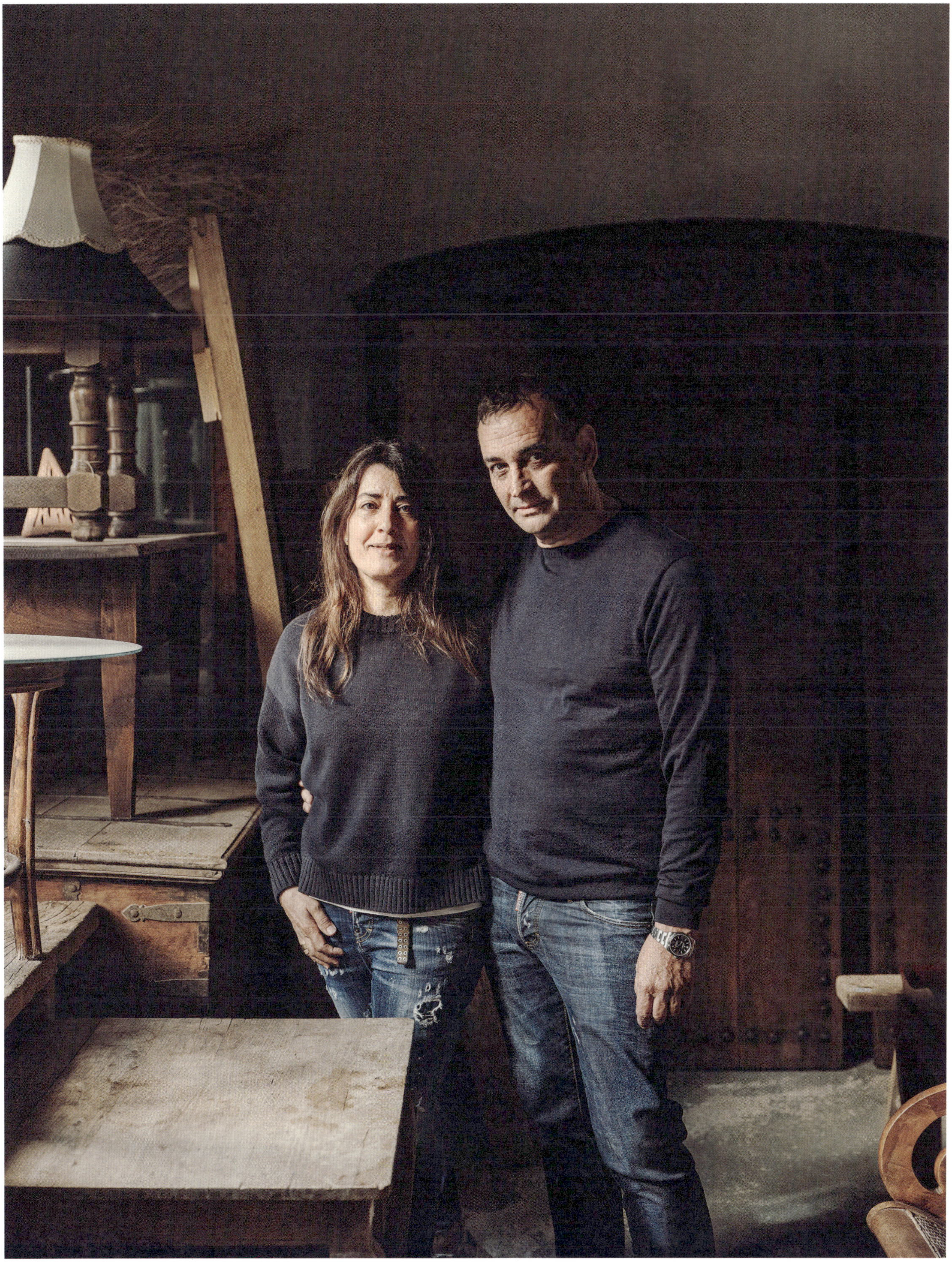

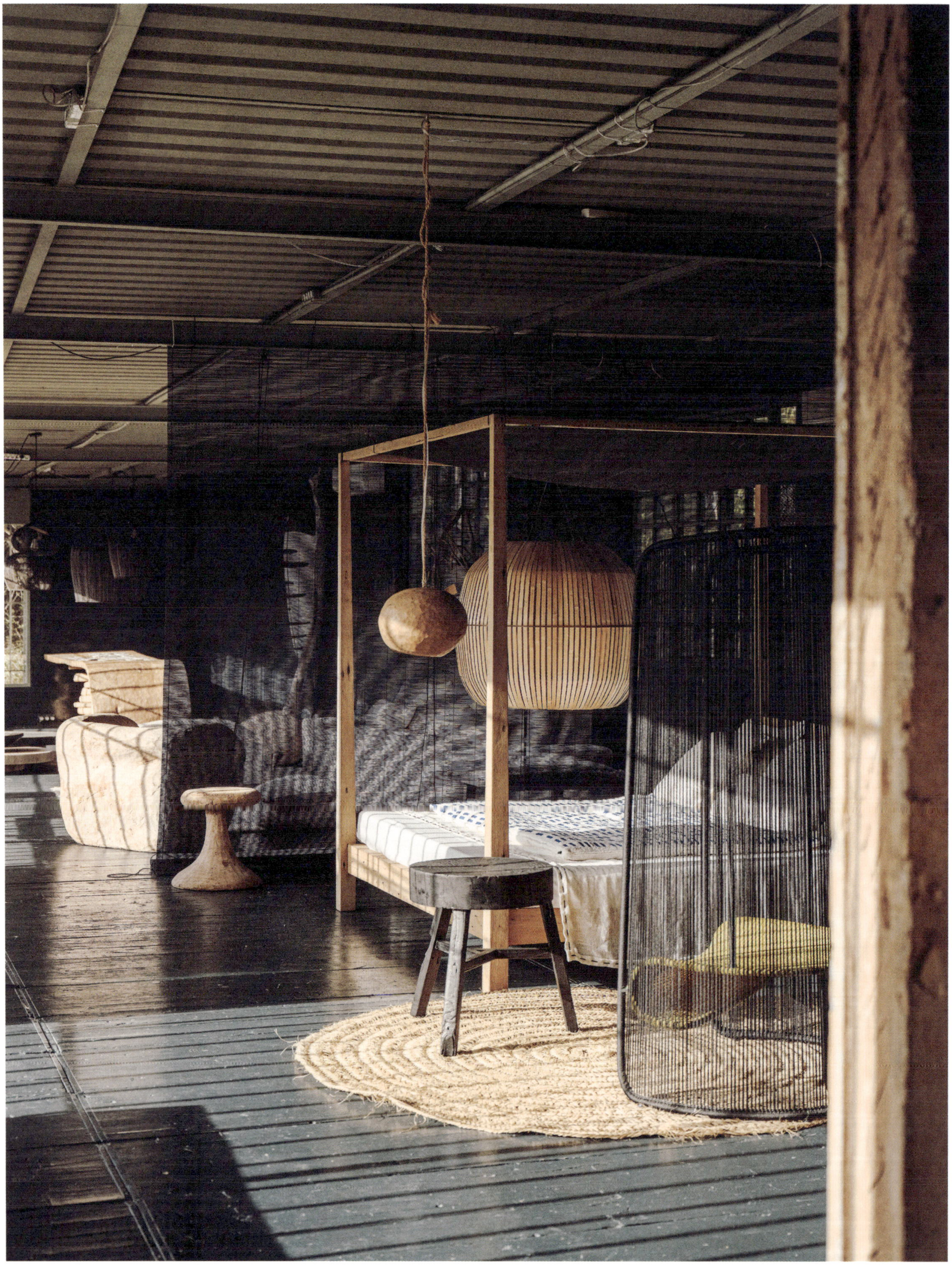

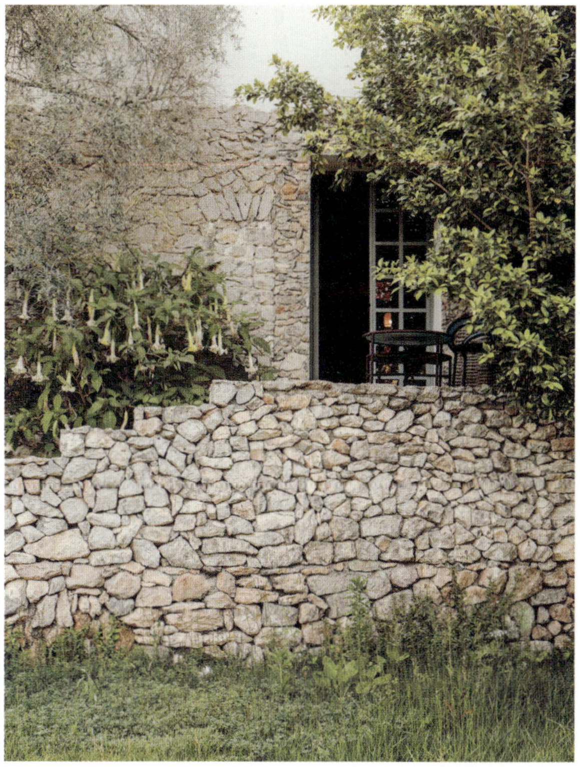

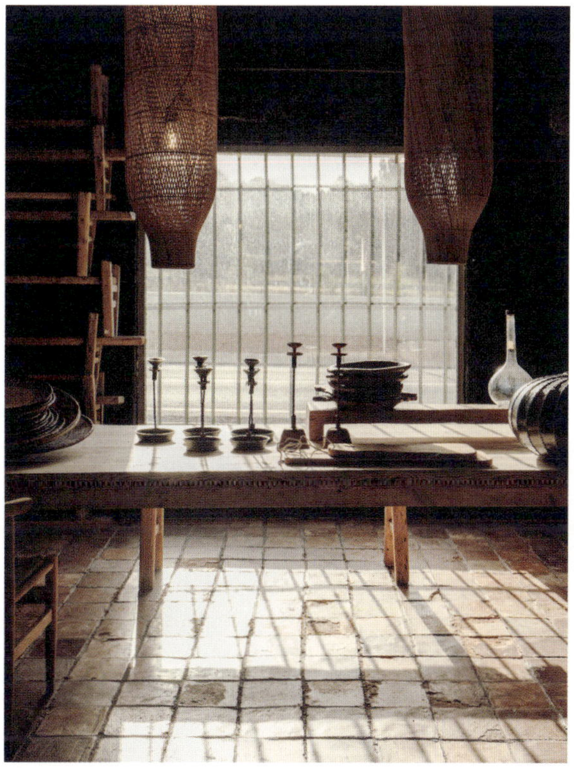

The showroom features a blend of in-house designs, restored antiques and curated brands. Accessed via stone steps (far left), the back garden adds to the space's charm and allure.

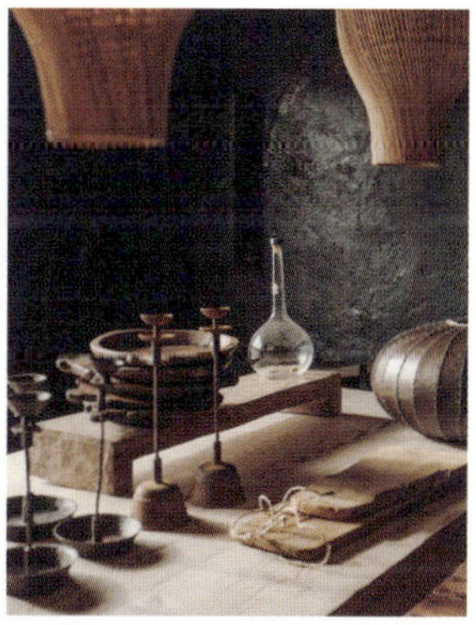

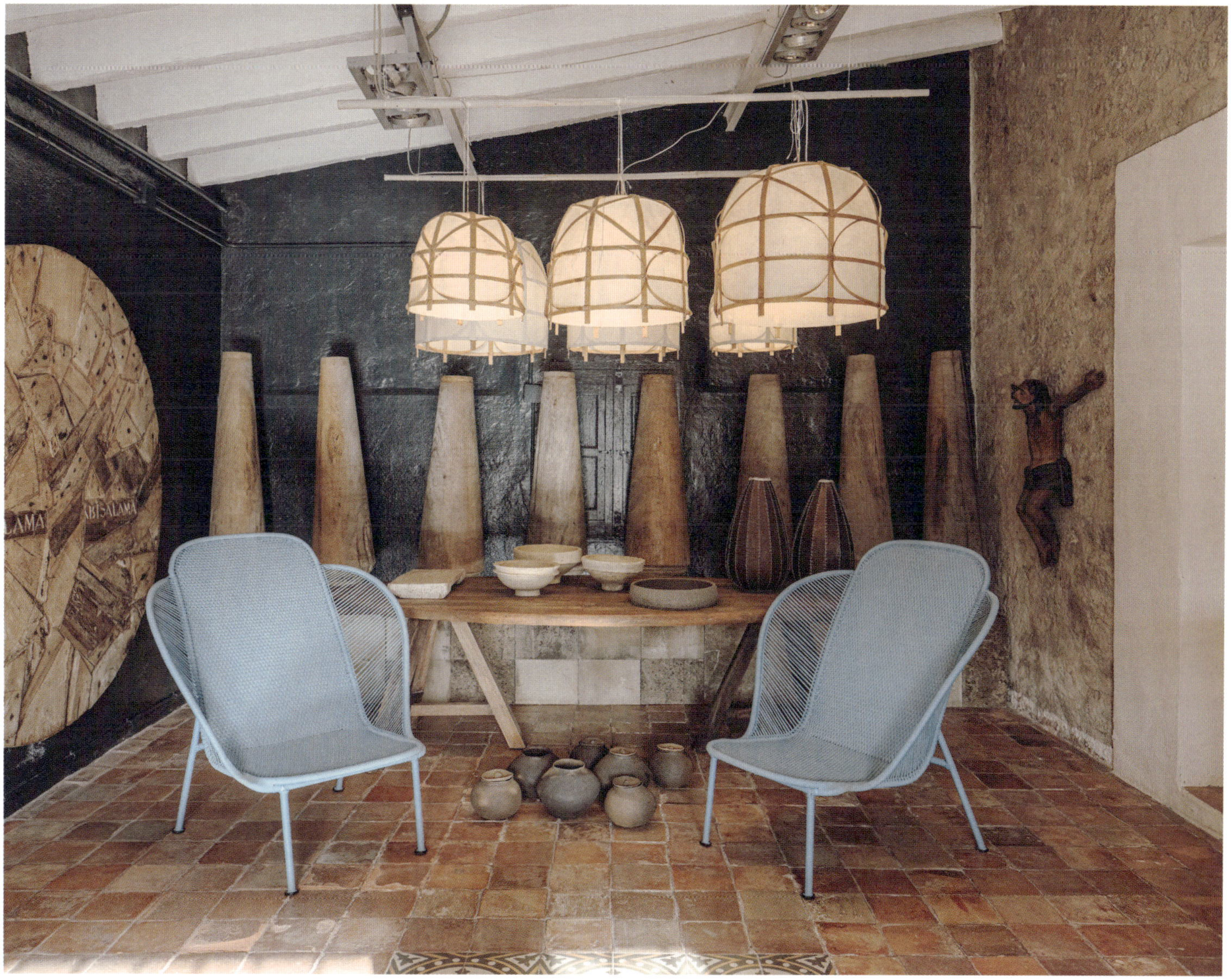

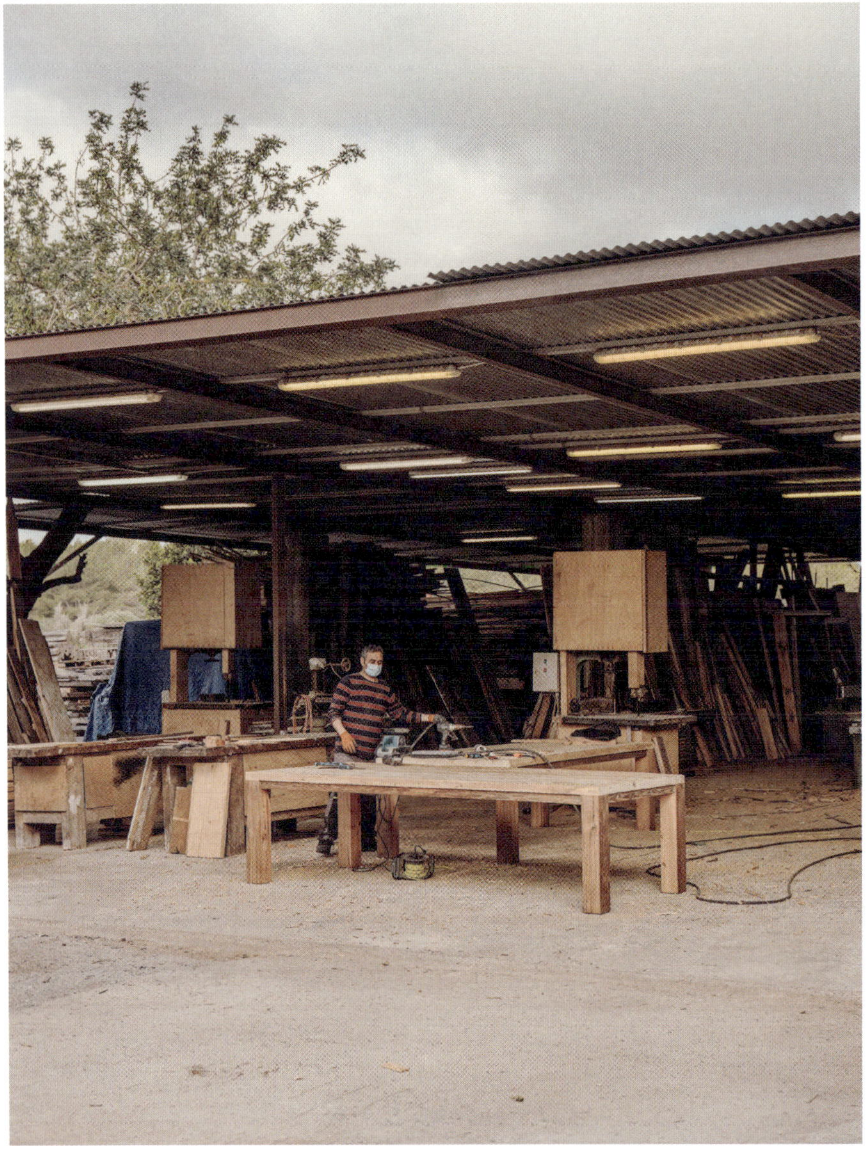

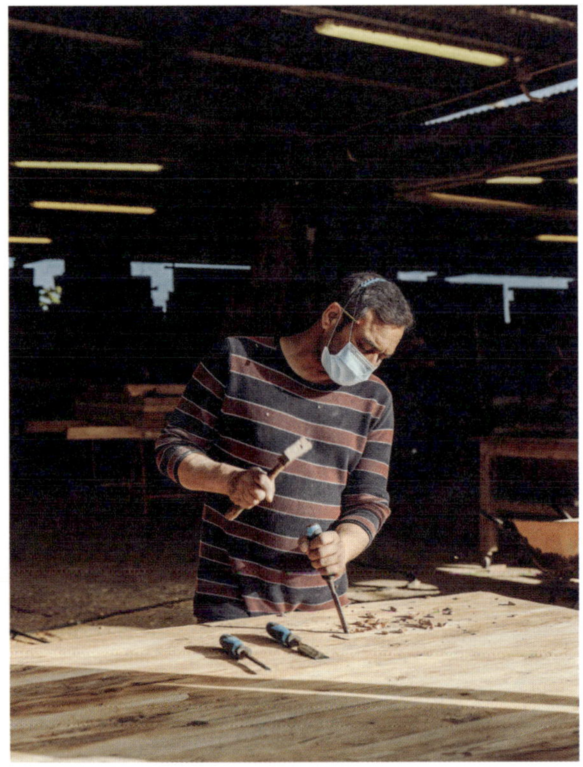

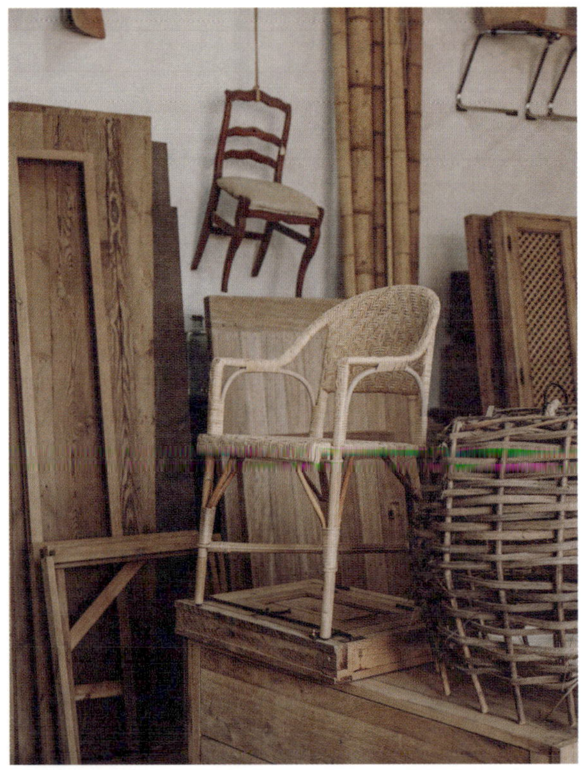

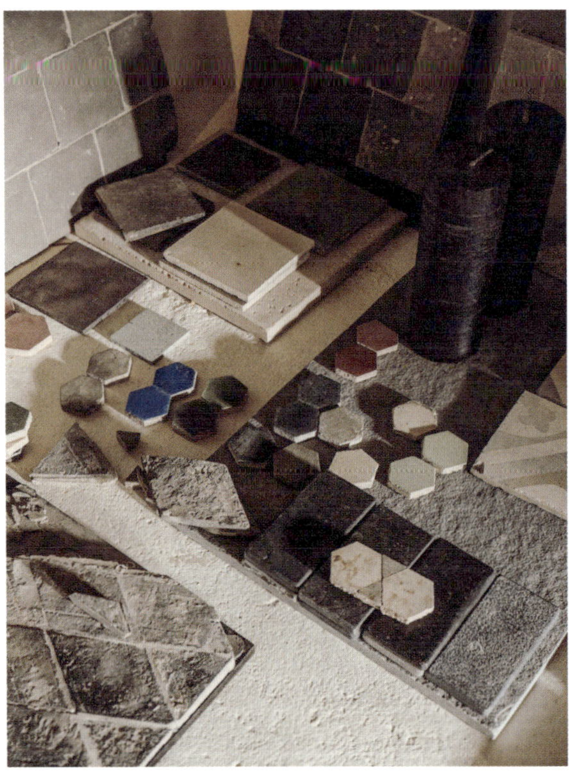

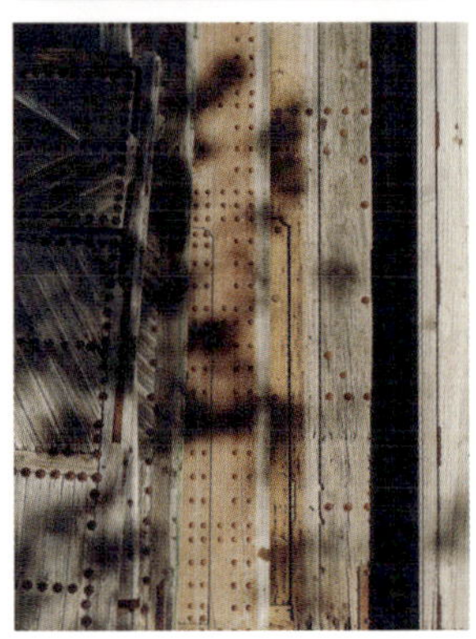

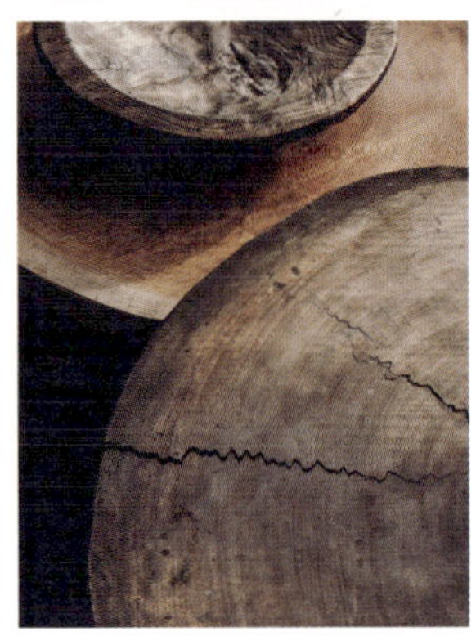

Working mostly manually, the Can Castello workshop maintains the originality of the wooden elements. The target is to adapt the recovered furniture to the current needs of their clients and at the same time to create one-off, timeless pieces.

Right: For their projects, Pura and José collect special tiles and stones, which are displayed in the material samples room.

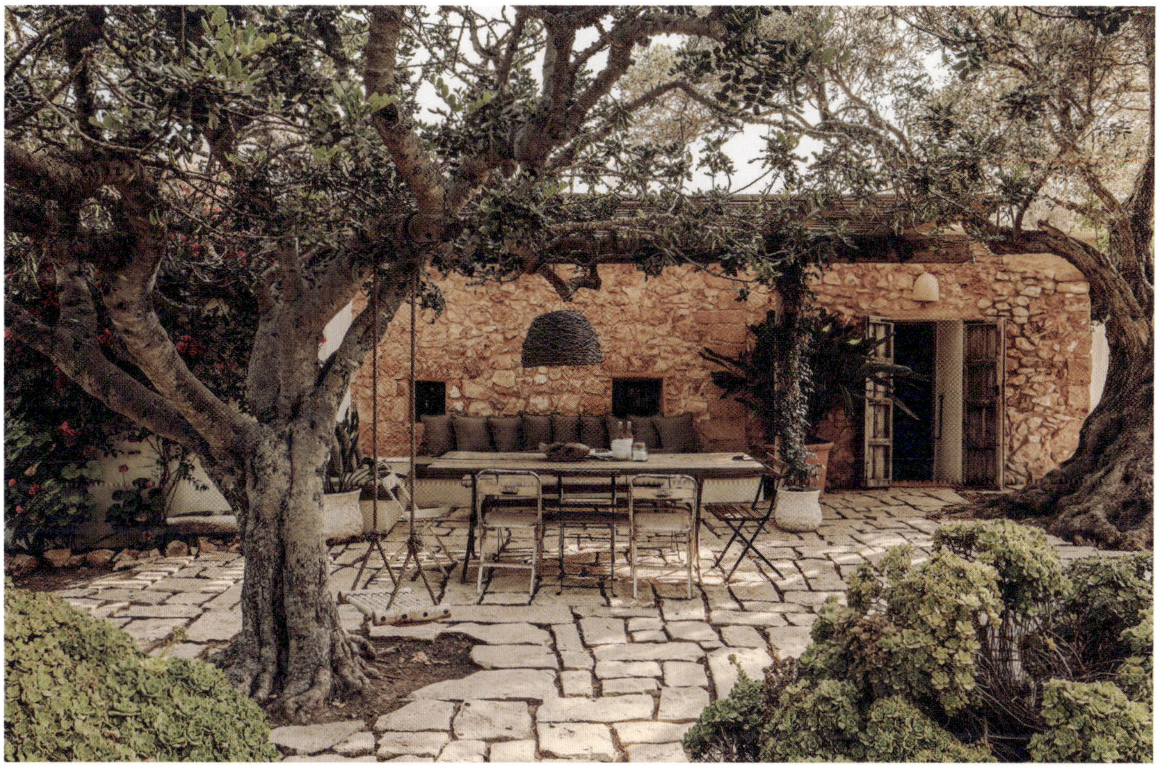

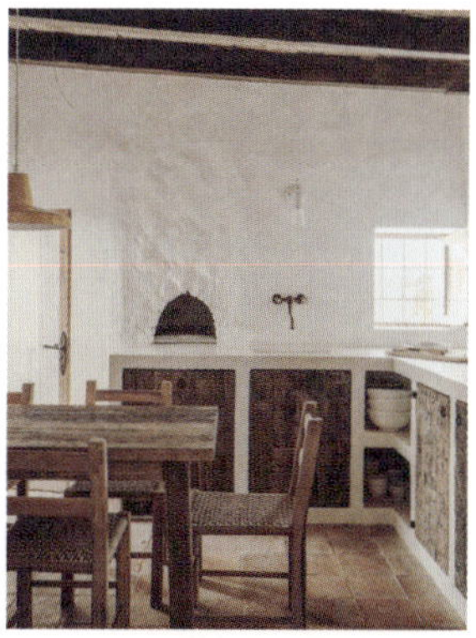

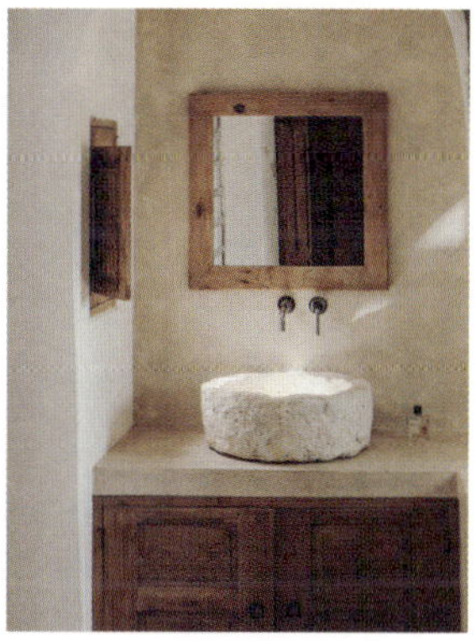

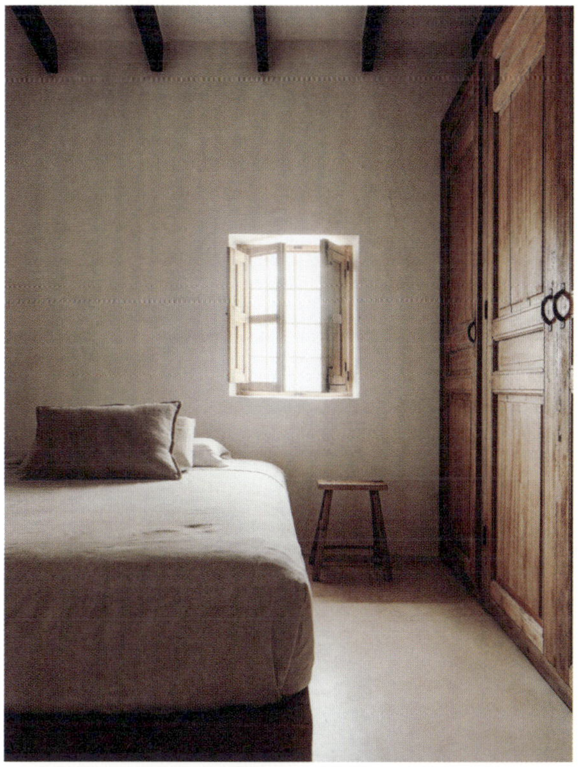

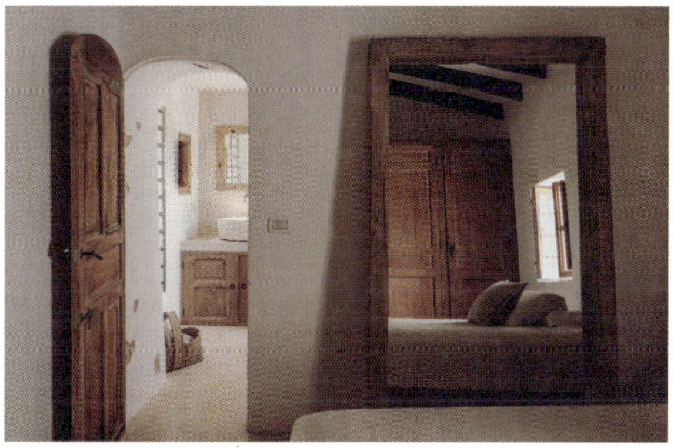

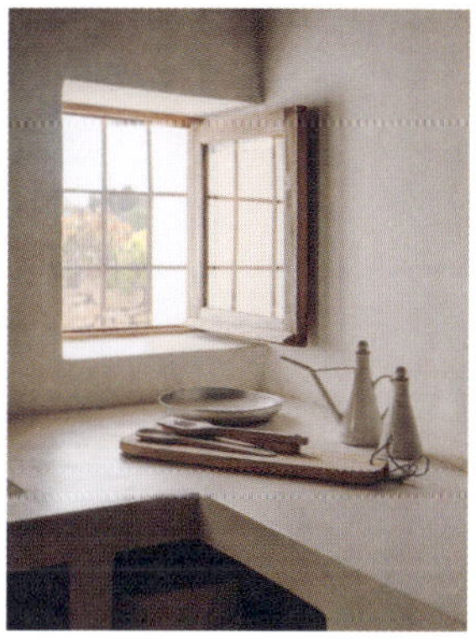

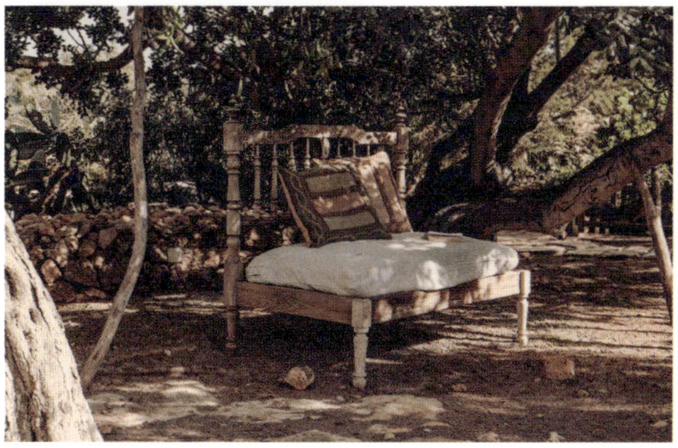

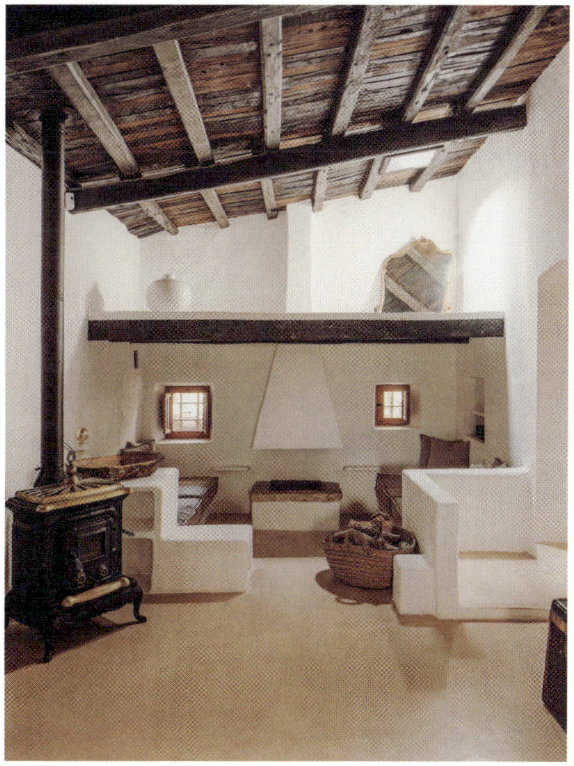

Can Castello's restoration project in Formentera honours the original features of the house, while introducing microcement, natural stone and handcrafted furniture from Pura and José's workshop.

SAN RAFAEL
sumeriacreations.com

SUMERIA CREATIONS

STAGE DESIGN

When Rabten van Oorschot arrived in Ibiza from The Netherlands at the age of eighteen, he made a living as a fire artist on Benirràs beach. That work led to invitations to perform in private houses, and he then received bookings for large corporate events around the world. He even toured with Cirque du Soleil.

Nowadays, in his mid-thirties, the Dutchman occasionally wows friends with his fire-breathing, but he no longer does it professionally. 'It's tough, always working at night and inhaling so much paraffin', he says.

Since he left fire-breathing behind, Rabten has made his name designing stage sets for clubs and events, from the vibrant nightlife scene in Ibiza to many festivals around the globe, including the infamous Burning Man in the Nevada desert.

Sumeria Creations was set up in 2016 and is based in San Rafael, north of Ibiza Town. Its neighbours are other small workshops, including one that repairs wooden boats.

Rabten is responsible for the timber construction of sets, while his partner, Nicolas Estrella, who used to make boat sails, sews together the shading systems.

'The magic of our stages is that we have the combination of building of the skeleton of the stages by hand, our computer-programmed CNC cutting machine to create the interiors, and the sewn element', says Rabten. 'Hardly anyone else in Ibiza offers this combination.'

Sumeria Creations has been behind many of Ibiza's most spectacular club nights and events, including Woomoon at Cova Santa in San José. But the island's commercial club scene has not recovered since the Covid pandemic.

In contrast, private events for Ibiza's wealthy residents are booming. An event at a private house can last from just one day to four days. 'We make stages and chill-out areas, and we can transform the setting into a themed environment. Everything is produced on demand', Rabten explains.

Some private clients follow up an event in Ibiza with one in their home town. That could be in London, UK, or in Tulum, Mexico. Sumeria Creations also works on electronic music events around the world, through commissions from the Paris-based event agency We Are Us. Those commissions have taken Rabten to El Palacio de Bellas Artes in Medellín, Colombia; to the Hôtel Salomon de Rothschild in Paris; and to Venice's leading casino.

'I produce everything in Ibiza and ship the parts to the festivals. If the event is in Europe, we pack everything into our van and go. It takes time, but it's cheaper than hiring a courier company and it's more interesting', says Rabten.

The hardest job of all, according to Rabten, is Burning Man, where he is one of tens of thousands of 'Burners' who gather to build Black Rock City, a temporary community in the desert. For several years, Sumeria Creations has designed and built 'camps' on site. 'You must take all your equipment to the middle of the desert, and if you forget a single screw, you're in trouble', Rabten says. 'After the event, everything has to be dismantled, and you can't leave any trace behind. It's hard, but very inspiring and a good learning process.'

Rabten's ambition is to design the massive centrepiece temple at Burning Man one year, or another stage elsewhere of that size. ***CD***

Business partners Rabten van Oorschot (on left) and Nicolas Estrella stand outside their workshop in San Rafael, where they create elaborate stage sets and installations for events and festivals.

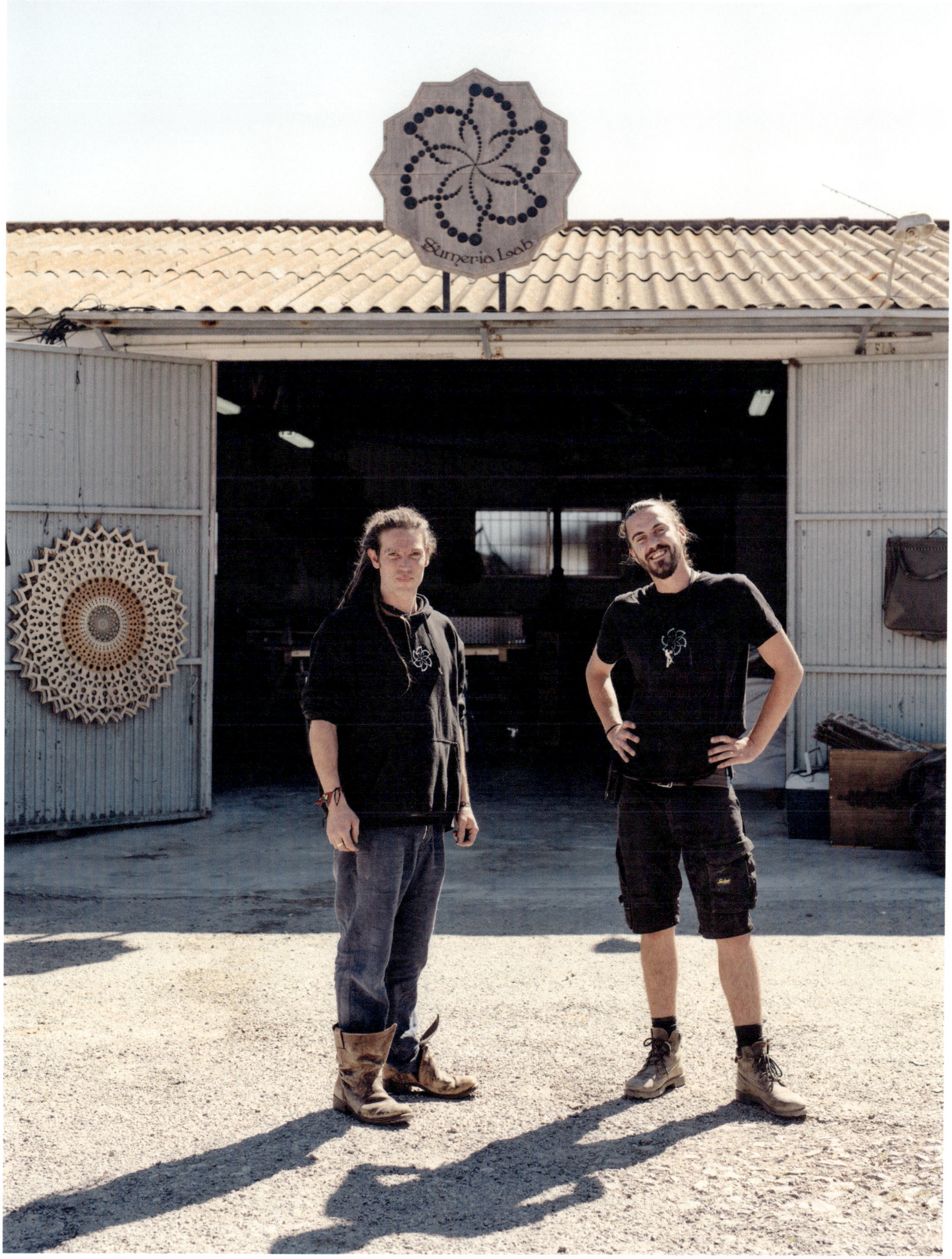
Sumeria Laab

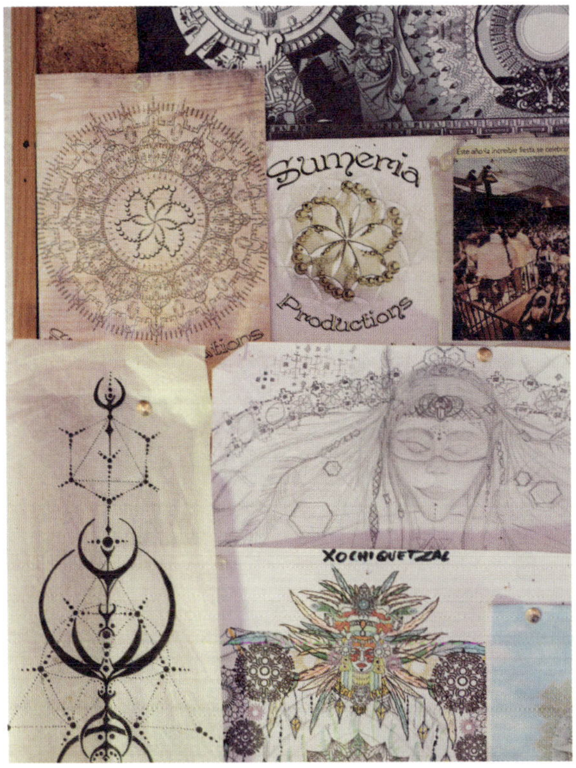

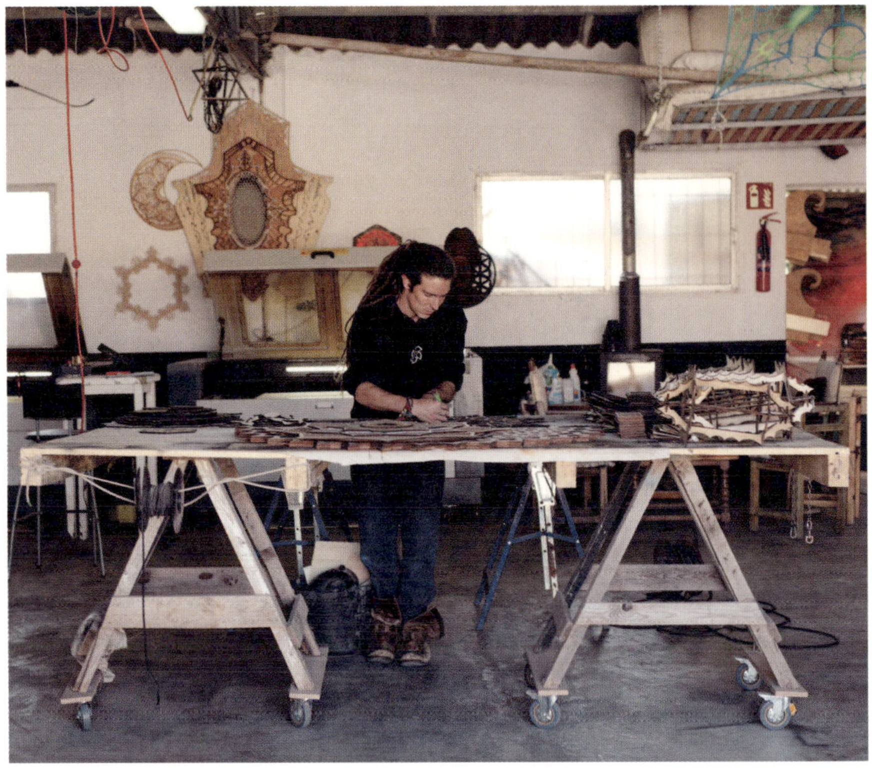

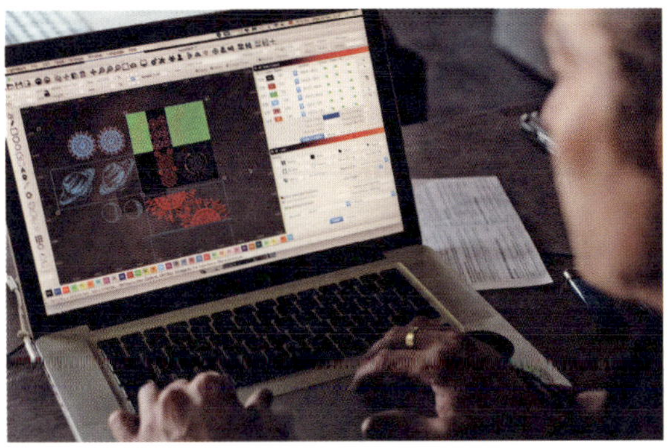

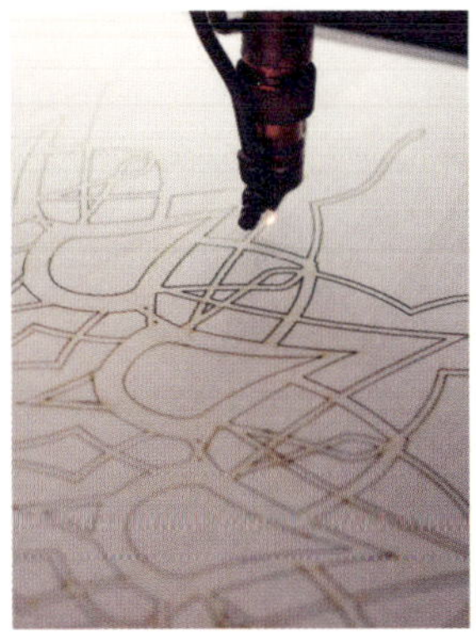

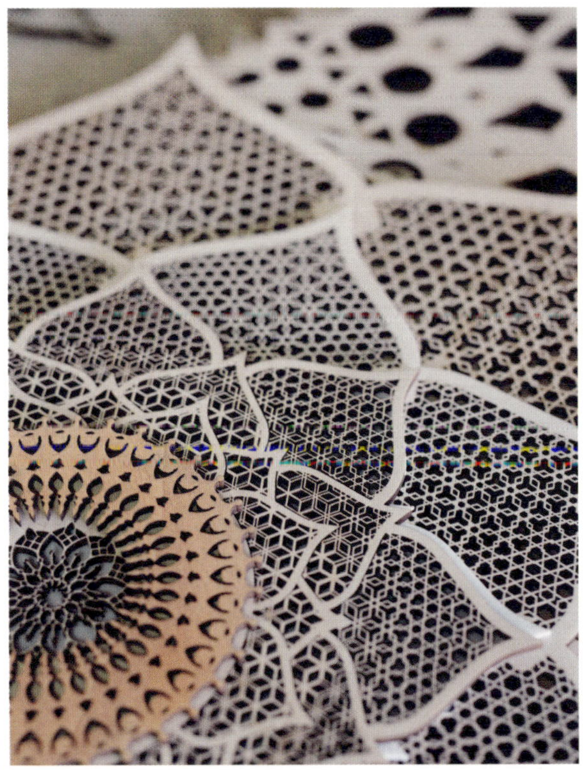

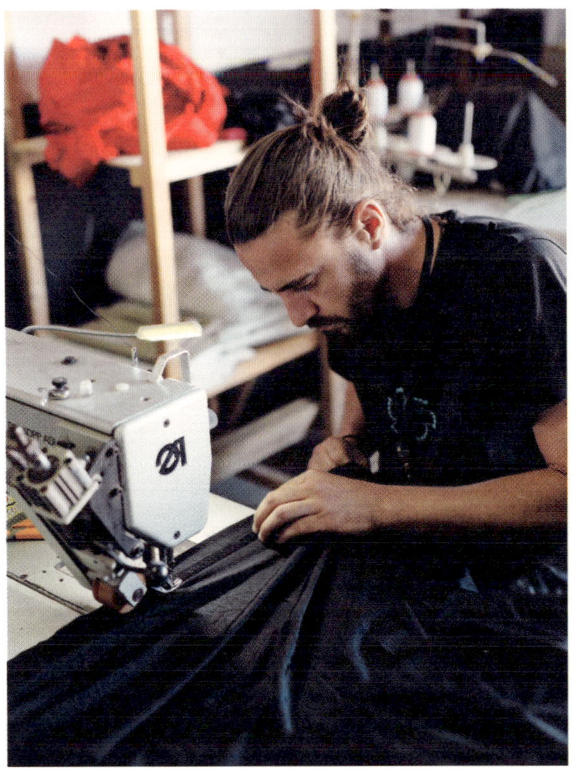

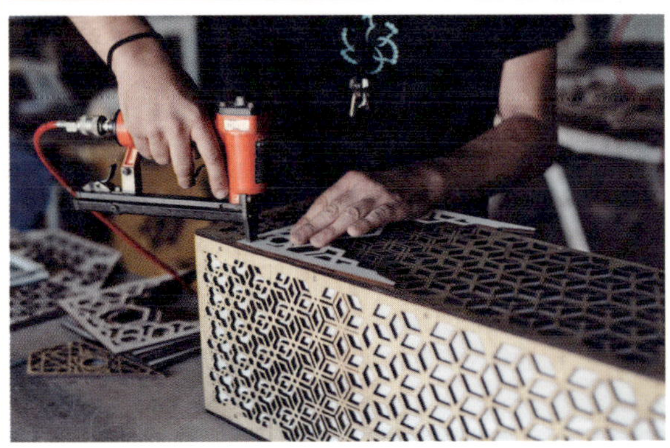

While Rabten is responsible for design, and programmes the CNC cutting machine to create intricate patterns in wood, Nicolas uses his background in sailmaking to stitch the fabric elements.

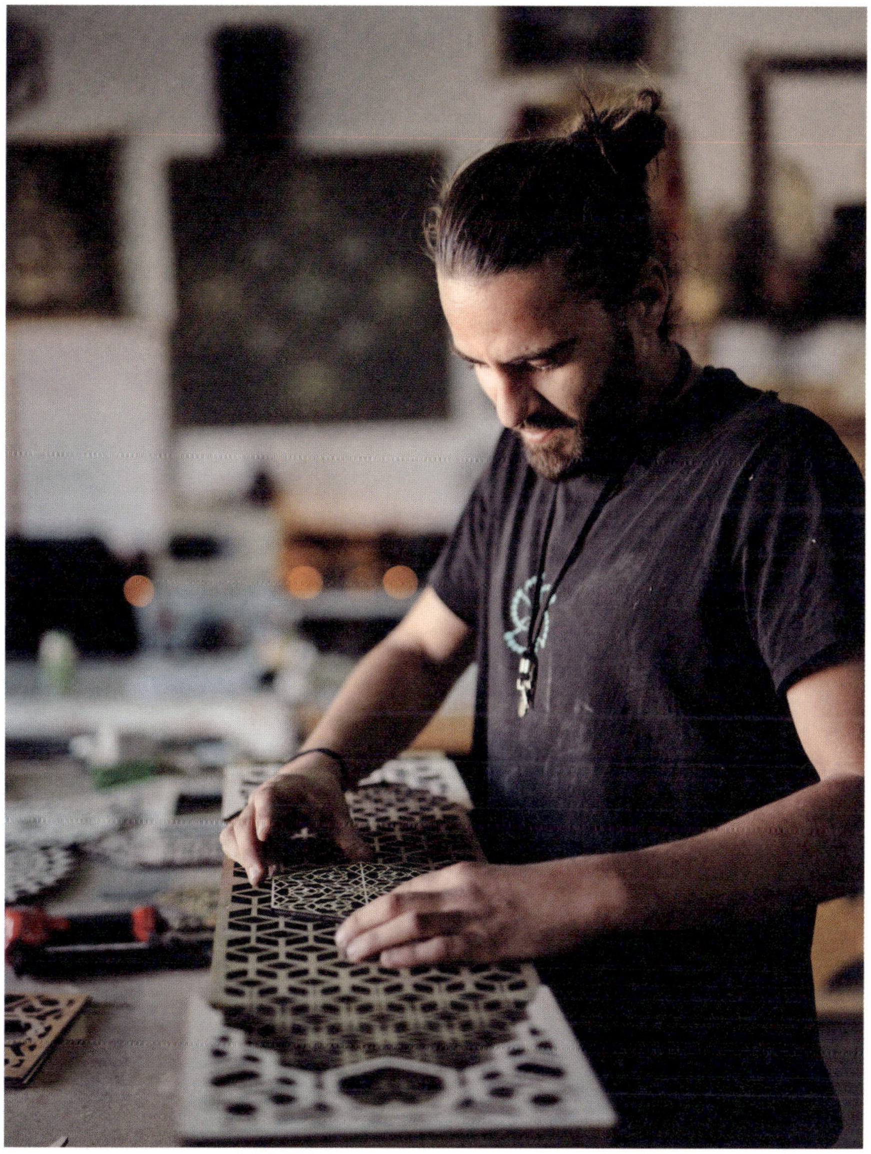

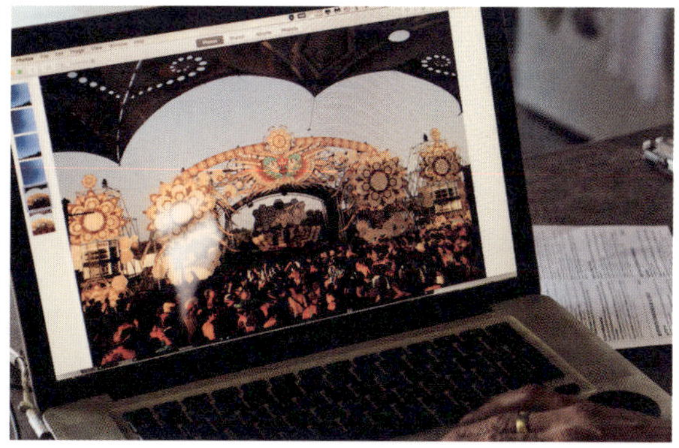

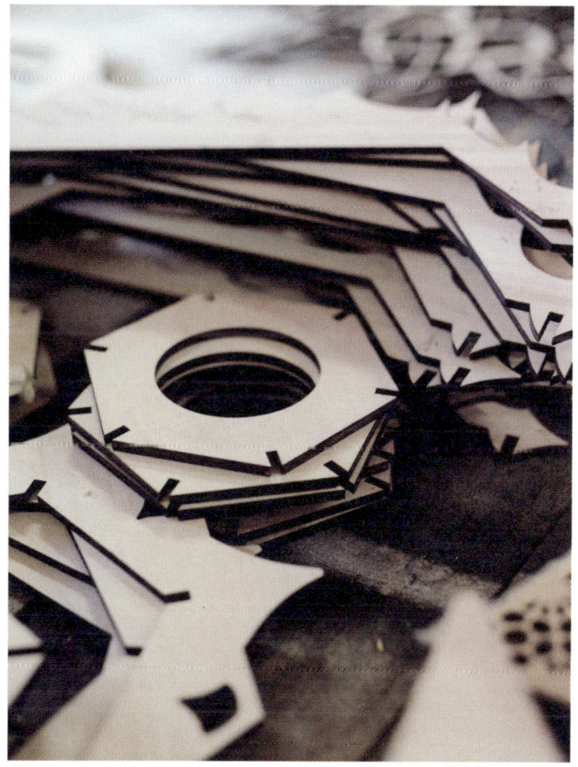

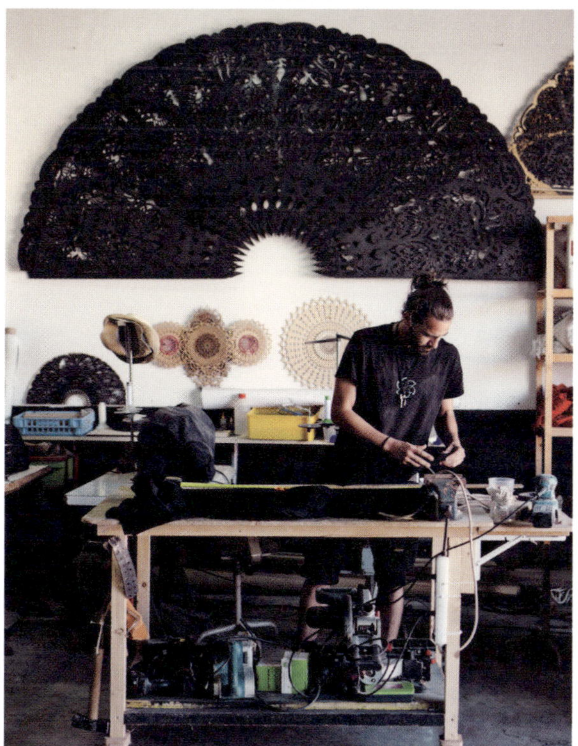

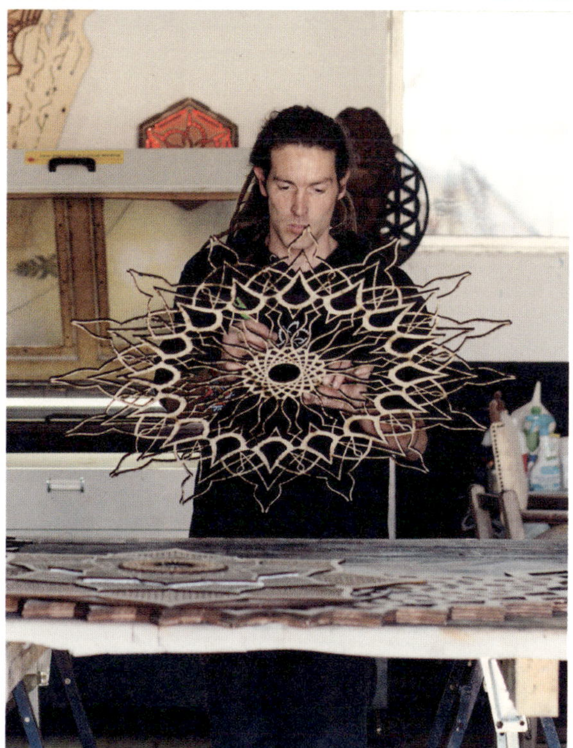

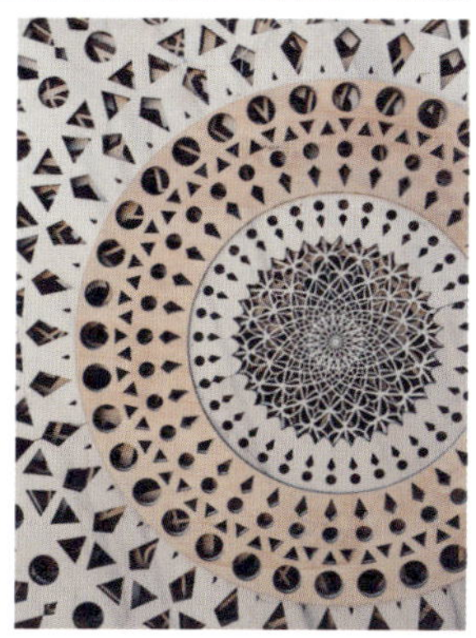

In his designs, Rabten often uses the mandala, a spiritual and ritual symbol in Hinduism and Buddhism. Once installed, such creations are often illuminated by a laser show.

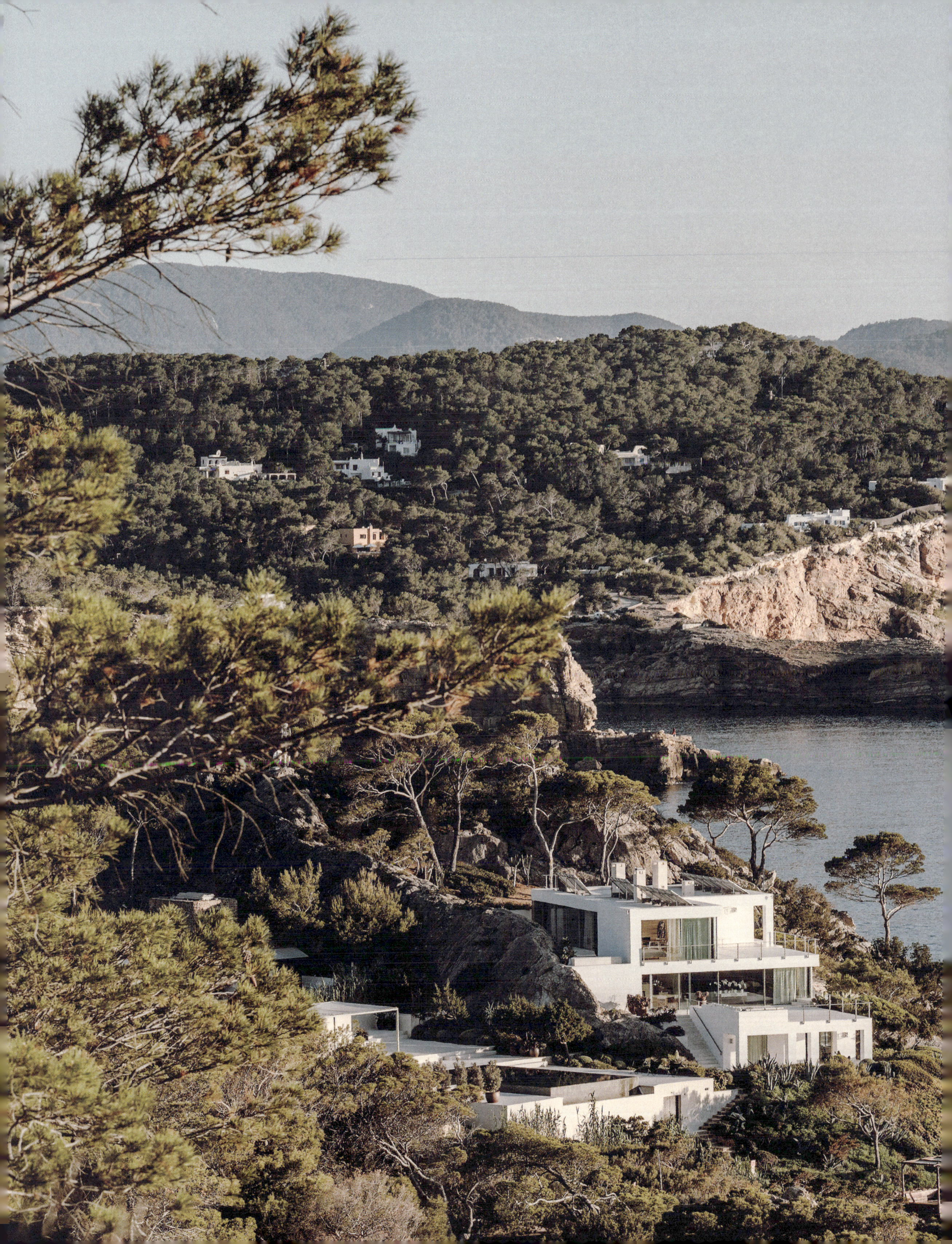

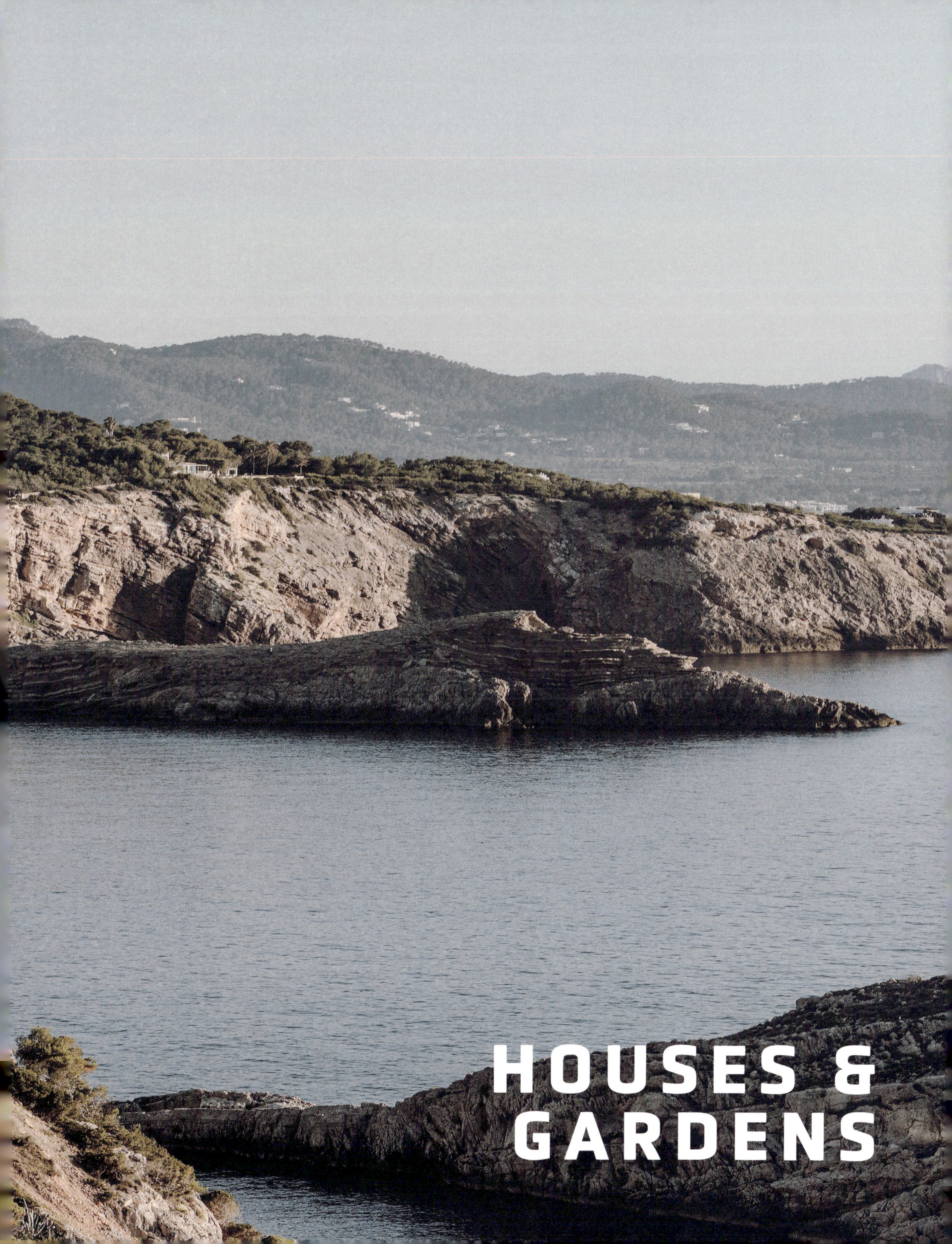

HOUSES & GARDENS

VICENT 'PALERMET' MARÍ SERRA

PRESERVATION

Vicent Marí Serra is the descendant of a long line of Ibicenco men whose sobriquet, Palermet, is a diminutive of the Sicilian place name Palermo and a nod to Ibiza's ancient migratory routes. A constructor, historian and champion of Ibizan rural heritage, Palermet is also a master esparto weaver, having learnt at the knee of his paternal grandfather, Pep Palermet. In 1962 Pep was the last quarryman at Sa Pedrera de Cala d'Hort, now commonly known as Atlantis. Along with many other traditional methods, weaving was a fundamental process on the island for thousands of years. On the uninhabited island of s'Espartar, off the south-western coast of Ibiza, esparto grass has been harvested since time immemorial. Today very few weavers remain. 'My grandfather and I would row out to s'Espartar in July to cut the grass, leaving it to dry in the sun', recalls Palermet. 'It then needed to be soaked for twenty-eight to forty days. Historically, it was soaked in vast nets in the sea, but in recent years we have used tanks on land because boats and divers disturb the bundles.'

As the grass is soaked, natural fermentation occurs and breaks down the toughest part of the stem. This part is stripped away to reveal soft fibres that are then split into thirteen or fifteen strands and plaited. Once a plait is finished, it is sewn into shape. Traditionally, women made delicate, intricate pieces and men made rougher pieces to be used on the farm. The origins of the esparto on s'Espartar remain a mystery: the grass is native to North Africa, and it is thought that the grassland may be the remnant of a Roman plantation. The basketry techniques are Palaeolithic in origin and similar to those found across the African continent.

Examples of Palermet's woven pieces can be found in the ethnographic museum close to Ses Païsses de Cala d'Hort/Ses Hisendes d'en Sorà, a historic finca that Palermet has been restoring since 2008. The property was originally a farm owned by the aristocratic Sorà family, whose primary residence was in Dalt Vila. The inhabitants were farm workers whose role would have involved forest-clearing, charcoal-burning and the cultivation of almond crops for export. The techniques used by Palermet at Ses Païsses de Cala d'Hort are the same as those used when the house was built more than 200 years ago. 'Historically, a finca was constructed using only materials that could be carried from nearby. Walls were built from limestone rocks and a lime mortar. Posidonia – a marine plant native to the waters of Ibiza and Formentera – was used, along with ash and clay, in the construction of the roofs', he explains.

In times past, lime played a vital role in remote areas of Ibiza such as Cala d'Hort, and each house would have had its own kiln. Palermet has restored the two kilns found at the finca in order to create his own mortar. Such rural traditions have been lost since Ibiza underwent a cultural shift in the 1960s from country to city life and daily tasks began to fall out of custom. 'When people leave the fields and go to live in San Antonio or Ibiza Town, they lose their connection to the earth. When the connection is gone, the wisdom and knowledge go with it. Our rural techniques have been in use for centuries, and it is heartbreaking to see them vanish in a few short years', laments Palermet.

As the historic farming community continues to age, it is undoubtedly a difficult time for Ibiza's fragile rural heritage. Palermet, however, is confident that a renewed interest in rural life and regeneration will help to preserve the island's ancient farming and construction methods. 'These techniques take years to learn, and I understand that such use of time is no longer economically viable. But if we unite as an island now, we can preserve our history for future generations. That is what I hope for.' ***MB***

Vicent Palermet is an advocate of Ibiza's cultural heritage and traditional techniques. He is engaged in restoring historic buildings, supporting museums with his craft and practising sustainable agriculture.

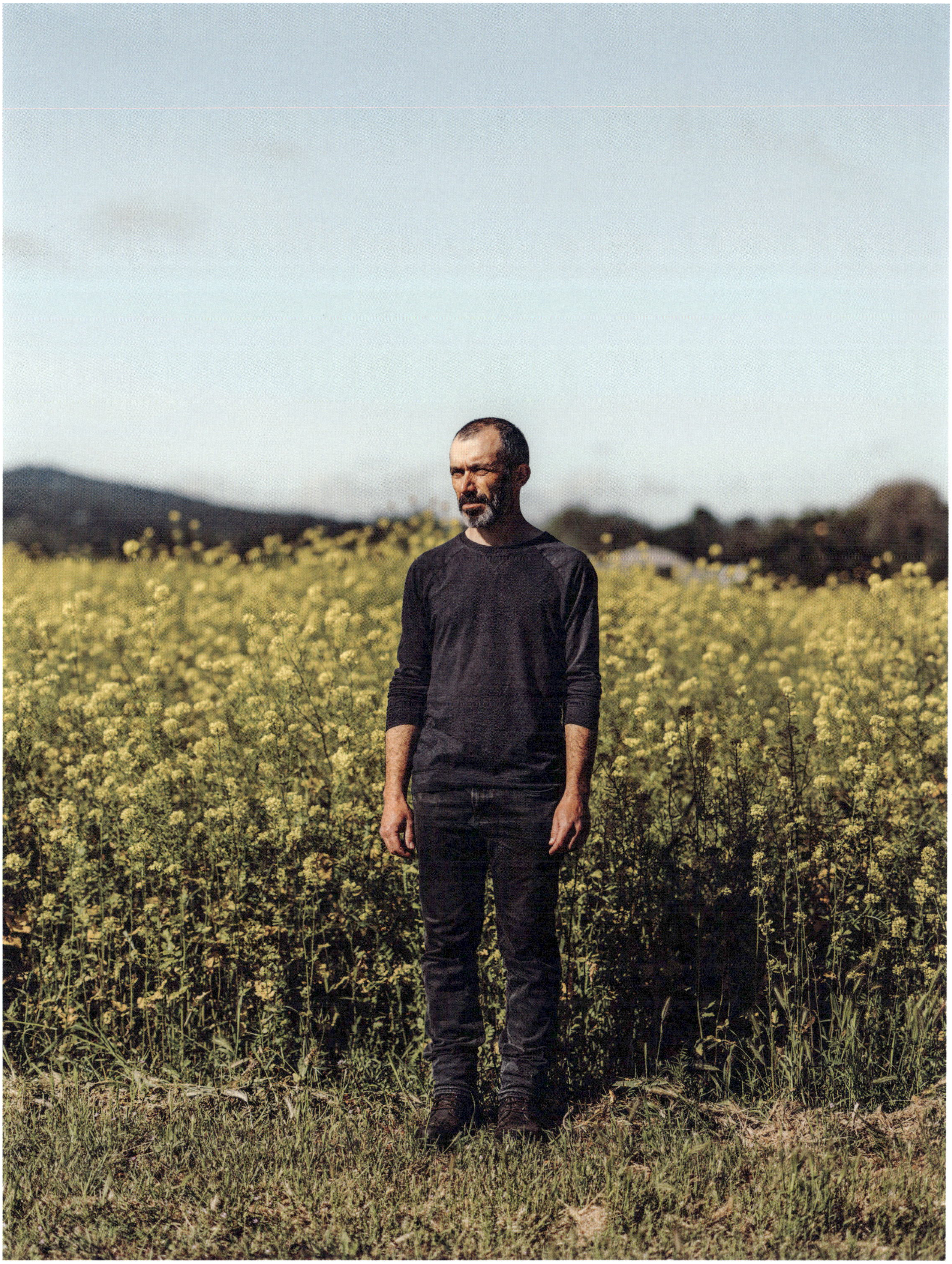

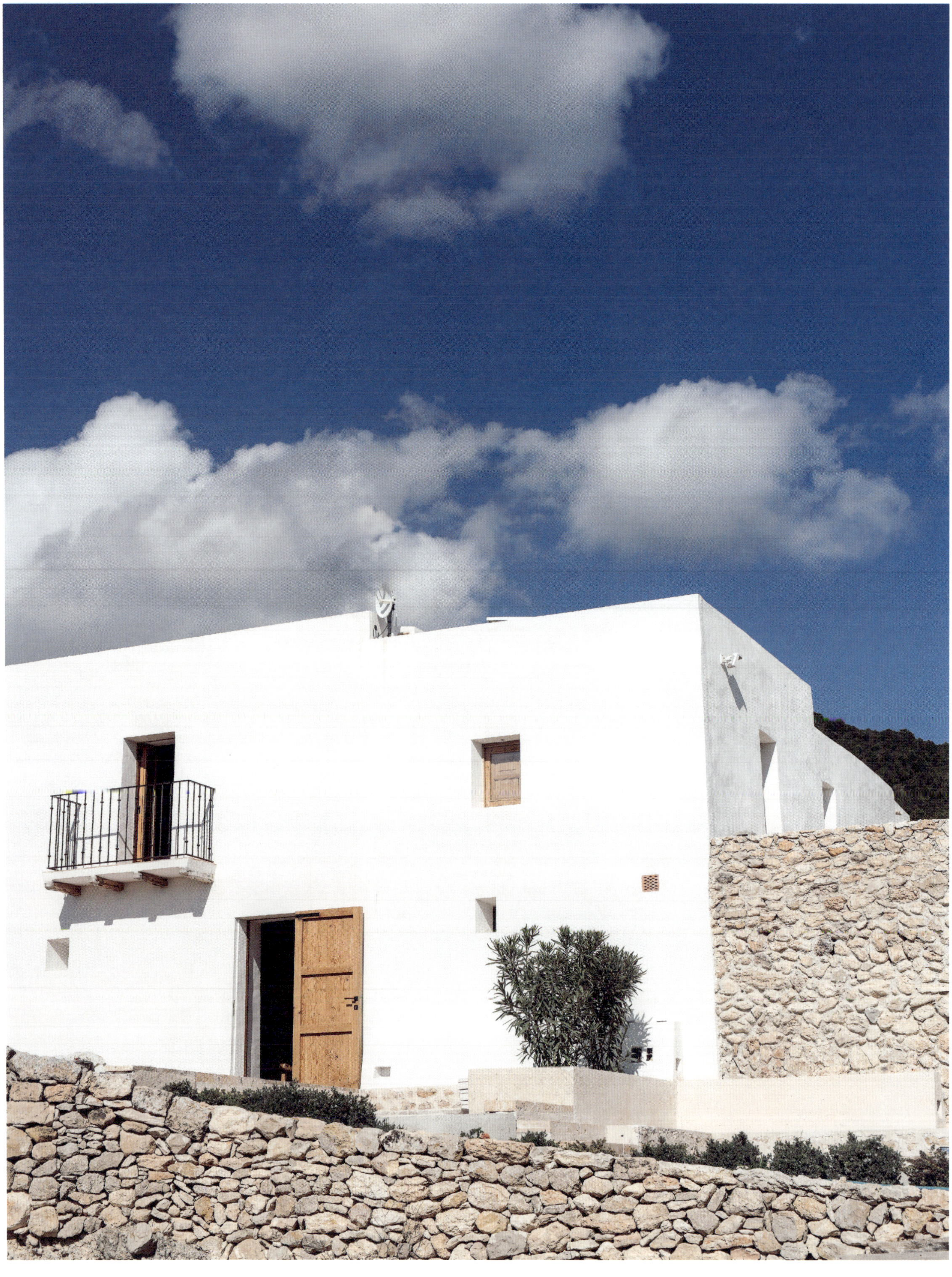

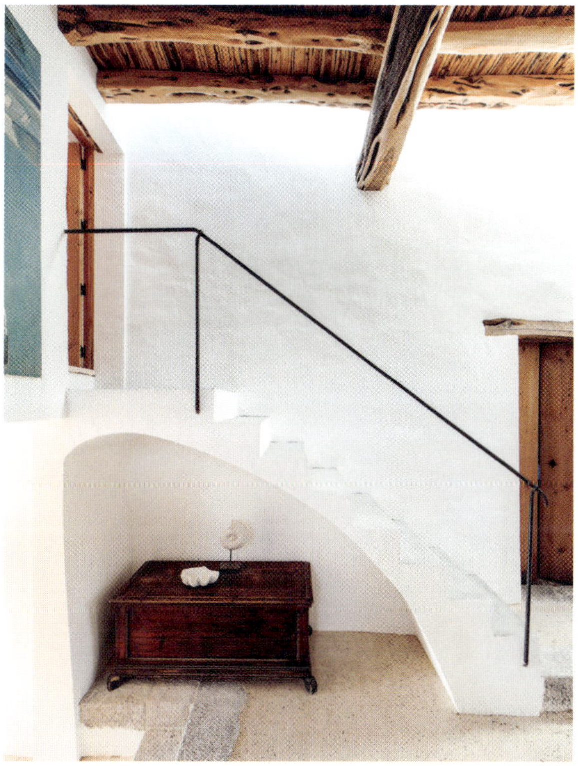

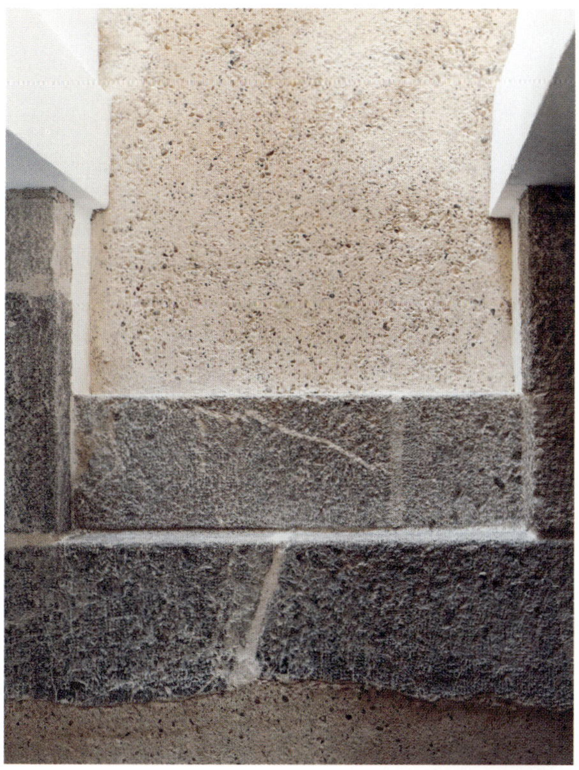

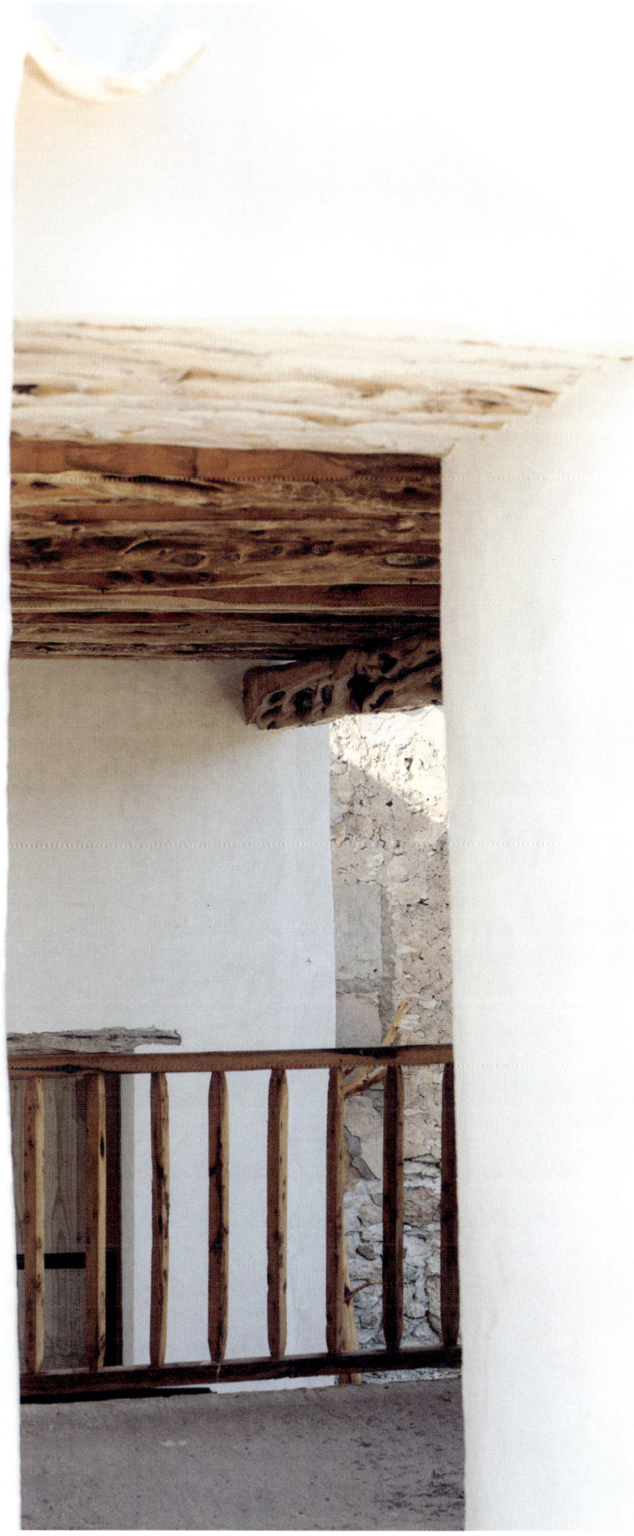

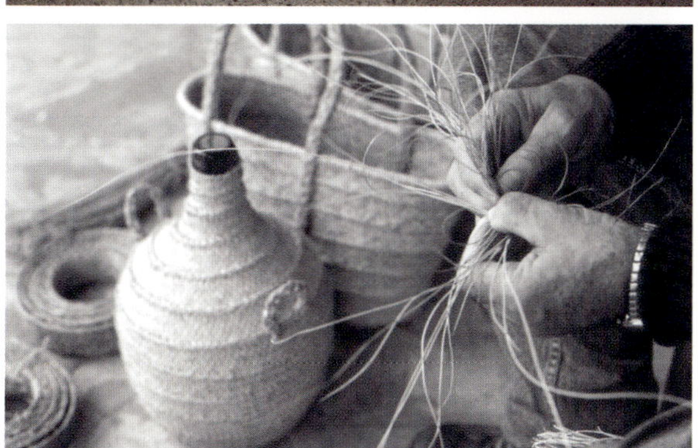

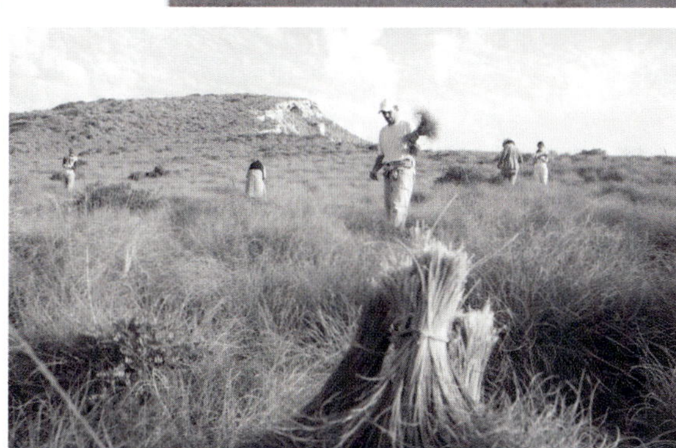

Opposite and above: Palermet has undertaken restoration work on the finca Ses Païsses de Cala d'Hort/Ses Hisendes d'en Sorà to preserve its historical value.

Far left: Woven works made by Palermet from esparto grass.

Left: Palermet harvests the grass on s'Espartar.

JESÚS
ecodisseny.info

ECODISSENY

PERMACULTURE & LANDSCAPE DESIGN

Pioneering, pragmatic and opinionated, Marcos Tur Witt has a love of the land that is the driving force behind his daily work. The son of two visionary artists, he left Ibiza as an optimistic, aspiring young designer, only to return shocked by the wasteful, consumptive habits of city-dwellers. He has been nudging people towards more sustainable systems and practices ever since. Specializing in permaculture, his landscape-design firm, Ecodisseny, promotes the idea that an appreciation of the past informs 'a retro-progressive path' for the future. Ibiza is an island long buffeted by outside influences, but Marcos's path is a quest for equilibrium and a plea to restore our relationship with Earth.

'I'm from the countryside, from the light, the sun, the sea', says Marcos, recalling his childhood. 'We ate limpets from the beach, blackberries from the field and apples from the orchard. It was a very different life.' His job at a Madrid interior-design firm was a stark contrast. 'When you're young, the city's culture and exhibitions feel wonderful, but there's also a part that feels aggressive and shocks your system', he says, explaining that urban life did not quite add up. 'There was a lot wrong with it all.'

Marcos returned to Ibiza disillusioned, but an invitation to see the Japanese natural farmer Masanobu Fukuoka at a conference in Mallorca became an emotional circuit breaker. 'The experience touched me very deeply', he recalls. 'I missed the plane home and spent a week fertilizing a farm with the group who had organized Fukuoka's visit.' Marcos began studying permaculture in earnest and in 2005 helped to set up Ibiza's first permaculture association.

'The key to redesigning human spaces on the island – or indeed around the globe – is to create a paradigm shift, working with a more systemic vision of the world, which is a great network of interrelationships', Marcos explains. 'Everything is connected.'

Marcos's projects fulfil this brief, resulting in complex elemental ecosystems where every leaf, stone and drop of water has been carefully considered within a larger seasonal puzzle. For example, for the architect Jaime Romano's revamp of the island villa Sa Ferradura, Marcos reforested the islet with native plant species, creating a seamless skyline with the surrounding pine-covered coast.

'There is definitely a duality with my approach', Marcos explains. 'On one side, there's my activism as an environmentalist, where I combine the whole package of permaculture, energy systems, water, landscaping and natural restoration with the message of reconnecting to nature. Then there's my ability to design and create contemporary things.'

Underlying all of this is a life philosophy that has evolved into an appeal for common sense: 'We cannot forget that we're still living beings integrated into a biosphere and that we're important figures in this biosphere. We cannot continue to live disconnected.'

Marcos's 'retro-progressive' recipe honours the essence of past traditions and culture while integrating technological advances in microbiology and regenerative agriculture. 'Human societies cannot follow the technological path if they do not first embrace the return to land and nature, the connection with the elements', he says. 'We must begin to resacralize the earth, the sky, the sea, the wind, the air and our ancestors – all of the cultural, tribal wisdom, which we seem to have lost.'

For Marcos, the essence of change is awareness. 'Ultimately, meeting Fukuoka changed my life', he says. 'I hadn't been interested in agriculture until then, but he talked about it through the prism of philosophy; he talked about energy, the cosmic seed. Something clicked, and there it was: a sudden awareness.' Much like the story of his mother and father – a partnership between a teacher and a painter (see pp. 190–93) – Marcos's vision and vocation form a marriage of the abstract and the avant-garde. ***LA***

Marcos Tur Witt is a staunch proponent of permaculture, and argues that an improved climate can be achieved only by adopting a more systemic vision. Each garden project becomes a small step towards a more fertile, caring, considerate future.

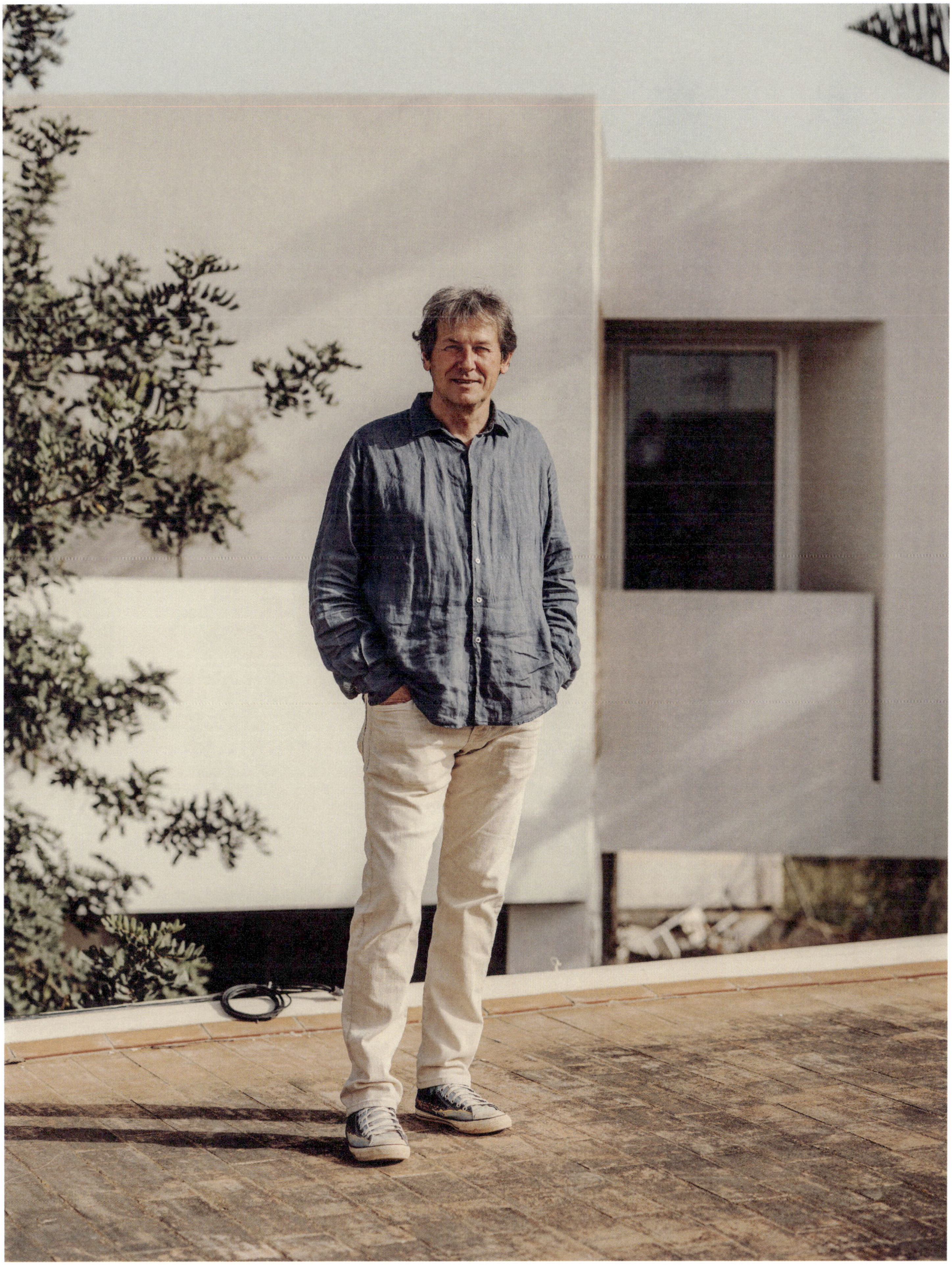

Ecodisseny's studio is housed in a building that was completed in 2015. The courtyard (bottom centre) serves as both welcoming entrance and central artery, connecting the studio and gallery with the original house (see pp. 190–93).

Sitting just behind the ornamental lily pond (opposite), a small subterranean canal recycles the waste water into the garden.

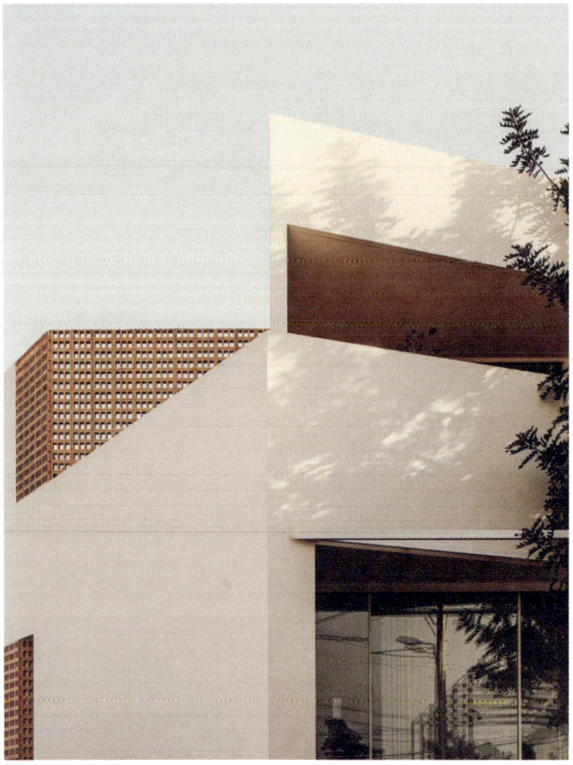

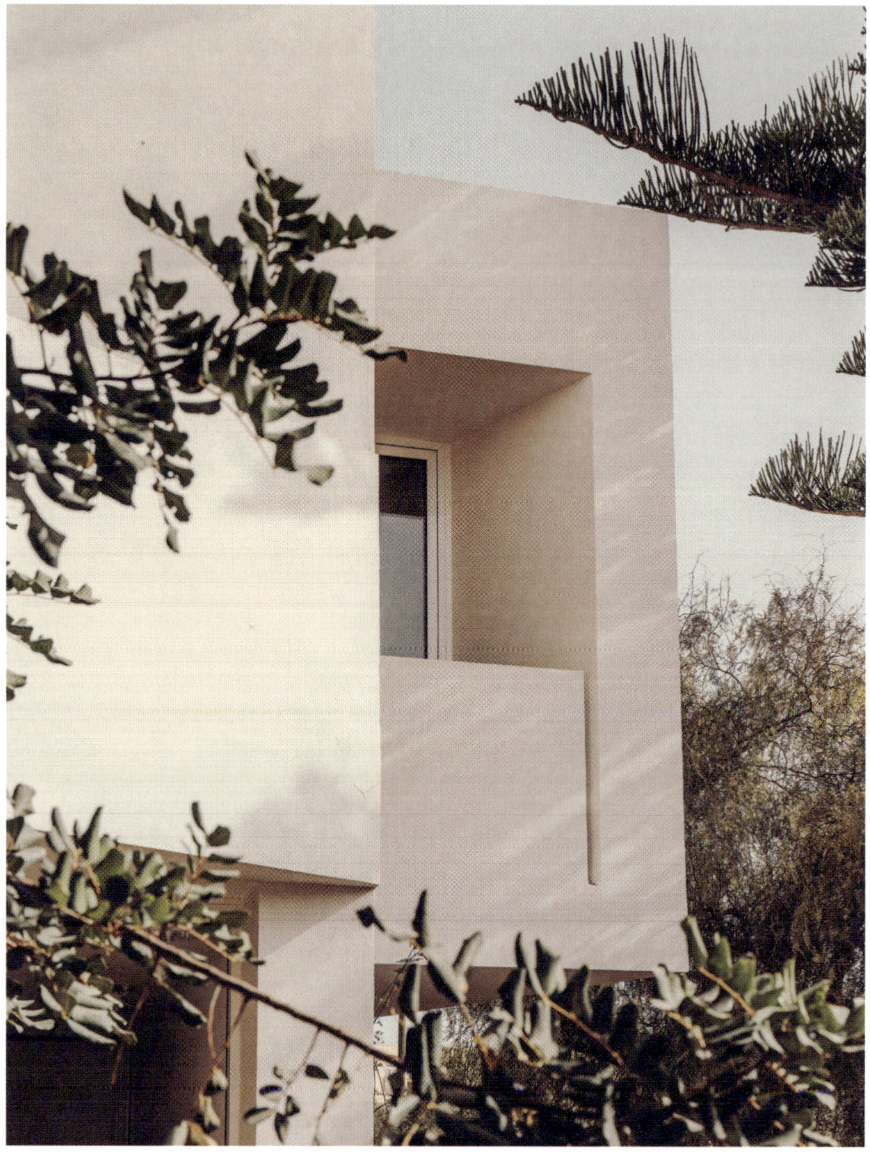

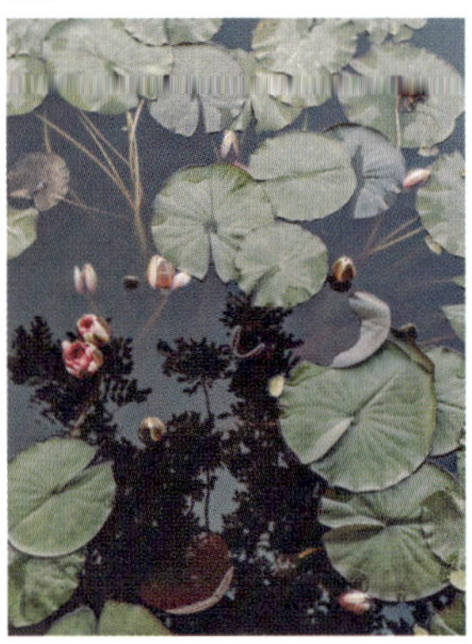

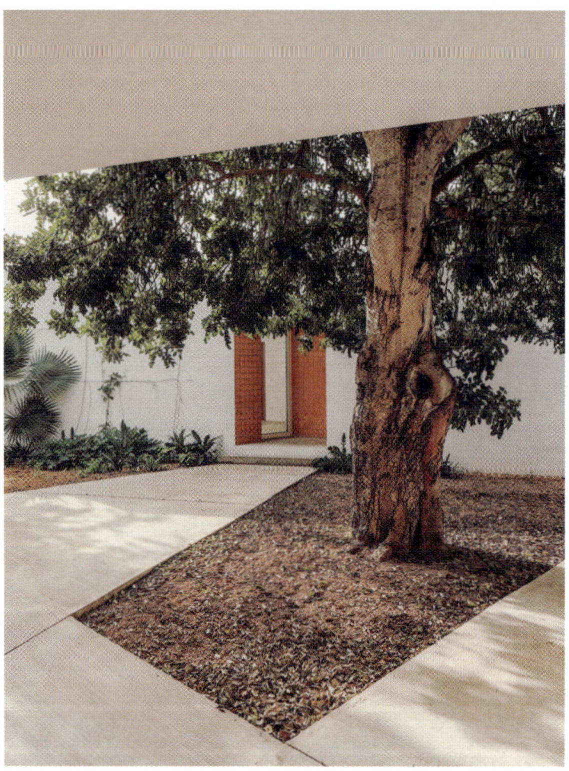

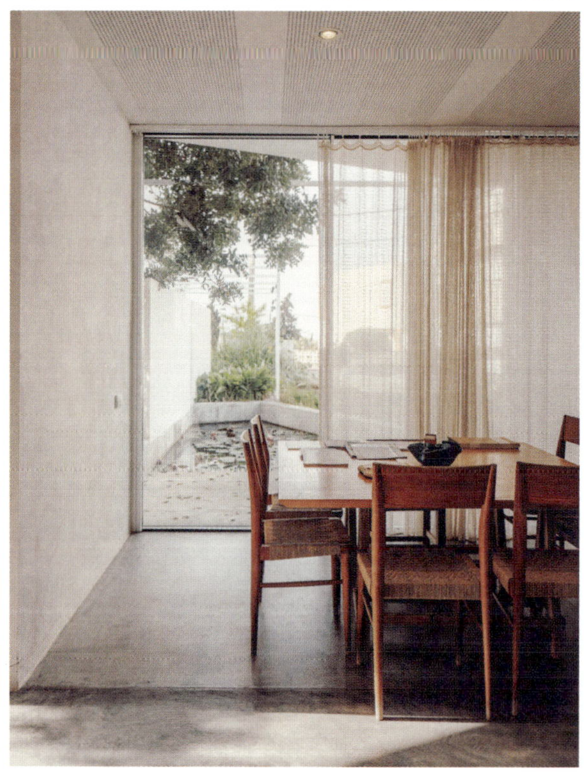

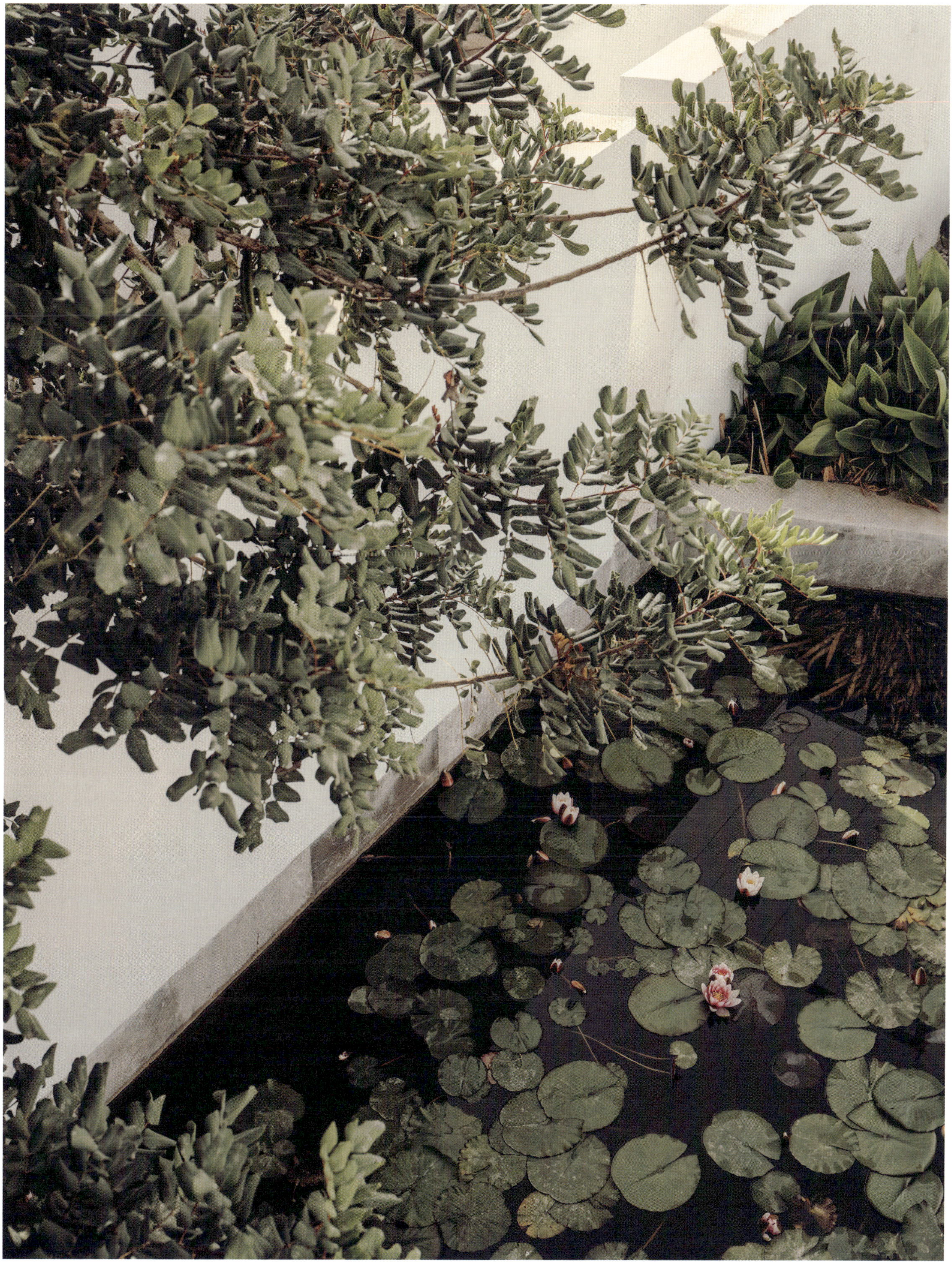

JESÚS
estuditurcosta.com

ESTUDI TUR COSTA

ATELIER & GALLERY

The tale of the Turs is deftly woven into Ibiza's creative tapestry. Part love story, part coming-of-age trajectory, it survives as a parable of the power of art to inspire new visions for the future. At the epicentre of this story is the family home. Designed and built by the architect Erwin Broner (pp. 234–37) in 1971, Rafael Tur Costa and Anneliese Witt's residence became an instant incubator of creativity. With a new modern building adding a combined art gallery, work studio and home for their son Marcos Tur Witt (see pp. 188–89), the family's creative legacy has continued to expand and inspire.

The artist Rafael Tur Costa was born in Ibiza in 1927, and his early works reflected the island's natural beauty through a realist and expressionist lens. When he met his soulmate, Anneliese Witt, a German-born artist schooled in the avant-garde, his way of seeing was forever changed. Anneliese introduced Rafael to the alluring world of abstraction, and together they went on to spearhead an entire movement of progressive thinkers, makers and builders.

Rafael became Ibiza's pre-eminent abstract painter and was awarded the Gold Medal, the Ibizan government's highest honour, just before his death in 2020. Anneliese was one of the island's most celebrated modern ceramicists. Passionate about safeguarding intergenerational wisdom, in 1977 she founded the pioneering children's art academy Infantart, which cultivated successive generations of local artists and makers.

The pair's modernist-influenced home was the final house built in Ibiza by the visionary German architect Broner. Located on the edge of the village of Jesús, it was completed at the beginning of the 1970s – a wildly contradictory decade that saw the ailing Franco dictatorship on the mainland contrasted with a modern movement of self-actualization sweeping across the Balearic Islands. Their new home became a focal point for the progressive thinkers and avant-garde artists who already gathered around the couple.

'There are many different tribes living here. And in Ibiza they coexist', says Marcos, who grew up seeing a colourful congregation around the family kitchen table. Now an established permaculturalist, Marcos witnessed how Ibiza's famed sense of well-being was intrinsically connected to nature. 'A grand part of the attraction is the light, the sea, the air, nature, the flowers', he says. 'This natural immersion is what binds creative souls to the island.'

Marcos is the sort of person who effortlessly swerves from the high-minded perspective of an artist to the heartfelt pleas of an activist, and his combined office-studio and art gallery, Estudi Tur Costa, sits alongside the family home and hosts seasonal exhibitions that showcase the new guard of Balearic art. It is the perfect platform for a man who often resembles a politico-philosopher; sharing stories, airing frustrations and then proffering groundbreaking solutions.

'It is evident that the great predator of the world is this machine of infinite consumerism and exponential growth on a finite planet. But we can't keep growing when we're already at breaking point', insists Marcos, who believes that the original build endures as a paragon of innovation. 'The real question is, how can we move towards a new paradigm of collaboration and symbiosis?'

'We need to keep nurturing our connection to the elements, to create this new paradigm; one where there is a respect and veneration for life', says Marcos. Enduring as a multidisciplinary gallery and workspace, Estudi Tur Costa keeps the door open to questions and conversations about Ibiza's past and future. And, more than fifty years later, people are still gathering here to ruminate on ideas of achievable change. ***LA***

Estudi Tur Costa was founded by Marcos Tur Witt and his parents. It promotes the life's work of Rafael Tur Costa and Anneliese Witt while strengthening the island's cultural and ecological values through exhibitions, lectures and conferences.

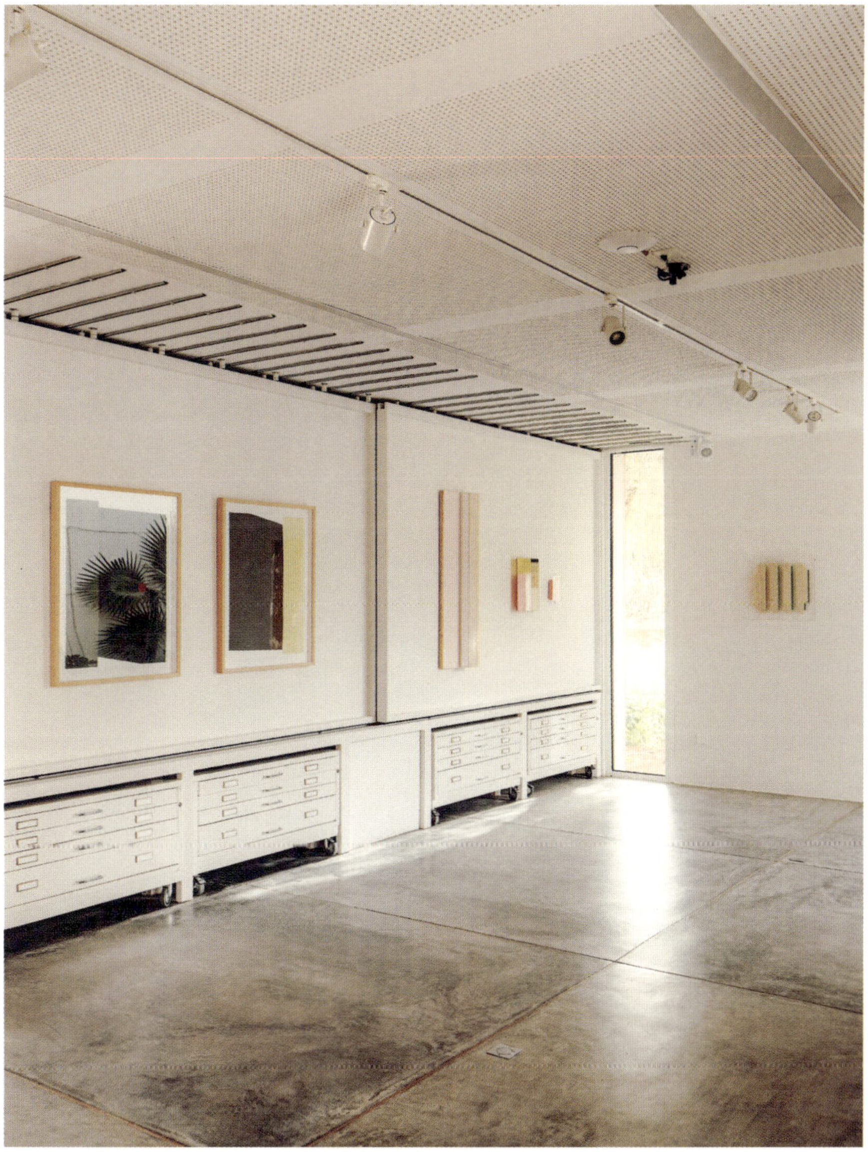

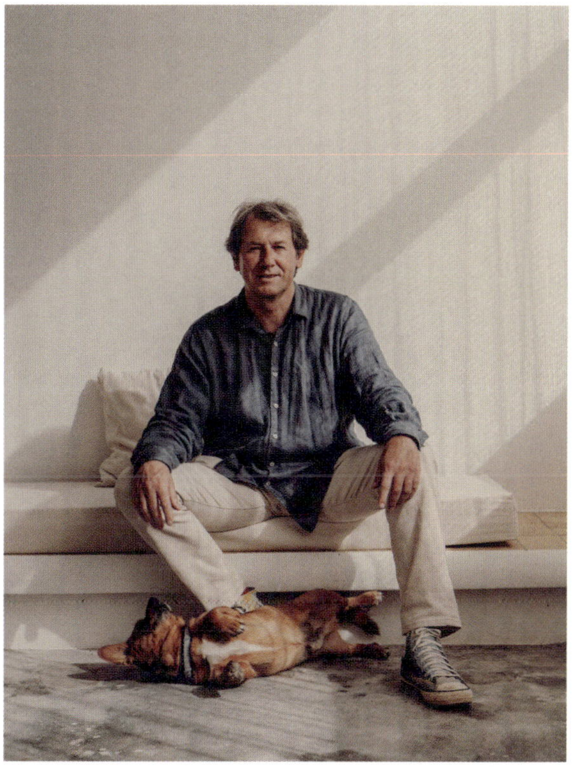

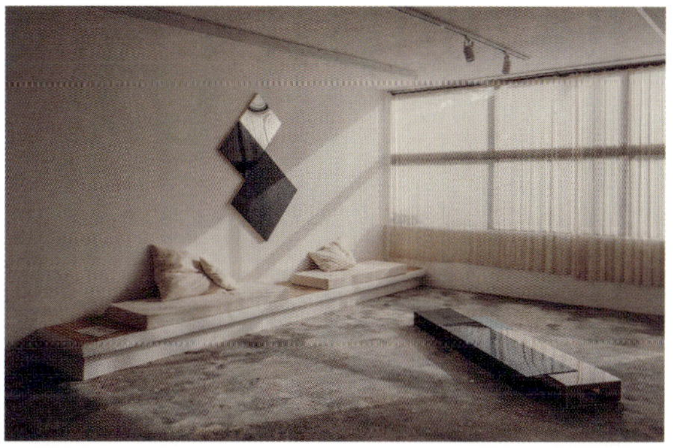

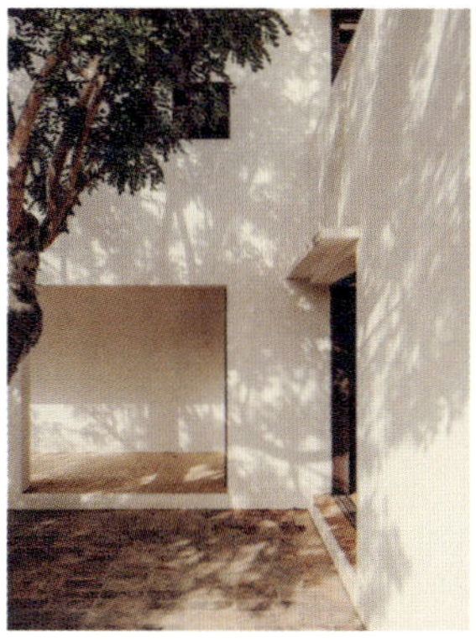

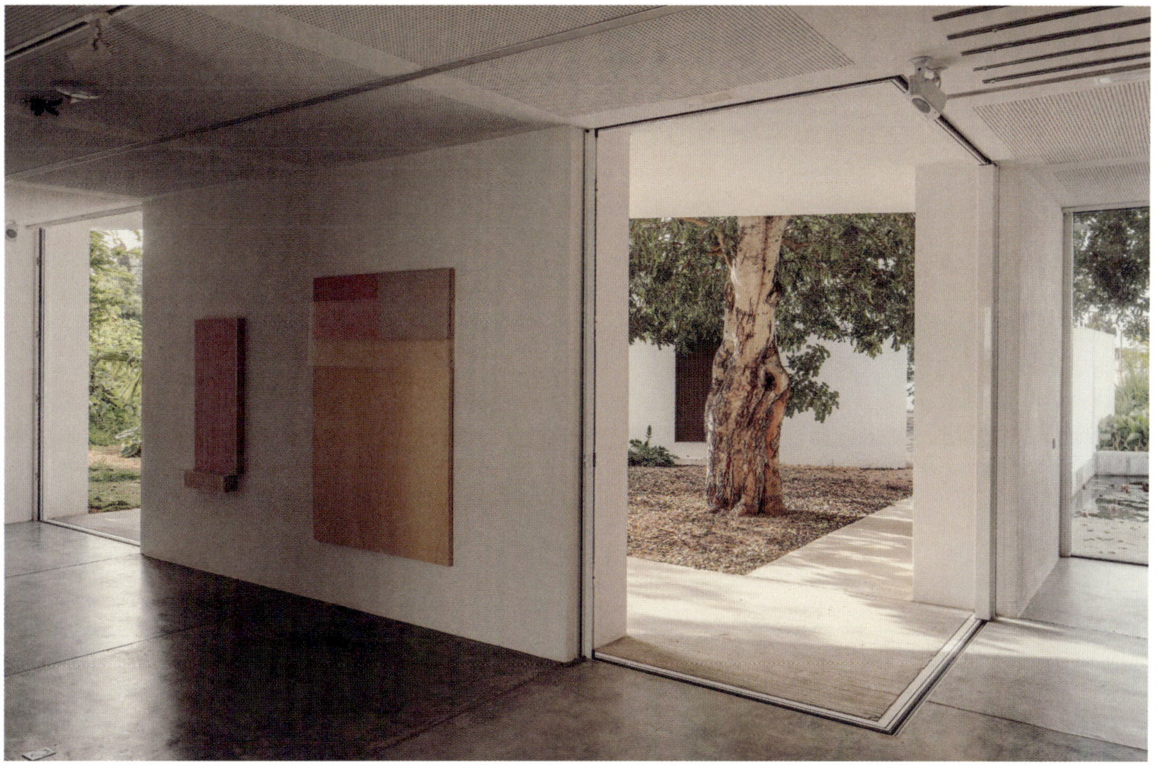

Works by the Ibicenco artist Bonet Vallribera inside the Estudi Tur Costa gallery space. Exhibitions change on a regular basis.

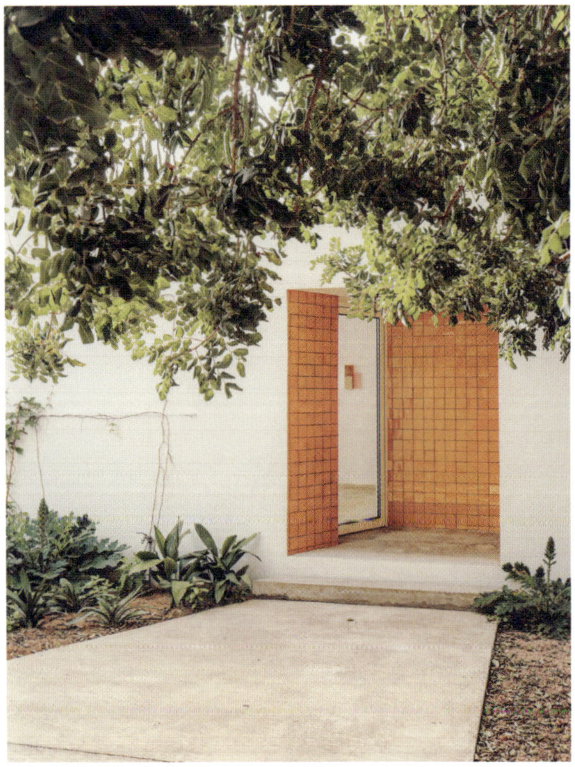

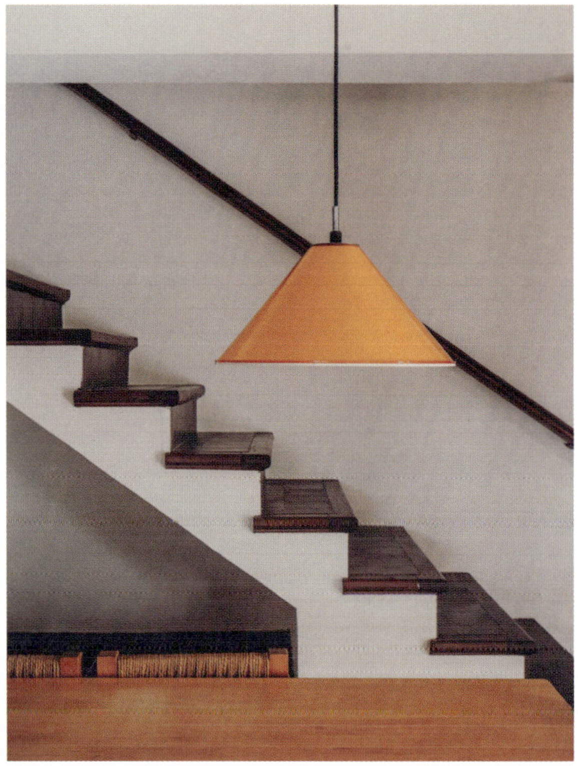

Opposite: Through the work of the artist collective Cuina de Fang and other regular workshops, the ceramicist Anneliese Witt's atelier still brims with life, creativity and malleable clay.

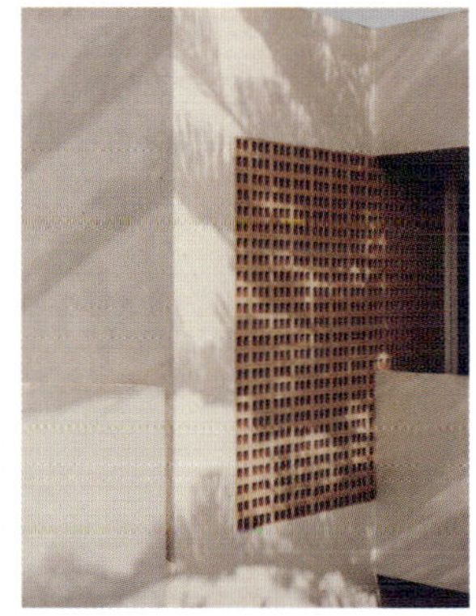

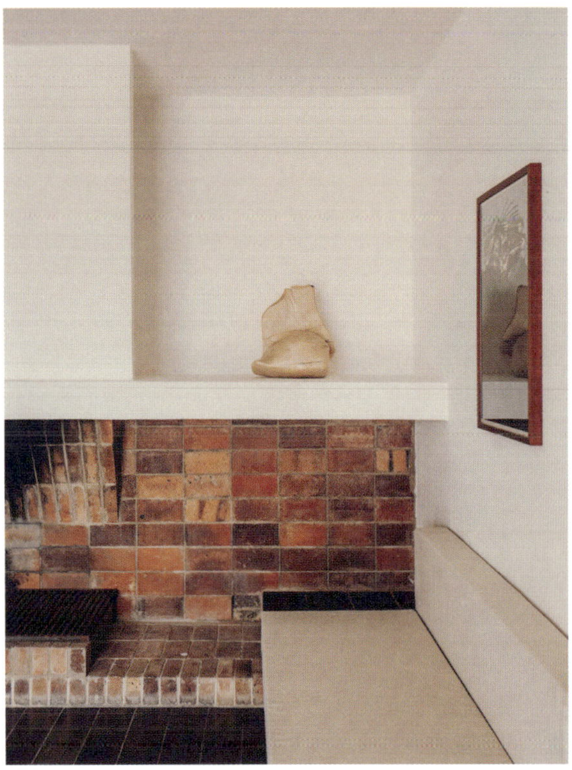

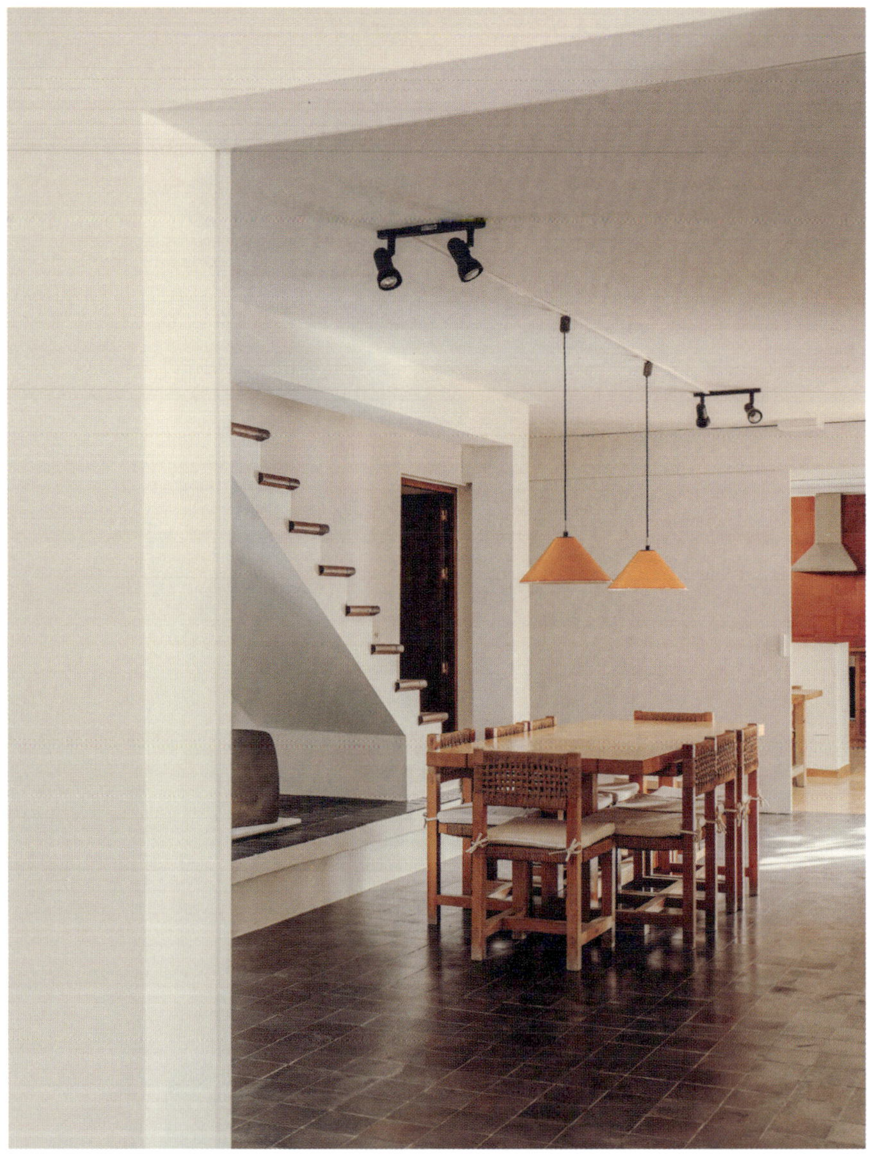

The interiors of Rafael and Anneliese's original house fuse traditional Ibizan furniture with modern Bauhaus-style elements, such as bold, ochre-coloured lampshades.

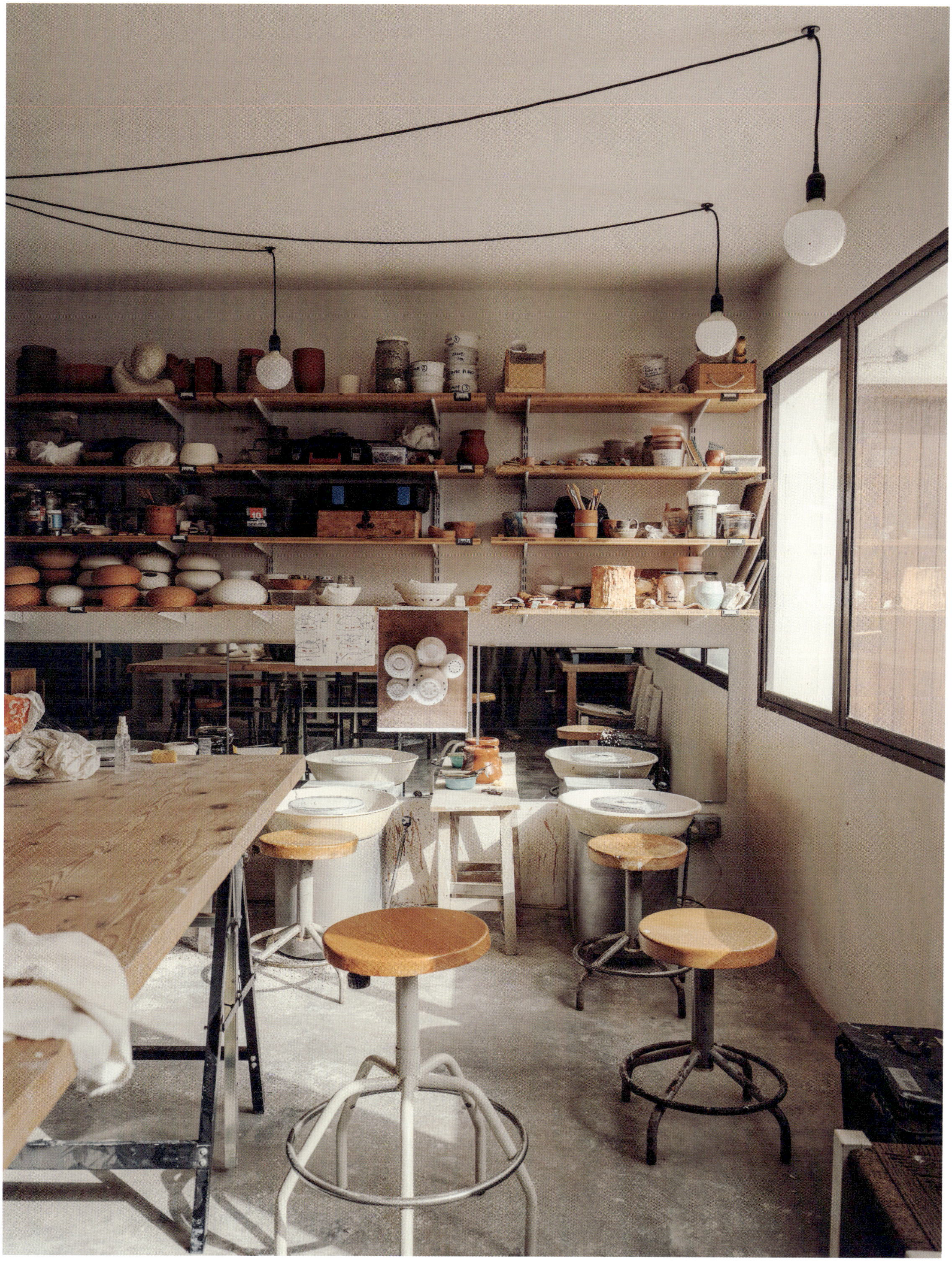

IBIZA TOWN
@masedo_jardines

JUAN MASEDO

LANDSCAPE ARCHITECTURE

Graceful, stylish and quietly charming, the Madrileño landscape gardener Juan Masedo cuts a singular figure on the island. A keen plant enthusiast in his early years, on his arrival in Ibiza in 1995 he quickly fell under the delicate tutelage of the Italian rose expert and author Orietta Sala, whose eye for relaxed and natural planting is unsurpassed. Juan's own much-photographed Ibiza garden demonstrates his signature mix of texture and shape, creating a dialogue between static and moving plants. This play of movement and light gives his gardens a fluid, almost filmic quality. 'When I'm designing a garden, I have a creative intuition that I understand in a truly pictorial way', he says. 'I have the same feeling as if I were beginning a painting, with the same attention to colour, balance and volume. In that way, I suppose I am an artist of the landscape.'

Thanks to the success of his own garden, Juan enjoyed significant early commissions and was responsible for the overhaul of the gardens at Can Pep Simó, the protected development designed by the Catalan modernist Josep Lluís Sert (see pp. 239–41). He now works with Ibiza's finest local architects, including Jordi Carreño at Estudio Vila 13 (pp. 216–21). 'The island and its history, nature and architecture provide all the inspiration that I need. Each project, each home, is its own world, and the specific conditions of the location create the sense of place', he says, adding that 'the plants must harmonize with the island's own ecosystem, both in the choice of species and in the plants' natural size and development'.

Climate resilience has also become a vital consideration. Water is a scarce natural resource in Ibiza, and the use of such drought-resistant plants as the California pepper tree and Australian rosemary is key to creating a garden that can withstand the island's blinding summer heat without intervention. 'It is crucial to me that the planting thrives to become part of the living environment; that it grows and develops in harmony with its surroundings and does not detract from the raw nature or the landscape', Juan explains.

One of the landscape architect's signatures is to create a complex depth of field that suggests the entering and exiting of different garden worlds. Meandering pathways are framed by native plants – lavender, bougainvillea, Spanish daisies – to create a striking visual effect that encourages the eye to travel through and beyond the immediate picture and into the distance. Lawns are studded with olive and carob trees in a manner that recalls the ancient terraces of Ibiza's rural farming heritage. Needle grasses billow in the breeze, reflecting flickering sunlight back on to coleonema, euphorbia and the majestic *chumbera*, or prickly pear, an icon of rural Ibiza transplanted from America in the sixteenth century.

While the overall effect is one of an authentic natural world, Juan's planting is in fact a precise endeavour that seeks to elevate the raw island elements. He returns to projects over and over to learn and to grow with the garden. As he says: 'A garden is never finished. It is a process, a journey, a lifelong creation that must be nurtured and supported like a child. To see each individual garden through the many phases of its life is an honour and a privilege. I watch and learn every day, and I never cease to see the wonder. I am as much a student of my craft as I am a master.' ***MB***

In harmonizing with the ecosystem of Ibiza, Juan Masedo creates multilayered spaces that connect with the island's raw natural elements.

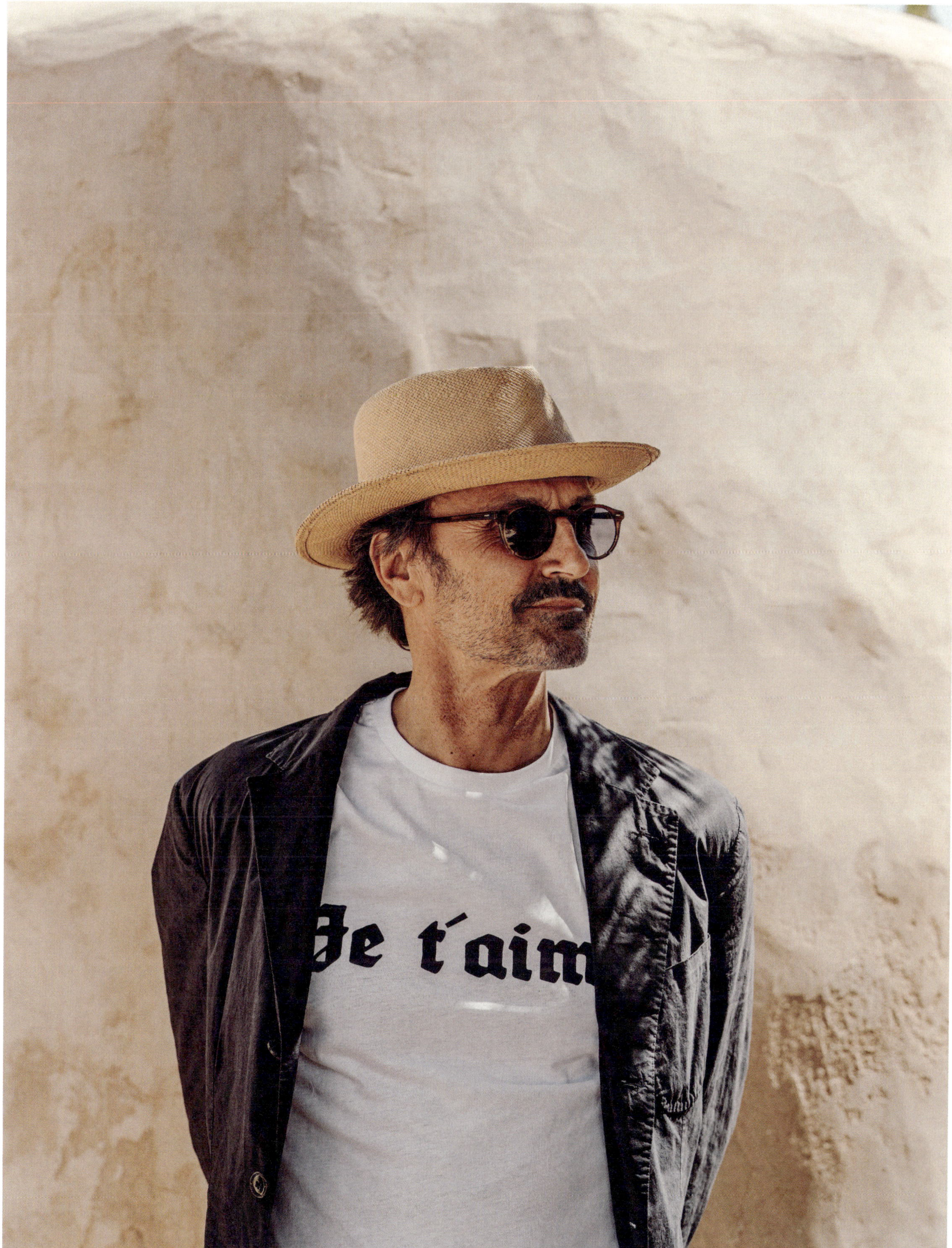

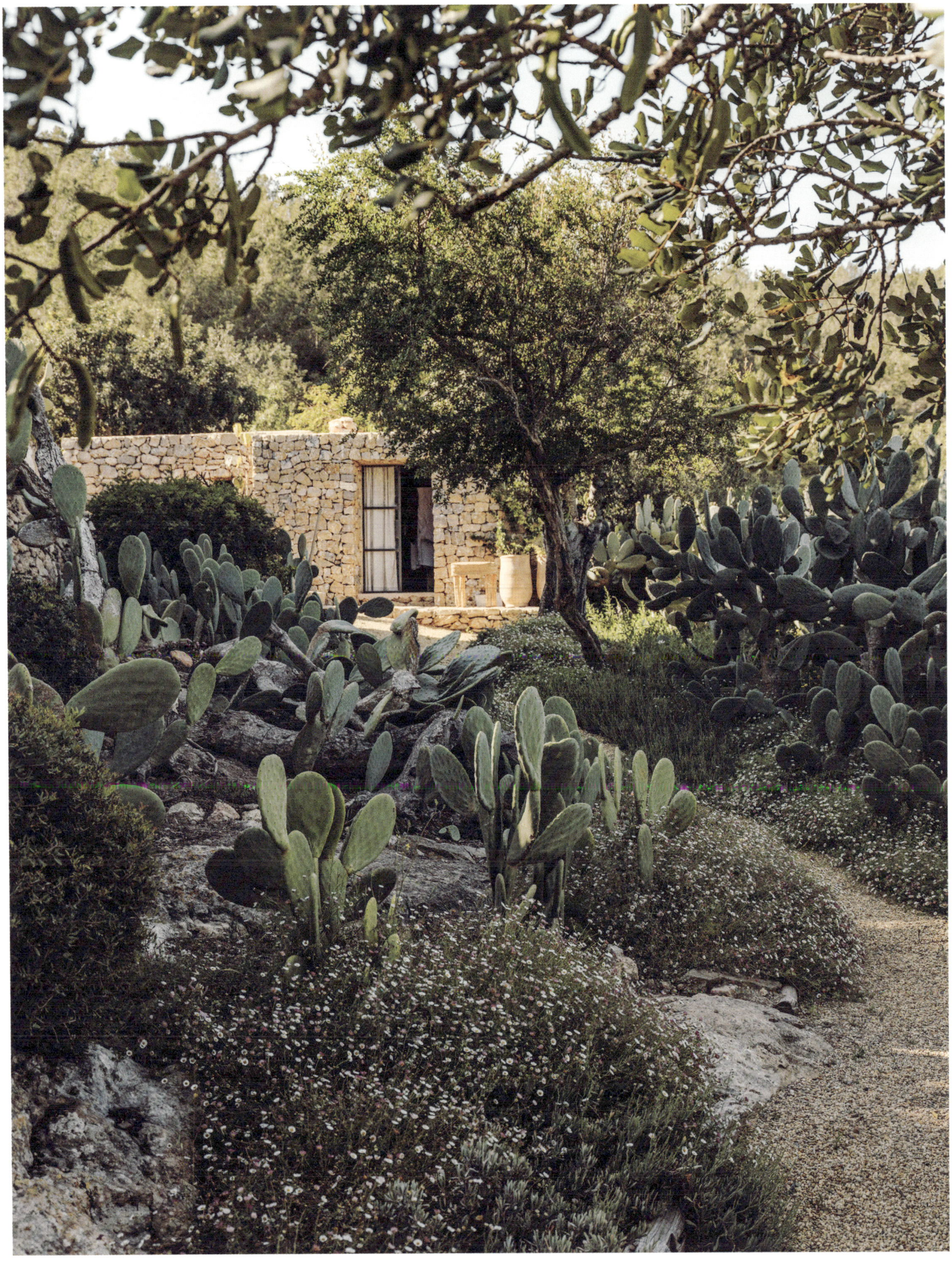

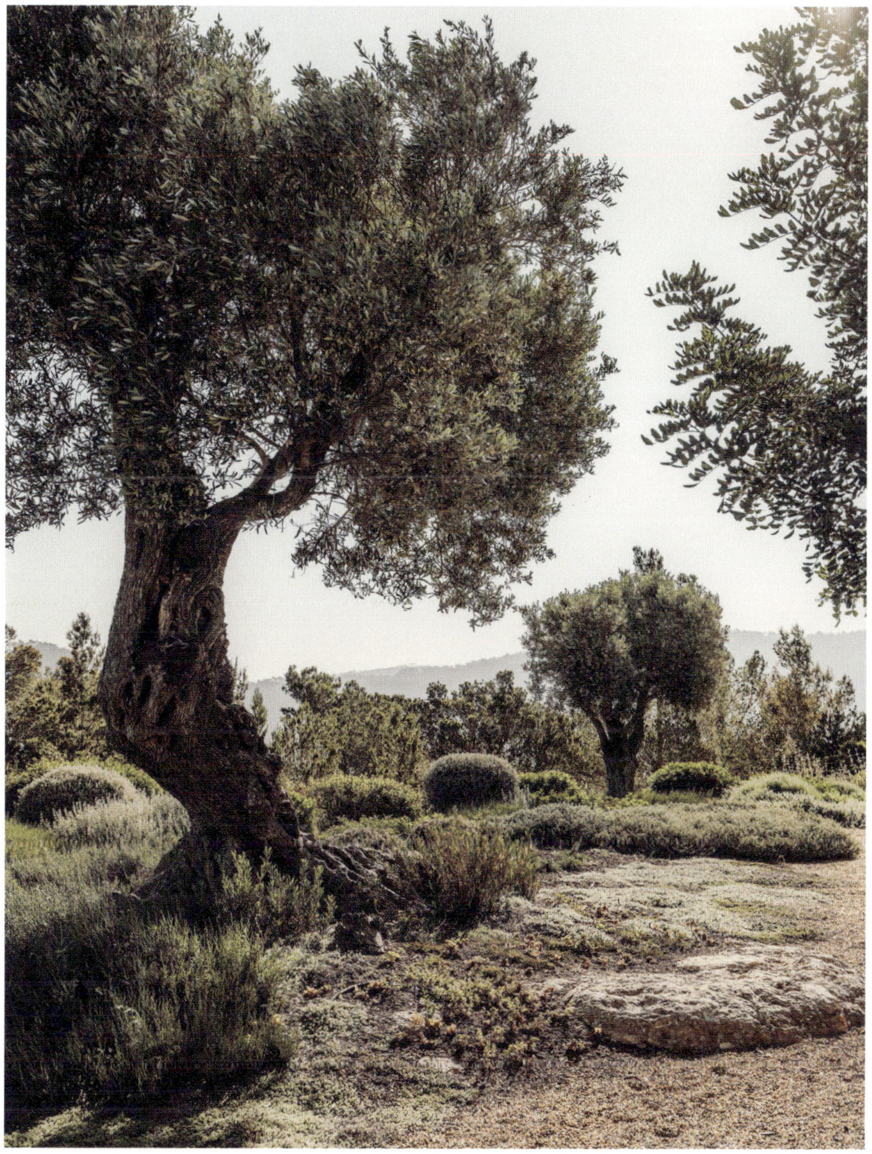

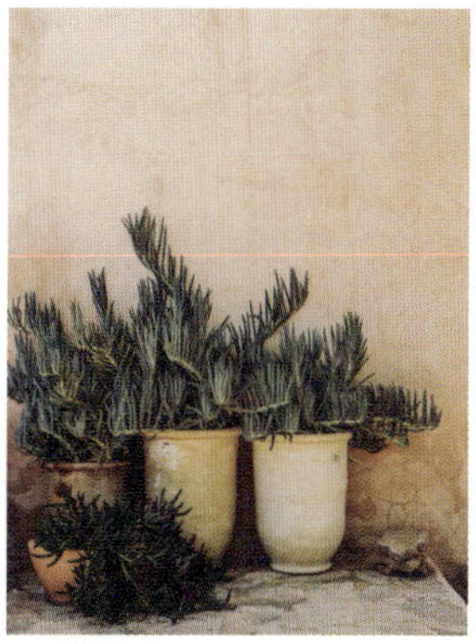

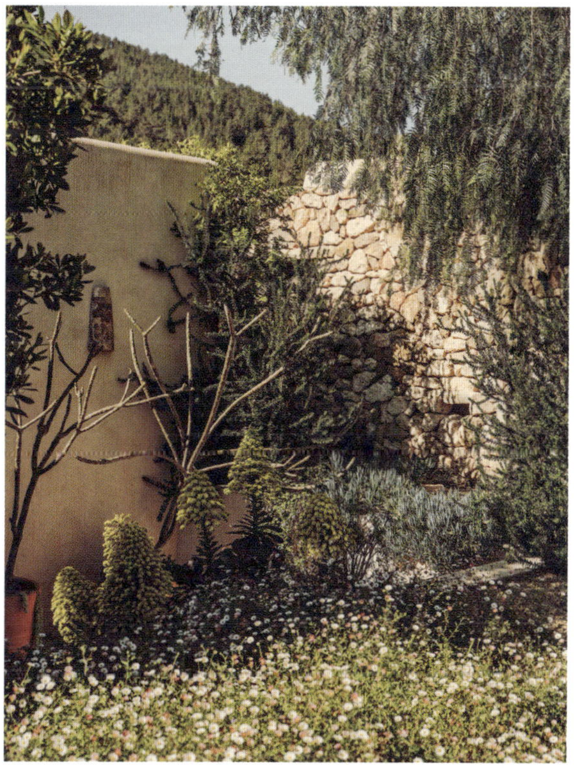

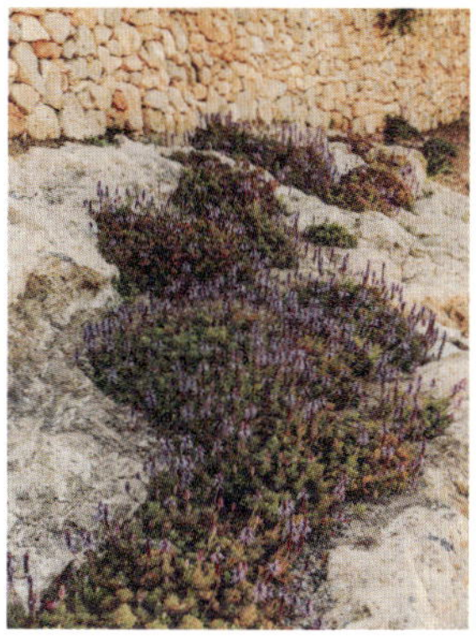

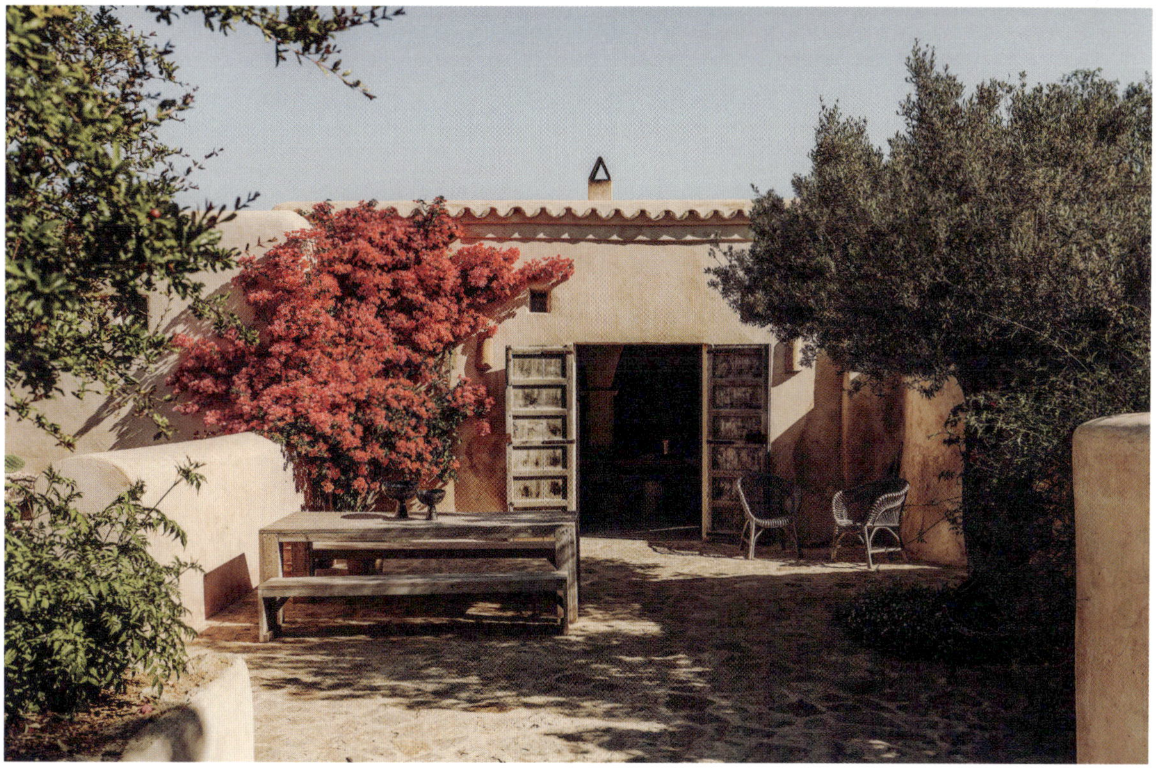

Bougainvillea (right) and the chumbera (prickly pear) cactus (opposite) are characteristic of Ibizan gardens. This property is situated close to San Juan.

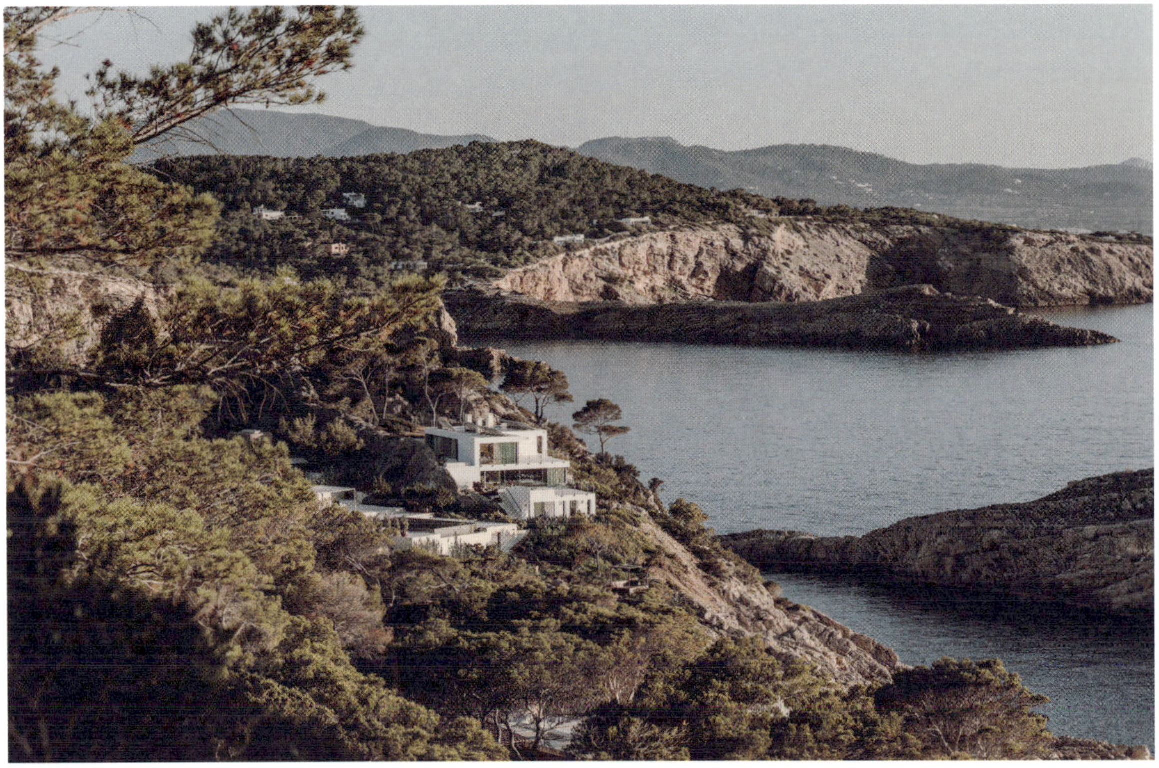

At this property near Cala Salada, native plants appear to grow from within the structure itself, softening the knife-like stone edges and giving the sense that nature is reclaiming the man-made.

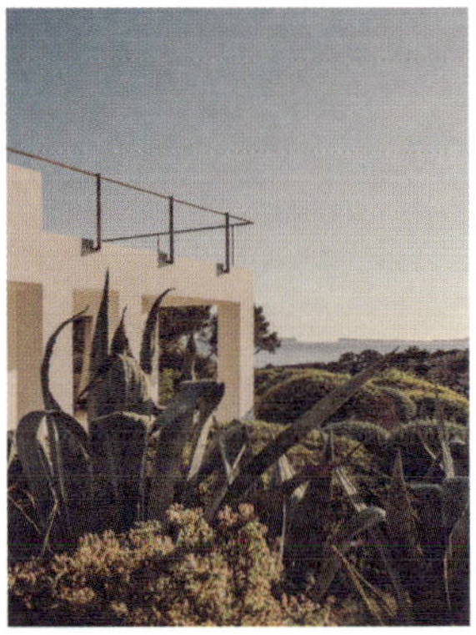

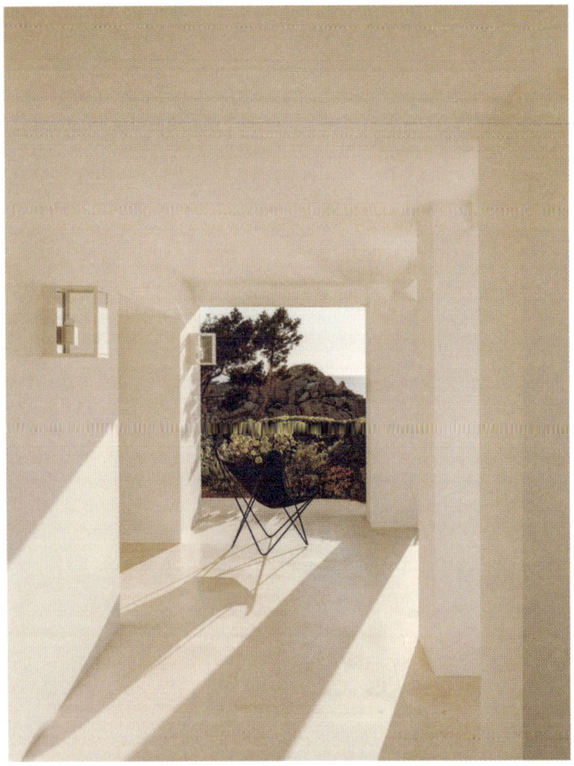

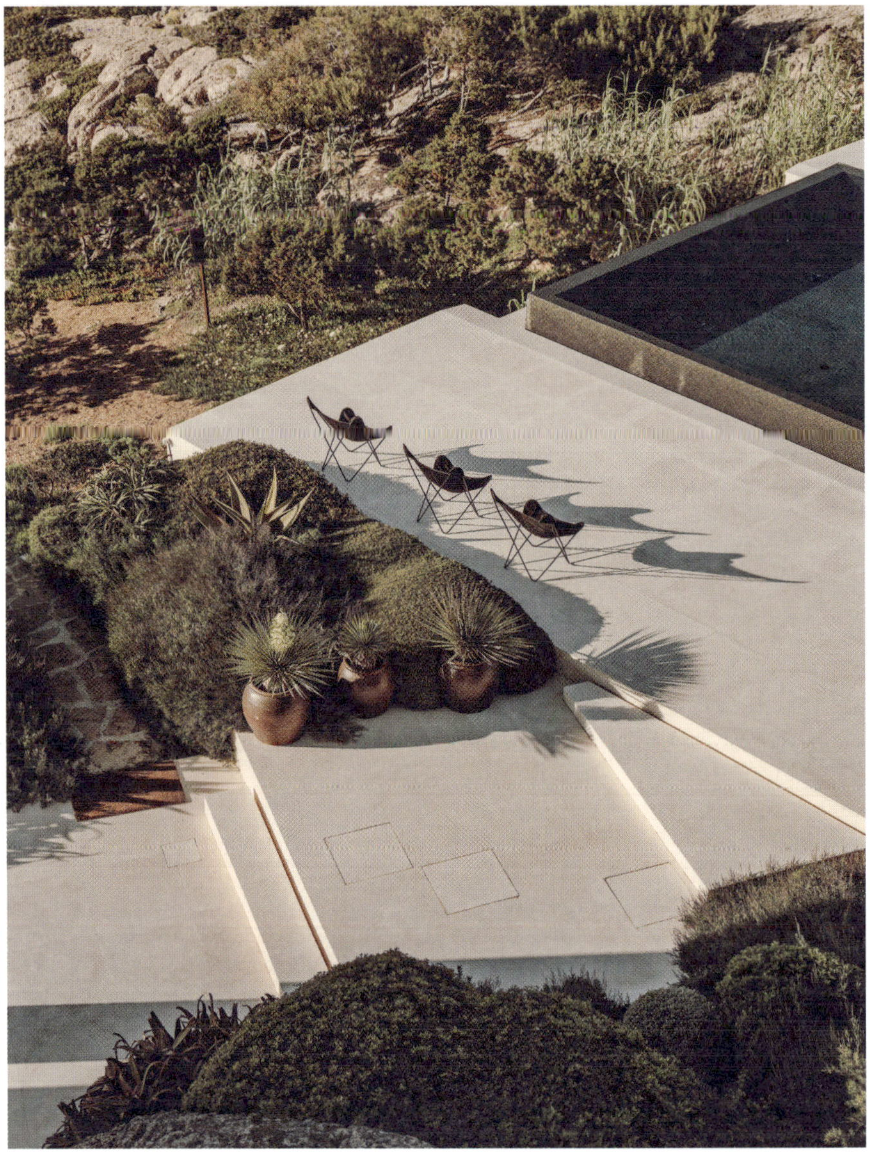

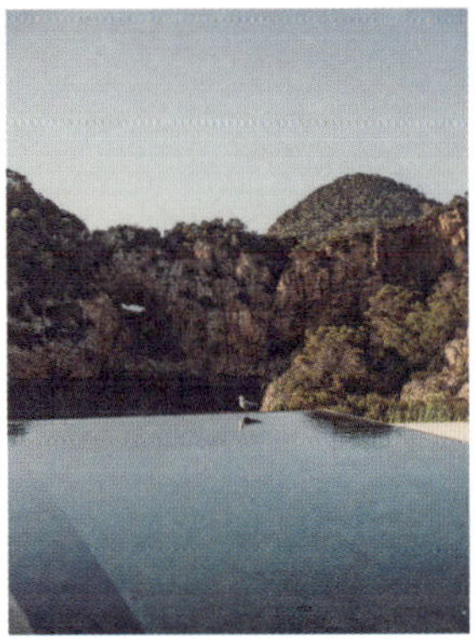

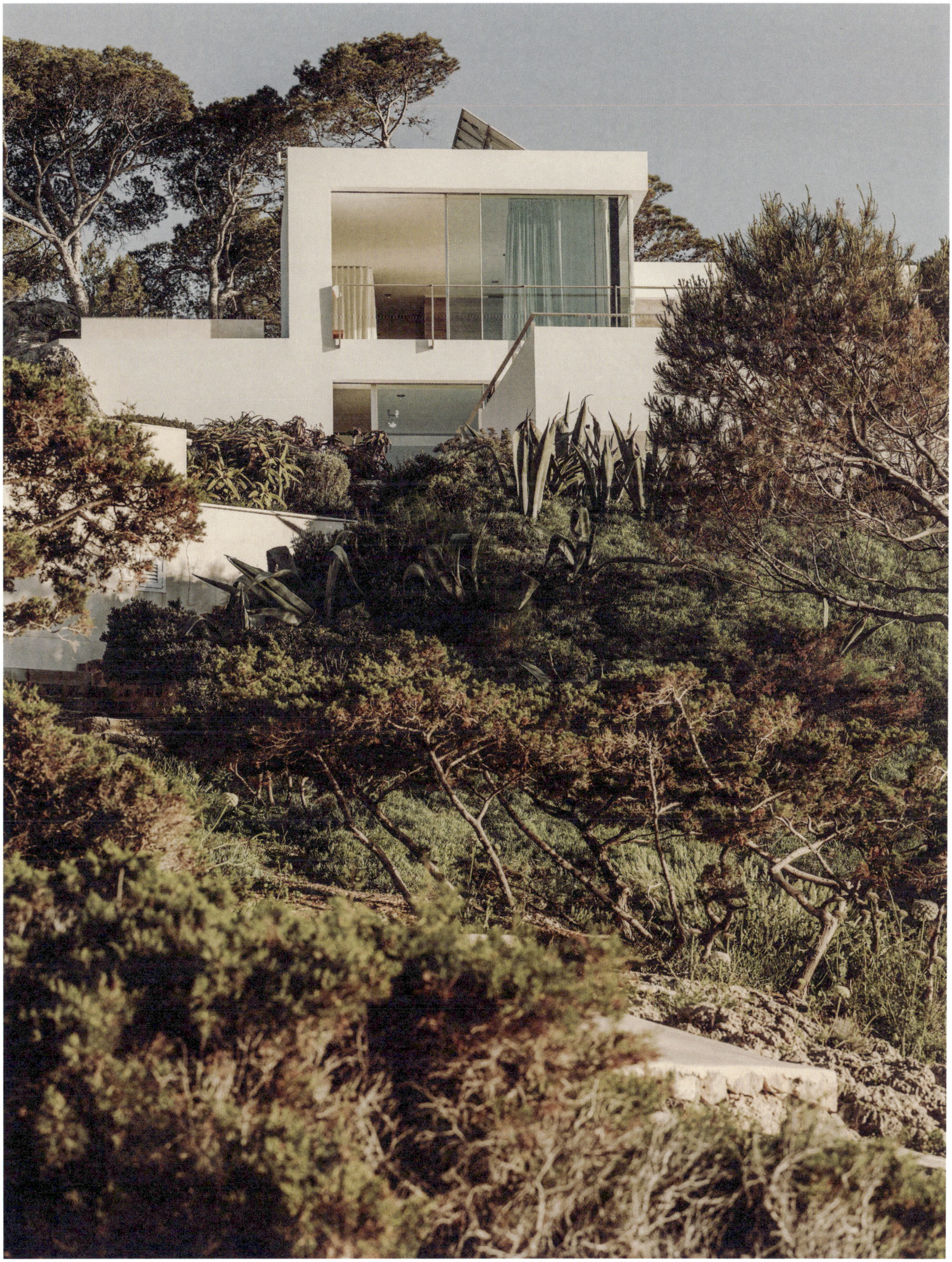

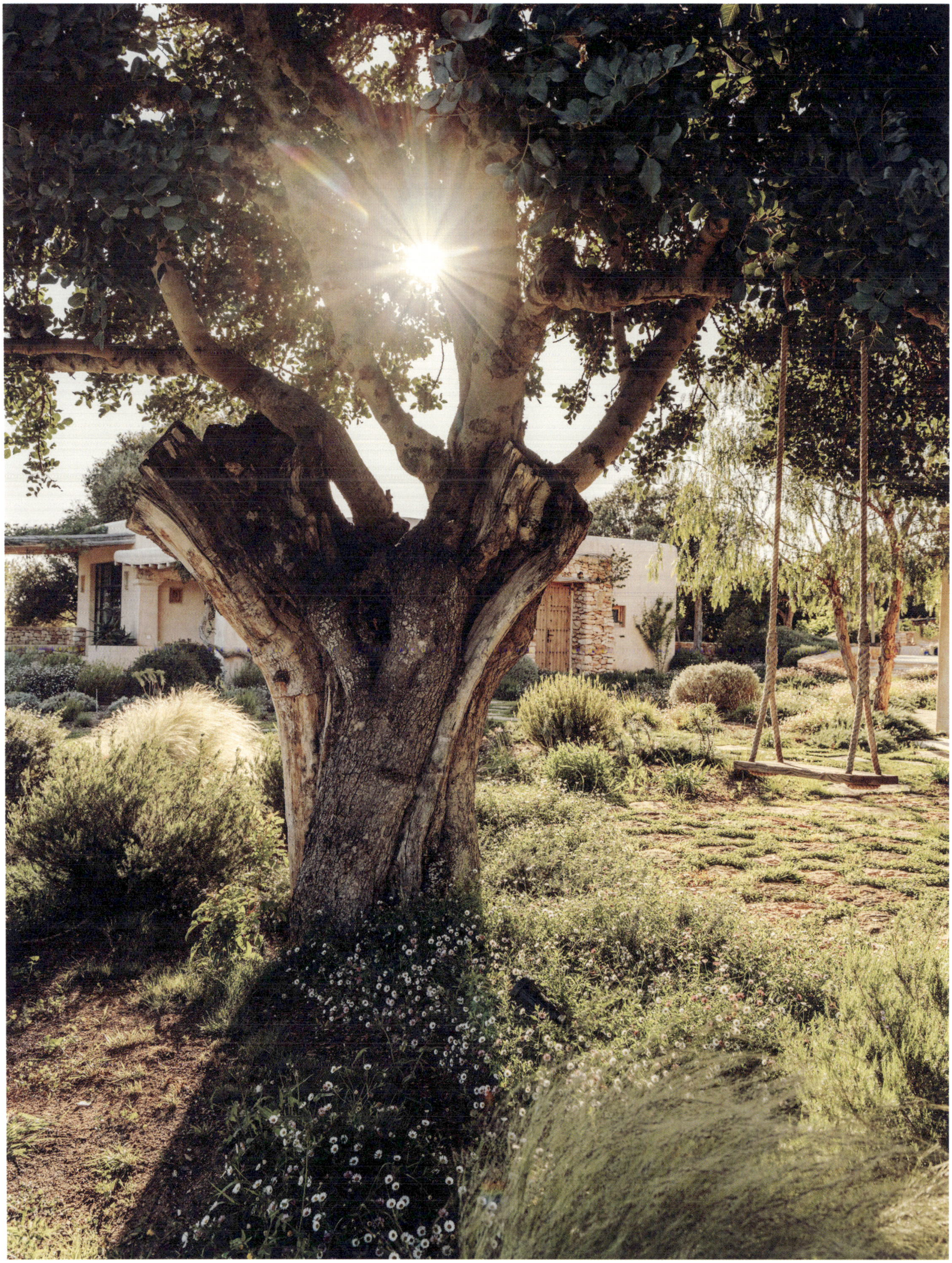

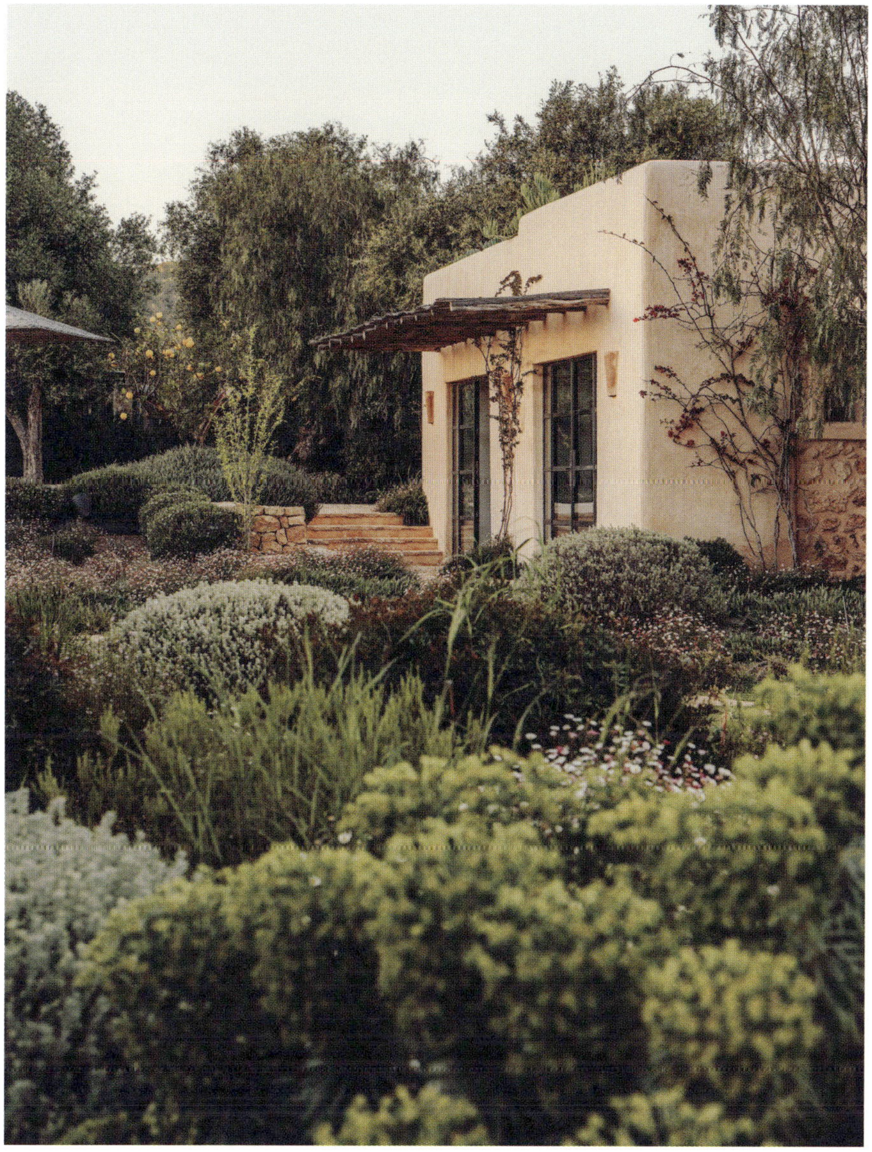

The garden of this property close to San José demonstrates Juan's signature mix of texture and shape and a dialogue between static and moving plants. The play of light and reflections on the leaves also assume a role in this complex narrative.

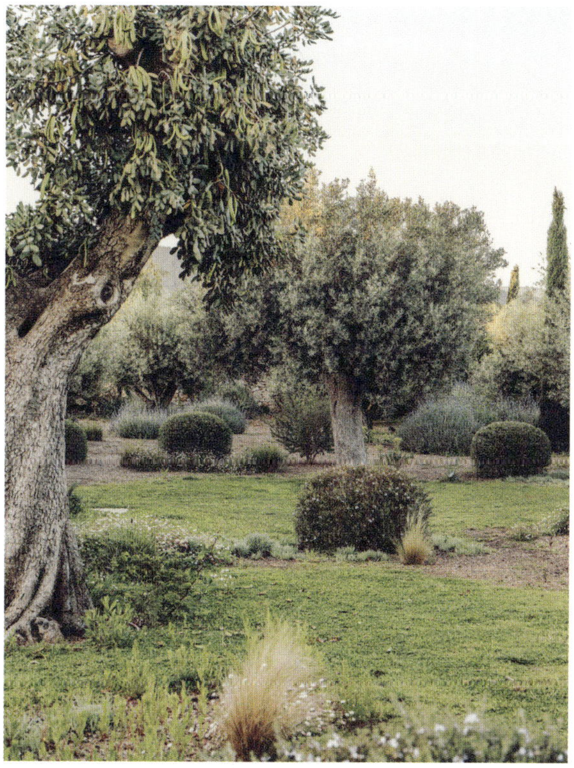

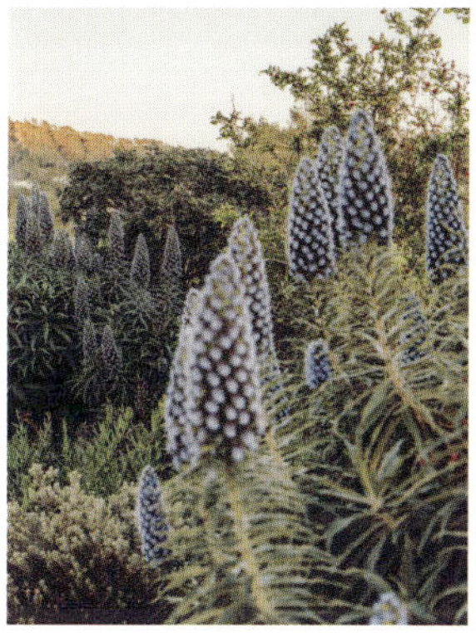

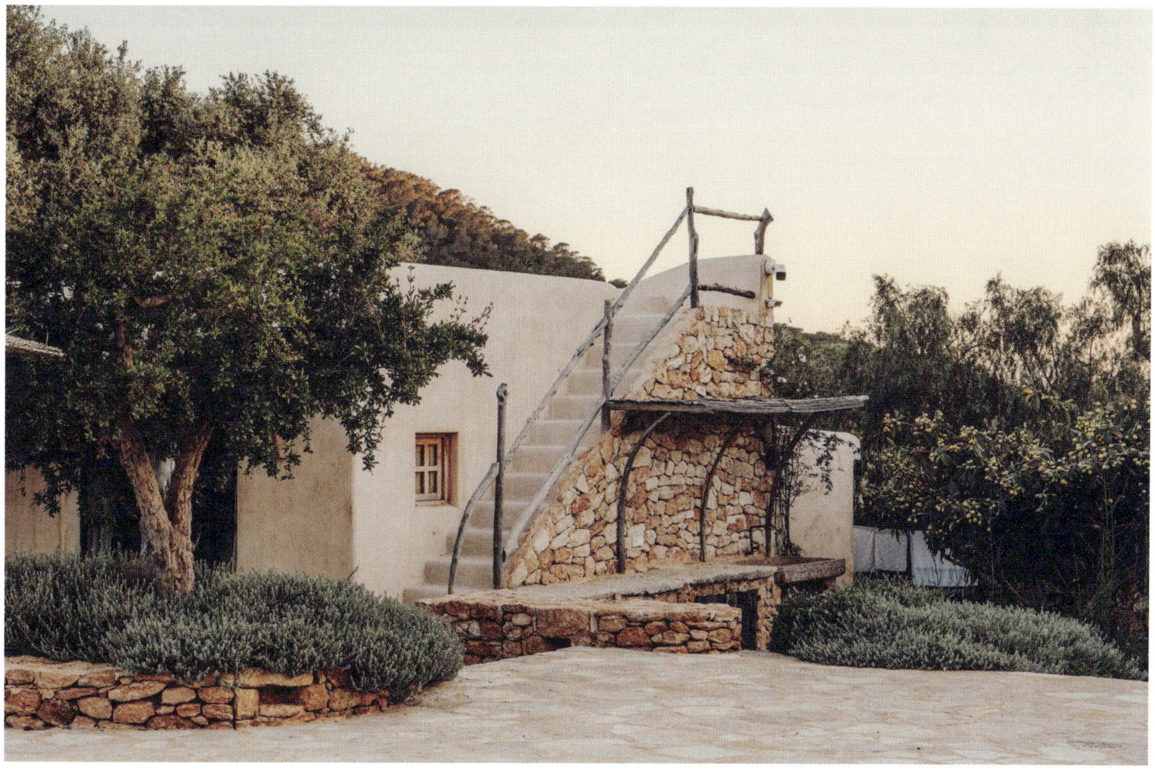

Above: The tall blue spikes of echium are among the first flowers to bloom in spring.

SANTA GERTRUDIS
@estudio_laterna

ESTUDIO LATERNA

LANDSCAPE ARCHITECTURE

'Gardens are complex ...', begins Andrea Sánchez, as if proffering an omen before recounting a mysterious tale. 'Gardens communicate; they move, get sick, live and die. They also yearn for love, to thrive and reproduce.' The Chilean landscape designer, who seeds, plants and nurtures her vision alongside her husband, Ricardo Jarpa, sees each garden as a 'living installation'. Gardens, she reminds us, are also habitats; abundant, resilient and ever-evolving: 'Similar to a house, they have many junctures, becoming somewhere to lose yourself, but also somewhere that is memorable.'

Memory is big business for Laterna. The studio became a formal venture in 2004, taking its name from the magic lantern, a device that projects whimsical connotations of creativity, dialogue and communication. Andrea describes her gardens as 'emotional landscapes', and each project takes root following an in-depth conversation. As Ricardo explains: 'They are like psychological meetings, where we extricate sentimental information from the client, then connect the sensations of youth to smells, sounds and spaces.' These can come to life in the form of citrus trees that re-create the aromas of a childhood home or the trickling water of a bespoke fountain that reminds people of past seaside adventures.

Conversations with wise Ibicenco old-timers help to reclaim fading customs. The superstitious planting of the ruta shrub (also known as the common rue or herb-of-grace) at the entrance to a home was thought to fend off 'bad vibes'. Laterna honours such local traditions as if they were sacred rituals. 'We imagine and re-create stories', says Andrea. 'People see themselves reflected in them.'

Having studied landscape design in Chile, Andrea travelled to Bonn, Germany, to hone her expertise. In the year 2000 a job opportunity at a Chilean-owned nursery in Ibiza fast-tracked her landscaping career because her language proficiency made her popular with the business's predominantly German clientele. Ricardo arrived on the island that same year, and their blossoming romance soon became entwined with collaborative garden design.

'You must place trust in the process', explains Andrea, who works with an extensive network of biologists, engineers and birdscapers, as well as forest authorities and technicians, to create a complex bed of biodiversity and healthy soil. These botanical investigations are then connected to such high-minded artistic concepts as *Beatus ille*, a 'Renaissance man' aspiration related to a simple, detached life in the countryside. At the luxury-villa development Sabina Ibiza, on the west coast of the island, a sprawling yet interconnected garden 'embraces many languages to become one language'. For Andrea's work at the home of the renowned photographer Andreas Gursky, the house's Herzog & de Meuron renovation served as a point of departure, with minimalist and abstract patterns replicated in the garden to amplify the ambience.

A new studio space in Santa Gertrudis signifies a more visible stage in the couple's growth cycle. Andrea secured the disused warehouse after much detective work. A refurbishment that lasted almost two years resulted in the recoating of the interiors with traditional limestone. A massive semi-subterranean, multidisciplinary space combines a gallery, an inspirational library focused on art and design, and an area for cultural events. A long-neglected adjoining plot of land is now a well-manicured public park that showcases Laterna's caring, connection-building approach.

'A garden isn't just a decorative thing', explains Andrea. 'Gardens are intricate places for infinite dialogues. It goes deeper than mere aesthetic beauty, because gardens connect to the heart of the beholder.' ***LA***

With so many interpretations, perspectives and expectations connected to the home, Andrea Sánchez and Ricardo Jarpa of Estudio Laterna turn landscaping into an exercise in empathy, while still ensuring each plant-based circulatory system thrives in a way that also keeps the house alive.

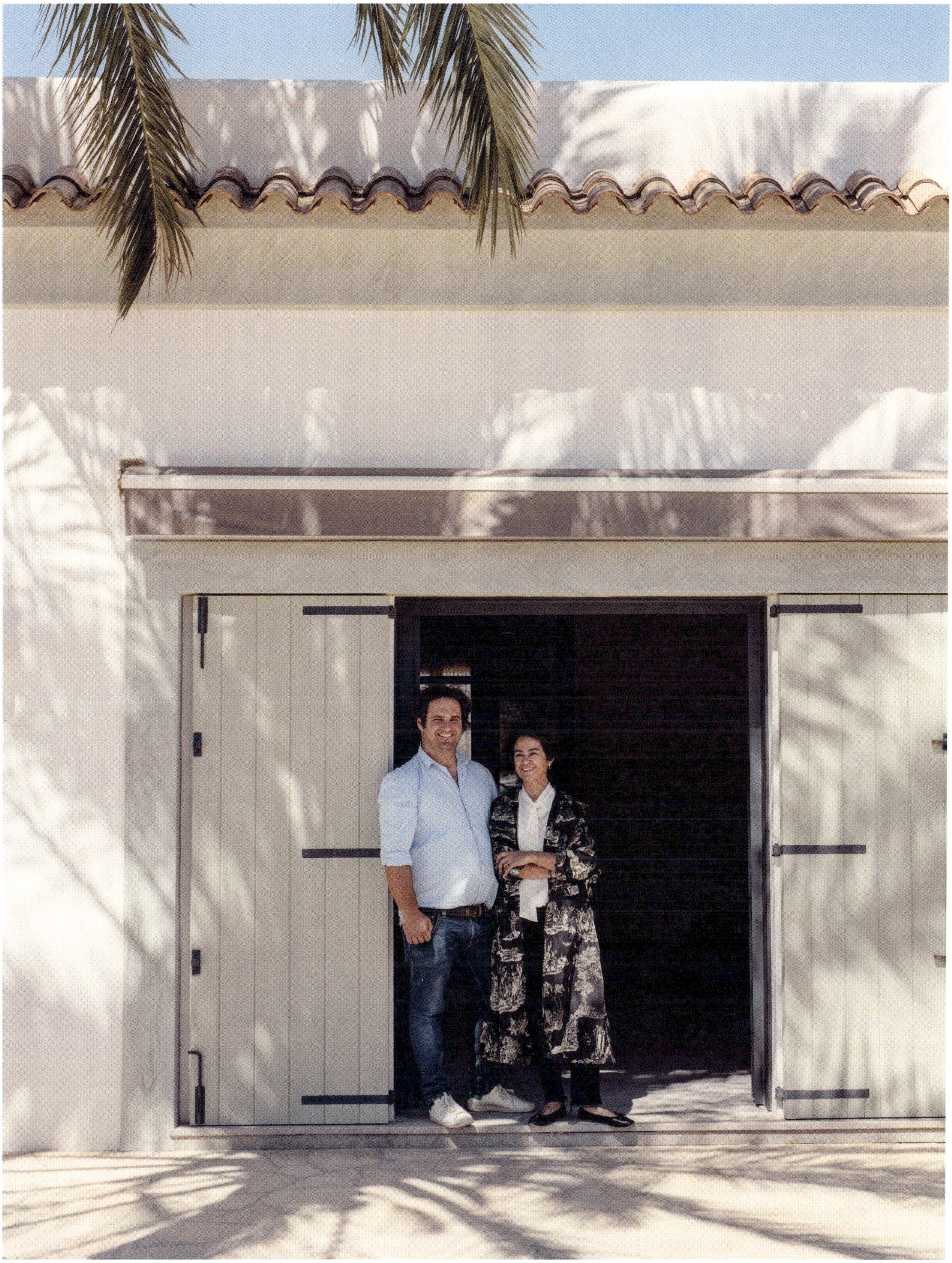

The office is renovated with natural materials, such as limestone on the walls. The statement desk (right) is by Can Castello (pp. 170–75). A water-filled sculpture (below) by Majoral (pp. 42–45) graces the studio's main entrance.

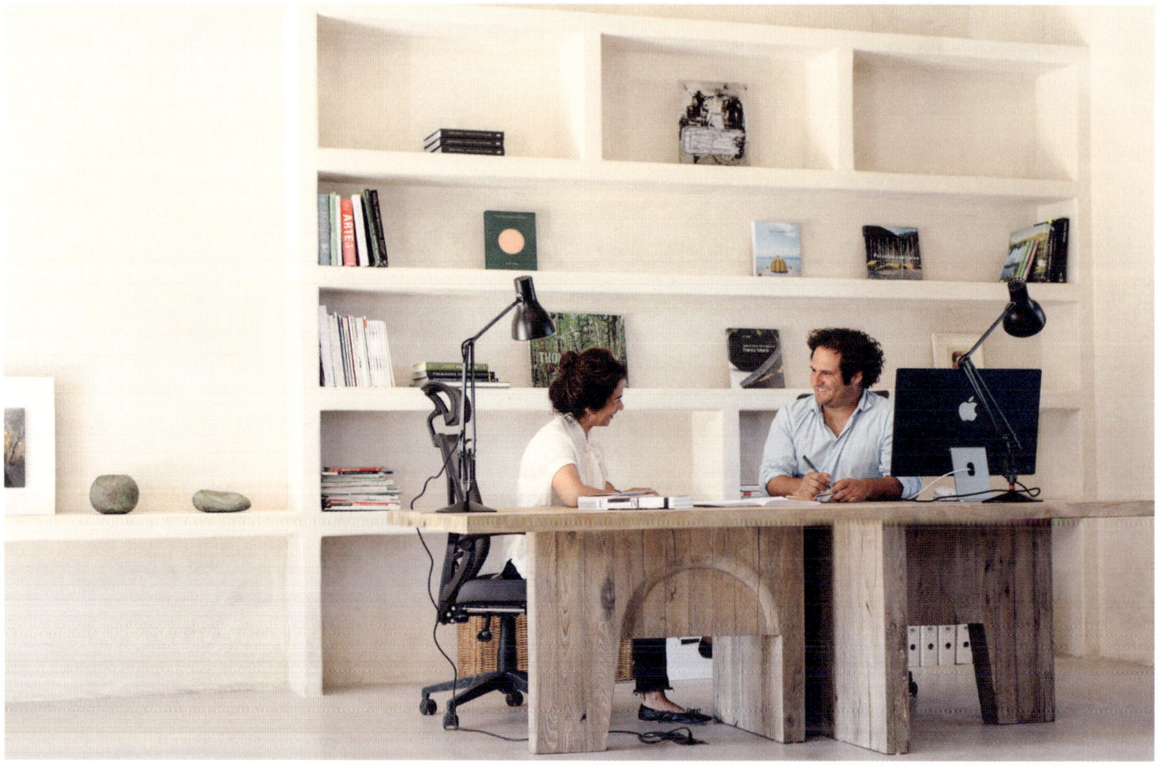

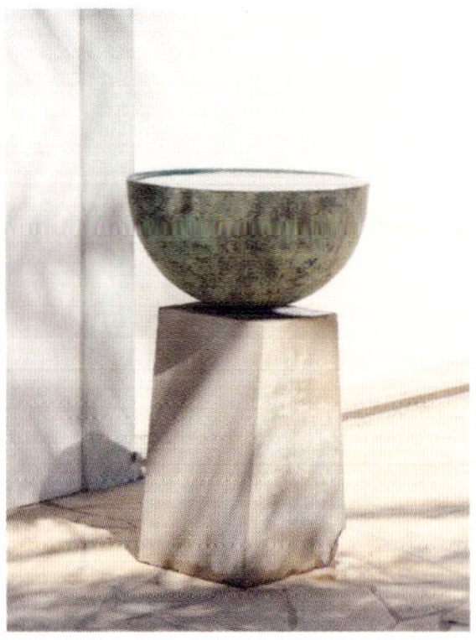

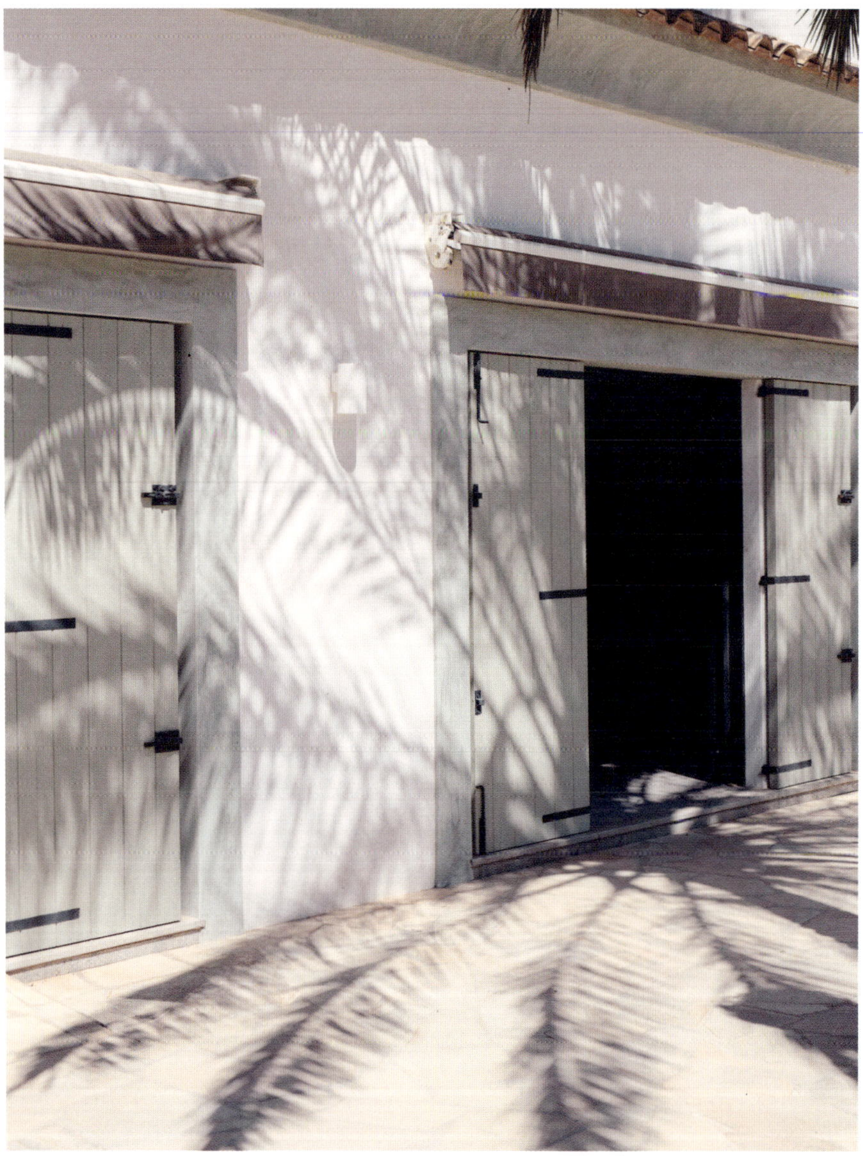

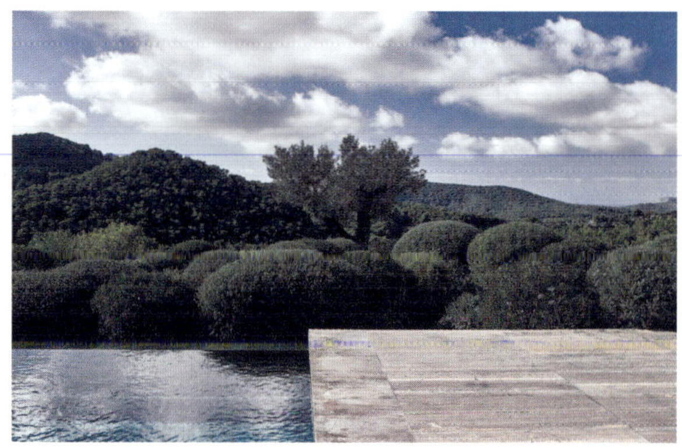

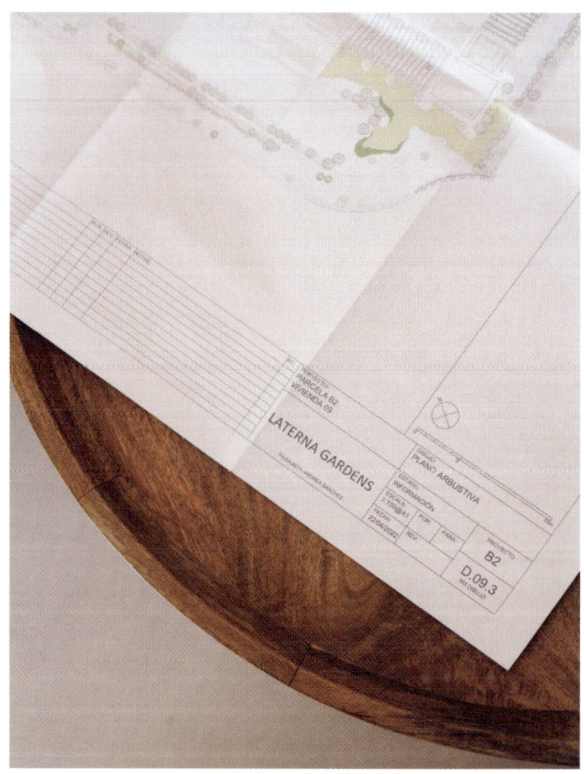

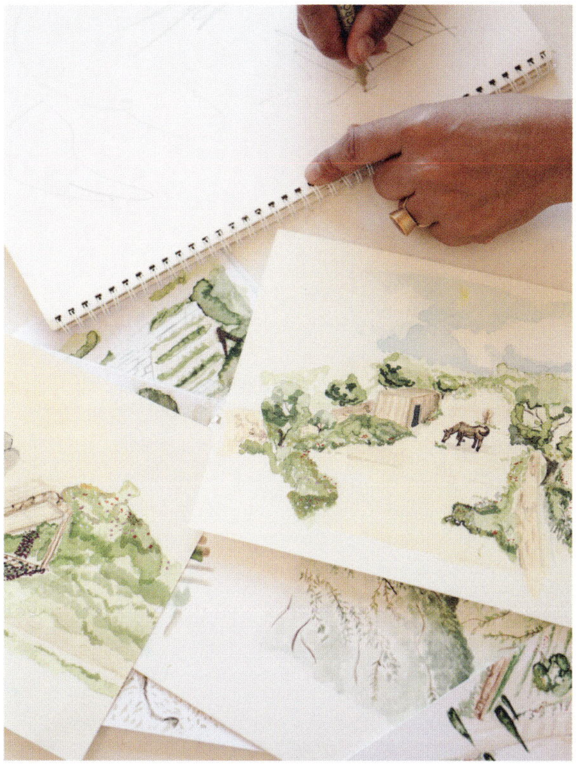

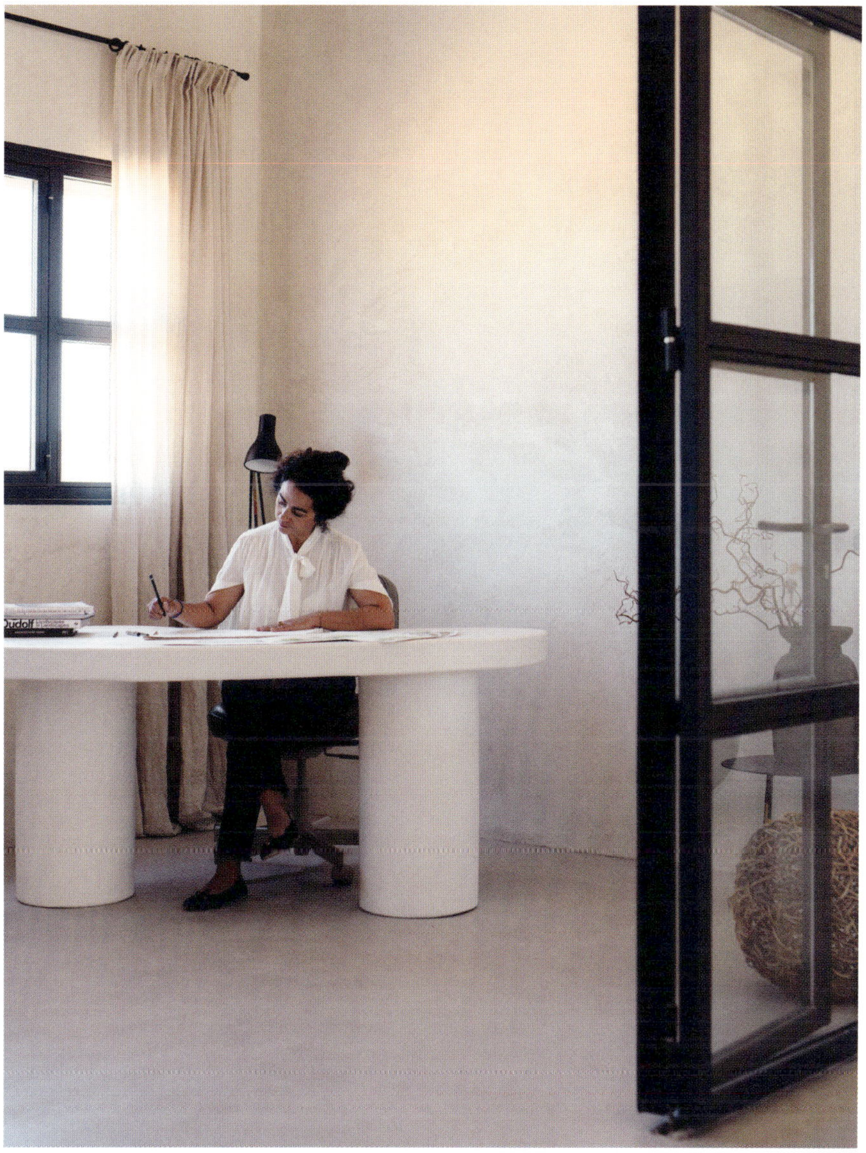

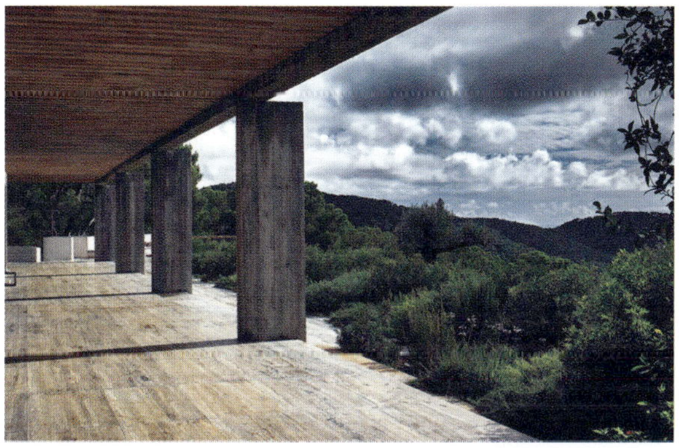

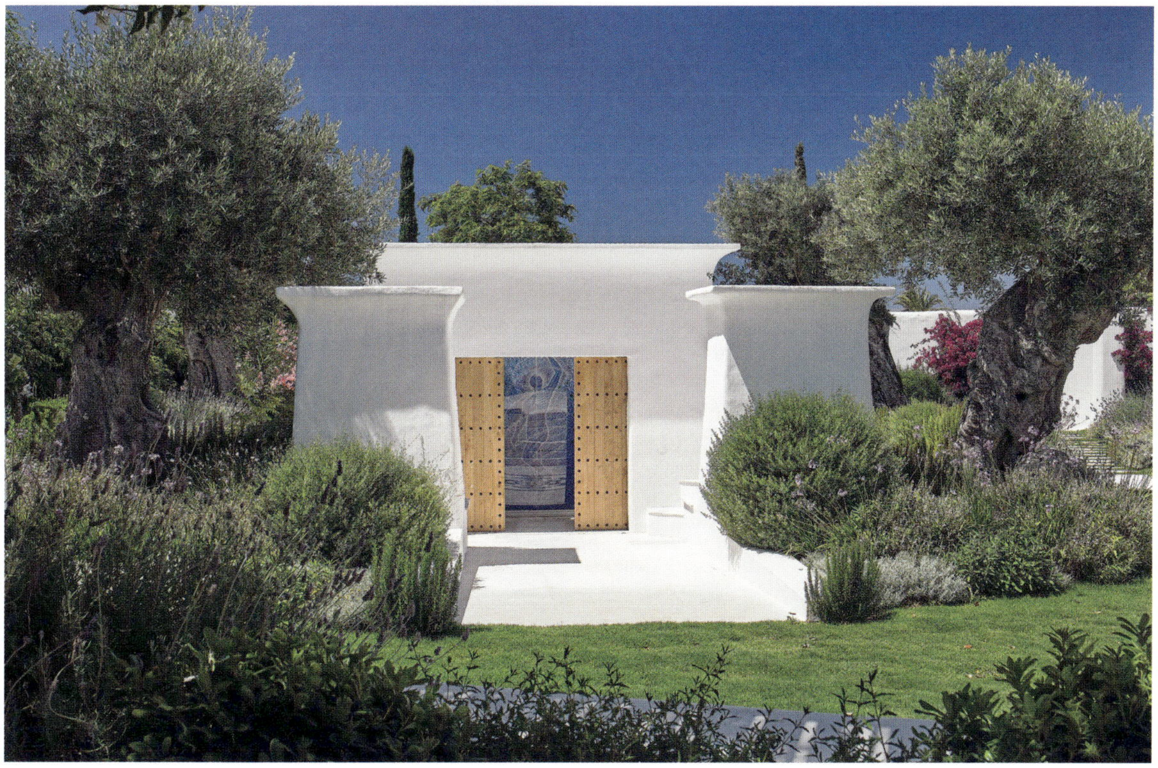

Opposite, centre; above, left; and overleaf: Many of Laterna's gardens – all featured here are in the San José area – blend seamlessly into the natural landscape. The studio's designs feature drought-resistant plants that are capable of surviving the Balearic summer heat.

Top left: Andrea uses watercolour drawings to help visualize her projects.

Left: At Sabina Ibiza, Laterna's garden designs complement the work of such prominent island architects as Blakstad Design Consultants *(pp. 208–15).*

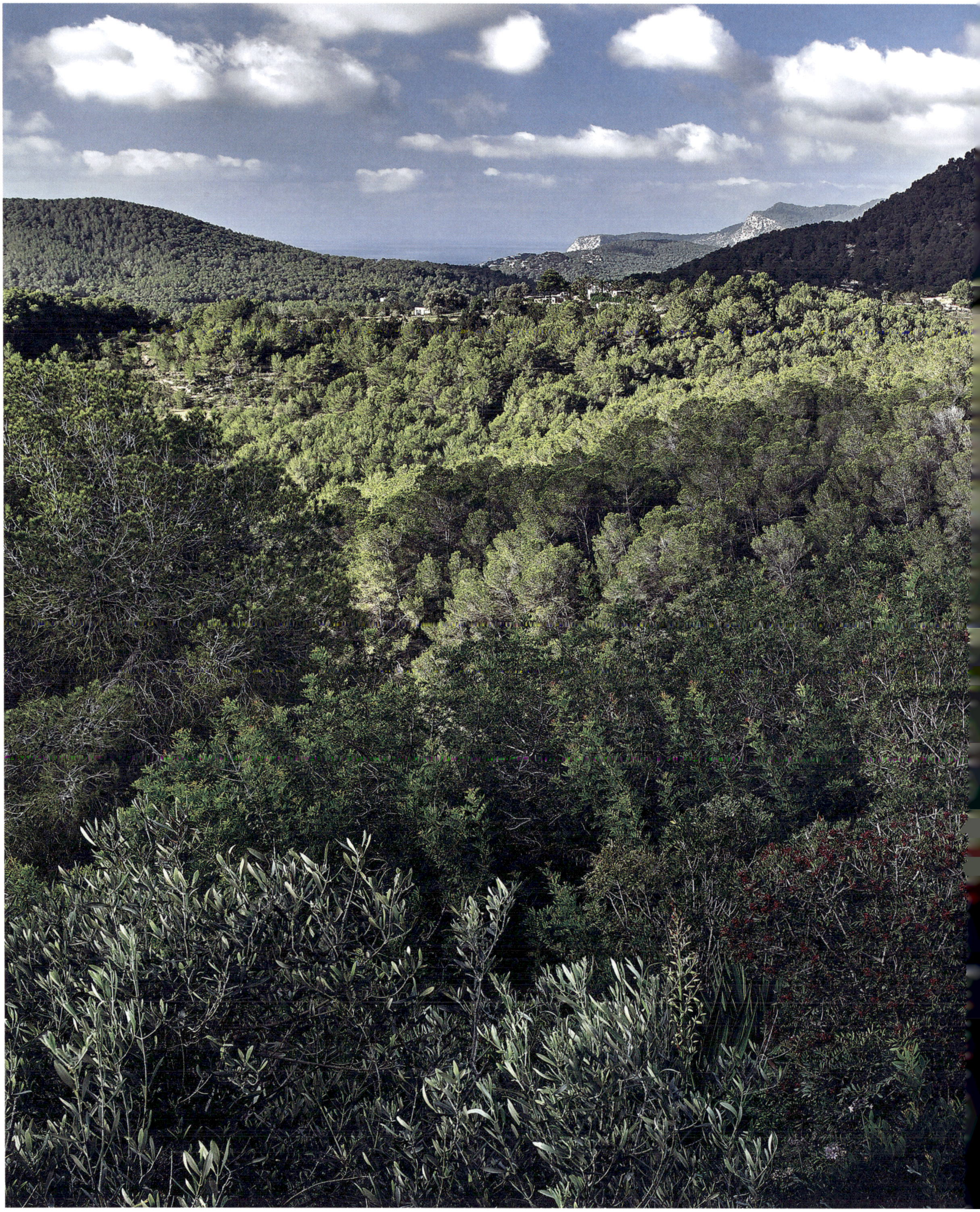

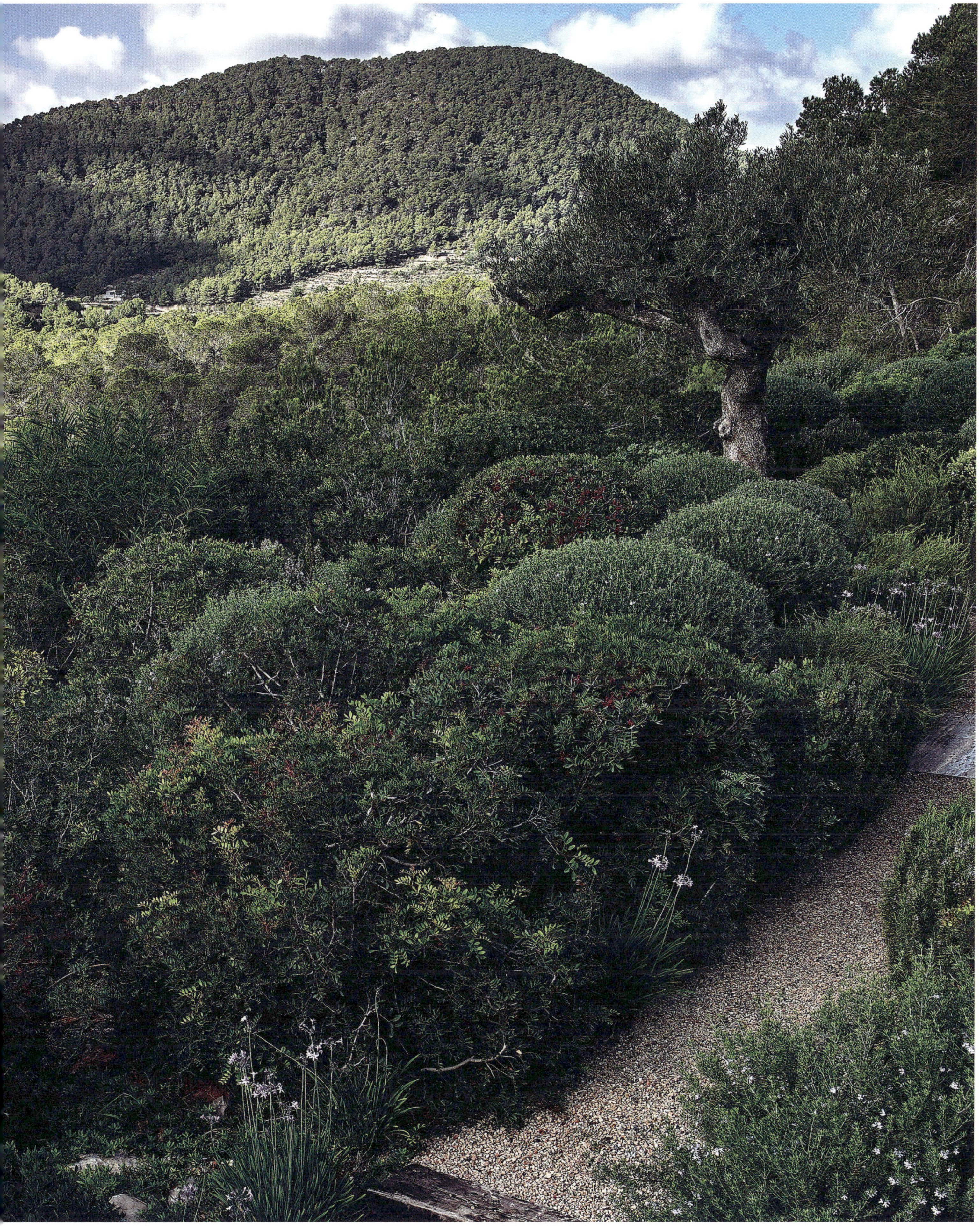

SAN CARLOS
blakstadibiza.com

BLAKSTAD DESIGN CONSULTANTS

ARCHITECTURE & INTERIOR DESIGN

Every legacy casts a long shadow. For the Blakstads, a life's work also became a source of light. In 1956, when Rolph and Mary Blakstad sailed into Ibiza's port en route to Mallorca, the island's charm persuaded them to drop anchor permanently. Rolph was captivated by the almost primordial landscape, and his initial curiosity about the architecture of Ibiza quickly developed into a fully fledged passion.

The family's future in Ibiza played a significant part in safeguarding the island's past. It began with Rolph's fascination with the ancient-looking farmhouses, which caught his film-maker's eye. He had grown up in Vancouver, Canada, where his Norwegian father, an architect, ensured that Rolph was well versed in Vignola's *Five Orders of Architecture* by the age of nine. Years later, on founding his architectural firm, Blakstad Design Consultants, in 1967, Rolph regarded building as a more dynamic, constructive sort of documentary. His career played out as a spirited effort to preserve misunderstood, centuries-old traditions and to proselytize a wider audience, particularly those concerned by the wave of tourism-fed modernization sweeping the island.

The theme of education extends across the entire family. In 1973 Mary founded the Morna Valley School in the former Blakstad home. The couple's two sons, Nial and Rolf, took the helm of the architecture firm and continue to defend Ibiza's timeless vernacular.

'My father's vision was always very pragmatic', explains Rolf. 'He never expected everybody to live like farmers. He studied the origins of architecture, taking wisdom and knowledge accumulated over thousands of years and applying it to the present day.'

However, every pioneer experiences some form of pushback, especially when challenging stiff conventions. 'My father didn't have an academic background, having studied painting and fine arts, but this gave him a certain liberty to tackle so-called "crazy" ideas', says Rolf. 'In the eighth chapter of his book [*La casa eivissenca/ The House of Ibiza*, written in 1996, first published in Catalan in 2013], he talks quite mystically about energies. No academic could possibly publish a paper like that!'

While Rolph occasionally ruffled feathers with his enthusiasm for traditional Ibizan architecture, his son Rolf carefully eschews the label of 'saviour' or 'guardian'. He prefers to draw the conversation around the focus of his father's work: shared, sustainable, generations-old values for living.

For this reason, the Blakstad name endures. Not simply because the family firm continues to develop its architectural vision through the design and construction of new homes and the restoration of others, but also because its work stands as a reminder of the home's connection to humanity's much grander history: houses that stand as monuments to the unshakeable bonds that bind our collective past – and future. ***LA***

Rolf Blakstad continues his father Rolph's vision, meaning that the family name has become a byword for preservation and provenance, blending traditional elements with modern functionality.

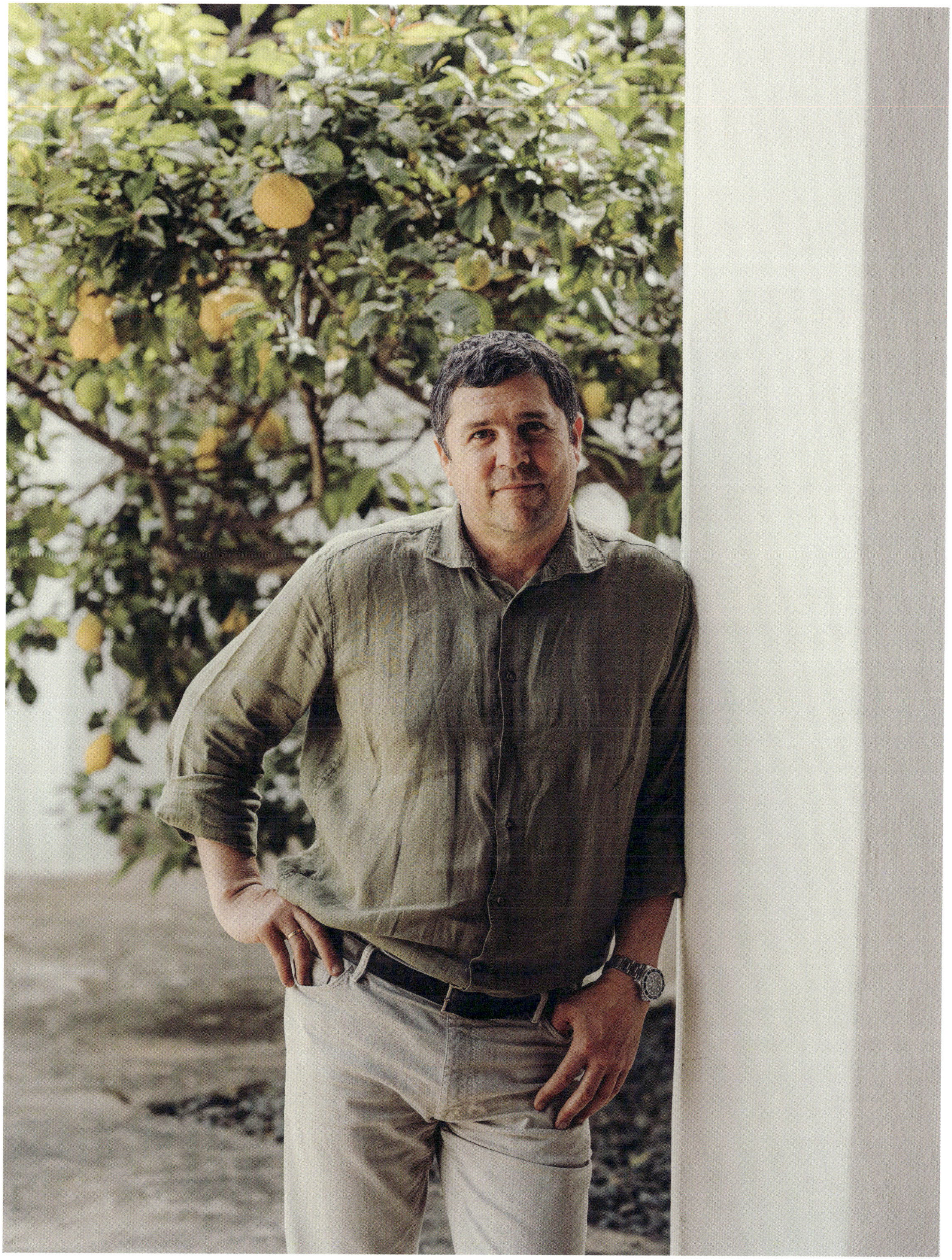

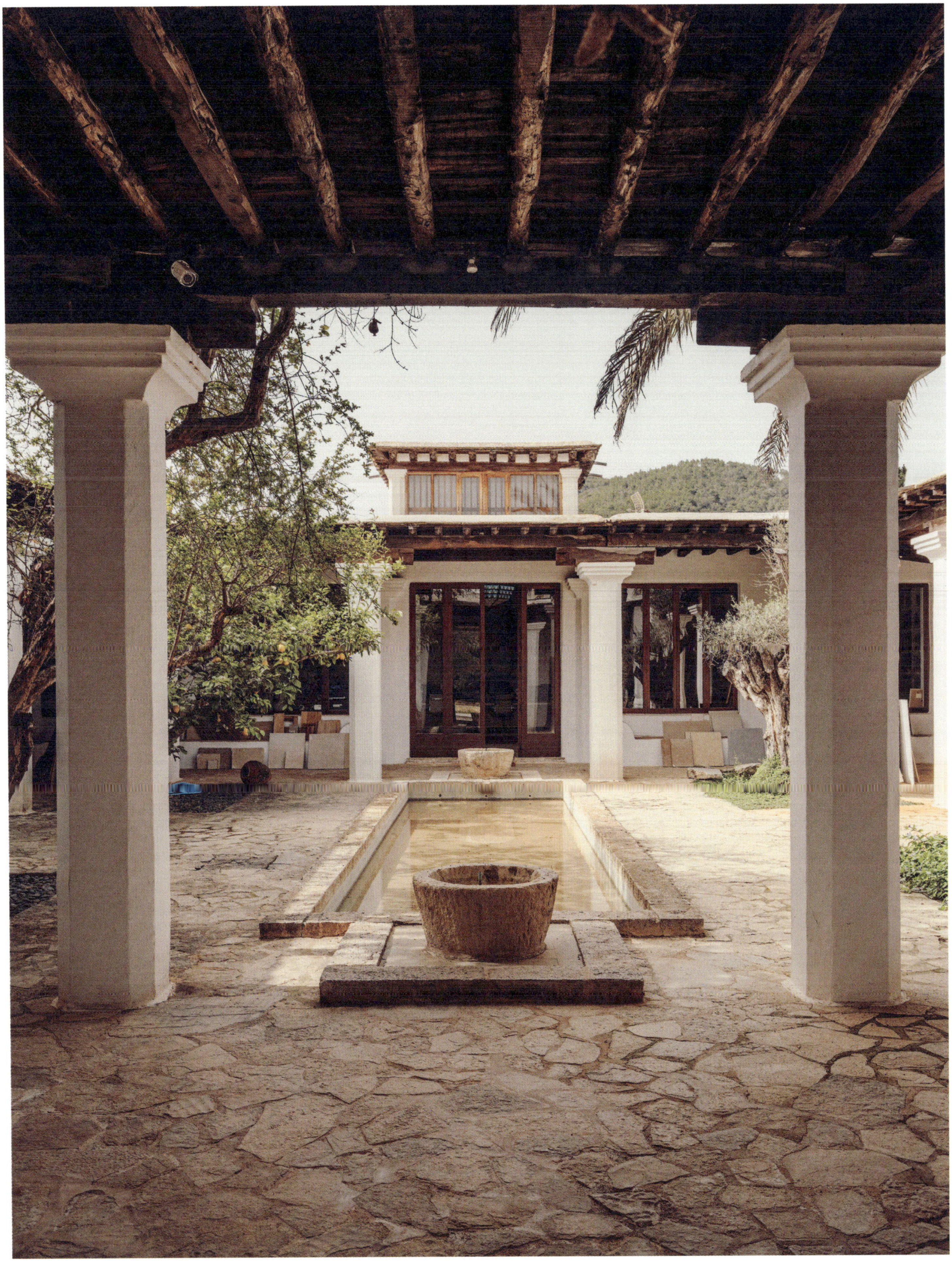

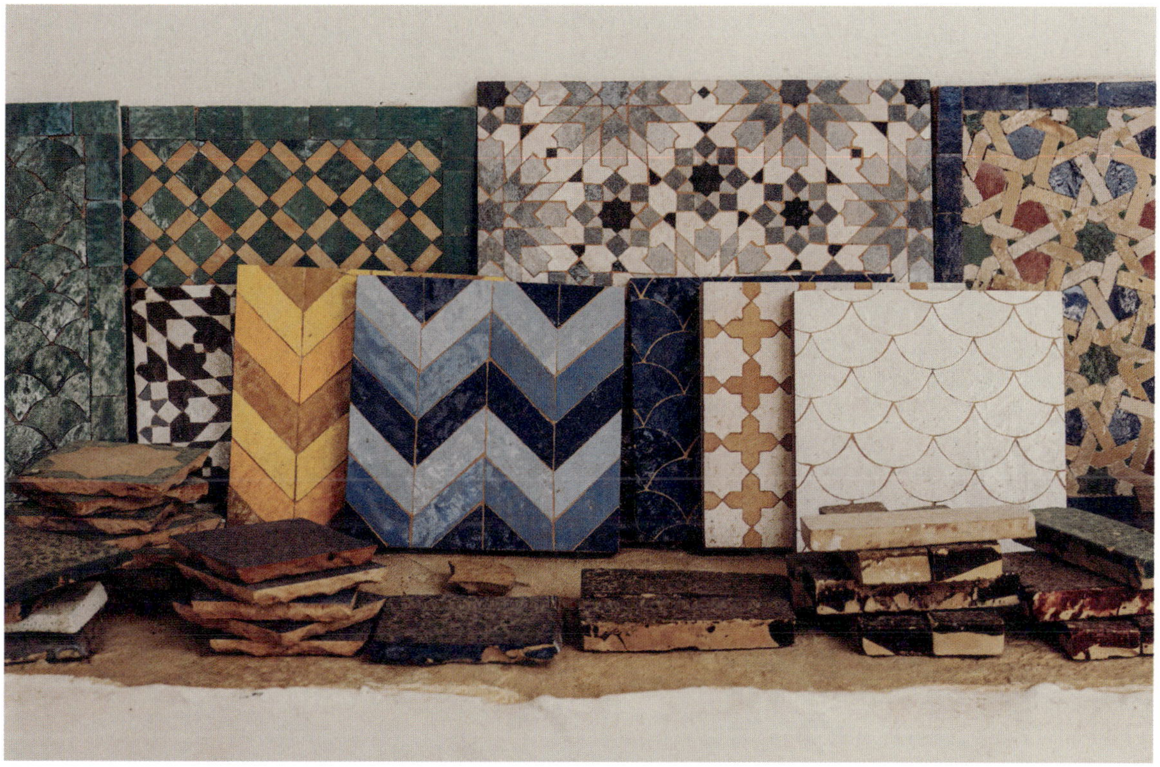

An extensive collection of material samples and books about architecture, art, international culture and landscape design fill the library shelves and overflow into other spaces.

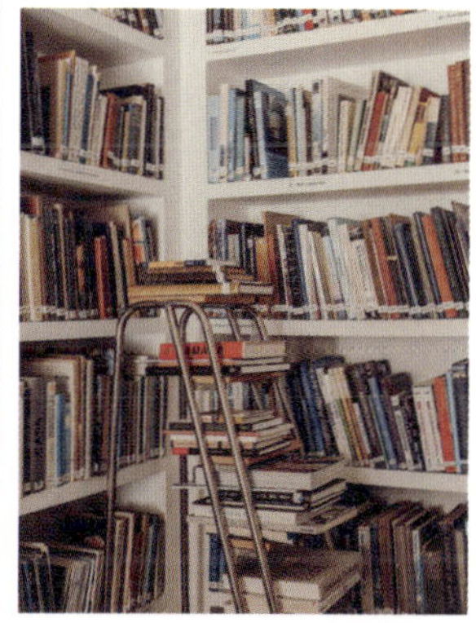

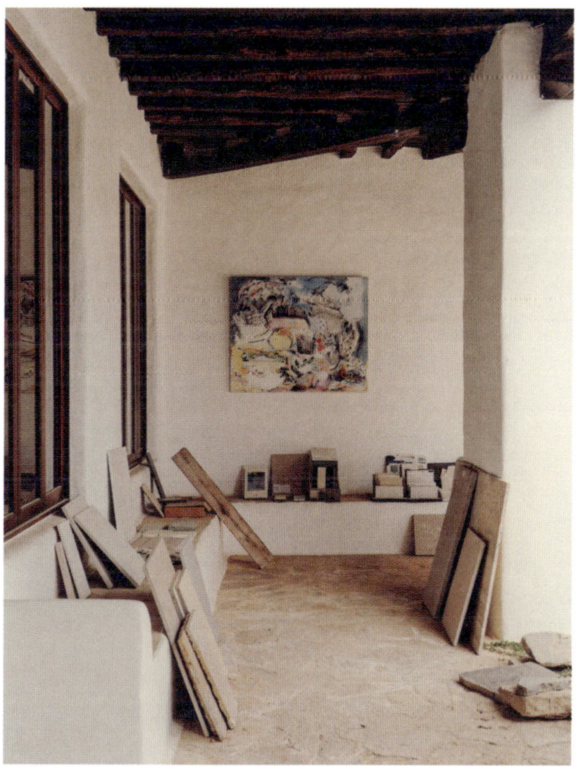

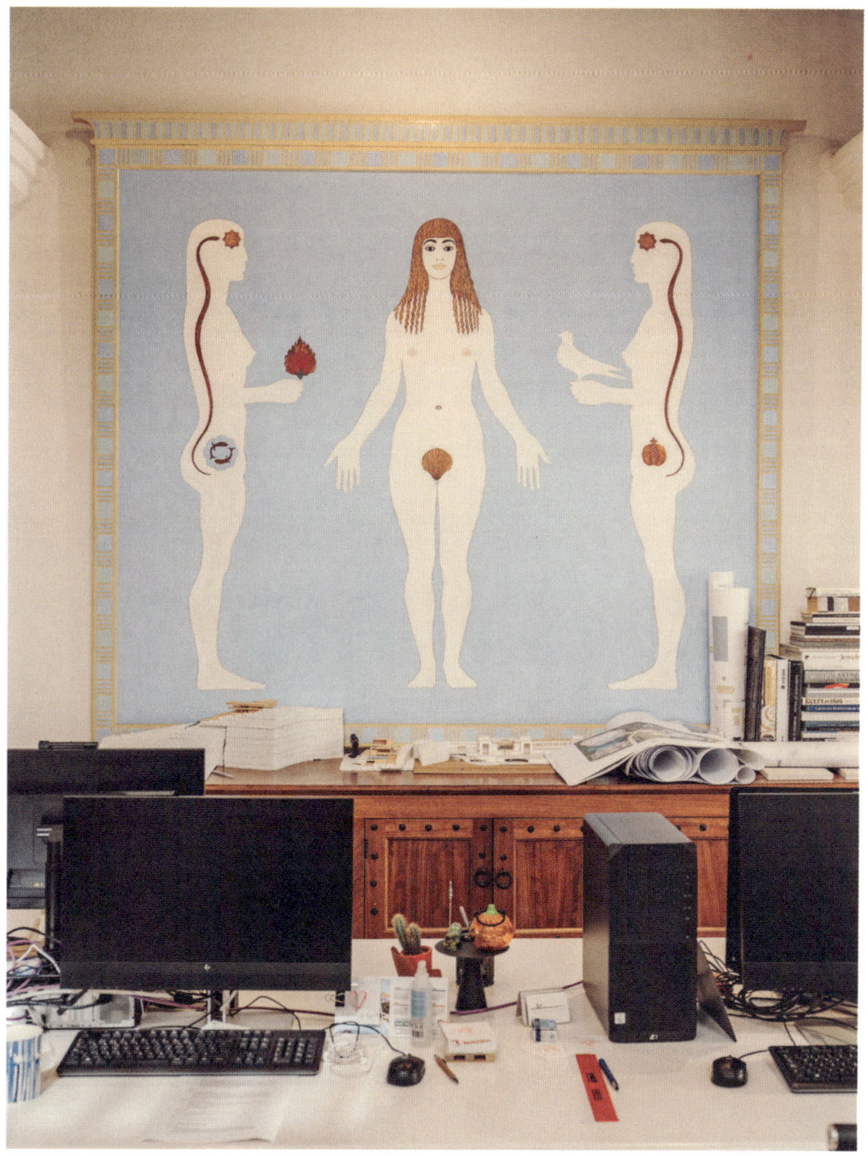

The Blakstad office (entrance shown opposite) is located in the Morna Valley, between Santa Eulalia and San Carlos. A painting by Rolph Blakstad (right) hangs behind the desks.

Overleaf: The clubhouse of Sabina Ibiza, designed by Blakstad.

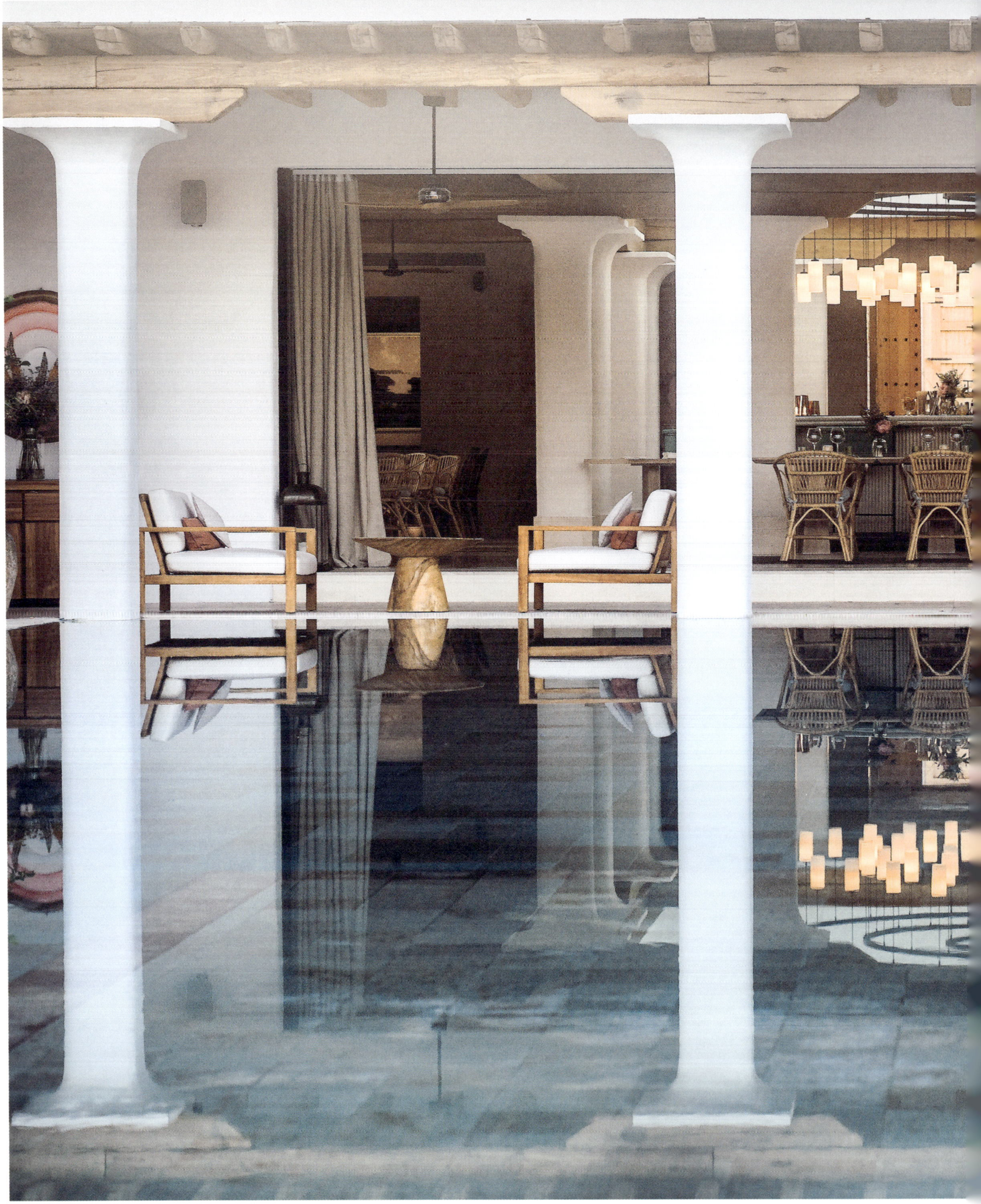

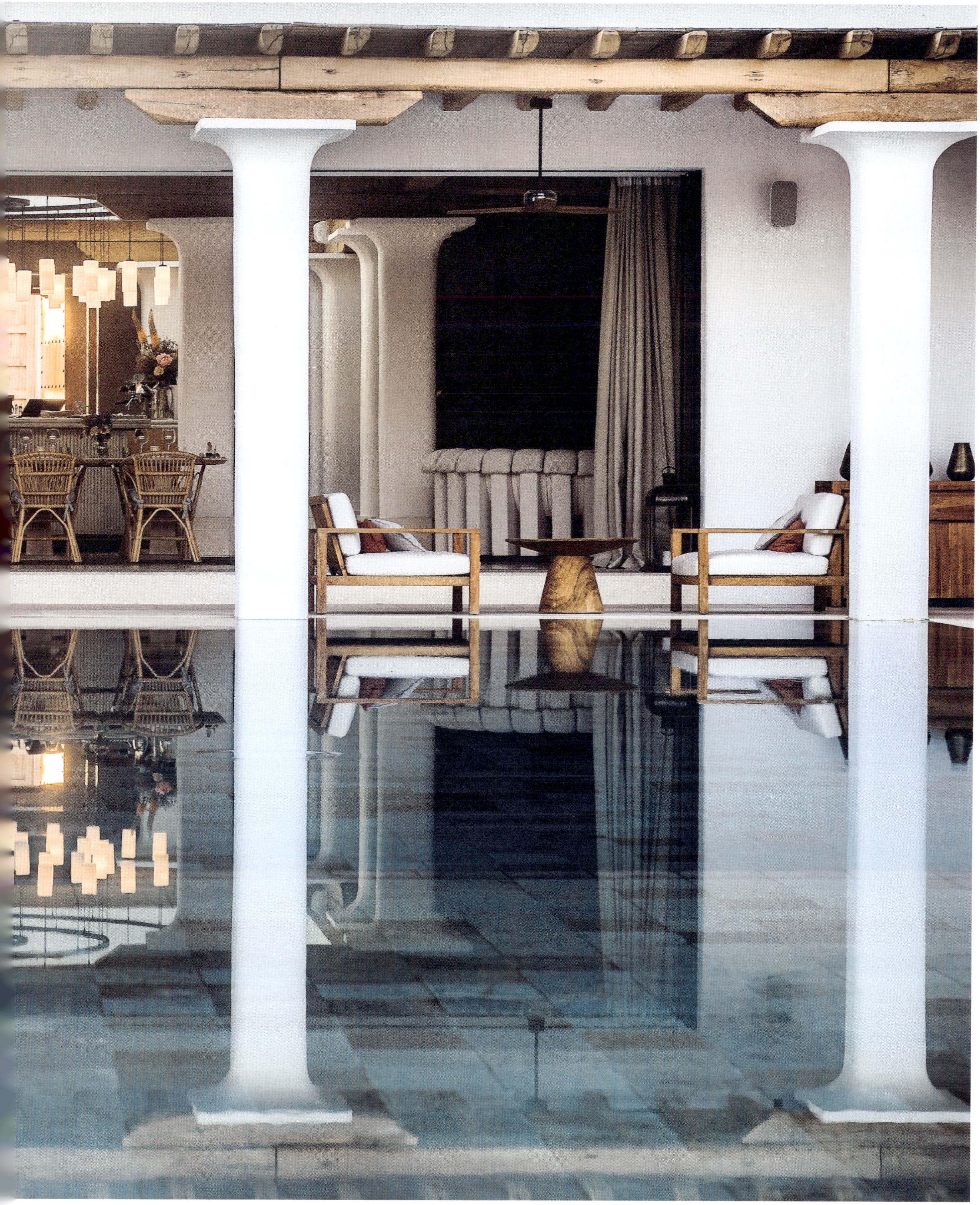

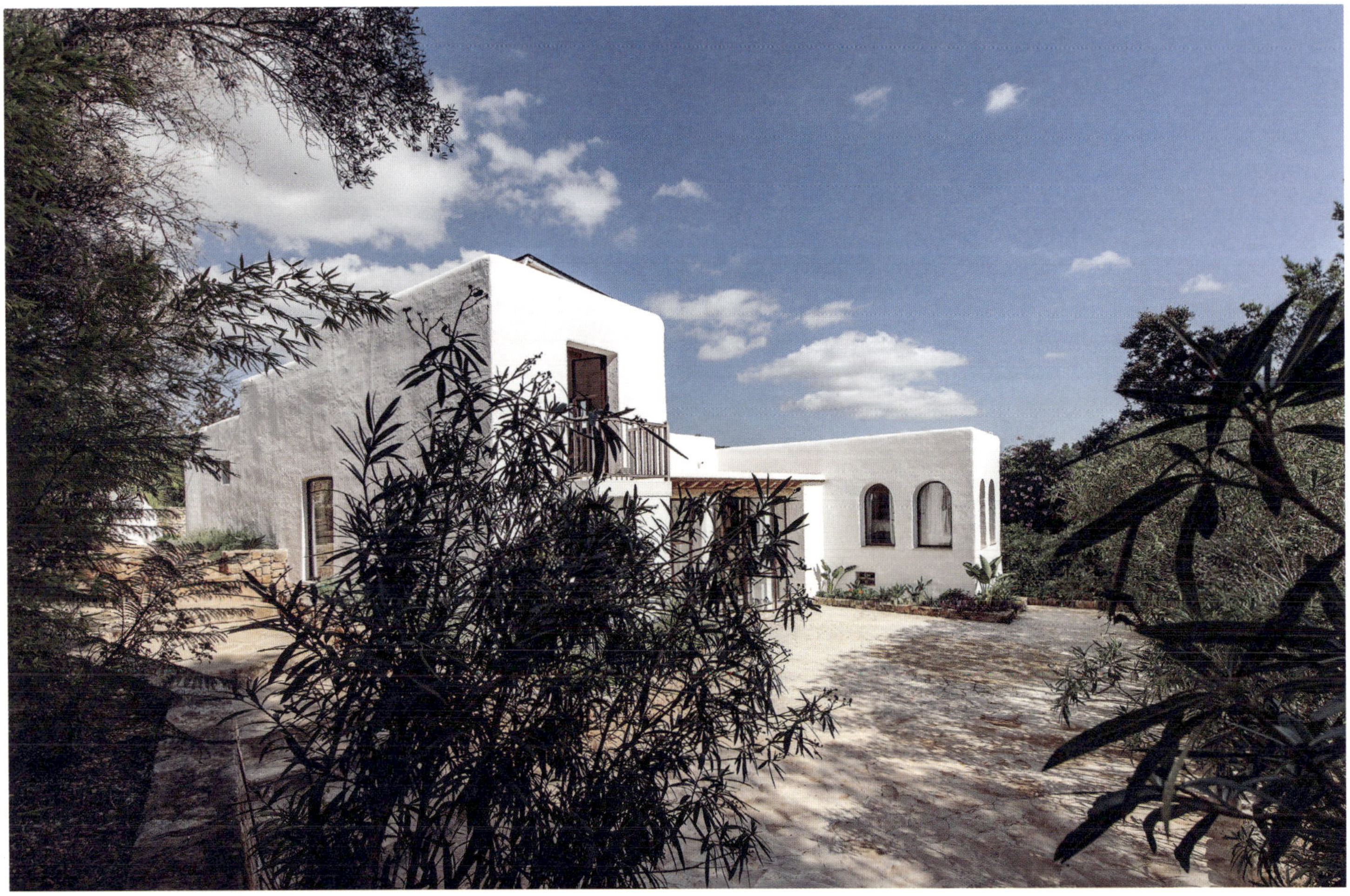

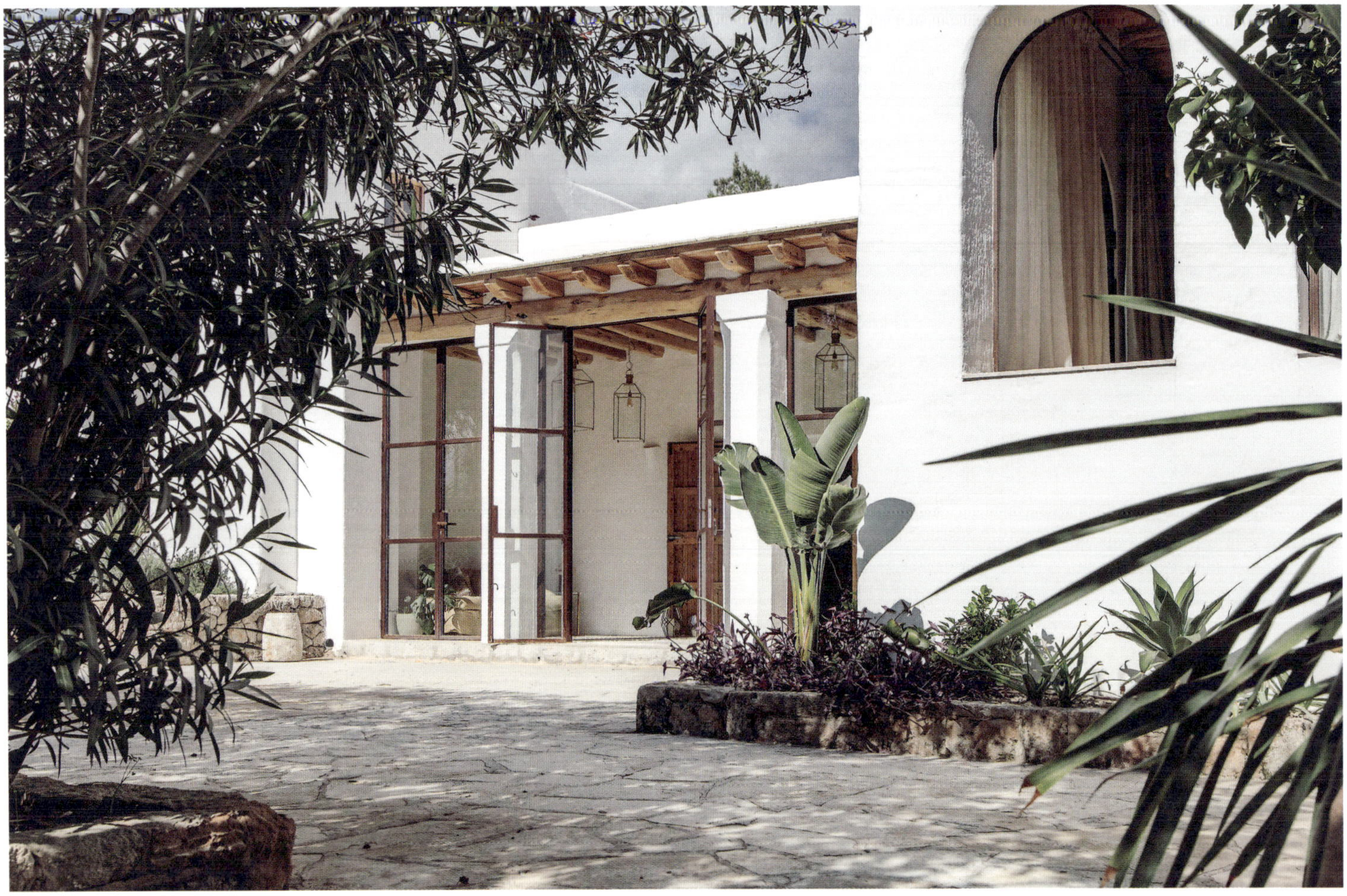

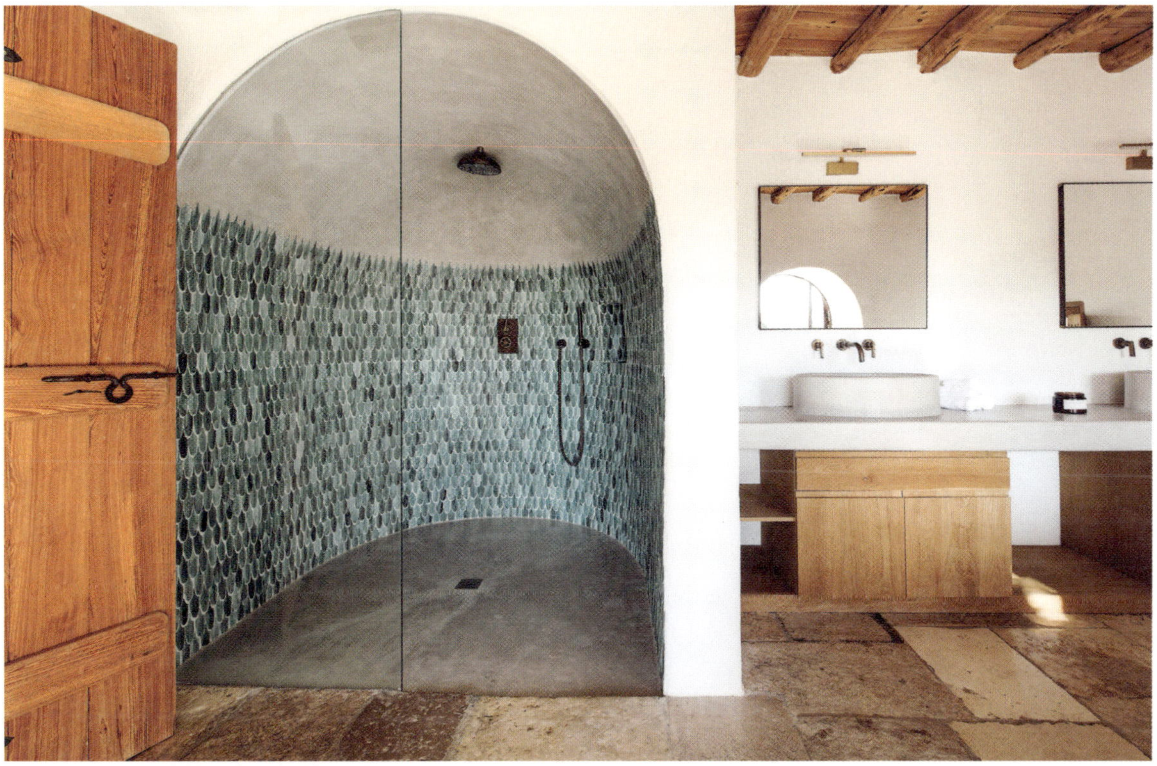

Finca Cullet, near Santa Gertrudis, designed by Blakstad for Harry Clark. Harry worked closely with Blakstad to create her ideal home, and she has lived happily with her family in this once-ramshackle farmhouse since 2012.

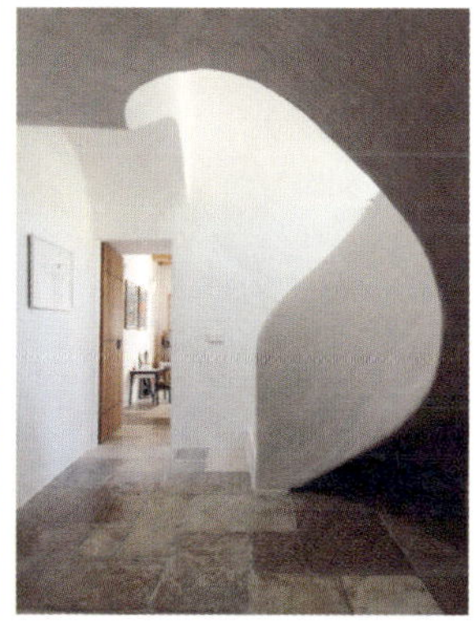

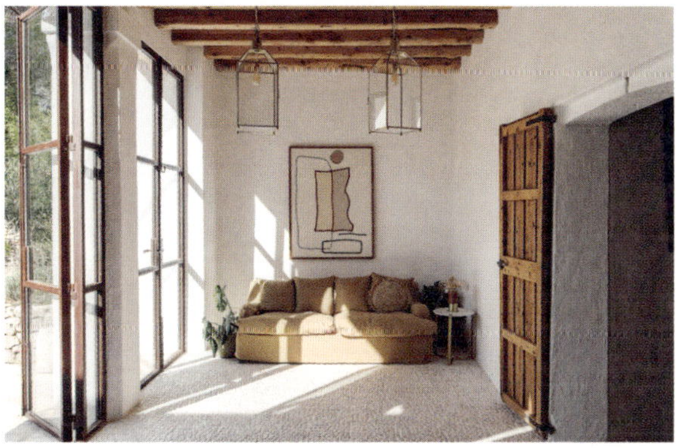

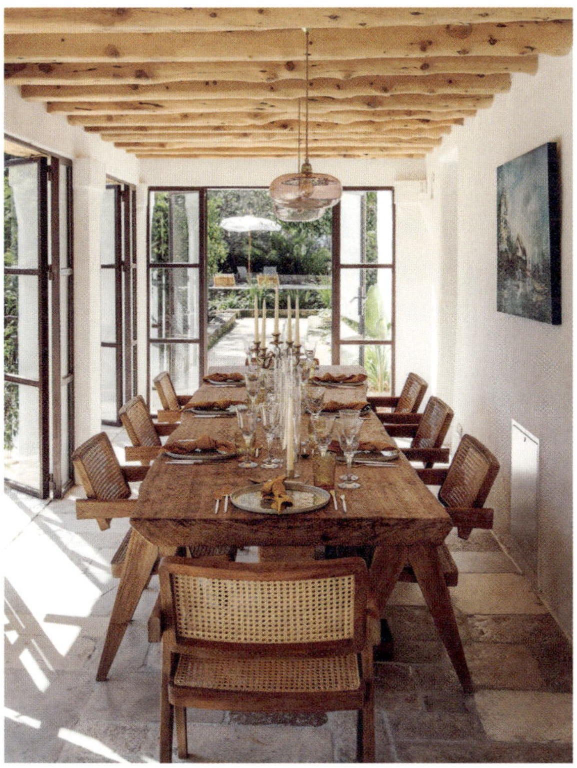

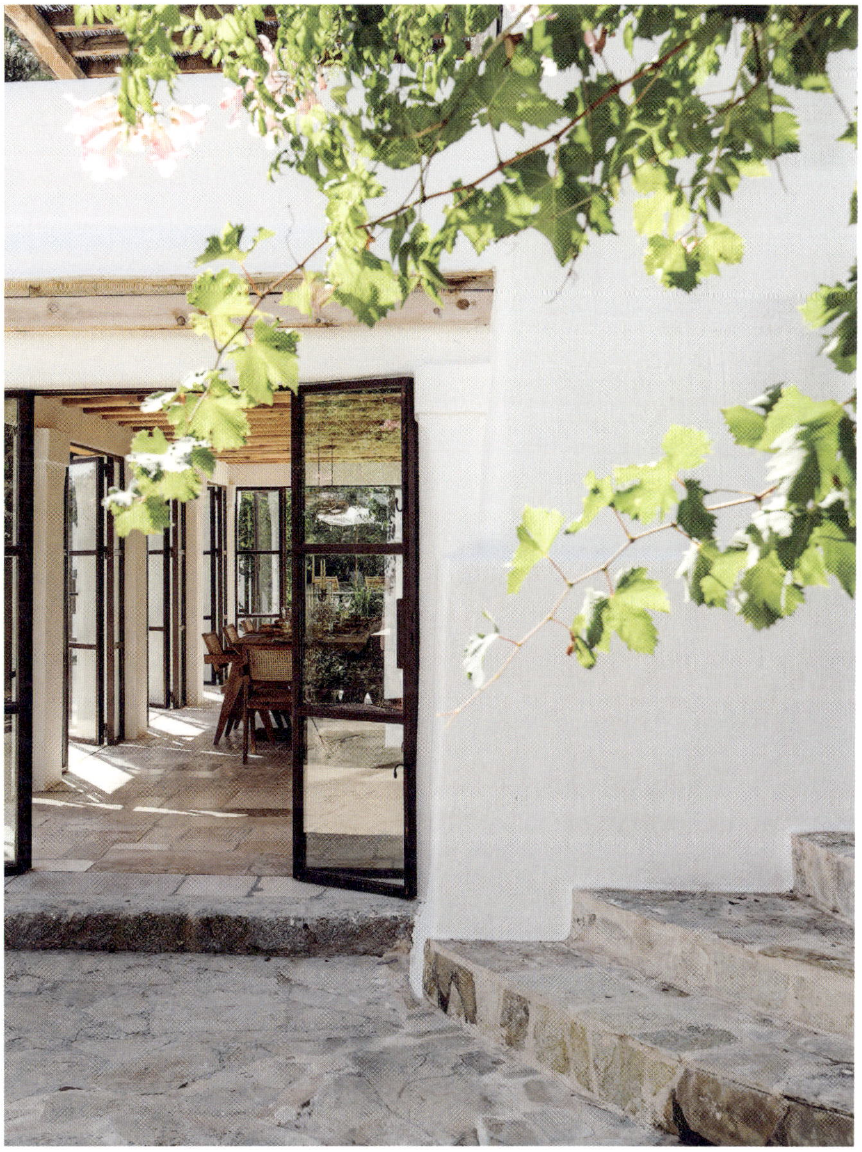

ESTUDIO VILA 13

ARCHITECTURE

Creative expression is our timestamp on the gradual construction of history. So says Jordi Carreño, an architect whose own trajectory is stitched together like an imaginative patchwork, spanning castles, nightclubs, modern homes and much-loved hospitality venues. Jordi was born in Ibiza, and his Ibicenco family history stretches back generations. His great-grandfather even built the first proper hotel on the island, El Montesol, in 1933. The idea that architecture and design can shape the future resonated with Jordi from a young age.

Jordi's first major project – the restoration of the castle wall in Dalt Vila in 2003 – unearthed centuries of learning about Ibiza's constructed history. Taking a full decade to complete, it became instrumental in shaping his future perspective. 'Much like that wall, I believe we all must add our own layer, being respectful of what we find, but always contributing something new that identifies with today', he explains. 'Finding this balance is what interests me most. How much to add? What deserves respect? A good project finds a way to properly answer both of these questions.'

Founded in 2009, Jordi's studio, Vila 13, feels like a free-flowing incubator of ideas. It favours a non-hierarchical structure, where all members of a young, inventive team contribute to the creation of concepts, then together solve the puzzle of bringing them to life. 'From Salvador Dalí to the forms of ant mounds, we reference pop culture, trips to other countries, and traditions from the island', Jordi says. His renovation of Hï Ibiza nightclub (formerly Space), Playa d'en Bossa, was inspired by the set design of *Star Wars*: serving as the VIP area, disc-shaped platforms cascade towards the main dance floor. 'Memories create ideas that I drag into my architecture', Jordi explains.

In the early years after the turn of the millennium, Jordi also spearheaded the movement to internationalize and innovate the island's hotels, winning a European Hotel Design Award in 2013 for the bold, sustainable vision of the Ushuaïa Tower Hotel, Playa d'en Bossa.

Unpretentious, unrelenting and a committed team player, Jordi Carreño personifies the open-hearted attitude of many Ibicencos. The result is a résumé of wildly diverse designs that are impossible to fit into one standard-issue box. 'Other studios may be much clearer with their identity, but I'm just not capable of repeating the same thing over and over again', he admits. 'Instead of just reinventing the wheel, I prefer to go the extra mile, adding something special. That is what keeps me feeling alive.' This eclectic approach to architecture reaffirms his equally constructive view that, in Ibiza, it does not matter where you come from; the important thing is what you are willing to contribute. ***LA***

Jordi Carreño's family has a long-standing association with the island's architecture. His practice, Estudio Vila 13, provides innovative designs for hotels, clubs and private residences, resulting in award-winning concepts.

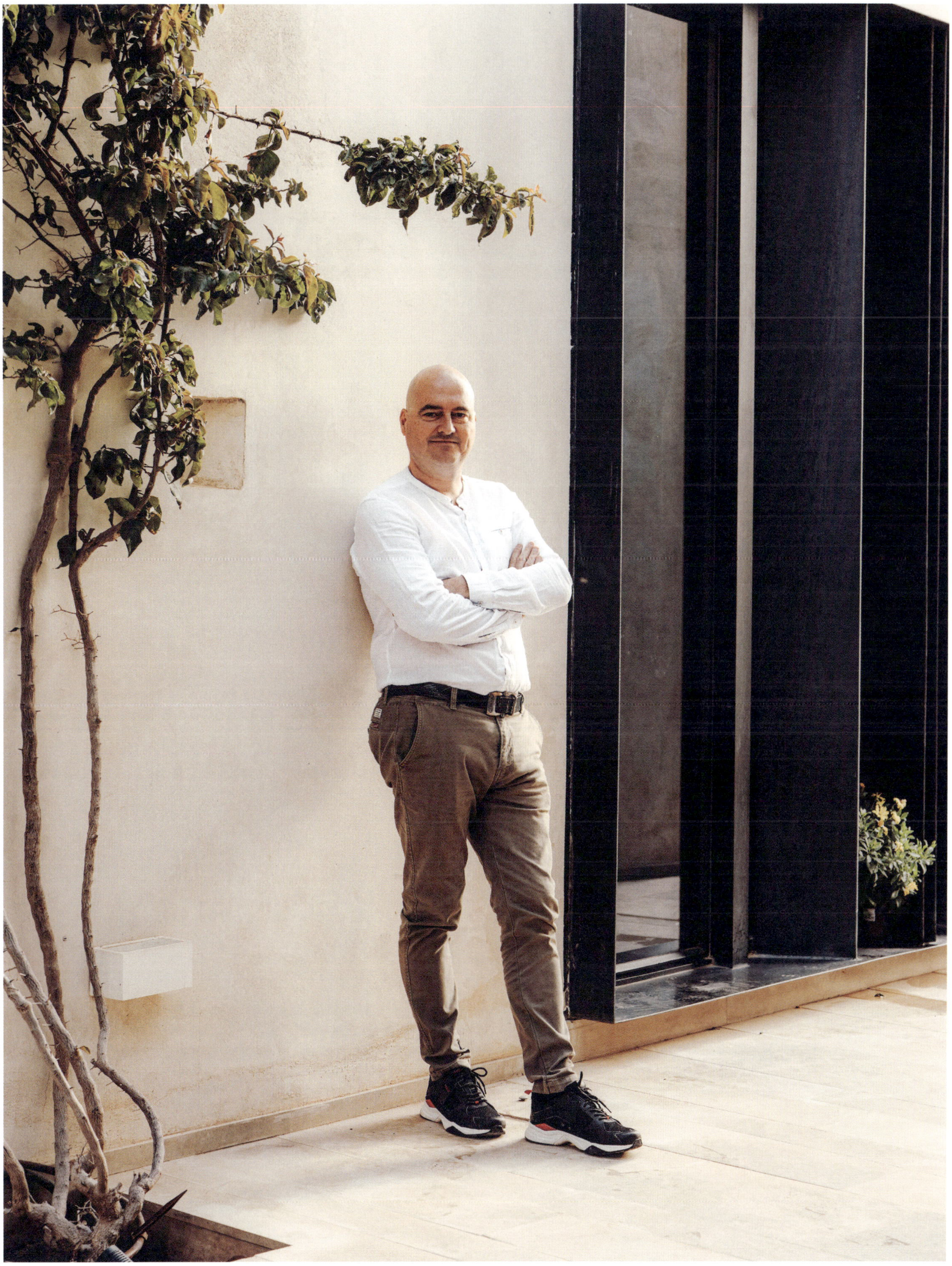

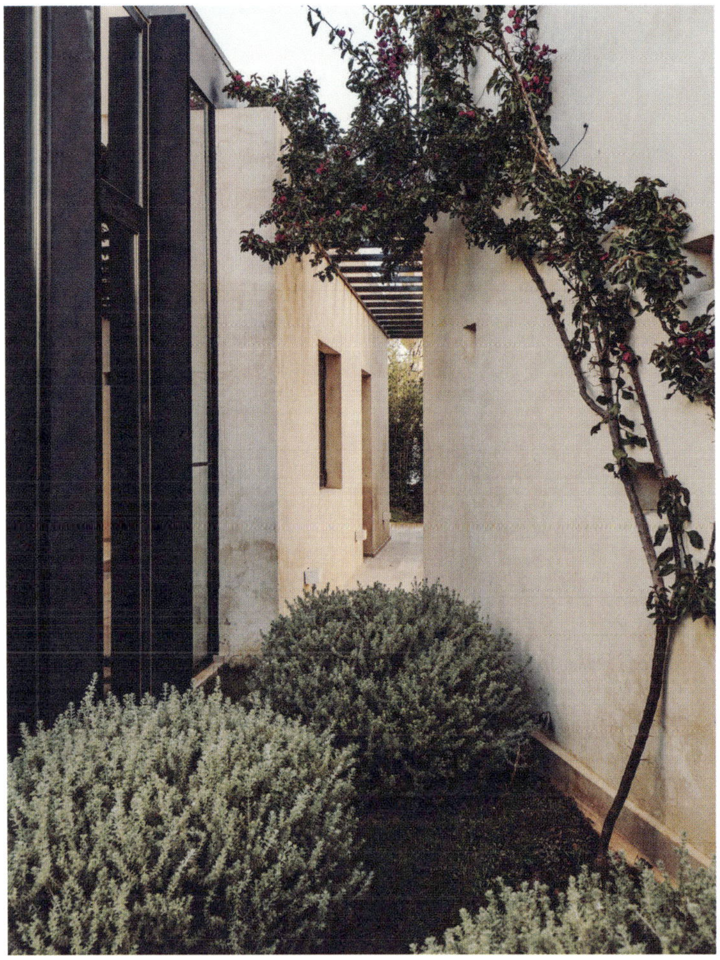
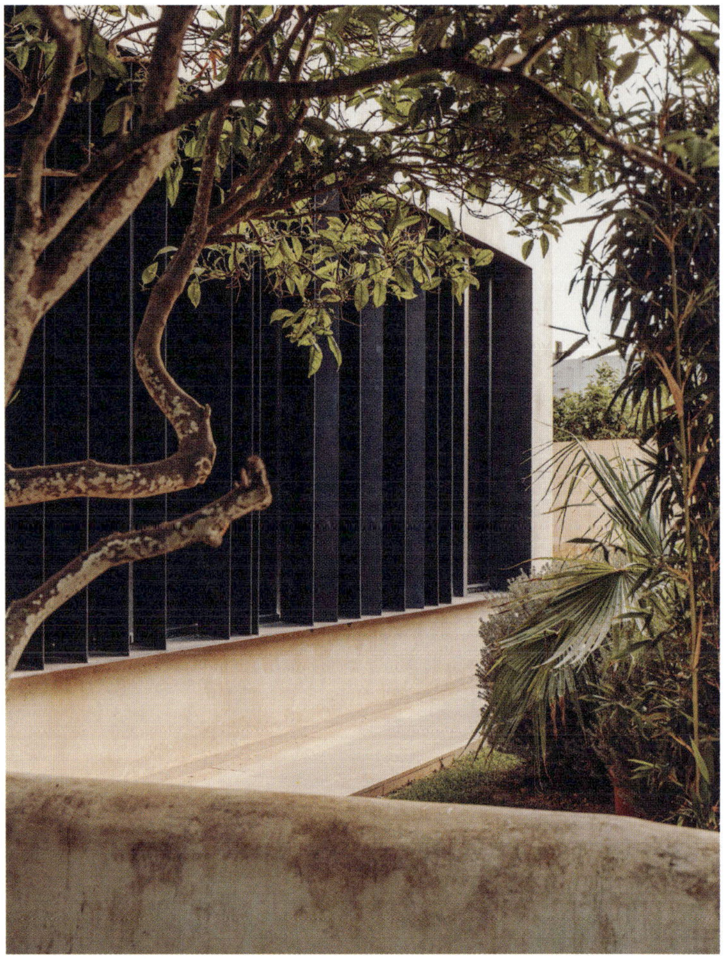
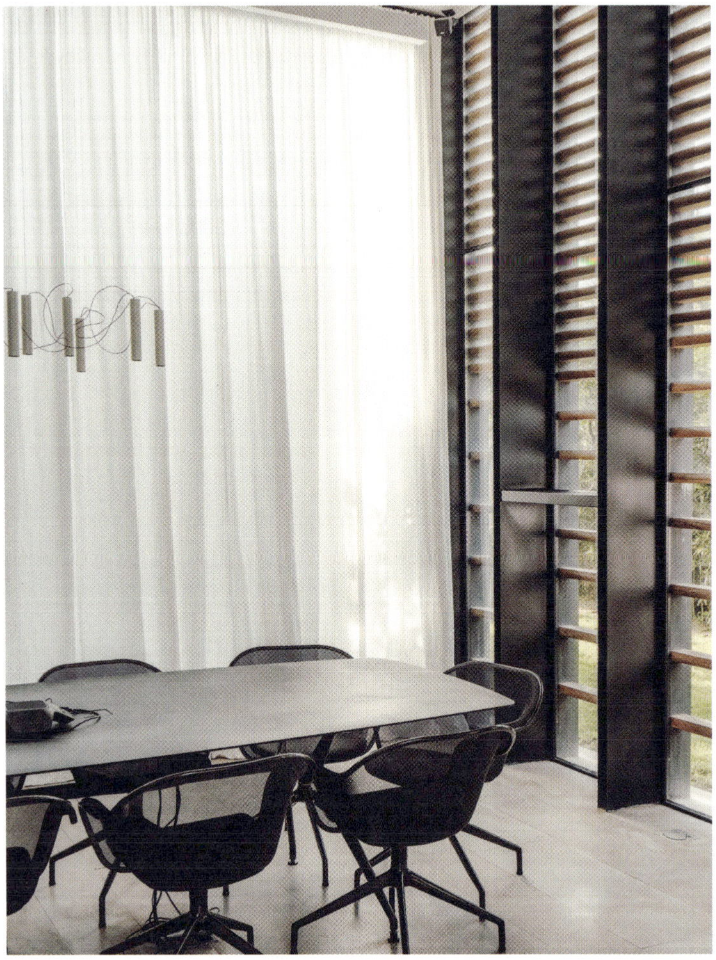
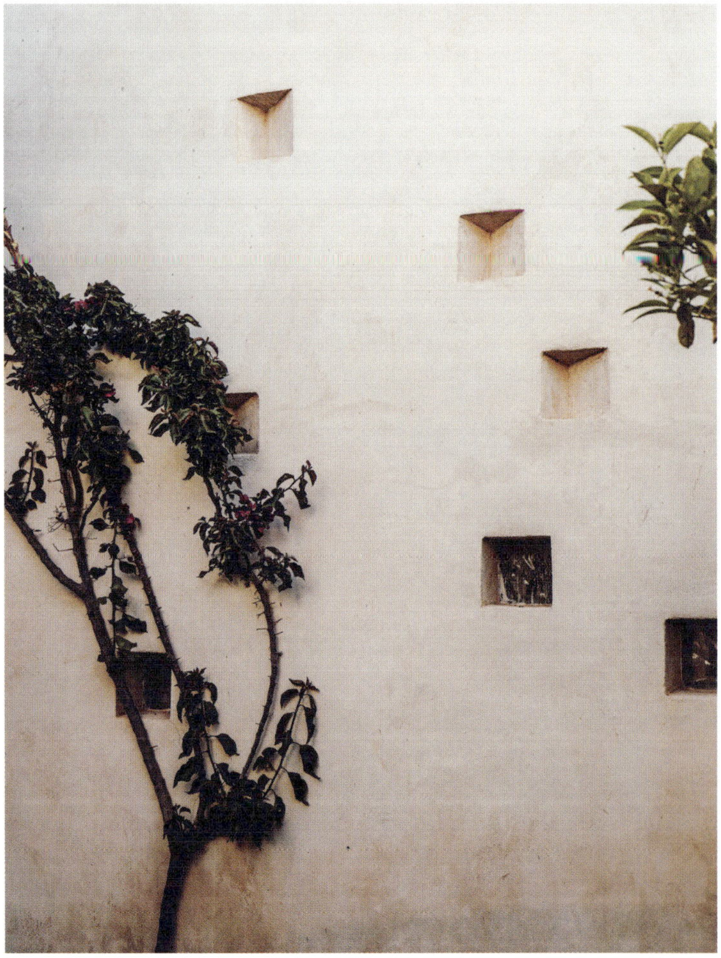

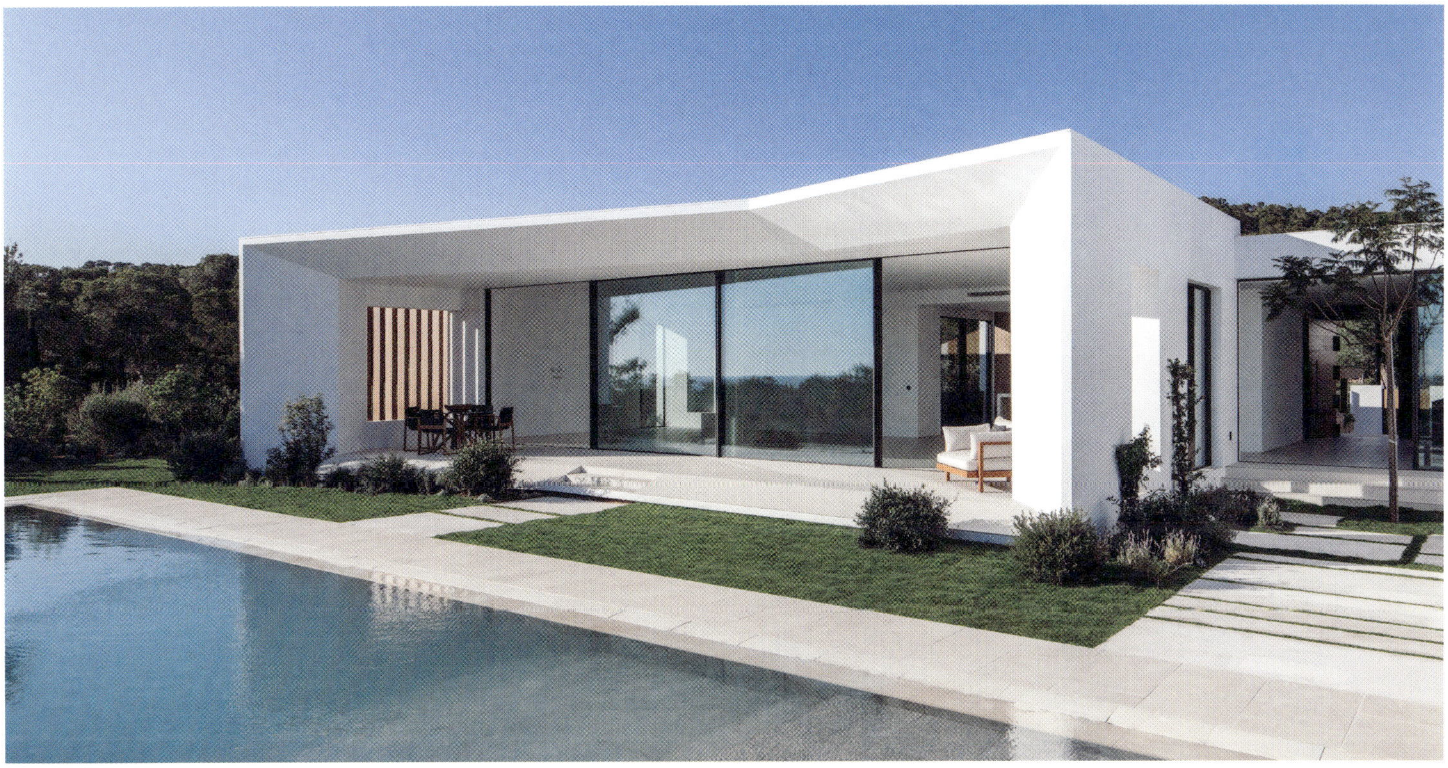

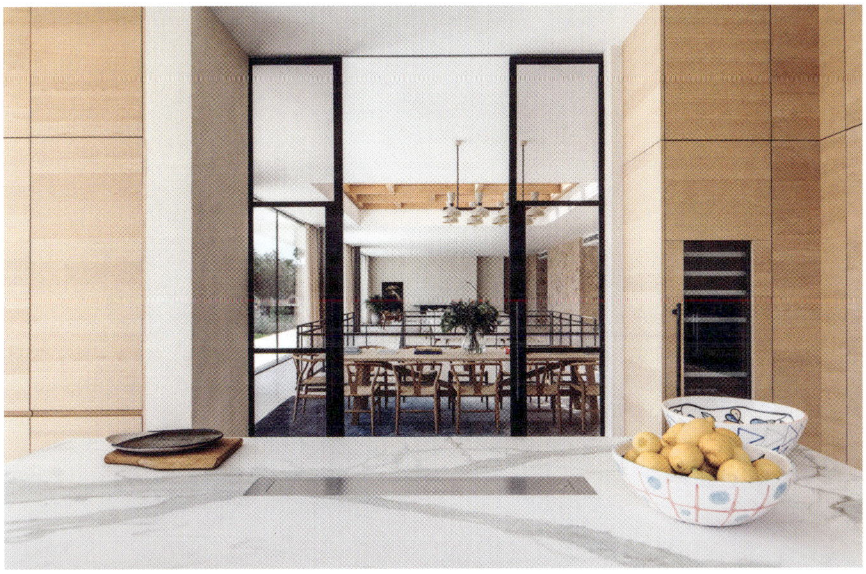

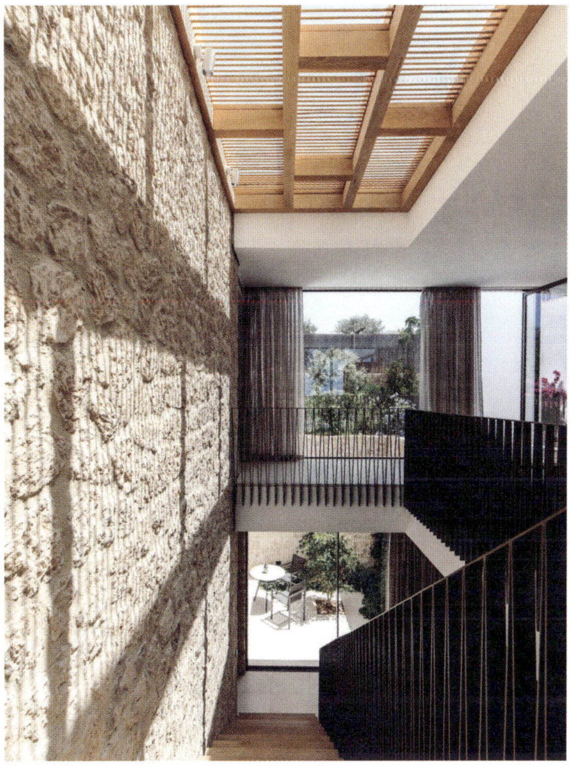

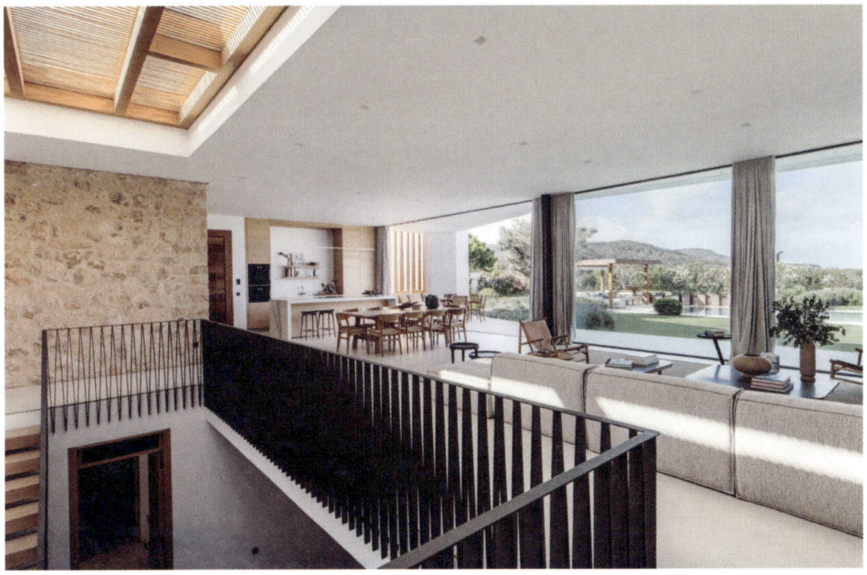

Opposite: Now based in Ca na Negreta, Estudio Vila 13 is named after its original location in Dalt Vila, the old part of Ibiza Town.

This page and overleaf: A private villa at Sabina Ibiza, the luxury complex on the west coast of the island whose master plan was also developed by Jordi.

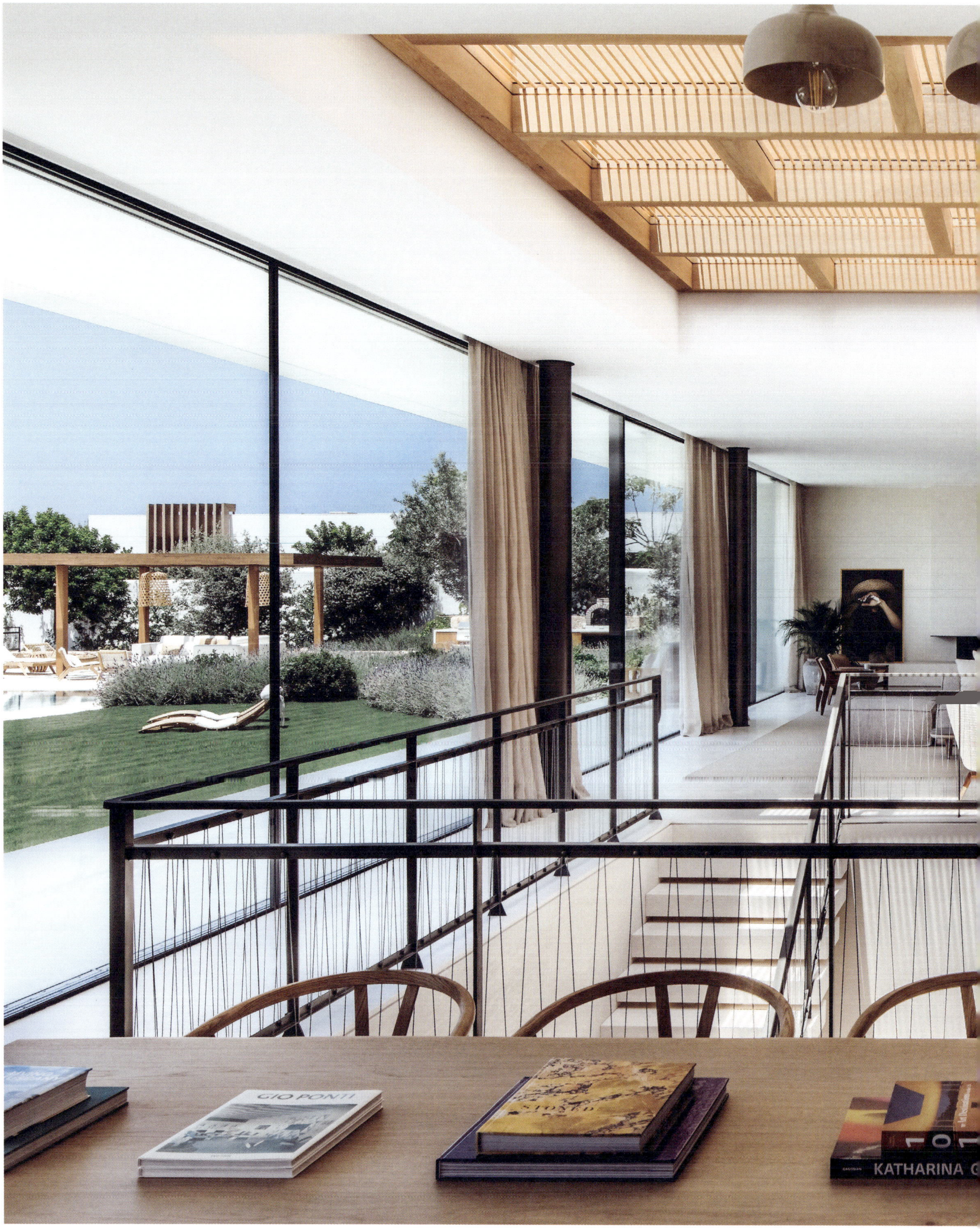
GIO PONTI
STONED
KATHARINA

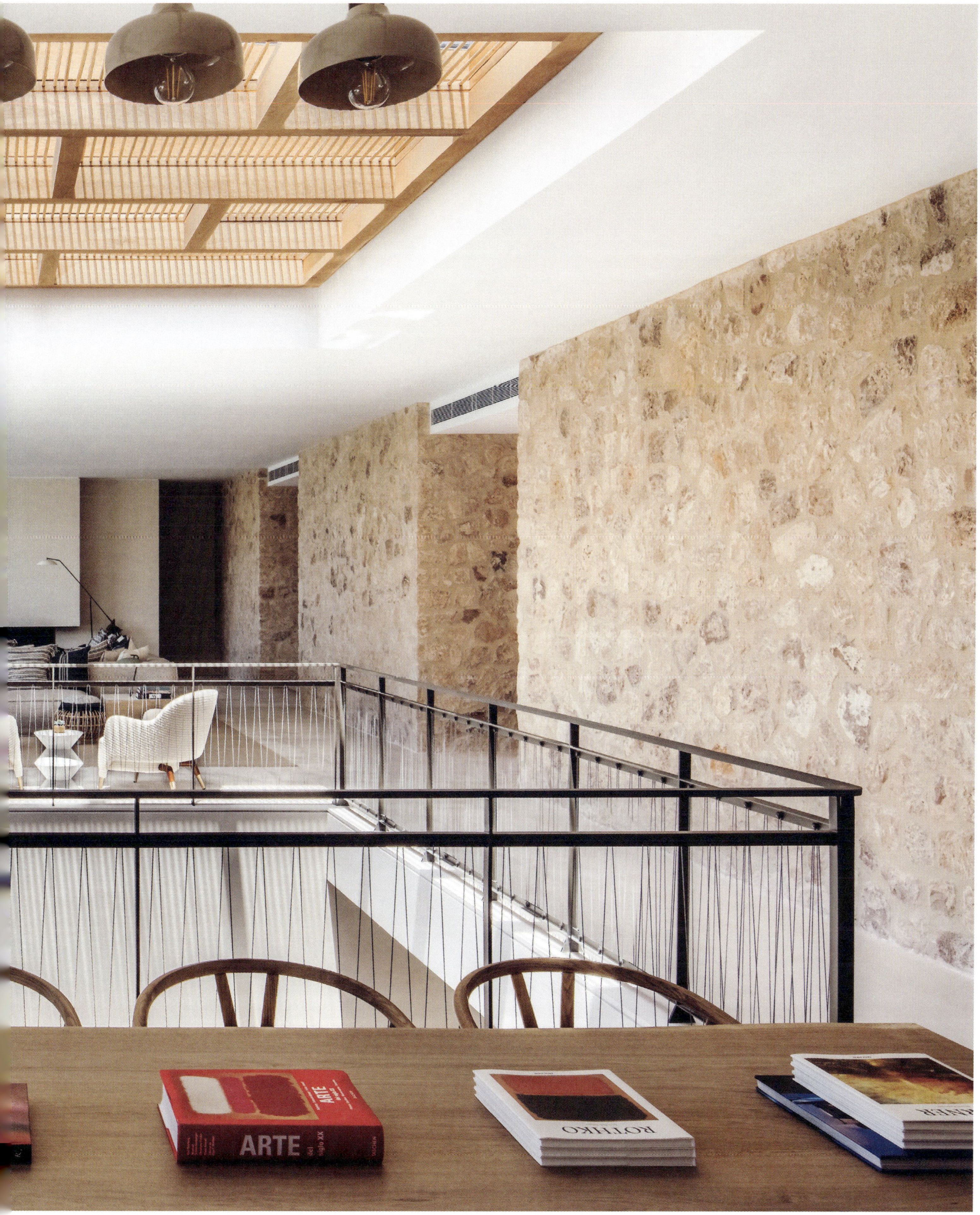
ARTE
ARTE
TASCHEN
ROTHKO

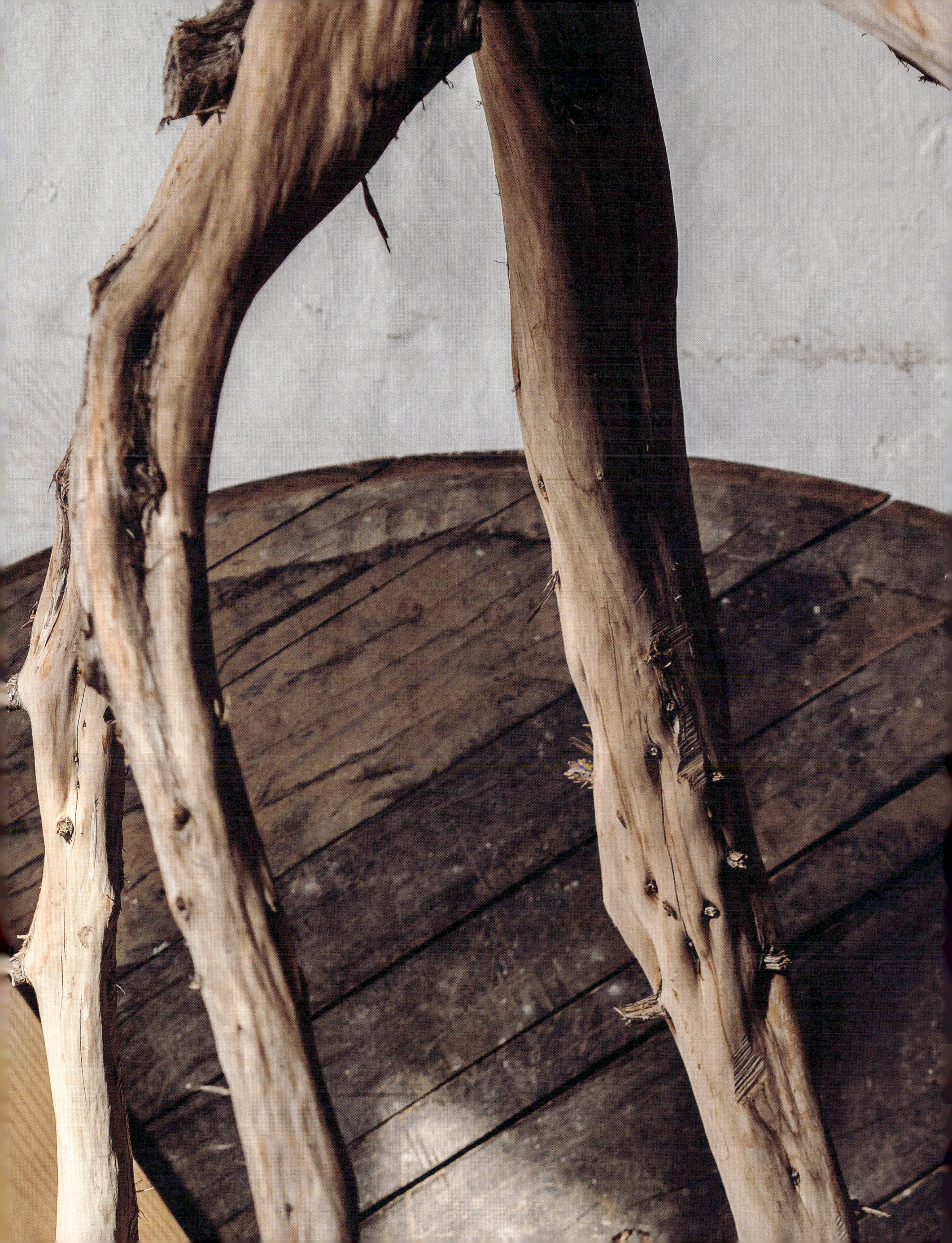

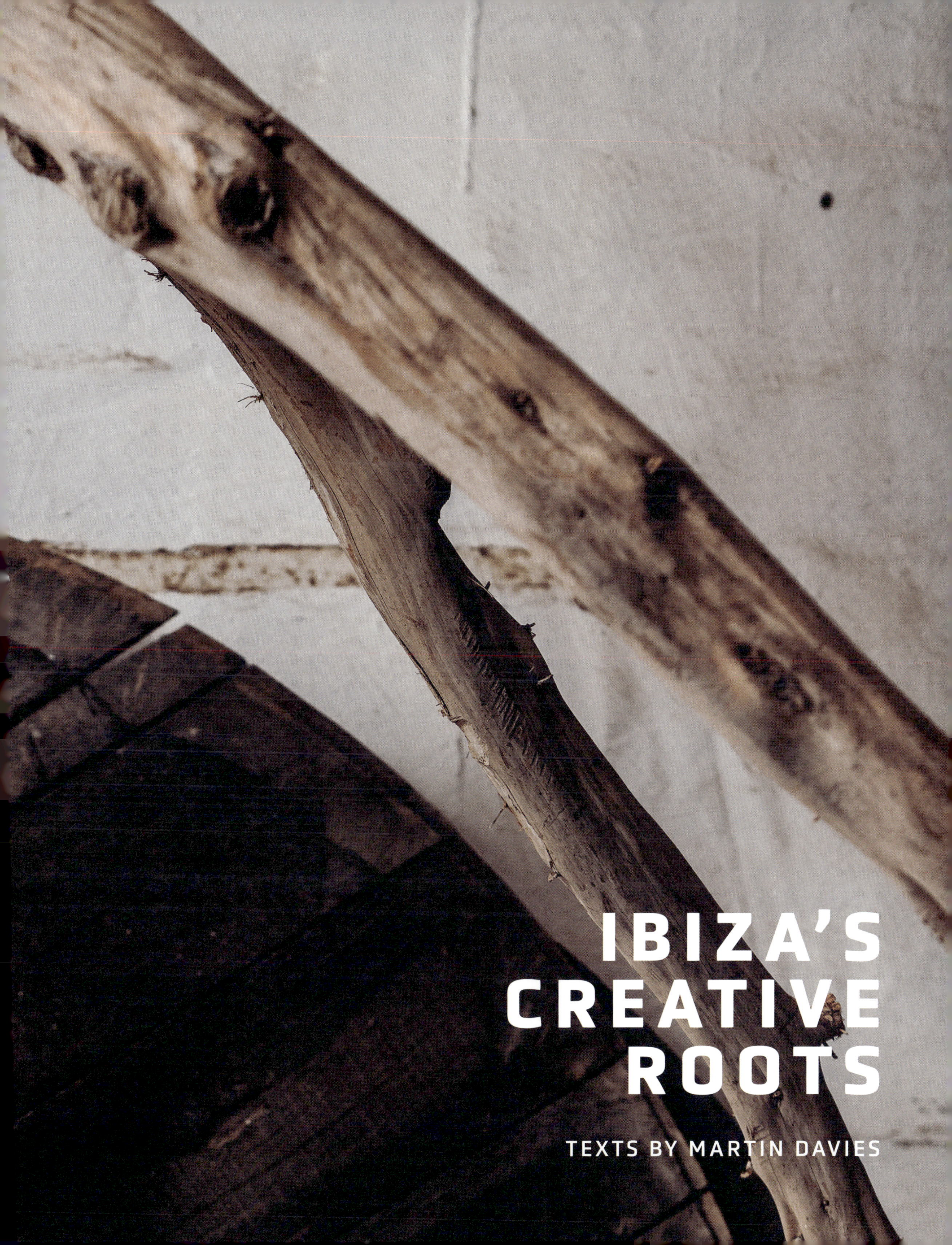

IBIZA'S CREATIVE ROOTS

TEXTS BY MARTIN DAVIES

ART AND CRAFTS IN IBIZA

THE UNTOLD STORY

BEGINNINGS, 1912–36 For more than a century, Ibiza's alluring capital, picturesque landscapes, exquisite light and colourful inhabitants have inspired artists from all around the world, while its cosmopolitan atmosphere and unique café culture have enriched and emboldened them in countless other ways. The island's artistic potential first came to light with three painters from Catalonia – Joan Llaverias, Santiago Rusiñol and Laureano Barrau – in the summer of 1912, the year the harbour's new quay was completed. Ibiza had long been notorious for violence among competing suitors, but Rusiñol, an acclaimed author as well as artist, did much to dispel the *leyenda negra* by coining a new nickname, 'la Isla Blanca', in the pages of the *Diario de Ibiza*. His main aim had been to dig for archaeological treasure in the newly uncovered Punic necropolis, but he also found time to produce five paintings in Ibiza Town, including *Patio azul* (1913), which appeared in an exhibition at the Museo de Bellas Artes de Bilbao in 2020.

Over the following decade the local scene began to crystallize around the 'patriarch' of Ibizan painting, Narcís Puget Viñas, who had studied photography as well as fine art in Barcelona and Madrid. In 1916 he opened the island's first art school – at Paseo de Vara de Rey 6 – where many leading local artists subsequently trained, among them José Tarrés Palau, Antoni Marí Ribas ('Portmany'), Vicent Ferrer Guasch and the painter's own son, Narcís Puget Riquer. The Sociedad Cultural Ebusus in Vara de Rey displays several works by Tarrés, who became the first Ibicenco to hold a solo exhibition when he inaugurated Galería Maria Ferst near the Old Market in 1933.

As word spread, a steady stream of talent, much of it from Spain's Levante coastline, found its way to Ibiza, including Rigoberto Soler from Alcoy and Fernando Viscaí from Valencia. *Costumbrismo* was then the country's leading artistic and literary movement, documenting exotic customs in far-flung provinces. Ibiza's unusual architecture and folklore made it a place of special pilgrimage, and Joaquín Sorolla himself spent a fortnight on the island in September 1919. The resulting masterwork, *Los contrabandistas* (The smugglers), was commissioned by the tobacco king Thomas Fortune Ryan and ranks among the *chefs d'œuvre* of Balearic Impressionism. In 2019 it was exhibited for the first time in the National Gallery in London, ending a century of undeserved neglect.

Along with townscapes and landscapes, Ibiza's colourful traditions remained for six decades a favourite subject among Spanish – and occasionally foreign – artists. In 2007 one of Dalt Vila's most striking palazzos was remodelled as a museum to promote the Puget legacy (father and son). The most prolific and successful *costumbrista* painters include Barrau, Soler (both based in Santa Eulalia) and José Chico Prats, who was born in Barcelona to an Ibicenco mother. One of his canvases graces the cover of Juan Cabot Llompart's *Ibiza y sus pintores* (1979), the only book so far published on this largely uncharted subject.

Four illustrators deserve a special mention, above all the Habsburg archduke Ludwig Salvator (visited Ibiza in 1867) and the Frenchman Gaston Vuillier (1889). Their ethnographic erudition and graphic skill have made their respective books, *Die alten Pityusen* (1869) and *Les Îles oubliées* (1893), lasting beacons of Balearic scholarship and art. Two neglected Britons complete our roll call of pioneering illustrators: the Scotsman Alexander Stuart Boyd, whose exquisite pen-drawings and colour plates appeared in *The Fortunate Isles* (1911) by his wife, Mary Stuart Boyd; and Katharine Clausen, whose brilliant artwork fills the pages of *Voyage and Discovery* (1933) by her husband, Conor O'Brien.

The first foreign painter to settle in Ibiza was the Dane Jan Bjørn Willumsen. Following an exploratory visit, he spent five years in San Antonio (1922–26) working on highly realistic canvases of *payesos*, courtship rituals and folk dancing. A second pioneer from the north, the Berliner Kurt Leyde (1923), produced striking landscapes and genre paintings in Ibiza Town and Santa Eulalia. These two were followed by a growing band of talented artists from Europe and further afield.

In 1932–33 New Zealand's leading modernist, Frances Hodgkins, spent seven months sketching and painting around Ibiza Town in a bold, semi-abstract style after falling under the spell of Matisse and Derain during travels round Europe. Paintings inspired by Ibiza feature prominently in books devoted to her legacy, highlighting the impact the White Island had on creative souls who came ashore. The Dadaist Raoul Hausmann, who had abandoned avant-garde art by the time he arrived in 1933, worked on an ambitious experimental novel published in 1969 as *Hyle: Ein Traumsein in Spanien* (Hyle: A dream life in Spain); his later reputation rests largely on his magnificent photographs of San José farmhouses and neighbours, as well as on his observations on Pityusan architecture and folklore. Ibiza's growing artistic reputation was curtailed, however, by the outbreak of the Spanish Civil War in July 1936 and the hasty departure of nearly all its foreign residents.

LOCAL CONSOLIDATION, ABSTRACTION AND RIVAL GROUPINGS, 1940–70 By 1939 the struggle in Spain had reached its conclusion, but storm clouds were now gathering beyond the Pyrenees, and a handful of artists opted to return. They included two figurative painters who later turned to abstraction, Will Faber from Germany

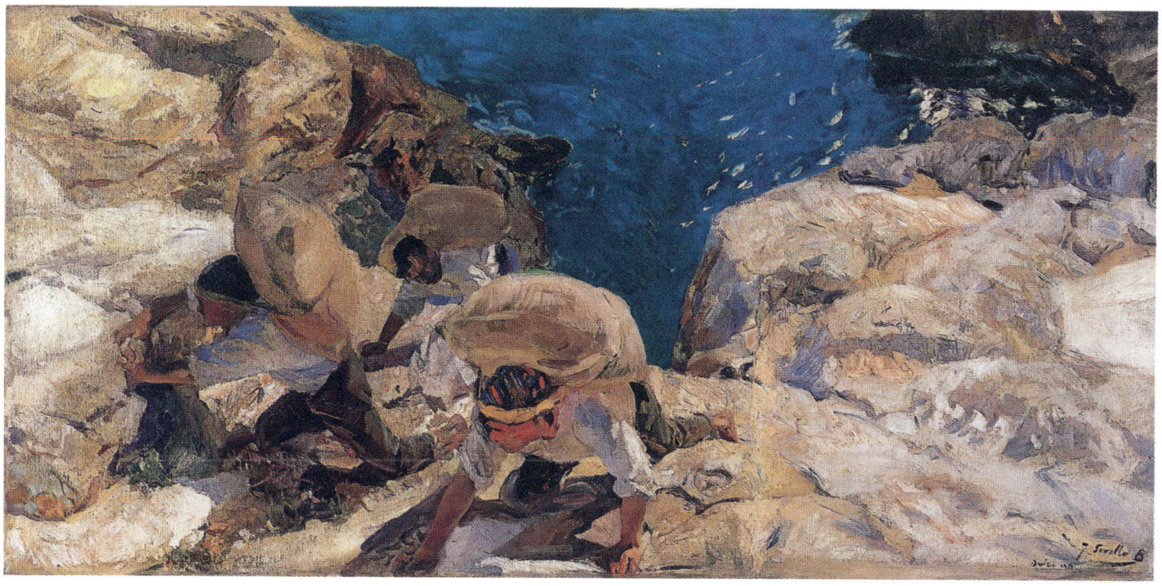

Los contrabandistas by Joaquín Sorolla, 1919. This late masterwork was painted on a cliff edge beyond the southern walls of Dalt Vila's upper citadel. Although the painter had received this unusual commission from the American 'tobacco king' Thomas Fortune Ryan back in 1913, it was Ibiza's dramatic coastline and strong tobacco-smuggling traditions that finally provided him with his long-sought-after inspiration.

and Bertil Sjöberg from Sweden, as well as the Swiss Concrete artist Hans Hinterreiter, whose sophisticated geometric compositions made him Ibiza's first, and arguably foremost, abstract artist. All three settled near Cala Gració in San Antonio, a secluded cove that became a haven for creative visitors in the mid-twentieth century.

In 1940 a forgotten blossoming of local art began when Ibizan painters decided to hold annual Salones de Arte at the Sociedad Cultural Ebusus in Vara de Rey during the island's patron saint festivities in early August. Over the following decade they reached out to art circles in Palma and Mahon, leading to group exhibitions on neighbouring islands. By 1956 the salon numbered forty-three participants, many of them foreigners, earning Ibiza a new nickname as the 'Island of Painters'.

Among the first British artists to take up residence was the cartoonist and portraitist Leslie Grimes, whose Dalt Vila palazzo remained a gathering place for artists and writers over several decades after his arrival in 1952. A dozen of Grimes's townscapes were later made into postcards, and in 2000 the Fundación Barceló in Palma singled him out for a posthumous exhibition and catalogue, the only painter in Ibiza to receive this special tribute (also awarded to Sorolla).

In 1953 the island was flooded with Swedish artists fleeing the rising cost of living in Paris. With the exception of Sjöberg, few gained a lasting reputation, although a brilliant colourist from nearby Finland, Anita Snellman, who in 1961 settled close to Cala de Boix, enjoys considerable standing in Scandinavia, backed by an art foundation that she set up in 1979. The cheapness of Ibiza, its mild climate, scenic beauty and laid-back social scene on the fringes of Fascist Spain combined chicness with a certain frisson. It compared favourably with European cities still recovering from war damage, and in September 1953 Spain signed the Pact of Madrid with the United States, a mutual defence agreement that opened the door to international tourism and eroded official hostility towards the avant-garde. The artistic liberty associated with Abstract Expressionism, it has emerged, was used by the CIA and the Congress for Cultural Freedom (1950–67) in their propaganda war against the Communist bloc. German artists, including those returning to Europe after American exile, led the way in Ibiza, keen to distance themselves from the taint of Socialist Realism prescribed by the Nazi and Soviet regimes.

Interest in the island's non-figurative art scene was sparked by an exhibition held in Barcelona's Sala Gaspar, *Seis artistas alemanes en Ibiza*, which opened in September 1955. This was sponsored by Club 49, a group of Catalan impresarios keen to further artistic and politico-linguistic change in Spain's eastern provinces. Curt Lahs, Erwin Broner, Erwin Bechtold, Hans Laabs, Hans Krause and Heinz Trökes exhibited their latest abstract works, making this the first show of Ibizan 'Informalism' (art created by chance) – a veritable bridgehead for pure self-expression within the borders of Francoist Spain. The growing reputation of Ibiza lent an air of cosmopolitan sophistication to this pioneering exhibition of cutting-edge art.

A year prior to the Barcelona exhibition, Galería El Corsario had opened in a Dalt Vila hotel established by the German Anna von Osterburg, along with her manager/partner, former Swiss Nazi journalist René Fonjallaz. This was where the architect Broner, a German-born modernist of Jewish ancestry, launched Ibiza's first abstract-art collective in 1959. Broner had explored Ibiza thoroughly in the 1930s, while prolonged spells in New York and California during the '40s provided first-hand experience of transatlantic trends. Grupo Ibiza 59 (1959–64) was composed of six very different German abstract painters (Broner, Bechtold, Laabs, Trökes, Katja Meirowsky and Egon Neubauer) and three others: Sjöberg, Robert Munford (Massachusetts) and the ceramicist Antonio Ruiz (Soria, Spain). Their densely worked canvases have little obvious connection with Ibiza's landscapes or culture, reflecting instead the existential angst of an era when thermonuclear war hovered over mental horizons in the West. The group's one exhibition outside Ibiza took place in 1961 at the Haus am Waldsee in Berlin, but after going their separate ways its members were represented in *Inspiration Ibiza*, held at the Leicester Galleries in London in 1964.

Grupo Ibiza 59 has a dedicated room next to the entrance of the Museu d'Art Contemporani d'Eivissa (MACE), reflecting its pioneering role in Balearic abstract art.

Partly in response to the aesthetic revolution sweeping in from outside, four Ibizan painters led by Vicent Ferrer Guasch came together in 1962 to form the Grup Puget, advocating a more diverse pictorial agenda. The group's other members were Antoni Marí Ribas ('Portmany'), Antoni Pomar and Vicent Calbet. Between 1962 and 1964 they staged shows in Ibiza's Caixa de Pensions, in Vara de Rey, and Palma's Cercle de Belles Arts, but disbanded in the latter year to pursue individual paths. Another favoured venue for traditional artists was Galería Tanit in La Marina, run by Dutch consul Hans van Praag and his wife, Lied. This quiet sanctuary remained open from 1957 to 1989, enhanced by a café and lending library.

As the 1960s progressed, three new galleries opened in Dalt Vila to promote the ascendant Informalism and provide an occasional venue for works of a more-or-less figurative nature. Leading the way, at Calle Obispo Torres 13 (now Calle Major, close to the Museu Puget), was Galería Ivan Spence, to which Grupo Ibiza 59 transferred its annual shows shortly after the venue opened its doors in 1961. During fourteen years, Spence's legendary gallery staged 142 solo exhibitions and numerous group shows, making Ibiza a veritable hub and spearheading avant-garde trends not just in the Balearics but in Spain as a whole.

Catering for native artists, another Dalt Vila venue, Galería Xaim, functioned sporadically from 1963 to 1967 under two Ibicenco managers, Dolores Palau and Lourdes Marí. Regular exhibitors included Rafael Tur Costa, who had embraced abstract art in 1955 when Curt Lahs of the Hochschule für Bildende Künste in Berlin brought over a group of students. Not only was the Ibicenco painter's future wife, the ceramicist Anneliese Witt, among them, but also the trip led to the seminal 'German artists in Ibiza' exhibition in Barcelona. As the first non-figurative artist born on the island, Tur Costa has enjoyed recognition as far afield as Japan.

Galería Van der Voort lasted longer than any of its predecessors, from 1968 to 1984. It was managed initially by the American Carl van der Voort, who had previously run Ivan Spence's premises in Dalt Vila. This was the most avant-garde gallery of all, and after its revival in 1987 under Catalina (Cati) Verdera, it maintained a strong presence at Madrid's annual art fair, ARCO (1996–2004), as well as at other international gatherings in Frankfurt, Barcelona, Miami and Chicago. Among the hundreds of contemporary artists who exhibited beneath its magnificent stone vault, one in particular, the German Eduard Micus, conferred an unusual legacy on Ibiza with his Espacio Micus (founded 1989), situated above the Jesús–Cala Llonga road. For more than three decades, its high-ceilinged spaces have promoted experimental art, and occasionally craft, in an idyllic rural setting.

One of the key local figures in the 1950s and '60s was the Berlin-born art dealer Ernesto Ehrenfeld (arrived 1952), who in April 1965 at Galería El Corsario organized a major collective exhibition featuring Miguel Rivera Bagur, David Walsh, Fumiko Matsuda, Bella Brisel and Greta Lund. Other well-known figures during that decade and the following one included Carlos Sansegundo, Manuel Hernández Mompó, Pierre Dmitrienko, Zush (Albert Porta i Muñoz, Ivan Spence's son-in-law and briefly manager of his gallery), Voldemar Boberman, Ignacio Agudo Clará, Frank 'El Punto' (Frank Ludwig Schaefer), Jussara (de Oliveira Heberle), Sarah Nechamkin and James Taylor.

Ibizan graphic art was given a boost in 1964 with the first international Bienal de Ibiza. By 1972 it had become the Ibizagrafic biennial under the management of the American artist Don Kunkel. The event attracted such influential figures as Antoni Tàpies (in 1972) as well as a surprising number of Japanese artists, and in 1979 led to the fully functioning establishment of MACE. For nearly half a century the museum has been a major force in the promotion of contemporary experimental art. Directed since 1990 by Elena Ruiz Sastre, it reopened in 2012 after a five-year-long refurbishment.

HIPPIES, CRAFTS AND OTHER ARTS SINCE 1970 By the late 1960s Ibiza's capital and coastal resorts were being transformed by mass tourism, which caused many artists to retreat inland for inspiration – to San Agustín, San Carlos, San Miguel and San Juan. The influx of hippies from every corner of the world also introduced a different aesthetic, one based on crafts rather than art, and centred on communes and workshops in fincas in the countryside. A major event was the Elmyr de Hory scandal, which unfolded over ten years from early 1967 and recast Ibiza as a shady workshop of ersatz art. How many School of Paris pastiches were painted at the Hungarian's Puig des Molins addresses remains unknown, but with the publication of *Fake! The Story of Elmyr de Hory, the Greatest Art Forger of Our Time* (1969), the slippery conman became a poster boy for bogus provenance. (His associate Réal Lessard made similar claims in a rambling memoir published in France and Argentina.) De Hory's biographer, Clifford Irving, followed up his success with a memoir supposedly dictated by Howard Hughes, which hit the headlines in 1972, and the island's reputation for artistic fakery was capped by Orson Welles's film *F for Fake* (1973).

The popularity of naïf painting soared around this time, thanks to the arrival of several women artists from Germany, Argentina and Brazil, among them Margot Tate, Uta Wohlfarth, Jussara and Ingeborg Gauger. The first primitive painters in Ibiza were two men who adopted the style in the 1950s and '60s: the American former boxer Charlie Orloff and Toni Torres from Sa Penya. Torres was known as 'Es Loco des Terrat' (the madman of the roof) after his attempt to parachute to the square beneath his house with the aid of an umbrella. Both artists found eager markets in the United States and Switzerland, and in 1984 a Torres townscape appeared on the cover of the 'Ibizee' special of the Dutch weekly *Vrij Nederland* (9 June), credited to 'Crazy Tony' Torres. The bright colours, simplified forms and gentle rural themes of naïf art helped to reawaken interest in Ibiza's disappearing traditions, which had largely been ignored by artists following the ever-changing fads of Greenwich Village, Chelsea and SoHo.

The island's material culture struck an especially deep chord with foreigners busy restoring abandoned farmhouses: not only the subtly curving rooflines and ever-harmonious volumes, but also the geometric carvings and painted designs on household artefacts, motifs cut into dower chests or woven into chair seats, and mysterious murals emerging from forgotten spring chambers or beneath multiple layers of whitewash on walls and door frames.

The Canadian Rolph Blakstad and the Belgian Philippe Rotthier are the best-known instigators of this revival of island folkways, but two others also deserve recognition: the Belgian illustrator Valérie Gevers, whose detailed drawings transformed Rotthier's *Ibiza: Le Palais paysan* (1984, co-authored with Ferdinand Joachim) into a local bestseller (Catalan edn, 1991); and Pía García de la Cruz, the indefatigable editor and photographer behind the Taller d'Estudis de l'Hàbitat Pitiús (Workshop of Studies of the Pityusan Habitat, usually referred to as TEHP), founded in 1985 with the photographer Pere Planells Coarasa. Blakstad's *The House of Ibiza* (2020), which was first published in Catalan in 2013 (the year after his death) as *La casa eivissenca*, is celebrated above all for his breathtaking illustrations of almost every aspect of traditional architecture.

The resurgent crafts movement formed a prevalent part of the island's artistic landscape during the 1970s. One early initiative, near San Miguel, was Can Tirurit, which opened its doors in 1975 as a 'Centro de artesanía y desarrollo de la creatividad' (Centre for crafts and developing creativity). Courses included weaving, sewing, macramé, leather, woodwork, metalwork and candle-making. For four years the finca became the island's arts and crafts hub, while also acquiring a name as a centre for meditation.

Over in San Carlos in 1973, Ibiza's original hippy market began tentatively when the management of Hotel Club Punta Arabí installed five temporary stalls (there are now 500 every Wednesday in summer) to showcase crafts made by local *peludos*, or 'hairy ones'. Las Dalias followed suit in February 1985 with a Saturday *mercadillo*, now a key tourist attraction alongside Dalt Vila, Es Vedrà and the giant nightclubs. In 1999 Ibiza Town inaugurated its famous Medieval Fair, which features stalls for Ibicenco artisans as well as for veteran foreigners such as the Israeli instrument-maker Yaron Marko.

In 1976 San Rafael joined the crafts network when three ceramicists – Miguel Ángel Ratto ('Kinoto', from Argentina), Julio Bauzá (Uruguay) and Carlos Icardi (Uruguay) – opted for this village on account of Bernard Leach's advice to find central locations for pottery studios. In 1990 it was declared a 'Zone of Artisanal Interest' by the Balearic Comissió d'Artesania, but after fifty years only one workshop remains in business. In 2002 the Espai Cultural Can Portmany opened in a colonial-style house built by Joan Gómez Ripoll ('Campos'), and ten years later San Rafael established its own crafts market.

Moda Adlib was set up in May 1971 by the Yugoslav 'princess' Smilja Mihailovitch to promote gauzy white dresses with a 'mainstream hippy' feel. About twenty labels are now affiliated to this collective (today known as Adlib Ibiza), which stages a major fashion show each summer sponsored by the Consell Insular d'Eivissa. Ibiza's biggest fashion label, Paula's, was founded in 1972 (one year after Moda Adlib) by the German Armin Heinemann in a tiny shop in Calle de la Virgen and was named after his daughter. With his American partner, Stuart Rudnick, Heinemann has staged ballets and operas involving Cuban companies, and their remarkable achievements over many decades are documented in a lavish volume, *Paula's Ibiza: 25* (1997).

Our knowledge and understanding of the island's cultural past are still changing rapidly as forgotten figures and artworks surface via online auctions and in exhibitions, articles and books. These are exciting times to be producing, collecting, curating and researching art made in Ibiza. The exchanges between local, mainland Spanish and foreign practitioners are what have made this artistic narrative enlightening and inspiring. Ibiza's intrinsic beauty, its ever-evolving culture and its unending capacity to broaden horizons mean that it will continue to play a vital role in Spanish and European art for the foreseeable future.

TANIT

A GODDESS REVISITED AND REINVENTED

Tanit – or Tinnit, as she was called 2000 years ago – was, along with Baal Hammon, chief deity of ancient Carthage from roughly 480 BCE to 140 BCE, as shown by invocations to the divine couple found on thousands of engraved stelae (tombstones) dug up in the city's tophet (infant graveyard) from 1921 onwards. The female head present on most Carthaginian coins from that era is generally thought to belong to her, while several experts believe she was also the heavenly guardian of Ibiza. However, coins from 'Ybshm (Iboshim, the Phoenician name for the island) until well after the birth of Christ are invariably stamped with feather-crowned Bes, an Egyptian dwarf god who may have also given Ibiza its name. Experts remain sharply divided on this matter.

Tanit was worshipped as an astral and fertility goddess at a remarkable hillside shrine in north-eastern Ibiza called Es Culleram. The cave's tutelary deity was originally thought to be Astarte, the consort of Melqart, but sixteen years after its discovery in 1907 a bronze plaque engraved with Tanit's name was found among rubble from earlier digs. The inscription dates from the second century BCE and commemorates a major rebuilding carried out at the sacred site. Deep inside the cave, archaeologists came across quantities of sheep and goat bones and broken crockery, plus well over 1000 votive figurines, testifying to springtime sacrifices over a lengthy period to petition for abundant harvests and fecund herds. The Greek-style cylinder (*kalathos*) nearly always present on Tanit's head represents a basket of mysterious sacred objects, potent symbols of plenitude and regeneration. A later shrine or temple to Tanit may have been erected on the summit of Cap des Llibrell, above Cala Llonga, where a sacrificial stone altar was dug up in 1987. The altar was adorned with two sculpted lion heads, perhaps representing Tanit's lesser-known attribute of warrior goddess. The site dates from around the time of the Second Punic War (218–201 BCE) and doubtless served as an important lookout.

Carthaginian religion remains a tantalizing and elusive subject, one on which future archaeological discoveries will undoubtedly broaden our severely limited knowledge. When the Romans destroyed the North African metropolis at the end of the Third Punic War (149–146 BCE), the city's libraries were handed over to 'petty kings' of adjoining territories, after which they completely disappear from sight. An agricultural manual taken to Rome has been passed down in Latin fragments, but the only other surviving Punic work consists of eighteen lines of Hanno's *Periplus* (translated into Greek), which describe a voyage around the west coast of Africa around 500 BCE. Carthaginians did not write on clay tablets such as the ones that have shone a bright light on ancient Mesopotamia, while their papyri have succumbed to damp and insects, unlike similar documents dug up in the Egyptian desert. In Ibiza only a handful of Punic inscriptions have surfaced over the past century or so, nearly all of them names. Two engraved dedications that mention Melqart, chief god of Tyre, turned up at a rescue dig in 2003 in Vía Púnica, Ibiza Town, where a shrine may once have existed.

To fill the immense gap of religious fact, a flood of Tanit folklore has sprouted on the mystic grapevine, tales of shady provenance: sacred prostitution, infant sacrifices, ceremonies in remote springs, farmhouse niche-shrines, a temple on Es Vedrà. On closer examination, these nearly always turn out to be literary or artistic conjecture, but what is clear is that Tanit has struck a deep chord in our eclectic and unequivocally feminist age. A beautiful, wavy-haired bust made in Sicily around 300 BCE, probably representing Demeter originally, has long been Ibiza's favourite image of Tanit (it was discovered in Puig des Molins necropolis in 1913).

In this hothouse atmosphere, archaeologists and technical papers are as necessary as ever to remind us about the authentic Punic goddess, and academic hypotheses are emerging that are just as fascinating as those suspect suppositions. Since 2007 a group of archaeologists and historians based at the University of Seville, and working closely with Ibiza's Archaeological Museum, has carried out a study of the 1422 artefacts (including 1114 terracottas) found at Es Culleram, now scattered among fifteen Spanish museums and an unspecified number of private collections. With backing from the Spanish Ministry of Science and Innovation, the research project headed by María Cruz Marín Ceballos, 'Tinnit en Ibiza: La cueva de Es Culleram', has arrived at some surprising conclusions.

First, far from signposting sacred prostitution, fertility symbols (e.g. lotus flowers, sacrificial piglets) on the terracotta figurines point to rites of passage for young women of marriageable age. The iconography is similar to well-documented Sicilian models, and mirrors growing links between Greek and Carthaginian religion in this period. Tanit rose to prominence in the Punic heartlands just as cultural imports from the Hellenistic world were rising sharply, including Greek gods (specifically Demeter and Persephone) and their rites.

Regarding child sacrifice, the archaeological community has long been deeply divided about what this really entailed. On stelae found in central North Africa, Sicily, Sardinia and Malta (the 'Circle of Tophet'), Tanit and her consort, Baal Hammon, were invoked and thanked with the burnt remains of new-born children and small animals. Many believe this simply reflects high infant mortality in the ancient world, with bereaved parents enacting special cremation ceremonies to petition the aid of Tanit and Baal Hammon on behalf of their lost offspring who were negotiating the

Tanit, one of the chief deities of Punic Carthage, venerated in ancient Ibiza as an astral, fertility and warrior goddess. This wavy-haired bust, now a global icon, was discovered in Puig des Molins in 1913 and is now on display in the nearby museum. Analysis points to a Sicilian origin and the Greek goddess Demeter as the original inspiration. In recent years Tanit has become very popular in Ibiza both as an ageless symbol of spiritual renewal and as an eye-catching emblem for commerce and fashion; in some circles, she has also taken on the role of guardian (or rather resuscitator) of Ibiza's springs.

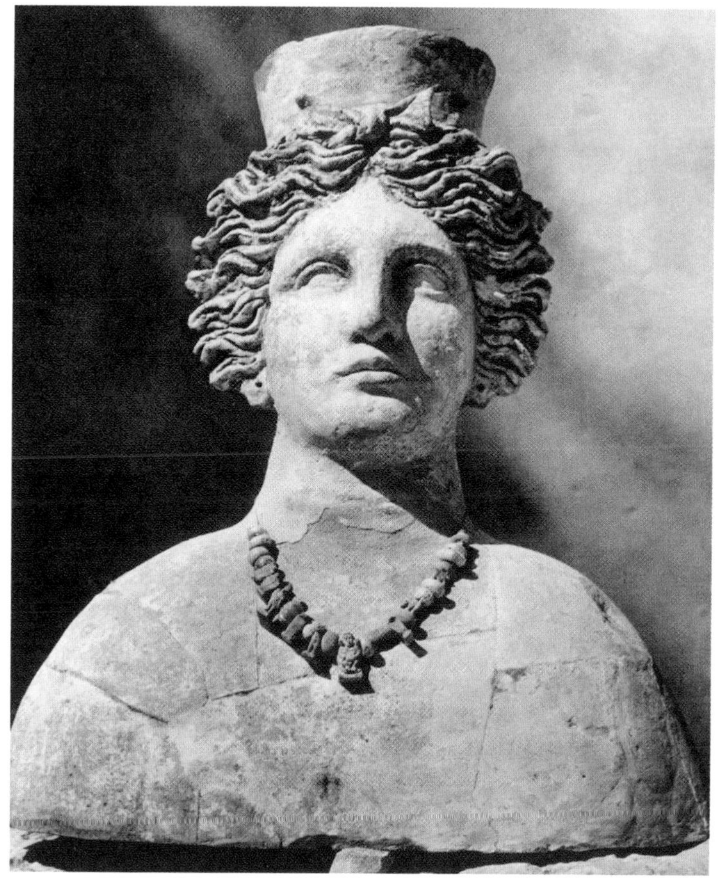

perilous path to the afterlife. The Punic caduceus is the usual sign of such divine protection, a symbol common among Es Culleram's winged figurines, where it also denotes medicine and good health.

Tophets are altogether absent in Ibiza and mainland Spain, so the idea of infant sacrifices has been ruled out for the west Carthaginian sphere. The so-called 'Sign of Tanit', a mysterious symbol that seems connected with eternal life and/or molk sacrifice rather than with any specific deity, crops up on countless stelae in the central Mediterranean 'Circle of Tophet', where Tanit also carried the honorific title 'Face of Baal Hammon' (i.e. intermediary). But this famous sign is rare in ancient Ibiza, and in a hundred years of excavations, little more than a dozen examples have been discovered, usually on small objects that could have come from afar, such as amulets. The symbol is nowhere to be seen at Es Culleram, Tanit's foremost shrine in the western Mediterranean, not on one of its 1400-plus artefacts. So its enormous popularity in modern Ibiza has nothing to do with the worship of Tanit/Tinnit on the island in ancient times.

And what about the fountains of the goddess? Again, not a single Ibizan spring or well has yielded an object with any connection to Tanit. Her so-called sign is thought by many to have adorned a spring chamber west of Santa Gertrudis, Font d'en Miquelet, but this is a simple case of 'idea inflation' during the heyday of alternative Ibiza. A photograph now in Ibiza's Archaeological Museum (taken in 1971 by its former director, Jordi Fernández, while preparing his BA dissertation) clearly shows the same space occupied by a painted rosette, a typical piece of Ibizan folk decoration from around 1800. Let us remind ourselves that Tanit, an astral divinity above all, was venerated in lofty sanctuaries, where her prime symbols included vulture feathers, the crescent moon and Venus, the sacred evening star/planet. When the Romans gave her a new name, it was Juno Caelestis – 'Juno of the Heavens'.

A temple on Es Vedrà can be dismissed (there are no Punic remains on that myth-spawning island), but was Tanit ever worshipped in Ibizan farmhouses? As in the case of the Santa Gertrudis spring, the notion rests on dubious evidence: two long-vanished wall-niches, one with cross-like emblems and the other depicting a skirted female, both interpreted as signs of Tanit. As noted above, that symbol was very rare in Punic Ibiza, and could not have survived intact for 2000 years, following the disappearance of Punic religion, successive invasions, a possible depopulation in the Dark Ages and several religious makeovers. Another icon cited in support of Tanit house-shrines is a similar-looking 'portable shrine' from Carthage engraved with Tanit signs and sun discs. Featured in Rolph Blakstad's book *The House of Ibiza* (2013/2020), this was actually an amalgamation of several illustrations found in *El culto a Tanit en Ebysos* (1970) by Antonio Planells Ferrer. No such object ever existed in Carthage or outside the fertile imagination of its ingenious – and somewhat mischievous – creator.

The Tanit team from Seville have one final surprise up their sleeves, perhaps the most remarkable of all: eighteen of the terracottas found at Es Culleram are incense burners in the shape of a female head bearing a crenellated mural crown. They believe this represents 'Tinnit-Gad', a goddess or daemon of fortune. The castellated Gad is often regarded as a protector of cities, usually linked with another deity, and as the name is inscribed immediately after Tanit's on the plaque at Es Culleram, this suggests that 'Tinnit-Gad' was a patron goddess of Iboshim. Her shrine on the distant hillside thus becomes a sort of symbolic boundary marker, indicating the limits of the political, territorial and economic influence of Iboshim.

But this could all change once more with a new discovery on a building site in town or somewhere deep in Ibiza's rolling countryside, and the religious goalposts would shift all over again. The all-powerful divinity who protected ancient seafarers like her great Phoenician predecessor, Melqart, and her psychopompic role, guiding souls on their journey into the afterlife, have likewise yet to receive the attention they merit. Meanwhile, Tanit's new-found role as guardian of Ibiza's springs and of refurbished (or new-built) country villas soars via the internet and coffee-table books, in which delightful drawings and mystic mosaics of the 'Sign of Tanit' abound. Our Lady of Carthage is heading west once again, and Ibiza lies at the very heart of her modish revival.

THE IBICENCO FARMHOUSE

AN ARCHETYPE OF AESTHETIC BALANCE AND SUSTAINABILITY

Deep in the interior of the White Island, flat-roofed farmhouses dot wooded slopes and nestle in every fertile valley. Many have picturesque porches and 'balconies' (drying lofts) where aromatic herbs once hung in bunches side by side with red peppers, tomatoes and the odd line of laundry. Flat rooflines are broken by triangular chimneys and curved waterspouts, while the swelling volume to one side marks the bread oven, in which enormous loaves were baked in batches every week. Outside the main door, the pyramidal roof of the cistern's pulley-house was formerly crowned by an elaborately carved wooden cross, highlighting the primordial blend of superstition and belief that permeated rural life. Only a handful of these crosses survived the whirlwinds of civil war and massive change that came in the wake of package tourism.

Over the past century, architects and artists from around the world have been drawn to these unique and marvellously diverse farmhouses, captivated by their forms and enthralled by their simple beauty. We have mentioned the porches with their light and shade, and the drying lofts with their accents of bright colour, but equally enchanting is the way an entire dwelling seems to grow out of the terraces on either side, the whitewashed *casement* (i.e. the farmhouse) blending in with its honey-toned *corrales* (animal pens). Then there is the 'box' effect – as if an artful giant set down blocks of different sizes, each harmonizing perfectly with its companions. Moving down in scale, tiny windows with wooden crossbars, dripstones topping walls, flagstones in patios, gates with horizontal bars, even the rough-and-ready masonry patterns in the animal pens – all provide eye-catching detail. Wood offsets stone, while horizontals are softened by curves, domes, pyramids and triangles. Everything has its counterpart, and the whole is laid out on a scale that seems superbly tailored to human requirements. It is little wonder that Ibiza once lacked what is usually seen as fine art: the aesthetic needs of its inhabitants were satisfied by an exquisite architectural 'dialogue' between every man-made feature and the surrounding landscape.

But the vernacular farmhouses were not as simple as they first appeared to visitors from abroad: the plain walls, for instance, were more than 1 metre (39 in.) thick (to keep out heat and cold), two walls raised in parallel with a rubble core. The 'box' effect owed much of its subtle appeal to a gentle convex taper as walls rose up, and the taper had its counterpart in a slightly concave roofline. As for the 'humble' flat roof, this (above a complex joist-and-beam structure) consisted of four layers: ceiling slats, seaweed, wood ash and clay. It required regular maintenance – weeding, topping up with clay and whitewashing of the parapet – to prevent rainwater ingress. Whitewashing of the entire house was also a time-consuming process, carried out annually by the women of the household.

The ground layout of these apparently archaic dwellings has been the focus of considerable attention since the mid-1930s, but until recently few investigators were aware that the farmhouse underwent dramatic changes during the eighteenth and nineteenth centuries. In the majority of dwellings, construction appears to have begun with two low-ceilinged units at the back for storage and sleeping, followed by a large rectangular kitchen perpendicular to the small bedrooms. The bread oven projected from one of the walls of the kitchen, the considerable height of which permitted smoke to circulate and rise before exiting from apertures in the roof (smoke hoods arrived only in the late nineteenth century). The kitchen can be identified thanks to its distinctive triangular chimney openings, one directly above the oven 'door'. The unheated *porxo* (main room) also had a tapering hood against one wall to prevent smoke entering from the kitchen. Produce-drying shelves often extended from this attractive fixture to walls on either side.

In Ibiza's oldest farmhouses, however, the rectangular kitchen is frequently found at the back of the house, parallel to the *porxo* and slightly offset. The reason why the layout underwent such a dramatic change has not been firmly established, although the alteration seems to have occurred in the wake of sweeping agricultural reforms and population growth in the late eighteenth and early nineteenth centuries. The new 'L' arrangement (with lateral kitchen) certainly facilitated house expansion: the 'L' could be transformed into a 'U' by adding a wing (often double-storeyed) on the opposite side, creating in turn a space in the middle for a high-roofed *porxo* or distributor, parallel to the two small back rooms.

The name *porxo* points to another change that occurred during the course of the nineteenth century, namely the filling-in of the southern wall of the high-ceilinged porch that formerly stood at the heart of the Ibicenco farmhouse. This created a new 'living room' – enclosed by walls on every side, with the main house entrance on the south side. The *porxo* thus replaced the true porch, with its generous post-and-lintel (rectilinear) openings or large arches (occasionally a single arch). As the house grew in size and agricultural yields such as grains, legumes and almonds increased, this fully enclosed space became necessary for storing implements and bulging sacks of produce, for holding family gatherings (above all, the great *matança* feast held in autumn/winter) and for accommodating internal staircases. Larger than the kitchen, the

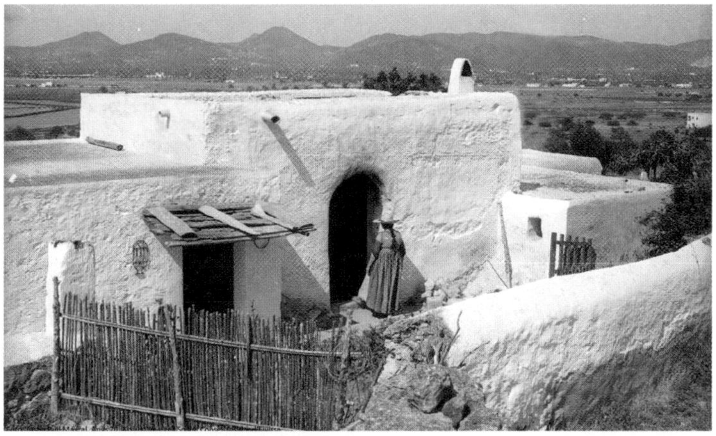

Left: A simple house near Salinas with no porch. Photograph by Josep Buil Mayral, 1970s.

Below: A typical eighteenth- or nineteenth-century farmhouse near San Carlos with a domed bread oven and a substantial double-storey porxet *(porch). Photograph by Ilse Mayer Gehrken, c. 1965.*

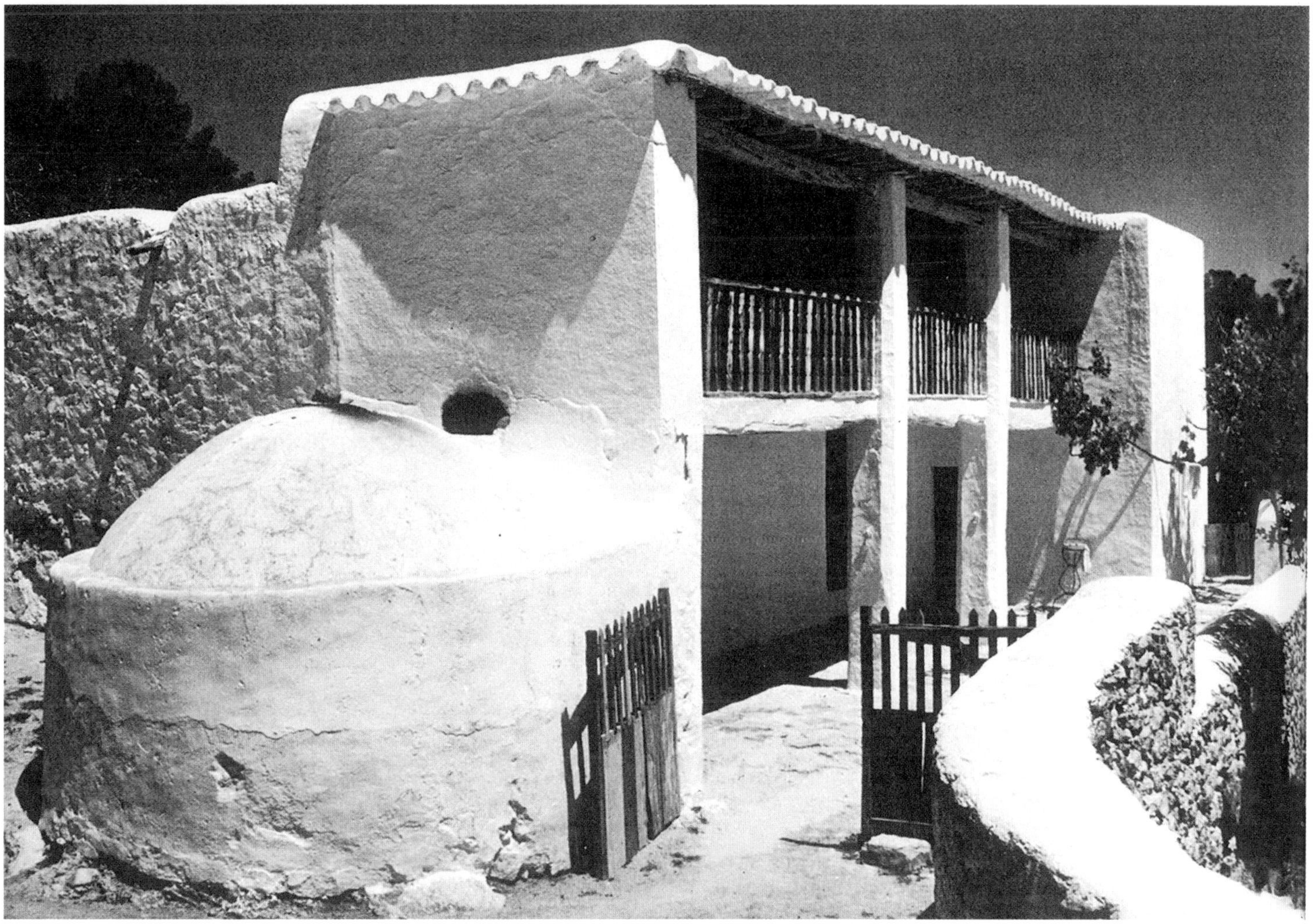

new multipurpose space had one major defect: in times gone by, its large openings to the south had provided ample light, making it ideal for domestic activities. Thus a new porch (a *porxet*, or 'little porch') was raised outside the front door, this structure being often double-storeyed and suitable for keeping produce, as well as for drying and hanging peppers, tomatoes, garlic and other staples. By the 1990s barely a dozen houses in Ibiza retained the old-style open *porxo*, and one of the last to survive is Can Prats in Sa Vorera, San Antonio, captured by Rolph Blakstad around 1968 in a series of stunning black-and-white photographs.

Whatever its plan, the island's vernacular was perfectly adapted to a way of life that is now on the verge of complete disappearance: to storing olive oil, wine, sausages and agricultural implements; to drying figs, tomatoes and almonds; to providing effective year-round protection from hot days, chilly nights and torrential rain. Dozens of books and hundreds of articles have examined these extraordinary dwellings, the origins of which are still shrouded in mystery. In 1869 the Austrian archduke Ludwig Salvator wrote that a recent census (1860) had recorded 4244 houses on the island, of which 245 were uninhabited. Few of these fabulous fincas – as termed by foreigners, the word means 'estate' – have not seen major alterations in recent decades, but that is nothing new: the Ibicenco farmhouse was always growing, adapting and reinventing itself, and continues to do so into the twenty-first century.

LEARNING FROM THE VERNACULAR

MODERN ARCHITECTURES IN IBIZA

For a century after Archduke Ludwig Salvator blazed a brilliant trail in 1867, almost every writer and painter who explored Ibiza left a description or artwork that paid homage to the island's remarkable farmhouses. In 1912 it was dubbed the 'White Island' partly in honour of its gleaming fincas, while in the 1930s a handful of bright-eyed architects from Catalonia, Germany and Switzerland became convinced that they had stumbled across the forgotten roots of the International Style. Civil war and exile delayed the transformation of theory into practice, but the determination of these Young Turks to blend the two house types bore fruit in the 1960s and early '70s, when a dozen modernist villas appeared on the wooded slopes of Can Pep Simó. These beautifully proportioned dwellings now form an aesthetic oasis above the suburban sprawl of glass and reinforced concrete.

VISITING ARCHITECTS IN THE 1930s Josep Lluís Sert (pp. 238–41), Le Corbusier's leading disciple south of the Pyrenees and a founding member of the Grupo de Arquitectos y Técnicos Españoles para el Progreso de la Arquitectura Contemporánea (GATEPAC), was among the first to notice a resemblance between the box-like buildings springing up all over Europe and Ibiza's flat-roofed farmhouses. Spain at this time was lagging behind in the rationalist revolution, so the ornament-free vernacular on Catalonia's own doorstep seemed the answer to the prayers of these go-ahead architects: a timeless Mediterranean house type with a strong echo of the latest aesthetic credo; a pattern book in stone that consecrated the sacred new shibboleths of simplicity, functionalism and light. With any luck, the Bauhaus would soon be beating a path to *their* door!

The Mediterraneanist gospel expounded by Sert and his associates was reinforced by fieldwork carried out in Ibiza by two kindred souls fresh from the powerhouses of the north, Erwin Broner (pp. 234–37) and Richard von Waldkirch (1905–1991). Graduates of what is now the Hochschule für Technik Stuttgart, they were fully versed in new architectural doctrines, to which they made their own significant contribution – the first accurate plans of Ibizan farmhouses (published in *A.C.*, no. 21, 1936). Unfortunately, Broner's early projects in Ibiza survive only in blueprints and photographs. His café-bar and bathing establishment at Talamanca (1934) was bombed in the Civil War, while a promising scheme for holiday houses never got beyond the drawing board.

CIVIL WAR, EXILE AND RETURN Franco's final victory in 1939 brought an abrupt end to almost all avant-garde activities in Spain. Sert and Broner (who both spoke English) went into exile in New England and California, while Germán Rodríguez Arias (1902–1987) opted for Chile, one of several Latin American havens popular among the fleeing Republicans. Josep Torres Clavé, Sert's one-time partner in two unrealized Ibiza projects (a hotel and a beach house), was killed in action in the closing months of the struggle. For a decade or more it looked as if Ibiza's brief spell in the limelight had been only a passing fad. Concrete blocks and the occasional Bauhaus-style balcony were the closest the island came to cutting-edge design during these years. The story has a final twist, however; a tribute to the unfailing magnetism of Ibiza for those of a curious, creative disposition.

The Milanese architect Luigi Figini was the first signed-up modernist to pay a visit after the Civil War, exploring the island thoroughly during a ten-day 'mission' in September 1949. Two years later his handsomely illustrated article about the surprisingly modern echoes of Ibiza's vernacular appeared in the influential Italian journal *Domus*, which was shining a bright light once more in avant-garde circles. It is surely significant that Broner returned just a few months later, in February 1952, before settling permanently in March 1959. Rodríguez Arias moved back from Chile in 1956 and was soon engaged on prestigious commissions in Ibiza Town, including the giant Banco de Crédito Balear and Cine Serra buildings at opposite ends of Vara de Rey. Sert, tying up his Fondation Maeght project in Provence, now chose Ibiza as a European summer pied-à-terre and in 1960 designed a three-storey double studio next to the ramparts of Dalt Vila. From its roof terrace his eye was drawn to a charming hillside on the far side of Talamanca that clearly had considerable potential.

THE BRONER LEGACY Throughout the 1960s, Broner built what has become an outstanding part of Ibiza's architectural heritage, twenty-four classic villas dotted around the island, largely for foreign clients. His impeccable credentials (including exile from European fascism), uncluttered interiors, simple lines and unerring proportions have made his *œuvre* a byword for modernist elegance on an island that has few iconic buildings from that period. On many sites he grafted new on to old, leaving intact side and back walls, but remodelling (removing) most of the original dwelling to bring in light as well as modern plumbing. Generous terraces with concrete overhangs partly disguised plate-glass façades, and white walls were left plain, with the occasional stretch of stone cladding to evoke traditional fincas and rustic *corrales*.

SERT AND CAN PEP SIMÓ Broner's fellow traveller from the 1930s was delighted to bask in Mediterranean sunlight after self-imposed exile in chilly Boston. The Catalan maestro's vertiginous rise in two professions – architecture and city planning – had left Broner somewhat in the shade, so it is fascinating to compare these different visionaries who devoted the end of their wide-ranging careers to substantial projects in Ibiza. Sert, a dean at Harvard for many years and in possession of a substantial inheritance, designed six summer villas for himself and his friends on the hillside he had glimpsed from the Dalt Vila studio. The site overlooked two idyllic bays next to Ibiza Town and had spectacular sunset views. Sert's Talamanca testament was completed with the help of long-time friend Rodríguez Arias, and included a string of holiday apartments just below named Es Fumerals (1970). Among the other villas in the *urbanización* were those designed and built by Rodríguez Arias (Casa Blanca, 1968; El Bungalow, 1969), Joseph Zalewski (Casa Zalewski, 1970) and Broner (Casa Dodane, 1971). The end result was a glorious modernist *pièce de résistance*, Ibiza's worthy answer to the celebrated Weissenhof Estate (1927) in Stuttgart. Few who have lingered as the lights flicker to life across the bay can deny the unique synthesizing genius of the man who dreamt it all up, or the rare talent of his architectural partners.

OTHER ARCHITECTS, 1970–2020 Over the past half century, Ibiza has become a testing ground for designers of ever-more ambitious villas, led by a stream of talented graduates from Barcelona's schools of architecture. Like their 1930s predecessors, they have drawn inspiration in varying degrees from Ibiza's architectural lexicon: stacked cubes, picturesque porches, airy loggias, external staircases and flagstoned patios. Leading names since the 1970s have included Raimon Torres, Elías Torres (no relation), Ricardo Bofill, Víctor Rahola, Jaime Romano and Jaime Serra Verdaguer. The prevailing tendency has been the International Style, reflecting academic curricula as well as the enduring legacy of GATEPAC and Broner.

The splendid sunsets of Ibiza's far west, transfigured each day by Es Vedrà's majestic 'keep' and the picturesque Ses Bledes group, have attracted dozens of architects since Karl Dudek designed his Casa de los Artistas in Cala Tarida (1961). Neither Broner nor Sert left their mark on this coastline (then barely accessible by road), and it was the Belgian André Jacqmain who led the way with a modernist holiday complex at Caló d'en Real (1973–93). His collaborators included fellow Belgians Philippe Rotthier and Cis Lenaerts, both of whom had already worked on Sert's Es Fumerals apartments. At that time, Lenaerts and his Ibicenco partner, Cati Verdera (later director of the Museu d'Art Contemporani d'Eivissa and manager of Galería Van der Voort), were investigating Ibizan farmhouses for their dissertations, and established a basic typology later borrowed by Rotthier for his influential book *Ibiza: Le Palais paysan* (1984, with Ferdinand Joachim).

A striking new initiative on this sought-after coastline is Sabina Ibiza, a luxury complex near Cala Tarida whose master plan was conceived by Jordi Carreño. Thirteen houses have been completed to date, including a villa by Jaime Romano and a clubhouse by Rolf Blakstad, out of a total of fifty villas, all by widely recognized names.

Broner and GATEPAC forged what might be called 'Balearic Internationalism' (Sert's villas owe a rarely mentioned debt to Mallorcan vernacular), but the island has also become an influential school and workshop for Ibizan traditionalism thanks to two much-fêted foreign residents, the Canadian Rolph Blakstad (1929–2012) and Philippe Rotthier (b. 1941), as well as the former's son Rolf. Their renovations and new builds, reviving the essential forms and features of Ibiza's anonymous master masons, have attracted considerable attention – and also commissions – from far and wide. After a hundred years of importing architectural fashions, Ibiza is now poised to become an exporter in the field.

Dozens of coffee-table books celebrate the White Island's luxurious villas and their breathtaking gardens, many hidden away in remote locations. Such books include *Mediterranean Houses: Balearic Islands* (1990), *Surprising Architecture: Ibiza* (2011), *Living in Style: Ibiza* (2014) and others devoted to individual practices with an eye on both clientele and posterity. The oft-bruited 'Ibiza Style' is perhaps difficult to pin down, spanning old and new, ethnic and industrial, shabby and chic, hippy and hipster. But its watchwords are still simplicity, beauty and functionalism, as they were in 1932, when Walter Benjamin suddenly made Ibiza's pared-down interiors the envy of a far richer nation. In a lengthy article that commanded the front page of the *Frankfurter Zeitung*, he reminded German readers of the aesthetic insights that the White Island can provide for open-minded souls who make the pilgrimage to its welcoming shores, irrespective of training or tendency:

Much can be gathered from these chairs as they stand there, unassuming in form but with strikingly beautiful cordwork. No collector could exhibit rugs from Isfahan or pictures by Van Dyck on his entrance walls with greater pride than the farmer does these chairs in the bare porxo. Moreover, they are not simply chairs. The moment a sombrero is hung over the back of one it changes its form. And in this new configuration the straw hat appears no less precious than the simple chair. In this way fishing net and copper kettle, rudder and earthenware jar, come together and are ready to change places and be reunited as the need arises a hundred times a day. They are all more or less precious, and the secret of their worth lies in the sobriety and sparseness of the living space they occupy.

Walter Benjamin, 'Raum für das Kostbare' (Room for the precious), Ibizenkische Folge (Ibicenco series), Frankfurter Zeitung*, 4 June 1932; author's translation*

ERWIN BRONER
(1898–1971)

APOSTLE OF THE AVANT-GARDE

Around 2010, articles, essays, dissertations and exhibition catalogues suddenly appeared – out of nowhere, it seemed – exploring the unique legacy of Erwin Broner, long-time promoter of modernism in the Pityuses and active in various artistic endeavours on both sides of the Atlantic. Born in Munich into a prosperous Jewish family, he trained at four of Germany's most prestigious art academies before political events sent him into permanent exile during the middle decades of his life (1933–59). He eventually settled in Ibiza with his third wife, Gisela, and immediately built a cliffhanging house-cum-studio (1960) on the protruding rock of Sa Penya, Ibiza Town. It was restored after his widow's death in 2005, and since 2010 has been managed by the Museu d'Art Contemporani d'Eivissa (MACE). In 2019 this architectural masterpiece, **Casa Broner**, was added to the distinguished Iconic Houses network, providing the late-flowering architect with posthumous international recognition. Broner's name, it should be said, resounds mainly among aficionados of Ibiza, to which can now be added a growing band of avant-garde architectural buffs. But why is he so esteemed on the White Island, and what is it about his legacy that has made him so popular today among fans of classic modernism all round the world?

There are six fields (indicated here by works or accomplishments in bold) in which this unassuming son of the Heilbronner banking dynasty (he changed his surname in 1944) became a catalyst for the cutting edge. To begin with, Broner was the first person to produce accurate plans and elevations of the Ibizan farmhouse, creating a **'typology' of rural dwellings** unmatched until the final years of the twentieth century. The resulting article, 'Ibiza (Baleares). Las viviendas rurales' was actually co-authored by Richard von Waldkirch (1905–1991), an enigmatic Swiss national whom Broner befriended while they were both studying architecture at what is now the Hochschule für Technik Stuttgart (1927–31). The seminal study appeared in 1936 in the trailblazing journal *A.C.: Documentos de actividad contemporánea*, with a cover photograph of an attractive San Jorge finca that later became the home of Clifford Irving while he was writing *Fake! The Story of Elmyr de Hory, the Greatest Art Forger of Our Time* (1969) and a fake autobiography of Howard Hughes. Broner also built De Hory's spectacular villa on the crest of Puig des Molins, La Falaise (1964), where the Hungarian forger/socialite entertained on a lavish scale, as seen in François Reichenbach's *Elmyr: The True Picture?* (1970), a BBC documentary plundered by Orson Welles for his film essay *F for Fake* (1973).

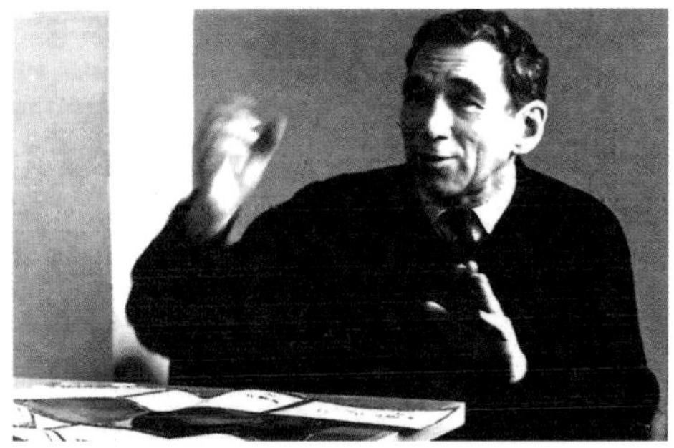

Erwin Broner, photographed in London in 1958. Casa Broner (below), where the architect lived from 1960 to 1971, is now a museum. It lies just off Calle de la Virgen, in the old fishermen's quarter of Sa Penya, Ibiza Town.

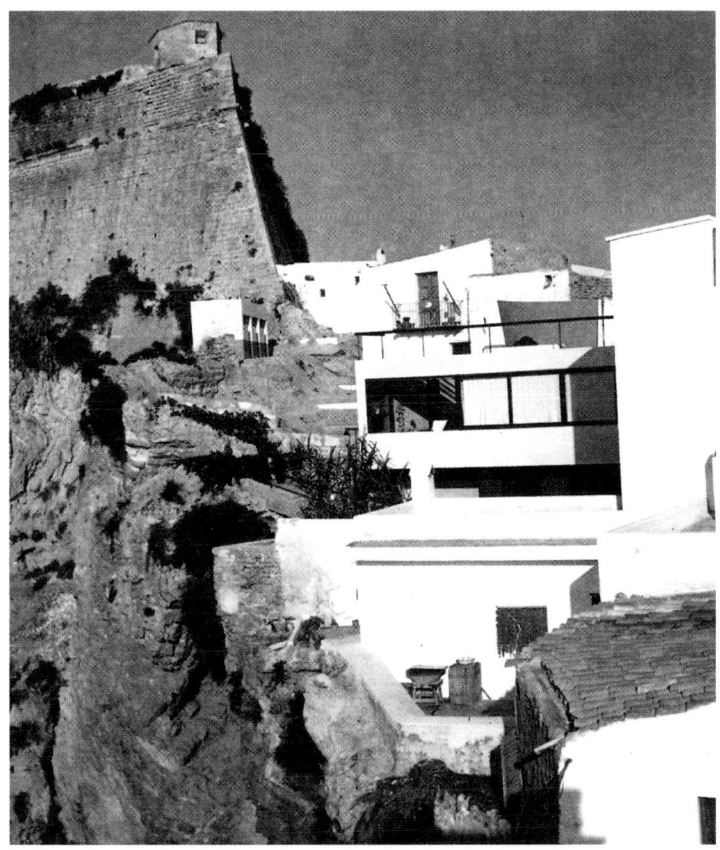

Broner's first period in Ibiza lasted from 1933 to 1935, and was also marked by the **island's first beach club**, Café-bar Playa Talamanca (1934). This was commissioned by another Jewish exile, the Czech Robert Hecht, and the final result appeared in the same issue of *A.C.* (as a double-page spread) – that classic Broner juxtaposition of ancient and modern. The Talamanca complex is often referred to as a 'bathing establishment' or 'bathing huts', but cubicles occupied a mere quarter of the entire complex: the *pièce de résistance* was a stylish 'terrace-bar-café-danzing' (as labelled on the plan) that gave directly on to the beach, an instant hit with foreign residents bussed over by motor launch. Our exiled German, a gifted violinist to boot, even played in the café's dance band when he was not engaged by Ibiza Town's cinemas: architectural commissions were still thin on the ground, and he had a wife and daughter (Anne/Nanna) to support.

Sadly, this remarkably innovative project (which included accommodation for Hecht and his wife) no longer exists; it was targeted by aerial bombers in the opening weeks of the Spanish Civil War (Hostal Talamanca occupies its site). But thanks to the *A.C.* article – six photographs plus plan – and a handful of archival materials, we can see just how visionary the scheme was. First, the terrace was completely open on one side, offering glorious views of the bay beyond while a sweeping concrete roof provided generous shade. To one side, an open staircase led to a rooftop terrace (both typical Broner features), where guests could sip drinks and enjoy meals. Greenery climbed trellises and overflowed from concrete flower beds, adding welcome colours to soften the dazzling walls. Even in black and white, we can daydream about this extraordinary water-lapped café, perhaps the coolest (and most acoustically discrete) beach club that has ever existed – in Spain or anywhere.

In 1935 the beach-bar visionary was obliged to pack his bags and set sail again, this time to Barcelona, where work was more plentiful for hand-to-mouth musicians. This was followed in turn by periods in Palestine (1937), Paris (1938), New York (1938–39, 1948–50) and – longest of all – California (1939–48). While visiting his brother in Palestine, the wanderer met Monica Bella Ullmann, a gifted textile designer and graduate of the Bauhaus (unlike Broner himself) who had studied with such leading figures as Wassily Kandinsky. Ullmann soon became his second wife, and their ten-year marriage entailed a close artistic collaboration and exchange of ideas. It was in California that Broner came into contact with the world of cinema, his lengthy artistic training leading to commissions in set design and the burgeoning cartoon industry. The experience bore late fruit in *The Little Island* (1958), Richard Williams's much-garlanded short (33 minutes) about three men who come to blows over their respective beliefs in Good, Truth and Beauty. Broner appears in the credits under 'Story and Timing Assistance'. The island in question was clearly based on Ibiza, or rather the part that accommodated its voluble café philosophers.

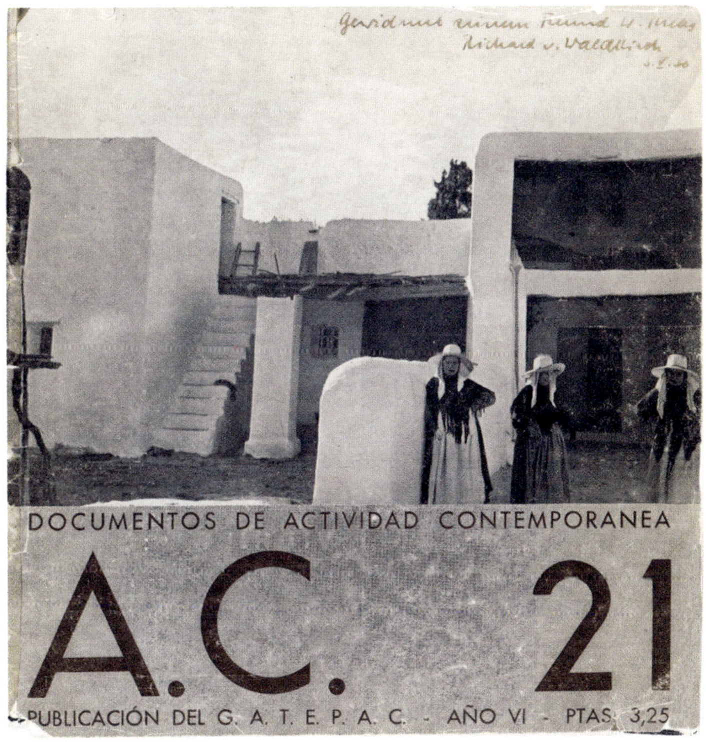

The journal A.C.: Documentos de actividad contemporánea *was published during the Second Spanish Republic by a group of avant-garde architects. Much of issue no. 21 (1936) was dedicated to Erwin Broner and Richard von Waldkirch's study of the Ibizan vernacular and to showcasing Broner's Talamanca beach club. Although usually attributed to Broner, the cover photograph was taken by his Swiss partner, von Waldkirch.*

Broner's overall impact on film-making – such as bringing American techniques to Paris and London – has yet to be properly assessed, and further discoveries may well be made in years to come.

Our subject's studies in Stuttgart, Munich and Dresden from 1919 to 1924 were dedicated to fine art, and his East Coast sojourn at the end of the American years brought him close to Abstract Expressionism, which was then taking Manhattan by storm. On his return to Ibiza in 1952, Broner plunged headlong into that art movement, as practitioner as well as promoter. When his oil painting *Ibiza paisaje* was shown in August at the annual group exhibition in the Salón de Ebusus (Vara de Rey), the *Diario de Ibiza* commented

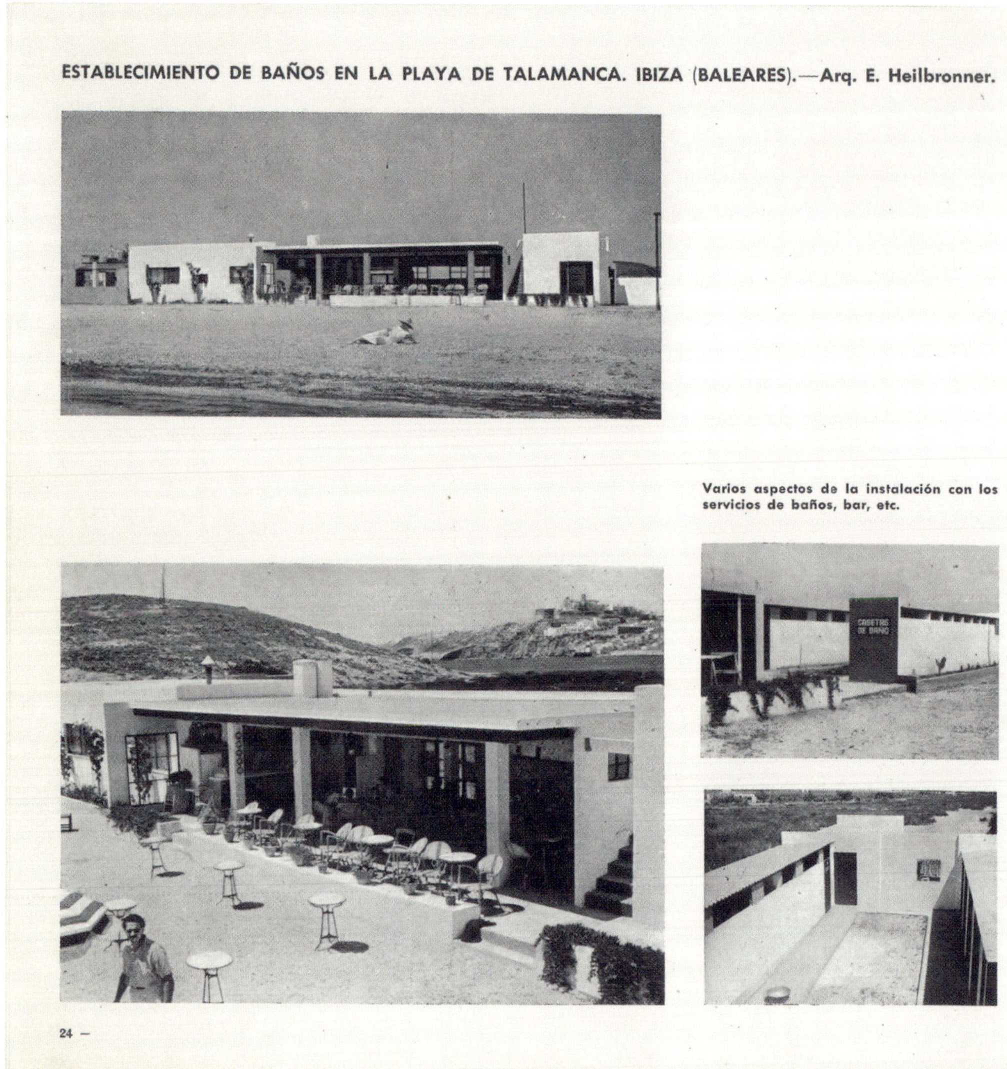
ESTABLECIMIENTO DE BAÑOS EN LA PLAYA DE TALAMANCA. IBIZA (BALEARES).—Arq. E. Heilbronner.

Varios aspectos de la instalación con los servicios de baños, bar, etc.

24 –

Designed in the International Style, Broner's Café-bar Playa Talamanca (1934) was Ibiza's first beach club.

that 'the sea appears to us of an extraordinary strangeness'; a few days later (13 August 1952), Broner's article 'Ideas sobre pintura moderna' appeared in the same newspaper. He was at the forefront of a small group of mostly German artists who played a key role in changing Ibizan attitudes to the new winds blowing in from North America and trendsetting capitals in northern Europe.

After further periods in California, then Paris and London (1953–59) to keep finances afloat by working on animated films, Broner was instrumental in the foundation of **Grupo Ibiza 59**, a modern-art collective that is an iconic name on the island. His forcefully articulated ideas about why Abstract Expressionism was the true 'new art' would resound throughout the Balearics and other parts of Spain for decades to come. With the exception of two exhibitions in 2019 and 2021, Broner's own pictorial legacy has generally attracted little attention: bold, spontaneous brushstrokes, an occasional collage and a surprising palette (green and turquoise – colours that are relatively rare in Ibizan abstraction – were clear favourites). A dozen of his paintings, all abstract, can be seen in MACE and on the walls of Casa Broner.

The biggest surprise was still to come, however. At the very end of his working life and right into his early seventies, Broner designed and built close to **thirty houses and apartments in Ibiza** (1960–71), his most enduring achievement beyond question. These modernist masterpieces have inspired two handsomely illustrated books, published in 1981 and 1994 by the Colegio de Arquitectos de Baleares (Balearic Architects' Association, with other cultural institutions), as well as the other works mentioned in the opening sentence. The villas and flats, more than half of them in and around the capital, were clearly inspired by Le Corbusier and such Bauhaus giants as Mies van der Rohe, and were mostly for foreign residents who were friends. Furnishings and fittings were designed by Broner, always displaying an innate respect and feeling for materials, proportion, simplicity and functionality – the essence of the Bauhaus creed. But Broner's architecture owes its greatest debt to Le Corbusier and Pierre Jeanneret's epoch-changing house at the Weissenhof Estate (1927) in Stuttgart. The house's ribbon windows, pilotis, roof terrace and bold horizontal lines are typical of nearly all of Broner's Ibizan projects, which also pay homage to the same modular perfection Le Corbusier found in the ancient Mediterranean – in Greece and North Africa, above all. In Broner's case, however, Ibiza's timeless farmhouses provided further lessons in functional simplicity, proportional balance and delightful architectural details. His ever-present external staircases owe a clear debt to the splendid example in the cover photograph

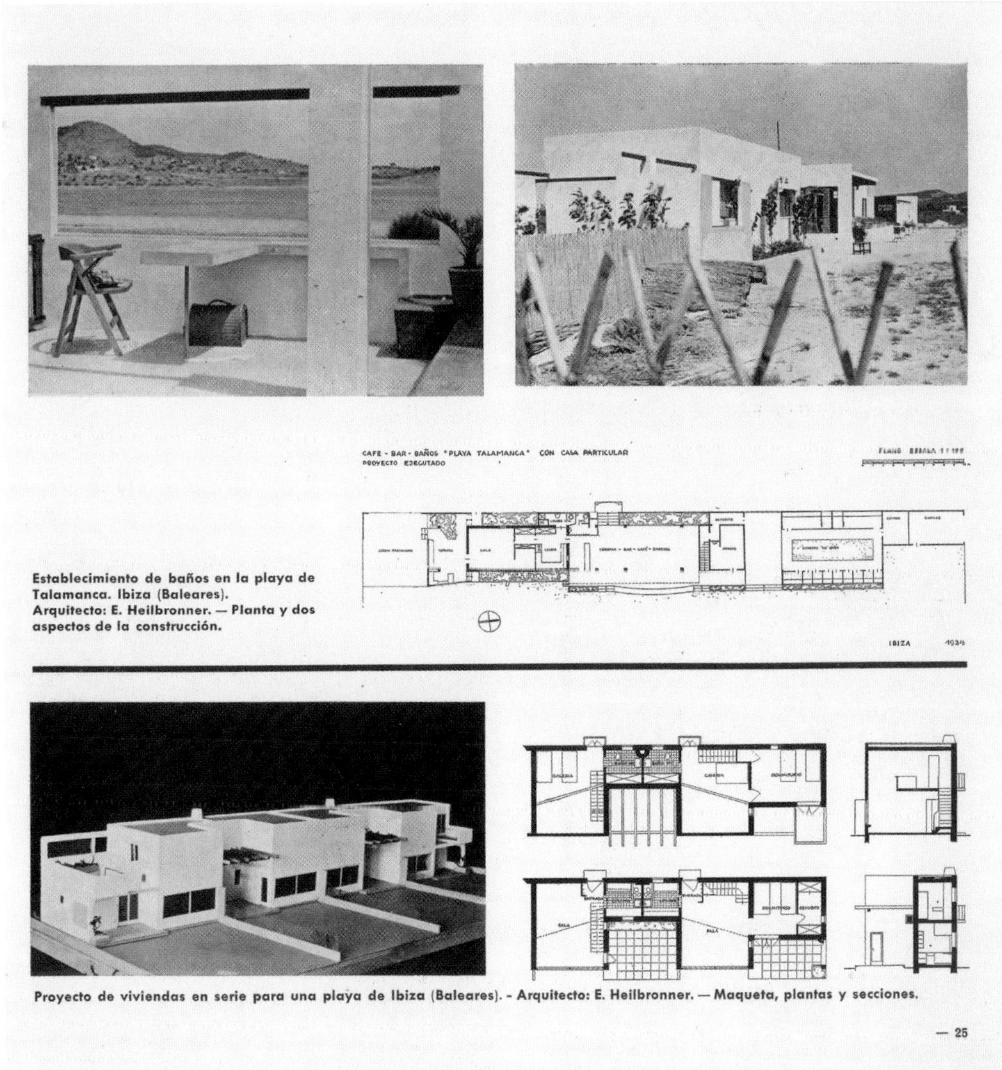
CAFE - BAR - BAÑOS "PLAYA TALAMANCA" CON CASA PARTICULAR
PROYECTO EJECUTADO

Establecimiento de baños en la playa de Talamanca. Ibiza (Baleares). Arquitecto: E. Heilbronner. — Planta y dos aspectos de la construcción.

IBIZA 1934

Proyecto de viviendas en serie para una playa de Ibiza (Baleares). - Arquitecto: E. Heilbronner. — Maqueta, plantas y secciones.

— 25

Left, top: Aerial bombing destroyed the Talamanca complex at the beginning of the Spanish Civil War (September 1936); all that remains are the photographs and plan, as published in A.C., and some archival material.

Left, bottom: Broner's model, floor plans and sections for a series of Ibizan beach houses, never built.

of issue no. 21 of *A.C.* (p. 235). His fondness for wooden pergolas likewise recalls the horizontal vine trellises that fronted several traditional fincas found in the same issue, while his generous porches, often with square columns, are far more *casa payesa* than Le Corbusier (in pre-touristic Ibiza, upper 'porches' were actually lofts for drying crops, rather than perches for enjoying views).

To sum up, Broner was a modernist who also championed traditional values, engaging deeply with the latter in a way that greatly enhanced his own designs. He was an exponent of what we now regard as the classically modern, whether in painting, architecture or any other medium. He repeatedly **defended Ibiza's urban spaces against insensitive planning**, and in 1965 wrote a powerful essay, 'Reflexiones sobre el futuro de Ibiza', which first appeared in print ten years after his death. He was the island's 'man for all seasons', displaying immense talent for whatever he turned his hand to. Other architects speak of his prodigious capacity for work, his attention to detail, his passion for purity and simplicity – character traits that resulted in complex dealings with some clients (but which architect has ever experienced otherwise?). His upbringing and his training in arts and architecture were both conservative and cutting edge, ensuring a remarkably diverse output over four busy decades. As in the case of many Jewish professionals brought up in Central Europe, classical music and literary masterpieces underpinned his education, and they are reflected in the serene, apparently effortless beauty of his œuvre, with childhood holidays in Greece and Italy imparting a sense of what is most enduring in human endeavours. His houses were built to last, and there is general consensus that his Ibizan legacy deserves preserving for future generations. We conclude with a passage from the 1965 essay that sums up Broner's humanistic and pragmatic philosophy, his practical yet creative modus operandi:

Ibiza's authentic and spiritual treasure (its scenery and ancient architecture) is an important part of its capital and a source of its fortune (a questionnaire to tourists about their reasons for coming to Ibiza would confirm this). But would any tourist like to sacrifice their physical comfort (running cold and hot water, electricity, heating facilities, lots of air and sun in their living room, etc. etc.) for those spiritual values? Our task is to combine, to synchronize these requirements and to find corresponding solutions.

Erwin Broner, 'Exposé of Some Ideas about the Future of Ibiza', 1965 essay first published in English in Erwin Broner, 1898–1971 *(1994), p. 188*

JOSEP LLUÍS SERT (1902–1983)

OUTSTANDING ARCHITECT AND MEDITERRANEANIST

One of the most influential architects and city planners of the last century, Josep Lluís Sert enjoyed a special connection with Ibiza and its timeless culture, one that was clearly evident at the very beginning and end of his brilliant career. This maverick disciple of Le Corbusier rose to prominence while still a student in Barcelona, campaigning vigorously for Spain's architectural modernization. Within two years of graduating from the city's Escuela Superior de Arquitectura, he co-founded the Grupo de Arquitectos y Técnicos Españoles para el Progreso de la Arquitectura Contemporánea (GATEPAC, 1930–37) and launched its epoch-making quarterly, *A.C.* The lasting impact of this cutting-edge journal, often cited along with its subtitle, *Documentos de actividad contemporánea* (1931–37, 25 issues), is borne out by two re-editions in single-volume facsimiles (1975, 2006) and a full Italian translation (with illustrations), published in 1978.

Ibiza's traditional farmhouses were singled out by Sert in five much-reproduced *A.C.* essays (1932–36), which brought the White Island to the attention of architects and designers all over southern Europe. The journal also showcased four modern projects conceived by Sert and others to cater for the island's pre-Civil War tourist boom, while several of his editorial pieces (penned anonymously) disseminated Le Corbusier's contentious theory that Mediterranean folk architecture was the true progenitor of modernism, the key to unravelling its pressing social, functional and aesthetic concerns. For Sert, Ibiza's fincas represented the gold standard: simple, white, cubic, unornamented, flexible (new rooms or wings easily added) and perfectly adapted to their surroundings. In short, they fitted the goals of modernism to a T, or so it seemed to city-based planners who had never actually built or lived in one.

Posterity has yet to reach a consensus about this complex – and on occasion starry-eyed – individual. For some, Sert represents the darker side of Brutalist modernism, characterized by a reliance on concrete and glass, the elimination of ornament (cornices and eaves banished), and anonymous blocks that tower into the sky or disappear along the shore. For others, he was a visionary who grafted the essence of *arquitectura popular* (traditional architecture) – simplicity, flexibility and human dimensions – on to monumental housing and leisure schemes. As urban populations soared, town halls and national governments became more committed to long-term planning, and in this light, Sert appears more of a humanizer in the mould of Morris or Ruskin, a socially minded architect grappling with runaway mechanization and metropolitan sprawl. The Anti-tuberculosis Clinic in Barcelona (1934–37) was an emblematic work of his early period, its focus on ventilation and sunlight making it a landmark in the treatment of this perennial scourge. But instead of looking to medieval arts and crafts for inspiration, Sert found it in the living folkways of the archipelago on his own doorstep.

The architect's personal trajectory is also full of paradoxes. He was born into a titled, privileged family whose wealth was based on textiles, and he had a celebrated uncle, Josep Maria Sert, who produced arresting murals for the Waldorf Astoria and the Rockefeller Center in New York, the League of Nations in Geneva and the Hôtel de Ville in Paris. As a young man, however, he turned his back on inherited wealth to become a lifelong Republican, married the daughter (Ramona Longás, known as Moncha) of the porter of one of his own projects, Calle Muntaner 342–348, and devoted his energies to improving the conditions of the labouring classes. Sert's adherence to principles made him the perfect candidate to design the Second Republic's Spanish pavilion at the 1937 Paris Expo, which led in turn to his permanent exile, first in New York (1939) and later Massachusetts.

Thanks partly to his links with world-class names – Le Corbusier and Walter Gropius, above all – the Catalan architect blossomed in America, becoming president of the Congrès Internationaux d'Architecture Moderne (CIAM, 1947–56) and dean of the Graduate School of Design at Harvard University (1953–69). His professional base remained in New York, where he founded Town Planning Associates (TPA, 1941–58) with Paul Lester Wiener, later joined by Paul Schulz. TPA is now known for its ambitious plans (rarely realized) to create manufacturing cities from scratch, mainly in Latin America. Its detailed blueprints had the financial backing of the US Department of State, which was keen to thwart overtures from European fascist and communist regimes towards its Latin American neighbours.

Several years after his mother's death in 1956, Sert came into a substantial inheritance, which allowed him to dust off the 1930s projects for the Balearics that had never borne fruit. Like Erwin Broner (another exiled architect whose career changed course in the United States, and who subsequently returned to Ibiza), Sert started off with a single scheme in Ibiza Town (1960–61, two stacked apartments), followed by six elegant holiday villas for himself, friends and associates on the pine-clad slopes of Can Pep Simó (1966–72). His leading contribution to this legendary *urbanización*, also known as Punta Martinet, was completed with Es Fumerals, a row of thirteen affordable three-storey apartments whose ground plans bear a close resemblance to the Ibiza Town flats. The result is widely recognized as a masterpiece, a rare example of modernism and Mediterraneanism rubbing shoulders serenely and superbly. The ochre façades nestle half-invisibly among the shrubs and trees, with splendid views of two bays, Dalt Vila and a substantial stretch of coastline. Five other architects contributed houses, often slightly smaller: Broner, Germán Rodríguez Arias (two), Jean Jacques Copetta (two), Joseph Zalewski and Sixte Illescas.

At this stage, Sert and his friends might well be said to have all but abandoned socialist housing, selling out to fellow globe-trotting second-homers. But to understand Can Pep Simó properly, we must look back thirty years, to five smaller weekend houses built by Sert and his young partner, Josep Torres Clavé (1906–1939), at Garraf (1934–35), south-west of Barcelona. The original model for the Garraf chalets was a *casa desmontable* (prefabricated house) that GATEPAC showcased in Barcelona in 1932 and made more permanent in *A.C.* issue no. 8 that same year. The article in *A.C.* was titled 'Two Types of Minimal Dwelling for the Beach', and revealed the envisaged island setting, as well as the importance of traditional materials and smaller dimensions, which placed these holiday chalets within the reach of middle-class pockets:

In the walls orientated east, north and west, use can be made of local materials, whether brick or stone. These houses, inspired by traditional ones that exist in Ibiza, were conceived for the Balearic Islands, where local, easily cut limestone is used for building walls.

When Sert began work at Can Pep Simó, he was still smarting from fairly heavy criticism: several of his American buildings had come under fire as being classic examples of Brutalist excess, and the global reputation of Brutalism needed lightening up. Two playful and imaginative Mediterranean showpieces from this period form a prequel to the Ibizan residential complex. The first, Joan Miró's workshop (now known as Sert's Studio/Taller Sert, 1956), a few miles west of Palma de Mallorca, is well known for its seagull-wing roof. The equally famous roofline of Fondation Maeght (1958–64), an art museum in Saint-Paul de Vence, Provence, is often likened to nuns' coifs, but is simply a pair of wittily upturned Catalan vaults.

Sharp-eyed observers have noticed parallels between Mallorca's farmhouses, ochre-coloured with ashlar-framed or painted doors and windows, and the façades of Can Pep Simó, where white bands surround windows and draw the eye towards rooflines (the cornice 'rediscovered'). Ibiza's farmhouses are generally whitewashed, but in the south-west (San José parish) there are many noteworthy exceptions, such as Ca na Rosa, below the bend on the Es Cubells road; Ses Païsses de Cala d'Hort, now an ethnographic museum; and Sa Païssa d'en Vergeret, where motorists catch their first glimpse of Es Vedrà. Sert may well have been inspired by these iconic Ibizan farms that merge discreetly with their surroundings. The rendered stone plinths on which his villas rest also evoke Ibizan houses, with their unwhitewashed side/back walls, as do the long wooden balustrades and horizontal pergolas (like many of Broner's houses). Intermediate spaces are an essential part of Sert's houses; generous, half-shaded terraces with views that invite both companionship and contemplation.

Until June 1975 Sert was denied admission to the architectural associations of both Catalonia and the Balearic Islands, so the plans for Can Pep Simó were signed by two prominent Catalan architects. Both had solid practices in Ibiza: Raimon Torres was the son of Sert's partner at Garraf, Josep Torres Clavé; Germán Rodríguez Arias was a long-time collaborator and associate in GATEPAC and on *A.C.* In 1981 the Consejo Superior de los Colegios de Arquitectos de España awarded Sert its Gold Medal, a belated recognition reaffirmed the following year by the Spanish Ministry of Culture, when it awarded him its Gold Medal for Merit in the Fine Arts.

Sert's long career was bookended by two ambitious Pityusan projects, neither of which reached fruition. The first was an immense 'Hotel en Ibiza', for which only the architect's drawing has survived (*c.* April 1933). This shows a giant, three-storey glass-and-concrete structure evidently planned for Talamanca and bearing a curious resemblance to two hotels that opened there some thirty years later: Hotel Argos (1965–67, by Josep Ribas González) and Hotel

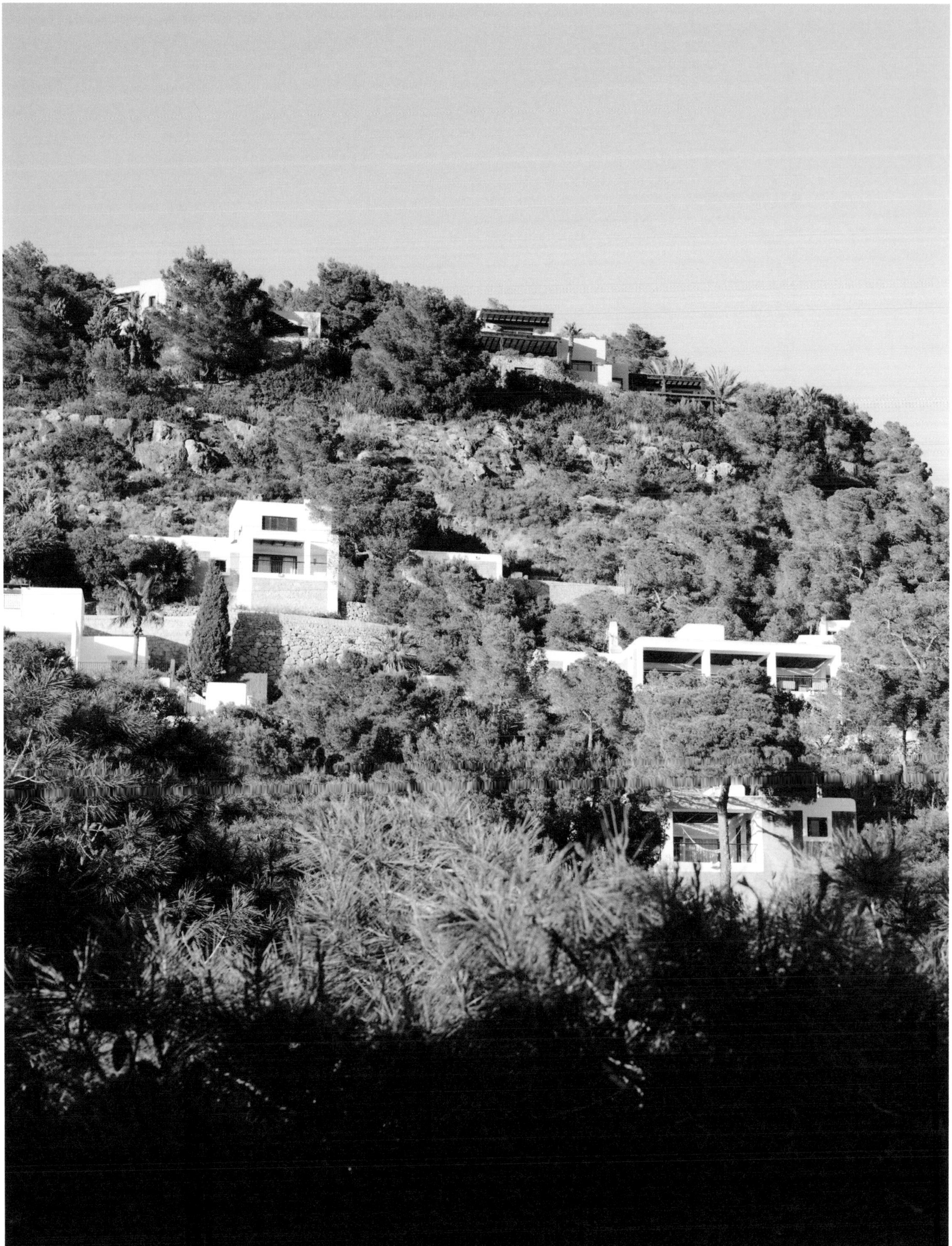

Nestled among the pines, the discreet and elegant villas designed by Josep Lluís Sert for himself and his friends at Can Pep Simó. Just below, Sert designed Es Fumerals, a row of thirteen affordable three-storey apartments. These modernist masterpieces offer stunning views of Dalt Vila and two bays.

Corso (1967–69, by Raimon Torres with Patricia Arklie). There is nothing remotely Ibizan in the 1933 project, with its gleaming glass-and-steel grid typical of the International Style.

The later unrealized scheme was the Cala d'en Serra holiday village (1970–71). Perched on the slopes of a magically secluded bay in San Juan, it was a 'non-speculative' tourist project that aimed to foster a different kind of tourism – cultural and sporting rather than hedonistic. The terraced structure was separated into various modules, and resembles an enormous amphitheatre, broken down into apartments for young families with children, rooms for couples and unattached singles, and accommodation for management and staff. Sporting facilities, workshops for arts and crafts, a cinema and a lending library completed the innovative master plan. Sert was approaching seventy at this stage and remained in the United States, while his trusted colleagues on the spot included Joan Prats (land purchase), Raimon Torres (fellow architect) and Antoni Ferran, *aparejador* (technical architect).

Work began on the kitchen, dining room and workshops of the Social Centre (i.e. the non-residential part), but then the money ran out, so that only the eerie concrete shell of the centre and the staff wing were completed. The stepped accommodation for holidaymakers on the north-western slopes was never built, but those familiar with Roca Llisa and its Amphitheatre flats by the shore can imagine how Cala d'en Serra might have looked. Incidentally, Roca Llisa, on the east coast of Ibiza, was conceived slightly earlier by a friend of Sert's, Joaquín Beltrán y Caralt, who contracted the Catalan architects Fernando Cavestany and Xavier Busquets. Here, too, a kind of artistic colony was envisaged, complete with craft studios, cafés, affordable housing and a Le Corbusier-type chapel – to be designed by Sert.

Traditional crafts were a passion of Sert's, and as a prolific author – *Can Our Cities Survive?* (1942) has been through thirty-one editions – he was asked to write the introduction (presented in four languages) to one of the most beautiful books ever published about Pityusan material culture, *Ibiza: Fuerte y luminosa/Ibiza: Strong and Luminous* (1967). The photographer was Joaquim Gomis, whose holiday home in Can Pep Simó was completed the same year as this book. Joan Prats Vallès, a well-known impresario and promoter of Mediterranean folk arts, was the series editor. The book contains one of Sert's most celebrated and lyrical passages:

> *This little island is a rare example of a physical environment where the land and patterns developed by agriculture, the buildings, the towns and the objects created by the local people through centuries of patient work, have come together as one entity and are part of a harmonious whole ... What has evolved through centuries in Ibiza is a lesson to the more developed countries – a lesson in measure, good manners and good taste. The inhabitants of big cities who have the facilities, means and tools of progress readily at hand have much to learn about the art of living from these self-educated people who have built such a harmonious environment. Is this due in part to the scarcity of materials and means? Or to the years of slow change, with time to think about things and to establish a real scale of values? Whatever the reasons, here is a healthy lesson worth studying for those concerned with the improvement of our environment.*
>
> *Josep Lluís Sert, 'Measure in Man-made Environment', in* Ibiza: Fuerte y luminosa/Ibiza: Strong and Luminous *(1967), pp. 19–23*

In a revealing interview in his Harvard home near the end of his life, the great Catalan exile revealed that in his youth he was more interested in painting and sculpture, but was persuaded by the family to pursue another profession, partly because they already had a successful artist in their midst, but also because 'painters didn't earn any money'. In 1932 he became one of the founding members of the Barcelona-based ADLAN group (Amics de l'Art Nou), and his lifelong friendship with Joan Miró bore fruit at the end of his career with the Fundació Joan Miró (1973–75), a distinctively skylighted building on the eastern flanks of Montjuïc in Barcelona.

But it was Ibiza, the perennial magnet for artists and dreamers, that best answered the deep longing Sert felt to steer a middle course between the demands of an industrialized world and society's need for beauty, harmony and the good life. It is fitting that he has come to rest in the cemetery adjoining the church of Jesús, just over a mile from his great Balearic 'testament', discreetly veiled by the twisting pines that overlook Talamanca Bay.

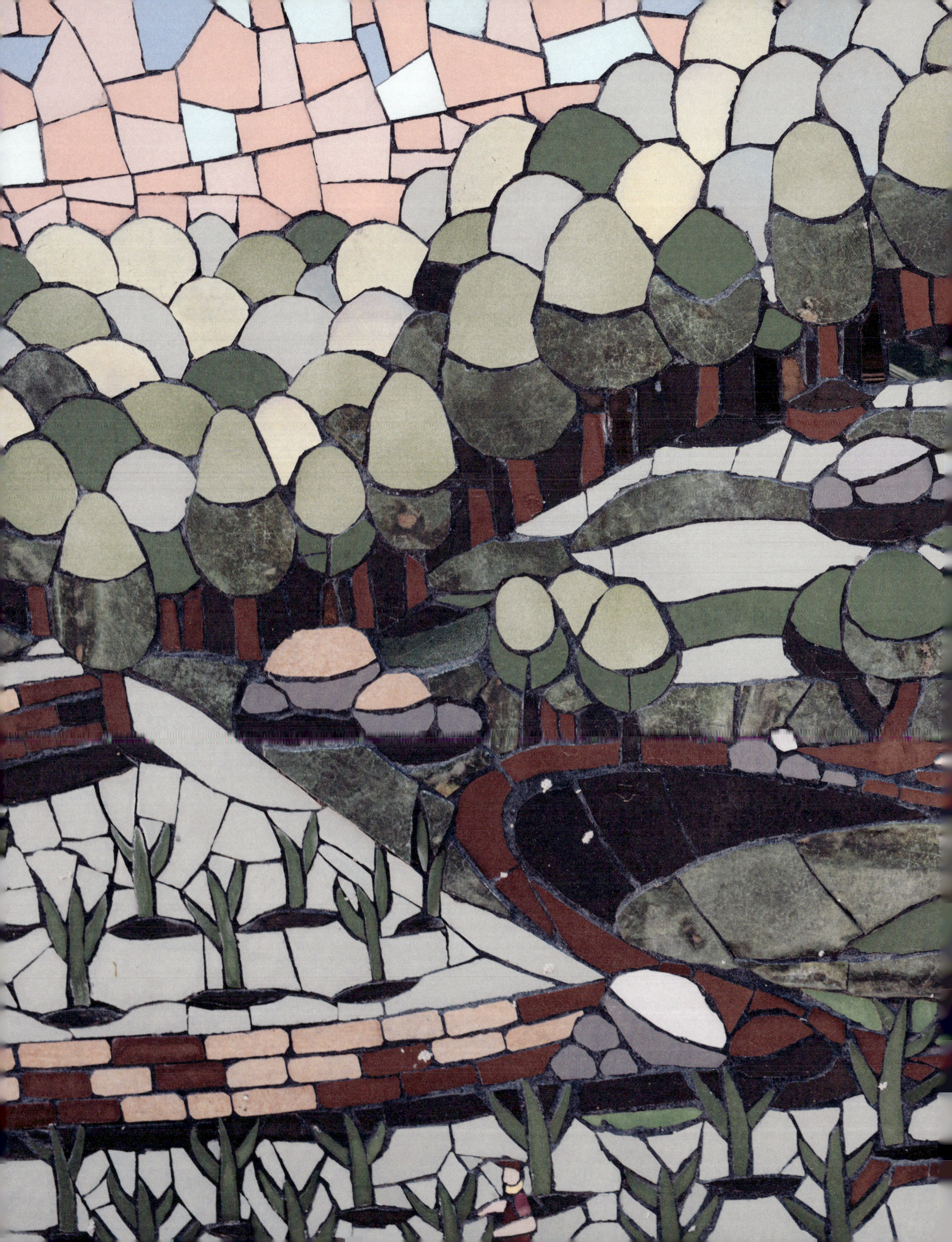

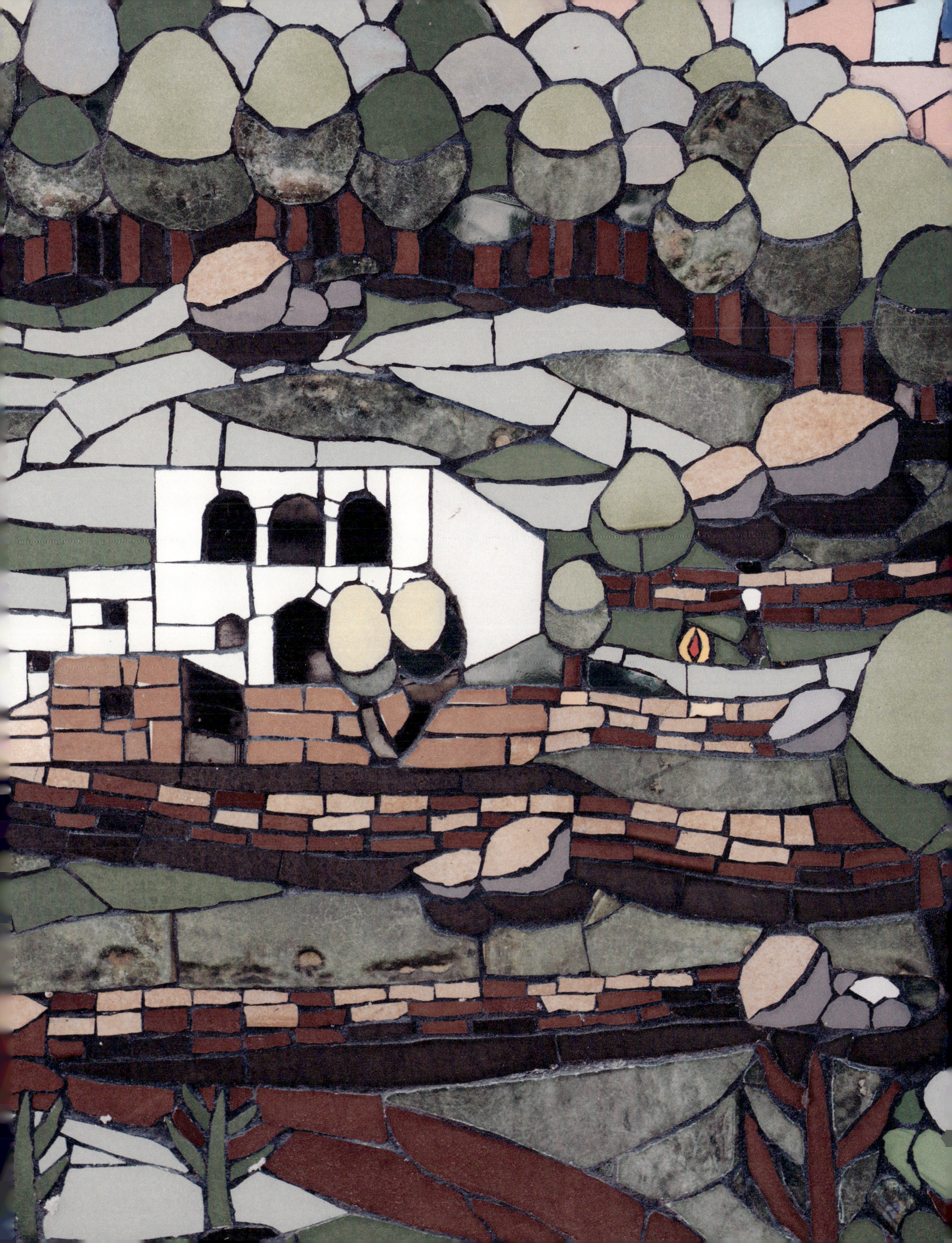

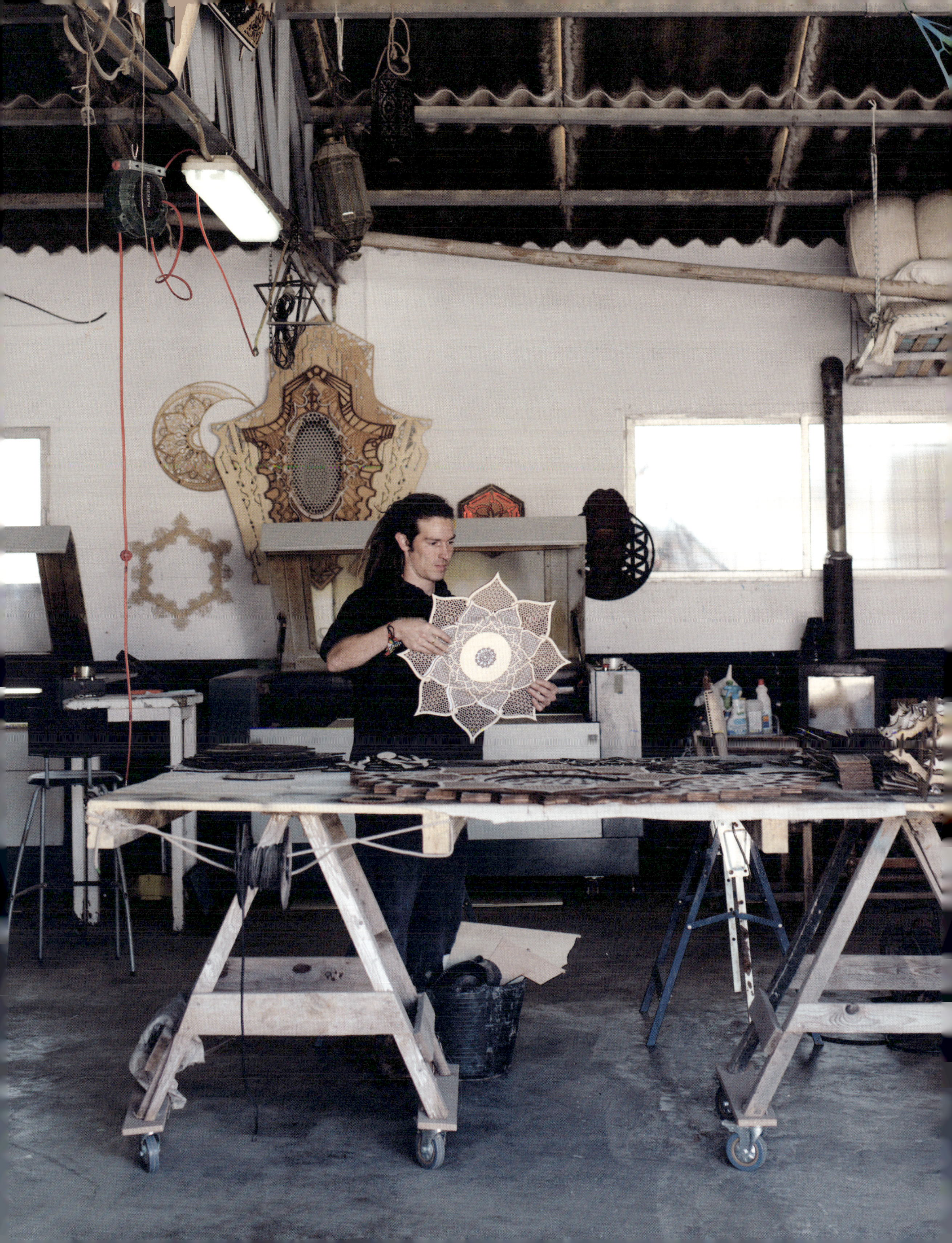

DIRECTORY

As well as the individuals and companies featured in this book, this list includes other creatives, craftspeople, businesses and cultural institutions in Ibiza.

FASHION & JEWELLERY
Bomé: bomeibiza.com (pp. 30–35)
Charo Ruiz: charoruiz.com
De La Vali: delavali.com
Delbes Ibiza: delbesibiza.es (pp. 18–23)
Elisa Pomar Ibiza: elisapomar.com (pp. 46–51)
Espardenyes Torres: espardenyesdeibiza.com (pp. 36–41)
Figtree Collection: figtree-collection.com (pp. 24–29)
La Galería Elefante: lagaleriaelefante.com
Majoral: majoral.com (pp. 42–45)
Natasha Collis: natashacollis.com
World Family Ibiza: worldfamilyibiza.com (pp. 52–57)

CRAFTS, WOODWORK & DESIGN
Can Castello: @cancastelloibiza (pp. 170–75)
Carpintería Thierry: @carpinteria_thierry (pp. 164–69)
Charlotte Ceramics: charlotteceramics.com
Indigo Artchitecture: indigoartchitecture.com (pp. 156–63)
Inés Ventós: inesventossoler-cabot.com (pp. 60–63)
Ladio Ceramics: ladio.eu (pp. 68–71)
María B.: @mariab.ceramics (pp. 72–75)
Sa Teulera: @sateulerapottery
Sumeria Creations: sumeriacreations.com (pp. 176–79)
Yvette Spowers: @yvettespowersceramics (pp. 64–67)

ART & CULTURE
Aline de Laforcade: alinedelaforcade.com (pp. 86–89)
Antonio Villanueva: antoniovillanueva.com (pp. 78–81)
Can Jay: canjayrecordingstudio.com (pp. 108–11)
Casa Broner: tourism.eivissa.es/what-to-see/cultural-visits/museums/casa-broner/
Clovis Neymo: @el__domo (pp. 104–107)
Espacio Micus: espacio-micus.com (pp. 94–99)
Estudi Tur Costa: estuditurcosta.com (pp. 190–93)
Galería También: @galeriatambien (pp. 100–103)
Museu d'Art Contemporani d'Eivissa: eivissa.es/mace/index.php/en/
Museu Puget: tourism.eivissa.es/what-to-see/cultural-visits/museums/the-puget-museum/
Parra & Romero: parra-romero.com
Prudence Dudan: @prudencedudan (pp. 90–93)
Sandra de Keller: @sandradekeller (pp. 82–85)
Ses 12 Naus: ses12naus.org
Violeta Galera: @violetagalera (p. 57)

FOOD & DRINK
Cafés Ibiza: cafesibiza.com (pp. 138–41)
Can Rei: @can___rei (pp. 130–33)
Can Rich: bodegascanrich.com (pp. 124–29)
Goldtooth: goldtoothaperitivo.com
Herbes Can Vidal: @herbescanvidal
Ibizkus: ibizkus.com
Juntos Farm: juntosfarm.com (pp. 118–23)
Juntos House: juntoshouse.com (pp. 118–23)
Marí Mayans: fmarimayans.com (pp. 114–17)
Meke Coffee Roasters: meke.coffee
Ojo de Ibiza: ojoibiza.com
Sal de Ibiza: saldeibiza.com (pp. 134–37)
Ses Cabretes: @sescabretes (pp. 150–53)
Terra Masia: terramasiaibiza.com
The Farm: @thefarmibiza (pp. 142–49)
The Floral Studio: @thefloralstudioibiza (pp. 142–49)

HOUSES & GARDENS
Art of Living: artof-living.info
Blakstad Design Consultants: blakstadibiza.com (pp. 208–15)
Carmen Straatsma: @carmenstraatsma
Casa Bedouin: casabedouin.com
Ecodisseny: ecodisseny.info (pp. 186–89)
Estudio Laterna: @estudio_laterna (pp. 202–207)
Estudio Vila 13: estudiovila13.com (pp. 216–21)
Florando Ando: @florando.ando
Ibiza Interiors: ibizainteriors.com
Juan Masedo: @masedo_jardines (pp. 194–201)
KsaR Living: ksarliving.com
Studio Anne-Fleur Aronstein: annefleuraronstein.com
Tanis Ibiza: @tanisibiza
Terravita: terravita.eu
Valerio Miragoli: @valeriomiragoli

AUTHOR BIOGRAPHIES

Liam Aldous
Liam Aldous is an Ibiza-based journalist, multidisciplinary writer and cultural curator. He has been the Spain correspondent for *Monocle* magazine since 2011, and he often collaborates with the fashion house Loewe to write books and direct films. During the Covid pandemic he directed creative content and a 'defiantly optimistic' narrative for The Smiley Company. In 2019 he founded ColourFeel, creating and curating inspirational, immersive, perspective-shifting experiences for companies and creatives around the world.

Maya Boyd
Maya Boyd is an award-winning Ibiza-based journalist, editor and brand consultant. She is the editorial director of *L'Officiel Ibiza* magazine and a contributor to *Condé Nast Traveller*. Having lived in Ibiza for long periods since she was a teenager, she has an intimate understanding of the island's history and heritage. She is the founder of the historical-interest forum Ibiza Insights. She began her career as the Ibiza correspondent for British *Vogue* and has written about the Balearic Islands for such publications as the *Daily Telegraph*, *The Guardian*, the *New York Times* and *House & Garden*. She is the author of several books about Ibiza and Formentera, including *Ibiza Bohemia* (2017).

Martin Davies
Martin Davies is a writer, translator and publisher who has lived in Ibiza since 1993. He completed a study of traditional Pityusan architecture in 1997, and three years later established Barbary Press, which has published titles on vintage photography, travel, archaeology, architecture, history, birdlife and early tourism in Ibiza. He has lectured widely and written some 200 articles on Ibizan history and culture for various publications, including *Arquitectura y espacio rural en Ibiza* (2002), *Secret Walks: Ibiza* (2015), *Enciclopèdia d'Eivissa i Formentera*, *Pacha Magazine* and Ibizahistoryculture.com.

Clare Dowdy
Clare Dowdy is a London-based journalist, author, curator and event moderator. She has written for publications including *Wallpaper*, *Wired*, *Monocle*, BBC.com, *The Guardian* and the *Financial Times*, in which she had a fortnightly column on design. She edits *Connections*, a quarterly magazine for electricians. She is a co-author of *Made in London: From Workshops to Factories*, published by Merrell in 2022.

Christopher English
Christopher English is a freelance writer specializing in the fields of food, travel, music, culture and community. For more than two decades he has contributed to a variety of publications, among them *The Guardian*, *Vice* and *Gourmet Traveller*. He has lived in Ibiza since 2007, after moving from Sydney to teach English and media studies at the island's international college.

Salva López
Salva López is an award-winning Barcelona-based photographer who specializes in lifestyle, interiors and portraiture. His work has featured in numerous publications, including the *Wall Street Journal*, *Monocle*, *Kinfolk*, *T Spain* and *Perdiz*. He has exhibited extensively, including in solo exhibitions such as *ILLA* at Wer-Haus in Barcelona in 2015 and *Skate Art Skate RIP* at FAD in Barcelona in 2009, and in group exhibitions such as Photo Phnom Penh in Cambodia and *Woman 3000* in Ukraine, both in 2010.

Ana Lui
Ana Lui is an experienced editorial and commercial photographer whose portfolio includes interiors, travel, portraiture and fine art. She has worked for *Condé Nast Traveller* magazine since 2018, and her love of travel and exploration continues to inspire her photography. She lived in Ibiza for fifteen years and is currently based in Mallorca.

PICTURE CREDITS

Key: l = left, r = right, t = top, c = centre, b = bottom

Archive Sal de Ibiza: 136–37 (except 136tr)
Archivo Majoral: 44cl, 44bl
Artefact/Alamy Stock Photo: 225
Aisha Bonet: 136tr
Josep Buil Mayral. Anys 70. Arxiu d'Imatge i So del Consell Insular d'Eivissa: 231t
Campañá–Puig Ferrán, Librería Verdera: 229
Joan Costa. Any 2005/2007. Arxiu d'Imatge i So del Consell Insular d'Eivissa: 185bl, 185br
Courtesy of Espacio Micus: 99c
Fons Enciclopèdia E i F (Rev. D'A). Arxiu d'Imatge i So del Consell Insular d'Eivissa: 234t, 234b
Albert Font: 44 (except cl, bl)
Sandra de Keller: 85c
Salva López: back cover cr and br, 73–75, 79–81, 101–103, 105–107, 143–49, 162, 171–75, 180–81, 183, 187–89, 191–93, 195–201, 209–11, 217–18
Ana Lui: front cover, back cover (except cr, br), 2, 4, 6–7, 8–9, 10–11, 12, 14, 16–17, 19–23, 25–29, 31–35, 37–41, 45, 47–51, 53–57, 58–59, 61–63, 65–67, 69–71, 76–77, 83–85 (except 85c), 87–89, 91–93, 95–99 (except 99c), 109–11, 112–13, 115–17, 119–23, 125–29, 131–33, 139–41, 151–53, 154–55, 157–61, 163, 165–69, 177–79, 184–85 (except 185bl, br), 203–205 (except 204c, 205c, b), 212–15, 219–21, 222–23, 240, 242–43, 244, 248–49, 250, 256
Martin Davies Collection: 235–37
Ilse Mayer Gehrken: 231b
Llibert Teixidó: 43
Conrad White: 204c, 205c, 205b, 206–207
Ben Wolf: 135

Additional Credits
14: *Las Pitiusas* by Sandra de Keller, © Sandra de Keller.
76–77: Untitled wire sculpture by Maria Catalán. *Vers l'avant*, sculpture by Martin Bialas. Other artworks, *Sin título*, by Eduard Micus.
85tl: *Las Pitiusas*, *La cal* and *Paredes del norte*, all by Sandra de Keller, © Sandra de Keller.
85c: *La payesa ibicenca* by Sandra de Keller, © Sandra de Keller.
85br: *Renault 4 Life/Es Vedrà* by Sandra de Keller, © Sandra de Keller.
99t: Untitled wire sculpture by Maria Catalán. *Vers l'avant*, sculpture by Martin Bialas. Other artworks, *Sin título*, by Eduard Micus.
99bl, br: *Sin título*, artworks by Eduard Micus.
102tc, 103bl: Ceramic wall sculptures by Natalie Rich Fernández, © Natalie Rich Fernández.
103tl: Pair of Easy Armchairs by Pierre Jeanneret, *c.* 1956, © ADAGP, Paris and DACS, London 2023. Set of three Totems floor lamps, Sun lamp and appliqué Sun sculpture, all white enamelled ceramic pieces by Georges Pelletier, © Georges Pelletier/Courtesy Antoine Jourdan/Galería También.
103tr: B17 bookshelf in French elm by Pierre Chapo, *c.* 1973.
103br: Student desk in teak by Pierre Jeanneret, *c.* 1960, © ADAGP, Paris and DACS, London 2023.
111tl: *Chair with Shadow* by Robert Arató. *Cabrita rosa* by Silvia Arató.
111c: Painting © Pepo Moreno.
121tr: Detail of mosaic mural by Lucas Pereyra.
144br: *Renault 4 Life/Che* by Sandra de Keller, © Sandra de Keller.
191tl: *Sin título 2*, *Sin título 1*, *Verticalidades*, *Sin título* and *Sin título*, all by Bonet Vallribera, © Bonet Vallribera.
191c: *Rombo negro* and *Hybrido II*, both by Bonet Vallribera, © Bonet Vallribera.
191br: *El descanso de la nostalgia* and *Dos rectangulos rosas*, both by Bonet Vallribera, © Bonet Vallribera.
211bl: *Céfiro* by Covadonga Pintada and Marina Franco.
211br: *Sin título* by Rolph Blakstad.
242–43: Detail of mosaic mural by Lucas Pereyra at Juntos House.

Every effort has been made to trace and contact copyright holders of the illustrations reproduced in this book. The publisher will be happy to correct in subsequent editions any errors or omissions that are brought to its attention.

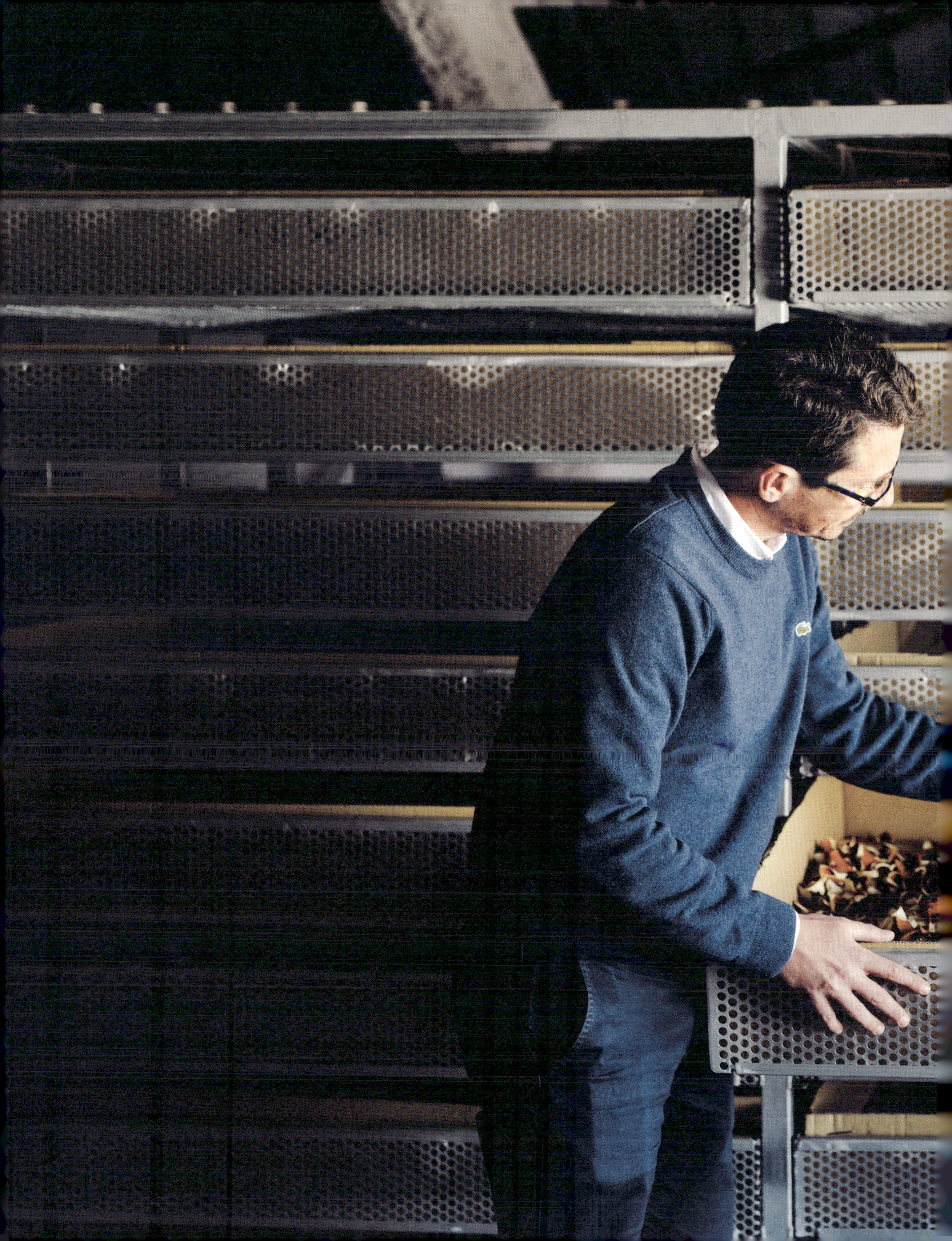

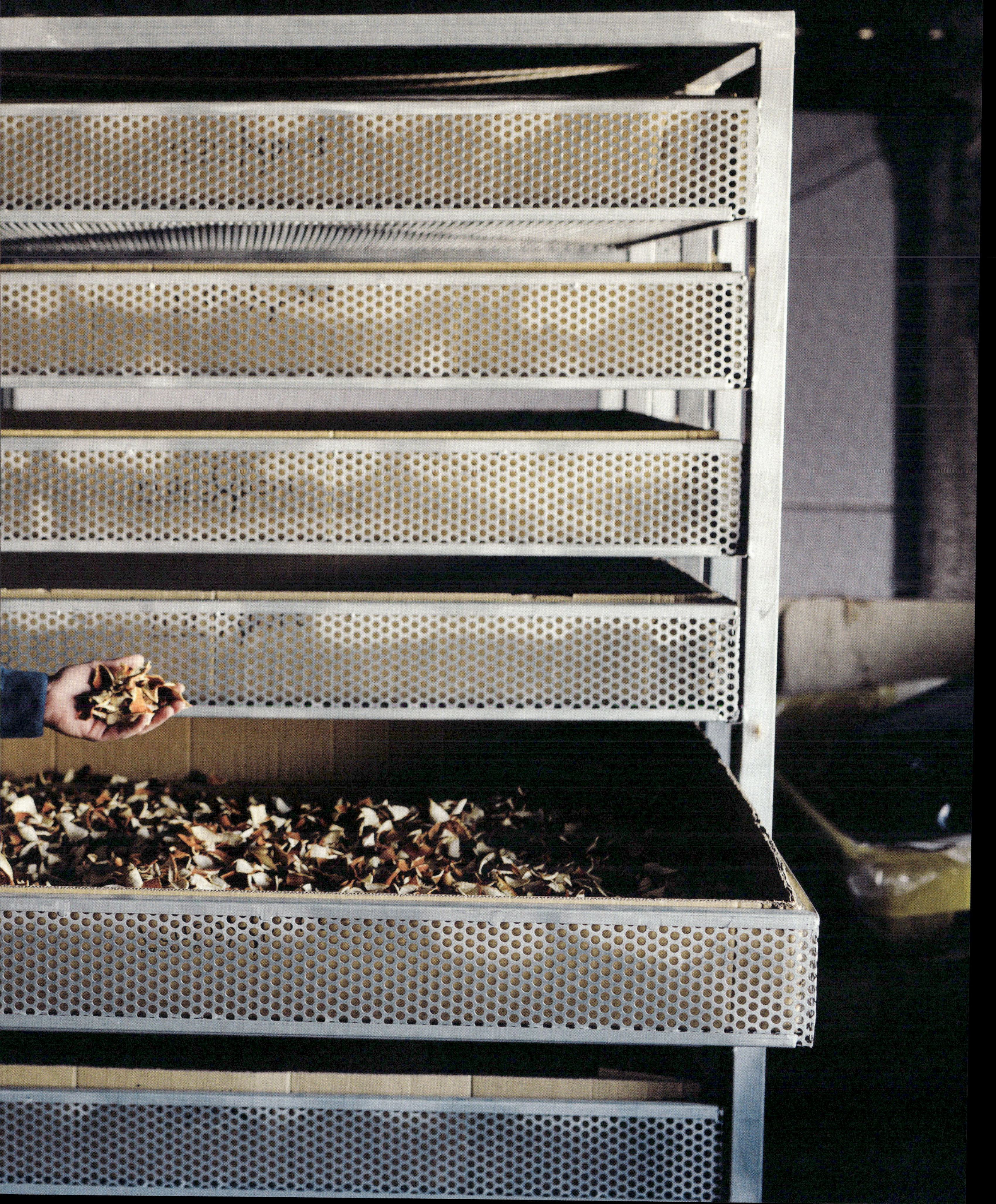

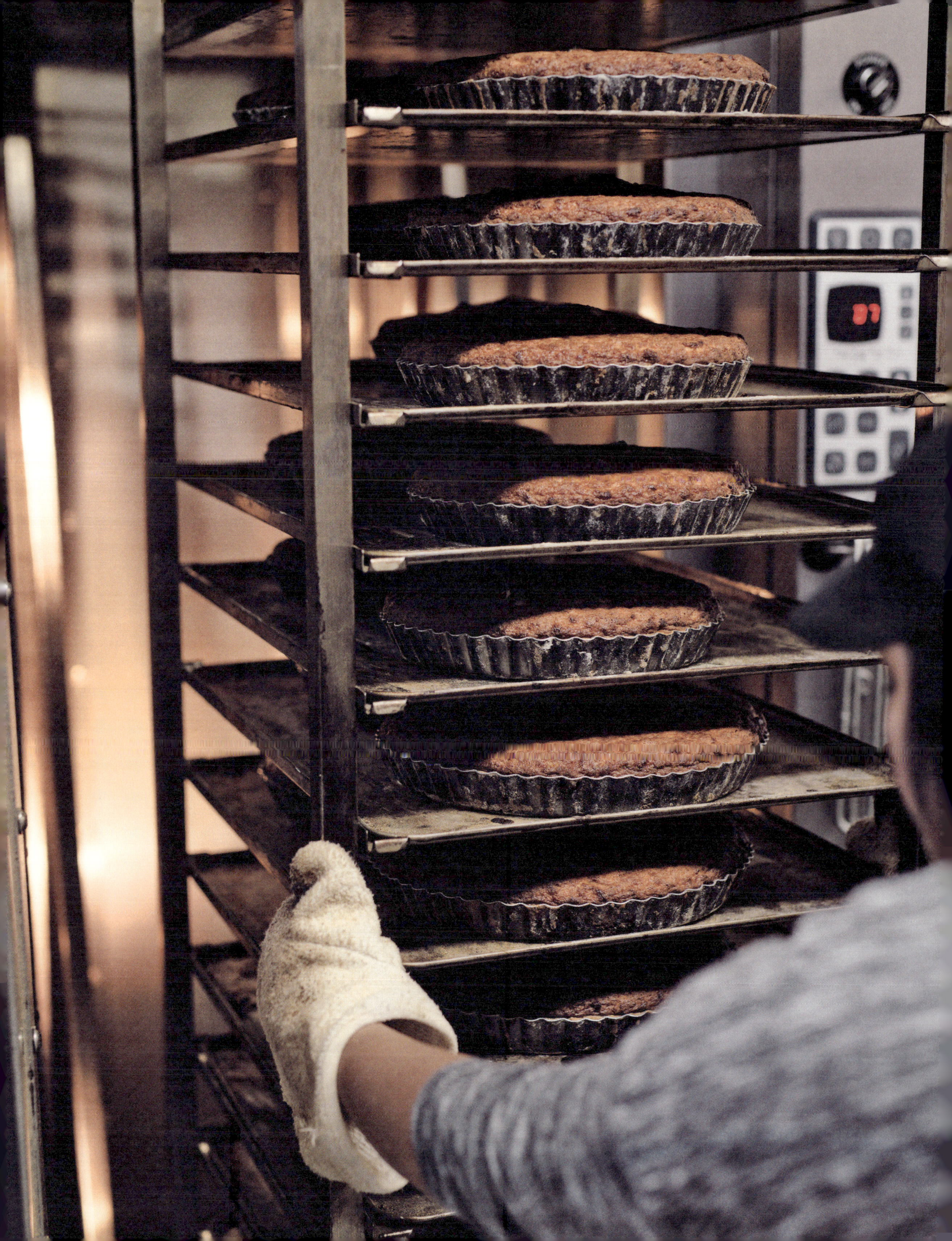

INDEX

Page numbers in *italic* refer to the illustrations.

First published 2024 by Merrell Publishers,
London and New York

Merrell Publishers Limited
70 Cowcross Street
London EC1M 6EJ

merrellpublishers.com

British Library Cataloguing in Publication Data.
A catalogue record for this book is
available from the British Library.

ISBN 978-1-8589-4713-6

Produced by Merrell Publishers Limited
Designed by Nathalie Hummer
Project-managed by Claire Chandler
Proofread by Barbara Roby
Indexed by Hilary Bird

Printed and bound in China

Front cover: Laura de Grinyo of Ladio Ceramics in front of her studio; see pp. 68–71.

Back cover (from left to right): Estudio Vila 13 (see pp. 216–21); Espardenyes Torres (see pp. 36–41); Carpintería Thierry (see pp. 164–69); Can Jay (see pp. 108–11); Marí Mayans (see pp. 114–17); María B. (see pp. 72–75); Ses Cabretes (see pp. 150–53); Clovis Neymo (see pp. 104–107).

Frontispiece: Enzo Billaud of Carpintería Thierry masterfully shapes a boat; see pp. 164–69.

Page 4: The vinyl library at Can Jay recording studio; see pp. 108–11.

Pages 6–7: Alba Esteva of Figtree Collection creates nature-based fashion underneath a carob tree; see pp. 24–29.

Pages 8–9: Pilar González of Ses Cabretes stirs goat's milk from her farm to produce cheese; see pp. 150–53.

Pages 10–11: Dario Bomé at work producing fine leather goods; see pp. 30–35.

Page 12: Liqueur production at the family company Marí Mayans; see pp. 114–17.

Page 14: *Las Pitiusas* by Sandra de Keller; see pp. 82–85.

Pages 242–43: Detail of mosaic mural by Lucas Pereyra at Juntos House; see pp. 118–23.

Page 244: Rabten van Oorschot of Sumeria Creations works on a mandala for his next stage design; see pp. 176–79.

Pages 248–49: Carlos Marí Mayans examines dried orange peel for the renowned Marí Mayans liqueurs; see pp. 114–17.

Page 250: *Flaó*, a local delicacy crafted at Can Rei for Ibiza's restaurants and delicatessens; see pp. 130–33.

Overleaf: Sonia Ferrer of Delbes Ibiza; see pp. 18–23.

CHAPTER OPENERS
Pages 16–17: Delbes Ibiza (see pp. 18–23); pages 58–59: Ladio Ceramics (see pp. 68–71); pages 76–77: Espacio Micus (see pp. 94–99); pages 112–13: Marí Mayans (see pp. 114–17); pages 154–55 and 222–23: Carpintería Thierry (see pp. 164–69); pages 180–81: Juan Masedo (see pp. 194–201).

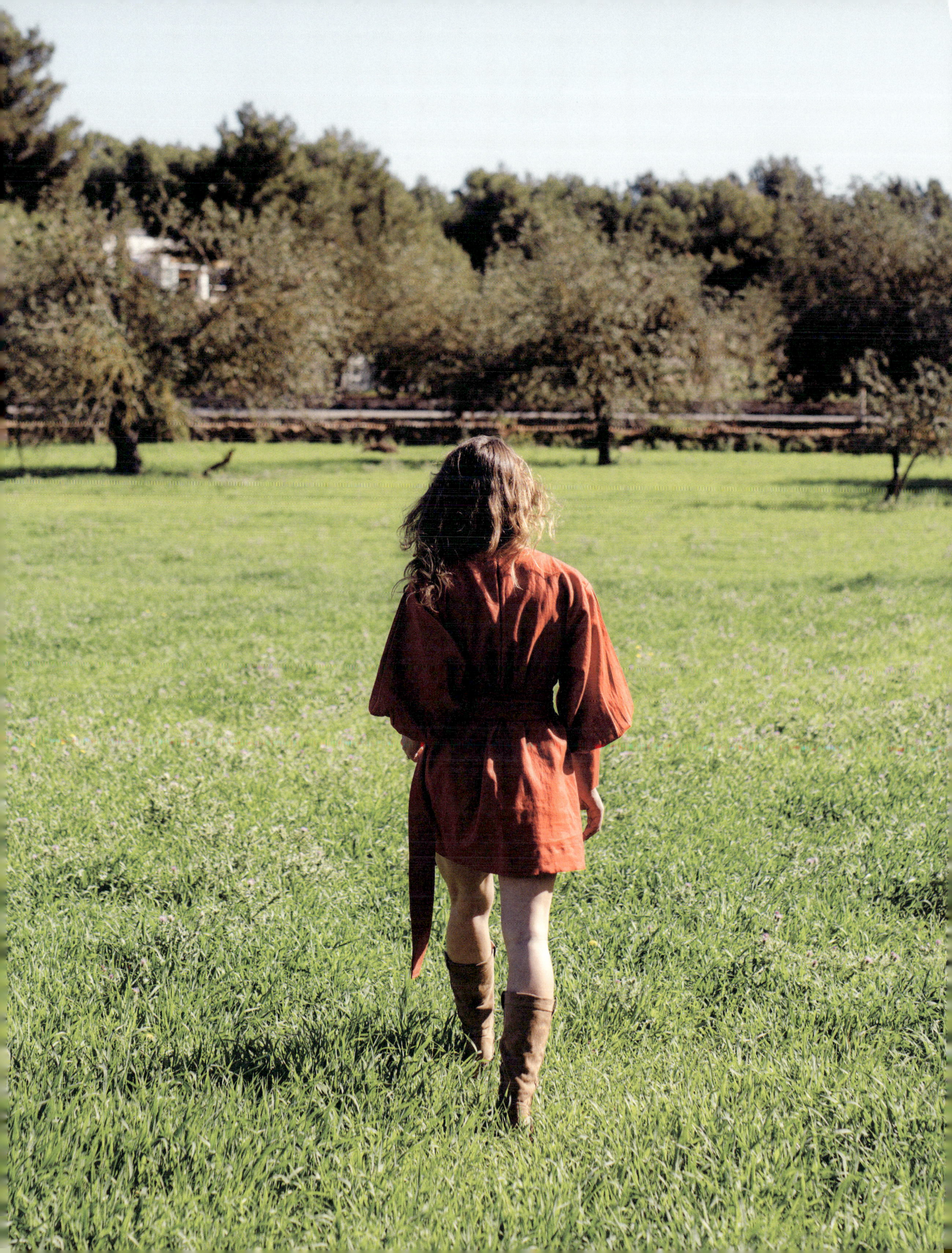